The Princeton Review

Cracking the New SAT

with Practice Tests on CD-ROM

ADAM ROBINSON, JOHN KATZMAN, AND
THE STAFF OF THE PRINCETON REVIEW

2006 EDITION

RANDOM HOUSE, INC.
NEW YORK

www.PrincetonReview.com

The Independent Education Consultants Association recognizes The Princeton Review as a valuable resource for high school and college students applying to college and graduate school.

The Princeton Review, Inc.
2315 Broadway
New York, NY 10024
E-mail: booksupport@review.com

ISBN 0-375-76486-0
ISSN 1551-6458

Editor: Suzanne Markert
Production Editor: Patricia Dublin
Production Coordinator: Jennifer Arias
Illustrations by: The Production Department of The Princeton Review

Manufactured in the United States of America.

9 8 7 6 5 4 3 2 1

2006 Edition

ACKNOWLEDGMENTS

An SAT course is much more than clever techniques and powerful computer score reports. The reason our results are great is that our teachers care so much about their kids. Many of them have gone out of their way to improve the course, often going so far as to write their own materials, some of which we have incorporated into our course manual as well as into this book. The list of these teachers could fill this page, but special thanks must be given to Lisa Edelstein, Thomas Glass, Len Galla, Rob Cohen, Fred Bernstein, and Jayme Koszyn.

For production and editing help, thanks to Dave Ragsdale, Allegra Viner, Graham Sultan, Morgan Chase, Andy Lutz, Ellen Mendlow, Jason Kantor, Jeff Rubenstein, Ryan Tozzi, Jennifer Arias, Patricia Dublin, Maria Dente, and Stephen White. Special thanks to Doug Pierce and Faisel Alam for their patience, intelligence, and expertise, and to Christine Parker and Peter Hanink for sharing their wealth of knowledge on this project and for leading the Diagpalooza crew, who created the practice tests and drills. For help updating the practice tests, thanks to Gary Bedford, Aaron Murray, Adam Cherensky, Adam Cadre, Graham Sultan, Doug Pierce, Neill Seltzer, Jennyfer Bagnell, Lois Lake Church, Stephanie Reeves, and Mariwyn Curtin. Special thanks also to Suzanne Markert, whose editorial intelligence and patience kept us all sane and steady.

The Princeton Review would never have been founded without the advice and support of Bob Scheller. Bob's program, Pre-test Review, provides the best sort of competition; his fine results make us work all the harder.

Finally, we would like to thank the people who truly have taught us everything we know about the SAT: our students.

Special thanks to Adam Robinson, who conceived of and perfected the Joe Bloggs approach to standardized tests and many of the other successful techniques used by The Princeton Review.

CONTENTS

Foreword

Welcome to the 2006 edition of *Cracking the New SAT*. If you are concerned about the recent changes to the SAT, relax. We've worked hard to make sure you are holding the most up-to-date book on the new test. If you concentrate on the techniques and strategies in this book, you will perform well on the SAT.

The Princeton Review was founded more than 20 years ago, based on a very simple idea: The SAT is not a test of intelligence, aptitude, how good of a person you are, or how successful you will be in life. The SAT simply tests how well you take the SAT. And performing well on the SAT (new or old) takes skill—skill that can be learned like any other.

This isn't the first time the SAT has changed. After we published the first edition of this book back in 1986, it hit the *New York Times* bestseller list. A few years later, Educational Testing Service (ETS), the company that publishes the SAT, changed the test. And now the SAT has changed again, this time because ETS was confronted with the possibility that one of its largest customers—the University of California system—would no longer use the SAT in its admissions processes.

Just because the SAT has changed again in response to pressure from outside sources does not mean it's becoming a better test, however:

> **It still doesn't measure anything.** It measures neither intelligence nor the stuff you're learning in high school. It doesn't predict college grades as well as your high school grades do, and the new 25-minute mini-essay, scored in 60 seconds, will certainly not measure how well you write.

> **It still underpredicts the college performance of women, minorities, and disadvantaged students.** In other words, this test can make it tougher, not easier, for many of you to get into and pay for college. Historically, women have done better than men in college but worse on the SAT. For a test that is used to help predict performance in college, that's a pretty poor record.

> **It's still coachable in all the worst ways.** Students in our course for the old test were getting 140-point average improvements, and we expect scores to improve by more than 250 points on the new test. But effective preparation for this test is much less about learning math, writing, or reasoning than it is what it's always been: learning how to take the test itself. A good test would encourage you to read Shakespeare; this test wouldn't even consider him to be an especially gifted writer.

Your preparation starts here. We at The Princeton Review spend millions of dollars every year improving our methods and materials. We have dozens of teachers covertly taking each SAT to make sure nothing slips by us. Each time the test changes, we change with it, improving and crafting our techniques so they work better than ever. This time is no exception: We're ready for the new test and we'll get you ready too.

Cracking the New SAT incorporates our observations, techniques, and strategies, and gives you the latest information possible. If you read this book carefully and work through the problems and practice tests included in the book, not only will you be thoroughly versed in the format of the new SAT and the concepts it tests, you will also have a sound overall strategy and a powerful arsenal of test-taking skills that you can apply to whatever you encounter on test day.

In addition to the thorough review in the book itself, we've tied the *Cracking the New SAT* book to drills and tests on our website—**PrincetonReview.com**—to make the book even more efficient at helping you to improve your scores. Before doing anything else, be sure to go to **PrincetonReview.com/cracking** and follow the log-in instructions to get set up. Once you've registered, you'll receive the most up-to-date information on the new SAT, detailed score reports for the tests in this book, exercises that will reinforce our techniques, and the opportunity to score your essays. You'll also get access to great information on college admissions, online applications, and financing.

The more you take advantage of the resources we've included in this book and the online companion tools that go with it, the better you'll do on the test. Read the book carefully and learn our strategies. Take full-length practice tests under actual timed conditions. Perhaps even study with a friend to stay motivated.

This test is challenging, but you're on the right track. Relax and work hard, and you can reach the SAT scores that your first-choice colleges want. We'll be with you all the way.

Good luck!

Andy Lutz
Vice President
The Princeton Review

Get More from *Cracking the New SAT* By Using Our Free Online Tools

Buyers of this book receive access to the latest in interactive test-preparation tools. Go to **www.PrincetonReview.com/cracking** to register for all the free services we offer to help you improve your test score and find the right college. Once you've logged on, you'll be able to:

- **Learn Key Test-Taking Skills Through Distance Learning Tools**. Some of the key lessons of *Cracking the New SAT* will be even clearer after you've spent a few hours seeing and hearing them presented online.

- **Analyze Your Performance on the Tests in This Book**. By logging on to our website and submitting your answers to the practice tests in this book, you can get personalized score reports that will help you focus your energy on specific areas where you may need help.

- **Submit Your Own Essay for Grading.** For a small fee, you can submit one or more of your *Cracking the New SAT* Practice Test Essays to our LiveGrader™ service for scoring by readers trained to follow the same scoring process used on the real SAT. You'll get scores for the essay and a detailed report on how you can improve your writing to get a higher score next time!

- **Practice New Techniques with Online Drills**. Once you've learned a new technique or concept, you can take online drills to practice and to gauge your mastery.

- **Research and Apply to the Best Colleges for You**. Through PrincetonReview.com, our award-winning college search site, you can access our complete library of information about U.S. colleges, manage your application process, and even apply electronically to more than 800 colleges.

YOU'RE IN COMPLETE CONTROL

Here's what you'll see once you've registered:

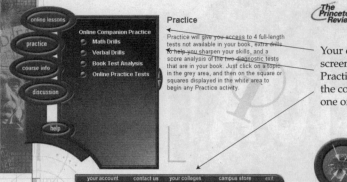

Your online tools are all brought together on one easy-to-use screen. Whether you're using the tests and drills located in the Practice area, the distance learning lessons in Online Lessons, or the college admissions tools in Your Colleges, you'll love every one of our well-organized online resources!

READING YOUR SCORE REPORT

After you take your extra practice exams, here's how to use your score report:

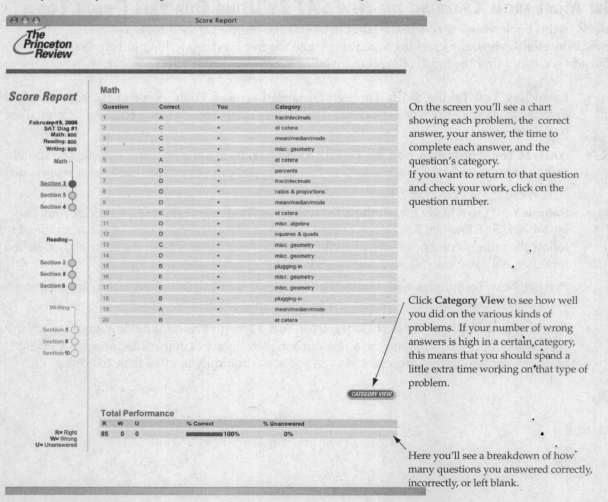

On the screen you'll see a chart showing each problem, the correct answer, your answer, the time to complete each answer, and the question's category.
If you want to return to that question and check your work, click on the question number.

Click **Category View** to see how well you did on the various kinds of problems. If your number of wrong answers is high in a certain category, this means that you should spend a little extra time working on that type of problem.

Here you'll see a breakdown of how many questions you answered correctly, incorrectly, or left blank.

PART **I**

Orientation

LET'S GET THIS PARTY STARTED!

You are about to unlock a vast repertoire of powerful strategies that have one and only one purpose: to help you get a better score on the SAT. This book contains the collected wisdom of The Princeton Review, which has spent over 20 years helping students achieve higher scores on standardized tests. We've devoted millions of dollars and years of our lives to cracking the SAT. It's what we do (twisted as it may be), and we want you to benefit from our expertise.

TO PREP OR NOT TO PREP?

Chances are you know someone who knows someone who scored a perfect or near-perfect score on the SAT without prepping. Yep, this friend-of-a-friend just walked into the test center and got a great score and now she's on her way to Harvard with a full scholarship. Hey, it *could* happen. But it's not a wise plan.

Would you show up for a basketball game or a swim meet if you'd missed every practice? Would you perform at a piano recital unprepared? Maybe you would consider it if you were a phenomenal athlete or a virtuoso—though even Michael Jordan and Mozart practiced. Yet thousands of students take the SAT each year without sufficient practice.

The SAT is a skill, and like any skill, it can be mastered. Unfortunately, many students assume that the SAT tests the same things as math or English class. However, this is not the case.

WHAT DOES THE SAT TEST?

Just because the SAT features math and reading problems, it does not mean that the test reflects what you learned in school. You can ace calculus or fancy yourself as the next William Faulkner, and still struggle with the SAT. The test writers claim that the test measures "reasoning ability," but actually, all the SAT measures is how well you take the SAT. It is most definitely *not* an intelligence test or an indicator of how good of a person you are.

IS THE SAT REQUIRED?

Many, but not all, colleges require the SAT. Even schools that don't usually recommend it because the test helps the colleges objectively compare applicants. For colleges, the SAT is an easy way of separating applicants. Large universities tend to place more importance on SAT scores, while smaller schools place slightly less importance on them.

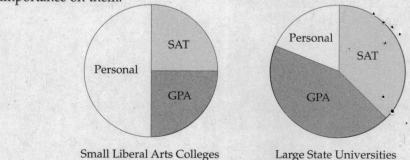

Small Liberal Arts Colleges   Large State Universities

Regardless of school size, your SAT score has a major impact on your college application. If your score falls well below that of the average applicant, the rest of your application will be more closely scrutinized. Think of the SAT as a first impression…and we all know what they say about first impressions.

WHO WRITES THE SAT?

Even though colleges and universities make extensive use of the SAT, they're not the ones who write the test. That task falls to the Educational Testing Service (ETS), a nonprofit company that is in the business of writing tests for college and graduate school admissions. ETS also writes tests for groups as diverse as butchers and professional golfers (who knew?).

ETS has oftentimes come under criticism for the SAT. Many educators argued that the test did not measure skills actually required for college. In fact, several years ago the University of California, one of the nation's largest university systems, decided that the SAT was an insufficient indicator for admissions. ETS scrambled to change the test. Hence, we have the "New" SAT.

THE NEW SAT

ETS unveiled the "New" SAT—which is really just a different test of how well you take the SAT—in 2005. The new test is almost an hour longer, requires you to write an essay, and tests grammar.

The New SAT (we'll just call it the SAT from now on) consists of:

- one 25-minute Essay section, requiring you to present your viewpoint on a topic

- two 25-minute Math sections, containing both multiple-choice questions and student-produced response questions (we call these "grid-ins")

- two 25-minute Critical Reading sections, made up of sentence completions and critical reading questions

- one 25-minute Writing section, containing error identification questions, improving sentences questions, and improving paragraphs questions

- one 20-minute Math section, including only multiple-choice questions

- one 20-minute Critical Reading section, again featuring sentence completions and critical reading questions

- one 10-minute Writing section focusing on improving sentences

- one 25-minute Experimental section on any of the above topics, other than the essay (there's no way to tell which section is the experimental, so treat every section as if it were scored)

SCORING ON THE SAT

You'll receive your score about two to four weeks after you take the test. The SAT is scored on a scale of 200 to 800, and each subsection—Math, Grammar, and Critical Reading—receives its own score. The three section scores are then totaled, for a combined score between 600 and 2400. The average SAT score is about a 500 per section, or a 1500 total.

You will also receive a percentile rank in addition to your scaled score. Your percentile rank tells you how you performed relative to others who have taken the test. If your score is in the sixtieth percentile, it means that you scored better than sixty percent of test takers.

One way of thinking of your SAT score is to imagine yourself in a line with 100 other students, all waiting to be seen by an admissions officer. However, the officer can't see every student—some students won't make it through the door. If your SAT score is in the fiftieth percentile, you'd have fifty other kids in front of you in line. Maybe you'll be seen, maybe not. Wouldn't it be nice to jump the line? If you can boost your SAT score, even by a couple of points, you move up the line and therefore increase your odds of being noticed.

This is where we come in. We can help you boost your score, move up in line, and ultimately increase your chances of being admitted to the college of your choice.

WHAT IS THE PRINCETON REVIEW?

The Princeton Review is the leader in test prep. Our goal is to help students everywhere crack the SAT. Ideally, we'd like the SAT to be eliminated altogether; we think the test is that bad. But until that happens, we'll content ourselves with aiding as many students as possible.

Starting from humble beginnings in 1981, The Princeton Review is now the nation's largest SAT preparation company. We give courses in over 500 locations and online, and publish best-selling books and software to get students ready for this test.

Our techniques work. We developed them after spending countless hours scrutinizing real SATs, analyzing them with computers, and proving our theories in the classroom. Our methods have been widely imitated, but no one achieves our score improvement.

THE PRINCETON REVIEW WAY

This book will show you how to crack the SAT by teaching you to:

- think like the test writers at ETS

- take full advantage of the limited time allowed

- find the answers to questions you don't understand by guessing intelligently

- avoid the traps that ETS has laid for you (and use those traps to your advantage)

Study

If you were getting ready to take a biology test, you'd study biology. If you were preparing for a basketball game, you'd practice basketball. So, if you're preparing for the SAT, study the SAT. ETS can't test everything (in fact, they test very little), so concentrate on learning what they *do* test.

ETS knows that our techniques work. For years, ETS claimed that the SAT couldn't be coached. But we've proven that view wrong, and ETS has struggled to find ways of changing the SAT so that The Princeton Review won't be able to crack it—in effect, acknowledging what our students have known all along: that our techniques really do work. The SAT has remained highly vulnerable to our techniques. And the "New" version of the SAT is even more susceptible to our methods. Read this book, work through the drills, take the practice tests, and you'll see what we mean.

HOW TO SCORE YOUR SAT PRACTICE TESTS

This book includes three practice tests. You can figure out your score on each of these tests with the same formula used by the College Board:

> # of questions you get correct –
> (# of questions you get incorrect ÷ 4) = Raw Score

The College Board then takes your raw score, along with the raw score of every other test taker in the country, and figures out a curve. Finally it assigns each raw score to a number on a scale of 200–800. This is your scaled score.

NOTE: Each test contains an unidentified, unscored, "experimental" section that varies from test to test. Questions from the experimental section are NOT included when calculating your raw or scaled scores.

To figure out your scaled score for each subject, use the scoring worksheet that follows every SAT practice test. Let's look at the subjects one at a time:

Writing

Step One   Count up the number of your correct answers for the two multiple-choice Writing sections. This is the number that goes in the first box.

Step Two   Count up the number of your incorrect answers for the multiple-choice Writing section. Divide this number by 4, and place this number in the second box.

Step Three   Subtract the second number from the first. This is your Raw Subscore. This is the number that goes in the third box.

Step Four   Look up the number from the third box in the Writing Multiple-Choice Subscore Conversion Table. This is your Scaled Subscore.

Step Five	The essay is scored on a scale from 2–12. It is based upon the score that two graders give you, each on a scale from 1–6. The number that you should put in the fourth box depends upon how it was scored. If your essay is self-graded on a 1–6 scale, then double that number so that it is from 2–12. If your essay was graded by The Princeton Review, then it already is on a 2–12 scale. Take your 2–12 grade and double it so that it is from 4–24. This is the number that goes in the fourth box.
Step Six	Add the fourth box to the third. This is your Raw Score. This number goes in the fifth box.
Step Seven	Look up the number from the fifth box in the SAT Score Conversion Table. This is your Scaled Score.

Critical Reading

Shortcuts

The Princeton Review's techniques are the closest thing there is to a shortcut to the SAT. However, there is no shortcut to learning these techniques.

Step One	Count up the number of your correct answers for the three Critical Reading sections of the test. This is the number that goes in the first box.
Step Two	Count up the number of your incorrect answers for the three Critical Reading sections of the test. Divide this number by 4. This is the number that goes in the second box.
Step Three	Subtract the second number from the first. This is your Raw Score. This is the number that goes in the third box.
Step Four	Look up the number from the third box in the SAT Score Conversion Table. This is your Scaled Score.

Math

Step One   Count up the number of correct grid-in answers. This is the number that goes in the first box.

Step Two   Count up the number of your correct answers for the multiple-choice questions in the three Math sections of the test. This is the number that goes in the second box.

Step Three   Count up the number of your incorrect answers for the multiple-choice questions in the three Math sections of the test. **Do NOT include any grid-in questions you may have answered incorrectly.** Divide this number by 4 and place this number in the third box.

Step Four   Subtract the third number from the second. This is your Raw Score. This is the number that goes in the fourth box.

Step Five   Look up the number from the fourth box in the SAT Score Conversion Table. This is your Scaled Score.

Are you ready? Let's get cracking!

Cracking the New SAT:
Basic Principles

HOW TO THINK ABOUT THE NEW SAT

Close your eyes for a moment and try to picture what goes on at ETS headquarters during a question-writing session. What images popped into your mind? If you imagined a room full of distinguished Nobel Prize-winning mathematicians and literary professors, you'd be way off base. If you saw some stuffy-yet-brilliant college professors, working hand-in-hand with the Department of Education, keep dreaming. How about a group of noble teachers and educators? Not even close.

The truth is that the SAT is written by a bunch of regular Joes whose jobs just happen to involve writing test questions. Why does this matter? Because you should always remember that the SAT is nothing special. It is simply a test. And with our help, you can master it.

WHAT ETS IS GOOD AT

The folks at ETS are quite good at writing standardized tests (it is their job, after all). They've been doing it for over 80 years, and they write tests for all sorts of programs. They have administered the test so many times that they know exactly how you will approach it. They know how you'll attack certain questions, what sort of mistakes you'll probably make, and even what answer you'll be most likely to pick. Kinda freaky, isn't it?

However, ETS's strength is also a weakness. Because the test is standardized, the SAT has to ask the same type of questions over and over again. Sure, the numbers or the words might change, but the basics don't. With enough practice, you can learn to think like ETS.

LEARN TO THINK LIKE ETS

Here's where we come in. This book will show you how to exploit the standardized format of the SAT. ETS uses the same tricks over and over again; once you become aware of them, you won't fall for them.

ETS also likes certain types of answers. If you notice, you aren't asked to pick the *correct* answer choice for each question on the SAT; instead, you are asked to select the *best* answer. What is the best answer? The best answer is simply what ETS says is the best answer. But don't worry, we'll tell you how to find it.

THE SAT ISN'T SCHOOL

Our job isn't to teach you math or English—leave that to your most knowledgeable and beloved school teachers. Instead, we're going to teach you the SAT. You'll soon see that the SAT involves a very different skill set.

Be forewarned that some of the approaches we're going to show you will seem weird or unnatural. In fact, if you tried to pull some of this stuff off in school, your teacher wouldn't be amused. But you must trust us. Try tackling the problems using our techniques, and keep practicing until they become easier. You'll see a real improvement in your score.

Now let's take a look at those techniques and get down to business.

CRACKING MULTIPLE-CHOICE QUESTIONS

What's the capital of Malawi?

Give up?

Unless you spend your spare time studying an atlas, you may not even know that Malawi is a tiny country in Africa, much less what its capital is. If this question came up on a test, you'd have to skip it, wouldn't you? Well, maybe not. Let's turn this question into a multiple-choice question—just like all the questions on the SAT Critical Reading and Grammar sections, and the majority of questions you'll find on the SAT Math section—and see if you can figure out the answer anyway.

1. The capital of Malawi is

    (A) Washington, D.C.
    (B) Paris
    (C) Tokyo
    (D) London
    (E) Lilongwe

The question doesn't seem that hard anymore, does it? Of course, we made our example extremely easy. (By the way, there won't actually be any questions about geography on the SAT.) But you'd be surprised by how many people give up on SAT questions that aren't much more difficult than this one just because they don't know the correct answer right off the top of their heads. "Capital of Malawi? Oh, no! I've never heard of Malawi!"

These students don't stop to think that they might be able to find the correct answer simply by eliminating all of the answer choices they know are wrong.

YOU ALREADY KNOW ALMOST ALL OF THE ANSWERS

All but a handful of the questions on the SAT are multiple-choice questions, and every multiple-choice question is followed by five answer choices. On every single multiple-choice question, one of those choices, and only one, will be the correct answer to the question. You won't have to come up with the answer from scratch. You only have to identify it.

How will you do that?

LOOK FOR THE WRONG ANSWERS INSTEAD OF THE RIGHT ONES

Why? Because wrong answers are usually easier to find. Remember the question about Malawi? Even though you didn't know the answer off the top of your head, you easily figured it out by eliminating the four obviously incorrect choices. You looked for wrong answers first.

In other words, you used the Process of Elimination, which we'll call POE for short. This is an extremely important concept, one we'll come back to again and again. It's one of the keys to improving your SAT score. When you finish reading this book, you will be able to use POE to answer many questions that you don't understand.

A Moral Dilemma

What if someone approached you moments before the SAT began and offered to give you the answers to the test? You'd be shocked. SHOCKED! Right? But what if we told you that the person making the offer was the proctor running the test? The fact is that every student who takes the test gets to see virtually all of the answers: They're printed in the test booklet, right underneath each question.

The great artist Michelangelo once said that when he looked at a block of marble, he could see a statue inside it. All he had to do to make a sculpture, he said, was to chip away everything that wasn't part of it. You should approach difficult SAT multiple-choice questions in the same way, by chipping away everything that's not correct. By first eliminating the most obviously incorrect choices on difficult questions, you will be able to focus your attention on the few choices that remain.

THIS ISN'T THE WAY YOU'RE TAUGHT TO THINK IN SCHOOL

SAT ≠ School

If the SAT is not like the tests you take in high school, then why do colleges want you to take it? Good question.

In school, your teachers expect you to work carefully and thoroughly, spending as long as it takes to understand whatever it is you're working on. They want you to prove not only that you know the answer to a question, but also that you know how to derive it. When your algebra teacher gives you a test in class, he or she wants you to work through every problem, logical step by logical step. You probably even have to show your work. If you don't know all the steps required to arrive at the solution, you may not receive full credit, even if you somehow manage to come up with the correct answer.

But the SAT is different. It isn't like school. You don't have to prove that you know why your answer is correct. The only thing ETS's scoring machine cares about is the answer you come up with. If you darken the right space on your answer sheet, you'll get credit, even if you didn't quite understand the question.

PROCESS OF ELIMINATION (POE)

There won't be many questions on the SAT in which incorrect choices will be as easy to eliminate as they were on the Malawi question. But if you read this book carefully, you'll learn how to eliminate at least one choice on virtually any SAT multiple-choice question, if not two, three, or even four choices.

What good is it to eliminate just one or two choices on a five-choice SAT question?

Plenty. In fact, for most students, it's an important key to earning higher scores. Here's another example:

2. The capital of Qatar is

(A) Paris
(B) Dukhan
(C) Tokyo
(D) Doha
(E) London

On this question you'll almost certainly be able to eliminate three of the five choices by using POE. That means you're still not sure of the answer. You know that the capital of Qatar has to be either Doha or Dukhan, but you don't know which.

Should you skip the question and go on? Or should you guess?

CLOSE YOUR EYES AND POINT

You've probably heard a lot of different advice about guessing on multiple-choice questions on the SAT. Some teachers and guidance counselors tell their students never to guess and to mark an answer only if they're absolutely certain that it's correct. Others tell their students not to guess unless they are able to eliminate two or three of the choices.

Both of these pieces of advice are incorrect.

Even ETS is misleading about guessing. Although it tells you that you *can* guess, it doesn't tell you that you *should*. In fact, if you can eliminate even one incorrect choice on an SAT multiple-choice question, guessing blindly from among the remaining choices will most likely improve your score. And if you can eliminate two or three choices, you'll be even more likely to improve your score by guessing.

THERE IS NO GUESSING PENALTY ON THE SAT

ETS tries to discourage students from guessing on multiple-choice questions by telling them that there is a "guessing penalty" in the way the test is scored. But this is not true. There is no penalty for guessing on the SAT. Even if you can't eliminate any of the choices, random guessing isn't going to hurt your score in the long run.

Your raw score is the number of questions you got right, minus a fraction of the number you got wrong (except on the grid-ins, which are scored a little differently). Every time you answer an SAT question correctly, you get one raw point. Every time you leave an SAT question blank, you get zero raw points. Every time you answer an SAT question incorrectly, ETS subtracts one-fourth of a raw point if the question has five answer choices, or nothing if it is a grid-in.

It is the subtracted fraction that ETS refers to as the "guessing penalty." But it's nothing of the sort. An example should help you understand.

Raw scores are a little confusing, so let's think in terms of money instead. For every question you answer correctly on the SAT, ETS will give you a dollar. For every multiple-choice question you leave blank, ETS will give you nothing. For every multiple-choice question you get wrong, you will have to give twenty-five cents back to ETS. That's exactly the way raw scores work.

What happens to your score if you select the correct answer on one question and incorrect choices on four questions? Remember what we said about money: ETS gives you a dollar for the one answer you guessed correctly; you give ETS a quarter for each of the four questions you missed. Four quarters equal a dollar, so you end up exactly where you started, with nothing—which is the same thing that would have happened if you had left all five questions blank.

In Fact, There's a Guessing Reward

Now, what if you were able to eliminate one incorrect choice on each of four questions? Random odds say you would get one question right—get a dollar—and miss the next three questions—give back 75 cents. You've just gained a quarter! In other words, there would be a guessing reward. All you would have to do to earn this reward is eliminate one choice, close your eyes, and take a shot.

Let's recap: If you eliminate nothing and guess, you break even (earn a dollar, give back four quarters). If you eliminate one or more answer choices, you gain points. So why would anyone hesitate to guess?

One of the most common misconceptions about the SAT is that you're better off leaving a multiple-choice question blank than "taking a chance" on getting it wrong. Some students even believe that they could earn a perfect score on the test by answering just four or five questions correctly and leaving all the others blank. They think they won't lose any points unless they give an answer that is actually wrong.

Nothing could be further from the truth.

In order to earn the highest scores on the SAT, you have to mark an answer for nearly every question, and just about every question you mark has to be correct. If you leave just one question blank in a Math section, for instance, the best Math score you can hope for is 780 or 790; if you leave forty questions blank, then the best score you can get is 400.

Why This Is True

Let's use money again to illustrate why this is true. When you take the SAT, you start the test with the equivalent of $2,400 ($800 Math, $800 Critical Reading, and $800 Writing) in the bank. If you answer all the questions on each section correctly, you get to keep all $2,400.

For every question you answer incorrectly, though, you lose $10. Now, here's the important part: For every question you leave blank, you still lose $8.

Because of the way ETS calculates raw scores on the SAT, an incorrect answer is only a tiny bit worse than a blank. The one thing you can be certain of is that if you leave a question blank, you are definitely going to lose $8, whereas if you guess, you have the possibility of keeping $10. If you guess incorrectly, you'll lose just $2 more than you would have if you hadn't guessed at all. And if you guess correctly, you'll get to keep your money. That's not much of a gamble, is it?

Credit for Partial Information

We hope we've been able to persuade you that guessing on multiple-choice questions isn't going to hurt you and that, if you learn to do it well, it will help you raise your score. If you're like most people, though, you probably still feel a little funny about it. Earning points for a guess probably seems a little bit like cheating or stealing: you get something you want, but you didn't do anything to earn it.

This is not a useful way to think about the SAT. It's also not true. Look at the following example:

3. The sun is a

    (A) main-sequence star
    (B) meteor
    (C) asteroid
    (D) white dwarf star
    (E) planet

If you've paid any attention at all in school for the past ten years or so, you probably know that the sun is a star. You can easily tell, therefore, that the answer to this question must be either A or D. You can tell this not only because it seems clear from the context that "white dwarf" and "main-sequence" are kinds of stars—as they are—but also because you know for a fact that the sun is not a planet, a meteor, or an asteroid. Still, you aren't sure which of the two possible choices is correct.

HEADS, YOU WIN A DOLLAR; TAILS, YOU LOSE A QUARTER

By using POE you've narrowed down your choice to two possibilities. If you guess randomly you'll have a fifty-fifty chance of being correct, like flipping a coin—heads you win a dollar, tails you lose a quarter. Those are extremely good odds on the SAT. But let's say that, in spite of everything we've told you, you just can't bring yourself to guess. You decide to leave the question blank.

Now, let's say there is a guy sitting next to you who is, to put it politely, no rocket scientist. When it comes to this question, he has no idea what the sun is: planet, asteroid, meteor—he's clueless. So he leaves the question blank, too.

Even though you know more about the sun than this guy, you both earn exactly the same score: zero. According to the SAT, you don't know any more about the sun than he does. (The answer, by the way, is A. And don't worry, there won't be any questions about astronomy on the SAT.)

If you were in class, this probably wouldn't happen. Your teacher might give you credit for knowing that the sun is some kind of star. In math class, your teacher probably gives you partial credit on a difficult problem if you set it up correctly, even if you make a silly mistake and get the wrong answer.

GUESSING INTELLIGENTLY WILL INCREASE YOUR SCORE

Guessing makes it possible to earn credit for partial information on the SAT. You won't know everything about every question on the test, but there will probably be a lot of questions about which you know something. Doesn't it seem fair that you should be able to earn some sort of credit for what you *do* know? Shouldn't your score be higher than the score of someone who doesn't know anything?

Of course, there are times you shouldn't guess. We will discuss these in the next chapter. However, if you spend any time working on a problem, you deserve to take a shot at the answer and possibly get credit. Guessing is only unfair if you don't do it—unfair to you, that is. Your SAT score won't be a fair indication of what you know unless you guess and earn some credit for partial information.

TEXTBOOK GRAFFITI

Write Now

Feel free to write all over this book, too. You need to get in the habit of making the SAT booklet your own. Start now by writing the names of the colleges you really want to attend in the margin below.

NUI Galway

University College Cork

University College Dublin

Brown

Weslyan

BU

At school you probably aren't allowed to write in your textbooks, unless your school requires you to buy them. You probably even feel a little peculiar about writing in the books you own. Books are supposed to be read, you've been told, and you're not supposed to scrawl all over them.

Because you've been told this so many times, you may be reluctant to write in your test booklet when you take the SAT. Your proctor will tell you that you are supposed to write in it—the booklet is the only scratch paper you'll be allowed to use; it says so right in the instructions from ETS—but you may still feel bad about marking it up.

DON'T BE RIDICULOUS!

Your test booklet is just going to be thrown away when you're finished with it. No one is going to read what you wrote in it and decide that you're stupid because you couldn't remember what 2 + 2 was without writing it down. Your SAT score won't be any higher if you don't make any marks in your booklet. In fact, if you don't take advantage of it, your score will probably be lower than it should be.

OWN YOUR TEST BOOKLET

You paid for your test booklet; act as though you own it. Scratch work is extremely important on the SAT. Don't be embarrassed about it. After all, writing in your test booklet will help you keep your mind on what you're doing.

- When you work on a geometry problem that provides a diagram, don't hesitate to write all over it. What if there's no diagram? Draw one yourself—don't simply try to imagine it. Keep track of your work directly on the diagram to help you avoid making careless mistakes.

- On sentence completion questions, you will often need to come up with your own word or two to help you answer a question. Write it down! Trying to retain information in your head leads to confusion and errors. Your test booklet is your scratch paper—use it.

- When you use POE to eliminate a wrong answer choice, physically cross off the answer choice in your test booklet. Don't leave it there to confuse you. You may often need to carefully consider two remaining answer choices. You want to be clear about which answer choices are left in the running.

- When you answer a question but don't feel entirely certain of your answer, circle the question or put a big question mark in the margin beside it. That way, if you have time later on, you can get back to it without having to search through the entire section.

You probably think of scratch paper as something that is useful only in arithmetic. But you'll need scratch paper on the SAT Critical Reading and Grammar sections, too. The Critical Reading sections of your booklet should be just as marked up as the Math ones.

TRANSFER YOUR ANSWERS AT THE END OF EACH GROUP

Scratch work isn't the only thing we want you to do in your test booklet. We also want you to mark your answers there. In the Sentence Completion sections, you should transfer your answers to the answer sheet when you come to the end of each group of questions. You should transfer your answers one page at a time in the Math, Grammar, and Critical Reading sections.

Doing this will save you a great deal of time, because you won't have to look back and forth between your test booklet and your answer sheet every few seconds. You will also be less likely to make mistakes in marking your answers on the answer sheet. However, be sure to give yourself enough time to transfer your answers. Don't wait until the last five minutes.

The only exception to this are the grid-ins, the ten non–multiple-choice math questions. You will need to grid each answer as you find it. We'll tell you all about grid-ins later in the book.

Mark Your Answer

When you take the SAT, you should mark all your answers in your test booklet, with a big letter in the margin beside each problem, and then transfer them later onto your answer sheet.

BASIC PRINCIPLES SUMMARY

1. When you don't know the right answer to a multiple-choice question, look for wrong answers instead. They're usually easier to find.

2. When you find a wrong answer choice, eliminate it. In other words, use POE, the Process of Elimination.

3. ETS doesn't care if you understand the questions on the SAT. All it cares about is whether or not you darken the correct space on your answer sheet.

4. There is no guessing penalty on the SAT. In fact, there is a guessing reward. If you can eliminate just one incorrect choice on an SAT multiple-choice question, you will most likely improve your score by guessing from among the remaining choices.

5. Leaving a question blank costs you almost as many points as answering it incorrectly.

6. Intelligent guessing on multiple-choice questions enables you to earn credit for partial information.

7. Do not hesitate to use your test booklet for scratch paper.

8. Transfer your answers to your answer sheet all at once when you reach the end of each group of questions in the Sentence Completion sections and one page at a time in the Math, Grammar, and Critical Reading sections (except for the grid-ins). And remember, give yourself enough time to transfer your answers; don't wait until the last five minutes.

CRACKING THE NEW SAT: BASIC PRINCIPLES ◆ 17

Cracking the New SAT: Advanced Principles

PUTTING THE BASIC PRINCIPLES TO WORK

In the preceding chapter, we reviewed some basic principles of the SAT. We showed you that it is possible to:

- find correct answers by using POE, the Process of Elimination, to get rid of incorrect choices
- take advantage of the SAT's "guessing reward"
- earn credit for partial information

But how will you know which answers to eliminate? And how will you know when to guess? In this chapter, we'll begin to show you. We will teach you how to:

- take advantage of the order in which questions are asked
- make better use of your time by scoring the easy points first
- use the Joe Bloggs principle to eliminate obviously incorrect choices on difficult questions
- find the traps that ETS has laid for you
- turn those traps into points

To show you how this is possible, we first have to tell you something about the way the SAT is arranged.

ORDER OF DIFFICULTY

If you have already taken a practice SAT, you may have noticed that the questions seem to get harder as each section progresses. This is not an accident; ETS purposely arranges the questions this way. Why? There are a couple of reasons.

First, starting students with easy questions can lead to a false sense of security. Chances are, after nailing the first three or four questions you start to think that you've got the test beat. That's exactly when ETS starts throwing some traps into the questions for the unwary or overconfident.

Second, the hard questions are the end of the section, when you have less time left. Knowing this, you may rush through the beginning of the section, making careless mistakes, just to get to the difficult and frustrating questions at the end.

Easy, Medium, Difficult

Think of each section as being divided into thirds. A third of the questions should be easy. Most test takers get these questions right. Another third of the questions are of medium difficulty. About half of the people taking the test get these questions right. The final third of the questions are difficult. Very few test takers answer these questions correctly.

The Math sections always follow this order of difficulty; thus, in a 20-question Math section, the first seven questions are easy, the next six are medium, and the final seven are difficult. Sentence completions follow a similar pattern, but unfortunately, questions in the Critical Reading and Writing sections are all jumbled up—they follow no particular order of difficulty.

THE PRINCETON REVIEW DIFFICULTY METER

Before you attack any SAT question, it is important to check out how difficult the question is. To remind you to do this, we will precede each math and sentence completion question in this book with The Princeton Review Difficulty Meter.

The Difficulty Meter divides each group of questions into thirds to indicate which questions are easy, which are medium, and which are hard. Before you begin working on an example, check the question number against the Difficulty Meter to determine how hard the question is.

Here's how the Difficulty Meter would look for a set of eight sentence completions:

SENTENCE COMPLETIONS		
1 2 3	4 5 6	7 8 **9**
EASY	MEDIUM	HARD

HOW WILL THIS HELP MY SCORE?

Knowing the difficulty level of a question can help you in several ways. Most importantly, it helps you make the best use of your time. Although in terms of difficulty the questions are definitely *not* created equally, each and every single question earns you exactly *one* point. ETS wants you to waste your time on the difficult questions, while missing easy points. Don't play their game. Do the easiest questions first, get as many points as you can, and then move on to the harder questions.

Furthermore, understanding the difficulty level of a question can help you to figure out ETS's trap answers. In order to do this, we first have to delve into the mind of a typical SAT test taker.

THE IMPORTANCE OF FEELING GOOD

The SAT is a timed test, and ETS doesn't give you a lot of time to work through every question. Plus, there's a tremendous amount of anxiety associated with taking the test. In a situation such as this, many students rely on a sense of what "feels" right when answering questions. Many times an answer choice just seems to scream out, "Pick me!"—and most students happily oblige. The problem is, in many of these cases, ETS is hoping you'll fall for a trap.

Easy to Be Hard

Remember, the SAT isn't a huge intellectual challenge; it's just tricky. When we talk about difficult questions on the SAT, we mean ones that people most often get wrong. Get your hands on an old SAT and look at some of the difficult math questions. Do any of them test anything you didn't learn in high school? Probably not. But do they all resemble the kind of straightforward questions you're used to seeing on a regular test? Probably not. ETS specializes in confusing and misleading test takers.

Rule #1
Answer easy questions first; save hard questions for last.

SHOULD YOU EVER PICK AN ANSWER THAT "FEELS" RIGHT?

Well, that depends on the difficulty level of the question (see, this whole discussion was leading somewhere). Consider this:

Rule #2

Easy questions tend to have easy answers; hard questions tend to have hard answers.

- On easy multiple-choice questions, ETS's answers seem right to high scorers, and right to virtually everyone: high scorers, low scorers, and average scorers.

- On medium questions, ETS's answers seem right to high scorers, wrong to low scorers, and sometimes right and sometimes wrong to average scorers.

- On hard questions, ETS's answers seem right to high scorers and wrong to everyone else.

When doing an easy question, you can trust your gut. But once you hit the medium and difficult questions, the answer that "feels right" is no longer the best answer.

MEET JOE BLOGGS

The "average test taker" always goes with his (or her) gut when taking the SAT. We've seen this average test taker so often that we've decided to give him a name: Joe Bloggs. Joe is the quintessential (good vocabulary word) American high school student. He has average grades and average SAT scores. There's a little bit of him in everyone, and there's a little bit of everyone in him. He isn't brilliant. He isn't dumb. He's just average.

And he's ETS's dream student.

HOW DOES JOE BLOGGS APPROACH THE SAT?

Joe Bloggs *always* trusts his gut. Regardless of the difficulty level of the question, he picks the answer that feels right. And of course, he ends up getting most of the easy questions right, about half of the medium questions right, and almost none of the difficult questions right. That makes ETS very happy.

Here's an example of hard question. Let's see how Joe tackles it:

20. Graham walked to school at an average speed of 3 miles an hour and jogged back along the same route at 5 miles an hour. If his total traveling time was 1 hour, what was the total number of miles in the round trip?

(A) 3

(B) $3\frac{1}{8}$

(C) $3\frac{3}{4}$

(D) 4

(E) 5

WHICH ANSWER DID JOE PICK?

This question is a number 20, meaning that it is one of the hardest questions in the section. Only about one student in ten answered this question correctly, and Joe certainly did not get it right. Can you guess which answer was screaming out for Joe to pick it? It was answer choice D, the choice that feels right. Joe read the question, looked at the numbers, and did some figuring. Unfortunately, Joe assumes that Graham spends exactly half the time traveling at 3 mph and the other half at 5 mph. Calculating the distance, he arrives at 4, exactly as ETS wanted him to do.

But hard questions never have easy answers. Joe didn't realize that the trip couldn't possibly take the same time in both directions (otherwise, the distance between his home and school would change). In the heat of the moment, Joe made a quick assumption and went right for the trap answer.

COULD ETS HAVE MADE THIS QUESTION EASIER?

Yes, by writing different answer choices.

Here's the same question with choices we have substituted to make the correct answer obvious:

1. Graham walked to school at an average speed of 3 miles an hour and jogged back along the same route at 5 miles an hour. If his total traveling time was 1 hour, what was the total number of miles in the round trip?

    (A) .01

    (B) .1

    (C) $3\frac{3}{4}$

    (D) 1,000

    (E) 10,000

When the problem is written this way, Joe Bloggs can easily see that the answer has to be C. It seems right to Joe, because all of the other answers seem obviously wrong.

Remember:

- An SAT question is easy if the correct answer seems correct to the average person—to Joe Bloggs.

- An SAT question is hard if the correct answer seems correct to almost no one.

THE JOE BLOGGS PRINCIPLE

When you take the SAT a few weeks or months from now, you'll have to take it on your own, of course. But suppose for a moment that ETS allowed you to take it with Joe Bloggs as your partner. Would Joe be of any help to you on the SAT?

YOU PROBABLY DON'T THINK SO

After all, Joe is wrong as often as he is right. He knows the answers to the easy questions, but so do you. You'd like to do better than average on the SAT, and Joe earns only an average score (he's the average person, remember). All things considered, you'd probably prefer to have someone else for your partner.

But Joe might turn out to be a pretty helpful partner, after all. Since his hunches are always wrong on difficult multiple-choice questions, couldn't you improve your chances on those questions simply by finding out what Joe wanted to pick, and then picking something else?

If you could use the Joe Bloggs principle to eliminate one, two, or even three obviously incorrect choices on a hard problem, couldn't you improve your score by guessing among the remaining choices?

ETS's Favorite Wrong Answers

Take another look at question 20. Answer choice D was included to lure Joe Bloggs into a trap. But it isn't the only trap answer choice. Other tempting choices are A and E. Why? Because they are numbers included in the question itself, and Joe Bloggs is most comfortable with familiar numbers. When ETS selects wrong answers to hard questions, it looks for three things:

1. The answer you'd get doing the simplest possible math. In this case, that's D.

2. The answer you'd get after doing some, but not all, of the necessary math.

3. Numbers that are already in the question itself (choices A and E).

ETS doesn't use all of these every time, but there's at least one in every set of difficult answer choices.

How to Navigate with a Broken Compass

If you were lost in the woods, would it do you any good to have a broken compass? It would depend on how the compass was broken. Suppose you had a compass that always pointed south instead of north. Would you throw it away? Of course not. If you wanted to go north, you'd simply see which way the compass was pointing and then walk in the opposite direction.

Joe Bloggs Is Like That Broken Compass

On difficult SAT questions, he always points in the wrong direction. If Joe Bloggs were your partner on the test, you could improve your chances dramatically just by looking to see where he was pointing, and then going a different way.

We're going to teach you how to make Joe Bloggs your partner on the SAT. When you come to difficult questions on the test, you're going to stop and ask yourself, "How would Joe Bloggs answer this question?" And when you see what he would do, you are going to do something else. Why? Because you know that on hard questions, Joe Bloggs is always wrong.

What if Joe Bloggs Is Right?

Remember what we said about Joe Bloggs at the beginning. He is the average person. He thinks the way most people do. If the right answer to a hard question seemed right to most people, the question wouldn't be hard.

Joe Bloggs is right on some questions: the easy ones. But he's always wrong on the hard questions.

Putting Joe Bloggs to Work for You

In the chapters that follow, we're going to teach you many specific problem-solving techniques based on the Joe Bloggs principle. The Joe Bloggs principle will help you:

- use POE to eliminate incorrect answer choices
- make up your mind when you have to guess
- avoid careless mistakes

The more you learn about Joe Bloggs, the more he'll help you on the test. If you make him your partner on the SAT, he'll help you find ETS's answers on problems you never dreamed you'd be able to solve.

Joe's Hunches

Should you always just eliminate any answer that seems to be correct? No! Remember what we said about Joe Bloggs:

1. His hunches are correct on easy questions.
2. His hunches are sometimes correct and sometimes incorrect on medium questions.
3. His hunches are always wrong on difficult questions.

On easy multiple-choice questions, pick the choice that Joe Bloggs would pick. On hard questions, be sure to eliminate the choices that Joe Bloggs would pick.

BECAUSE THIS IS SO IMPORTANT, WE'RE GOING TO SAY IT AGAIN

Here's a summary of how Joe Bloggs thinks:

Question Type	Joe Bloggs Looks For	Joe Bloggs Selects	Time Joe Spends	How Joe Does
Easy	the answer	the one that seems right	very little	mostly right
Medium	the answer	the one that seems right	not much	so-so
Difficult	the answer	the one that seems right	too much	all wrong!

YOU HAVE TO PACE YOURSELF

Rule #3

Any test taker scoring below 700 on either the Math section or the Critical Reading will hurt his or her score by attempting to answer every question.

There are some very difficult questions on the SAT that most test takers shouldn't even bother to read. On the difficult third of every group of questions, there are some questions that almost no one taking the test will understand. Rather than spending time beating your head against these questions, you should enter a guess quickly and focus your attention on questions that you have a chance of figuring out.

Since most test takers try to finish every section ("I had two seconds left over!"), almost every test taker hurts his or her score. The solution, for almost anyone scoring less than 700 on a section, is to slow down.

Most test takers could improve their scores significantly by attempting fewer questions and devoting more time to questions they have a chance of answering correctly. Slow down, score more.

SET THE RIGHT GOAL BEFOREHAND

It's very important to set realistic goals. If you're aiming for a 500 on the Critical Reading section, your approach to the SAT is going to be different from that of someone who is aiming for an 800. The following charts will give you some idea of what you realistically need to know in order to score at various levels on the SAT. Use the chart to gauge your progress as you work through practice tests like those in this book or in *11 Practice Tests for the New SAT & PSAT*.

Now before you decide you must get a 700 in Critical Reading no matter what, do a reality check: To date, what have you scored on the Critical Reading SAT? The Writing section? The Math? Whatever those numbers are, add 50–90 points to each to determine your goal score. Then get cracking! Work through this book, practice the techniques, and, after a time, take a timed practice test. If you achieve your goal score on the practice test, great! Could you have worked a little more quickly yet maintained your level of accuracy? If so, increase your goal by another 50 points.

In other words, you must set an attainable goal in order to see any improvement. If you scored a 400 on the last Math SAT you took, and you immediately shoot for a 700, you will be working too quickly to be accurate, and won't see any increase in your score. However, if you instead use the "460–500" pacing guide, you may jump from a 400 to a 480! After that you can work to score over a 500, etc.

Come back to these pages after each practice test you take to reassess your pacing strategy. Remember, accuracy is more important than speed. Finishing is not the goal; getting questions right is! Besides, all the hard problems are at the end. If you are missing easy questions due to your haste to get to the difficult questions, you are throwing points away.

By the way, you may notice that the following three charts present slightly different pacing strategies for the Math, Critical Reading, and Grammar sections. That's because on the Math section, it's even more important to take as much time as you need to get each problem right, rather than furiously working through absolutely every problem on the test. The numbers of questions listed in the charts represent how many questions you should do, not how many you need to get right.

Rule #4

Remember, accuracy is more important than speed.

MATH PACING CHART

To get (scaled score)	You need to earn: (raw points)	Attempt this many questions				
		20-question section	10-question section	Grid-Ins	15-question section	Total # of questions to attempt
350	7	6	2	2	2	12
400	12	7	3	3	4	17
450	19	9	4	4	6	23
500	25	11	5	5	8	29
550	32	14	6	6	10	36
600	38	16	6	7	13	42
650	44	18	7	8	15	48
700	47	all	all	9	all	53
750	52	all	all	all	all	54
800	54	all	all	all	all	54

CRITICAL READING PACING CHART

To get (scaled score)	You need to earn: (raw points)	Attempt this many questions			Total # of questions to attempt
		25-question section	25-question section	15-question section	
300	5	4	4	1	9
350	9	5	5	3	13
400	14	7	7	4	18
450	21	10	10	6	26
500	29	15	15	7	37
550	38	18	18	10	46
600	46	22	22	11	55
650	53	23	23	14	60
700	59	24	24	16	64
750	63	all	all	all	67
800	67	all	all	all	67

GRAMMAR PACING CHART

To get (scaled score)	You need to earn: (raw points)	Attempt this many questions		Total # of questions to attempt
		35-question section	14-question section	
35	5	10	5	15
40	11	13	7	20
45	17	18	8	26
50	22	22	9	31
55	27	26	10	36
60	31	27	11	38
65	36	31	all	45
70	40	all	all	49
75	44	all	all	49
80	49	all	all	49

ESTIMATED WRITING SCORES

If your scaled grammar score is	Depending on your essay score, your writing score will range from
40	280–500
45	300–540
50	340–580
55	380–620
60	420–660
65	460–710
70	510–750
75	540–780
80	650–800

ADVANCED PRINCIPLES SUMMARY

1. The problems in almost every group of questions on the SAT start out easy and gradually get harder. The first question in a group is often so easy that virtually everyone can find ETS's answer. The last question is so hard that almost no one can.

2. Because number one is true, you should never waste time trying to figure out the answer to a hard question if there are still easy questions that you haven't tried. All questions are worth the same number of points. Why not do the easy ones first?

3. Almost every group of questions on the SAT can be divided into thirds by difficulty as follows:

   - On the easy third of each group of questions, the average person gets all the answers right. The answers that seem right to the average person actually are right on these questions.

   - On the medium third of each group, the average person's hunches are right only some of the time. Sometimes the answers that seem right to the average person really are right; sometimes they are wrong.

   - On the difficult third, the average person's hunches are usually wrong. The answers that seem right to the average person on these questions invariably turn out to be wrong.

4. Joe Bloggs is the average student. He earns an average score on the SAT. On easy SAT questions, the answers that seem correct to him are always correct. On medium questions, they're sometimes correct and sometimes not. On hard questions, they're always wrong.

5. On hard questions, Joe Bloggs is your partner. Decide what Joe would do, then *do something else*. Cross off Joe Bloggs answers to increase your potential for guessing correctly.

6. Most test takers could improve their scores significantly by attempting fewer questions and devoting more time to questions they have a chance of answering correctly.

7. It's very important to set realistic goals. If you're aiming for a 500 on Critical Reading, your approach to the SAT is going to be very different from that of someone who is aiming for an 800.

8. After each practice exam, go back to the pacing chart. You may need to answer more questions on the next exam to earn the score you want.

WHAT DOES THE CRITICAL READING SECTION

PART $\mathbf{II}$

How to Crack the
Critical Reading Section

A FEW WORDS ABOUT WORDS

The SAT contains ten sections. Three of these will be Critical Reading sections.

Each of the three scored Critical Reading sections on the SAT contains two types of questions: sentence completions and critical reading. In sentence completion questions, you'll be given an incomplete sentence, along with several possible ways to complete it. In critical reading questions, you will be given a passage to read, followed by a series of questions asking you about the passage.

WHAT DOES THE CRITICAL READING SECTION TEST?

ETS says that the Critical Reading section tests "verbal reasoning abilities" or "higher order reasoning abilities." You may be wondering exactly what these statements mean, but don't sweat it—they're not true anyway. Critical reading questions test your ability to read and your familiarity with certain words. Strong vocabulary will help you understand what you are reading and allow you to write stronger essays. If you have a big vocabulary, you'll probably do well on the exam. If you have a small vocabulary, you'll have more trouble no matter how many techniques we teach you.

The best way to improve your reading is by practicing reading. Even certain periodicals—newspapers and some magazines—can improve your verbal performance if you read them regularly. Keep a notebook and a dictionary by your side as you read. When you encounter words you don't know, write them down, look them up, and try to incorporate them into your life. The dinner table is a good place to throw around new words.

Most of us have to encounter new words many times before we develop a firm sense of what they mean. You can speed up this process a great deal by taking advantage of Chapter 7, "Vocabulary." It contains a short list of words that are very likely to turn up on the SAT, a section on word roots, and some general guidelines about learning new words. If you work through it carefully between now and the time you take the test, you'll have a much easier time on the Critical Reading section. The more SAT words you know, the more our techniques will help you.

Read through Chapter 7 and sketch out a vocabulary-building program for yourself. You should follow this program every day, at the same time that you work through the other chapters of this book.

The techniques described in the other three Critical Reading chapters that follow are intended to help you take full advantage of your growing vocabulary by using partial information to attack hard questions. In a sense, we are going to teach you how to get the maximum possible mileage out of the words you know. Almost all students miss SAT questions that they could have answered correctly if only they had used our techniques.

Read What You Like

Some folks think it's necessary to read nothing but books on obscure subjects in order to build a better vocabulary. Not true. Identify something that interests you and find some books on that subject. You'll be spending time on something you enjoy, and hey, you just might learn something.

Joe Bloggs and the
Critical Reading Section

JOE BLOGGS AND THE CRITICAL READING SECTION

Joe Bloggs will be a big help to you on the Critical Reading section. Keep Joe Bloggs in mind as you take the SAT, and you will assuredly increase your score. Let's look at how you can use Joe on the Critical Reading sections.

JOE BLOGGS AND ORDER OF DIFFICULTY

The Critical Reading sections of the SAT contain two question types: sentence completions and critical reading. As we mentioned before, only the sentence completions follow a definitive order of difficulty. In general, the harder sentence completions test harder vocabulary words. Of course, there's no such thing as a "hard" word or an "easy" word—just words you know and words you don't know. Your best defense against Joe Bloggs answer choices is to increase your vocabulary.

A Reminder

On easy questions, the answers that seem right to Joe really are right; on hard questions, the answers that seem right to Joe are wrong.

No matter how many words you learn, though, you'll still run across words you don't know on the sentence completions. Not to worry: Joe Bloggs can once again guide you to the right answer. Here's an example of a difficult sentence completion:

SENTENCE COMPLETIONS

1 2 3 4 5 6 7 **8**
EASY   MEDIUM   HARD

8. The researchers believe their experimental and observational data furnish the ------- evidence that proves their hypothesis.

(A) trifling
(B) theoretical
(C) intuitive
(D) empirical
(E) microscopic

Analysis

This is a hard question. Only about eight percent of test takers answer it correctly. More than twice as many of them would have answered it correctly if they had simply closed their eyes and picked one of the choices at random. Why did the vast majority of test takers—including, of course, our friend Joe Bloggs—do so poorly on this question? They all fell into a cleverly laid trap.

Joe reads the sentence and sees that it is about scientists and hypotheses. Instantly, certain words and images spring into his mind. Joe starts looking through the answers for a word commonly associated with science, and he is immediately drawn to choices B and E. Hey, science experiments have to start with a theory, right? And scientists need microscopes to do their experiments, right? Yeah, that's the ticket....

Don't think like Joe! On hard questions, eliminate any choice or choices that you know will be attractive to Joe. We'll tell you more about how to do this as we go along. (Incidentally, the correct answer to this question is D.)

CAN JOE HELP ME ON CRITICAL READING PASSAGES?

Even though the critical reading passages don't have a strict order of difficulty, knowing how Joe Bloggs approaches this type of question will help you avoid traps and careless mistakes.

When Joe answers a critical reading question, he tends to answer from memory. He doesn't go back to the passage to verify his answer. In the Critical Reading chapter (Chapter 5), you'll learn the best way of approaching these problems. Keep in mind that the Princeton Review approach for finding the right answers is practically the opposite of the Joe Bloggs approach. Make sure you use our approach, not Joe's.

PUTTING JOE TO WORK ON THE CRITICAL READING SAT

Generally speaking, the Joe Bloggs principle teaches you to:

- trust your hunches on easy questions
- double-check your hunches on medium questions
- eliminate Joe Bloggs answers on difficult questions

The next few chapters will teach you how to use your knowledge of Joe Bloggs to add points to your SAT score.

Bloggs Magnets

Joe is irresistibly drawn to easy answer choices containing words that remind him of the question. Therefore, on hard sentence completions, you can eliminate such choices.

Sentence Completions

SAT SENTENCE COMPLETIONS: CRACKING THE SYSTEM

Sentence completions are sentences from which one or two words have been removed. Your job is to find the missing word or words. How will you do this? By finding the clue ETS has left for you in the sentence. Each sentence completion contains one or more clues that will tell you what goes in the blank(s). All you have to do is find the clues, and you've cracked the question.

MEMORIZE THE INSTRUCTIONS

Before we begin, take a moment to read the following set of instructions and answer the sample question that comes after it. Both appear here exactly as they do on the real SAT. Be certain that you know and understand these instructions before you take the SAT. If you learn them ahead of time, you won't have to waste valuable seconds reading them on the day you take the test.

Level of Difficulty

Set of Eight
1–3 Easy
4–6 Medium
7–8 Difficult

Each sentence below has one or two blanks, each blank indicating that something has been omitted. Beneath the sentence are five words or sets of words labeled A through E. Choose the word or set of words that, when inserted in the sentence, <u>best</u> fits the meaning of the sentence as a whole.

Example:

Medieval kingdoms did not become constitutional republics overnight; on the contrary, the change was -------.

(A) unpopular   (B) unexpected   (C) advantageous
    (D) sufficient   (E) gradual

Ⓐ Ⓑ Ⓒ Ⓓ ●

ETS's answer to this sample question is E.

Sentence completions appear in each of the test's Critical Reading sections. The questions will be arranged in groups of eight, six, and five sentences. Regardless of the number of sentence completions in a section, the questions will follow a rough order of difficulty: The first third will be easy and the last third will be the most difficult.

Because our techniques vary depending on the difficulty of the question, we have placed a Difficulty Meter before each example. Look at the meter to determine how hard the example is. And remember, the harder the question, the more you should doubt the obvious, Joe Bloggs answer choices.

Let's begin with an easy question. Try the following example. The answer choices have been removed so you can concentrate solely on the sentence. Read the sentence, look for the clue, and decide which word goes in the blank.

SENTENCE COMPLETIONS

① 2 3 4 5 6 7 8

EASY   MEDIUM   HARD

1. Even though it is a dead language, rather than fading away, Latin is now being -------.

Analysis

What word did you come up with? Probably something like *rediscovered* or *restored*. How did you decide that was the word that you needed? Because of the clue. The clue in the sentence is *rather than fading away*. It tells us that Latin is doing the opposite of *fading away*, like making a comeback.

Now that you have decided on the kind of word that goes in the blank, look at the following answer choices. Cross off the answers that are not close to yours (ones that don't mean *rediscovered* or *restored*), and pick the best answer.

(A) forgotten
(B) excavated
(C) mortified
(D) revitalized
(E) revealed

Answer choices A and C are out right away. You may find it hard to choose among B, D, and E, but think about which is closest to your word. Can a language be dug up? Not really, so get rid of B. Has Latin been hidden? No, so get rid of E.

The credited response is D.

But Why?

You may be wondering why we didn't just plug each answer into the sentence to see which one sounded right. That's because *all* the answers are designed to *sound* right. Look back to the question we just did. The sentence would sound just fine if you plugged in any one of those answer choices. But only one of them is ETS's answer.

More importantly, plugging each word into the sentence is how Joe Bloggs would solve the question. Does Joe get all sentence completion questions correct? No way. Joe doesn't know that ETS has given him a clue in the sentence that tells him exactly what the answer is. He just plugs in choices and takes a guess.

You, on the other hand, know the inside scoop. In each sentence, ETS must include a clue that reveals the answer. If it didn't, no one would agree on the right answer (there wouldn't *be* a right answer) and lots of people would sue.

CLUELESS

The following two examples will further illustrate what we've been talking about. The first is a sentence completion that has no clue. The second is virtually the same sentence, except with ETS's clue added. Which one of the following is easier?

I. The woman told the man, "You're very -------."

    (A) rich
    (B) correct
    (C) preposterous
    (D) cloistered
    (E) sick

II. The doctor told the man, "You're very -------."

    (A) rich
    (B) correct
    (C) preposterous
    (D) cloistered
    (E) sick

As you can see, questions I and II are identical, with the exception of a single word. And yet that word makes all the difference in the world. In question I, several of the choices are possible. In fact, this question cannot be answered (don't worry—you won't have one like this on the SAT). But in question II, the word *doctor* makes the answer E. The key word *doctor* determines ETS's answer.

ETS will put a clue in every sentence to indicate what goes in the blank. Find it! Once you do, use it to determine the missing word or words. Don't rely on the answer choices—ETS makes them as attractive as possible, so that the Joe Bloggses of the world get caught by trying to find an answer that sounds right. How can you avoid getting caught in the "sounds right" trap?

COVER UP

Sentence Completion Rule #1

Cover the answer choices until you come up with your own word.

Cover the answer choices before you begin each sentence completion. Place your hand (or your answer sheet) over the five answer choices so that you are not tempted to look at them too soon. Then, read the sentence and find ETS's clue. Decide what you think the word in the blank should be, and then use POE to get to ETS's answer.

Try another example:

4. The onset of the earthquake was gradual, the tremors occurring ------- at first, then with greater frequency.

Here's How to Crack It

The clue in any sentence completion is always a short, descriptive phrase that tells you what word goes in the blank. What is the clue in this sentence? Two things give you the full picture: *gradual* and *then with greater frequency.* Since we know the earthquake came on gradually and that the tremors later came with greater frequency, we can assume that the tremors occurred *infrequently* or *gradually* at first.

Now that you have a target word, use POE to get to ETS's answer:

(A) continuously
(B) intensely
(C) sporadically
(D) unexpectedly
(E) chronically

The only word that comes close to meaning *infrequently* or *gradually* is C, *sporadically.* This is ETS's answer.

GET A CLUE

Try the following example. Before you begin, cover up the answer choices. Then read the sentence and underline the clue. Fill in the blank with your own word, then use POE to get to ETS's answer.

```
SENTENCE COMPLETIONS
1  2  3  ④  5  6
EASY  MEDIUM  HARD
```

4. Some developing nations have become remarkably
   wealthy ------, using aid from other countries to build
   successful industries.

(A) populous
(B) dry
(C) warlike
(D) prosperous
(E) isolated

Here's How to Crack It

The clue in this sentence is *build successful industries*. It indicates that some nations "have become remarkably *successful*."

Let's look at each answer choice for a word that's close to *successful*:

(A) Does *populous* mean *successful*? No. Cross off this answer.
(B) Does *dry* mean *successful*? Not at all. Cross it off.
(C) Does *warlike* mean *successful*? Nope. Ditch it.
(D) Does *prosperous* mean *successful*? Sure does.
(E) Does *isolated* mean *successful*? Nope. Ditch it.

ETS's answer must be D.

SEARCHING FOR CLUES

If you are having trouble finding the clue, ask yourself two simple questions about each sentence:

1. What is the blank talking about?

2. What *else* does the sentence say about this?

For example, look back to the question we just did. What is the blank talking about? Some nations. What else does the sentence say about the nations? They were able to *build successful industries*. This must be the clue of the sentence because it refers to the same thing the blank refers to.

Find and underline the clue in the following sentence. Then fill in the blank with your own word. If you have any trouble, ask:

1. What is the blank talking about?

2. What *else* does the sentence say about its subject?

1. Shaquille O'Neal is such a physically intimidating basketball player that his opponents focus on his ------- and thus underestimate his surprising quickness.

Analysis

What is the blank talking about? Shaquille O'Neal. What else does the sentence say about Shaquille O'Neal? He is a *physically intimidating basketball player*. Therefore, his opponents focus on his *large size*.

PICK A WORD, ANY WORD

The word you come up with to fill the blank doesn't have to be an elegant word, or a hard word, or the perfect word. It doesn't even have to be a word; instead, it can be a phrase—even a clunky phrase—as long as it captures the correct meaning.

In an episode of *The Simpsons*, a lawyer couldn't think of the word *mistrial*, so he asked the judge to declare a "bad court thingie." *Bad court thingie* is an accurate enough substitute for *mistrial* on the SAT. With *bad court thingie* as your "word," POE will get you to *mistrial*.

RECYCLE THE CLUE

Instead of coming up with a different word for the blank, you can often just recycle the clue. If you can put the clue itself in the blank, you can be sure that you've put your finger on ETS's answer.

Is the blank always the same as the clue? Sometimes the blank is exactly the same, while other times it is exactly the opposite. You must use the rest of the sentence to determine if the blank and the clue are the same or opposite. In other words, you must be on the lookout for "trigger words."

TRIGGER WORDS

Very often on sentence completions, the most important clue to ETS's answer is a trigger word: a single revealing word or expression that lets you know exactly where ETS is heading. About half of all SAT sentence completions contain trigger words. Combining trigger words with your clue makes filling in the blank a breeze.

Trigger words can either change the direction the sentence is going in or keep it the same. The most important change-direction trigger words are *but, though,* and *although*. These are words that "change the direction" of a sentence. The most important same-direction trigger words are *and* and *because*. These are words that maintain the direction of a sentence.

Change-direction trigger words are more common on the SAT than same-direction trigger words. Both provide terrific clues that you can use to find ETS's answer. To see what we mean, take a look at the following incomplete sentences. For each one, fill in a few words that complete the thought in a plausible way. There's no single correct answer. Just fill in something that makes sense in the context of the entire sentence:

I really like you, *but*_____.

I really like you, *and*_____.

Here's how one of our students filled in the blanks:

I really like you, *but I'm going to leave you.*

I really like you, *and I'm going to hug you.*

Analysis

In the first sentence, the word *but* indicates that the second half of the sentence will contradict the first half. Because the first half of the sentence is positive, the second half must be negative. I like you, *but* I'm going to leave you. The sentence "changes direction" after the trigger word *but*.

If you were directing *Romeo and Juliet*, you'd have to hold auditions in order to find actors. You wouldn't look at all the actors in the world before reading the play, would you? For the role of Juliet, you'd be looking for someone suited to the part. Everybody else would be sent packing.

Sentence completions are the same. You have to read the sentence first and decide what kind of word would fit best *before* you look at the answer choices available. Then, like the director, you would pick the answer choice that is most like what you want and eliminate the ones that are different.

In the second sentence, the word *and* indicates that the second half of the sentence will confirm or support the first half. Because the first half of the sentence is positive, the second half must be positive as well. I like you, *and* I'm going to hug you. In this case, the sentence continues in the same direction after the trigger word *and*.

OTHER TRIGGERS

Two other same-direction triggers to look for include punctuation triggers, particularly colons and semicolons, and time triggers. Punctuation triggers are important becase they divide the sentence into two pieces: one part with the blank and one without. Most of the time, the part that does not contain the blank is the clue to what kind of word belongs in the blank. Time triggers denote a change in the sentence with a passage of time and help you fill in the blank with the proper word.

DRILL 1

Circle the trigger word (if there is one) and underline the clue in each of the following sentences. Then, write your own word in the blank. If you have trouble finding the clue, ask yourself, "What is the blank talking about?" and "What else does the sentence say about this?" Don't worry if you can't think of a single, perfect word for the blank; use a phrase that catches the meaning. Once you've finished these questions, go on to Drill 2 and use POE to find ETS's answer. Answers can be found on page 336.

1. Because theaters refused to show it when it was first released, *Citizen Kane* was ------- failure, though now it is considered one of the greatest American films ever made.

6. Ironically, many of the family-owned small businesses located in the newly revitalized neighborhood downtown are so threatened by increasing rents that they may be ------- by the very economic redevelopment that the city has pursued for so long.

7. When will Hollywood directors stop producing technically slick but emotionally ------- movies and begin creating films filled with authenticity and poignancy?

DRILL 2

Here are the same questions, this time with the answer choices. Refer to your notes from Drill 1 and make a choice for each question. Remember to use POE. Answers can be found on page 336.

1. Because theaters refused to show it when it was first released, *Citizen Kane* was ------- failure, though now it is considered one of the greatest American films ever made.

   (A) a revolutionary
   (B) a personal
   (C) a commercial
   (D) an aesthetic
   (E) a perennial

6. Ironically, many of the family-owned small businesses located in the newly revitalized neighborhood downtown are so threatened by increasing rents that they may be ------- by the very economic redevelopment that the city has pursued for so long.

   (A) buttressed
   (B) bankrupted
   (C) hindered
   (D) ameliorated
   (E) relieved

7. When will Hollywood directors stop producing technically slick but emotionally ------- movies and begin creating films filled with authenticity and poignancy?

   (A) polished
   (B) vacuous
   (C) rich
   (D) sophisticated
   (E) unrefined

AND THEN THERE WERE TWO

About half of all sentence completions contain two blanks. Many students fear these questions because they look long and intimidating. But two-blank sentence completions are no more difficult than single-blank sentence completions. The key is to take them one blank at a time.

To crack two-blank sentence completions, read the sentence, circling the trigger word(s) and underlining the clue(s), keeping in mind that there may be a clue for *each* blank. Then fill in whichever blank seems easier to you. Once you have filled in one of the blanks, go to the answer choices and check just the words for that blank, using POE to get rid of answers that are not close to yours. Then go back to the other blank, fill it in, and check the remaining choices. You do not need to check both words at one time. If one of the words doesn't work in a blank, then it doesn't matter what the other word is. One strike and the answer is out.

When eliminating answers, draw a line through the entire answer choice. That way you won't get confused and check it again when you are checking the other blank. Even if you do fill in both blanks the first time you read the sentence, only check one blank at a time. It is much easier to concentrate on one word than on a pair of words. Sometimes you'll be able to get rid of four choices by checking only one blank, and you won't even need to check the other blank.

Here's an example of a two-blank sentence completion:

SENTENCE COMPLETIONS
1 2 3 4 **5** 6 7 8
EASY   MEDIUM   HARD

5. While the ------- student openly questioned the teacher's explanation, she was not so ------- as to suggest that the teacher was wrong.

    (A) complacent . . suspicious
    (B) inquisitive . . imprudent
    (C) curious . . dispassionate
    (D) provocative . . respectful
    (E) ineffectual . . brazen

Here's How to Crack It

Let's start with the first blank. The clue is *openly questioned*, and we can simply recycle the clue and put *questioning* in the blank. Now let's take a look at the first-blank words in the answer choices and eliminate any words that are definitely not a good match for *questioning*. Eliminate choices A and E because *complacent* and *ineffectual* have nothing to do with *questioning*. All we want to do at this point is eliminate any words that are way off base. Then we can move on to the second blank.

The clue for the second blank is *suggest that the teacher was wrong*. How would you describe a student who accuses the teacher of being wrong? *Bold* or *rude*, maybe? Look at the remaining choices and get rid of any second words that don't mean something like *bold* or *rude*. C is out—*dispassionate* does not mean *bold* or *rude*. Also, D is out, since this student is anything but *respectful*. ETS's answer must be B.

Notice that we only had to eliminate one of the words in each answer choice in order to get rid of the entire choice. Attacking this question using POE also made it easier because we could eliminate four answers without much trouble. If four answers are wrong, the one that's left must be ETS's answer.

Shoe Store

If you were shopping for shoes and found a pair you liked, you'd ask the clerk to bring you a pair in your size to try on. Say you tried the right shoe first. If it felt horrible, would you even bother to try the left shoe on? No, because even if the left shoe was comfy, you'd have to wear it with the right shoe, which you already know causes you unspeakable pain. You would look for another pair of shoes. Two-blank sentence completions are like shoes. If one doesn't fit, there's no point trying the other one. Half bad is all bad.

THE TRICKY ONES

Every now and then, the clue for one of the blanks in a two-blank sentence completion turns out to be the other blank. What? How can ETS get away with making the clue a *blank*?

Don't worry—if ETS has decided to use one blank as the clue for the other blank, you know it has inserted another way for you to find the answer. Let's look at an example:

6. Most of Rick's friends think his life is unbelievably
   -------, but in fact he spends most of his time on
   ------- activities.

    (A) fruitful . . productive
    (B) wasteful . . useless
    (C) scintillating . . mundane
    (D) varied . . sportive
    (E) callow . . simple

Here's How to Crack It

The trigger word in this sentence is *but*. We gather from the sentence that most of Rick's friends think his life is one way, but in fact it is another. We cannot tell if his friends think his life is great and busy while it's really lousy and slow, or vice versa. However, we do know that our blanks are opposites: the first is positive while the second is negative *or* the first is negative while the second is positive.

Knowing this is enough to get us to ETS's answer. Let's look at each answer choice, keeping in mind that we need a pair of words that are opposites:

    (A) *Fruitful* is positive, *productive* is positive.
        Eliminate this choice.
    (B) *Wasteful* is negative, *useless* is negative. Cross
        it off.
    (C) *Scintillating* is positive, *mundane* is negative.
        Keep it.
    (D) *Varied* is positive, *sportive* is positive. Cross it
        off.
    (E) *Callow* is negative, *simple* is neutral. A
        possibility, but not great.

ETS's answer is C: Rick's life may look *scintillating*, but he spends most of his time on *mundane* activities. If the clue of one of the blanks is the other blank in a two-blank sentence completion, look for the trigger word and determine the relationship between the blanks. Then use POE to find ETS's answer.

Vocab

Don't eliminate words you've never seen before or cannot readily define. Or, in the words of Bob Dylan, "Don't criticize what you can't understand."

ARE YOU A GOOD WORD OR A BAD WORD?

Notice in the last example that we didn't use *words* to fill in the blanks; instead, we looked for positive and negative. On difficult sentence completions, you may find it hard to determine what the word in the blank is supposed to be. However, you will usually have an idea if that word should be a good word (something positive) or a bad word (something negative). Knowing whether a blank is positive or negative can help you eliminate answer choices. If you are unable to come up with your own word, use + or – to get rid of answers and make smart guesses.

Here's an example:

```
        SENTENCE COMPLETIONS
    1  2  3  4  5  6  7  8
      EASY      MEDIUM   HARD
```

8. Ruskin's vitriolic attack was the climax of the
   ------- heaped on paintings that today seem
   amazingly -------.

   (A) criticism . . unpopular
   (B) ridicule . . inoffensive
   (C) praise . . amateurish
   (D) indifference . . scandalous
   (E) acclaim . . creditable

Here's How to Crack It

A Gentle Reminder

Your aim is to eliminate wrong answers. Get rid of as many incorrect choices as you can, guess from among the remaining choices, and then move on.

A *vitriolic* attack is something bad (and so is simply an *attack*, if you don't know what *vitriolic* means). The climax of a vitriolic attack must also be bad, and therefore the first blank must be a bad word. Already we can eliminate choices C and E (and possibly choice D). We don't have to worry about the second word in these answer choices because we already know that the first word is wrong.

Now look at the second blank. The first part of the sentence says that Ruskin thought the paintings were very bad; today, *amazingly*, they seem—what? Bad?

No! The word in the second blank has to be a *good* word. Choices C and E are already crossed out. We can now also eliminate choices A and D (without bothering to look at the first words again) because the second blank words are bad words. The only choice left is B—ETS's answer. You've correctly answered a very hard question simply by figuring out whether the words in ETS's answer were good or bad. Not bad!

The good-word/bad-word method is also helpful when you have anticipated ETS's answer but haven't found a similar word among the choices. Simply decide whether your anticipated answer is positive or negative, then determine whether each of the answer choices is positive or negative. Eliminate the choices that are different, and you'll find ETS's answer.

WHAT ABOUT JOE?

As you know, the last few questions in each group of sentence completions will be quite difficult. On these hard questions, you will find it useful to remember the Joe Bloggs principle and eliminate choices that you know would attract Joe. Here's an example:

keeping out

5. The policy of benign ------- was based upon the assumption that citizens were better off when the government kept out of their daily affairs.

    (A) regulation
    (B) engagement
    (C) neglect
    (D) democracy
    (E) coercion

Here's How to Crack It

Joe Bloggs is attracted to choices containing words that remind him of the subject matter of the sentence. The words in sentence that Joe notices are *citizens* and *government*—words relating to politics. Which answers attract his attention? Choices A and D. You can therefore eliminate both.

What's the clue in this sentence? It's the phrase *kept out of their daily affairs*. By recycling the clue, you can anticipate the correct answer: "The policy of benign *keeping out of citizens' daily affairs* was based on...." Which answer choice could mean something similar to that? Only C, *neglect*.

How Hard Is It?

Let's assume you've tried everything: You've looked for the clue and trigger, tried to anticipate ETS's answer, eliminated the Joe Bloggs answers, and used the good-word/bad-word technique. You still can't find ETS's answer. What should you do?

Remember order of difficulty: Easy questions have easy answers and hard questions have hard answers. Joe Bloggs tends to avoid choices containing words whose meaning he doesn't understand. As a result, we can be fairly certain that on easy questions (which Joe gets right) ETS's answer will contain easy words. However, on hard questions (which Joe gets wrong) ETS's answer will contain hard words, ones that Joe would never pick.

And an easy word will usually not be ETS's answer on a hard question.

When you come down to the wire and need to guess on the hardest couple of sentence completions, simply pick the hardest choice—the one with the weirdest, most difficult words. Eliminate any choice whose word or words you can define, and guess from among what's left. No problem!

Important!

Eliminating Joe Bloggs attractors should always be the first thing you do when considering answer choices on a hard sentence completion. If you don't eliminate them immediately, you run the risk of falling for them as you consider the various choices.

DRILL 3

The following two questions contain only the answer choices—not questions—from tough sentence completions. These are both numbers eight out of eight—in other words, the hardest problems in the section. Practice your POE skills by eliminating the easy answer choices, then guess the hardest, weirdest answer choices. Answers can be found on page 336.

Answers can be found on page 336.

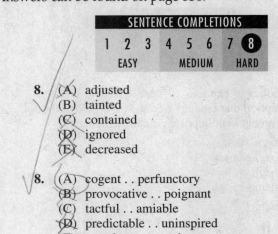

8. (A) adjusted
   (B) tainted
   (C) contained
   (D) ignored
   (E) decreased

8. (A) cogent . . perfunctory
   (B) provocative . . poignant
   (C) tactful . . amiable
   (D) predictable . . uninspired
   (E) mundane . . trenchant

DRILL 4

Putting It All Together

Take all the techniques you've learned and put them into practice. Don't forget to underline your clues and circle your triggers! The numbers reflect where in the section each question would appear. Answers can be found on page 338.

Answers can be found on page 338.

2. Instead of being ------- by piles of papers, some college admissions officers are trying to ------- the application process by utilizing computers to simplify the procedure.

   (A) hindered . . facilitate
   (B) bolstered . . retard
   (C) disappointed . . arrest
   (D) quickened . . accelerate
   (E) offended . . innovate

5. In National Park Ranger Nevada Barr's novel *Blind Descent*, the ------- must rescue the endangered victim of a ------- caving accident.

   (A) adventurer . . secondary
   (B) philanderer . . fictional
   (C) protagonist . . perilous
   (D) globetrotter . . coincidental
   (E) adversary . . hazardous

Easy to Be Hard

How to exploit the order of difficulty on sentence completions:

1. On easy questions, be very suspicious of hard choices.
2. On hard questions, be very suspicious of easy choices.

6. Weather conditions can cause leaves to appear so ------- that they resemble ------- human skin.

- (A) lustrous . . opaque
- (B) verdant . . scarred
- (C) ashen . . sanguine
- (D) wizened . . withered
- (E) obsolete . . nascent

7. The nonprofit organization was searching for a ------- new employee, one who would courageously support the goals of the organization and become devoted to helping other people.

- (A) querulous
- (B) novice
- (C) proficient
- (D) magnanimous
- (E) lavish

SENTENCE COMPLETIONS SUMMARY

1. Cover the answer choices. Learn to anticipate ETS's answer by filling in each blank before you look at the answer choices. If you look at the answer choices first, you will often be misled.

2. Always look for the clue—the key word or words that you need to fill in the blank(s)—and underline it.

3. If you have trouble finding the clue, ask yourself:

   - What is the blank talking about?

   - What else does the sentence say about this subject?

4. Look for trigger words—revealing words or expressions that give you important clues about the meanings of sentences—and circle them. The most important negative trigger words are *but*, *though*, and *although*. These are words that "change the direction" of a sentence. The most important positive trigger words are *and* and *because*. These are words that maintain the direction of the sentence.

5. Fill in the blank with any word or phrase that will help you get to ETS's answer. Don't worry if you need to use a clunky or an awkward phrase. If you can, recycle the clue. If you can't come up with any words for the blank, use + or –. Use POE to get to ETS's answer.

6. Attack two-blank sentence completions by focusing on one blank at a time. Use the same techniques you would use on one-blank questions. If you can eliminate either word in an answer choice, you can cross out the entire choice. If the clue for one of the blanks is the other blank, use the trigger word to determine the relationship between the blanks.

7. Never eliminate a choice unless you are sure of its meaning.

8. Eliminate Joe Bloggs answers. On difficult questions, Joe is attracted to answers containing easy words that remind him of the subject matter of the sentence. Learn to recognize these words and be extremely suspicious of the answer choices in which they appear.

9. Take advantage of the order of difficulty. Easy sentence completions have easy answers, hard ones have hard answers. If you can do nothing else on a hard sentence completion, simply pick the choice with the hardest or weirdest words.

Critical Reading

SAT CRITICAL READING: CRACKING THE SYSTEM

The majority of points you can score on the Critical Reading section of the SAT (over two thirds of them) are, unsurprisingly, from critical reading questions. You'll be given a reading passage, followed by a series of questions directly relating to the passage.

Critical reading questions come in two formats: short (under 50 lines) and long (over 50 lines). While you should approach them the same way, short passages tend to have more general questions, whereas long passages tend to have more specific questions. In this chapter, we're going to focus on long passages.

1. Read for what you need.
2. Eliminate answer choices that could not possibly be correct.
3. Take advantage of your common sense.
4. Use your inside knowledge (about how ETS thinks).
5. Make better use of your limited time by skipping a difficult passage.

MEMORIZE THE INSTRUCTIONS

Before we begin, take a moment to read the following set of instructions, which appears exactly as it does on the real SAT.

> The passage below is followed by questions based on its content. Answer the questions following each passage on the basis of what is <u>stated</u> or <u>implied</u> in that passage and in any introductory material that may be provided.

Be sure that you know and understand these instructions before you take the SAT. If you learn them ahead of time, you won't have to waste valuable seconds reading them on the day you take the test.

JUST THE QUESTIONS, PLEASE

The least important part of critical reading is the passage. No, really. The name of the section implies that you will be doing lots of reading, but it doesn't tell you that most of the reading you'll be doing is of the questions. Critical reading is *not* about learning something new and interesting—it's about scoring points by answering questions correctly.

Many students have difficulty with critical reading because they place too much emphasis on the passage and not enough on the questions. In actuality, you could probably answer many questions more effectively if you never read the passage at all.

Look at the following question. Without so much as a glance at a passage, use your common sense and knowledge of ETS to cross off impossible answers. Then take a guess at ETS's answer.

The Fact Bank

Somebody once asked notorious thief Willie Sutton why he robbed banks. "Because that's where the money is," he replied. While cracking critical reading is safer and slightly more productive than larceny, the same principle applies: Concentrate on the questions and answer choices because that's where the points are. The passage is just a place for ETS to stash facts and details. You'll find them when you need to. What's the point of memorizing all 67 pesky details about plankton if ETS only asks you about 12?

18. The author believes that federal judges can sometimes be criticized for

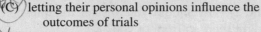

(A) failing to consider the meaning of the law
(B) ignoring the rights of defendants
(C) letting their personal opinions influence the outcomes of trials
(D) slowing the flow of court cases by caring too much about the requirements of justice
(E) forgetting that the Constitution is the foundation of the American legal system

Here's How to Crack It

The question wants to know what an *ETS author* might criticize a federal judge for. The answer, of course, is "not much." ETS is a very pro-American, pro-justice system organization. ETS is very careful to be respectful of the right people.

Let's look at each answer choice to see if it is possible:

(A) Could ETS criticize federal judges for "failing to consider the meaning of the law"? A federal judge doesn't consider the law? Not likely. This answer is not possible because it would never happen. Even though you have no idea what this passage is about, you can cross off this answer choice.

(B) Could ETS criticize federal judges for "ignoring the rights of defendants"? Another unlikely practice of a federal judge. Even if *you* have a jaded opinion of our federal legal system, ETS doesn't. This answer is not possible—cross it off.

(C) Could ETS criticize federal judges for "letting their personal opinions influence the outcomes of trials"? Although this answer seems a little more plausible, it's still pretty unlikely. Federal judges represent the epitome of impartiality, at least according to ETS. Keep it for now, but it is unlikely.

(D) Could ETS criticize federal judges for "slowing the flow of court cases by caring too much about the requirements of justice"? What a laudable error, huh? ETS could criticize them for this honorable mistake. Lookin' good as a choice.

(E) Could ETS criticize federal judges for "forgetting that the Constitution is the foundation of the American legal system"? Would a federal judge simply *forget* about the Constitution? Not likely. Cross this off.

Of the two choices remaining, the most reasonable guess is D. It is also ETS's answer.

GOOD ANSWER

You just answered a critical reading question correctly without ever seeing the passage it was associated with. What does that tell you about critical reading questions? It tells you that there's a lot more to answering a critical reading question than reading the passage. In fact, reading the passage is the least important part of answering critical reading questions.

Will you be answering lots of questions without reading the passage? No, for two reasons: 1) It takes longer to answer a question when you have no knowledge of the passage, and 2) Why should you answer the question this way when all the answers are right there in front of you?

OPEN-BOOK TEST

Critical reading is nothing more than an open-book test. If your history teacher tells you that Friday's exam is going to be an open-book test, what's your reaction? Most people do the "this is gonna be easy" dance when they are told that all the info they need to know will be right in front of them. Okay, you can sit down now.

Well, critical reading is exactly the same as an open-book test. What's more, you only have to scan a few paragraphs to find your answers. For each critical reading passage, you will do the following:

1. **Read What You Need.** Do a topic search so that you have a clue about the passage's topic and organization.

2. **Translate the Question.** Reword each question so you know exactly what you are being asked.

3. **Put Your Finger on the Answer.** Go back to the passage and find the exact location of the answer you are looking for.

4. **Answer the Question in Your Own Words.** Answer the question in your own words before you read any of the answer choices.

5. **Use POE.** Get rid of answers that are not close to yours.

SAMPLE PASSAGE AND QUESTIONS

Here is an example of what a critical reading passage and questions look like. We will use this passage to illustrate critical reading techniques. You may want to stick a paper clip on this page to make it easier to flip back to it.

Questions 16–21 are based on the following passage.

The following passage about the Mexican Revolution examines the interchange of power among various rebel leaders.

Revolutionaries can sometimes be their own worst enemies; such was certainly the case with the leaders of the Mexican Revolution. They began
Line their revolt by forcing General Porfirio Díaz into
5 exile in May of 1911. For the next seventeen years, control of the government passed from one rebel to the next as eight different leaders seized political power. Only one succeeded; the rest were either assassinated or exiled.
10   Díaz was the first to go. His dictatorship began in 1884, extended over four decades, and had seven successive, falsified re-elections. By the end of 1910, the economic deprivation and governmental exploitation that marked his reign had pushed the
15 population over the edge. Despite his attempts to secure power by eliminating all opponents, rebel forces led by Fransisco Madero surrounded Díaz and forced Díaz's exile into France. A provisional president was appointed until the October election,
20 which Madero won with 98 percent of the vote.
   Madero did not, however, maintain popular support; instead, his constituents criticized his attempts to ease the sufferings of farmers and urban workers, despite his best efforts to redistribute
25 the land and respond to increased strikes. An additional difficulty originated in the growing disparity between revolutionary factions. Each region within Mexico had its own concerns, with key issues including anti-clericalism, agrarian
30 reform, and educational goals and policies. Madero had initially received support and encouragement from the peasant rebel leader Emiliano Zapata. But, when the latter had reason to believe that Madero's interest in land and labor reform was not strong
35 enough, he became a prominent faction against the president's regime. In February of 1913, Zapata joined with other rebels and arrested the president. Only a few days later, Madero was killed in what most people believe to be an assassination. He was
40 succeeded by Victoriana Huerta.
   The initial optimism of yet another new presidency, however, did not last long. Zapata's forces in Morelos remained small and isolated, but another rebel, Venustiano Carranza, announced his

45 own revolt in March of 1913, refusing to recognize Huerta's government. This announcement split Mexico in thirds, with Zapata in Morelos, Huerta in Mexico City, and Carranza in the north. The United States supported the Carranza faction, and its
50 increased pressure forced Huerta into exile in July of 1914, when Carranza claimed limited control.
   When Carranza held a convention attempting to unite the various revolutionary forces holding sway over the country, he actually only succeeded in
55 driving them deeper into their individual corners of Mexico. Pancho Villa took over Mexico City and Carranza stationed his forces in Veracruz. Finally, with U.S. recognition of Carranza's government and the backing of a leading labor union, he
60 recaptured Mexico City, defeated Pancho Villa's army, and simultaneously brought an end to any possibility of cooperation among revolutionary factions. In 1917, Carranza won the presidential election, much to the chagrin of Pancho Villa and
65 Emiliano Zapata. Consequently, when Zapata denounced the president's reluctance to institute adequate labor reform in March of 1919, Carranza conspired to have the rebel leader assassinated. The murder, however, was only a harbinger of
70 Carranza's own future.
   Carranza's annunciation of his successor prompted Alvaro Obregón to unite the military, agrarian, and urban industrial workers against him. As his popularity waned, Carranza attempted to
75 flee to Veracruz, but was murdered by a turncoat member of his entourage. Interim president Adolfo de la Huerta governed from June to December of 1920, stepping down when Obregón won the December 1920 election.
80   In 1924, when he announced Plutarco Elias Calles as his successor, Obregón met some resistance from the former interim president. Huerta's revolt against Calles, however, actually aided the president by effectively weeding out the disloyal factions of his
85 military. Huerta was defeated and Calles, with the help of Obregón, continued making improvements in government spending and anti-clerical policy. In 1928, Obregón again ran for president, winning the election because he and Calles executed any
90 opposing voices. He "won" the election only to be murdered in Mexico City a few days later. His death marked the end of a revolution spanning nearly two decades—a revolution characteristically defined by the people who died for it.

16. In 1910, the Mexican people deposed General Díaz after a forty-year dictatorship because of

(A) poverty and political abuse
(B) unreasonable taxation and tariffs
(C) unfair representation and distribution of land
(D) lack of anti-clerical reform
(E) enforced social inequality

17. All of the following leaders of the Mexican Revolution were killed EXCEPT

(A) Alvaro Obregón
(B) Emiliano Zapata
(C) Fransisco Madero
(D) Venustiano Carranza
(E) Victoriana Huerta

18. As it is used in the passage, the word "harbinger" (line 69) means

(A) a plentiful yield
(B) an unexplained coincidence
(C) a shelter or house
(D) a prediction of things to come
(E) a period of political distress

19. Which of the following statements about the Mexican Revolution is NOT supported by the passage?

(A) It occurred over the course of nearly 20 years.
(B) Both economic and social issues were points of contention.
(C) Threats to revolutionary leaders did not come only from their political opponents.
(D) None of the elections during that time were fair.
(E) Certain aspects of the Revolution were affected by forces beyond the country's borders.

20. The author's attitude toward the Mexican revolutionary leaders could best be described as

(A) supportive
(B) suspicious
(C) mildly critical
(D) condemnatory
(E) apathetic

21. It can be most reasonably concluded from the passage that the author believes that revolutions are

(A) often most dangerous to the leaders who direct them
(B) a necessary ingredient for political progress
(C) more violent than they need to be
(D) never able to produce the changes for which they are fought
(E) always begun when a dictator becomes too aggressive

READ WHAT YOU NEED

What do you need to know about a critical reading passage before you head to the questions? Three things:

1. the author's point
2. the author's tone
3. the passage layout

Virtually every SAT reading passage has the same basic structure: The author has a point. Her primary purpose is to develop or explain this point. She does this by stating her point and then supporting it with details, facts, examples, metaphors, and secondary ideas. The author also has an attitude toward her subject (she may be *for* something, *against* something, or *neutral*), which she conveys in her tone or style.

You also need to get the gist of how the passage is organized. Remember our open-book test from history class? You may not go home and study for that open-book test, but it would behoove you to organize your notes a bit so you can find answers in a timely fashion. The same holds true for critical reading passages. You want a sense of where the author put stuff so you can find answers easily.

To access the initial stuff you need from a passage quickly and easily, you're going to do a topic search. To do a topic search, read:

- **The blurb.** Most critical reading passages are introduced by a brief italicized paragraph that gives you some idea of what the passage is about. Read it carefully.

- **The first few sentences of the first paragraph.** Get an idea of what the author is saying. Once you feel you have a clue, jot down a note and move on.

- **The first sentence of the remaining paragraphs.** Jot down a note next to each paragraph so you have a handle on the passage structure.

- **The last sentence.** Read the last sentence so you know how the passage winds up. Jot down a note to yourself about the author's overall point and tone.

TOPIC SEARCH TEST DRIVE

Flip back to our sample passage on page 57 and try a topic search. Be sure to jot down quick notes to yourself so you know what's going on. Then flip back here to see how you did.

Passage Types

Critical reading passages come from four broad subject areas:

1. Science: discoveries, controversies, or other topics in physics, chemistry, astronomy, biology, medicine, botany, zoology, and the other sciences

2. Humanities: excerpts from essays about art, literature, music, philosophy, or folklore; discussions of artists, novelists, or historical figures

3. Social sciences: topics in politics, economics, sociology, or history

4. Narrative: usually excerpts from novels, short stories, or humorous essays (We have yet to see a poem on the SAT.)

ETS usually includes a passage involving a historically overlooked community or social group. This "ethnic" passage, as we call it, is usually either a social science or humanities passage.

Here's How to Crack It

First, read the blurb:

> *The following passage about the Mexican Revolution examines the interchange of power among various rebel leaders.*

This sets you on the right track. Now read the first sentence of the passage:

> Revolutionaries can sometimes be their own worst enemies; such was certainly the case with the leaders of the Mexican Revolution.

As you read, the following phrases ought to attract your attention: *revolutionaries; their own worst enemies; leaders of the Mexican revolution.* The author's point is right here: "Revolutionaries who became leaders during the Mexican Revolution caused problems for themselves." Don't sweat the details. Move on.

The structure of this passage is so straightforward that you won't even need much more than the first sentence of each body paragraph to be able to follow it. The second paragraph describes a leader named Diaz, the third paragraph describes one named Madero, and each successive paragraph tells you something about a different leader.

Remember: You aren't looking for details right now. You're looking for the author's point, and you're getting a sense of how the passage is put together. The author is writing about the various fates of leaders of the Mexican Revolution—that's enough for now.

The last paragraph describes the end of the revolutionary period and what happened to the last leader. Don't worry too much about the details. Just jot down what you know:

- The author's point: Leaders of the Mexican Revolution caused problems for themselves.
- The author's tone: neutral-critical

WHY WRITE IT DOWN?

As you know, when you take a test under pressure, it's easy to forget stuff, lose your focus, and then feel rushed and out of control. The more you write in your test booklet, the less likely you are to do a mental drift or lose information that "you know you saw *somewhere* in the passage." On critical reading it is imperative that you jot down notes as you go along so you can easily find the info you need when you go back.

HEAD FOR THE QUESTIONS

Your initial search should only take a minute or two. Once you have a clue about the author's point and the layout of the passage, head for the questions.

Unlike the other sections of the SAT, critical reading questions are *not* arranged in order of difficulty. They are, however, arranged in roughly chronological order. In other words, a question about the first paragraph will come before a question about the second paragraph, and so on. Most of the questions you'll encounter will ask for specific details from the passage. For the most part, you will answer critical reading questions in the order they are given.

TRANSLATING

The most important reading you will do on the Critical Reading section of the test is when you read the questions. ETS has gone out of its way to make critical reading questions hard to understand. Therefore, before you go searching for answers to any question, put the question in "English" so you know what you are being asked.

Take a look at the following question. What are you being asked?

> 1. According to the passage, the "language of
>   bureaucracy" and the "language of liberation" are
>   alike in that they take into account which one of the
>   following?

Let's simplify this a bit. "According to the passage..." means look at the passage. Cross off this phrase since it is extra and simply adds confusion. "The 'language of bureaucracy' and the 'language of liberation' are alike...." How are these two languages similar?

The rest of the sentence is fluff ("in that they take into account") followed by a *see the answer choices* phrase ("which one of the following"). Cross off the last part of the sentence. To answer this question, you need to know how the two languages mentioned are similar.

Flip back to our passage on page 57. Read each question and translate it. If there is anything about the question you find confusing, put it into "English." Cross out unnecessary phrases. Make sure you know exactly what you are being asked. When you finish, flip back here to see how you did.

What the Questions Really Ask

16. Why did the Mexican people remove General Díaz from power in 1910?

17. Which leader was not killed?

18. Clear as written

19. Four of the answer choices we know to be true of the Mexican Revolution; which one do we NOT know is true?

20. What is the author's attitude toward the revolutionaries?

21. What does the author believe about revolutions?

Now let's talk about how to answer each of these questions.

In the Form of a Question

One way ETS confuses test takers is by replacing questions with incomplete sentences: "The primary purpose of the passage is..." instead of "What is the primary purpose of the passage?" Many students find it easier to understand what ETS is driving at if they rephrase those incomplete sentences as questions beginning with "What" or "Why." "What" questions ask for things (facts, ideas). "Why" questions ask for reasons.

CRITICAL READING ◆ 61

GIVE IT THE FINGER

Once you know what a question is asking, you can head back to the passage to find the answer. For the most part, the only way to answer critical reading questions correctly is to put your finger on the answer in the passage. Use the notes you jotted down as you searched the passage to help you locate the answers you need. Once you find the part of the passage that contains your answer, translate it into "English." In other words, *answer the question in your own words* before you look at any answer choices.

Translate the following passage excerpt into "English."

The painters made the already good looking west even prettier using light

> The luminist school of American landscape painting drenched the monumental vistas of the American West in golden, surreal light, transforming already striking scenes into glimpses of Utopia.

In other words, "luminist school painters used lots of light to paint scenes of the West, making the scenes even more beautiful."

They Don't Care What You Know

More than one million students take the SAT every year. They can't all have studied the same subjects, so ETS can't expect you to know anything it hasn't told you. This is important to remember on specific questions. All you have to do is find something the passage already states.

ANSWER THE QUESTION

Answering the questions in your own words before looking at any answer choices will keep you from getting trapped by ETS's distractor answers. You can bet that Joe Bloggs isn't answering the questions in his own words. In fact, Joe is reading the passage slowly and carefully, trying to memorize a bunch of facts he hardly understands, and then trying to answer a bunch of questions he hardly understands without going back to the passage. He's sunk from the start.

You, on the other hand, have already searched the passage, translated the question, and are now ready to find your answer. How can you do this?

Questions often contain clues that point to the answer in the passage. In addition to your notes, you can use these clues to zero in on the answers you are looking for.

LINE REFERENCES

The best clue that ETS gives you for finding the answer within a passage is a *line reference*. The majority of the questions in each Critical Reading section will refer to some line or lines in the passage. For example, ETS might ask you to determine what a passage says about "new research in the field of genetics" in "lines 21–25."

Line reference questions will be phrased something like this:

> According to paragraph 3 (lines 34–50), scientists studied the comet in order to

> In lines 56–75, the narrator is primarily concerned with

The author uses the quote from Johnson's book (line 79) to demonstrate that

According to paragraph 2, the new species of penguins are an "important find" (line 20) because they are

These line references will be a big help when you go back to the passage to look for ETS's answer, because they tell you approximately where to look. We say approximately because, of course, ETS never makes your life that easy. If ETS refers to lines 33–36, the answer may actually be in lines 31–32, or in lines 37–39.

Read at least five lines above and five lines below the lines mentioned in the question in order to be sure that you've found ETS's answer, which will be a paraphrase of what you've just read.

VOCABULARY IN CONTEXT (VIC)

ETS also uses line reference questions to test vocabulary. For example, a question may ask you for the meaning of the word *stupefying* in line 12. Attack these questions aggressively, handling them in exactly the same way we've taught you to handle sentence completions. Even if you don't know the meaning of the word, the context should enable you to eliminate several incorrect choices using POE. Here's our step-by-step strategy:

1. Cover the answer choices so that you won't be influenced by them.

2. Go to the passage and read the sentence that contains the word being tested.

3. Draw a line through the word with your pencil. Read the sentence again and come up with your own word for the blank (just as you would on a sentence completion). If you don't come up with a word on your first try, read one sentence before and one sentence after. Using the context will give you clues.

4. Once you've settled on your own word, uncover the answer choices and use POE to eliminate those choices that are not like your word.

It is very important to use this method in answering these questions. If you simply plug in the choices in this case—Joe Bloggs's favorite technique—you may fall into a trap. ETS's answer will often be a secondary meaning of the word they asked you to define. If you go straight to the choices, you may be irresistibly attracted to one that might be correct in a different context, but is dead wrong in this one. Covering up the answer choices will eliminate temptation. Don't get careless.

Take another look at question 18 from our sample passage.

Heads Up

ETS will try to trip you up by asking questions that seem to have one answer but actually have another. Often the real answer will be hiding behind a trigger word. In writing questions, ETS looks for places in the passage where meanings change. ETS thinks of each of these changes as a trap for a careless reader—for Joe Bloggs. If you pay attention to the trigger words, you will be able to avoid many of ETS's traps. See the Sentence Completions chapter for a review of trigger words.

Vocabulary in Context: The Student's Friend

Since VIC questions are little more than sentence completions, you really don't have to find the main idea of the passage or anything else in order to answer them. Even if you don't plan to answer every critical reading question, you should still try every VIC question. They're short, predictable, and don't require you to read very much. And they earn you the same point you'd earn answering a longer, more complicated question.

18. As it is used in the passage, the word "harbinger" (line 69) means

    (A) a plentiful yield
    (B) an unexplained coincidence
    (C) a shelter or house
    (D) a prediction of things to come
    (E) a period of political distress

Here's How to Crack It

Cover up the answer choices, then find the word in the passage and lightly draw a line through it. Now proceed as though you were trying to anticipate ETS's answer for a sentence completion question.

Here's the sentence you are trying to complete:
"The murder, however, was only a _____ of Carranza's own future."

The word that is missing has something to do with Carranza's future, but what? If you take a quick look at the sentences before and after this one, you see that Carranza was part of an assassination, and eventually was killed himself. So the best fit for the missing word might be *a sign of future events*. Now look at the answer choices.

    (A) Nothing like the word you anticipated. There isn't any mention of Carranza receiving or gaining anything that could be described as plentiful.

    (B) Nothing like the word you anticipated. There isn't any indication here that anything is unexplained. In fact, the author *does* explain what happened. Eliminate this one.

    (C) Nothing like the word you anticipated.

    (D) This one is just right! This is ETS's answer.

    (E) Nothing like the word you anticipated. This may seem tempting since there is certainly a great deal of bad goings-on described, but we need a more specific word referring to the future here.

Lead Words

Some questions in the Critical Reading sections will not have line references, but will still point to a specific place in the passage. For these questions, ETS gives a different clue that tells you where to look for the answer. For example, if a question asked about the author's opinion of the "volcano theory," you would naturally go back to the passage and find the lines that mention the volcano theory. Every specific question that does not have a line reference has a word or phrase that you can use to find ETS's answer in the passage. We call these *lead words*. In our example, *volcano theory* would be the lead words for the question.

Lead word questions are phrased like this:

The author suggests that science fiction writers have a tendency to

According to the passage, which of the following is a feature of architecture in the 1960s?

The author of the passage suggests that she was able to sell her first painting because

In the passage, the invention of the microchip was similar to

In each of the questions above, there is a phrase—*science fiction writers, architecture in the 1960s, sell her first painting, invention of the microchip*—that you could use as lead words to find ETS's answer in the passages. And you won't have to search the whole passage to find where the lead words are mentioned. Since questions about a passage are in chronological order, you can use line reference questions that come before and after a lead word question to help you locate your answer.

As with line references, once you find the lead words in the passage, you must read at least five lines above and five lines below the line that contains the lead words. Keep reading until you can put your finger on ETS's answer. Answer the question in your own words, then eliminate answers that don't match yours.

Take another look at question 16 from our sample passage.

16. In 1910, the Mexican people deposed General Díaz after a forty-year dictatorship because of

(A) enforced social inequality
(B) unreasonable taxation and tariffs
(C) unfair representation and distribution of land
(D) lack of anti-clerical reform
(E) poverty and political abuse

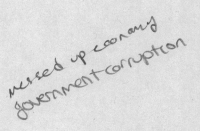

messed up economy government corruption

Here's How to Crack It

Our translated question asks: "Why did the Mexican people remove General Díaz from power in 1910?" This question doesn't have a specific line reference, but it has some excellent lead words: *1910* and *Díaz*. Where do you see the date 1910? In line 13 in the second paragraph. Go back and read what you need. Once you have a paraphrased answer, go through each answer choice and use POE.

(A) This is ETS's answer. The paragraph says that people were angered by *economic deprivation and governmental exploitation.*

(B) Eliminate. This isn't really mentioned anywhere in the passage.

(C) Eliminate. This is mentioned in the passage, but about Madero, not Díaz.

(D) Eliminate. This is also mentioned in the passage, but about Madero, not Díaz.

(E) Eliminate. Nowhere does it say that Díaz enforced social inequality.

THE AUTHOR'S POINT

There are some questions that ask general stuff about the passage. Usually, these questions want to know the author's main idea, tone, etc. Do you need to go back to the passage to answer these questions? No. You already know the author's point from your topic search. Simply use that information plus the information you gather from answering specific questions to answer any general questions you come across.

Let's look at number 21 from our sample passage.

Cross It Off

On critical reading questions, it is very likely that you may need to read a few of the answer choices more than once. To avoid confusion, be sure you cross off each answer entirely when you eliminate it. That way, if you have two or three choices you are considering, you can easily tell which choices are left in the running and which you have eliminated.

21. It can be most reasonably concluded from the passage that the author believes that revolutions are
   (A) often most dangerous to the leaders who direct them
   (B) a necessary ingredient for political progress
   (C) more violent than they need to be
   (D) never able to produce the changes for which they are fought
   (E) always begun when a dictator becomes too aggressive

Here's How to Crack It

Our translated question asks, "What does the author believe about revolutions?" Answer the question in your own words before you read the choices. We said earlier that the passage was about revolutionaries causing trouble for themselves, so we want something that sums up this idea.

Let's look at each answer choice:

(A) Looks good, but be sure to go through all the answer choices just to be safe. You never know when there might be something better lurking somewhere!

(B) This answer may look good, but is a Joe Bloggs answer. It may seem as if the author is suggesting there is a connection between progress and revolution, but it isn't really stated anywhere. Also, this answer uses extreme wording: *necessary* is pretty strong, and is unlikely to be the correct answer.

(C) This may also be tempting, since the passage focuses on the deaths of so many people, and you may even personally agree with this statement. But nowhere does the author discuss how much violence would be appropriate.

(D) The author never really talks about what the desired changes were, or whether they were eventually achieved. We would need more information for this to be right.

(E) There is no connection made between aggressive leaders and revolutions. Really there is no discussion of why revolutions start in the first place. Let's get rid of it.

ETS's answer is A. Answering the question in your own words before looking at the answer choices saved you from picking the Joe Bloggs answers. Be sure to have a good idea of the answer to a question in your mind before you read any answer choices.

Now try number 20 from our sample passage:

20. The author's attitude toward the Mexican revolutionary leaders could best be described as

(A) supportive
(B) suspicious
(C) mildly critical
(D) condemnatory
(E) apathetic

*[handwritten: What does the author think about mex. revolutionary leaders?
They got themselves in trouble]*

Here's How to Crack It

The question asks for the author's attitude or tone, which we said earlier was neutral-critical. You can therefore cross off any extreme or positive choices. This eliminates answers A and D. What about E? Can an author be *apathetic*? If she didn't care about this subject, she would hardly write about it, now would she? *Apathetic* is never the author's tone. Cross off E.

You are now down to B and C. *Suspicious* is negative, but doesn't make much sense in this context. Does the author indicate she thinks that the revolutionaries are up to something bad, but lacks proof? Not really. Our author mostly just told the story of what happened to each of the revolutionaries, and suggests that things turned out as they did because the leaders acted in certain ways. C is the best answer.

You can see these kinds of questions on shorter critical reading passages. In fact, questions about the author's tone pop up frequently, since they are so general. Take a look at this example:

Most people date chemical and biological warfare to the beginning of the twentieth century, when German forces used mustard gas during World War I to devastate
Line their enemies. Soldiers' nerves were ruined, their skin
5 was burned, and they permanently lost their eyesight. But this type of warfare is actually far older; it was commonly used in the ancient world. Legend has it that during a third-century siege of Hatra, in present day Iraq, the inhabitants filled clay pots with scorpions and dropped
10 them on the heads of the invading Romans. The terror inspired by such a weapon completely demoralized the Romans, superior in technology and manpower, just as through clever management, David beat Goliath.

11. The author's attitude toward the defense of Hatra can best be described as

[handwritten: impressed]

(A) somewhat impressed at the technological innovations of the formerly inferior inhabitants
(B) slightly scornful of the crudity of the techniques in comparison with more modern technologies
(C) horrified, due to the fact that the existence of such historical precedents suggest that war will never end
(D) completely neutral; the author is determined to treat the subject in an academic manner
(E) ambivalent as to its value insomuch as war is no longer conducted at such a primitive level

Here's How to Crack It

As we mentioned, ETS likes its authors to be neutral or slightly positive in tone. Armed with just this information, you can eliminate choices C and E (because ambivalence implies that one doesn't care). Now consider this passage, where the author refers to the Hatrans' cleverness and likens them to David beating Goliath. (Even if you don't know who these folks are, the word *clever* tells you that the author thought well of them.) Choice B is incorrect because no comparison or contrast is made, so that leaves us with either choice A or D. The reason D is incorrect is because the author lets a personal viewpoint to come through by suggesting that the defense of Hatra was clever. Therefore choice A is correct.

Let's try another (same passage, different type of question):

12. The example of mustard gas in World War I is used in order to
    (A) discount the idea that biological and chemical warfare are modern inventions
    (B) prove that modern and ancient warfare are actually identical
    (C) dramatize the horror of modern warfare, and suggest that it must not be allowed to continue
    (D) offer a particularly compelling and seemingly foundational image of chemical warfare
    (E) support the claim that World War I was one of the most violent wars ever

Here's How to Crack It

First, translate the question: Why did the author use the example of mustard gas? Now let's find what the passage says about mustard gas: "Most people date chemical and biological warfare to the beginning of the twentieth century," making the mustard gas the apparent origin of such warfare. This does not validate choice A because the example is not used to disprove anything. On the contrary, it's providing the apparent origin; therefore, the correct answer is D. There is no comparison made for choice B, nor any dramatization for choice C, and clearly no support for choice E.

THE TOUGH STUFF

As we mentioned, you will answer most critical reading questions in the order in which they appear. However, there are some critical reading questions that are harder and more time-consuming to answer than the others. These will be your "later" questions.

Later questions ask you for a lot more than just some basic information from the passage. If you read a question that sounds time-consuming, save it for later. Also, if you read a question and have no clue where to find the answer in the passage, save it for later. The information you learn from answering the other questions about a passage will often make these *later* questions a little easier to do.

There are a few types of *later* questions that come up frequently on a test. Let's take a look at them.

Do It Later

Look at question 17 from our sample passage:

17. All of the following leaders of the Mexican Revolution were killed EXCEPT

(A) Alvaro Obregón
(B) Emiliano Zapata
(C) Fransisco Madero
(D) Venustiano Carranza
(E) Victoriana Huerta

When we translated our question, we took into account what the word EXCEPT means in a question. EXCEPT in a question means that *four* of the choices you read will be true, while only *one* of the answers will be false. Your job is to identify the false answer choice. This takes a bit more time to find, since you have to find the four that are "wrong" to know which one is "right."

To crack an EXCEPT question, first go back to the passage. For question 17, we need to read the details surrounding the deaths of each leader listed in the answers. Don't rely on your memory! Do back to the passage as many times as you need to. As you discover which leaders were killed, label the corresponding answer choice "T" for true. The one that isn't true is the answer you are looking for.

Here's How to Crack It

Let's look at each answer choice:

(A) True. Alvaro Obregón was killed just a few days after taking office (lines 90–91).

(B) True. Emiliano Zapata was killed by political enemies (lines 65–68).

(C) True. It is believed that Fransisco Madero was assassinated in 1913 (lines 36–38).

(D) True. Venustiano Carranza was killed by one of his own people (lines 74–76).

(E) False. Victoriana Huerta stepped down in 1920, but there is no indication that he was killed.

What is the answer to this question? Use the *Sesame Street* method: One of these things is not like the others. ETS's answer is E.

Notice that even though this question wasn't more difficult than others you've answered, it was more time-consuming. Leave these questions for later—do them after you've done the shorter, easier questions about the passage.

EXCEPT . . . NOT!

ETS's EXCEPT/LEAST/NOT questions are big time-wasters. Think about it: You're really answering four questions for the price of one. Most of these questions expect you to find four pieces of information in the passage, but only reward you with one measly point. Do them last, if at all.

EXCEPT . . . NOT!

There's another reason why you should answer EXCEPT/LEAST/NOT questions last. Once you've answered all the other questions, you have a good idea of what facts in the passage are important to ETS and where to find them. By answering other questions, you may also have gathered information that you can use to eliminate wrong answers on EXCEPT/LEAST/NOT questions. You're the one taking the test; make it work for *you*.

I, II, III QUESTIONS

Occasionally on the SAT, you will find a question like the following:

29. According to the author, which of the following characteristics is (are) common to both literature and biology?

    I. They are concerned with living creatures.
    II. They enrich human experience.
    III. They are guided by scientific principles.

    (A) I only
    (B) II only
    (C) III only
    (D) I and III
    (E) I, II, and III

We call these "I, II, III questions." We could also call them "triple true/false questions," because you are really being asked to determine whether each of three separate statements is true or false. These questions are very time-consuming, and you will receive credit only if you answer all three parts of the question correctly. Therefore, you should save them for last. Still, these questions are excellent for educated guessing because you can improve your odds dramatically by using POE.

As is usually true on the SAT, the key to success is taking one step at a time. Consider each of the numbered statements individually. If you discover that it's true, you can eliminate any choice that does not contain it. If you discover that it is false, you can eliminate any choice that does contain it.

For example, suppose you know from reading the passage that statement II is false. That means you can eliminate two choices, B and E. Since B and E both contain II, neither can be correct. (Similarly, if you know that one of the statements is correct, you can eliminate any answer choice that does not contain it.) Incidentally, ETS's answer in this case is C.

THE POWER OF COMMON SENSE

Now try question 19 from our sample passage:

19. Which of the following statements about the Mexican Revolution is NOT supported by the passage?

    (A) It occurred over the course of nearly 20 years.
    (B) Both economic and social issues were points of contention.
    (C) Threats to revolutionary leaders did not come only from their political opponents.
    (D) None of the elections during that time were fair.
    (E) Certain aspects of the Revolution were affected by forces beyond the country's borders.

Here's How to Crack It

You'll have to use the whole passage to answer this question. Remember, the NOT in the question acts just like EXCEPT: You will want to use the true/false method to label the choices and eliminate down to the correct answer.

Let's look at each answer choice:

(A)   True. This is stated in both the introduction and the conclusion.

(B)   True. If you skim the passage, you can spot the word *economic* (line 13) pretty easily. *Educational goals* are also mentioned, and are a good example of a social issue that affected the course of the revolution.

(C)   True. Venustiano Carranza was assassinated by someone from his own group.

(D)   Not sure. You probably aren't able to find anything in the passage about this, so you may be reluctant to label it.

(E)   True. The United States played a role in the revolution when it supported Carranza and his followers.

So, you found four, but can't find evidence for D. Do you need to go looking for more information? No. ETS's answer is D. Since you know that the other four are true, and can point to specific information in the passage as proof, you can feel pretty confident in choosing D. Besides, very often on NOT or EXCEPT questions the "correct" answer is something that isn't in the passage at all, so expect that sometimes you have no evidence for what turns out to be the credited answer.

Use the Power

What else made answer choice D on the last question so wrong? The word *none* made the answer choice quite extreme—it means that *not a single election during the entire revolution* was fair. Even if you weren't sure you had all the info you needed, common sense says that such an all-inclusive statement is unlikely to be true.

Don't underestimate the power of common sense. When the ETS team gets together to write up questions and answer choices, it takes them quite a while to come up with the "perfect" ETS answer. If they want to get their work done, they can't spend all day writing tricky wrong answer choices. They just need to make sure the other four choices are clearly wrong. That's where your common sense comes into play.

Stupid Answers

The Critical Reading section of the SAT is filled with stupid answers—answers that can't possibly be ETS's answer. Don't assume that you are trying to find the "best" answer from a pool of five good answer choices. Rather, you are trying to find the "least wrong" answer from a pool of pretty bad answer choices. That's why you can sometimes answer a question without even reading the passage to which it refers.

Look at the following example:

16. According to the passage, all of the following are true of living organisms EXCEPT

- (A) They are able to reproduce themselves.
- (B) They are past the point of further evolution.
- (C) They are capable of growth.
- (D) They respond to stimuli.
- (E) They are characterized by a capacity for metabolism.

Here's How to Crack It

If you know even a little about biology, you will probably be able to answer this question without reading the passage. (Remember that on this question you are asked to look for a statement that is *not* true.) Now let's consider each choice in turn.

- (A) The ability to reproduce is one of the obvious differences between living things and nonliving things. Rocks don't reproduce. Eliminate.

- (B) Have living organisms stopped evolving? Of course not. This must be ETS's answer.

- (C), (D), and (E)

    These are all part of the standard biological definition of life. Eliminate.

Without even reading the passage, you could figure out which one of the answer choices had to be ETS's answer.

Buzzwords

Avoid answer choices that contain the following words:
must
always
impossible
never
cannot
each
every
totally
all
solely
only

DON'T GO TO EXTREMES

Likewise, answers that use extreme language or express information that could be argued with are not going to be ETS's answer. If even one percent of the 1.5 million students who take the SAT each year were able to raise a plausible objection to ETS's answer to a question, ETS writers would have to spend all their time arguing with students. In order to keep this from happening, they try to make the answers impossible to argue with.

How does ETS do that? Let's look at an example:

Which of the following statements is impossible to argue with?

- (A) The population of the world is 4.734 billion people.
- (B) The population of the world is quite large.

Analysis

Statement A sounds precise and scientific; statement B sounds vague and general. Which is impossible to argue with?

Statement B, of course! Does anyone know exactly what the population of the world is? What if some experts say that the population of the world is 4.732 billion people? Doesn't the population of the world change from minute to minute? A number that is correct today will be wrong tomorrow. It's easy to think of dozens of reasons why statement A could be wrong.

Statement B, on the other hand, is so vague and general that no one could argue with it. Anyone can see that it is true. If it were ETS's answer to an SAT critical reading question, no one would be able to quibble with it.

Let's look at an example. Assume that you've already eliminated some of the choices. You can answer this question now without even reading the passage.

27. With which of the following statements would the author of the passage probably agree?

(A) No useful purpose is served by examining the achievements of the past.
(B) A fuller understanding of the present can often be gained from the study of history.
(C) [eliminated]
(D) [eliminated]
(E) Nothing new ever occurs.

Here's How to Crack It

Which of these statements are too extreme? Choices A and E. Choice A says that studying the past has *no* useful purpose. This statement is absolute. Once you find just one exception to the statement, you've proven the statement false. Therefore, the author of the passage probably wouldn't be any more likely to agree with it than we would.

Similarly, choice E says that nothing new ever occurs. This, too, is an extreme statement. Therefore, it's easy to raise objections to it. Nothing new ever occurs? Not even once in a while? Surely there must be an exception somewhere. This statement is easy to attack. If we find a single small exception, we have proven the statement wrong.

Choice B, however, is so general and vague that no one could argue with it. A single example would be enough to prove it correct. It must be ETS's answer.

Here's a silly example that makes the point:

20. With which of the following statements would the weather forecaster probably agree?

(A) It will begin raining tomorrow at 3:36.
(B) Tuesday's low temperature will be 38 degrees.
(C) Next year's snowfall will total 45 inches.
(D) Tomorrow may be cooler than today.
(E) Next month will be the wettest month of the year.

Choose Vague

The vague choice is usually correct. And the specific choice is usually incorrect. So when you are trying to decide between two choices, both of which seem good, the more specific choice will be much easier to poke holes in. And a choice that is easier to poke holes in will most likely be the wrong choice.

Do I Offend?

Often ETS will include a passage on the test that talks about a particular ethnic group—normally a group that has been subjugated by our culture. They allegedly put these passages in to make certain groups feel "more comfortable" with the test. Of course, a critical reading passage doesn't make any student feel more comfortable with an exam that's riddled with biases. However, it does make critical reading a bit easier. If the test writers choose to include an "ethnic" passage, they will most certainly use a positive, inspirational tone. Keep their objective in mind if you see a passage about a traditionally discriminated-against group. Cross off any answers that are offensive or insulting to the group being discussed.

Dual Passage Strategy

1. Read the blurb
2. Passage 1
   (A) Read what you need
   (B) Attack the passage 1 questions
3. Passage 2
   (A) Read what you need
   (B) Attack the passage 2 questions
4. Attack the questions about both passages.

Here's How to Crack It

This question and the answer choices don't refer to an actual reading passage, of course. But even without seeing a passage (or knowing a weather forecaster), you ought to be able to tell that D is the only statement with which our imaginary weather forecaster, or anyone else, would probably agree. *Tomorrow may be cooler than today* is vague enough to be true no matter what. It may be cooler tomorrow, or it may not. All the bases are covered. The other four statements, by contrast, are so specific and absolute that no weather forecaster could make them. If a television weather forecaster said, "It will begin raining tomorrow at 3:36," your reaction would be, "Oh, yeah? How do you know?"

If a statement says that something is always true, then you need to find only one exception in order to prove it wrong. If a statement says that every child ordered a hot dog, then you need to find only one child with a hamburger to prove it wrong. These words are highly specific, and therefore make the choices that contain them easier for you to attack and, very likely, to eliminate.

WEIRD PASSAGES

NARRATIVES

Some passages you read will be more like stories than like passages. These passages are called "narratives." Why do you care? Because it is tough to do a topic search on a narrative. If you read the blurb of a passage and it sounds like it is going to be an excerpt from a story, use a "trigger search" to read what you need. In other words, go through the passage circling trigger words and reading the info that comes after each trigger. (See the Sentence Completions chapter for a review of trigger words.) Then attack the questions as usual, looking for answers around the trigger words.

DUAL PASSAGES

Sometimes you will be given two passages for the price of one. You will be asked questions about the first passage, questions about the second passage, and questions about both. Do these passages one at a time. Read the blurb, then read what you need for passage 1. Then, answer the passage 1 questions (they will come first).

After you finish the passage 1 questions, go back and read what you need for passage 2. Do the passage 2 questions. Finally, do the questions that involve both passages.

SKIP IT

You've probably noticed by now that critical reading takes longer than any other question type on the SAT. Depending on where you are scoring, it may be to your benefit to skip some or all of a passage. Remember, easy questions are worth just as many points as hard questions. Rushing through sentence completions to get to critical reading will hurt your accuracy and cost you points.

THE TAIL END

Whether or not you are doing all the critical reading questions, you should definitely do them last of all the question types. In the 25-minute Critical Reading sections, critical reading questions will come after sentence completions. Be sure to do all the sentence completions you plan to do before you begin critical reading. If you run out of time on critical reading, no problem—all the easy stuff is already done.

The 20-minute Critical Reading section consists solely of critical reading. Work this section smartly, not rushing to get through but rather working to answer questions correctly. You can do just as well on critical reading as you can on sentence completions if you remember to:

- read what you need
- translate the questions
- put your finger on the answers
- answer the questions in your own words
- use POE

DRILL 1

Use the dual passage on the next page to put it all together. Review your strategy for attacking a dual passage before you begin, then crack this passage. Remember, the questions are more important than the passage. Focus on answering questions correctly by putting your finger on each answer in the passage and answering the questions in your own words before looking at any answer choices. Use your common sense and POE to avoid ETS's traps. Answers can be found on page 337.

Critical Reading Takes Time

If you were offered a job that paid $10 an hour and another that paid $10 a minute, which one would you choose? Be good to yourself and do critical reading last.

[handwritten at top: The "request for the Hawaiian islands ~~was~~ to be admitted to the US was unexpected, and politicians etc didn't know what to do, but in the end most business men supported it]

In 1959, the Hawaiian Islands were admitted into the United States as the fiftieth state. Both of the following passages discuss the United States' annexation of Hawaii.

[handwritten left margin: Be neutral]

Passage 1

On January 28, 1893, Americans read in their evening newspapers a bulletin from Honolulu, Hawaii. Two weeks earlier, said the news report, a
Line group of American residents had overthrown a
5 young native queen and formed a provisional government. Marines from the U.S.S. *Boston* had landed at the request of the American minister in order to protect lives and property. Violence had ended quickly. The rebels were in full control and
10 were said to have enthusiastic support from the populace. Most noteworthy of all, they had announced the intention of asking the United States to annex the islands.

The proposal was not as startling as it might
15 have seemed. Most of the large landowners in the islands were Americans or the children of Americans. So, too, were the men who grew, refined, and shipped the sugar that was Hawaii's principal export. In addition, many of the
20 kingdom's Protestant clergymen, lawyers, bankers, factory owners, and other leading personages were also American citizens. Though numbering only two thousand of the island's total population of around ninety thousand, these Americans had
25 already given Hawaii the appearance of a colony. This influence could be seen as far back as 1854 when they nearly persuaded a native monarch to request annexation by the United States. Subsequently, the American element helped secure
30 tariff reciprocity from the United States while the island ceded a naval station to the United States. *[handwritten: gave]* Such measures sparked enough concern by the United States to lead presidents from Tyler on down to periodically warn European powers
35 against meddling in Hawaiian affairs. Thus, by 1893, the new proposal might have been characterized as simply a plan to annex a state already Americanized and virtually a protectorate.

Nonetheless, the proposition came
40 unexpectedly, and neither politicians nor journalists knew quite what to make of it. Editorials and comments from Capitol Hill were at first noncommittal. The molders of public opinion seemed intent on learning what mold the public
45 wanted.

San Francisco's leading Republican and Democratic dailies, the *Chronicle* and *Examiner*, declared that Hawaii should certainly be accepted as a state. On January 29, the *Chronicle* reported a
50 poll of local businessmen demonstrating overwhelming support for this view. Some businessmen focused on potential profits. Claus Spreckels, for example, who owned Hawaii's largest sugar plantation, hoped to obtain the two-
55 cent-a-pound bounty paid by the United States government to domestic sugar producers. In addition, he anticipated increased freight for his Oceanic Steamship line as well as more plentiful and cheaper raw sugar for his California Sugar
60 Refinery Company.

Businessmen elsewhere on the Pacific coast followed their lead. San Diego, for example, was virtually the property of the Spreckels family. Moreover, in Los Angeles, Fresno, and San Jose,
65 the Spreckelses were allied, to some extent, in the battle against the railroad with merchants, bankers, warehouse owners, real estate dealers, and contractors; and the Chambers of Commerce of Portland and Seattle had long cooperated with that
70 of San Francisco in pressing for national policies advantageous to the West. It was not long before businessmen all along the coast were reported as favoring annexation.

Passage 2

President Cleveland was opposed to annexation
75 throughout his term of office. He believed taking the Islands was immoral, and without his support annexationists had no hope. The Provisional Government, however, did not cease to push its cause in Washington—in fact, the vocal
80 commissioner Lorrin Thurston pushed so hard that he was declared *persona non grata*.

When the Cleveland administration rejected annexation, it requested that the Provisional Government restore the monarchy. This request
85 created additional hard feelings in Hawaii, and the new government flatly refused to comply. For a time it appeared that American forces might be called upon to wrest power from the Provisional Government, but the request was not unduly
90 pressed by the United States and tensions soon eased. The Provisional Government now became the Republic of Hawaii. A new constitution was written and the Islands settled down to await more favorable times.
95 As a consequence of Cleveland's decision, a battle of words raged across the U.S. in the nation's newspapers. Many newspapers supported the royalists while others hailed the Republic. In San Francisco, the *Call* warned that
100 the annexation of Hawaii "will be the open door through which the least desirable elements in Japan

[handwritten bottom: Many ~~support~~ opposed the annexation]

[handwritten bottom: Tone: Neutral/critical to annexation]

will enter upon American citizenship." The *New York Journal and Advertiser* thought Hawaii belonged to the United States: "The acquisition of
105 Hawaii is an imperative patriotic duty."

The most powerful opponent of annexation was the sugar trust, which was comprised of the sugar refiners. The sugar trust was divided into Eastern and Western camps, with Claus Spreckels
110 controlling the West. The refiners subsidized many of the nation's sugar planters. The refiners, therefore, were able not only to name the price mainland farmers received for their crops, but also to control the retail price of sugar as well. The
115 admission of Hawaii created many questions, and the refiners feared a loss of their monopoly control. Perhaps high-grade Hawaiian sugars would not need refining. Certainly all hopes of a tariff barrier would be gone; and it was possible that
120 Hawaiian sugar could be produced at lower costs. All of these things loomed as threats.

The sugar trust lobby in Washington was a powerful one, and its weight was felt in Congress. The lobbyists also conducted a campaign
125 aimed at turning the American public against acquisition of the islands. One of their favorite suggestions was that a popular vote on annexation be taken in Hawaii. This the Republic of Hawaii wanted to avoid at all costs.

1. In passage 1, what event occurred "two weeks earlier" (line 3) than January 28, 1893?

   (A) Hawaii became the fiftieth state of the United States.
   (B) The United States annexed the Hawaiian islands.
   (C) American rebels seized governmental control of the Hawaiian islands.
   (D) Marines from the U.S.S. *Boston* arrived to protect the young native queen from rebels.
   (E) Angry Hawaiian natives rebelled against American rule in Honolulu.

2. According to the second paragraph of passage 1, Americans on the Hawaiian islands

   (A) outnumbered native islanders by about 88,000
   (B) were largely in opposition to the American proposal of an annexation of the islands
   (C) already owned all the land, and thus rightly usurped the power of the monarchy
   (D) had established themselves there in such a way that annexation seemed the next likely step
   (E) were reluctant to establish a tariff reciprocity that would make it difficult to export sugar

3. The word "ceded," as used in line 31, most nearly means

   (A) sowed with new plants
   (B) took as tax
   (C) paid as tax
   (D) donated as charity
   (E) gave over

4. In describing the response of the "molders of public opinion," (line 43) the author of passage 1 suggests that they

   (A) persuaded the United States government to annex the Hawaiian islands
   (B) really had little to do with the public's opinion on annexation
   (C) were unfamiliar with the politics of the Hawaiian islands
   (D) wanted to learn about the events that took place on the islands
   (E) never spoke out on the possible annexation of Hawaii

5. In passage 1, the author mentions Claus Spreckels in order to

   (A) present an example of how businessmen would profit from the annexation of Hawaii
   (B) demonstrate that some people in the United States were opposed to annexation
   (C) prove that Hawaiians were predominantly in favor of statehood
   (D) further the argument concerning the ambiguity of public opinion
   (E) show the role that Americans played in Hawaii

6. All of the following served as reasons that Claus Spreckels supported annexation EXCEPT
    (A) the two-cent-a-pound bounty
    (B) more plentiful sugar for his refineries
    (C) support for the railroads
    (D) cheaper sugar for his refineries
    (E) more cargo for his steamship line to carry

7. According to the first paragraph of passage 2, in order for Hawaii to be annexed, the annexationists needed
    (A) additional funding
    (B) the support of the president
    (C) to overthrow the Provisional Government
    (D) to eliminate the sugar monopoly
    (E) to gain the backing of major United States newspapers

8. Passage 2 suggests that the Provisional Government of Hawaii
    (A) often caved in to pressure from the mainland
    (B) was merely a puppet of American economic interests
    (C) received a large amount of support from the American government
    (D) persisted despite resistance from the American government
    (E) was completely representative of the people of Hawaii

9. The third paragraph of passage 2 implies that public opinion as expressed in newspapers on the issue of Hawaii's annexation was
    (A) solidly in favor of annexation
    (B) overwhelmingly opposed to annexation
    (C) unvoiced, and therefore neither favored nor opposed annexation
    (D) split between support for and opposition to annexation
    (E) limited to only a few public elites

10. The discussion of Hawaiian sugars in lines 106–114 suggests that these products were
    (A) clearly superior to domestic sugars
    (B) faced with a high tariff upon entry to the United States
    (C) not controlled by the American sugar trust
    (D) more expensive than domestic products
    (E) not required to undergo a refining process similar to that undergone by domestic sugars

11. The final paragraph of passage 2 implies that a popular vote on annexation taken in Hawaii would
    (A) have overwhelming success
    (B) most likely fail to gain enough votes for annexation
    (C) have been the political method of choice for the Republic of Hawaii
    (D) not present a true representation of public sentiment
    (E) result in the demise of the Republic of Hawaii

12. Which of the following does the author of passage 2 cite as possible opposition to annexation that is not mentioned by the author of passage 1?
    (A) The exiled Hawaiian monarchy
    (B) Marines from the U.S.S. *Boston*
    (C) Politicians and journalists
    (D) The *Chronicle* and *Examiner*
    (E) The president of the United States

13. One major difference between the two passages is that
    (A) while both authors analyze the same events, they appear to reach different conclusions concerning the possibility of Hawaii's annexation
    (B) the author of the first passage fails to provide specific examples of public sentiment similar to those presented in the second passage
    (C) one passage focuses on support for annexation, while the other emphasizes resistance
    (D) the authors disagree over how much Hawaii had already become Americanized
    (E) the authors arrive at different conclusions concerning the importance of sugar as an import

CRITICAL READING SUMMARY

1. Critical reading questions account for more than two-thirds of all the points on the Critical Reading section.

2. The passage is the least important part of every group of critical reading questions.

3. Begin by reading what you need. Do a topic search (or a trigger word search on narratives) to determine:
   - the author's point
   - the author's tone
   - the passage layout

4. On critical reading, the questions are *not* presented in order of difficulty.

5. Translate the questions into "English." You can't answer a question if you don't understand what you are being asked.

6. Put your finger on the answer. Go back to the passage and find the answer to each specific question.

7. Use line references and lead words to help you find ETS's answer in the passage. Always read <u>five lines above</u> and <u>five lines below</u> the line reference or the lead words.

8. Answer the questions in your own words before you read ETS's answers. You will avoid Joe Bloggs answer choices by knowing what the answer is before you read any of the choices.

9. Use POE to get rid of choices that don't match yours. Cross out incorrect choices as you go. You should have a definite sense of zeroing in on ETS's answer. If you don't cross out incorrect choices, you'll waste time and energy rereading wrong answer choices.

10. Eliminate answer choices that have extreme wording (*must*, etc.) or violate common sense.

11. Be careful on EXCEPT/LEAST/NOT questions. ETS's answer is the choice that is *not* true. Use the true/false technique. Do these questions last.

12. I, II, III questions are also very time-consuming and should therefore be saved for last. Still, eliminating choices is easy and straightforward.

13. Treat dual passages as two separate passages. The majority of the questions won't require you to think of any connection whatsoever between the two passages.

14. To read what you need for a narrative passage, do a trigger word search. Circle the trigger words and look for important information around the trigger words.

15. It's okay to run out of time on the Critical Reading section. Most people do. If you are working at the proper pace, the questions you don't have time to tackle are questions you might have missed, anyway.

6

Short Reading

SAT SHORT READING: CRACKING THE SYSTEM

The SAT already tests you on long passages, so why bother testing you on short passages, as well? If you think it seems pretty pointless, we wholeheartedly agree with you.

However, ETS has a different perspective. The short reading passages are supposed to test what ETS has termed "analogous" or "extended" reasoning: basically, your ability to draw conclusions from what you've read. In reality, though, the short reading passages aren't so different from the long reading passages. In fact, for many of the questions, you'll follow the same exact approach you used in Chapter 5. As for the rest? We're going to show you how to do the following:

1. Read **both** questions first.

2. Actively read the passage.

3. Answer the question in your own words.

4. Use POE to find the best answer.

Although short reading passages precede the long passages, you'll follow the same directions given at the beginning of the section. So don't forget to memorize them before test day! Now let's see what a short reading passage looks like:

> For centuries, citizens have waved banknotes like the monetary flags of their respective nations. Many newly emergent states in Latin American and Africa took great
> Line pride in establishing a currency system that visibly
> 5 expressed their independence from former colonial rulers. Despite the political value of having one's own currency, some of these countries have recently adopted the United States dollar as a means of improving their economies. Ecuador replaced the *sucre* in an attempt
> 10 to halt hyperinflation, while El Salvador relinquished the *colón* in order to increase the efficiency of its many commercial transactions with the U.S. economy. This economic gamble, in which countries surrender control of their monetary system in the hope of achieving greater
> 15 stability, has not been universally popular. Among those who view money as a national symbol, adoption of the dollar represents a step back into the colonial past.

16. The author uses the simile "waved banknotes like the monetary flags of their respective nations" in order to

    (A) highlight the symbolism of currency in many centuries
    (B) compare the appearance of currency and flags in respective nations
    (C) explain the attitude of Latin Americans and Africans toward currency
    (D) suggest a function for banknotes other than commercial transactions
    (E) describe the role of currency as a tangible national symbol

17. It can be most reasonably inferred from the passage that

(A) no African country has considered adopting the dollar as its currency

(B) the Ecuadorian *sucre* has suffered from extreme inflation in the past

(C) adopting the dollar is an effective means of improving Latin American economies

(D) newly emergent countries need their own currencies to escape the colonial past

(E) having one's own currency is of greater political value than economic value

Here's How to Crack It

Even though this short passage will be a quicker read, you still should check out the questions first. The first one asks why the author uses a particular simile while the second question asks us to draw an inference. Question 17 is one of those "extended" reasoning-type questions we mentioned earlier. It's going to require a bit more work, so we'll focus on the first question. Now, *actively* read the passage. By that, we mean read the passage expressly in order to answer the question. The first sentence is the simile the question asks about. That's good. Keep reading, and stop when you can answer why the author included that sentence. The next sentence helps: Apparently currency can be a symbol of a nation's independence. The next couple of sentences discuss what happens when a country surrenders its currency. We're not concerned about that, so skim through those lines. At the end, we read once again about money as a national symbol.

It appears that the author used a simile to show how currency can be a national symbol. Go to the answers and use POE. Choice A misreads the "for centuries" introduction, while choice B is unsupported because there is no comparison of physical appearances in the passage. Choice C incorrectly limits the symbolism to Latin Americans and Africans, and choice D reads the comparison literally, misunderstanding the goal of a simile. What are we left with? Choice E correctly compares the currency with a national symbol.

Now On to the Next Question...

Question 17 is more challenging because you won't find the answer directly stated in the passage; we have no clear idea what ETS wants us to infer. But we can use the answer choices to help us. Take a look at choice A, and then actively read the passage—does it tell us whether African countries have considered adopting the dollar? Nope, so we can't infer it. How about choice B? The passage states, "Ecuador replaced the *sucre* in an attempt to halt hyperinflation." Choice B is looking pretty good at this point. Let's check the rest just to be sure. Lines 12–13 of the passage say that adopting the dollar is a gamble, so C is wrong. Choice D states that countries "need" to have a currency in order to escape colonialism, but the passage doesn't state that at all. Nor can we find any support for choice E. So choice B is it—we can safely infer that the *sucre* must not have been doing too well, since it was replaced. This kind of inference question is just one way the SAT tests "extended reasoning."

WELCOME TO THE TWISTED WORLD OF EXTENDED REASONING

Extended reasoning questions come in the following tasty flavors:

1. Inference questions

2. Weaken/Strengthen questions

3. Author Agree/Respond questions

4. Literary Device questions

5. Similar Situation/Relationship questions

We'll take a look at these questions one by one and tell you how to crack them. Note that these question types are not exclusive to the short reading passages. They may turn up in the long reading passages as well. Follow the exact same approach, regardless of where you encounter these questions.

INFERENCE QUESTIONS

How often does someone ask you make an inference? Unless you're a detective or a scientist, you probably don't spend a lot of time drawing inferences. A true inference is a conclusion based on the available evidence. For example, upon learning that you have two term papers due on the same day, you may *infer* that your teachers are out to get you. While that may or may not be true, it's not the kind of inference for which ETS is looking.

When ETS asks you to infer something, you are in fact being asked to select an answer that *must* be true based on the information in the passage. Wrong answers will either not be mentioned at all in the passage, or will go beyond the information given. For example, if the passage states that a man walks in and his hair is wet, can you infer that it's raining outside? Not according to ETS. That would be beyond the information given. All you can infer is that the man's hair is not dry.

Let's see how this applies to the questions. Try this:

> The Peloponnesian War, which began in 431 BC and
> lasted for 30 years, was perhaps the first modern war
> in Western history. Previously, wars had been routine
> *Line* local affairs, begun after the crops had been planted,
> 5 and decided by a single skirmish so that the warriors
> were generally home for the fall harvest. This was a
> new kind of war: the first "global" conflict involving
> two superpowers. Not only was its scope and duration
> unprecedented, but it also had the novel attributes of
> 10 starting with a sneak attack, seeming unwinnable to both
> sides, and precipitating the slaughter of civilians as a
> matter of course.

14. It can be inferred from the passage that

    (A) the Peloponnesian War was fought all over the world
    (B) both sides in this war had powerful weapons
    (C) most prior wars lasted only a few months
    (D) the combatants were primarily farmers
    (E) neither side was declared victorious by the treaty that was signed

Here's How to Crack It

As we saw before, there is no way to dissect the passage based on the question alone. Instead, we'll use the answer choices to guide our reading. Start with answer choice A. Do we know that the war was fought "all over the world?" Not based on the passage. Joe Bloggs might be fooled by the use of the term "global conflict," but we're sure you weren't tempted by it. Answer choice B also goes beyond the information given; yes, the Peloponnesian War was a significant event, but the passage never mentions the kind of weapons used. Now look at choice C. Can you support that answer? The passage states that before the Peloponnesian War, wars were "decided by a single skirmish." This is what ETS is looking for when it asks you to draw an inference. Choice D is wrong because no mention is made of who fought in the war, while E mentions a treaty that the passage doesn't discuss at all.

Ready for another one? Here it goes:

> For years scientists have tried to discover cures for
> depression. Right now, a combination of talk-therapy
> and drug-therapy is used by most diagnosed patients.
> *Line* However, new research into the biochemistry of food
> 5   reveals that what we eat has a profound impact on how
> we behave. Some scientists postulate that omega-3 fatty
> acids, found in fish, flaxseed, and soy products, increase
> the brain's resistance to depression. Over one-third of the
> brain is fatty tissue, and this compilation of fats, including
> 10   omega-3s, might increase the production of serotonin, a
> chemical necessary to stave off depression. The brains
> of depressed patients generally show depleted omega-3
> levels as compared with the brains of control patients.
> The role of omega-3s in brain chemistry is not fully
> 15   understood, but further research hopes to prove the mood-
> food link once and for all.

12. It can be inferred from the passage that

(A) omega-3 acids can replace traditional drug
      regimens
(B) serotonin is found in omega-3–rich foods
(C) populations with high fish consumption show
      lower levels of depression
(D) the American diet's high starch content
      encourages depression
(E) omega-3 acids can replace traditional fats in
      the brain

Here's How to Crack It

This is another opportunity to use some aggressive POE. Answer choice A is over-generalizing; the research is not definitive. Does the passage state that omega-3s contain serotonin? Nope, they only increase the production of it, so cross off choice B. If you picked choice D or E, you're probably working too hard—nothing supporting those answers can be found anywhere in the passage. Choice C is the best.

WEAKEN/STRENGTHEN QUESTIONS

Weaken/Strengthen questions require you to argue for or against a given argument. First you need to figure out the exact point the author is making. If a question asks you to strengthen the author's conclusion, you must find the answer choice that supports the point. A weaken question requires you to attack or disprove the author's point.

Let's give it a go:

> Because Western classical music encompasses such a variety of styles, media, and composers and spans more than a thousand years, it is difficult to identify the genre's
> *Line* primary characteristics. A monastic chant that relies
> 5 solely on the human voice and an orchestral symphony that requires multiple instruments are both classical, yet neither sounds remotely like the other. Even the title of "classical" is misleading, given that music historians uniformly recognize the years from 1750 to 1827 A.D. as
> 10 the Classical era of classical music. Despite this inability to definitively pinpoint the nature of classical music, people of all musical backgrounds continue to find the label useful. After all, how many listeners would fail to recognize that Bizet's opera *Carmen* is a classical piece
> 15 and that Andrew Lloyd Webber's musical *Cats* is not?

[Handwritten margin note: The label "classical" isn't very specify but is useful]

19. The author's argument is most weakened by which of the following statements?

    (A) Few people listen to classical music on a regular basis.
    (B) Most people have difficulty distinguishing operas from musicals.
    (C) Andrew Lloyd Webber has composed orchestral symphonies in the past.
    (D) Some orchestral performances utilize the human voice.
    (E) Music historians do not consider musicals part of the classical tradition.

Here's How to Crack It

In order to tackle this type of question, we must first figure out the author's point or conclusion. Look for a statement of the author's opinion. What is the author of this passage trying to convince us of? The author wants us to believe that "people of all backgrounds continue to find the label useful." Since this is a weaken question, we want to attack the author's conclusion. The correct answer will make us believe that the "classical" label is *not* useful to people of all backgrounds. Once again, POE is our best bet. Answer choice A states that few people listen to classical music; however, this doesn't really say whether the label is useful. Eliminate it. Choice B states that most people cannot distinguish operas from musicals. Would the label be useful to these people? Probably not. If these people cannot tell the difference between musicals and operas, the label won't be much use to them.

Choices C and D don't affect the conclusion. Choice E indicates that musicals are not part of the classical tradition; this actually *supports* the conclusion. If some types of music don't belong in the classical category, then a label would be useful. Therefore the correct answer is B.

Try another:

Even casual fans of the sport of baseball are likely to recognize the impact Babe Ruth had on the sport. Of course, Ruth's feats on the baseball diamond are well-documented: Ruth is among the all-time leaders in home
Line
5   runs, runs batted in, and walks. In addition, Ruth helped the New York Yankees win seven pennants. But what few people realize is the significant impact Babe Ruth had off the field. His larger-than-life persona and his distinctive physical appearance captured the imaginations of fans of
10 all ages and helped to revitalize the sport of baseball.

8. The author's argument would be most strengthened if it were true that

(A) Babe Ruth was not popular with fans until after he was traded to the New York Yankees
(B) no player holds as many records as does Babe Ruth
(C) Babe Ruth was the first player elected to the Baseball Hall of Fame
(D) attendance at baseball games was significantly lower prior to Babe Ruth's playing career than attendance was during it
(E) many fans were upset when Babe Ruth's records were subsequently broken

Here's How To Crack It

What is the author trying to convince us of? Apparently, Babe Ruth had a big impact on baseball and helped to revitalize the sport. The question wants us to strengthen this conclusion, so we need to find an answer that will make us more likely to believe the author. Choice A says that Ruth was popular, but it doesn't say how he helped to revitalize the sport. Answer choice B doesn't affect the conclusion at all. Choice C makes it obvious that Ruth was a great player, but again doesn't address how he revitalized the sport. In choice D, we see that attendance at baseball games increased during Ruth's career. This would support the author's conclusion. And while choice E might be true, it doesn't relate to the author's main point. Therefore D is the best answer.

AUTHOR AGREE/RESPOND QUESTIONS

These are fun little questions. Here, ETS wants us to figure out what the author would most likely agree with or how the author would respond to a particular point. Since it is unlikely that you are able to read the author's mind, the answer to these questions has to be in line with the main point of the passage. As on inference questions, you must be careful not to go beyond the information given in the passage.

Have a go at this question:

> The annals of scientific history are filled with names of great import. August names such as Mendeleev, Darwin, and Einstein dominate their respective fields, and the
> *Line* majority of science textbooks sing their praises as well.
> 5 But what of the names J.L. Meyer, A.R. Wallace, and Hermann Minkowski? These names are not revered, but instead have been relegated to the dustbin of science, known only to the most diligent of scientific scholars. Yet these men independently developed
> 10 theories on the periodic nature of the elements, on the theory of evolution, and on the theory of relativity, often at practically the same time as their better known contemporaries. It is a mere whim of historical chance that we choose to remember some scientists but not others
> 15 of equal importance.

16. The author would most likely agree with which one of the following statements?

    (A) Scientific breakthroughs must be seen not as the product of an individual scientist but as the result of multiple individuals.
    (B) Science textbooks should give as much attention to Meyer, Wallace, and Minkowski as they do to Mendeleev, Darwin, and Einstein.
    (C) No scientific advances should ever be attributed to one scientist.
    (D) Scientific history is not entirely correct when it ascribes certain scientific achievements to individual scientists.
    (E) Mendeleev, Darwin, and Einstein should not receive credit for their discoveries.

Here's How to Crack It

The question wants us to figure out what the author would most likely agree with. Read the passage actively, looking for the main idea. The passage indicates that certain scientists are highly regarded for their achievements, while others are not. Now use POE on the answer choices. Choice A is close, but it uses the word *must*, which is too extreme. We don't know that the author would agree with choice B because the author doesn't state how much attention the other scientists should receive. Choice C is also too strong. Choice D is more wishy-washy (which is a good thing on the SAT) and is similar to the main idea of the passage. Answer choice E is wrong because the author never says that those scientists shouldn't receive credit, only that the credit should be shared. Therefore, D is the best answer.

PASSAGE PAIRS

Oftentimes, short reading passages will come in pairs. In these cases, you can almost bet on a question asking you how one author would respond to the other (unfortunately, the author never just tells the other one to cram it).

Take a look at these two passages:

Passage 1

Dreams of sending a manned mission to Mars are unlikely to come to fruition without the implementation of what NASA terms In Situ Resource Utilization (ISRU)
Line strategies: the use of Martian resources to support the
5 expedition. Scientists believe that the Martian landscape could yield the rocket fuel, energy, water, and oxygen necessary for a sustained human presence on the Red Planet. Without the use of ISRUs, the cost of transporting fuel, materials, and vital supplies from Earth would be
10 prohibitive, not to mention potentially dangerous. Despite the eagerness of scientists to explore Mars, no one would advocate sending explorers some forty million miles from Earth with no viable way of returning.

Passage 2

While sending a person to Mars would certainly
15 represent a triumph of human ingenuity and courage, the current state of technology makes such a mission unlikely in the near future. Some optimists argue that we can simply apply the lessons learned in sending people to the Moon to this more formidable situation. But there
20 are forty million miles separating Mars from Earth, a vast distance. As one scientist stated, "A distress message from the Moon would reach Earth in 1.8 seconds. But that same message would take almost 10 minutes to reach us from Mars. The time lag could be fatal." With so many pressing
25 scientific issues here on Earth, time and money should not be spent on a mission that would contribute more to human vanity than to scientific progress.

18. The author of Passage 2 would most likely respond to the author of Passage 1's proposal to use ISRUs by

(A) arguing that the scientific value of ISRUs has been overstated

(B) agreeing that ISRUs could make a manned trip to Mars possible

(C) rejecting the assertion that ISRUs are the only reasonable solution to the problem of providing fuel and oxygen for a manned mission to Mars

(D) confirming that ISRUs may make a manned mission to Mars safer for explorers

(E) asserting that the technology necessary for ISRUs is not sufficiently developed to make a mission to Mars feasible

Here's How To Crack It

The key to cracking this type of question is to stick with the main idea and to use some aggressive POE. The main idea of Passage 1 is that ISRUs can make a mission to Mars possible. However, Passage 2 argues that a mission to Mars isn't possible due to the limits of current technology. Choice A is out because the issue isn't the scientific value of the ISRU; the issue is whether the technology works. Choice B is the opposite of what the author of Passage 2 would believe. Choice C rejects the use of ISRUs, but the author of Passage 1 doesn't assert that the ISRUs are the only way to solve the problem. The author of Passage 2 believes a trip to Mars is too dangerous and so wouldn't believe choice D. It looks like E is best.

LITERARY DEVICE QUESTIONS

While the SAT is most definitely not a literature test, ETS will occasionally toss around some fancy sounding literature terms. Don't worry, though: You won't have to know what a synecdoche is (go ahead, look it up). ETS will only test you on the most basic literary terms. Here's a recap of the types of terms that you might see on the test:

- **Metaphor**: A metaphor uses one word or concept to symbolize a seemingly unrelated word or concept.

  Example: He is the bomb. The SAT is a joke.

- **Simile**: A simile makes a comparison by using the words *like* or *as*.

  Example: Her brown eyes were like pools of fresh mud. His back was as hairy as a warthog's.

- **Personification**: Just as the word sounds, personification attaches human thoughts, behaviors, or feelings to nonhuman objects.

  Example: The wind clawed me with its horrible, bitterly cold fingernails.

- **Rhetorical Question:** A rhetorical question is a device used for persuasive effect.

  Example: You didn't think that your SAT scores would matter for the rest of your life, did you?

- **Hyperbole:** A hyperbole is a deliberate exaggeration.

  Example: I've probably done at least a million SAT problems in the last week.

- **Irony:** Irony is the use of words to express the opposite of their literal meaning. It can also be a situation in which the actual outcome is incongruous with the expected outcome.

  Example: I just can't wait to get started on my homework—it's only going to take, oh, six hours to do.

Of course, if you aren't comfortable with these terms, feel free to skip these questions; there aren't likely to more than a couple of them anyway. Remember, you are in control of the test. But before you decide to skip ahead, give this one a try:

> A sugar molecule known as *hyaluronan* is perhaps the most diligent compound available to modern medicine. Since 1980, it has been used to treat humans in a variety
> *Line* of ways: to protect the cornea during eye surgery,
> 5 to reduce arthritic inflammation, and to prevent the formation of scar tissue after surgery. Hyaluronan occurs naturally in humans, but it was originally discovered in the eyes of cows in the 1930s. At the time, there was no commercially viable way to extract hyaluronan
> 10 to test its therapeutic potential. Years later, scientists not only discovered the compound was contained in rooster combs but also developed a method to extract it from them. Veterinarians used hyaluronan for years before the extraction method patent was sold to a major
> 15 pharmaceutical company in 1980.

14. Which of the following phrases provides the best example of personification?

   (A) "sugar molecule"
   (B) "diligent compound"
   (C) "protect the cornea"
   (D) "the eyes of cows"
   (E) "contained in rooster combs"

Here's How to Crack It

Personification? Even without a refresher on literary terms, we bet you could figure this one out. You can eliminate choice A; the sugar molecule isn't doing anything remotely humanlike. Choice B, however, makes the compound diligent—diligence is a human trait. Keep it. Choice C is wrong, since the molecule isn't choosing to protect the cornea, and D is wrong because cows do have eyes, just like humans do. Choice E is wrong because once again, nothing humanlike is implied.

SIMILAR SITUATION/RELATIONSHIP QUESTIONS

For this type of question, ETS wants to you to match the situation or relationship found in the passage with a similar case in the answer choices. These questions can seem weird because the answer choices may discuss situations that are not mentioned at all in the passage. But the details aren't important—only the general type of situation or relationship.

Here's an example:

> The word *telescope* literally means "far-seeing," but
> all telescopes do not "see" in the same way. While the
> most common types of telescope use a system of mirrors
> *Line* and lenses to gather light from distant objects, other
> 5 telescopes employ very different ways of seeing. Radio
> telescopes, for example, do not see at all; rather, they
> use antennae to pick up radio waves emitted by celestial
> objects. Other telescopes, such as X ray telescopes,
> infrared telescopes, and ultraviolet telescopes, can see
> 10 wavelengths imperceptible to the human eye. NASA's
> next major telescope project, the James Webb Space
> Telescope—heralded as a "breakthrough" in telescope
> technology—will rely on a combination of these types of
> viewing methods.

17. The relationship between the traditional telescope
and the radio telescope, as described in the passage,
is most similar to which of the following?

(A) the relationship between the horseshoe crab,
which is not a crustacean, and a crab, which is
a member of the crustacean family

(B) the relationship between the sea snake, a
venomous species of snake that lives in the
sea, and the king cobra, a venomous species
of snake that lives on land

(C) the relationship between the spider monkey,
a small monkey with a prehensile tail, and
a howler monkey, a large monkey with a
prehensile tail

(D) the relationship between the penguin, a
species of bird that cannot fly, and the eagle, a
species of bird that can fly long distances

(E) the relationship between the cougar and
mountain lion, members of the same species
that are known by different names

Here's How to Crack It

From the answer choices, it appears that none of them makes sense. After all, the
passage is about telescopes and the answer choices talk about animals. What's
the deal? Forget about the details of the choices and focus instead on the basic
situation. According to the passage, the radio telescope is a type of telescope that
isn't really a telescope at all. Find the answer that has the same relationship. In
choice A, we have a type of crab that really isn't a crab at all. That's exactly what
we're looking for. Choice B details the relationship between two types of snakes
that live in two different environments. That's not what we want. Choice C makes
an issue about the size relationship between the two monkeys, but the passage
doesn't relate the size of the optic telescope to that of the radio telescope. Choice D
talks about members of a species, one which has a specific ability and one which
lacks it. That's doesn't match either. Choice E describes a situation in which one
species has two different names, but again that's not the same as the situation in
the passage. The best answer is A.

DRILL 1

Use the following short critical reading passages to put together everything you've learned. Review your strategy for attacking these paragraph-length passages and focus on cracking the questions. Remember to avoid ETS's trap answers that misrepresent the passage, aren't common sense, or go to extremes. Try to answer the questions in your own words before looking at the answer choices. Then use POE to get to the least stinky answer choice. Answers can be found on page 337.

Critical Reading Strategy

1. Carefully read and translate the questions.
2. Forage in the passage for answers.
3. Paraphrase the answer to the question.
4. Use POE.

> The passage below is followed by questions based on its content. Answer the questions on the basis of what is <u>stated</u> or <u>implied</u> in the passage and in any introductory material that may be provided.

Adopting a completely computerized voting system is unfeasible. If ballots are recorded only in a machine's memory with no physical proof, a recount becomes
Line
5 impossible. Vigilant election officials may ensure integrity and security at the polls, yet accidental or malicious errors could be introduced into software long before election day. If a voter chooses "X," but the machine records "Y," there is no way to recover the intended vote. If computers
10 are used in voting, there should also be a paper ballot that permits voters to verify their choices. This ballot would allow the voter's intent to be confirmed at any later date. Advances in technology are beneficial and should be integrated into the voting process to improve accessibility
15 and ease of ballot casting, but we should not reject paper ballots entirely.

14. The tone of the author in the above article is one of

    (A) unbiased neutrality
    (B) reasoned opposition
    (C) unabashed defiance
    (D) hesitant support
    (E) optimistic fervor

15. All of the following reasons not to adopt an entirely computerized voting system are given in the passage EXCEPT

    (A) both paper ballot and electronic voting systems are by nature insecure
    (B) a machine may make a mistake in recording a person's intended vote
    (C) even the best election officials may be unable to judge the integrity of software
    (D) a lack of physical evidence renders a post-election recount impractical
    (E) tampering or mistakes in the computer program could remain undiscovered until it is too late

Terra-cotta, or "baked earth," is an artistic medium that was used widely during the Roman Empire. Originally used for architecture, terra-cotta was transformed into
Line an artistic material during the Renaissance. Sculptors in
5 particular began to use the fired clay to make "bozzetti," rough drafts of sculptures that would later be created out of stone, bronze, or other more traditional materials. These rough drafts, however, often created more interest than the finished works. During the eighteenth century,
10 art aficionados began collecting terra-cotta models for exhibition in their homes and at salons. Collectors maintained that the models presented a more accurate representation of an artist's talent, and created a sustainable market for larger sculptures. The trend was
15 so successful that these "rough drafts" often commanded higher selling prices than the original pieces.

16. In context, the word "medium" in the first sentence most nearly means

(A) material
(B) average
(C) method
(D) bozzetti
(E) implement

17. It can be inferred from the passage that

(A) collectors were not interested in owning finished sculptures
(B) terra-cotta was not used to make artistic miniatures
(C) terra-cotta was readily available to sculptors
(D) artists preferred their rough drafts to their finished sculptures
(E) terra-cotta was no longer used for architecture after the Renaissance

After more than thirty years of study, Japanese researchers claim to have identified a new species of baleen whale. In 1970, nine adult whales were killed in
Line the Indian Ocean for research purposes. Through recent
5 DNA analysis of samples from these whales, the Japanese scientists obtained what they believe is sufficient data to identify a new species. Aside from differences in both internal and external physical features, there were significant differences between the genetic material of
10 these whales and that of the most similar species of whale used for comparision, the fin whale. Other researchers in this field have cautiously pointed out that DNA comparisions with seven other similar species were not conducted.

18. According to the passage, the Japanese researchers

   (A) ignored genetic data from seven similar species
   (B) would have identified the new species in 1970 if DNA analysis had been available
   (C) chose the fin whale for comparison because of its physical size
   (D) compared the DNA of nine separate whales to that of the fin whale
   (E) had the nine whales killed to obtain samples of genetic material

19. The author's primary purpose is to

   (A) exemplify how the scientific process functions
   (B) criticize the Japanese researchers for incomplete analysis
   (C) show how slowly Japanese scientists proceed
   (D) justify the killing of whales for research
   (E) indicate a valuable utilization of DNA analysis

Charles Marie de la Condamine, a French scientist, introduced the idea for the rubber eraser to Europe in 1736. Condamine brought natural "India" rubber from
Line South America to the Institute de France in Paris for study.
5 The Indian tribes in South America had used the rubber as an adhesive—for headdresses and other costume pieces— but Europeans later adapted the material as erasers. In 1770, it is said that an English engineer, Edward Naime, writing at home, accidentally picked up a chunk of this
10 rubber instead of the breadcrumbs commonly used then to remove pencil marks, and discovered its possibilities as an erasing tool. He eventually sold his "rubber squares" throughout the continent. The only inadequacy of these early erasers was that, like food, they spoiled
15 quickly—a problem that remained until 1839, when Charles Goodyear learned to "cure" the rubber to prevent spoilage, and the new and improved eraser became even more popular.

20. According to the passage, who was first responsible for popularizing rubber erasers in Europe?

    (A) Charles Goodyear
    (B) Charles Marie de la Condamine
    (C) Institute de France in Paris
    (D) Indian tribes in South America
    (E) Edward Naime

21. It can be inferred that which of the following must be true of 1770?

    (A) "India" rubber was available outside the Institute de France.
    (B) Charles Goodyear was still working on a way to "cure" rubber.
    (C) The Institute de France was no longer experimenting with the "India" rubber.
    (D) Breadcrumbs were the only erasing tools available to Europeans.
    (E) Europeans bought rubber squares to wipe away pencil marks.

In 1965, Houston's Astrodome became the first stadium
to use artificial turf, named AstroTurf® in its honor. The
fake grass was first developed for playground areas
Line in inner cities. The Ford Foundation had conducted
5 studies of physical fitness levels among young men in
the military, and they found that those who came from
suburban areas were generally stronger and faster because
they had more grassy areas to use for sports. At the same
time, the Chemstrand Company was developing durable
10 flooring materials for public buildings. Chemstrand
eventually tested artificial turf on the grounds of a high
school in Providence, Rhode Island, in a project funded
by the Ford Foundation. It was the first successful use of
the artificial grass before it was christened in Houston.

22. In the last sentence, the word "christened" most
nearly means

    (A) used
    (B) blessed
    (C) named
    (D) debuted
    (E) popularized

23. According to the passage, most inner city children

    (A) joined the military less often than suburban
        children
    (B) could not afford to live near grassy areas in
        the city
    (C) had less access to areas with AstroTurf than
        most suburban children
    (D) were generally weaker and slower than most
        suburban children
    (E) had fewer playground areas than suburban
        children

Some critics say the demise of the short-lived Women's
United Soccer Association (WUSA) was due to an
apathetic and declining fan base. They are wrong. The
Line core group of fans remained constant for all three seasons
5 of WUSA's existence. Soccer fans of all ages and both
sexes were regulars at the matches. Families, single
collegiate men, and middle-aged women all purchased
season tickets during the inaugural season and renewed
them each year. Corporate sponsorships increased and
10 the association's expenses decreased each year of the
league's existence. Even so, the WUSA repeatedly posted
excessive losses each year. Management deficiencies
and malfeasance were the causes of the WUSA's early
departure from the ranks of professional women's sports
15 in the United States.

24. The overall tone of this passage is
    (A) analytical
    (B) equivocal
    (C) apathetic
    (D) speculative
    (E) assured

25. The author most likely would agree with which of
    the following statements?

    (A) Professional women's sporting leagues cannot
        succeed in the United States.
    (B) The WUSA needed managerial changes
        and additional corporate sponsorships to
        survive.
    (C) The WUSA needed to do a better job of
        maintaining spectator interest.
    (D) The WUSA could have succeeded by making
        managerial changes.
    (E) The players needed to work harder to improve
        their game to entice people to attend.

SHORT READING SUMMARY

1. Short reading passages account for roughly eight to ten questions on the SAT.

2. Approach short reading passages by reading the questions first.

3. Actively read the passage, looking for the answer to the question. Paraphrase it, and then go to the answer choices to find one that matches.

4. Most short reading questions are similar to the types of questions found on the long reading passages.

5. Some of the short reading questions are designed to test "extended reasoning."

6. The questions for short reading passages are not arranged in order of difficulty.

7. Regardless of the question type, the best answer will still be supported by the passage.

8. Follow the same POE guidelines given for long reading passages when eliminating answers.

Vocabulary

WORDS, WORDS, WORDS

A great way to improve your reading and essay-writing skills is to improve your vocabulary. The more words you know on the test, the easier it will be. It's as simple as that. For this reason, it's important that you get to work on your vocabulary *immediately*.

THE HIT PARADE

The Hit Parade list consists of those words that show up most often on the SAT. Each word on the list is accompanied by its definition, a pronunciation guide, and a sentence that uses the word. Your vocabulary-building program should start with these words.

LEARN THE WORDS IN GROUPS

The Hit Parade has been arranged by groups of related words. Learning groups of related words can better help you remember each word's meaning. Even when you don't remember the exact meaning of a word, you may remember what group it is from. This will give you an idea of the word's meaning, which can help you use POE to get to an answer.

Make each group of words a part of your life. Rip out one of the group lists, carry it around with you, and use the words throughout your day. For example, on Monday you may feel like using words of *disdain* (see the "Negative Statements" list), but on Friday you may wish to be more *affable* (see the "Friendliness" list).

DON'T MEMORIZE THE DICTIONARY

Only a tiny percentage of all the words in the English language are ever used on the SAT. Generally speaking, the SAT tests the kinds of words that an educated adult—your English teacher, for example—would know without having to look them up. It tests the sorts of words that you encounter in your daily reading, from a novel in English class to the newspaper.

HOW TO MEMORIZE NEW WORDS

Here are three effective methods for learning new words.

1. **Flash Cards:** You can make your own flash cards out of 3×5 index cards. Write a word on one side and the definition on the other. Then quiz yourself on the words, or practice with a friend. You can carry a few cards around with you every day and work on them in spare moments, like when you're riding on the bus.

2. **The Image Approach:** The image approach involves letting each new word suggest a wild image to you, then using that image to help you remember the word. For example, the word *enfranchise* means "to give the right to vote." *Franchise* might suggest to you a McDonald's franchise. You could remember the new word by imagining people lined up to vote at a McDonald's. The weirder the image, the better you'll remember the word.

3. **Mnemonics:** Speaking of "the weirder, the better," another way to learn words is to use mnemonics. A mnemonic is a device or trick, such as a rhyme or a song, that helps you remember something. *In fourteen hundred ninety-two Columbus sailed the ocean blue* is a mnemonic that helps you remember a date in history. The funnier or the stranger you make your mnemonic, the more likely you are to remember it. Write down your mnemonics (your flash cards are a great place for these).

Even if you are not able to think of a mnemonic for *every* Hit Parade word, sometimes you'll end up learning the word just by thinking about the definition long enough.

LOOK IT UP

Well-written general publications—like the *New York Times* and *Sports Illustrated*—are good sources of SAT words. You should read them on a regular basis. When you come across a new word, write it down, look it up, and remember it. You can make flash cards for these words as well.

Before you can memorize the definition of a word you come across in your reading, you have to find out what it means. You'll need a real dictionary for that. ETS uses two dictionaries in writing the SAT: the *American Heritage Dictionary* and *Webster's New Collegiate Dictionary*. You should own a copy of one or the other. (You'll use it in college, too—it's a good investment.)

Keep in mind that most words have more than one definition. The dictionary will list these in order of frequency, from the most common to the most obscure. ETS will trip you up by testing the second, third, or even the fourth definition of a familiar-sounding word. For example, the word *pedestrian* shows up repeatedly on the SAT. When ETS uses it, though, it never means a person on foot—the definition of *pedestrian* you're probably most familiar with. ETS uses it to mean common, ordinary, banal—a *secondary* definition.

Very often, when you see easy words on hard SAT questions, ETS is testing a second, third, or fourth definition that you may not be familiar with. The Hit Parade will help prepare you for these tricks. So grab those index cards and get ready to improve your vocabulary!

COMMUNICATION

assertion   uh SUR shun
> *a declaration or statement*
>> We could not believe John's assertion that he had never seen *Star Wars*.

clarity   KLAR uh tee
> *clearness in thought or expression*
>> Carol spoke with such clarity that her two-year-old son understood exactly what she wanted him to do.

cogent   KO jent
> *convincing; reasonable*
>> Christina's argument was so cogent that even her opponents had to agree with her.

coherent   ko HEER ent
> *logically connected*
>> The old prospector's story was not coherent; he rambled on about different things that had nothing to do with each other.

cohesive   ko HEE siv
> *condition of sticking together*
>> Erik's essay was cohesive because each point flowed nicely into the next point.

didactic   dy DAK tik
> *intended to instruct*
>> The tapes were entertaining and didactic because they both amused and instructed children.

discourse   DIS kors
> *verbal expression or exchange; conversation*
>> Their discourse varied widely; they discussed everything from Chaucer to ice fishing.

eloquence   EH lo kwens
> *the ability to speak vividly or persuasively*
>> Cicero's eloquence is legendary; his speeches were well-crafted and convincing.

emphasize   EM fuh size
> *to give special attention to something, to stress*
>> During English class, our instructor emphasized the importance of learning vocabulary.

fluid   FLOO id
> *easily flowing*
>> The two old friends' conversation was fluid; each of them was able to respond quickly and easily to what the other had to say.

implication   im pli KAY shun

  the act of suggesting or hinting

  When your mother says, "Where were you raised, in a pigsty?" the implication is that you should clean your room.

lucid   LOO sid

  easily understood; clear

  Our teacher does a good job because he provides lucid explanations of difficult concepts.

pundit   PUN dit

  an authority who expresses his/her opinions

  The political pundit has made many predictions, but few of them have come true.

rhetoric   RET uh rik

  the art of using language effectively and persuasively

  Since they are expected to make speeches, most politicians and lawyers are well versed in the art of rhetoric.

◣ DECISIONS

arbiter   AHR bih ter

  a judge who decides a disputed issue

  An arbiter was hired to settle the Major League Baseball strike because the owners and players could not come to an agreement.

biased   BYE ist

  prejudiced

  A judge should not be biased, but should weigh the evidence fairly before making up her mind.

exculpate   EKS kul payt

  to free from guilt or blame

  When the gold coins discovered in his closet were found to be fake, Dr. Rideau was exculpated and the search for the real thief continued.

impartial   im PAR shul

  not in favor of one side or the other, unbiased

  The umpire had a hard time remaining impartial; his son was pitching for the home team, and this made it difficult to call the game fairly.

incontrovertible   in kon truh VERT uh bul

  indisputable; not open to question

  The videotape of the robbery provided incontrovertible evidence against the suspect—he was obviously guilty.

integrity   in TEG rit ee
trustworthiness; completeness
> The integrity of the witness was called into question when her dislike
> for the defendant was revealed—some jurors suspected that she was not
> being entirely truthful.

jurisprudence   jer is PROO duns
the philosophy or science of law
> Judges and lawyers are longtime students of jurisprudence.

objectivity   ahb jek TIV ih tee
treating facts without influence from personal feelings or prejudices
> It is important that a judge hear all cases with objectivity, so that her
> personal feelings do not affect her decision.

penitent   PEN ih tunt
expressing remorse for one's misdeeds
> His desire to make amends to the people he had wronged indicated
> that he was truly penitent, so the parole board let him out of the peni-
> tentiary.

plausible   PLAWZ ih bul
seemingly valid or acceptable; credible
> Keith's excuse that he missed school yesterday because he was captured
> by space aliens was not very plausible.

substantiated   sub STAN shee ay tid
supported with proof or evidence; verified
> The fingerprint evidence substantiated the detective's claim that the
> suspect had been at the scene of the crime.

vindicated   VIN duh kayt id
freed from blame
> Mrs. Layton was finally vindicated after her husband admitted to the
> crime.

PRIDE

condescending   kon de SEND ing
treating people as weak or inferior
> Robert always looked down on his sister and treated her in a conde-
> scending manner.

contemptuous   kun TEMP choo us
feeling hatred; scornful
> She was so contemptuous of people who wore fur that she sprayed red
> paint on their coats.

despotic   des PAHT ik
exercising absolute power; tyrannical
> He was a despotic ruler whose every law was enforced with threats of
> violence or death.

dictatorial   dik tuh TOR ee ul

domineering; oppressively overbearing

> The coach had a dictatorial manner and expected people to do whatever he demanded.

disdain   dis DAYN

(n.) contempt, scorn
(v.) to regard or treat with contempt; to look down on

> I felt nothing but disdain for the person who stole my lunch—what a jerk!

haughty   HAW tee

arrogant; vainly proud

> His haughty manner made it clear that he thought he was better than everyone else.

imperious   im PEER ee us

arrogantly domineering or overbearing

> She had a very imperious way about her; she was bossy and treated others as if they were beneath her.

patronizing   PAY truh ny zing

treating in a condescending manner

> Patrick had such a patronizing attitude that he treated everyone around him like a bunch of little kids.

DIFFICULT SITUATIONS

convoluted   kon vuh LOO tid

intricate; complex

> The directions were so convoluted that we drove all around the city and got lost.

cryptic   KRIP tik

difficult to comprehend

> The writing on the walls of the crypt was cryptic; none of the scientists understood it.

futile   FEW tul

having no useful purpose; pointless

> It is futile to try to explain the difference between right and wrong to your pet.

impede   im PEED

to slow the progress of

> The retreating army constructed barbed-wire fences and destroyed bridges to impede the advance of the enemy.

obscure   ub SKYUR

(adj.) relatively unknown
(v.) to conceal or make indistinct

Scott constantly makes references to obscure cult films, and no one ever gets his jokes.

The man in front of me was so tall that his head obscured my view of the movie.

quandary   KWAHN dree

a state of uncertainty or perplexity

Morgan was in a quandary because he had no soap with which to do his laundry.

NEGATIVE CHARACTERISTICS

dilatory   DIL uh tor ee

habitually late

Always waiting until the last moment to do his work, Stephen was a dilatory student.

indolent   IN duh lunt

lazy

Mr. Lan said his students were indolent because none of them had done their homework.

insipid   in SIP id

uninteresting; unchallenging

That insipid movie was so boring and predictable that I walked out.

listless   LIST luss

lacking energy

Since she is accustomed to an active lifestyle, Mary feels listless when she has nothing to do.

torpor   TOR per

laziness; inactivity; dullness

The hot and humid day filled everyone with an activity-halting torpor.

RELATIONSHIPS

alienated   AY lee en ay tid

removed or disassociated from (friends, family, or homeland)

Rudolph felt alienated from the other reindeer because they never let him join in their reindeer games.

alliance   uh LY uhns

a union of two or more groups

The two countries formed an alliance to stand against their common enemy.

disparity dis PAR uh tee

inequality in age, rank, or degree; difference

There is a great disparity between the rich and poor in many nations.

servile SER vil

submissive; like a servant

Cameron's servile behavior finally ended when he decided to stand up to his older brother.

suppressed suh PREST

subdued; kept from being circulated

The author's book was suppressed because the dictator thought it was too critical of his regime.

BEAUTY

embellish em BELL ish

to make beautiful by ornamenting; to decorate

We embellished the account of our vacation by including descriptions of the many colorful people and places we visited.

florid FLOR id

describing flowery or elaborate speech

The candidate's speech was so florid that although no one could understand what he was talking about, they all agreed that he sounded good saying it.

opulent AHP yuh lunt

exhibiting a display of great wealth

Dances at the king's palace are always very opulent affairs because no expense is spared.

ornate or NAYT

elaborately decorated

The carved wood was so ornate that you could examine it several times and still notice things you had not seen before.

ostentatious ah sten TAY shus

describing a showy or pretentious display

Whenever the millionaire gave a party, the elaborate decorations and enormous amounts of food were always part of her ostentatious display of wealth.

poignant POYN yunt

profoundly moving; touching

The most poignant part of the movie was when the father finally made peace with his son.

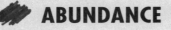

ABUNDANCE

ebullience   ih BOOL yuns
intense enthusiasm
> A sense of ebullience swept over the crowd when the matador defeated the bull.

effusive   eh FYOO siv
emotionally unrestrained; gushy
> Gwyneth was effusive in her thanks after winning the Oscar; she even burst into tears.

egregious   uh GREE jus
conspicuously bad or offensive
> Forgetting to sterilize surgical tools before an operation would be an egregious error.

flagrant   FLAY grunt
extremely or deliberately shocking or noticeable
> Burning the flag shows flagrant disrespect for the country.

frenetic   freh NEH tik
wildly excited or active
> The pace at the busy office was frenetic; Megan never had a moment to catch her breath.

gratuitous   gruh TOO ih tus
given freely; unearned; unwarranted
> The film was full of gratuitous sex and violence that was not essential to the story.

superfluous   soo PER floo us
extra; unnecessary
> If there is sugar in your tea, adding honey would be superfluous.

FULL ON

ample   AM pul
describing a large amount of something
> Because no one else wanted to try the new soda, Minesh was able to have an ample sample.

comprehensive   kahm pre HEN siv
large in scope or content
> The final exam was comprehensive, covering everything that we had learned that year.

copious   KO pee us
plentiful; having a large quantity
> She had taken copious notes during class, using up five large notebooks.

permeated   PER mee ay tid

spread or flowing throughout

> After I had my hair professionally curled, the scent of chemicals permeated the air.

pervasive   per VAY siv

dispersed throughout

> The pervasive smell of baking bread filled the house and wafted onto the back porch.

prodigious   pruh DIJ us

enormous

> The shattered vase required a prodigious amount of glue to repair.

replete   ruh PLEET

abundantly supplied; filled to capacity

> After a successful night of trick-or-treating, Dee's bag was replete with Halloween candy.

POSITIVE SITUATIONS

alleviate   uh LEEV ee ayt

to ease a pain or a burden

> John took aspirin to alleviate the pain from the headache he got after taking the SAT.

asylum   uh SY lum

a place of retreat or security

> The soldiers sought asylum from the bombs in the underground shelter.

auspicious   aw SPISH us

favorable; promising

> Our trip to the beach had an auspicious start; the rain stopped just as we started the car.

benevolent   buh NEV uh lunt

well-meaning; generous

> She was a kind and benevolent queen who was concerned about her subjects' well-being.

benign   buh NINE

kind and gentle

> Uncle Ben is a benign and friendly man who is always willing to help.

emollient   eh MOHL yunt

(adj.) softening and soothing
(n.) something that softens or soothes

> His kind words served as an emollient to the pain she had suffered.

mollify   MAHL uh fy
> *to calm or soothe*
>> Anna's apology for scaring her brother did not mollify him; he was mad at her all day.

reclamation   rek luh MAY shun
> *the act of making something useful again*
>> Thanks to the reclamation project, the once unusable land became a productive farm.

sanction   SANK shun
> *to give official authorization or approval*
>> The students were happy when the principal agreed to sanction the use of calculators in math classes.

LIES

dubious   DOO bee us
> *doubtful; of unlikely authenticity*
>> Jerry's claim that he could fly like Superman seemed dubious—we didn't believe it.

fabricated   FAB ruh kay tid
> *made; concocted in order to deceive*
>> Fabio fabricated the story that he used to play drums for Metallica; he had never actually held a drumstick in his life.

hypocrisy   hih POK ruh see
> *the practice of pretending to be something one is not; insincerity*
>> People who claim to be vegetarian but eat chicken and fish are guilty of hypocrisy.

slander   SLAN der
> *false charges and malicious oral statements about someone*
>> After the radio host stated that Monica was a space alien, she sued him for slander.

spurious   SPUR ee us
> *not genuine; false, counterfeit*
>> The sportscaster made a spurious claim when he said that the San Antonio Spurs were undefeated.

CUNNING

astute   uh STOOT
> *shrewd; clever*
>> Kelly is financially astute; she never falls for the tricks that credit card companies play.

camouflage   KAM uh flahzh

to hide by blending in with surroundings

> The smugglers did not want the trail to their hideout discovered, so they camouflaged the entrance with branches and vines.

clandestine   klan DES tin

secretive

> The spies planned a clandestine maneuver that depended on its secrecy to work.

coup   KOO

a brilliantly executed plan

> It was a coup when I talked the salesperson into selling me this valuable cuckoo clock for five dollars.

disingenuous   dis in JEN yoo us

not straightforward; crafty

> Mr. Gelman was rather disingenuous; although he seemed simply to be asking about your health, he was really trying to figure out why you'd been absent.

ruse   ROOZ

a crafty trick

> The offer of a free cruise was merely a ruse to get people to listen to their sales pitch.

stratagem   STRAT uh jem

a clever trick used to deceive or outwit

> Planting microphones in the gangster's home was a clever, but illegal, stratagem.

surreptitiously   sur ep TISH us lee

done by secretive means

> Matt drank the cough syrup surreptitiously because he didn't want anyone to know that he was sick.

wary   WAIR ee

on guard; watchful

> My father becomes wary whenever a salesman calls him on the phone; he knows that many crooks use the phone so that they can't be charged with mail fraud.

wily   WY lee

cunning

> The wily coyote devised all sorts of clever traps to catch the roadrunner.

UNCERTAINTY

ambiguous   am BIG yoo us

open to more than one interpretation

His eyes were an ambiguous color: Some people thought they were brown and some thought they were green.

ambivalent   am BIV uh lunt

simultaneously having opposing feelings; uncertain

She had ambivalent feelings about her dance class: On one hand, she enjoyed the exercise, but on the other hand, she thought the choice of dances could be more interesting.

apathetic   ap uh THET ik

feeling or showing little emotion

When the defendant was found guilty on all charges, her face remained expressionless and she appeared to be entirely apathetic.

arbitrary   AR bih trayr ee

determined by impulse rather than reason

The principal made the arbitrary decision that students could not wear hats in school without offering any logical reason for the rule.

capricious   kuh PREE shus

impulsive and unpredictable

The referee's capricious behavior angered the players because he was inconsistent in his calls; he would call a foul for minor contact, but ignore elbowing and kicking.

equivocate   eh KWIV uh kayt

to avoid making a definite statement

On critical reading questions, I choose answers that equivocate; they use words such as *could* or *may* that make them hard to disprove.

indifferent   in DIF rent

not caring one way or the other

The old fisherman was completely indifferent to the pain and hunger he felt; his only concern was catching the enormous marlin he had hooked.

spontaneous   spon TAY nee us

unplanned; naturally occurring

Delia is such a good musician that she can create a song spontaneously, without having to stop and think about it.

whimsical   WIM zuh kul

subject to erratic behavior; unpredictable

Egbert rarely behaved as expected; indeed, he was a whimsical soul whose every decision was anybody's guess.

SMALLNESS

inconsequential   in kahn suh KWEN shul
unimportant
> The cost of the meal was inconsequential to Quentin because he wasn't paying for it.

superficial   soo per FISH ul
concerned only with what is on the surface or obvious; shallow
> The wound on his leg was only superficial, even though it looked like a deep cut.

tenuous   TEN yoo us
having little substance or strength; shaky; unsure, weak
> Her grasp on reality is tenuous at best; she's not even sure what year it is.

trivial   TRIH vee ul
of little importance or significance
> Alex says he doesn't like trivia games because the knowledge they test is trivial; he prefers to spend his time learning more important things.

POSITIVE CHARACTERISTICS

assiduous   uh SID yoo us
hard-working
> Spending hours in the hot sun digging out every tiny weed, Sidney tended her garden with assiduous attention. ⎯⎯⎯

compelling   kum PEL ing
forceful; urgently demanding attention
> By ignoring the problems in the city, the mayor gave people a very compelling reason to vote him out of office.

diligent   DIL uh jent
marked by painstaking effort; hard-working
> With a lot of diligent effort, they were able to finish the model airplane in record time.

dogged   DOG id
stubbornly persevering
> Her first few attempts resulted in failure, but her dogged efforts ultimately ended in success.

endure   en DUR
to put up with; to survive a hardship
> It was difficult to endure the incredibly boring lecture given in class the other day.

intrepid in TREH pid

courageous; fearless

The intrepid young soldier scaled the wall and attacked the enemy forces despite being outnumbered fifty to one.

maverick MAV uh rik

one who is independent and resists adherence to a group

In *Top Gun*, Tom Cruise was a maverick; he often broke the rules and did things his own way.

obdurate AHB dur ut

stubborn; inflexible

Leanna was so obdurate that she was unwilling to change her way of thinking on even the most minor issues.

obstinate AHB stin ut

stubbornly adhering to an opinion or a course of action

Even though he begged them constantly, Jeremy's parents were obstinate in their refusal to buy him a motorcycle.

proliferate pro LIF er ayt

to grow or increase rapidly

Because the number of fax machines, pagers, and cell phones has proliferated in recent years, many new area codes have been created to handle the demand for phone numbers.

tenacity ten ASS uh tee

persistence

With his overwhelming tenacity, Clark was finally able to get an interview with Brad Pitt for the school newspaper.

vitality vy TA lih tee

energy; power to survive

After a few days of rest, the exhausted mountain climber regained her usual vitality.

DIRECTION

assimilation uh sim il AY shun

to absorb; to make similar

The unique blend of Mexican culture was formed by the assimilation of the cultures of the Native Americans and the Spanish.

consensus kun SEN sus

general agreement

After much debate, the committee came to a consensus; although they differed on minor points, the members all agreed on the major issue.

context   KAHN tekst

circumstances of a situation; environment

The senator complained that his statements had been taken out of context and were therefore misleading; he said that if the newspaper had printed the rest of his speech, it would have explained the statements in question.

derived   de RYVD

copied or adapted from a source

Many SAT questions are derived from older questions—the details may have been changed, but the same basic concept is being tested.

incumbent   in KUM bunt

imposed as a duty; obligatory

Since you are the host, it is incumbent upon you to see that everyone is having fun.

inevitable   in EV ih tuh bul

certain to happen, unavoidable

Gaining a little extra weight during the wintertime is inevitable, especially after the holidays.

malleable   MAL ee uh bul

easily shaped or formed; easily influenced

Gold is malleable; it is easy to work with and can be hammered into very thin sheets.

subdue   sub DOO

to restrain; to hold back

It took four officers to subdue the fugitive because he fought like a madman.

KNOWLEDGE

acquired   uh KWY erd

developed or learned; not naturally occurring

A love of opera is an acquired taste; almost nobody likes it the first time he or she hears it.

conception   kun SEP shun

the ability to form or understand an idea

Most people have no conception of the enormous amount of genetic information present in a single living cell.

conviction   kun VIK shun

a fixed or strong belief

Although he privately held on to his convictions, threats by the church caused Galileo to publicly denounce his theory that the earth orbited the sun.

dogmatic   dog MAT ik

stubbornly adhering to insufficiently proved beliefs

Doug was dogmatic in his belief that exercising frequently boosts one's immune system.

enlightening   en LYT uh ning

informative; contributing to one's awareness

The Rosetta Stone was enlightening because it allowed linguists to begin to translate Egyptian hieroglyphs, whose meanings had previously been a mystery.

impression   im PREH shun

a feeling or understanding resulting from an experience

It was my impression that I was supposed to throw a curve ball, but I must have been wrong because the catcher didn't expect it.

intuition   in too ISH un

the power of knowing things without thinking; sharp insight

It is said that some people have intuition about future events that allows them to predict disasters.

misconception   mis kun SEP shun

an incorrect understanding or interpretation

His belief that storks bring babies was just one of his many misconceptions.

perception   per SEP shun

awareness; insight

The detective's perception of people's hidden feelings makes it easy for her to catch liars.

perspective   per SPEK tiv

point of view

People from the North and South viewed the Civil War from different perspectives—each side's circumstances made it difficult for them to understand the other side.

profound   pro FOWND

having great depth or seriousness

There was a profound silence during the ceremony in honor of those who died during World War II.

TRAITS

inherent   in HER ent

inborn; built-in

One of the inherent weaknesses of the SAT is that a multiple-choice test, by definition, cannot allow students to be creative in their answers.

innate   in AYT

possessed at birth; inborn

Cats have an innate ability to see well in the dark; they are born with this skill, and do not need to develop it.

inveterate   in VET uh rit

long established; deep-rooted; habitual

Stan has always had trouble telling the truth; in fact, he's an inveterate liar.

omnipotent   om NIP uh tent

all-powerful

He liked to think that he was an omnipotent manager, but he really had very little control over anything.

proximity   prahk SIM ih tee

closeness

I try to sit far away from Roxy—I don't like sitting in proximity to her because she wears too much perfume.

MOVEMENT

elusive   il OO siv

difficult to capture, as in something actually fleeting

The girl's expression was elusive; the painter had a hard time recreating it on the canvas.

emigrate   EM ih grayt

to leave one country or region and settle in another

Many Jews left Russia and emigrated to Israel after it was founded in 1948.

transient   TRAN zhunt

passing away with time; passing from one place to another

Jack Dawson enjoyed his transient lifestyle; with nothing but the clothes on his back and the air in his lungs, he was free to travel wherever he wanted.

transitory   TRAN zih tor ee

short-lived or temporary

The sadness she felt was only transitory; the next day her mood improved.

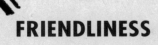

FRIENDLINESS

affable   AF uh bul

easy-going; friendly

We enjoyed spending time with Mr. Lee because he was such a pleasant, affable man.

amenable   uh MEEN uh bul

responsive; agreeable

> Since we had been working hard all day, the group seemed amenable to my suggestion that we all go home early.

camaraderie   kahm RAH duh ree

goodwill between friends

> There was great camaraderie among the members of the team; they were friends both on and off the field.

cordial   KOR jul

friendly; sincere

> Upon my arrival at camp, I received a warm and cordial greeting from the counselors.

facetious   fuh SEE shus

playfully humorous

> Although the teacher pretended to be insulting her favorite students, she was just being facetious.

NEGATIVE FEELINGS

impinge   im PINJ

hinder; interfere with

> By not allowing the students to publish a newspaper, the school was impinging upon their right to free speech.

lament   luh MENT

express grief for; mourn

> After Beowulf had been killed by the dragon, the Geats wept and lamented his fate.

melancholy   MEL un kah lee

sadness; depression

> Joy fell into a state of melancholy when her Smashing Pumpkins CD got scratched.

sanction   SANK shun

(n.) an economic or military measure put in place to punish another country

> In 1962, The United States imposed economic sanctions on Cuba to protest Castro's dictatorship; travel and trade between the countries are severely restricted to this day.

truncated   TRUN kay tid

shortened; cut off

> The file Chris downloaded from the Internet was truncated; the end of it was missing.

ART

aesthetic   es THET ik

having to do with the appreciation of beauty

The arrangement of paintings in the museum was due to aesthetic considerations; as long as paintings looked good together, it didn't matter who painted them or when they were painted.

anthology   an THAH luh jee

a collection of literary pieces

This anthology contains all of Shakespeare's sonnets, but none of his plays.

contemporary   kun TEM po rare ee

current, modern; from the same time

Contemporary music is very different from the music of the 1920s. Pocahontas and Shakespeare were contemporaries; they lived during the same time, though not in the same place.

dilettante   dih luh TAHNT

one with an amateurish or superficial understanding of a field of knowledge

You can't trust Betsy's opinion because she's just a dilettante who doesn't understand the subtleties of the painting.

eclectic   uh KLEK tik

made up of a variety of sources or styles

Lou's taste in music is eclectic because he listens to everything from rap to polka.

excerpt   EK serpt

a selected part of a passage or scene

We read an excerpt from *Romeo and Juliet* in which Juliet says, "Romeo, Romeo, wherefore art thou Romeo?"

genre   ZHAHN ruh

describing a category of artistic endeavor

Gene enjoyed only science fiction movies; in fact, he never went to see anything that was not in that genre.

medley   MED lee

an assortment or a mixture, especially of musical pieces

At the concert, the band played a medley of songs from its first album, cutting an hour's worth of music down to five minutes.

mural   MYUR ul

a large painting applied directly to a wall or ceiling surface

The mural on the wall of the library showed the signing of the Declaration of Independence.

narrative NAR uh tiv

(adj.) characterized by the telling of a story
(n.) a story

> Tina gave us a running narrative of the game, since she was the only one who could see over the fence.

parody PAR uh dee

an artistic work that imitates the style of another work for comic effect

> *Mad* magazine is famous for its parodies of popular movies, such as *Star Bores* and *The Umpire Strikes Out*.

realism REE uh liz um

artistic representation that aims for visual accuracy

> Her photographs have a stark realism that conveys the true horror of the war.

virtuoso ver choo OH so

a tremendously skilled artist

> Some people say that Eddie Van Halen is a guitar virtuoso because of his amazing ability—others say that his music is just noise.

TEMPERAMENT

decorous DEK er us

proper; marked by good taste

> The class was well-behaved and the substitute was grateful for their decorous conduct.

equanimity ek wuh NIM uh tee

the quality of being calm and even-tempered; composure

> She showed great equanimity; she did not panic even in the face of catastrophe.

modest MAH dist

quiet or humble in manner or appearance

> Although Mr. Phillips is well off financially, he lives in a modest, simple home.

propriety pruh PRY uh tee

appropriateness of behavior

> Anyone who blows his nose on the tablecloth has no sense of propriety.

prudent PROO dunt

exercising good judgment or common sense

> It wouldn't be prudent to act until you've considered every possible outcome.

serene suh REEN

calm

> The quiet seaside resort provided a much-needed vacation in a serene locale.

staid   STAYD

unemotional; serious

> Mr. Carver had such a staid demeanor that he stayed calm while everyone else celebrated the team's amazing victory.

stoic   STOW ik

indifferent to pleasure or pain; impassive

> Not one to complain, Jenny was stoic in accepting her punishment.

NEGATIVE STATEMENTS

condemn   kun DEM

to express strong disapproval of; denounce

> Homer condemned Mayor Quimby for allowing the schoolchildren to drink spoiled milk; he was outraged and let the mayor know it.

discredit   dis CRED it

to cause to be doubted

> The claim that π is exactly equal to 3 can be discredited simply by careful measurement.

disparage   dis PAR uj

to speak of in a slighting way or negatively; to belittle

> Glen disparaged Wanda's work as being careless and unoriginal.

pejorative   puh JOR uh tiv

describing words or phrases that belittle or speak negatively of someone

> Teachers should refrain from using such pejorative terms as "numbskull" when dealing with students who need encouragement.

plagiarism   PLAY juh riz um

the act of passing off the ideas or writing of another as one's own

> The author was accused of plagiarism when an older manuscript was discovered that contained passages that she had used, word for word, in her own book.

vilify   VIL uh fye

to make vicious statements about

> Chad issued a series of pamphlets that did nothing but vilify his opponent, but his cruel accusations were not enough to win him the election.

MORE NEGATIVE CHARACTERISTICS

brittle   BRIT ul

easily broken when subjected to pressure

> That antique vase is so brittle that it might break at any moment.

brusque BRUSK

rudely abrupt

Mr. Weir was a brusque teacher who didn't take time to talk to or listen to his students.

caustic KAW stik

bitingly sarcastic or witty

She had a very caustic wit and she seldom told a joke without offending someone.

feral FEAR ul

savage; untamed

Although Murphy was usually timid, he joined the feral cats who lived in the woods after his owner deserted him.

fractious FRAK shus

quarrelsome; unruly

Leonard was a fractious child who disagreed with everything and refused to listen.

incorrigible in KOR ij uh bul

unable to be reformed

Sasha is absolutely incorrigible; no matter how many times you punish her, she goes right ahead and misbehaves.

ingrate IN grayt

an ungrateful person

It is a true ingrate who can accept favor after favor and never offer any thanks.

insolent IN suh lunt

insulting in manner or speech

It was extremely insolent of him to stick his tongue out at the principal.

notorious no TOR ee us

known widely and usually unfavorably; infamous

Al Capone was a notorious gangster in the 1930s; he was feared throughout America.

pugnacious pug NAY shus

combative; belligerent

Lorenzo was a pugnacious child who settled his differences by fighting with people.

reprehensible rep ree HEN si bul

worthy of blame

It was reprehensible of the girls to spit their gum in their teacher's water bottle; they had detention for a week.

EVIL

deleterious   del uh TEER ee us

having a harmful effect; injurious

> Although it may seem unlikely, taking too many vitamins can actually have a deleterious effect on your health.

enmity   EN muh tee

mutual hatred or ill will

> There was great enmity between the opposing generals, and each one wanted to destroy the other.

heinous   HAY nus

hatefully evil; abominable

> To murder someone in cold blood is a heinous crime.

malfeasance   mal FEEZ uns

misconduct or wrongdoing, especially by a public official

> The mayor was accused of malfeasance because of his questionable use of public funds.

malice   MAL is

extreme ill will or spite

> It was clear that he was acting with malice when he disconnected the brakes in his business partner's car.

putrid   PYOO trid

rotten

> He threw his lunch in the bottom of his locker every day and had a putrid mess by the end of the year—rotten bananas, moldy sandwiches, and curdled milk were some of the more disgusting ingredients.

rancorous   RANK er us

hateful; marked by deep-seated ill will

> They had such a rancorous relationship that no one could believe that they had ever gotten along.

toxic   TAHK sik

poisonous

> Since many chemicals are toxic, drinking from random flasks in the chemistry lab could be hazardous to your health.

AGE

archaic   ar KAY ik

characteristic of an earlier period; old fashioned

> "How dost thou?" is an archaic way of saying "How are you?"

hackneyed   HACK need

worn-out through overuse; trite

> All my mom could offer in the way of advice were hackneyed old phrases that I'd heard a hundred times before.

medieval   med EE vul

referring to the Middle Ages, old fashioned

His ideas about fashion were positively medieval; he thought that a man should always wear a coat and tie, and a woman should always wear a dress.

obsolete   ahb suh LEET

no longer in use; old fashioned

Eight-track tape players are obsolete because albums aren't released in that format anymore.

DULLNESS

austere   aw STEER

without decoration; strict

The gray walls and bare floors provided a very austere setting.

mediocrity   mee dee AH krit ee

the state or quality of being average; of moderate to low quality

Salieri said that he was the patron saint of mediocrity because his work could never measure up to Mozart's.

mundane   mun DAYN

commonplace; ordinary

We hated going to class every day because it was so mundane; we never did anything interesting.

ponderous   PAHN duh rus

extremely dull

That 700-page book on the anatomy of the flea was so ponderous that I could not read more than one paragraph.

prosaic   pro ZAY ik

unimaginative; dull

Rebecca made a prosaic mosaic—it consisted of only one tile.

sedentary   SEH dun tair ee

not migratory; settled

Galatea led a sedentary existence; she never even left her home unless she had to.

ANXIETY

apprehension   ap reh HEN shun

anxiety or fear about the future

My grandmother felt apprehension about nuclear war in the 1960s, so my grandfather built a bomb shelter in the backyard to calm her fears.

harbinger HAR bin jer
something that indicates what is to come; a forerunner
> When it is going to rain, insects fly lower, so cows lie down to get away from the insects; therefore, the sight of cows lying down is a harbinger of rain.

ominous AH min us
menacing; threatening
> The rattling under the hood sounded ominous, because we were miles from the nearest town and would have been stranded if the car had broken down.

premonition prem uh NISH un
a feeling about the future
> Luckily, my premonition that I would break my neck skiing was unfounded; unluckily, I broke my leg instead.

timorous TIM uh rus
timid; fearful about the future
> Tiny Tim was timorous; he was afraid that one day he would be crushed by a giant.

trepidation trep uh DAY shun
uncertainty; apprehension
> We approached Mrs. Fielding with trepidation because we didn't know how she would react to our request for a field trip.

NEW THINGS

innovative IN no vay tiv
introducing something new
> The shop on the corner has become known for its innovative use of fruit on its pizzas.

naïve nah YEEV
lacking sophistication
> It was naïve of him to think that he could write a novel in one afternoon.

nascent NAY sunt
coming into existence; emerging
> If you study Nirvana's first album, you can see their nascent abilities that were brought to maturity on their second recording.

novel NAH vul
strikingly new or unusual
> Mei's novel approach to the problem stunned the scientific community; no one had ever thought to apply game theory to genetics.

novice   NAH vis
    a beginner
        Having only played chess a couple of times, Jamal was a novice compared to the contestants who had been playing all their lives.

➤ OPENNESS

candor   KAN der
    sincerity; openness
        It's refreshing to hear Candice's honesty and candor—when asked about her English teacher, she says, "I can't stand her!"

frank   FRANK
    open and sincere in expression; straightforward
        When Frank lost my calculator, he was frank with me; he admitted losing it without trying to make up some excuse.

➤ NATURAL PHENOMENA

arid   AR id
    describing a dry, rainless climate
        Since they receive little rain, deserts are known for their arid climates.

conflagration   kahn fluh GRAY shun
    a widespread fire
        The protesters burned flags, accidentally starting a fire that developed into a conflagration that raged out of control.

nocturnal   nok TER nul
    of or occurring in the night
        Owls are nocturnal animals because they sleep during the day and hunt at night.

sonorous   SAH nuh rus
    producing a deep or full sound
        My father's sonorous snoring keeps me up all night unless I close my door and wear earplugs.

➤ RESPECT

catalog   KAT uh log
    (v.) to make an itemized list of
        He decided to catalog his expenses for the week, hoping that this list would show him where he could cut back his spending.

exemplary eg ZEM pluh ree
commendable; worthy of imitation
> Jay's behavior was exemplary; his parents wished that his brother Al were more like him.

facile FAS ul
done or achieved with little effort; easy
> Last night's math homework was such a facile task that I was done in ten minutes.

fastidious fas TID ee us
possessing careful attention to detail; difficult to please
> Since Kiera was so fastidious, she volunteered to proofread our group's report.

hierarchy HY er ar kee
a group organized by rank
> With each promotion raising him higher, Archie moved up in his company's hierarchy.

idealize eye DEE uh lyze
to consider perfect
> The fans had idealized the new star pitcher; they had such unrealistically high expectations that they were bound to be disappointed.

laudatory LAW duh tor ee
giving praise
> The principal's speech was laudatory when he congratulated the students on their SAT scores.

paramount PAR uh mount
of chief concern or importance
> The workers had many minor complaints, but the paramount reason for their unhappiness was the low pay.

venerated VEN er ay tid
highly respected
> Princess Diana was venerated for her dedication to banning land mines around the world; people today still sing her praises.

meticulous muh TIK yuh lus
extremely careful and precise
> The plastic surgeon was meticulous; he didn't want to leave any scars.

pragmatic prag MAT ik
practical
> Never one for wild and unrealistic schemes, Amy took a pragmatic approach to research.

solvent SAHL vunt
able to pay one's debts
> After five years of losing money, the business has finally solved its financial problems and become solvent.

IDEAS

abstract   ab STRAKT

not applied to actual objects

"Justice" is an abstract concept, because it is merely an idea.

apparatus   ap uh RAT us

equipment; a group of machines

The physics lab housed a cumbersome apparatus that has since been replaced by a much smaller and more accurate piece of equipment.

paradigm   PAR a dym

an example or model

The current educational paradigm has students engaged in discovery-based learning, whereas the older model had teachers lecturing and students merely taking notes.

phenomenon   feh NAH meh nahn

an unusual, observable event

The phenomenon of lightning remained unexplained until scientists discovered electricity.

rational   RASH un ul

logical; motivated by reason rather than feeling

While Joe is more impulsive, Ari is more rational because he thinks things through rather than acting on his feelings.

theoretical   thee oh RET ih kul

lacking application or practical application

Theoretical physics is concerned with ideas, whereas applied physics is concerned with using those ideas.

WORK

cartographer   kar TAH gruh fer

one who designs or makes maps

Until the nineteenth century, European cartographers knew very little about the interior of Africa and had to leave it blank on their maps.

vocation   vo KAY shun

an occupation or profession

Tristan has always been interested in maps, so he chose a vocation as a cartographer in the army.

OTHER WORDS

As important as Hit Parade words are, they aren't the only words on the SAT. As you go about learning the Hit Parade, you should also try to incorporate other new words into your vocabulary. The Hit Parade will help you determine what kinds of words you should be learning—good solid words that are fairly difficult but not impossible.

One very good source of SAT words is your local paper. Get it, read it, write down the words you don't know, and look them up. (You just may learn something about the world as well.) No one ever got dumber by reading.

Roots

Many of the words in the English language were borrowed from other languages at some point in our history. Words that you use every day contain bits and pieces of ancient Greek and Latin words that meant something similar. These bits and pieces are called "roots." The dictionary describes each word's roots by giving its etymology—a "minihistory" of where it came from. For example, the *American Heritage Dictionary* gives the following etymology for *apathy*, a word on the Hit Parade: "Greek *apatheia*, for *apathés*, without feeling: *a-*, without + *pathos*, feeling." Similar-sounding words, like *pathos*, *pathetic*, *sympathy*, and *empathy*, are all related and all have to do with feeling.

Many people say the best way to prepare for the SAT is simply to learn a lot of roots. Students who know a lot of roots, they say, will be able to "translate" any unfamiliar words they encounter on the test. There is some truth in this; the more you know about etymology, the easier it will be to build your vocabulary. But roots can also mislead you. The hardest words on the SAT are often words that seem to contain a familiar root, but actually do not. For example, *audacity*, a hard word sometimes tested on the SAT, means "boldness or daring." It has nothing to do with sound, even though it seems to contain the root *aud-* from a Latin word meaning "to hear"—as in *audio*, *audiovisual*, or *auditorium*. *Audacity* really comes from the Latin word *audax*, "courageous."

Still, learning about roots can be helpful—if you do it properly. You should think of roots not as a code that will enable you to decipher unknown words on the SAT, but as a tool for learning new words and making associations between them. For example, *eloquent*, *colloquial*, and *circumlocution* all contain the Latin root *loqu/loc*, which means "to speak." Knowing the root and recognizing it in these words will make it easier for you to memorize all of them. You should think of roots as a tool for helping you organize your thoughts as you build your vocabulary.

The worst thing you can do is try to memorize roots all by themselves, apart from words they appear in. In the first place, it can't be done. In the second place, it won't help.

HIT PARADE OF ROOTS

Just as the Hit Parade is a list of the most frequently tested words on the SAT, the Hit Parade of Roots is a list of the roots that show up most often in SAT vocabulary words. You may find it useful in helping you organize your vocabulary study. When approaching the Hit Parade of Roots, focus on the words, using the roots simply as reminders to help you learn or remember the meanings. When you take the SAT, you may be able to prod your memory about the meaning of a particular word by thinking of the related words that you associate with it.

The roots on the Hit Parade of Roots are presented in order of their importance on the SAT. The roots at the top of the list appear more often than the roots at the bottom. Each root is followed by a number of real SAT words that contain it. (What should you do every time you don't know the meaning of a word on the Hit Parade of Roots? Look it up!) Note that roots often have several different forms. Be on the lookout for all of them.

CAP/CIP/CEIPT/CEPT/CEIV/CEIT (take)

capture	exceptionable
intercept	susceptible
receptive	deception
recipient	conception
incipient	receive
perceptive	conceit
percipient	accept
anticipate	emancipate
except	precept
exceptional	

GEN (birth, race, kind)

generous	homogeneous
generate	heterogeneous
degenerate	genealogy
regenerate	indigenous
genuine	congenital
congenial	gender
ingenious	engender
ingenuous	genre
ingenue	progeny

DIC/DICT/DIT (tell, say, word)

predicament	malediction
condition	benediction
dictate	extradite
dictator	verdict
abdicate	indict
predict	diction
contradict	dictum
addict	

SPEC/SPIC/SPIT (look, see)

perspective	spectrum
aspect	specimen
spectator	introspection
spectacle	respite
suspect	conspicuous
speculation	circumspect
suspicious	perspicacious

SUPER/SUR/SUM (above)

surpass	supercilious
superficial	superstition
summit	superimpose
superlative	supersede
supernova	superfluous

TENT/TENS/TEND/TENU (stretch, thin)

tension	contention
extend	distend
tendency	tenuous
tendon	attenuate
tent	portent
tentative	tendentious
contend	

TRANS (across)

transfer	transitory
transaction	transient
transparent	transmutation
transgress	transcendent
transport	intransigent
transform	traduce
transition	

DOC/DUC/DAC (teach, lead)

conduct	document
reduce	docile
seduce	didactic
conducive	indoctrinate
inductee	traduce
doctrine	induce

CO/CON/COM (with, together)

company	contrition
collaborate	commensurate
conjugal	conclave
congeal	conciliate
congenial	comply
convivial	congruent
coalesce	

VERS/VERT (turn)

controversy	aversion
convert	extrovert
revert	introvert
subvert	inadvertent
inversions	versatile
divert	adversity
diverse	

LOC/LOG/LOQU (word, speech)

eloquent	colloquial
logic	eulogy
apology	loquacious
circumlocution	dialogue
monologue	prologue
neologism	epilogue
philology	

SEN (feel, sense)

sensitive	consent
sensation	dissent
sentiment	assent
sensory	consensus
sensual	sentry
resent	sentinel

DE (away, down, off)

denounce	delineate
debility	deface
defraud	devoid
decry	defile
deplete	desecrate
defame	derogatory

NOM/NOUN/NOWN/NAM/NYM (name, order, rule)

name	astronomy
anonymous	ignominy
antonym	renown
nominate	misnomer
economy	nomenclature
renounce	

CLA/CLO/CLU (shut, close)

closet

claustrophobia

enclose

disclose

include

conclude

exclusive

preclude

recluse

seclude

cloister

VO/VOC/VOK/VOW (call)

voice

vocal

provocative

advocate

equivocate

vocation

convoke

vociferous

irrevocable

evocative

revoke

avow

MAL (bad)

malicious

malady

dismal

malfunction

malign

malcontent

malodorous

malefactor

malevolent

malediction

maladroit

FRA/FRAC/FRAG (break)

fracture

fraction

fragment

fragmentary

fragile

frail

refraction

refractory

infraction

infringe

fractious

OB (against)

objective	obstinate
obsolete	obliterate
oblique	oblivious
obscure	obsequious
obstruct	obfuscate

SUB (under)

submissive	subordinate
subsidiary	sublime
subjugation	subtle
subliminal	subversion
subdue	subterfuge

AB (from, away)

abandon	abstain
abhor	absolve
abnormal	abstemious
abstract	abstruse
abdicate	abrogate

GRESS/GRAD (step)

progress	degrade
regress	downgrade
retrogress	aggressor
retrograde	digress
gradual	transgress

SEC/SEQU (follow)

second	execute
sequel	subsequent
sequence	prosecute
consequence	obsequious
inconsequential	

PRO (much, for, a lot)

prolific	prodigal
profuse	protracted
propitious	proclivity
prodigious	propensity
profligate	prodigy

QUE/QUIS (ask, seek)

inquire	querulous
question	acquire
request	acquisitive
quest	acquisition
query	exquisite

SACR/SANCT/SECR (sacred)

sacred	sacrosanct
sacrifice	consecrate
sanctuary	desecrate
sanctify	sacrament
sanction	

SCRIB/SCRIP (write)

scribble	proscribe
describe	ascribe
script	inscribe
postscript	circumscribe
prescribe	

PATHY/PAS/PAT (feeling)

apathy	compassion
sympathy	compatible
empathy	dispassionate
antipathy	impassive
passionate	

DIS/DIF (not)

dissonance

dispassionate

discrepancy

disparate

disdain

diffident

dissuade

disparage

dismay

CIRCU (around)

circumference

circuitous

circulation

circumscribe

circumstance

circumvent

circumnavigate

circumlocutory

PART III

How to Crack the Math Section

A FEW WORDS ABOUT SAT MATH

Three of the nine scored sections on the SAT are Math sections. Two of the scored Math sections will last 25 minutes each; the third will last 20 minutes.

The math questions on your SAT will be drawn from the following four categories:

1. Arithmetic
2. Basic algebra
3. Geometry
4. Basic algebra II

The math questions on your SAT will appear in two different formats:

1. Regular multiple-choice questions
2. Grid-ins

Other than the essay, grid-ins are the only non–multiple-choice questions on the SAT; instead of selecting ETS's answer from among several choices, you will have to find ETS's answer independently and mark it in a grid. The grid-ins on your test will be drawn from arithmetic, algebra, and geometry, just like regular SAT math questions. But this format has special characteristics, so we will treat it separately.

WHAT DOES THE MATH SAT MEASURE?

ETS says that the Math SAT measures "mathematical reasoning abilities" or "higher-order reasoning abilities." But this is not true. The Math section is merely a brief test of arithmetic, algebra, and a bit of geometry. By a "bit" we mean just that. The principles you'll need to know are few and simple. We'll show you which ones are important. Most of them are listed for you at the beginning of each section.

ORDER OF DIFFICULTY

As was true of the sentence completion questions, questions on the Math section are arranged in order of difficulty. The first question in each section will be the easiest in that section, and the last will be the hardest; in this case, harder doesn't mean tougher—it means trickier. In addition, the questions within the grid-in question groups will also be arranged in order of difficulty. The difficulty of a problem will help you determine how to attack it.

YOU DON'T HAVE TO FINISH

We've all been taught in school that when you take a test, you have to finish it. If you only answered two-thirds of the questions on a high school math test, you probably wouldn't get a very good grade. But as we've already seen, the SAT is not at all like the tests you take in school. Most students don't know about the difference, so they make the mistake of doing all the problems on each Math section of the SAT.

Since they only have a limited amount of time to answer all the questions, most students are always in a rush to get to the end of the section. At first, this seems reasonable, but think about the order of difficulty for a minute. All the easy questions are at the beginning of a Math section, and the hard questions are at the end. So when students rush through a Math section, they're actually spending less time on the easier questions (which they have a good chance of getting right), just so they can spend more time on the harder questions (which they have very little chance of getting right). Does this make sense? Of course not.

Here's the secret: On the Math section, you don't have to answer every question in each section. In fact, unless you're trying to score 600 or more, you shouldn't even look at the difficult last third of the Math questions. The fact is, most students can raise their math scores by concentrating on getting all the easy and medium questions correct. In other words...

SLOW DOWN!

Most students do considerably better on the Math section when they slow down and spend less time worrying about the hard questions (and more time working carefully on the easier ones). Haste causes careless errors, and careless errors can ruin your score. In most cases, you can actually *raise* your score by answering *fewer* questions. That doesn't sound like a bad idea, does it? If you're shooting for an 800, you'll have to answer every question correctly. But if your target is 550, you should ignore the hardest questions in each section and use your limited time wisely.

To make sure you're working at the right pace in each Math section, refer to the Math Pacing Chart on page 27. The chart will tell you how many questions you need to answer in each section in order to achieve your next score goal.

THE PRINCETON REVIEW APPROACH

We're going to give you the tools you need to handle the easier questions on the Math section, along with several great techniques to help you crack some of the more difficult ones. But you must concentrate first on getting the easier questions correct. Don't worry about the difficult third of the Math section until you've learned to work carefully and accurately on the easier questions.

When it does come time to look at some of the harder questions, the Joe Bloggs principle will help you once again; this time to zero in on ETS's answer. You'll learn what kinds of answers appeal to Joe in math, and how to avoid those answers. Just as you did in the Critical Reading section, you'll learn to use POE to find ETS's answer by getting rid of obviously incorrect answers.

Generally speaking, each chapter in the Math section of this book begins with the basics and then gradually moves into more advanced principles and techniques. If you find yourself getting lost toward the end of the chapter, don't worry. Concentrate your efforts on principles you can understand but still need to master.

Better Than Average

If you got 70% on a math test in school, you'd feel pretty lousy—that's a C minus, below average. But the SAT is not like school. Getting 42 out of 60 questions correct (70%) would give you a math score of about 600—100 points *above* the national average.

FUNDAMENTALS

Although we'll show you which mathematical concepts are most important to know for the SAT, this book cannot take the place of a basic foundation in math. For example, if you discover as you read this book that you have trouble working with fractions, you'll want to go back and review the fundamentals. Our drills and examples in this book will refresh your memory if you've gotten rusty, but if you have serious difficulty with the following chapters, you should consider getting extra help. For this purpose, we recommend our own *Math Smart*, which is designed to give you a thorough review of all the fundamental math concepts that you'll need to know on the SAT. Always keep in mind that the math tested on the SAT is different from the math taught in school. If you want to raise your score, don't waste time studying math that ETS never tests.

CALCULATORS

Students are permitted (but not required) to use calculators on the SAT. You should definitely bring a calculator to the test. It will be extremely helpful to you, as long as you know how and when to use it and don't get carried away. We'll tell you more about calculators as we go along.

BASIC PRINCIPLES OF SAT NUMBERS

Before moving on, you should be certain that you are familiar with some basic terms and concepts that you'll need to know for the Math SAT. This material isn't at all difficult, but you must know it cold. If you don't, you'll waste valuable time on the test and lose points that you easily could have earned.

INTEGERS

Integers are the numbers that most of us are accustomed to thinking of simply as "numbers." They can be either positive or negative. The positive integers are:

$$1, 2, 3, 4, 5, 6, 7, \text{ and so on}$$

The negative integers are:

$$-1, -2, -3, -4, -5, -6, -7, \text{ and so on}$$

Zero (0) is also an integer, but it is neither positive nor negative.

Note that positive integers get bigger as they move away from 0, while negative integers get smaller. In other words, 2 is bigger than 1, but –2 is smaller than –1. This number line should give you a clear idea of how negative numbers work.

```
      ↑
    — 4
    — 3
    — 2
    — 1
    — 0
    — −1
    — −2
    — −3
    — −4
      ↓
```

You should also remember the types of numbers that are *not* integers. Here are some examples:

−2.7, .625, 15.898, −9.8

Basically, integers are numbers that have *no* fractions or decimals. So if you see a number with a fraction or decimal, it's *not* an integer.

DISTINCT NUMBERS

You might see problems on the SAT that mention "distinct numbers." Don't let this throw you. All ETS means by distinct numbers is different numbers. For example, the set of numbers 2, 3, 4, and 5 is a set of distinct numbers, whereas 2, 2, 3, and 4 would not be a set of distinct numbers because 2 appears twice. Easy concept, tricky wording.

DIGITS

There are ten digits:

0, 1, 2, 3, 4, 5, 6, 7, 8, 9

All integers are made up of digits. In the integer 3,476, the digits are 3, 4, 7, and 6. Digits are to numbers as letters are to words.

The integer 645 is called a "three-digit number" for obvious reasons. Each of its digits has a different name depending on its place in the number:

5 is called the *units* digit

4 is called the *tens* digit

6 is called the *hundreds* digit

Negative Land

Think of integers as steps on a staircase leading up from the cellar (the negatives), through a doorway (zero), and above the ground (the positives). Five steps down (−5) is farther below ground than four steps down (−4) because you're one step farther away from the cellar door (0). Integers are like stairs, because when climbing stairs, you can't use a fraction of a step.

Thus the value of any number depends on which digits are in which places. The number 645 could be rewritten as follows:

$$6 \times 100 = 600$$
$$4 \times 10 = 40$$
$$+ 5 \times 1 = + 5$$
$$645$$

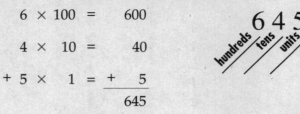

POSITIVE AND NEGATIVE

There are three rules regarding the multiplication of positive and negative numbers:

1. pos × pos = pos
2. neg × neg = pos
3. pos × neg = neg

ODD AND EVEN

Even numbers are integers that can be divided evenly by 2. Here are some examples of even numbers:

−4, −2, 0, 2, 4, 6, 8, 10, and so on

You can always tell at a glance whether a number is even: It is even if its final digit is even. Thus 999,999,999,992 is an even number because 2, the final digit, is an even number.

Odd numbers are integers that cannot be divided evenly by 2. Here are some examples of odd numbers:

−5, −3, −1, 1, 3, 5, 7, 9, and so on

You can always tell at a glance whether a number is odd: It is odd if its final digit is odd. Thus, 222,222,222,229 is an odd number because 9, the final digit, is an odd number.

Several rules always hold true with odd and even numbers:

even + even = even	even × even = even
odd + odd = even	odd × odd = odd
even + odd = odd	even × odd = even

FACTORS

The factors of a number are all of the numbers by which it can be divided evenly. For example, the factors of 30 are 1, 2, 3, 5, 6, 10, 15, and 30.

MULTIPLES

A multiple of a number is any product of an integer and the given number. For example, 20, 50, 180, and 370 are all multiples of 10.

REMAINDERS

If a number cannot be divided evenly by another number, the number left over at the end of the division is called the remainder. For example, 25 cannot be divided evenly by 3; 25 divided by 3 is 8 with 1 left over. The 1 is the remainder. Decimals are not remainders.

CONSECUTIVE INTEGERS

Consecutive integers are integers listed in increasing order of size without any integers missing in between. For example, –1, 0, 1, 2, 3, 4, and 5 are consecutive integers; 2, 4, 5, 7, and 8 are not. Nor are –1, –2, –3, and –4 consecutive integers, because they are decreasing in size.

PRIME NUMBERS

A prime number is a positive integer that can be divided evenly only by itself and by 1. For example, the following are all the prime numbers less than 30: 2, 3, 5, 7, 11, 13, 17, 19, 23, 29. (Note: 1 is not prime.)

DIVISIBILITY RULES

You may be called upon to determine whether one number can be divided evenly by another. To do so, use your calculator. If the result is an integer, the number is evenly divisible. Is 4,569 divisible by 3? Simply punch in the numbers on your calculator. The result is 1,523, which is an integer, so you have determined that 4,569 is indeed divisible by 3. Is 1,789 divisible by 3? The result on your calculator is 596.33333, which is not an integer, so 1,789 is not divisible by 3. (Integers don't have decimal points with digits after them.)

STANDARD SYMBOLS

The following standard symbols are used frequently on the SAT:

SYMBOL	MEANING
=	is equal to
≠	is not equal to
<	is less than
>	is greater than
≤	is less than or equal to
≥	is greater than or equal to

Leftovers

Don't try to figure remainders on your calculator. On your calculator, 25 divided by 3 is 8.3333333, but .3333333 is not the remainder. The remainder is 1.

Prime Time

Here are a few important facts about prime numbers:
- 0 and 1 are not prime numbers.
- 2 is the smallest prime number.
- 2 is the only even prime number.
- Not all odd numbers are prime: 1, 9, 15, 21, and many others are *not* prime.

The SAT Formula

Why would ETS give you all those geometric formulas on the test? Because the SAT is not really a geometry test. ETS doesn't care about geometric proofs because it doesn't want to spend the money grading proofs. So, the test writers dress up arithmetic and algebra with the occasional geometric figure. You need to know some rules of geometry, but not the way you do in a real geometry class.

FINALLY, THE INSTRUCTIONS

Each of the three scored Math sections on your SAT will begin with the same set of instructions. These instructions include a few formulas and other information that you may need to know in order to answer some of the questions. You must learn these instructions ahead of time. You should never have to waste valuable time referring to them during the test.

Still, if you do suddenly blank out on one of the formulas while taking the test, you can always refresh your memory by glancing back at the instructions. Be sure to familiarize yourself with them thoroughly ahead of time, so you'll know which formulas are there.

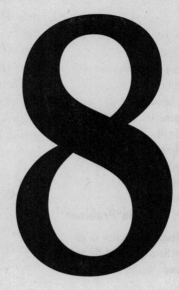

Joe Bloggs and
the Math Section

HEY, JOE!

Joe Bloggs has already been a big help to you on the Critical Reading section of the SAT. By learning to anticipate which answer choices would attract Joe on difficult questions, you now know how to avoid careless mistakes and eliminate obvious incorrect answers.

You can do the same thing on the SAT Math section. In fact, Joe Bloggs answers are even easier to spot on math questions. ETS is quite predictable in the way it writes incorrect answer choices, and this predictability will make it possible for you to zero in on its answers to questions that might have seemed impossible to you before.

HOW JOE THINKS

No Problem

Joe Bloggs is attracted to easy solutions arrived at through methods that he understands.

As was true on the SAT Critical Reading section, Joe Bloggs gets the easy questions right and the hard questions wrong. In Chapter 2, we introduced Joe by showing you how he approached a particular math problem. That problem, you may remember, involved the calculation of total miles in a trip. Here it is again:

PROBLEM SOLVING
1 2 3 4 5 6 7 8 9 10 11 12 13 14 15 16 17 18 19 **20**
EASY   MEDIUM   HARD

20. Graham walked to school at an average speed of 3 miles an hour and jogged back along the same route at 5 miles an hour. If his total traveling time was 1 hour, what was the total number of miles in the round trip?

(A) 3

(B) $3\frac{1}{8}$

(C) $3\frac{3}{4}$

(D) 4

(E) 5

When we showed this problem the first time, you were just learning about Joe Bloggs. Now that you've made him your invisible partner on the SAT, you ought to know a great deal about how he thinks. Your next step is to put Joe to work for you on the Math sections.

Here's How to Crack It

This problem was the last in a 20-question Math section. Therefore, it was the hardest problem in that section. Naturally, Joe got it wrong.

The answer choice most attractive to Joe on this problem is D. The question obviously involves an average of some kind, and 4 is the average of 3 and 5, so Joe picked it. Choice D just seemed like the right answer to Joe. (Of course, it wasn't the right answer; Joe gets the hard ones wrong.)

Because this is true, we know which answers we should avoid on hard questions: answers that seem obvious or that can be arrived at simply and quickly. If the answer really were obvious and if finding it really were simple, the question would be easy, not hard.

Joe Bloggs is also attracted to answer choices that simply repeat numbers from the problem. This means, of course, that you should avoid such choices. In the problem about Graham's going to school, you can also eliminate choices A and E, because 3 and 5 are numbers repeated directly from the problem. Therefore, they are extremely unlikely to be ETS's answer.

We've now eliminated three of the five answer choices. Even if you couldn't figure out anything else about this question, you'd have a fifty-fifty chance of guessing correctly. Those are excellent odds, considering that we really didn't do any math. By eliminating answer choices that we knew were wrong, we were able to beat ETS at its own game. (ETS's answer to this question is C, by the way.)

Avoid Repeats

Joe Bloggs is attracted to answer choices that simply repeat numbers from the problem.

Putting Joe to Work on the Math SAT

Generally speaking, the Joe Bloggs principle teaches you to:

- trust your hunches on easy questions

- double-check your hunches on medium questions

- eliminate Joe Bloggs answers on difficult questions

The rest of this chapter is devoted to using Joe Bloggs to zero in on ETS's answers to difficult questions. Of course, your main concern is still to answer all easy and medium questions correctly. But if you have some time left at the end of a Math section, the Joe Bloggs principle can help you eliminate answers on a few difficult questions, so that you can venture some good guesses. And as we've already seen, smart guessing means more points. (In Chapter 13, you'll learn how he can help you with grid-ins.)

BASIC TECHNIQUES

Hard Questions = Hard Answers

As we've just explained, hard questions on the SAT simply don't have correct answers that are obvious to the average person. Avoiding the "obvious" choices will take some discipline on your part, but you'll lose points if you don't. Even if you're a math whiz, the Joe Bloggs principle will keep you from making careless mistakes.

Here's an example:

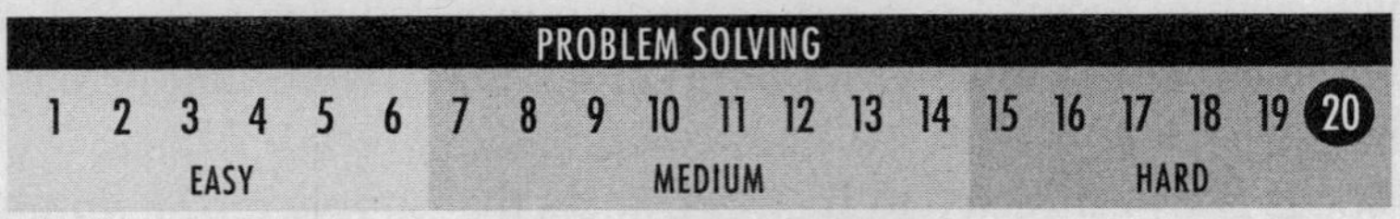

Joe Likes to Share

When it comes to the goofy "nonoverlapping region" questions, Joe's own good nature gets the best of him and he assumes that he must divide the figure evenly. That's why he likes to pick C on this problem. But, *nowhere does the question say the regions must be equal in size. Read carefully.*

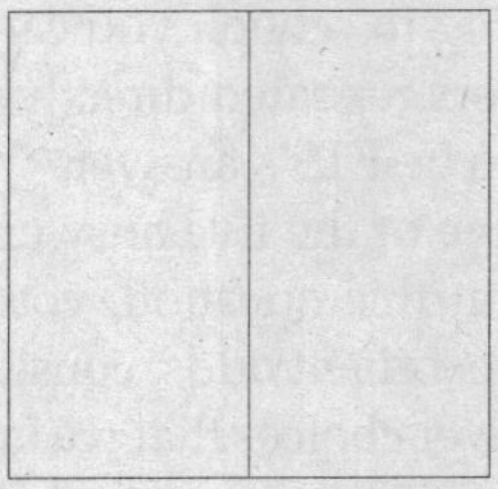

20. The figure above is a square divided into two nonoverlapping regions. What is the greatest number of nonoverlapping regions that can be obtained by drawing any two additional straight lines?

    (A) 4
    (B) 5
    (C) 6
    (D) 7
    (E) 8

Here's How to Crack It

This is the last question from a Math section. Therefore, it's extremely difficult. One reason it's so difficult is that it is badly written. (ETS's strengths are mathematical, not verbal.) Here's a clearer way to think of it: The drawing is a pizza cut in half; what's the greatest number of pieces you could end up with if you make just two more cuts with a knife?

The most obvious way to cut the pizza would be to make cuts perpendicular to the center cut, dividing the pizza into six pieces, like this:

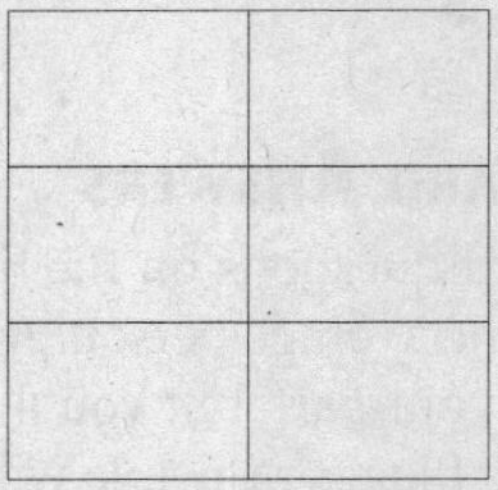

There, that was fast and easy. So that means 6 is ETS's answer, right? Wrong. That was too easy, which means that 6 can't possibly be ETS's answer, and choice C can be eliminated. If finding ETS's answer were that simple, Joe Bloggs would have gotten this question right and it would have been an easy question, not a difficult one.

Will this fact help you eliminate any other choices? Yes, because you know that if you can divide the pizza into at least six pieces, neither five nor four could be the greatest number of pieces into which it can be divided. Six is a greater number than either five or four; if you can get six pieces you can also get five or four. You can thus eliminate choices A and B as well.

Now you've narrowed it down to two choices. Which will you pick? You shouldn't waste time trying to find the exact answer to a question like this. It isn't testing any mathematical principle, and you won't figure out the trick unless you get lucky. If you can't use another of our techniques to eliminate the remaining wrong answer, you should just guess and go on. Heads you win a dollar, tails you lose a quarter. (ETS's answer is D. Our third technique, incidentally, will enable you to zero in on it exactly. Keep reading.)

In case you're wondering, here's how ETS divides the pizza:

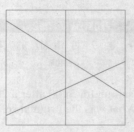

Here's another example:

PROBLEM SOLVING																			
1	2	3	4	5	6	7	8	9	10	11	12	13	14	15	16	17	**18**	19	20
EASY						MEDIUM								HARD					

18. A 50-foot wire runs from the roof a building to the top of a 10-foot pole 14 feet across the street. How much taller would the pole have to be if the street were 16 feet wider and the wire remained the same length?

(A) 2 feet
(B) 8 feet
(C) 14 feet
(D) 16 feet
(E) 18 feet

Here's How to Crack It

Which answer seems simple and obvious? Well, if the wire stays the same length, and the street is 16 feet wider, then it seems obvious that the pole would have to be 16 feet higher.

What does that mean? It means that we can eliminate choice D. If 16 feet were the correct answer, then Joe Bloggs would get this problem right and it would be an easy question, not one of the hardest in the section.

Choice C repeats a number from the problem, which means we can be doubly certain that it's wrong.

If you don't know how to do this problem, working on it further probably won't get you anywhere. You've eliminated two choices; guess and move on. (ETS's answer is B. Use the Pythagorean theorem—see Chapter 11.)

SIMPLE OPERATIONS = WRONG ANSWERS ON HARD QUESTIONS

Since Joe Bloggs doesn't usually think of difficult mathematical operations, he is attracted to solutions that use very simple arithmetic. Therefore, any answer choice that is the result of simple arithmetic should be eliminated on hard SAT math questions.

Here's an example:

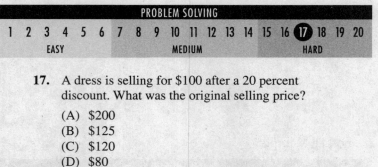

17. A dress is selling for $100 after a 20 percent discount. What was the original selling price?

    (A) $200
    (B) $125
    (C) $120
    (D) $80
    (E) $75

Here's How to Crack It

When Joe Bloggs looks at this problem, he sees "20 percent less than $100" and is attracted to choice D. Therefore, you must eliminate it. If finding the answer were that easy, Joe Bloggs would have gotten it right. Joe is also attracted to choice C, which is 20 percent more than $100. Again, eliminate.

With two Joe Bloggs answers out of the way, you ought to be able to solve this problem quickly. The dress is on sale, which means that its original price must have been more than its current price. That means that ETS's answer has to be greater than $100. Two of the remaining choices, A and B, fulfill this requirement. Now you can ask yourself:

(A) Is $100 20 percent less than $200? No. Eliminate.

(B) Is $100 20 percent less than $125? Could be. This must be ETS's answer. (It is.)

LEAST/GREATEST

Hard SAT math problems will sometimes ask you to find the least or greatest number that fulfills certain conditions. On such problems, Joe Bloggs is attracted to the answer choice containing the least or greatest number. You can therefore eliminate such choices. (ETS sometimes uses similar words that mean the same thing: *most, maximum, fewest, minimum,* and so on. The same rules apply to problems containing all such terms.)

Look at the square problem on page 152. The question asks you for the greatest number of regions into which the square can be divided. Which choice will therefore attract Joe Bloggs? Choice E. Eight is the greatest number among the choices offered, so it will seem right to Joe. Therefore, you can eliminate it.

Here's another example:

PROBLEM SOLVING																			
1	2	3	4	5	6	7	8	9	10	11	12	13	14	15	**16**	17	18	19	20
		EASY							MEDIUM							HARD			

16. If 3 parallel lines are cut by 3 nonparallel lines, what is the maximum number of intersections possible?

    (A)   9
    (B)   10
    (C)   11
    (D)   12
    (E)   13

Here's How to Crack It

The problem asks you for the *maximum*, or greatest number. What is the maximum number among the choices? It is 13; therefore, you can eliminate choice E. By the *simple = wrong* rule that we just discussed, you can also eliminate choice A. Joe's preference for simple arithmetic makes him think that the answer to this problem can be found by multiplying 3 times 3. The simple operation leads quickly to an answer of 9, which must therefore be wrong.

ETS's answer is D. Here's how it's found:

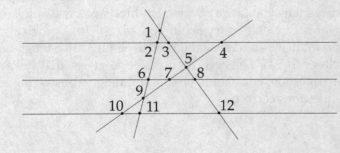

"IT CANNOT BE DETERMINED"

Occasionally on the Math section, the fifth answer choice on a problem will be:

(E)   It cannot be determined from the information
        given.

The Joe Bloggs principle makes these questions easy to crack. Why? Joe Bloggs can never determine the correct answer on difficult SAT problems. Therefore, when Joe sees this answer choice on a difficult problem, he is greatly attracted to it.

What Does This Mean?

It means that if "it cannot be determined" is offered as an answer choice on a difficult problem, it is usually wrong.

Here's an example:

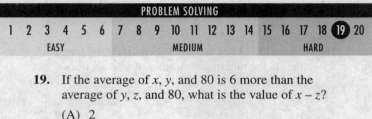

Easy/Medium

Don't automatically eliminate "it cannot be determined" on easy and medium problems. On medium problems, "it cannot be determined" has about one chance in two of being ETS's answer. So, if you are stuck on an easy or medium problem and "it cannot be determined" is one of the choices, pick it and move on. You will have one chance in two of being correct.

When Joe Bloggs picks "It cannot be determined from the information given" on a hard question, he's thinking, "If I can't get it, no one can."

19.   If the average of x, y, and 80 is 6 more than the average of y, z, and 80, what is the value of $x - z$?

(A) 2
(B) 3
(C) 6
(D) 18
(E) It cannot be determined from the information
        given.

Here's How to Crack It

This problem is the next-to-last question in a section. It looks absolutely impossible to Joe. Therefore, he assumes that the problem must be impossible to solve. Of course, he's wrong. Eliminate choice E. If E were ETS's answer, Joe would be correct and this would be an easy problem.

Choice C simply repeats a number from the problem, so you can eliminate that choice also. If you couldn't figure out anything else, you would have to guess. Since you already eliminated two answer choices, the odds are in your favor. (Remember, tails you lose a quarter, but heads you win a dollar.)

ETS's answer is D. Don't worry about how to solve this problem right now. It's only important that you understand how to eliminate Joe Bloggs answers in order to get closer to ETS's answer. If you have to guess, that's okay. Besides, that was a hard question; you should be concentrating on answering all the easy and medium questions correctly.

JOE BLOGGS AND MATH SUMMARY

1. Joe Bloggs gets the easy math questions right and the hard ones wrong.

2. On difficult problems, Joe Bloggs is attracted to easy solutions arrived at with methods he understands. Therefore, you should eliminate obvious, simple answers on difficult questions.

3. On difficult problems, Joe Bloggs is also attracted to answer choices that simply repeat numbers from the problem. Therefore, you should eliminate any such choices.

4. On difficult problems that ask you to find the least or greatest number that fulfills certain conditions, you can eliminate the answer choice containing the least or greatest number.

5. On difficult problems, you can almost always eliminate any answer choice that says, "It cannot be determined from the information given."

6. The point of Joe Bloggs is not to get to ONE answer choice, it's to improve your odds when you must guess, and eliminate answer choices that could distract you or seem right if you made a careless error.

The Calculator

THE CALCULATOR

You are allowed (but not required) to use a calculator when you take the SAT. You should definitely do so. A calculator can be enormously helpful on certain types of SAT math problems. This chapter will give you general information about how to use your calculator. Other math chapters will give you specific information about using your calculator in particular situations.

You'll need to bring your own calculator when you take the SAT. If you don't own one now, you can buy one for around $15, or you can ask your math teacher about borrowing one. If you do purchase one, buy it far enough ahead of time to practice with it before you take the test. Even if you now use a calculator regularly in your math class at school, you should still read this chapter and the other math chapters carefully and practice the techniques we describe.

Many students already own a graphing calculator. If you have one, great; if you don't, don't sweat it. Graphing calculators look fancy and have bigger screens (so you can see most of your work), but they are not necessary on the SAT. In fact, no calculators are. However, if you have one, it may simplify certain graphing problems on the SAT.

For the two or three graphing problems you are going to face, it's probably not worth the purchase. If you do decide to use one, keep in mind that it *cannot* have a QWERTY-style keyboard on it (like the TI-95). Most of the graphing calculators have typing capabilities, but since they don't have a typewriter-style keyboard, they are perfectly legal.

The only danger in using a calculator on the SAT is that you may be tempted to use it in situations in which it won't help you. Joe Bloggs thinks his calculator will solve all his difficulties with math. It won't. Occasionally, it may even cause him to miss a problem that he might have answered correctly on his own. Your calculator is only as smart as you are. But if you practice and use a little caution, you will find that your calculator will help you a great deal.

WHAT A CALCULATOR IS GOOD AT

Here is a complete list of what a calculator is good at on the SAT:

- Arithmetic
- Decimals
- Fractions
- Square roots
- Percentages
- Graphs (if it is a graphing calculator)
- Nothing else

We'll discuss the calculator's role in most of these areas in the next few chapters.

CALCULATOR ARITHMETIC

Adding, subtracting, multiplying, and dividing integers and decimals is easy on a calculator. You only need to be careful when you key in the numbers. A calculator will give you an incorrect answer to an arithmetic calculation only if you press the wrong keys. Here are two tips for avoiding mistakes on your calculator:

1. Check every number on the display as you key it in.

2. Press the *on/off* or *clear all* key after you finish each problem or after each separate step.

The main thing to remember about a calculator is that it can't help you find the answer to a question you don't understand. If you wouldn't know how to solve a particular problem using pencil and paper, you won't know how to solve it using a calculator, either. Your calculator will help you, but it won't take the place of a solid understanding of basic SAT mathematics.

Calculators Don't Think

Calculators crunch numbers and often save us a great deal of time and effort, but they are not a substitute for your problem-solving skills.

USE YOUR PAPER FIRST

Before you use your calculator, be sure to set up the problem or equation on paper; this will keep you from getting lost or confused. This is especially important when solving the problem involves a number of separate steps. The basic idea is to use the extra space in your test booklet to make a plan, and then use your calculator to execute it.

Working on scratch paper first will also give you a record of what you have done if you change your mind, run into trouble, or lose your place. If you suddenly find that you need to try a different approach to a problem, you may not have to go all the way back to the beginning. This will also make it easier for you to check your work, if you have time to do so.

Don't use the memory function on your calculator (if it has one). Because you can use your test booklet as scratch paper, you don't need to juggle numbers within the calculator itself. Instead of storing the result of a calculation in the calculator, write it on your scratch paper, clear your calculator, and move to the next step of the problem. A calculator's memory is fleeting; scratch paper is forever.

ORDER OF OPERATIONS

In Chapter 10, we will discuss the proper order of operations when solving equations in which several operations must be performed. Be sure you understand this information, because it applies to calculators as much as it does to pencil-and-paper computations. (We will teach you a mnemonic device that will enable you to remember this easily.) You must always perform calculations in the proper order.

Write Things Down

You paid for the test booklet; make the most of it. Keep track of your progress through each problem by writing down each step.

CALCULATOR SUMMARY

1. You should definitely use a calculator on the SAT.

2. Bring your own calculator when you take the test. You don't need a fancy one. Make sure your calculator doesn't beep (like the one on your cell phone) or have a typewriter-style keyboard.

3. Even if you already use a calculator regularly, you should still practice with it before the test.

4. Be careful when you key in numbers on your calculator. Check each number on the display as you key it in. Clear your work after you finish each problem or after each separate step.

5. A calculator can't help you find the answer to a question you don't understand. (It's only as smart as you are!) Be sure to use your calculator as a tool, not a crutch.

6. Set up the problem or equation on paper first. By doing so, you will eliminate the possibility of getting lost or confused.

7. Don't use the memory function on your calculator (if it has one). Scratch paper works better.

8. Whether you are using your calculator or paper and a pencil, you must always perform calculations in the proper order.

9. Make sure your calculator has fresh batteries at test time! Change them a day or two before.

Arithmetic

THERE ARE ONLY SIX OPERATIONS

There are only six arithmetic operations that you will ever need to perform on the SAT:

1. Addition (3 + 3)

2. Subtraction (3 – 3)

3. Multiplication (3 × 3 or 3 • 3)

4. Division (3 ÷ 3)

5. Raising to a power (3^3)

6. Finding a square root ($\sqrt{3}$)

If you're like most students, you probably haven't paid much serious attention to these topics since junior high school. You'll need to learn about them again if you want to do well on the SAT. By the time you take the test, using them should be automatic. All the arithmetic concepts are fairly basic, but you'll have to know them cold. You'll also have to know when and how to use your calculator, which will be quite helpful.

In this chapter, we'll deal with each of these six topics.

WHAT DO YOU GET?

You should know the following arithmetic terms:

- The result of addition is a *sum* or *total*.

- The result of subtraction is a *difference*.

- The result of multiplication is a *product*.

- The result of division is a *quotient*.

- In the expression 5^2, the 2 is called an *exponent*.

THE SIX OPERATIONS MUST BE PERFORMED IN THE PROPER ORDER

Do It Yourself

Some calculators automatically take order of operations into account, and some don't. Either way, you can very easily go wrong if you are in the habit of punching in long lines of arithmetic operations. The safe, smart way is to clear the calculator after every individual operation, performing PEMDAS yourself.

Very often, solving an equation on the SAT will require you to perform several different operations, one after another. These operations must be performed in the proper order. In general, the problems are written in such a way that you won't have trouble deciding what comes first. In cases in which you are uncertain, you only need to remember the following sentence:

Please **E**xcuse **M**y **D**ear **A**unt **S**ally, she limps from *left* to *right*.

That's **PEMDAS**, for short. It stands for **P**arentheses, **E**xponents, **M**ultiplication, **D**ivision, **A**ddition, **S**ubtraction. First you clear the parentheses; then you take care of the exponents; then you perform all multiplication and division at the same time, from *left* to *right*, followed by addition and subtraction, from *left* to *right*.

The following drill will help you learn the order in which to perform the six operations. First set up the equations on paper. Then use your calculator for the arithmetic. Make sure you perform the operations in the correct order.

DRILL 1

Solve each of the following problems by performing the indicated operations in the proper order. Answers can be found on page 338.

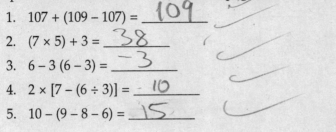

1. $107 + (109 - 107) =$ ___109___
2. $(7 \times 5) + 3 =$ ___38___
3. $6 - 3(6 - 3) =$ ___-3___
4. $2 \times [7 - (6 \div 3)] =$ ___10___
5. $10 - (9 - 8 - 6) =$ ___15___

Whichever Comes First

Addition and subtraction are interchangeable in the order of operations. Solve whichever operation comes first, reading left to right. The same is true of multiplication and division. And remember, if you don't solve in order from left to right, you could end up with the wrong answer! Example:
$24 \div 4 \times 6 = 24 \div 24 = 1$
wrong
$24 \div 4 \times 6 = 6 \times 6 = 36$
right

PARENTHESES CAN HELP YOU SOLVE EQUATIONS

Using parentheses to regroup information in SAT arithmetic problems can be very helpful. In order to do this, you need to understand a basic law that you have probably forgotten since the days when you last took arithmetic—*the distributive law*. You don't need to remember the name of the law, but you do need to know how it works.

THE DISTRIBUTIVE LAW

If you're multiplying the sum of two numbers by a third number, you can multiply each number in your sum individually. This comes in handy when you have to multiply the sum of two variables.

If a problem gives you information in "factored form"—$a(b + c)$—then you should distribute the first variable before you do anything else. If you are given information that has already been distributed—$ab + ac$—then you should factor out the common term, putting the information back in factored form. Very often on the SAT, simply doing this will enable you to spot ETS's answer.

For example:

Distributive: $6(53) + 6(47) = 6(53 + 47) = 6(100) = 600$

Multiplication first: $6(53) + 6(47) = 318 + 282 = 600$

You get the same answer each way, so why get involved with ugly arithmetic? If you use the distributive law, you don't even need to use your calculator.

The drill on the following page illustrates the distributive law.

DRILL 2

Rewrite each problem by either distributing or factoring, whichever is called for. Questions 3, 4, and 5 have no numbers in them, therefore, they can't be solved with a calculator. Answers can be found on page 338.

1. $(6 \times 57) + (6 \times 13) =$ _6(57+13) = 420_

2. $51(48) + 51(50) + 51(52) =$ _51(48+50+52) = 7650_

3. $a(b + c - d) =$ _ab+ac-ad_

4. $xy - xz =$ _x(y-z)_

5. $abc + xyc =$ _c(ab+xy)_

FRACTIONS

A FRACTION IS JUST ANOTHER WAY OF EXPRESSING DIVISION

Or Use Your Calculator

Another option for solving questions with fractions is to use your calculator.

The expression $\dfrac{x}{y}$ is exactly the same thing as $x \div y$. The expression $\dfrac{1}{2}$ means nothing more than $1 \div 2$. In the fraction $\dfrac{x}{y}$, x is known as the numerator (hereafter referred to as "the top") and y is known as the denominator (hereafter referred to as "the bottom").

ADDING AND SUBTRACTING FRACTIONS WITH THE SAME BOTTOM

To add two or more fractions that all have the same bottom, simply add up the tops and put the sum over the common bottom. For example:

$$\frac{1}{100} + \frac{4}{100} = \frac{1+4}{100} = \frac{5}{100}$$

Subtraction works exactly the same way:

$$\frac{4}{100} - \frac{1}{100} = \frac{4-1}{100} = \frac{3}{100}$$

ADDING AND SUBTRACTING FRACTIONS WITH DIFFERENT BOTTOMS

In school you were taught to add and subtract fractions with different bottoms by finding a common bottom. To do this, you have to multiply each fraction by a number that makes all the bottoms the same. Most students find this process annoying.

Fortunately, we have an approach to adding and subtracting fractions with different bottoms that simplifies the entire process. Use the example below as a model. Just multiply in the direction of each arrow, and then either add or subtract across the top. Lastly, multiply across the bottom.

$$\frac{1}{3} + \frac{1}{2} =$$

$$\frac{2}{} \qquad \frac{3}{}$$

$$\frac{1}{3} \diagdown \frac{1}{2}$$

$$\frac{2+3}{6} = \frac{5}{6}$$

That was easy, wasn't it? We call this procedure the *Bowtie* because the arrows make it look like a bowtie. Use the Bowtie to add or subtract any pair of fractions without thinking about the common bottom, just by following the steps above.

MULTIPLYING ALL FRACTIONS

Multiplying fractions is easy. Just multiply across the top, then multiply across the bottom.

Here's an example:

$$\frac{4}{5} \times \frac{5}{6} = \frac{20}{30}$$

When you multiply fractions, all you are really doing is performing one multiplication problem on top of another.

You should never multiply two fractions before looking to see if you can reduce either or both. If you reduce first, your final answer will be in the form for which ETS is looking.

$$\frac{63}{6} \times \frac{48}{7} = \frac{\overset{9}{\cancel{63}}}{6} \times \frac{48}{\cancel{7}_1} = \frac{\overset{9}{\cancel{63}}}{\cancel{6}_1} \times \frac{\overset{8}{\cancel{48}}}{\cancel{7}_1} =$$

$$\frac{9}{1} \times \frac{8}{1}$$

$$\frac{72}{1} = 72$$

REDUCING FRACTIONS

When you add or multiply fractions, you will very often end up with a big fraction that is hard to work with. You can almost always reduce such a fraction into one that is easier to handle.

Start Small

It is not easy to see that 26 and 286 have a common factor of 13, but it's pretty clear that they're both divisible by 2.

To reduce a fraction, divide both the top and the bottom by the largest number that is a factor of both. For example, to reduce $\frac{12}{60}$, divide both the top and the bottom by 12, which is the largest number that is a factor of both. Dividing 12 by 12 yields 1; dividing 60 by 12 yields 5. The reduced fraction is $\frac{1}{5}$.

If you can't immediately find the largest number that is a factor of both, find any number that is a factor of both and divide both the top and bottom by that. Your calculations will take a little longer, but you'll end up in the same place. In the previous example, even if you don't see that 12 is a factor of both 12 and 60, you can no doubt see that 6 is a factor of both. Dividing top and bottom by 6 yields $\frac{2}{10}$. Now divide by 2. Doing so yields $\frac{1}{5}$. Once again, you have arrived at ETS's answer.

DIVIDING ALL FRACTIONS

Just Do It

When dividing (don't ask why) just flip the last one and multiply.

To divide one fraction by another, invert the second fraction and multiply. To invert a fraction, simply flip it over. Doing this is extremely easy, as long as you remember how it works. Here's an example:

$$\frac{2}{3} \div \frac{4}{3} =$$

$$\frac{2}{3} \times \frac{3}{4} = \frac{6}{12} = \frac{1}{2}$$

Be careful not to cancel or reduce until after you flip the second fraction. You can even do the same thing with fractions whose tops and/or bottoms are fractions. These problems look quite frightening but they're actually easy if you keep your cool.

Here's an example:

$$\frac{\frac{4}{4}}{3} =$$

$$\frac{4}{1} \div \frac{4}{3} =$$

$$\frac{4}{1} \times \frac{3}{4} =$$

$$\frac{\cancel{4}}{1} \times \frac{3}{\cancel{4}} =$$

$$\frac{3}{1} = 3$$

CONVERTING MIXED NUMBERS TO FRACTIONS

A mixed number is a number like $2\frac{3}{4}$. It is the sum of an integer and a fraction. When you see mixed numbers on the SAT, you should usually convert them to ordinary fractions. Here's a quick and easy way to convert mixed numbers:

- Multiply the integer by the bottom of the fraction.
- Add this product to the top of the fraction.
- Place this sum over the bottom of the fraction.

For example, let's convert $2\frac{3}{4}$ to a fraction. Multiply 2 (the integer part of the mixed number) times 4 (the bottom of the fraction). That gives us 8. Add that to the 3 (the top of the fraction) to give us 11. Place 11 over 4 to give us $\frac{11}{4}$.

The mixed number $2\frac{3}{4}$ is exactly the same as the fraction $\frac{11}{4}$. We converted the one to the other because fractions are easier to work with than mixed numbers.

Just Don't Mix

For some reason, ETS thinks it's okay to give you mixed numbers as answer choices. On grid-ins, however, if you use a mixed number, ETS won't give you credit.

DRILL 3

Try converting the following mixed numbers. Answers can be found on page 338.

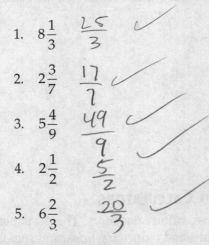

1. $8\frac{1}{3}$ $\frac{25}{3}$ ✓

2. $2\frac{3}{7}$ $\frac{17}{7}$ ✓

3. $5\frac{4}{9}$ $\frac{49}{9}$ ✓

4. $2\frac{1}{2}$ $\frac{5}{2}$

5. $6\frac{2}{3}$ $\frac{20}{3}$

COMPARING FRACTIONS

The SAT sometimes contains problems that require you to compare one fraction with another and determine which is larger. There are two ways to compare fractions: convert them to decimals or use the Bowtie.

Using the Bowtie to compare fractions is quick and easy. Let's say you are given a problem in which you need to determine which is bigger, $\frac{9}{10}$ or $\frac{10}{11}$.

As before, multiply in the direction of the arrows.

$$99 \quad\quad\quad 100$$
$$\frac{9}{10} \diagdown\diagup \frac{10}{11}$$

Notice that you don't need to multiply across the bottom when you are comparing fractions. Since 100 is bigger than 99, $\frac{10}{11}$ is bigger than $\frac{9}{10}$.

If you prefer, you can use your calculator to convert each fraction to a decimal. To do this, perform the division problem the fraction represents. Divide 9 by 10 on your calculator, which gives you 0.9. Then divide 10 by 11, which gives you 0.9090909. Which is bigger?

FRACTIONS BEHAVE IN PECULIAR WAYS

Joe Bloggs has trouble with fractions because they don't always behave the way he thinks they ought to. For example, because 4 is obviously greater than 2, Joe Bloggs sometimes forgets that $\frac{1}{4}$ is less than $\frac{1}{2}$. He becomes especially confused when the top is some number other than 1. For example, $\frac{2}{6}$ is less than $\frac{2}{5}$.

Joe also has a hard time understanding that when you multiply one fraction by another, you will get a fraction that is smaller than either of the first two. For example:

$$\frac{1}{2} \times \frac{1}{4} = \frac{1}{8}$$

$$\frac{1}{8} < \frac{1}{2}$$

$$\frac{1}{8} < \frac{1}{4}$$

A WORD ABOUT FRACTIONS AND CALCULATORS

It's possible to key fractions into many scientific calculators. These calculators allow you to add, subtract, multiply, divide, and reduce fractions, and some also convert mixed numbers to fractions and back again. If you know how to work with fractions on your calculator, go ahead and use it. While you should still understand how to work with fractions the old-fashioned way, your calculator can be a tremendous help if you know how to use it properly. If you plan to use your calculator on fraction problems, make sure you practice with your calculator before the test.

DRILL 4

If you have trouble on any of these problems, go back and review the information just outlined. Answers can be found on page 339.

1. Reduce $\dfrac{18}{6}$ _____ 3 _____

2. Convert $6\dfrac{1}{5}$ to a fraction _____ $\dfrac{31}{5}$ _____

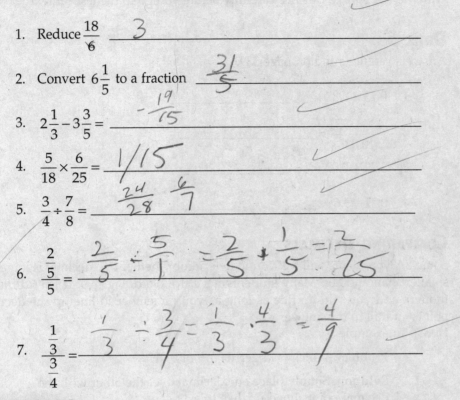

3. $2\dfrac{1}{3} - 3\dfrac{3}{5} =$ _____ $-\dfrac{19}{15}$ _____

4. $\dfrac{5}{18} \times \dfrac{6}{25} =$ _____ $1/15$ _____

5. $\dfrac{3}{4} \div \dfrac{7}{8} =$ _____ $\dfrac{24}{28}$ $\dfrac{6}{7}$ _____

6. $\dfrac{\frac{2}{5}}{5} =$ _____ $\dfrac{2}{5} \div \dfrac{5}{1} = \dfrac{2}{5} \cdot \dfrac{1}{5} = \dfrac{2}{25}$ _____

7. $\dfrac{\frac{1}{3}}{\frac{3}{4}} =$ _____ $\dfrac{1}{3} \div \dfrac{3}{4} = \dfrac{1}{3} \cdot \dfrac{4}{3} = \dfrac{4}{9}$ _____

DECIMALS

A DECIMAL IS JUST ANOTHER WAY OF EXPRESSING A FRACTION

Fractions can be expressed as decimals. To find a fraction's decimal equivalent, simply divide the top by the bottom. (You can do this easily with your calculator.) For example:

$$\frac{3}{5} =$$

$$3 \div 5 = 0.6$$

ADDING, SUBTRACTING, MULTIPLYING, AND DIVIDING DECIMALS

Manipulating decimals is easy with a calculator. Simply punch in the numbers—being especially careful to get the decimal point in the right place every single time—and read the result from the display. A calculator makes these operations easy. In fact, working with decimals is one area on the SAT where your calculator will prevent you from making careless errors. You won't have to line up decimal points or remember what happens when you divide. The calculator will keep track of everything for you, as long as you punch in the correct numbers to begin with. Just be sure to practice carefully before you go to the test center.

DRILL 5

Answers can be found on page 339.

1. $0.43 \times 0.87 =$ _____ .3741

2. $\dfrac{43 + 0.731}{0.03} =$ _____ 1457.7

3. $3.72 \div 0.02 =$ _____ 186

4. $0.71 - 3.6 =$ _____ -2.89

COMPARING DECIMALS

Some SAT problems will ask you to determine whether one decimal is larger or smaller than another. Many students have trouble doing this. It isn't difficult, though, and you will do fine as long as you remember to line up the decimal points and fill in missing zeros.

Here's an example:

Place Value

Compare decimals place by place, going from left to right.

Problem: Which is larger, 0.0099 or 0.01?

Solution: Simply place one decimal over the other with the decimal points lined up, like this:

0.0099
0.01

To make the solution seem clearer, you can add two zeros to the right of 0.01. (You can always add zeros to the right of a decimal without changing its value.) Now you have this:

0.0099
0.0100

Which decimal is larger? Clearly, 0.0100 is, just as 100 is larger than 99. (Remember that $0.0099 = \dfrac{99}{10,000}$, while $0.0100 = \dfrac{100}{10,000}$. Now the answer seems obvious, doesn't it?)

Analysis

Joe Bloggs has a terrible time on this problem. Because 99 is obviously larger than 1, he tends to think that 0.0099 must be larger than 0.01. But it isn't. Don't get sloppy on problems like this! ETS loves to trip up Joe Bloggs with decimals. In fact, any time you encounter a problem involving the comparison of decimals, you should stop and ask yourself whether you are about to make a Joe Bloggs mistake.

172 ◆ CRACKING THE NEW SAT

ABSOLUTE VALUE

The absolute value of a number is its distance from zero; since distances are positive values, all absolute values *must* be positive. The absolute value of a number is denoted by $|x|$. For example, if you see an expression such as $|-7 - 10| = x$, then x will be 17. Evaluate the stuff inside the bars and see how far that number is from zero. Just be careful with tricky minus signs: $-|-7 - 10|$ actually works out to be -3.

RATIOS AND PROPORTIONS

A RATIO IS A COMPARISON

Many students get extremely nervous when they are asked to work with ratios. But there's no need to be nervous. A ratio is a comparison between the quantities of ingredients you have in a mixture, be it a class full of people or a bowl of cake batter. Ratios can be written to look like fractions—don't get them confused.

The ratio of x to y can be expressed in the following three ways:

1. $\dfrac{x}{y}$

2. the ratio of x to y

3. $x:y$

PART, PART, WHOLE

Ratios are a lot like fractions. In fact, anything you can do to a fraction (convert it to a decimal or percentage, reduce it, etc.), you can do to a ratio. The difference is that a fraction gives you a part (the top number) over a whole (the bottom number), while a ratio typically gives you two parts (boys to girls, CDs to cassettes, sugar to flour), and it is your job to come up with the whole. For example, if there is one cup of sugar for every two cups of flour in a recipe, that's three cups of stuff. The ratio of sugar to flour is 1:2. Add the parts to get the whole.

Ratios vs. Fractions

Keep in mind that a ratio compares part of something to another part. A fraction compares part of something to the whole thing.

Ratio: $\dfrac{\text{part}}{\text{part}}$

Fraction: $\dfrac{\text{part}}{\text{whole}}$

RATIO TO REAL

If a class contains 3 students and the ratio of boys to girls in that class is 2:1, how many boys and how many girls are there in the class? Of course: There are 2 boys and 1 girl.

Now, suppose a class contains 24 students and the ratio of boys to girls is still 2:1. How many boys and how many girls are there in the class? This is a little harder, but the answer is easy to find if you think about it. There are 16 boys and 8 girls.

How did we get the answer? We added up the number of "parts" in the ratio (2 parts boys plus 1 part girls, or 3 parts all together) and divided it into the total number of students. In other words, we divided 24 by 3. This told us that the class contained 3 equal parts of 8 students each. From the given ratio (2:1), we knew that two of these parts consisted of boys and one of them consisted of girls.

An easy way to keep track of all this is to use a tool we call the *Ratio Box*. Every time you have a ratio problem, set up a Ratio Box with the information provided in the problem and use it to find ETS's answer.

Here's how it works:

Let's go back to our class containing 24 students, in which the ratio of boys to girls is 2:1. Quickly sketch a table that has columns and rows, like this:

	Boys	Girls	Whole
Ratio (parts)	2	1	3
Multiply By			
Actual Number			24

This is the information you have been given. The ratio is 2:1, so you have 2 parts boys and 1 part girls, for a total of 3 parts. You also know that the actual number of students in the whole class is 24. You start by writing these numbers in proper spaces in your box.

Your goal is to fill in the two empty spaces in the bottom row. To do that, you will multiply each number in the *parts* row by the same number. To find that number, look in the last column. What number would you multiply by 3 to get 24? You should see easily that you would multiply by 8. Therefore, write an 8 in all three blanks in the *multiply by* row. (The spaces in this row will always contain the same number, although of course it won't always be an 8.) Here's what your Ratio Box should look like now:

	Boys	Girls	Whole
Ratio (parts)	2	1	3
Multiply By	8	8	8
Actual Number			24

The next step is to fill in the empty spaces in the bottom row. You do that the same way you did in the last column, by multiplying. First, multiply the numbers in the boys column ($2 \times 8 = 16$). Then multiply the numbers in the girls column ($1 \times 8 = 8$).

Here's what your box should look like now:

	Boys	Girls	Whole
Ratio (parts)	2	1	3
Multiply By	8	8	8
Actual Number	16	8	24

Now you have enough information to answer any question that ETS might ask you. For example:

- What is the ratio of boys to girls? You can see easily from the ratio (parts) row of the box that the ratio is 2:1.

- What is the ratio of girls to boys? You can see easily from the ratio (parts) row of the box that the ratio is 1:2.

- What is the total number of boys in the class? You can see easily from the bottom row of the box that it is 16.

- What is the total number of girls in the class? You can see easily from the bottom row of the box that it is 8.

- What fractional part of the class is boys? There are 16 boys in a class of 24, so the fraction representing the boys is $\frac{16}{24}$, which can be reduced to $\frac{2}{3}$.

As you can see, the Ratio Box is an easy way to find, organize, and keep track of information on ratio problems. And it works the same no matter what information you are given. Just remember that all the boxes in the *multiply by* row will always contain the same number.

Here's another example:

PROBLEM SOLVING
1 2 3 4 5 6 7 8 9 (10) 11 12 13 14 15 16 17 18 19 20
EASY   MEDIUM   HARD

10. In a jar of red and green jelly beans, the ratio of green jelly beans to red jelly beans is 5:3. If the jar contains a total of 160 jelly beans, how many of them are red?
(A) 30
(B) 53
(C) 60
(D) 100
(E) 160

Here's How to Crack It
First, sketch out a Ratio Box:

	Green	Red	Whole
Ratio (parts)	5	3	8
Multiply By	20	20	20
Actual Number	100	60	160

What You Need

Always keep an eye on what you are being asked. You do not want to do more work than necessary. Question 10 never asks about green jelly beans, so leave that box empty.

Now find the multiplier. What do you multiply by 8 to get 160? You multiply 8 by 20. Now write 20 in each box on the *multiply by* row:

	Green	Red	Whole
Ratio (parts)	5	3	8
Multiply By	20	20	20
Actual Number			160

The problem asks you to find how many red jelly beans there are. Go to the red column and multiply 3 by 20. The answer is 60. ETS's answer is C. Notice that you would have set up the box in exactly the same way if the question had asked you to determine how many jelly beans were green. (How many are green? The answer is 5 × 20, which is 100.)

PROPORTIONS ARE EQUAL RATIOS

Some SAT math problems will contain two proportional, or equal, ratios from which one piece of information is missing.

Here's an example:

PROBLEM SOLVING		
1 2 3 4 ⑤ 6	7 8 9 10 11 12 13 14	15 16 17 18 19 20
EASY	MEDIUM	HARD

5. If 2 packages contain a total of 12 doughnuts, how many doughnuts are there in 5 packages?

   (A) 12
   (B) 24
   (C) 30
   (D) 36
   (E) 60

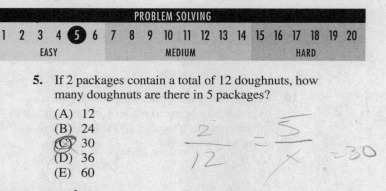

Here's How to Crack It

This problem simply describes two equal ratios, one of which is missing a single piece of information. Here's the given information represented as two equal ratios:

$$\frac{2 \text{ (packages)}}{12 \text{ (doughnuts)}} = \frac{5 \text{ (packages)}}{x \text{ (doughnuts)}}$$

Since ratios are fractions, we can treat them exactly like fractions. To find the answer, all you have to do is figure out what you could plug in for x that would make $\frac{2}{12} = \frac{5}{x}$. One way to do this is to cross-multiply:

$$\frac{2}{12} \diagdown \frac{5}{x}$$

so, $2x = 60$

$x = 30$

ETS's answer is C.

Careful

You can only cross-multiply across an equal sign. You can't reduce across an equal sign.

DIRECT AND INDIRECT VARIATION

This is a somewhat new concept for the SAT, but has been consistently tested on the SAT Math IC and Math IIC Subject Tests. Direct variation problems, a fancy term for proportions, are the same as what you've just seen: If one quantity grows or decreases by a factor, the other quantity grows or decreases by the same factor. Indirect variations (also known as *indirect proportions*) are just the opposite of that. As one quantity grows or decreases, the other quantity decreases or grows by the same factor. The key to both of these is figuring out that factor.

What's in a Name?

When you see *variation*, think *proportion*.

The main formula you want to remember for indirect proportions is:

$$x_1 y_1 = x_2 y_2$$

Try one:

15. The amount of time it takes to consume a buffalo carcass is inversely proportional to the number of vultures. If it takes 12 vultures 3 days to consume a buffalo, how many fewer hours will it take if there are 4 more vultures?

    (A) $\dfrac{1}{4}$

    (B) $\dfrac{3}{4}$

    (C) 18

    (D) 24

    (E) 54

Here's How to Crack It

For inverse proportions, follow the formula. First, convert the days: 3 days is equal to 72 hours. Now set up the equation: (12 vultures)(72 hours) = (16 vultures)(x). We solve to get $x = 54$, which is 18 fewer hours. The answer is C.

PERCENTAGES

PERCENTAGES ARE FRACTIONS

There should be nothing frightening about a percentage. It's just a convenient way of expressing a fraction whose bottom is 100.

Percent means "per 100," or "out of 100." If there are 100 questions on your math test and you answer 50 of them, you will have answered 50 out of 100, or $\dfrac{50}{100}$, or 50 percent. To think of it another way:

$$\frac{\text{part}}{\text{whole}} = \frac{x}{100} = x \text{ percent}$$

MEMORIZE THESE PERCENTAGE-DECIMAL-FRACTION EQUIVALENTS

$$0.01 = \frac{1}{100} = 1 \text{ percent} \qquad\qquad 0.25 = \frac{1}{4} = 25 \text{ percent}$$

$$0.1 = \frac{1}{10} = 10 \text{ percent} \qquad\qquad 0.5 = \frac{1}{2} = 50 \text{ percent}$$

$$0.2 = \frac{1}{5} = 20 \text{ percent} \qquad\qquad 0.75 = \frac{3}{4} = 75 \text{ percent}$$

CONVERTING PERCENTAGES TO FRACTIONS

To convert a percentage to a fraction, simply put the percentage over 100 and reduce. For example:

$$80 \text{ percent} = \frac{80}{100} = \frac{8}{10} = \frac{4}{5}$$

Another Way

You can also convert fractions to percentages by cross-multiplying:

$$\frac{3}{4} = \frac{x}{100}$$

$$4x = 3(100)$$

$$x = \frac{3(100)}{4}$$

$$x = 75$$

CONVERTING FRACTIONS TO PERCENTAGES

Since a percentage is just another way to express a fraction, you shouldn't be surprised to see how easy it is to convert a fraction to a percentage. To do so, simply use your calculator to divide the top of the fraction by the bottom of the fraction, and then multiply the result by 100. Here's an example:

Problem: Express $\frac{3}{4}$ as a percentage.

Solution: $\frac{3}{4} = 0.75 \times 100 = 75$ percent.

Converting fractions to percentages is easy with your calculator.

CONVERTING PERCENTAGES TO DECIMALS

To convert a percentage to a decimal, simply move the decimal point *two places to the left*. For example: 25 percent can be expressed as the decimal 0.25; 50 percent is the same as 0.50 or 0.5; 100 percent is the same as 1.00 or 1.

CONVERTING DECIMALS TO PERCENTAGES

To convert a decimal to a percentage, just do the opposite of what you did in the preceding section. All you have to do is move the decimal point *two places to the right*. Thus, 0.5 = 50 percent; 0.375 = 37.5 percent; 2 = 200 percent.

The following drill will give you practice working with fractions, decimals, and percentages.

DRILL 6

Fill in the missing information in the following table. Answers can be found on page 339.

	Fraction	Decimal	Percent
1.	$\frac{1}{2}$	.5	50%
2.	$\frac{3}{1}$	3.0	300%
3.	1/200	.005	0.5
4.	$\frac{1}{3}$	.3	33.3%

WHAT PERCENT OF WHAT?

Problem: What number is 10 percent greater than 20?

Solution: We know that 10 percent of 20 is 2. So the question really reads: What is 2 greater than 20? The answer is 22.

Analysis

Joe Bloggs gets confused on questions like this. You won't if you take them slowly and solve them one step at a time. The same holds true for problems that ask you what number is a certain percentage less than another number. What number is 10 percent less than 500? Well, 10 percent of 500 is 50. The number that is 10 percent less than 500, therefore, is 500 − 50, or 450. You will see the words *of*, *is*, *product*, *sum*, and *what* pop up a lot in the Math sections of the SAT. Don't let these words fool you because they all translate into simple math functions. Look at the "Translate" sidebar for The Princeton Review's translation of some terms, and get to know them. It will save you time on the test and make your life with the SAT much nicer.

Translate

On a math test like the SAT, we can convert (or translate) words into arithmetic symbols. Here are some of the most common:

Word	Symbol
is	=
of	× (multiply)
percent	/100
what	*n* (variable)

WHAT PERCENT OF WHAT PERCENT OF WHAT?

On harder SAT questions, you may be asked to determine the effect of a series of percentage increases or decreases. The key point to remember on such problems is that each successive increase or decrease is performed on the result of the previous one.

Here's an example:

PROBLEM SOLVING																			
1	2	3	4	5	6	7	8	9	10	11	12	13	14	**15**	16	17	18	19	20
		EASY							MEDIUM							HARD			

Bite-Size Pieces

Always handle percentage problems in bite-size pieces: one piece at a time.

15. A business paid $300 to rent a piece of office equipment for one year. The rent was then increased by 10 percent each year thereafter. How much will the company pay for the first three years it rents the equipment?

    (A) $920
    (B) $960
    (C) $990
    (D) $993
    (E) $999

Here's How to Crack It

You are being asked to find a business's total rent for a piece of equipment for three years. The easiest way to keep from getting confused on a problem like this is to take it one step at a time. First, make an outline of exactly what you have to find out.

Year 1:

Year 2:

Year 3:

Write this down in the margin of your test booklet. There's one slot for each year's rent; ETS's answer will be the total.

You already know the number that goes in the first slot: 300, because that is what the problem says the business will pay for the first year.

What number goes in the second slot? 330, because 330 equals 300 plus 10 percent of 300.

Now, here's where you have to pay attention. What number goes in the third slot? Not 360! (Cross out choice C!) The rent goes up 10 percent each year. This increase is calculated from the previous year's rent. That means that the rent for the third year is $363, because 363 equals 330 plus 10 percent of 330.

Now you are ready to find ETS's answer:

Year 1: 300

Year 2: 330

Year 3: 363 (underlined)

993

ETS's answer is thus choice D, $993.

WHAT PERCENT OF WHAT PERCENT OF . . . YIKES!

Sometimes you may find successive percentage problems in which you aren't given actual numbers to work with. In such cases, you need to plug in some numbers.

Here's an example:

PROBLEM SOLVING																			
1	2	3	4	5	6	7	8	9	10	11	12	13	14	15	16	**17**	18	19	20
EASY						MEDIUM									HARD				

17. A number is increased by 25 percent and then decreased by 20 percent. The result is what percent of the original number?

(A) 80
(B) 100
(C) 105
(D) 120
(E) 125

Here's How to Crack It

Using the Joe Bloggs principle, you ought to be able to eliminate three choices right off the bat: A, D, and E. Joe loves easy answers. Choices A, D, and E are all equal to 100 plus or minus 20 or 25. All three choices seem right to Joe for different reasons. This is a difficult question, so answers that seem right to Joe must be eliminated. Get rid of them.

A somewhat more subtle Joe Bloggs attractor is choice C. Joe thinks that if you increase a number by 25 percent and then decrease by 20 percent, you end up with a net increase of 5 percent. He has forgotten that in a series of percentage changes (which is what we have here), each successive change is based on the result of the previous one.

We've now eliminated everything but choice B, which is ETS's answer.

Could we have found it without Joe's help? Yes. Here's how: You aren't given a particular number to work with in this problem—just "a number." Rather than trying to deal with the problem in the abstract, you should immediately plug in a number to work with. What number would be easiest to work with in a percentage problem? Why, 100, of course.

1. 25 percent of 100 is 25, so 100 increased by 25 percent is 125.

2. Now you have to decrease 125 by 20 percent, 20 percent of 125 is 25, so 125 decreased by 20 percent is 100.

3. 100 (our result) is 100 percent of 100 (the number you plugged in), so ETS's answer, once again, is B.

AVERAGES

WHAT IS AN AVERAGE?

On the SAT, the average (also called *arithmetic mean*) of a set of *n* numbers is simply the sum of all the numbers divided by *n*. In other words, if you want to find the average of three numbers, add them up and divide by 3. For example,

the average of 3, 7, and 8 is $\frac{(3+7+8)}{3}$, which equals $\frac{18}{3}$, or 6.

That was an easy example, but ETS does not always write average questions with clear solutions. That is, ETS doesn't always give you the information for averages in a way that is easy to work with. For that reason, we have a visual aid, like the Ratio Box for ratios, that helps you organize the information on average questions and find ETS's answer.

We call it the *Average Pie*. Here's what it looks like:

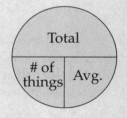

The *total* is the sum of all the numbers you're averaging, and the *number of things* is the number of elements you're averaging. Here's what the Average Pie looks like using the simple average example we just gave you.

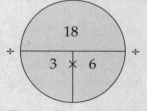

Here's how the Average Pie works mathematically. The line in the middle means *divide*. If you know the total and the number of things, just divide to get the average (18 ÷ 3 = 6). If you know the total and the average, just divide to get the number of things (18 ÷ 6 = 3). If you know the average and the number of things, simply multiply to get the total (6 × 3 = 18). The key to most average questions is finding the total.

Here's another simple example:

Problem: If the average of three test scores is 70, what is the total of all three test scores?

Solution: Just put the number of things (3 tests) and the average (70) in the pie. Then multiply to find the total, which is 210.

Total

When calculating averages and means, always find the total. It's the one piece of information that ETS loves to withhold.

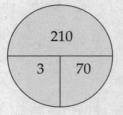

Here's another example:

Problem: What's the average of 10, 10, 10, and 50?

Solution: Simply add up the numbers to find the total, which is 80. The number of things is 4. Then just divide to find the average, which is 20.

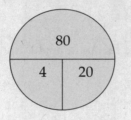

AVERAGES: ADVANCED PRINCIPLES

To solve most difficult average problems, all you have to do is fill out one or more Average Pies. Most of the time you will use them to find the total of the number being averaged. Here's an example:

Problem: Suppose a student has an average of 80 on four tests. If the student scores a 90 on the fifth test, what is her average on all five?

Solution: To find the average of all five tests, you need the total score. You need to start by finding the total of the first *four* tests. Draw an Average Pie and write in the average of the first four tests (80), and the number of things (4):

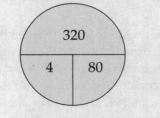

$4 \times 80 = 320$

$320 + 90 = 410$

$\frac{410}{5} = 82$

$Avg \times \# \ of \ things = total$

Then multiply to find the total, which is 320. Now, find the total of all five tests by adding the fifth score to the total of the first four: 320 + 90 = 410. Now draw another Average Pie to find the average of all five tests. Write in the total (410), and the number of things (5). Then divide to find the average: 82.

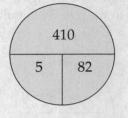

Now let's try a difficult question:

20. If the average (arithmetic mean) of eight numbers is 20, and the average of five of these numbers is 14, what is the average of the other three numbers?

(A) 14
(B) 17
(C) 20
(D) 30
(E) 34

Here's How to Crack It

Start by drawing an Average Pie for all eight numbers; then multiply to find the total.

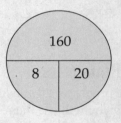

The total of the eight numbers is 160. Now draw another Average Pie for five of the numbers.

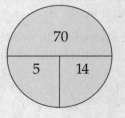

The total of those five numbers is 70. (Remember, those are five out of the original eight numbers.) To find the average of the other three numbers, you need the total of those three numbers. You have the total of all eight numbers, 160, and the total of five of those numbers, 70, so you can find the total of the other three by subtracting 70 from 160. That means the total of the three remaining numbers is 90. It's time to create one more Average Pie to find the average of those three numbers.

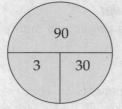

The average is 30, so ETS's answer is D.

On the SAT, you'll also need to know two other topics related to averages: *median* and *mode*.

What Is a *Median*?

The median of a group of numbers is the number that is exactly in the middle of the group when the group is arranged from smallest to largest, as on a number line. For example, in the group 3, 6, 6, 6, 6, 7, 8, 9, 10, 10, 11, the median is 7. Five numbers come before 7 in the group, and 5 come after. Remember it this way: *median* sounds like *middle*.

Median Median

To find the median of a set containing an even number of items, take the average of the two middle numbers.

What Is a *Mode*?

The mode of a group of numbers is the number in the group that appears most often. In the group 3, 4, 4, 5, 7, 7, 8, 8, 8, 9, 10, the mode is 8, because it appears three times while no other number in the group appears more than twice. Remember it this way: *mode* sounds like *most*.

EXPONENTS AND SQUARE ROOTS

Exponents Are a Kind of Shorthand

Many numbers are the product of the same factor multiplied over and over again. For example, $32 = 2 \times 2 \times 2 \times 2 \times 2$. Another way to write this would be $32 = 2^5$, or "thirty-two equals two to the fifth power." The little number, or *exponent*, denotes the number of times that 2 is to be used as a factor. In the same way, $10^3 = 10 \times 10 \times 10$, or 1,000, or "ten to the third power," or "ten cubed." In this example, the 10 is called the *base* and the 3 is called the *exponent*. (You won't need to know these terms on the SAT, but you will need to know them to follow our explanations.)

Multiplying Numbers with Exponents

When you multiply two numbers with the same base, you simply add the exponents. For example, $2^3 \times 2^5 = 2^{3+5} = 2^8$.

Dividing Numbers with Exponents

When you divide two numbers with the same base, you simply subtract the exponents. For example, $\dfrac{2^5}{2^3} = 2^{5-3} = 2^2$.

Warning

The rules for multiplying and dividing exponents do not apply to addition or subtraction:
$2^2 + 2^3 = 12$
$(2 \times 2) + (2 \times 2 \times 2) = 12$
It does not equal 2^5 or 32.

Raising a Power to a Power

When you raise a power to a power, you multiply the exponents. For example, $(2^3)^4 = 2^{3 \times 4} = 2^{12}$.

Calculator Exponents

You can compute simple exponents on your calculator. Make sure you have a scientific calculator with a y^x key. To find 2^{10}, for example, simply use your y^x key, punching 2 in for the y value and 10 in for the x value. This may be especially useful if you are asked to compare exponents.

The Peculiar Behavior of Exponents

Raising a number to a power can have quite peculiar and unexpected results, depending on what sort of number you start out with. Here are some examples:

- If you square or cube a number greater than 1, it becomes larger. For example, $2^3 = 8$.

- If you square or cube a positive fraction smaller than one, it becomes smaller.

  For example, $= \left(\dfrac{1}{2}\right)^3 = \dfrac{1}{8}$.

- A negative number raised to an even power becomes positive. For example, $(-2)^2 = 4$.

- A negative number raised to an odd power remains negative. For example, $(-2)^3 = -8$.

You should also have a feel for relative sizes of exponential numbers without calculating them. For example, 2^{10} is much larger than 10^2. ($2^{10} = 1{,}024$; $10^2 = 100$.) To take another example, 2^5 is twice as large as 2^4, even though 5 seems only a bit larger than 4.

SQUARE ROOTS

The radical sign ($\sqrt{\ }$) indicates the positive square root of a number. For example, $\sqrt{25} = 5$.

The Only Rules You Need to Know

Here are the only rules regarding square roots that you need to know for the SAT:

1. $\sqrt{x}\sqrt{y} = \sqrt{xy}$. For example, $\sqrt{3}\sqrt{12} = \sqrt{36} = 6$

2. $\sqrt{\dfrac{x}{y}} = \dfrac{\sqrt{x}}{\sqrt{y}}$. For example, $\sqrt{\dfrac{5}{4}} = \dfrac{\sqrt{5}}{\sqrt{4}} = \dfrac{\sqrt{5}}{2}$

3. $\sqrt{x}$ = positive root only. For example, $\sqrt{16} = 4$

Note that rule 1 works in reverse: $\sqrt{50} = \sqrt{25} \times \sqrt{2} = 5\sqrt{2}$. This is really a kind of factoring. You are using rule 1 to factor a large, clumsy radical into numbers that are easier to work with.

Careless Errors

Don't make careless mistakes. Remember that the square root of a number between 0 and 1 is *larger* than the original number. For example, $\sqrt{\frac{1}{4}} = \frac{1}{2}$, and $\frac{1}{2} > \frac{1}{4}$.

INTEGER AND RATIONAL EXPONENTS

So far we've only dealt with positive integers for exponents, but they can be negative integers as well as fractions. The same concepts and rules apply, but the numbers just look a little weirder. Keep these concepts in mind:

- Negative exponents are a fancy way of writing reciprocals:

$$x^{-n} = \frac{1}{x^n}$$

- Fractional exponents are a fancy way of taking roots and powers:

$$x^{\frac{y}{z}} = \sqrt[z]{x^y}$$

PROBABILITY

Probability is a mathematical expression of the likelihood of an event. The basis of probability is simple. The likelihood of any event is discussed in terms of all of the possible outcomes. To express the probability of a given event, x, you would count the number of possible outcomes, count the number of outcomes that give you what you want, and arrange them in a fraction, like this:

$$\text{Probability of } x = \frac{\text{number of outcomes that are } x}{\text{total number of possible outcomes}}$$

Every probability is a fraction. The largest a probability can be is 1; a probability of 1 indicates total certainty. The smallest a probability can be is 0, meaning that it's something that cannot happen. Furthermore, you can find the probability that something WILL NOT happen by subtracting the probability that it WILL happen from 1. For example, if the weatherman tells you that there is a 0.3 probability of rain today, then there must be a 0.7 probability that it won't rain, because $1 - 0.3 = 0.7$. Figuring out the probability of any single event is usually simple. When you flip a coin, there are only two possible outcomes, heads and tails; the probability of getting heads is therefore 1 out of 2, or $\frac{1}{2}$. When you roll a die, there are six possible outcomes, 1 through 6; the odds of getting a 6 is therefore $\frac{1}{6}$. The odds of getting an even result when rolling a die are $\frac{1}{2}$ since there are 3 even results in 6 possible outcomes.

Here's an example of a probability question:

PROBLEM SOLVING																			
1	2	3	4	5	6	7	8	9	10	11	**12**	13	14	15	16	17	18	19	20
EASY									MEDIUM						HARD				

12. A bag contains 7 blue marbles and 14 marbles that are not blue. If one marble is drawn at random from the bag, what is the probability that the marble is blue?

(A) $\dfrac{1}{7}$

(B) $\dfrac{1}{3}$

(C) $\dfrac{1}{2}$

(D) $\dfrac{2}{3}$

(E) $\dfrac{3}{7}$

Here's How to Crack It

Here, there are 21 marbles in the bag, 7 of which are blue. The probability that a marble chosen at random would be blue is therefore $\dfrac{7}{21}$, or $\dfrac{1}{3}$. The correct answer is B.

PERMUTATIONS

A permutation is an arrangement of objects of a definite order. The simplest sort of permutations question might ask you how many different arrangements are possible for six different chairs in a row, or how many different four-letter arrangements of the letters in the word FUEL are possible. Both of these simple questions can be answered with the same technique.

Just draw a row of boxes corresponding to the positions you have to fill. In the case of the chairs, there are six positions, one for each chair. You would make a sketch like this:

Then, in each box, write the number of objects available to be put into that box. Keep in mind that objects put into previous boxes are no longer available. For the chair-arranging example, there would be six chairs available for the first box; only five left for the second box; four for the third, and so on until only one chair remained to be put into the last position. Finally, just multiply the numbers in the boxes together, and the product will be the number of possible arrangements, or permutations.

$$\boxed{6}\ \boxed{5}\ \boxed{4}\ \boxed{3}\ \boxed{2}\ \boxed{1} = 720$$

There are 720 possible permutations of a group of six chairs. This number can also be written as 6!. That's not a display of enthusiasm—the exclamation point means *factorial*. The number is read "six factorial," and it means $6 \times 5 \times 4 \times 3 \times 2 \times 1$, which equals 720. A factorial is simply the product of a series of integers counting down to 1 from the specified number. For example, the number 70! means $70 \times 69 \times 68 \dots 3 \times 2 \times 1$.

The number of possible arrangements of any group with n members is simply $n!$. In this way, the number of possible arrangements of the letters in FUEL is 4!, because there are four letters in the group. That means $4 \times 3 \times 2 \times 1$ arrangements, or 24. If you sketched four boxes for the four letter positions and filled in the appropriate numbers, that's exactly what you'd get.

ADVANCED PERMUTATIONS

Permutations get a little trickier when you work with smaller arrangements. For example, what if you were asked how many two-letter arrangements could be made from the letters in FUEL? It's just a modification of the original counting procedure. Sketch two boxes for the two positions. Then fill in the number of letters available for each position. As before, there are four letters available for the first space, and three for the second; the only difference is that you're done after two spaces:

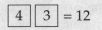

$$\boxed{4}\ \boxed{3} = 12$$

As you did before, multiply the numbers in the boxes together to get the total number of arrangements. You should find there are twelve possible two-letter arrangements from the letters in FUEL.

That's all there is to permutations. The box-counting procedure is the safest way to approach them. Just sketch the number of positions available, and fill in the number of objects available for each position, from first to last—then multiply those numbers together.

Try one:

17. Hal wrote 7 essays in his English class. He wants to put all 7 essays in his portfolio and is deciding in what order to place the essays. In how many different orders can Hal arrange his essays?

    (A)   49
    (B)   420
    (C)   5,040
    (D)   5,670
    (E) 10,549

Here's How to Crack It

There are seven essays that could be first. Once an essay is selected for first place, there are six left that could be second, then five that could be third, four that could be fourth, three that could be fifth, two that could be sixth, and one that will be last. Multiply all of those choices together: $7 \times 6 \times 5 \times 4 \times 3 \times 2 \times 1 = 5{,}040$.

$$\boxed{7}\ \boxed{6}\ \boxed{5}\ \boxed{4}\ \boxed{3}\ \boxed{2}\ \boxed{1} = 5{,}040$$

ARITHMETIC SUMMARY

1. There are only six arithmetic operations tested on the SAT: addition, subtraction, multiplication, division, exponents, and square roots.

2. These operations must be performed in the proper order (PEMDAS), beginning with operations inside parentheses.

3. Apply the distributive law whenever possible. Very often, this is enough to find ETS's answer.

4. A fraction is just another way of expressing division.

5. You must know how to add, subtract, multiply, and divide fractions. And don't forget that you can also use your calculator.

6. In any problems involving large or confusing fractions, try to reduce the fractions first. Before you multiply two fractions, for example, see if it's possible to reduce either or both of the fractions.

7. If you know how to work out fractions on your calculator, use it to help you with questions that involve fractions. If you intend to use your calculator for fractions, make sure you practice. You should also know how to work with fractions the old-fashioned way.

8. A decimal is just another way of expressing a fraction.

9. Use a calculator to add, subtract, multiply, and divide decimals.

10. A ratio can be expressed as a fraction, but ratios are not fractions. A ratio compares parts to parts; a fraction compares a part to the whole.

11. Use a ratio box to solve ratio questions.

12. Direct proportion is $\dfrac{x_1}{y_1} = \dfrac{x_2}{y_2}$. Indirect proportion is $x_1 y_1 = x_2 y_2$.

13. A percentage is just a convenient way of expressing a fraction whose bottom is 100.

14. To convert a percentage to a fraction, put the percentage over 100 and reduce.

15. To convert a fraction to a percentage, use your calculator to divide the top of the fraction by the bottom of the fraction. Then multiply the result by 100.

16. To convert a percentage to a decimal, move the decimal point two places to the left. To convert a decimal to a percentage, move the decimal point two places to the right.

17. In problems that require you to find a series of percentage increases or decreases, remember that each successive increase or decrease is performed on the result of the previous one.

18. To find the average (or arithmetic mean) of several values, add up the values and divide the total by the number of values.

19. Use the Average Pie to solve problems involving averages. The key to most average problems is finding the total.

20. The median of a group of numbers is the number that is exactly in the middle of the group when the group is arranged from smallest to largest, as on a number line.

21. The mode of a group of numbers is the number in the group that appears most often.

22. Exponents are a kind of shorthand for expressing numbers that are the product of the same factor multiplied over and over again.

23. To multiply two exponential expressions with the same base, add the exponents.

24. To divide two exponential expressions with the same base, subtract the exponents.

25. To raise one exponential expression to another power, multiply the exponents.

26. When you raise a positive number greater than 1 to a power greater than 1, the result is larger. When you raise a positive fraction less than 1 to an exponent greater than 1, the result is smaller. A negative number raised to an even power becomes positive. A negative number raised to an odd power remains negative.

27. When you're asked for the square root of any number $\sqrt{x}$, you're being asked for the positive root only.

28. Here are the only rules regarding square roots that you need to know for the SAT:

    a. $\sqrt{x} \times \sqrt{y} = \sqrt{xy}$

    b. $\sqrt{\dfrac{x}{y}} = \dfrac{\sqrt{x}}{\sqrt{y}}$

    c. $x^{-n} = \dfrac{1}{x^{n}}$

    d. $x^{\frac{y}{z}} = \sqrt[z]{x^{y}}$

29. Probability is expressed as a fraction:

$$\text{Probability of } x = \frac{\text{number of outcomes that are } x}{\text{total number of possible outcomes}}$$

30. To find permutations, or possible orders of objects, use factorials. A factorial is the whole series of integers counting down from the given number, all multiplied together.

11

Algebra:
Cracking the System

SAT ALGEBRA: CRACKING THE SYSTEM

The SAT generally tests algebra concepts that you probably learned in the eighth or ninth grade. So unless you suffer from arithmophobia (fear of numbers), you are probably pretty familiar with the level of math on the test. In fact, many people who take the SAT are currently taking math classes, such as calculus or trigonometry, that cover topics far more advanced than those on the SAT.

The SAT Math section tests not only your math skills, but also your reading skills. It is important that you read the questions carefully and translate the words in the problem into mathematical symbols.

Here are some words and their equivalent symbols:

WORD	SYMBOL
is	=
of, times, product	×
what (or any unknown value)	any letter (x, k, b)
more, sum	+
less, difference	−
ratio, quotient	÷

Here are two examples:

Words: 14 is 5 more than some number

Equation: $14 = 5 + x$

Words: If one-eighth of a number is 3, what is one-half of the same number?

Equation: $\frac{1}{8} n = 3, \frac{1}{2}n = ?$

Later in the chapter we're going to show you some extremely important techniques for bypassing a great majority of the algebra on the test, but first we need to go over some of the basics. If you feel comfortable with your algebra skills, feel free to skip ahead.

BASIC PRINCIPLES: FUNDAMENTALS OF SAT ALGEBRA

Many problems on the SAT require you to work with variables and equations. In algebra class you learned to solve equations by "solving for x" or "solving for y." To do this, you isolate x or y on one side of the equal sign and put everything else on the other side. The good thing about equations is that, to isolate the variable, you can do anything you want to them—add, subtract, multiply, divide, square—provided you perform the same operation to all the numbers in the equation.

Hence, the golden rule of equations:

> Whatever you do to the numbers on one side of the equals sign, you must do to the numbers on the other side of it as well.

Let's looks at a simple example of this rule:

1. If $2x - 15 = 35$, what is the value of x?

Here's How to Crack It

You want to isolate the variable. First, add 15 to each side of the equation. Now you have the following:

$$2x = 50$$

Divide each side of the equation by 2. Thus, x equals 25.

SOLVING EQUATIONS

On the SAT, you usually won't need to solve equations this way. Oftentimes, there is a shortcut.

Problem: If $2x = 5$ and $3y = 6$, then $6xy = ?$

Math-class solution:

1. Find x.

2. Find y.

3. Multiply 6 times x times y.

Using this procedure, you find that $x = \dfrac{5}{2}$ and $y = 2$. Therefore, $6xy = (6)\dfrac{5}{2}(2)$, or 30.

The Princeton Review solution:
You notice that $6xy$ equals $(2x)(3y)$. Therefore, $6xy$ equals $(5)(6)$, or 30.

Analysis

Finding direct solutions will save you time. ETS expects you to perform long, complicated calculations on the SAT. You should always stop and think for a moment before beginning such a process. Look for a trick—a shortcut to the answer.

Here's another example:

> If a, b, c, and d are integers and $ab = 12$,
> $bc = 20$, $cd = 30$, and $ad = 18$, then $abcd = ?$

Here's How to Crack It

If you try to solve this the math-class way, you'll end up fiddling forever with the equations, trying to find individual values for a, b, c, and d. Once again, you may get the correct answer, but you'll spend an eternity doing it.

This problem is much simpler if you look for a direct solution. The first thing to notice is that you have been given a lot of information you don't need. For example, the problem would have been much simpler to answer if you had been given only two equations: $ab = 12$ and $cd = 30$. You should know that $(ab)(cd) = abcd$, which means that $abcd = (12)(30)$, which means that the answer is 360.

SOLVING SIMULTANEOUS EQUATIONS

Sometimes on the SAT you will be asked to find the value of an expression based on two given equations. To find ETS's answer on such problems, simply add or subtract the two equations.

Here's an example:

$$\text{If } 4x + y = 14 \text{ and } 3x + 2y = 13, \text{ then } x - y = ?$$

Stack 'Em

Don't solve simultaneous equations on the SAT the way you would in school (by multiplying one equation by one number, and then adding or subtracting). We have rarely seen an SAT on which simultaneous equations had to be solved this way. Just stack 'em, and add 'em or subtract 'em.

Here's How to Crack It

You've been given two equations here. But instead of being asked to solve for a variable (x or y), you've been asked to solve for an expression ($x - y$). Why? Because there must be a direct solution.

In math class, you're taught to multiply one equation by one number and then subtract equations to find the second variable. Or you're taught to solve one equation for one variable in terms of the other and to substitute that value into the second equation to solve for the other variable, and, having found the other variable, to plug it back into the equation to find the value of the first variable.

Forget it. There's a better way. Just add or subtract the two equations; either addition or subtraction will produce an easy answer. Adding the two equations gives you this:

$$
\begin{array}{r}
4x + y = 14 \\
+ 3x + 2y = 13 \\
\hline
7x + 3y = 27
\end{array}
$$

This doesn't get us anywhere. So try subtracting:

$$
\begin{array}{r}
4x + y = 14 \\
- 3x + 2y = 13 \\
\hline
x - y = 1
\end{array}
$$

The value of $(x - y)$ is precisely what you are looking for, so this must be ETS's answer.

SOLVING INEQUALITIES

Warning!

When you multiply or divide an inequality by a negative number, you must reverse the inequality sign.

In an equation, one side equals the other. In an inequality, one side does not equal the other. The following symbols are used in inequalities:

$\ne$ is not equal to

$>$ is greater than

$<$ is less than

$\ge$ is greater than or equal to

$\le$ is less than or equal to

Solving inequalities is pretty much like solving equations. You can collect similar terms, and you can simplify by doing the same thing to both sides. All you have to remember is that if you multiply or divide both sides of an inequality by a negative number, the direction of the inequality symbol changes. For example, here's a simple inequality:

$$x > y$$

Now, just as you can with an equation, you can multiply both sides of this inequality by the same number. But if the number you multiply by is negative, you have to change the direction of the symbol in the result. For example, if we multiply both sides of the inequality above by –2, we end up with the following:

$$-2x < -2y$$

SIMPLIFYING EXPRESSIONS

If a problem contains an expression that can be factored, you should factor it immediately. For example, if you come upon a problem containing the expression $2x + 2y$, you should factor it immediately to produce the expression $2(x + y)$.

If a problem contains an expression that is already factored, you should multiply it out according to the distributive law to return it to its original unfactored state. For example, if you come upon a problem containing the expression $2(x + y)$, you should unfactor it by multiplying through to produce the expression $2x + 2y$.

Here are five worked examples:

1. $4x + 24 = 4(x) + 4(6) = 4(x + 6)$

2. $\dfrac{10x - 60}{2} = \dfrac{10(x) - 10(6)}{2} = \dfrac{10(x - 6)}{2} = 5(x - 6) = 5x - 30$

3. $\dfrac{x + y}{y} = \dfrac{x}{y} + \dfrac{y}{y} = \dfrac{x}{y} + 1$

4. $2(x + y) + 3(x + y) = (2 + 3)(x + y) = 5(x + y)$

5. $p(r + s) + q(r + s) = (p + q)(r + s)$

MULTIPLYING POLYNOMIALS

Multiplying polynomials is easy. Just be sure to use FOIL (first, outer, inner, last):

$$(x + 2)(x + 4) = (x + 2)(x + 4)$$
$$= (x \times x) + (x \times 4) + (2 \times x) + (2 \times 4)$$
$$\text{FIRST OUTER INNER LAST}$$
$$= x^2 + 4x + 2x + 8$$
$$= x^2 + 6x + 8$$

Something to Hide

Because factoring or unfactoring is usually the key to finding ETS's answer on such problems, learn to recognize expressions that could be either factored or unfactored. This will earn you more points. ETS likes to hide the answers in factors.

COMBINE SIMILAR TERMS FIRST

In manipulating long, complicated algebraic expressions, combine all similar terms before doing anything else. In other words, if one of the terms is $5x$ and another is $-3x$, simply combine them into $2x$. Then you won't have as many terms to work with. Here's an example:

$$(3x^2 + 3x + 4) + (2 - x) - (6 + 2x) =$$
$$3x^2 + 3x + 4 + 2 - x - 6 - 2x =$$
$$3x^2 + (3x - x - 2x) + (4 + 2 - 6) =$$
$$3x^2$$

EVALUATING EXPRESSIONS

Sometimes ETS will give you the value of one of the letters in an algebraic expression and ask you to find the value of the entire expression. All you have to do is plug in the given value and see what you come up with.

Here is an example:

Problem:

If $2x = -1$, then $(2x - 3)^2 = ?$

Solution:

Don't solve for x; simply plug in -1 for $2x$, like this:

$$(2x - 3)^2 = (-1 - 3)^2$$
$$= (-4)^2$$
$$= 16$$

SOLVING QUADRATIC EQUATIONS

To solve quadratic equations, remember everything you've learned so far: Look for direct solutions and either factor or unfactor when possible.

Here's an example:

$$\text{If } (x + 3)^2 = (x - 2)^2, \text{ then } x = ?$$

Here's How to Crack It

Since both sides of the equation have been factored, you should unfactor them by multiplying them out:

Left: $(x + 3)(x + 3) = x^2 + 6x + 9$

Right: $(x - 2)(x - 2) = x^2 - 4x + 4$

Therefore: $x^2 + 6x + 9 = x^2 - 4x + 4$

Now you can simplify. Eliminate the x^2's, since they are on both sides of the equal sign. Move the x's to the left and the numbers to the right to give you:

$$10x = -5$$

$$x = -\frac{1}{2}$$

Here's another example:

If $x^2 - 4 = (18)(14)$, then what could x be?

Here's How to Crack It

$x^2 - 4$ is actually a common quadratic expression: $x^2 - y^2$. Since $x^2 - y^2 = (x + y)(x - y)$, that means $x^2 - 4$ can be factored in the same way:

$$x^2 - 4 = (x + 2)(x - 2)$$

Therefore: $(x + 2)(x - 2) = (18)(14)$

Notice that each side of the equation consists of two terms multiplied by each other. Set the corresponding parts equal to each other and see what you get.

$$(x + 2) = 18$$

$$(x - 2) = 14$$

Both equations work if x is 16 (–16 also solves the original problem).

SOLVING QUADRATIC EQUATIONS SET TO ZERO

If $ab = 0$, what do you know about a and b? You know that at least one of them has to equal 0. You can use this fact in solving some quadratic equations. Here's an example:

What are all the values of x for which
$x(x - 3) = 0$?

Here's How to Crack It

Because the product of x and $(x - 3)$ is 0, you know that x or $(x - 3)$—or both of them—has to equal 0. To solve the problem, simply ask yourself what x would have to be to make either expression equal 0. The answer is obvious: x could be either 0 or 3.

Three Common Quadratics box:

Three Common Quadratics

$(x + y)(x - y) = x^2 - y^2$
$(x + y)^2 = x^2 + 2xy + y^2$
$(x - y)^2 = x^2 - 2xy + y^2$

PRINCETON REVIEW ALGEBRA, OR, HOW TO AVOID ALGEBRA ON THE SAT

Now that you've reviewed the basics of algebra, it's time for some Princeton Review algebra. At The Princeton Review, we like to avoid algebra whenever possible. You read that correctly: We're going to show you how to avoid doing algebra on the SAT. Now, before you start crying and complaining that you love algebra and couldn't possibly give it up, just take a second to hear us out. We have nothing against algebra—it's very helpful when solving problems, it works all the time, it impresses your friends—but on the SAT, using algebra can actually hurt your score. And we don't want that.

BUT ALGEBRA WOULD NEVER HURT ME!

We know it's difficult to come to terms with this. But if you use algebra on the SAT, you're doing exactly what ETS wants you to do. You see, when the test writers design the problems on the SAT, they expect the students to use algebra to solve them. ETS builds little traps into the problems to take advantage of that fact. But if you don't use algebra, there's no way you can fall into those traps.

Plus, when you avoid algebra, you have one other powerful tool at your disposal: your calculator! Even if you have a super-fancy calculator that plays games and doubles as a global positioning system, chances are it doesn't do algebra. Arithmetic, on the other hand, is easy for your calculator. It's practically what calculators were invented for.

Our goal, then, is to turn all the algebra on the SAT into arithmetic. We do that using something we call *Plugging In*.

PLUGGING IN THE ANSWER CHOICES (PITA)

Algebra uses letters to stand for numbers, but no one else does. You don't go to the grocery store to buy x eggs or y gallons of milk. Most people think in terms of numbers, not letters that stand for numbers.

You should think in terms of numbers on the SAT as much as possible. On many SAT algebra problems, even very difficult ones, you will be able to find ETS's answer without using any algebra at all. You will do this by working backward from the answer choices instead of trying to solve the problem using math-class algebra.

Plugging In the Answer Choices is a technique for solving word problems in which the answer choices are all numbers. Many so-called algebra problems on the SAT can be solved simply and quickly by using this powerful technique.

In algebra class at school, you solve word problems by using equations. Then, if you're careful, you check your solution by plugging in your answer to see if it works. Why not skip the equations entirely by simply checking the five solutions ETS offers on the multiple-choice questions? One of these has to be correct. You don't have to do any algebra, you will seldom have to try more than two choices, and you will never have to try all five. Note that you can only use this technique for questions that ask for a specific amount.

Here's an example:

8. The units digit of a 2-digit number is 3 times the tens digit. If the digits are reversed, the resulting number is 36 more than the original number. What is the original number?

(A) 26
(B) 31
(C) 36
(D) 62
(E) 93

Here's How to Crack It

Don't waste time fumbling around all the possible digit combinations. (There are only three, but it can take a while to figure that out.) ETS has limited your decision to five choices—they've already done almost all the work.

What you want to do is look at each answer choice to see if it fulfills the conditions stated in the problem. If it doesn't, you can use POE to get rid of it.

Plugging In on this problem is a piece of cake. You simply take the stated conditions one at a time and try them out against the answer choices.

The first condition stated in the problem is that the units (or ones) digit of the number you are looking for is three times the tens digit. Now you look at the choices:

(A) Is 6 three times 2? Yes. A possibility.

(B) Is 1 three times 3? No. Eliminate.

(C) Is 6 three times 3? No. Eliminate.

(D) Is 2 three times 6? No. Eliminate.

(E) Is 3 three times 9? No. Eliminate.

The answer is A. You found it without even testing the other conditions stated in the problem. Mark your answer and move on.

When you plug in on a question, don't select an answer until you've either tested all the conditions or eliminated all but one of the choices. In this problem, if there had been another choice whose units digit was three times its tens digit, you would have had to move on to the next condition.

Here's another example:

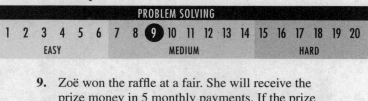

9. Zoë won the raffle at a fair. She will receive the prize money in 5 monthly payments. If the prize was $496 and each payment is half as much as the previous month's payment, then what is the amount of the first month's payment?

(A) $256
(B) $96
(C) $84
(D) $16
(E) $4

Here's How to Crack It

To solve this question the ETS way, you need to set up an equation like this:

$$p + \frac{1}{2}p + \frac{1}{4}p + \frac{1}{8}p + \frac{1}{16}p = 496$$

Forget it! That's way too much time and effort, plus there's too much room for mistakes—heck, look at all those fractions! Why not try one of the answers on for size?

Numeric answers on the SAT are always given in order of size. Thus when you are plugging in on a problem like this, you should always start out with the number in the middle—choice C. If that number turns out to be too small, you can try a bigger number next; if it's too big, try a smaller number. That way you save time and don't need to duplicate your effort.

Let's look at what happens when you try C: If the payments halve each month, Zoë will receive 84 + 42 + 21 + 10.5 + 5.25—you don't even need to add these to know that the total is going to be way too small. You need to eliminate this choice, along with D and E. Try again with either A or B.

Which one should you try? Well, since C was WAY too small, why not A, the bigger of the two? If it works, you'll pick it; if it doesn't, you'll eliminate it and pick B.

Here's what you get when you try choice A: 256 + 128 + 64 + 32 + 16 = 496. The answer must be A!

PLUGGING IN: ADVANCED PRINCIPLES

Plugging In is the same on difficult problems as it is on easy and medium ones. You just have to watch your step and make certain you don't make any careless mistakes or fall for Joe Bloggs answers.

Which Way?

Sometimes, it's hard to tell which way to go after eliminating C—higher or lower. Don't fret, just move. Find a choice with an easy-to-manipulate number. It may turn out to be wrong, but it won't take long to find out. It may also tell you whether to go higher or lower.

Here's one of our examples:

PROBLEM SOLVING

1 2 3 4 5 6 7 8 9 10 11 12 13 14 **15** 16 17 18 19 20

EASY   MEDIUM   HARD

15. Out of a total of 154 games played, a baseball team won 54 more games than it lost. If there were no ties, how many games did the team win?

    (A) 94
    (B) 98
    (C) 100
    (D) 102
    (E) 104

Here's How to Crack It

What's the Joe Bloggs answer here? It is choice C. Be careful!

To solve the problem all you have to do is plug in. You've eliminated choice C already, so start with D. If the team won 102 games, how many games did it lose? It lost 52 (154 − 102 = 52). Is 102 (wins) 54 greater than 52 (losses)? No. 102 − 52 = 50. You need more wins to make the problem come out right. That means that ETS's answer must be E. (It is.)

Here's another example we created:

17. Committee A has 18 members and Committee B has 3 members. How many members from Committee A must switch to Committee B so that Committee A will have twice as many members as Committee B?

    (A) 4
    (B) 6
    (C) 7
    (D) 9
    (E) 14

Here's How to Crack It

This problem represents one of the most difficult principles tested in the SAT math section. Only a small percentage of students gets it right. But if you plug in, you won't have any trouble.

This problem is about two committees, so the first thing you should do is quickly draw a picture in your test booklet to keep from getting confused:

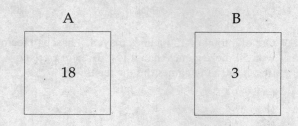

Now plug in the answer choices, starting with answer choice C. If you move 7 members out of Committee A, there will be 11 members left in A and 10 members in B. Is 11 twice as many as 10? No, eliminate.

As you work through the choices, keep track of them, like this:

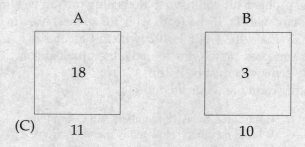

Choice C didn't work. To make the question work out right, you need more members in Committee A and fewer in Committee B. In other words, you need to try a smaller number. Try the smallest one, choice A. Moving 4 members from Committee A will leave 14 in A and 7 in B. Is 14 twice as many as 7? Yes, of course. This is ETS's answer.

Hey, Smarty!

If you think you can improve your SAT Math score without learning to plug in, you're in for an unpleasant surprise. Seriously, this technique applies strictly to the SAT, and it works.

Just bear in mind: This is a multiple-choice test; the correct answers are already right there on the page.

PLUGGING IN YOUR OWN NUMBERS

Plugging In the Answer enables you to find ETS's answer on problems whose answer choices are all numbers. What about problems whose answer choices contain letters? On these problems, you will usually be able to find the answer by plugging in your own numbers.

Plugging In is easy. It has three steps:

1. Pick numbers for the letters in the problem.

2. Use *your* numbers to find an answer to the problem.

3. Plug your numbers from step 1 into the answer choices to see which choice equals the answer you found in step 2.

THE BASICS OF PLUGGING IN YOUR OWN NUMBERS

This sort of Plugging In is simple to understand. Here's an example:

PROBLEM SOLVING

1 2 **3** 4 5 6 7 8 9 10 11 12 13 14 15 16 17 18 19 20
EASY   MEDIUM   HARD

3. If Jayme will be j years old 3 years from now, then in terms of j, how old was Jayme 5 years ago?

   (A) $j - 8$
   (B) $j - 5$
   (C) $j - 3$
   (D) $j + 5$
   (E) $j + 8$

Here's How to Crack It

First, pick a number for j. Pick something easy to work with, like 10. In your test booklet, write 10 directly above the letter j in the problem, so you won't forget.

If $j = 10$, then Jayme will be 10 years old in 3 years. That means that she is 7 right now. Since the problem asked you how old she was 5 years ago, just calculate $7 - 5 = 2$. She was 2! Write a nice big 2 in you test booklet and circle it. The correct answer will be the choice that, when you plug in 10 for j, equals 2.

Now let's plug in!

Plug in 10 for j in A and you get $10 - 8$, or 2. This is the number that you are looking for, so this must be the right answer! Go ahead and try the other choices just to make sure that you're right and to practice Plugging In.

Here's another example:

PROBLEM SOLVING

1 2 3 4 5 6 7 8 9 10 11 **12** 13 14 15 16 17 18 19 20
EASY   MEDIUM   HARD

12. The sum of four consecutive positive even integers is x. In terms of x, what is the sum of the two middle integers?

    2, 4, 6, 8,

    10

    (A) $\dfrac{x - 12}{4}$

    (B) $\dfrac{x - 6}{2}$

    (C) $2x + 6$

    (D) $\dfrac{x}{2}$

    (E) $\dfrac{x^2 - 3x}{4}$

Here's How to Crack It

Let's pick four numbers: 2, 4, 6, and 8. The sum of these four is 20, so $x = 20$; write that in your test booklet. The middle two numbers, 4 and 6, add up to 10; this is your target number, circle it. We are looking for the choice that will equal 10 when we plug in 20. Let's try each choice:

(A) $\dfrac{20 - 12}{4} = 2$ Nope!

(B) $\dfrac{20 - 6}{2} = 7$ Nope!

(C) $2(20) + 6 = 46$ Too big!

(D) $\dfrac{20}{2} = 10$ Looks good. This is the correct answer.

(E) $\dfrac{20^2 - 3(20)}{4} = ?$ Waaaay too big!

WHICH NUMBERS?

Be Good

"Good" numbers make a problem less confusing by simplifying the arithmetic. This is your chance to make the SAT easier.

Although you can plug in any number, you can make your life much easier by plugging in "good" numbers—numbers that are simple to work with or that make the problem easier to manipulate. Picking a small number, such as 2, will usually make finding the answer easier. If the problem asks for a percentage, plug in 10 or 100. If the problem has to do with minutes, try 60. If you plug in wisely, you can sometimes eliminate computation altogether.

Except in special cases, you should avoid plugging in 0 and 1; these numbers have weird properties. Using them may allow you to eliminate only one or two choices at a time. You should also avoid plugging in any number that appears in the question or in any of the answer choices.

Many times you'll find that there is an advantage to picking a particular number, even a very large one, because it makes solving the problem easier.

Here's an example:

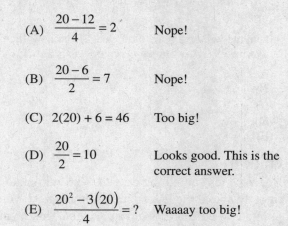

14. If 60 equally priced downloads cost x dollars, then how much do 9 downloads cost?

(A) $\dfrac{20}{3x}$

(B) $9x - 60$

(C) $\dfrac{20x}{3}$

(D) $60x + 9$

(E) $\dfrac{3x}{20}$

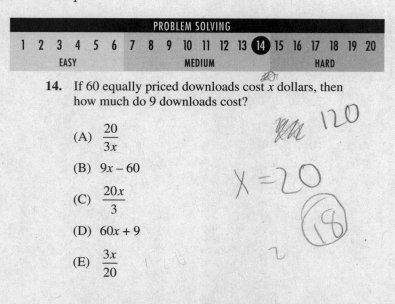

Here's How to Crack It

Should you plug in 2 for x? You could, but plugging in 120 would make the problem easier. After all, if 60 downloads cost a total of $120, then each download costs $2. Write $x = 120$ in your test booklet.

If each download costs $2, then 9 downloads cost $18. Write an 18 in your test booklet and circle it. You are looking for the answer choice that works out to 18 when you plug in $120 for x. Let's try each choice:

(A) $\dfrac{20}{3(120)} \neq 18$

(B) $9(120) - 60 \neq 18$

(C) $\dfrac{20(120)}{3} \neq 18$

(D) $60(120) + 9 \neq 18$

(E) $\dfrac{3(120)}{20} = 18!!!$ Here's your answer.

Here's another example:

PROBLEM SOLVING																			
1	2	3	4	5	6	7	8	9	10	11	12	13	14	15	16	17	18	19	20
	EASY								MEDIUM							HARD			

20. A watch loses x minutes every y hours. At this rate, how many hours will the watch lose in one week?

(A) $7xy$

(B) $\dfrac{7y}{x}$

(C) $\dfrac{x}{7y}$

(D) $\dfrac{14y}{5x}$

(E) $\dfrac{14x}{5y}$

Here's How to Crack It

This is an extremely difficult problem for students who try to solve it the math-class way. You'll be able to find the answer easily, though, if you plug in carefully.

What should you plug in? As always, you can plug in anything, but if you select numbers wisely, you'll make things easier on yourself. There are three units of time in this problem: minutes, hours, and weeks. If we plug in 60 for x, we can get it down to two, because 60 minutes equal an hour. Write $x = 60$ in your test booklet.

We can also make things easier for ourselves by plugging in 24 for y. There are 24 hours in a day. What we are saying so far is that the watch loses 60 minutes every 24 hours. In other words, it loses an hour a day. Write $y = 24$ in your test booklet.

At this rate, how many hours will the watch lose in a week? It will lose 7, obviously, because there are 7 days in a week. Write 7 in your test booklet and circle it. We are looking for the answer choice that equals 7 when we plug in 60 for x and 24 for y.

Now let's check each choice:

(A) $7xy = (7)(60)(24)$. Common sense, not computation, tells us that this is way too big. Eliminate.

(B) $7\dfrac{y}{x} = \dfrac{(7)(24)}{(60)} = \dfrac{168}{60} = 2.8$. Eliminate.

(C) $\dfrac{x}{7y} = \dfrac{(60)}{(7)(24)} = \dfrac{60}{168} = 0.35714$. Eliminate.

(D) $\dfrac{14y}{5x} = \dfrac{(14)(24)}{(5)(60)} = \dfrac{336}{300} = 1.12$. Eliminate.

(E) $\dfrac{14x}{5y} = \dfrac{(14)(60)}{(5)(24)} = \dfrac{840}{120} = 7$. This is ETS's answer.

INEQUALITIES

Weird Numbers

As you may have noticed, some numbers have uncommon properties. Because of this, we plug them in only under certain circumstances, usually when solving:

- Inequalities
- MUST BE problems

Plugging In works on problems containing inequalities, but you will have to follow some different rules. Plugging in one number is often not enough; to find ETS's answer, you may have to plug in several numbers, including weird numbers like: $-1, 0, 1, \dfrac{1}{2}$, and $-\dfrac{1}{2}$.

The five numbers just mentioned all have special properties. Negatives, fractions, 0, and 1 all behave in peculiar ways when, for example, they are squared. Don't forget about them!

Sometimes you can avoid plugging in altogether by simplifying. Here's an example:

PROBLEM SOLVING		
1 2 3 4 5 6 7 **8** 9 10 11 12 13 14 15 16 17 18 19 20		
EASY	MEDIUM	HARD

What Are the Weird Numbers?

- Fractions
- Negatives
- Big numbers
- 1 and 0

8.   If $-3x + 6 \geq 18$, which of the following must be true?

(A) $x \leq -4$
(B) $x \leq 6$
(C) $x \geq -4$
(D) $x \geq -6$
(E) $x = 2$

Here's How to Crack It

The inequality in the problem can be simplified quite a bit:

$$-3x + 6 \geq 18$$
$$-3x \geq 12$$
$$-x \geq 4$$

We're close to one of the answer choices, but not quite there yet. Multiply both sides by –1 to make x positive. *Remember to change the direction of the inequality sign!*

$$x \leq -4$$

So choice A is ETS's answer.

OTHER SPECIAL CASES

Sometimes SAT algebra problems will require you to determine certain characteristics of a number or numbers. Is x odd or even? Is it small or large? Is it positive or negative?

On questions like this, you will probably have to plug in more than one number and/or plug in weird numbers, just as you do on problems containing inequalities. Sometimes ETS's wording will tip you off. If the problem states only that $x > 0$, you know for certain that x is positive but you don't know that x is an integer. See what happens when you plug in a fraction.

Here are some other tip-offs you should be aware of:

If the problem asked for this	and you plugged in this	also try this, just to be sure
an integer	3	1, 0, or –1
a fraction	$\frac{1}{4}$	$-\frac{1}{4}$
two even numbers	2, 4	2, –2
a number	an integer	a fraction
a number	an even number	an odd number
a number	a small number	a huge number
a multiple of 7	7	7,000 or –7
consecutive numbers	1, 2, 3	–1, 0, 1
$x^2 = 4$	2	–2
$xy > 0$	(2, 4)	(–2, –4)
$x = 2y$	(4, 2)	(–4, –2) or (0, 0)

Gator!

Think of the inequality sign as the mouth of a hungry alligator. The alligator eats the bigger number.

Must Be True

Try the following problem:

18. If $x - y$ is a multiple of 3, then which of the following must also be a multiple of 3?

(A) $y - x$

(B) $\dfrac{y - x}{2}$

(C) $\dfrac{x + y}{2}$

(D) $x + y$

(E) xy

Here's How to Crack It

Since there are variables in the answer choices, we will plug in. First plug in easy numbers that make the given statement ($x - y$ is a multiple of 3) true. Let's make $x = 6$ and $y = 3$. The question asks which of the following must also be a multiple of 3. Let's plug in our numbers, and cross off any answer choices that are not multiples of 3.

(A) $3 - 6 = -3$ is a multiple of 3, so keep it.

(B) $\dfrac{3 - 6}{2}$ is not a multiple of 3. Cross it off.

(C) $\dfrac{6 + 3}{2}$ is not a multiple of 3. Cross it off.

(D) $6 + 3 = 9$. Keep it.

(E) $(6)(3) = 18$. Keep it.

Since this question asks for something that *must* be true and we are left with three answer choices, we must plug in again. The question asks us for a multiple of 3. The first time we plugged in, we used two other multiples of three ($x = 6$ and $y = 3$) to satisfy the first condition. Let's now use two numbers that make the initial statement true but are *not* multiples of 3. Plug in 5 for x and 2 for y. Now check the answers we didn't eliminate the first time:

(A) $2 - 5 = -3$. It still works, so keep it.

(D) $5 + 2 = 7$. Cross it off.

(E) $(5)(2) = 10$. Cross it off.

The answer is A.

A Little Terminology

Here are some words that you will need to know to follow this chapter. The words themselves won't show up on the SAT, so after you finish the chapter you can forget about them.

Term: An equation is like a sentence, and a term is the equivalent of a word. For example, 9×2 is a term in the equation $9 \times 2 + 3x = 5y$.

Expression: If an equation is like a sentence, then an expression is like a phrase or a clause. An expression is a combination of terms and mathmatical operations with no equal or inequality sign. For example, $9 \times 2 + 3x$ is an expression.

Polynomial: A polynomial is any expression containing two or more terms. Binomials and trinomials are both known as polynomials.

PLUGGING IN: ADVANCED PRINCIPLES

As you have just learned, you should plug in whenever you don't know what a number is. But you can also plug in when you have numbers that are too big, too ugly, or too inconvenient to work with. On such problems you can often find the answer simply by using numbers that aren't as ugly as the ones you've been given.

Here's an example:

PROBLEM SOLVING

| 1 2 3 4 5 6 | 7 8 9 10 11 12 13 14 | 15 **16** 17 18 19 20 |
| EASY | MEDIUM | HARD |

16. In a marathon, runners who finish 1st through 75th receive gift certificates; those who finish 76th and higher do not. If 312 runners participated in the race, how many did NOT receive gift certificates?

    (A) 75
    (B) 76
    (C) 235
    (D) 236
    (E) 237

Here's How to Crack It

This is a number 16—a difficult question. Finding the answer has to be harder than simply subtracting 76 from 312 to get 236, which means that C has to be wrong. Cross it out. (You can also immediately eliminate A and B as they are way too small.)

One way to find the answer would be to count this out by hand. But to count from 76 to 312 would take forever. You can achieve the same result by using simpler numbers instead.

It doesn't matter which numbers you use. How about 7 and 11? The difference between 7 and 11 is 4. But if you count out the numbers on your hand—7, 8, 9, 10, 11—you see that there are 5 numbers. In other words, if we were looking at runners 7 through 11, the number of runners would have been 1 greater than the difference between 7 and 11. The answer therefore will be 1 greater than the difference between 76 and 312, in other words, E.

Here's another example:

PROBLEM SOLVING

| 1 2 3 4 5 6 | 7 8 9 10 11 12 13 14 | 15 16 17 **18** 19 20 |
| EASY | MEDIUM | HARD |

18. $2^{23} - 2^{22} =$

    (A) 2^1
    (B) $2^{\frac{23}{22}}$
    (C) 2^{22}
    (D) 2^{23}
    (E) 2^{45}

Factoring with Exponents

We can also solve question 18 by factoring 2^{22} out of the parentheses, giving us a new expression: $2^{22}(2^1 - 1) = 2^{22}(2 - 1) = 2^{22}(1) = 2^{22}$

Here's How to Crack It

These are big, ugly, inconvenient exponents. No wonder this question is a number 18. But you'll be able to solve it if you plug in easier numbers.

Instead of 2^{23}, let's use 2^4. And instead of 2^{22}, let's use 2^3. Now we can rewrite the problem: $2^4 - 2^3 = 16 - 8 = 8 = 2^3$.

Our answer is the second of the two numbers we started with. ETS's answer, therefore, must be the second number we started with, or 2^{22}, which is choice C. (If you don't believe this always works, try it with 2^3 and 2^2, and with 2^5 and 2^4, or any other similar pair of numbers. By the way, choices A and B are Joe Bloggs answers.)

That wasn't to bad! Now that you know how to crack SAT Algebra, let's move on to some of the harder stuff.

ADVANCED PRINCIPLES OF SAT ALGEBRA

SOLVING RATIONAL EQUATIONS

A rational equation is basically a fraction with a polynomial in the numerator and a polynomial in the denominator. Rational equations look scary, but there are very simple ways of solving them. One way is to factor out like terms and then cancel. All in all, ETS can't get too messy here, so they will keep the math nice and tidy.

Try one:

18. If $\dfrac{x^2 + 6x - 16}{x^2 - 5x + 6} = \dfrac{-6}{x^2 - 2x - 3}$, then which of the

following could be a value of x?

(A) −7
(B) −5
(C) 0
(D) 6
(E) 16

Here's How to Crack It

What's the quickest way? PITA! Start with answer choice C and plug in 0 for x. Does everything work out? In this case, it doesn't. Keep trying other answer choices until you find one that works. Choice A does, so that's the correct answer choice. See? These are all bark and no bite.

SOLVING RADICAL EQUATIONS

Radical equations are just what the name suggests: an equation with a radical ($\sqrt{}$) in it. Whereas these aren't brand new to the SAT, ETS has not put the variable under the radical sign…until now. Not to worry, just remember to get rid of the radical first by raising both sides to that power.

For example, $7\sqrt{x} + 23 = 11$ is a radical equation. First, combine the terms, by subtracting 23 from both sides, which leaves us with: $7\sqrt{x} = -22$.

To get rid of the radical, simply raise both sides to the second power. That leaves us with: $49x = 484$. Now divide both sides by 49, and $x = 9.878$.

SOLVING EQUATIONS

In algebra class you learned to solve equations by "solving for x" or "solving for y." To do this, you isolate x or y on one side of the equal sign and put everything else on the other side. This is a long, laborious process with many steps and many opportunities for mistakes.

On the SAT, you usually won't need to solve equations this way. You've already learned how to plug in. On the few problems where these techniques don't apply, you should be able to find direct solutions. To demonstrate what we mean, we'll show you the same problem solved two different ways.

Problem:

If $2x = 5$ and $3y = 6$, then $6xy = ?$

FUNCTIONS

When you learned about functions in algebra class, you probably talked about "f of x," or $f(x)$.

The SAT is a little different. It tests functions, but sometimes in a peculiar way. On occasion, instead of using $f(x)$, it uses funny little symbols to stand for operations. For example, you might be used to seeing $f(x)=3x + 10$. Sometimes on the SAT, you'll see that written as $Hx = 3x + 10$. They really are saying the same thing. So, if you understand functions, then this shouldn't be a huge deal; just remember to follow your rules of the function. If you don't understand functions, just follow what we tell you.

In a function problem, an arithmetic operation is defined, and then you are asked to perform it on a number, a pair of numbers, or an ordered pair of numbers. All you have to do is keep your wits about you, use your booklet as scratch paper, and do what the function tells you to. A function is like a set of instructions: follow it and you'll find ETS's answer.

Here's an example:

Predictable Functions

There are usually two or three function problems on every SAT. The last one will be extremely difficult. If you're not trying to score in the 700s, you should probably skip it. On the others, work very, very carefully.

PROBLEM SOLVING
1 2 3 4 5 6 7 8 9 10 11 12 13 **14** 15 16 17 18 19 20
EASY　　　　　　　　　MEDIUM　　　　　　　　HARD

14. If $x \# y = \dfrac{1}{x-y}$, what is the value of $\dfrac{1}{2} \# \dfrac{1}{3}$?

(A) 6

(B) $\dfrac{6}{5}$

(C) $\dfrac{1}{6}$

(D) -1

(E) -6

Here's How to Crack It

Finding ETS's answers is just a matter of simple substitution. Just substitute $\frac{1}{2}$ and $\frac{1}{3}$ for x and y in the function.

$$\frac{1}{2} \# \frac{1}{3} = \frac{1}{\frac{1}{2} - \frac{1}{3}}$$

$$= \frac{1}{\frac{1}{6}}$$

$$= 6$$

ETS's answer, therefore, is choice A.

Let's try a pair of functions:

Questions 16–17 refer to the following definition:

For all integers x, let $\odot\, x = x^2$ if x is negative, and let $\odot\, x = 2x$ if x is positive.

						PROBLEM SOLVING													
1	2	3	4	5	6	7	8	9	10	11	12	13	14	15	**16**	17	18	19	20
		EASY							MEDIUM							HARD			

16. $\underset{25}{\odot}(-5) - \underset{10}{\odot}5 =$ 15

    (A) −10
    (B) −5
    (C)   0
    (D)   10
    (E)   15

						PROBLEM SOLVING													
1	2	3	4	5	6	7	8	9	10	11	12	13	14	15	16	**17**	18	19	20
		EASY							MEDIUM							HARD			

17. What is the value of $\odot(-(\odot x)) - \odot(\odot x)$ when x is equal to -3?

    (A) −18
    (B) −12
    (C)   0
    (D)   18
    (E)   63

$$\odot(-(\odot -3)) - \odot(\odot -3)$$

$$81 - 18 =$$

Here's How to Crack Them

If you are given two function problems that refer to the same definition, the second one will be significantly harder than the first. You should feel free to skip the second one if you are having trouble with functions. Let's look at number 16 first.

If x is negative, we are to square it. In this case, our first term is –5. –5 squared equals 25. If x is positive, multiply it by 2. Our second term is 5 so multiply it times 2 to get 10. We now have 25 – 10, or 15. ETS's answer is E.

Number 17 is a bit messier. Just pull it apart one piece at a time. Do your parentheses first, from the inside out. In this problem we are told that x equals –3. Fill –3 in for x:

$$\odot(-(\odot -3)) - \odot(\odot -3)$$

In the first term, square –3 to get 9. Get rid of the parentheses and you have –9. Square that and you have 81.

In the second term, square –3 to get 9. Multiply 9 times 2 (since 9 is positive) and you have 18. 81 minus 18 equals 63. The answer is E.

A function is essentially a mapping relation. The function takes in a value and maps it to only one output value. Two different input values can create overlapping or same outputs; however, one input value cannot have two different outputs. That is to say, mathematically, $f(3) = 7$ and $f(5) = 7$ is completely acceptable, but $f(3) = 7$ and $f(3) = 22$ is not.

DOMAIN AND RANGE

The set of all possible inputs to a function is known as its *domain* and the set of all possible outputs is known as its *range*. As we just stated, the inputs, or x values, make up the domain of a function, for which that function is defined (most commonly meaning there is no zero in the denominator). The outputs, or $f(x)$ (also the y values), make up the range of the function. The questions you will see on these concepts deal mostly with what values are outside the domain (where the function is undefined) or range (what the function cannot equal). That means the easiest way to solve function questions is by plugging in the answers.

Most functions aren't too particular about what you put into them, so you can work with almost any value. For example, if you have a function like this one, $f(x) = \dfrac{x}{x-3}$, then the function can accept any value other than three (three minus three produces a zero in the denominator which, as we know in math, is the greatest faux pas). Here are a couple of things that would make your function undefined:

- zero in the denominator
- taking the even root (square root, fourth root, sixth root, etc.) of a negative number

Just as with domain, some functions don't have hugely restricted ranges. In the function $f(x) = 2x + 5$, the range is all real numbers. The range of almost any linear function will be the set of all real numbers. The one exception you need to be on the lookout for is when $f(x)$ equals a number (a constant); the range in this case is whatever that constant is (i.e., if $f(x) = 7$, then the range is $\{y: y = 7\}$).

Here are a few of things that would limit your range:

- Even exponents must produce non-negative numbers.

- Square roots and other even roots produce non-negative numbers.

- Absolute values produce non-negative numbers.

Let's take a closer look at a domain/range question:

17. If $f(x) = \dfrac{1}{(x)(x-4)}$, then which of the following represents the domain of $f(x)$?

(A) $\{x \neq 0\}$
(B) $\{x \neq 1\}$
(C) $\{x \neq 4\}$
(D) $\{x \neq 0, 4\}$
(E) All real numbers

Here's How to Crack It

Remember the domain is the set of values (inputs for x's) for which the function is defined. The easiest way to tackle this particular question is to plug in the answer choices and see which ones give you a zero in the denominator. Start with choice C; does it give you a zero? Yes, so 4 is NOT in the domain (eliminate choices B and E) but should be in the answer. Next try 0. Again, we get a zero in the denominator, so you can safely eliminate A and C. The domain includes all numbers EXCEPT 0 and 4, which makes the correct answer D.

THE REASON WE BOUGHT GRAPH PAPER...

Why did the math folks come up with functions? To graph them, of course! On the SAT, however, you won't be asked to draw pretty graphs (how would they score them?) or graph functions on your calculator (remember, ETS claims you do not need a calculator to solve any of the problems on the SAT). What ETS will do is show you a graph and ask you questions regarding it.

If you're not altogether comfortable with graphs, feel free to skip the oddball graphing question, but for most of you, these are not even half as frustrating as, say, fractions. The reason you are asked function questions is to test whether or not you can figure out the relationship between a function and its graph. To tackle these questions, you need to know that the independent variable, the x, is on the (what else?) x-axis and the dependent variable, the $f(x)$, is on the y-axis. For example, if you see a function of $f(x) = 7$, then you need to understand that this is a graph of a horizontal line where $y = 7$.

Another type of function question you might be asked is how the graph of a function would shift if you added a value to it. Again, there are not going to be a lot of these questions, so feel free to skip the few that appear if you don't feel comfortable answering them.

Here is a quick guide (c is a constant) for the graph of $f(x) = x^2$:

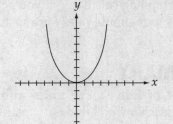

For $f(x) + c$, the graph will shift up c units. Like this:

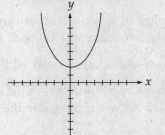

Conversely, $f(x) - c$ will shift the graph down by c units:

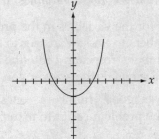

For $f(x + c)$, the graph will shift c units to the left:

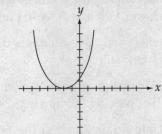

For $f(x - c)$, the graph will shift to the right by c units:

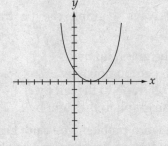

You may have realized how easy these problems would become if you simply put them into your graphing calculator. If you've got one, type in the function; if not, remember the four simple rules for transforming graphs (number 11 below).

ALGEBRA SUMMARY

1. Don't "solve for x" or "solve for y" unless you absolutely have to. (Don't worry; your math teacher won't find out.) Instead, look for direct solutions to SAT problems. ETS never uses problems that *necessarily* require time-consuming computations or endless fiddling with big numbers. There's almost always a trick—if you can spot it.

2. If a problem contains an expression that can be factored, factor it. If it contains an expression that already has been factored, unfactor it.

3. To solve simultaneous equations, simply add or subtract the equations.

4. When an algebra question has numbers in the answer choices, plug in each of the numbers in the answer choices into the problem until you find one that works.

5. Plugging in your own numbers is the technique for multiple-choice problems whose answer choices contain variables. It has three steps:

    i. Pick numbers for the variables in the problem.
    ii. Use your numbers to find an answer to the problem.
    iii. Plug your numbers from step 1 into the answer choices to see which choice equals the answer you found in step 2.

6. When you plug in, use "good" numbers—ones that are simple to work with and that make the problem easier to manipulate.

7. Plugging In works on problems containing inequalities, but you will have to be careful and follow some different rules. Plugging in one number is often not enough; to find ETS's answer, you may have to plug in several numbers.

8. You can also plug in when you have numbers that are too big, too ugly, or too inconvenient to work with.

9. Learn to recognize SAT function problems. Sometimes they have funny symbols. Solve them like playing "Simon says"—do what you are told.

10. Domain is what goes into a function and the range is what comes out. Remember, the domain must always keep the function defined (no zeros in the denominator).

11. Memorize the four ways a graph can be transformed by adding a constant:

    i. $f(x) + c$ shifts the graph up by c.
    ii. $f(x) - c$ shifts the graph down by c.
    iii. $f(x + c)$ shifts the graph to the left by c.
    iv. $f(x - c)$ shifts the graph to the right by c.

12. If you come across a word problem you can't beat by Plugging In, simply translate the problem into an equation and solve it.

12
Geometry

SAT GEOMETRY: CRACKING THE SYSTEM

About a third of the math problems on the SAT will involve geometry. Fortunately, you won't have to prove theorems or memorize tons of terms and formulas. That's right, every formula you'll need is on the first page of each Math section on the test, in the box entitled, "Reference Information."

In this chapter we will teach you:

- the fundamental facts you must know to solve SAT geometry problems

- The Princeton Review's approach to handling even the hardest problems

- how to use Ballparking to find ETS's answers and avoid careless mistakes

- how to use Plugging In effectively on geometry problems

THE PRINCETON REVIEW WAY

The key to cracking SAT geometry is to gather all the available information in the problem. The best way to do that is to follow these simple steps:

1. **Know the rules!** The SAT doesn't require any advanced geometric knowledge, but you will have to know the basics backwards and forwards.

2. **Fill in the missing info.** SAT geometry problems almost always leave out important information. Fill it in!

3. **Write down any formulas required.** All the area and volume formulas that you need will be provided. Write 'em down and fill in the values that you know.

4. **Solve for any missing info.** After you fill in the formula, solve.

Some problems won't require you to work through all the steps. For easier geometry problems, you might only need steps one and two. For harder problems, you may need all four steps. Either way, get in the habit of looking for missing information and filling it into the diagram.

Let's get started with step one: learning the basic rules.

BASIC PRINCIPLES: FUNDAMENTALS OF SAT GEOMETRY

The SAT doesn't test any really difficult geometry, but you will need a thorough knowledge of several fundamental rules. You will use these fundamentals in applying the techniques that we will teach you later in the chapter. You don't need to linger over these rules if you have already mastered them. But be sure you understand them completely before you move on. Some of these rules will be provided in the instructions on your SAT, but you should know them before you go to the test center. Consulting the instructions as you work is a waste of time. (On the other hand, if the Pythagorean theorem suddenly vaporizes from your brain while you are taking the test, don't hesitate to peek back at the instructions.)

We divide SAT geometry into five basic topics:

1. Degrees and angles
2. Triangles
3. Circles
4. Rectangles and squares
5. Odds and ends

DEGREES AND ANGLES

1. A circle contains 360 degrees.

Every circle contains 360 degrees. Each degree is $\frac{1}{360}$ of the total distance around the outside of the circle. It doesn't matter whether the circle is large or small; it still has exactly 360 degrees.

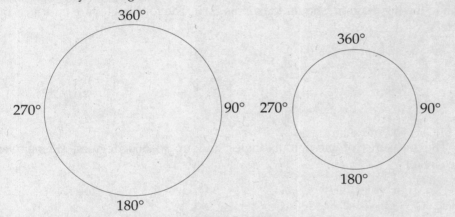

2. When you think about angles, remember circles.

An angle is formed when two line segments extend from a common point. If you think of the point as the center of a circle, the measure of the angle is the number of degrees enclosed by the lines when they pass through the edge of the circle. Once again, the size of the circle doesn't matter; neither does the length of the lines.

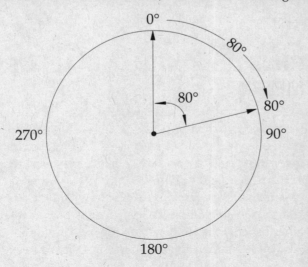

3. A line is a 180-degree angle.

You probably don't think of a line as an angle, but it is one. Think of it as a flat angle. The following drawings should help:

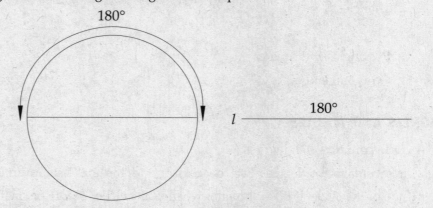

4. When two lines intersect, four angles are formed.

The following diagram should make this clear. The four angles are indicated by letters.

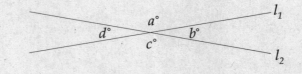

The measures of these four angles add up to 360 degrees. (Remember the circle.)

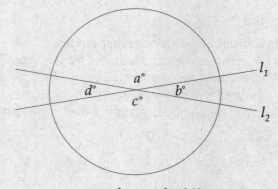

$$a + b + c + d = 360$$

If two lines are perpendicular to each other, each of the four angles formed is 90 degrees. A 90-degree angle is called a *right angle*.

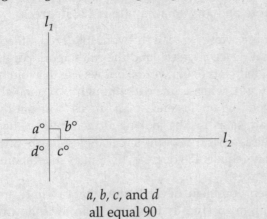

a, b, c, and d
all equal 90

perpendicular (*adj.*) meeting at right (90°) angles

The little box at the intersection of the two lines is the symbol for a right angle. If the lines are not perpendicular to each other, then none of the angles will be right angles.

If two lines are perpendicular, then their slopes are negative reciprocals; i.e., if ℓ_1 has a slope of 2 and ℓ_2 is perpendicular to ℓ_1, then ℓ_2 must have a slope of $-\dfrac{1}{2}$.

5. **When two lines intersect, the angles opposite each other will have the same measures.**

Such angles are called *vertical angles*. In the following diagram, angles a and c are equal; so are angles b and d. The total of all four angles is still 360 degrees.

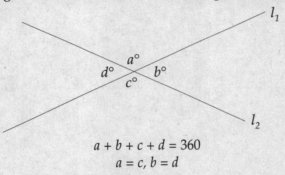

$a + b + c + d = 360$
$a = c$, $b = d$

It doesn't matter how many lines you intersect through a single point. The total measure of all the angles formed will still be 360 degrees.

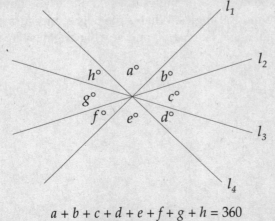

$a + b + c + d + e + f + g + h = 360$
$a = e$, $b = f$, $c = g$, $d = h$

6. **When two parallel lines are cut by a third line, all of the small angles are equal, all of the big angles are equal, and the sum of any big angle and any small angle is 180 degrees.**

Parallel lines have the same slope.

At The Princeton Review, we call this concept "Fred's theorem." Parallel lines are two lines that never intersect, and the rules about parallel lines are usually taught in school with lots of big words. But we like to avoid big words whenever possible. Simply put, when a line cuts through two parallel lines, two kinds of angles are created: big angles and small angles. You can tell which angles are big and which are small just by looking at them. All the big angles look equal, and they are. The same is true of the small angles. Lastly, any big angle plus any small angle always equals 180 degrees. (ETS likes rules about angles that add up to 180 or 360 degrees.)

In any geometry problem, never assume that two lines are parallel unless the question or diagram specifically tells you so. In the following diagram, angle a is a big angle, and it has the same measure as angles c, e, and g, which are also big angles. Angle b is a small angle, and it has the same measure as angles d, f, and h, which are also small angles.

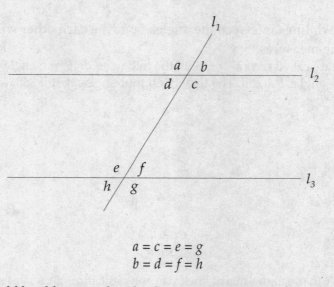

$$a = c = e = g$$
$$b = d = f = h$$

You should be able to see that the degree measures of angles a, b, c, and d add up to 360 degrees. So do those of angles e, f, g, and h. If you have trouble seeing it, draw a circle around the angles. What is the degree measure of a circle? Also, the sum of any small angle (such as d) and any big angle (such as g) is 180°.

TRIANGLES

1. Every triangle contains 180 degrees.

The word *triangle* means "three angles," and every triangle contains three interior angles. The measure of these three angles always adds up to exactly 180 degrees. You don't need to know why this is true or how to prove it. You just need to know it. And we mean *know* it.

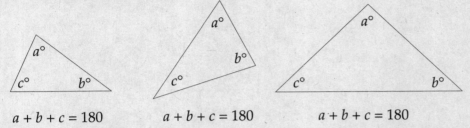

$$a + b + c = 180 \qquad a + b + c = 180 \qquad a + b + c = 180$$

2. An equilateral triangle is one in which all three sides are equal in length.

Because the angles opposite equal sides are also equal, all three angles in an equilateral triangle are equal, too. (Their measures are always 60 degrees each.)

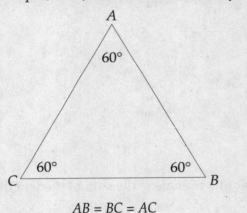

$$AB = BC = AC$$

Your Friend the Triangle

If ever you are stumped by a geometry problem that deals with a quadrilateral, hexagon, or circle, look for the triangles that you can form by drawing lines through the figure.

3. An isosceles triangle is one in which two of the sides are equal in length.

The angles opposite those equal sides are also equal because, as we just mentioned, angles opposite equal sides are also equal.

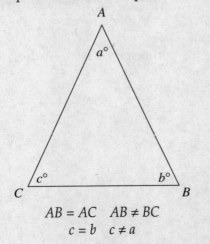

$$AB = AC \quad AB \neq BC$$
$$c = b \quad c \neq a$$

4. **A right triangle is a triangle in which one of the angles is a right angle (90 degrees).**

The longest side of a right triangle, which is always opposite the 90° angle, is called the *hypotenuse*.

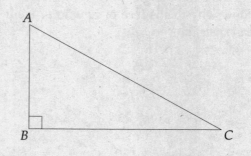

AC is the hypotenuse.

Some right triangles are also *isosceles*. The angles in an isosceles right triangle always measure 45°, 45°, and 90°.

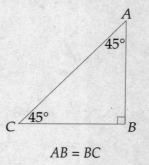

AB = BC

5. **The perimeter of a triangle is the sum of the lengths of its sides.**

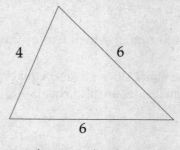

perimeter = 4 + 6 + 6 = 16

6. The area of a triangle is $\frac{1}{2}$ base $\times$ height.

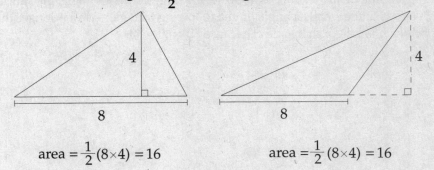

$$\text{area} = \frac{1}{2}(8 \times 4) = 16 \qquad\qquad \text{area} = \frac{1}{2}(8 \times 4) = 16$$

The Pythagorean Theorem

The Pythagorean theorem states that in a right triangle, the square of the hypotenuse equals the sum of the squares of the other two sides. As we told you earlier, the hypotenuse is the longest side of a right triangle; it's the side opposite the right angle. The square of the hypotenuse is its length squared. Applying the Pythagorean theorem to the following drawing, we find that $c^2 = a^2 + b^2$.

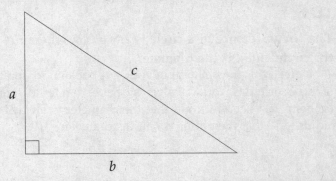

If you forget the Pythagorean theorem, you can always look it up in the box at the beginning of the Math section. Very often, however, you won't need to use the Pythagorean theorem to find ETS's answer because ETS writes very predictable geometry questions involving right triangles. ETS has two favorites:

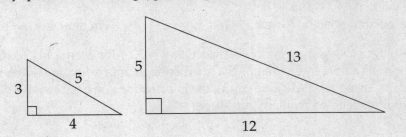

If you memorize these two sets of Pythagorean triplets (3-4-5 and 5-12-13), you'll often be able to find ETS's answer without using the Pythagorean theorem. If ETS gives you a triangle with a side of 3 and a hypotenuse of 5, you know right away that the other side has to be 4. ETS also uses right triangles with sides that are simply multiples of the Pythagorean triplets. For example, ETS likes right triangles with sides of 6, 8, and 10. These sides are simply the sides of a 3-4-5 triangle multiplied by 2.

Pythagorean Theorem:

$a^2 + b^2 = c^2$, where c is the hypotenuse of a right triangle. Learn it, love it.

Your Friend the Rectangle

Be on the lookout for problems in which the application of the Pythagorean theorem is not obvious. For example, every rectangle contains two right triangles. That means that if you know the length and width of the rectangle, you also know the length of the diagonal, which is the hypotenuse of both triangles.

Angle-Side Relationships in Triangles

The longest side of any triangle is opposite the largest interior angle; the shortest side is opposite the smallest angle. In the following triangle, side a is longer than side b, which is longer than side c, because 80 > 60 > 40.

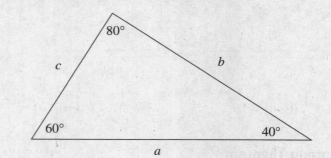

Another Relationship

It is simply impossible for the third side of a triangle to be longer than the total of the other two sides. Nor can the third side of a triangle be shorter than the difference between the other two sides. Imagine a triangle with sides a, b, and c:

$$a - b < c < a + b.$$

The same rule applies to isosceles and equilateral triangles. An isosceles triangle, remember, is one in which two of the sides are equal in length; therefore, the angles opposite those sides are also equal. In an equilateral triangle, all three sides are equal; so are all three angles.

CIRCLES

Some Formulas

Area = πr^2
Circumference = $2\pi r$ or πd
Diameter = $2r$

1. **The circumference of a circle is $2\pi r$ or πd, where r is the radius of the circle and d is the diameter.**

You'll be given this information in your test booklet, so don't stress over memorizing these formulas. You will always be able to refer to your test booklet if you forget them. Just keep in mind that the diameter is always twice the length of the radius (and that the radius is half the diameter).

circumference = $2 \times \pi \times 5 = 10\pi$ circumference = 10π

In math class you probably learned that $\pi = 3.14$ (or even 3.14159). On the SAT, $\pi = 3^+$ (a little more than 3) is a good enough approximation. Even with a calculator, using $\pi = 3$ will give you all the information you need to solve difficult SAT multiple-choice geometry questions.

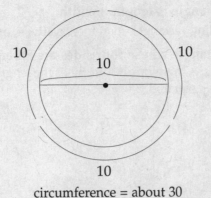

circumference = about 30

2. The area of a circle is πr^2, where r is the radius of the circle.

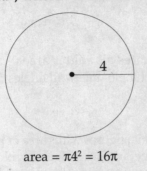

area = $\pi 4^2 = 16\pi$

3. A tangent is a line that touches a circle at exactly one point. Any radius drawn from that tangent point forms a 90-degree angle.

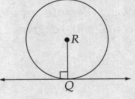

RECTANGLES AND SQUARES

1. The perimeter of a rectangle is the sum of the lengths of its sides. Just add them up.

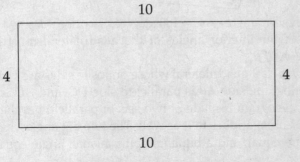

perimeter = 10 + 4 + 10 + 4 = 28

Little Boxes

Here's a progression of quadrilaterals from least specific to most specific:

quadrilateral = 4-sided figure
↓
parallelogram = a quadrilateral in which opposite sides are parallel
↓
rectangle = a parallelogram in which all angles = 90 degrees
↓
square = a rectangle in which all sides are equal

2. The area of a rectangle is length × width.
The area of the preceding rectangle, therefore, is 10×4, or 40.

3. A square is a rectangle whose four sides are all equal in length.
The perimeter of a square, therefore, is four times the length of any side. The area is the length of any side squared.

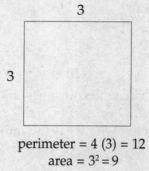

$$\text{perimeter} = 4\,(3) = 12$$
$$\text{area} = 3^2 = 9$$

4. In rectangles and squares all angles are 90-degree angles.
It can't be a square or a rectangle unless all angles are 90 degrees.

POLYGONS

Polygons are two-dimensional figures with three or more straight sides. Triangles and rectangles are both polygons. So are figures with five, six, seven, eight, or any greater number of sides. The most important fact to know about polygons is that any one of them can be divided into triangles. This means that you can always determine the sum of the measures of the interior angles of any polygon.

For example, the sum of the interior angles of any four-sided polygon (called a *quadrilateral*) is 360 degrees. Why? Because any quadrilateral can be divided into two triangles, and a triangle contains 180 degrees. Look at the following example:

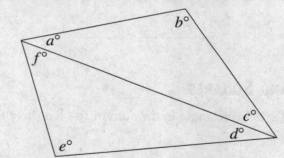

In this polygon, $a + b + c = 180$ degrees; so does $d + e + f$. That means that the sum of the interior angles of the quadrilateral must be 360 degrees ($a + b + c + d + e + f$).

A *parallelogram* is a quadrilateral whose opposite sides are parallel. In the following parallelogram, side AB is parallel to side DC, and AD is parallel to BC. Because a parallelogram is made of two sets of parallel lines that intersect each other, Fred's theorem applies to it as well: The two big angles are equal, the two small angles are equal, and a big angle plus a small angle equals 180 degrees.

In the figure below, big angles A and C are equal, and small angles B and D are equal. Also, since A is a big angle and D is a small angle, $A + D = 180$ degrees.

VOLUME

ETS will occasionally ask a question that will require you to calculate the volume of a rectangular solid (a box or a cube). The formula for the volume of a rectangular solid is length × width × height. Since length, width, and height are equal in a cube, the volume of a cube can be calculated simply by cubing (where do you think they get the name?) the length of any edge of the cube.

Volume = 8 × 4 × 3 = 96

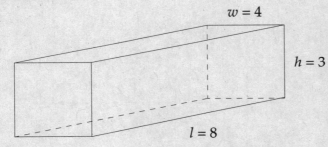

Volume = 3^3 = 27

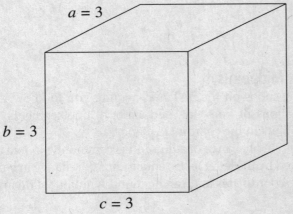

No Sweat

In the rare case when ETS asks you to find the volume of a figure other than a rectangular solid, the formula will either be provided with the question or will appear in the instructions.

GRIDS

If you've ever looked for a particular city on a map in an atlas, you're probably familiar with the idea behind grids. You look up Philadelphia in the atlas's index and discover that it is located at D5 on the map of Pennsylvania. On the map itself you find letters of the alphabet running along the top of the page and numbers running down one side. You move your finger straight down from the D at the top of the page until it is at the level of the 5 along the side, and there you are: in Philadelphia.

Grids work the same way. The standard grid is shaped like a cross. The horizontal line is called the *x-axis*; the vertical line is the *y-axis*. The four areas formed by the intersection of the axes are called *quadrants*. The location of any point can be described with a pair of numbers (x, y), just the way you would point on a map: $(0, 0)$ are the coordinates of the intersection of the two axes (also called the *origin*); $(1, 2)$ are the coordinates of the point one space to the right and two spaces up; $(-1, 5)$ are the coordinates of the point one space to the left and five spaces up; $(-4, -2)$ are the coordinates of the point four spaces to the left and two spaces down. All these points are located on the diagram on the next page.

Zones

A grid has four distinct zones, called *quadrants*:

Quadrant I is the upper right-hand corner, where *x* and *y* are both positive.

Quadrant II is the upper left-hand corner, where *x* is negative and *y* is positive.

Quadrant III is the lower left-hand corner, where *x* and *y* are both negative.

Quadrant IV is the lower right-hand corner, where *x* is positive and *y* is negative.

Sometimes, pinning down a coordinate's quadrant is all you need to do to find ETS's answer.

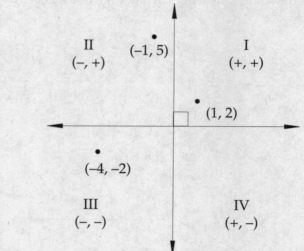

Distance and Midpoints

Some of the questions on the SAT may require you to know the properties of slope, the equations of lines, the midpoints of line segments, or the distance between two points in the coordinate plane.

Slope is the rate of change of a line and is commonly known as the "rise over run." It's denoted by the letter *m*. Essentially, it's the change in *y*-coordinates over the change in *x*-coordinates and can be found with the following formula:

$$m = \frac{(y_2 - y_1)}{(x_2 - x_1)}$$

The **midpoint** formula gives the midpoint of ST, with points S (x_1, y_1) and T (x_2, y_2). It's simply the average of the x-coordinates and the y-coordinates. In our example, the midpoint would be $\dfrac{(x_1 + x_2)}{2}, \dfrac{(y_1 + y_2)}{2}$.

The **distance** formula looks quite complicated. The easiest way to solve the distance between two points is to connect them and form a triangle. Then use the Pythagorean theorem. Many times, the triangle formed is one of the common Pythagorean triples (3-4-5 or 5-12-13).

$$\sqrt{(x_2 - x_1)^2 + (y_2 - y_1)^2}$$

BASIC PRINCIPLES: PRACTICE

Okay, now that you've mastered the rules, you're ready to knock out some problems.

Warm up with this one:

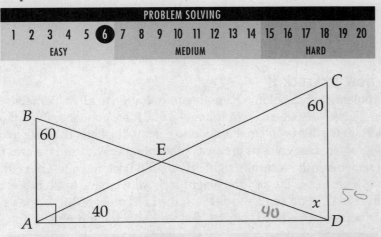

6. What is the value of x in the figure above?

  (A) 20
  (B) 30
  (C) 40
  (D) 50
  (E) 60

Here's How To Crack It

Look at the way ETS presents the problem. We have two triangles, but only two angles are given in each figure. Let's start filling in the missing information. Triangle *ABD* has a 90-degree angle and a 60 degree angle. What's missing? Write 30 degrees in for the third angle. Now let's move to triangle *ACD*. This figure has angle measurements of 60 and 40. Fill in the missing third angle of 80. Now we have enough information to solve the problem. Angle *D* is 80 degrees and part of it is 30, so the leftover part, x, must be 50. D is the correct answer.

Here's another one:

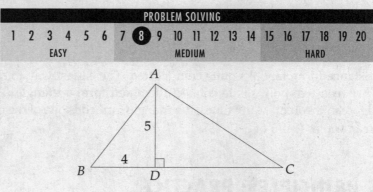

8. If the area of $\triangle ABC$ in the figure above is 30, what is the length of DC?

(A) 2
(B) 4
(C) 6
(D) 8
(E) 12

Here's How To Crack It

In this problem, there's not much missing information to fill in. Perhaps you filled in the missing 90-degree angle in triangle *ABD*. If so, good job. Even though it's not important for this problem, it's good to get into the habit of filling in information. The problem also gives us the area of the triangle. Write out the area formula. (You do remember the formula, right? If not, flip back to page 229.) Fill in what you know. The area is 30, and the height is 5. All we have to do is solve for the base, which is 12. If *BC* is 12 and *BD* is 4, then *DC* must be 8.

Now you're warmed up. Let's try a more challenging problem:

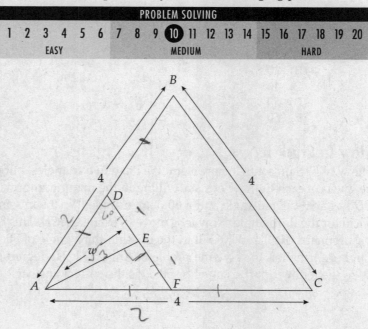

10. Triangle ABC is equilateral and angle AEF is a right angle. D is the midpoint of AB, F is the midpoint of AC, and E is the midpoint of DF. What is the value of w?

(A) 1

(B) $\sqrt{3}$

(C) 2

(D) $2\sqrt{2}$

(E) $2\sqrt{3}$

Here's How To Crack It

This problem has a lot more going on in it. But if we take it piece by piece, we'll crack it. Let's start filling in some information. The first thing the problem tells us is that triangle ABC is equilateral. Mark 60 degree angles on the figure. Next, we see that angle AEF is a right angle. Write that in as well. The problem also conveniently tells us that D and F are the midpoints of AB and AC, respectively. Therefore, AD and AF are 2. Finally, the last piece of information reveals that E is the midpoint of DF; mark DE and EF as equal.

Now, what do we have? Triangle AEF is a right triangle, with a hypotenuse of 2 and a leg of 1. Hmm, perhaps the good ol' Pythagorean theorem can help us. Plug the numbers into the theorem, and you'll see that the answer is B.

BALLPARKING

You may be thinking, "Wait a second, isn't there an easier way?" By now, you should know that of course there is, and we're going to show you. On many SAT geometry problems, you won't have to calculate an exact answer. Instead, you can estimate an answer choice. We call this *Ballparking*.

Ballparking is extremely useful on SAT geometry problems. At the very least, it will help you avoid careless mistakes by immediately eliminating answers that could not possibly be correct. In many problems, Ballparking will allow you to find ETS's answer without even working out the problem at all.

For example, on many SAT geometry problems, you will be presented with a drawing in which some information is given and you will be asked to find some of the information that is missing. In most such problems, ETS expects you to apply some formula or perform some calculation, often an algebraic one. But you'll almost always be better off if you look at the drawing and make a rough estimate of ETS's answer (based on the given information) before you try to work it out.

The basic principles you just learned (such as the number of degrees in a triangle and the fact that $\pi \approx 3$) will be enormously helpful to you in ballparking on the SAT. You should also know the approximate values of several common square roots. Be sure to memorize them before moving on. Knowing them cold will help you solve problems and save time, even if your calculator has a square root function.

Pictures

Unless otherwise stated, the diagram ETS supplies you with is drawn to scale.

Square Roots

$$\sqrt{1} = 1$$
$$\sqrt{2} \approx 1.4$$
$$\sqrt{3} \approx 1.7+$$
$$\sqrt{4} = 2$$

You will also find it very helpful if you have a good sense of how large certain common angles are. Study the following examples.

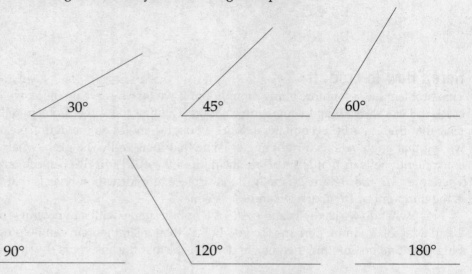

To get a little practice using the material you've memorized to help you ballpark, do the following drill.

DRILL 1

Ballpark the following values. Use estimates for $\sqrt{2}, \sqrt{3}$, and π (rather than using your calculator) to figure out each value. Answers can be found on page 340.

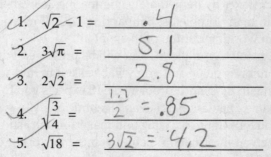

1. $\sqrt{2} - 1 =$ _____ .4_____
2. $3\sqrt{\pi} =$ _____ 5.1_____
3. $2\sqrt{2} =$ _____ 2.8_____
4. $\sqrt{\dfrac{3}{4}} =$ $\dfrac{1.7}{2} = .85$
5. $\sqrt{18} =$ $3\sqrt{2} = 4.2$

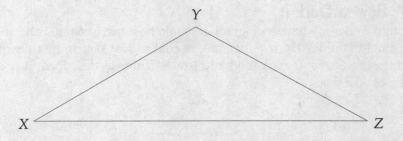

6. In the figure above, given $XY = 16$, estimate all the angles and the lengths of the other sides.

HOW HIGH IS THE CEILING?

If your friend stood next to a wall in your living room and asked you how high the ceiling was, what would you do? Would you get out your trigonometry textbook and try to triangulate using the shadow cast by your pal? Of course not. You'd look at your friend and think something like this: "Dave's about 6 feet tall. The ceiling's a couple of feet higher than he is. It must be about 8 feet high."

Your ballpark answer wouldn't be exact, but it would be close. If your mother later claimed that the ceiling in the living room was 15 feet high, you'd be able to tell her with confidence that she was mistaken.

You'll be able to do the same thing on the SAT. Every geometry figure on your test will be drawn exactly to scale unless there is a note in that problem telling you otherwise. That means you can trust the proportions in the drawing. If line segment A has a length of 2 and line segment B is exactly half as long, then the length of line segment B is 1. All such problems are ideal for ballparking.

WHEN YOU CAN'T MEASURE, SKETCH AND BALLPARK

You will sometimes encounter geometry problems that have no diagrams, or that have diagrams containing only partial information. In these cases, you should use the given information to sketch a complete diagram and then use your drawing as a basis for ballparking. Don't hesitate to fill your test booklet with sketches and scratch work: This is precisely what you are supposed to do. Finding ETS's answer will be much harder, if not impossible, if you don't take full advantage of the information ETS gives you.

Here's an example:

> ### The Correct Choice
> Remember that the SAT is a multiple-choice test. This means that you don't always have to come up with an answer; you just have to identify the correct one from among the five choices provided.

PROBLEM SOLVING																			
1	2	3	4	5	6	7	8	9	10	11	12	13	14	15	**16**	17	18	19	20
		EASY							MEDIUM							HARD			

16. All faces of a cube with a 4-meter edge are covered with striped paper. If the cube is then cut into cubes with 1-meter edges, how many of the 1-meter cubes have striped paper on exactly one face?
    (A) 24
    (B) 36
    (C) 48
    (D) 60
    (E) 72

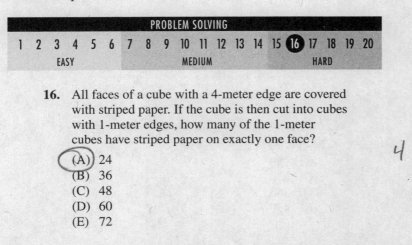

Here's How to Crack It

This problem doesn't have a diagram. It would be much easier to solve if it did. What should you do? Draw a diagram, of course! Just sketch the cube quickly in your test booklet and mark it off into 1-meter cubes as described. Your sketch might look like this:

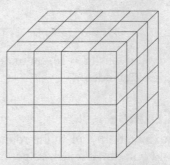

You should be able to see that there are four cubes on each side of the big cube that will have striped paper on only one face (the four center cubes—all the other cubes have at least two exterior sides). Since a cube has six sides, this means that ETS's answer is choice A.

PLUGGING IN

As you learned in Chapter 11, Plugging In is one of the most powerful techniques for solving SAT algebra problems. It is also very useful on geometry problems. On some problems, you will be able to plug in ballpark values for missing information and then use the results either to find ETS's answer directly or to eliminate answers that could not possibly be correct.

Here's an example:

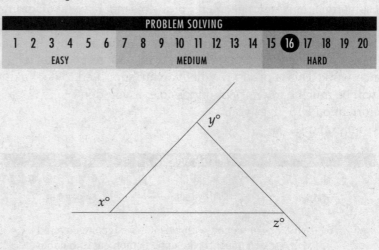

16. In the figure above, what is the value of $x + y + z$?

(A) 90
(B) 180
(C) 270
(D) 360
(E) 450

Here's How to Crack It

We don't know the measures of the interior angles of the triangle in the drawing, but we do know that the three interior angles of any triangle add up to 180, and 180 divided by 3 is 60. Now, simply plug in 60 for the value of each interior angle.

This doesn't give you ETS's answer directly; the problem does not ask you for the sum of the interior angles. But Plugging In does enable you to find ETS's answer. Look at the redrawn figure:

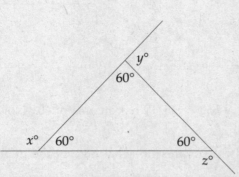

If the marked interior angle is 60, what must x be? Remember that every line is a 180-degree angle. That means that the measure of x must be $180 - 60$, or 120. You can now do the same thing for the other two angles. Using this method you find that x, y, and z each equal 120. That means that $x + y + z = 360$. ETS's answer, therefore, is choice D.

Ballparking like this won't always give you ETS's exact answer, but it will usually enable you to eliminate at least three of the four incorrect choices. Other kinds of geometry problems also lend themselves to Plugging In.

Here's another example:

20. The base of triangle T is 40% less than the length of rectangle R. The height of triangle T is 50% greater than the width of rectangle R. The area of triangle T is what percent of the area of rectangle R?

    (A) 10
    (B) 45
    (C) 90
    (D) 110
    (E) 125

Here's How to Crack It

This is a really hard problem. You should recognize that A, C, and D are Joe Bloggs answers and should be eliminated. Even if you don't see this, you'll still be able to find the right answer by sketching and Plugging In.

Alternate Solution

You can also solve problem 16 by ballparking. Angle x looks like it's about 135 degrees; angle y looks like about 100 degrees; angle z looks like about 120. You don't have to be very precise. What does that add up to? 355. Not bad!

When Plugging In, always use numbers that are easy to work with. Let's say the length of the rectangle is 10; that means that the base of the triangle, which is 40% smaller, is 6. Now if we plug 4 in for width of rectangle *R*, then the height of triangle *T* is 6. You should come up with two sketches that look like this:

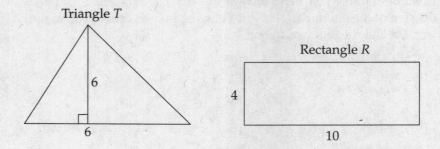

Triangle *T*

Rectangle *R*

T has an area of $\frac{1}{2}bh$, or 18. *R* has an area of 40. Now set up the translation:

$$18 = \frac{x}{100}(40)$$ where x represents what percent the triangle was of the rectangle. Solve for x and you get 45. (If you're not sure how to set up a percent, we'll show you in the next chapter.)

As you can see, advanced geometry problems actually don't involve any advanced principles. Rather, these problems are harder simply because they combine multiple concepts (and therefore require a lot more work). However, if you follow The Princeton Review's strategy—and know your basic rules—you should have a pretty good handle on these.

Let's give another difficult one a shot:

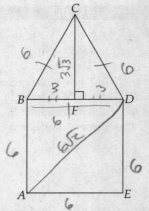

14. In the figure above, *BCD* is an equilateral triangle, F is the midpoint of *BD*, and $CF = 3\sqrt{3}$. What is the length of the diagonal of square *ABDE*?

(A) $3\sqrt{2}$
(B) $3\sqrt{3}$
(C) 6
(D) $6\sqrt{2}$
(E) $6\sqrt{3}$

Here's How to Crack It

First, you should fill in the missing angles on triangle *BCD*. It looks like we have a 30-60-90 right triangle for *FCD*. This is one of ETS's favorite triangles. In fact, the test writers love it so much that they provide all the information you need to know about in the beginning of each Math section. Even so, it might be helpful to memorize the relationship of sides in the 30:60:90 triangle. If the smallest side, which is opposite the 30-degree angle, is x, then the hypotenuse will be $2x$. The medium-length side opposite the 60-degree angle will be $x\sqrt{3}$.

Conveniently, the side opposite the 60-degree angle is $3\sqrt{3}$. Therefore, x must be 3. And if side *DF* is 3, then so too must be side *BF*. You've now discovered that the side of the square is 6; you're in the home stretch. Since you need the diagonal of the square, you can use the Pythagorean theorem. $6^2 + 6^2 = c^2$. Solving for the diagonal, you should get $6\sqrt{2}$.

Had enough? Maybe we should try one more:

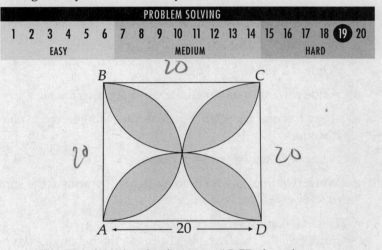

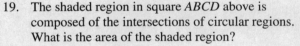

19.   The shaded region in square *ABCD* above is composed of the intersections of circular regions. What is the area of the shaded region?

    (A) 20π
    (B) $40(\pi - 2)$
    (C) $200(\pi - 2)$
    (D) 100π
    (E) 400π

Here's How To Crack It

This problem is a nightmare. Notice the difficulty level—it's right up there at the top. But even the most difficult problems can be cracked if you know how to approach them. Instead of doing all of the math, which would take ages, let's engage in a little Ballparking. Start with what you know: You have a square with a side length of 20. The question asks for the area of the circle-shaped portions. The entire area of the square is 400. Ballpark the amount of the picture taken up by the shaded region; it looks to be around half. So we need an answer around 200. Let's go to the choices:

(A) $20\pi \approx 60$ TOO SMALL
(B) $40(\pi - 2) \approx 40$ TOO SMALL
(C) $200(\pi - 2) \approx 200$ LOOKS GOOD!
(D) $100\pi \approx 314$ TOO BIG
(E) $400\pi \approx 1200$ WAY TOO BIG!

The answer is C.

You may think that this isn't the "right" way to do the problem, but that's the not the issue. The goal is to get as many points as possible, by any means possible. In most areas of your life, we wouldn't recommend that sort of mindset, but for the SAT it's okay.

GEOMETRY SUMMARY

1. Degrees and angles:

   a. A circle contains 360 degrees.

   b. When you think about angles, remember circles.

   c. A line is a 180-degree angle.

   d. A line continues on indefinitely in both directions.

   e. A ray has one endpoint, but continues indefinitely in one direction.

   f. A line segment has two endpoints.

   g. When two lines intersect, four angles are formed; the sum of their measures is 360 degrees.

   h. Fred's theorem: When two parallel lines are cut by a third line, the small angles are equal, the big angles are equal, and the sum of a big angle and a small angle is 180 degrees.

2. Triangles:

   a. Every triangle contains 180 degrees.

   b. An equilateral triangle is one in which all three sides are equal in length, and all three angles are equal in measure (60 degrees).

   c. An isosceles triangle is one in which two of the sides are equal in length, and the two angles opposite the equal sides are equal in measure.

d. A right triangle is one in which one of the angles is a right angle (90 degrees).

e. The perimeter of a triangle is the sum of the lengths of its sides.

f. The area of a triangle is: $\frac{1}{2}bh$.

g. The height *must* form a right angle with the base.

h. The Pythagorean theorem states that in a right triangle, the square of the hypotenuse equals the sum of the squares of the other two sides. Remember ETS's favorite Pythagorean triplets (3-4-5 and 5-12-13).

i. The longest side of any triangle is opposite the largest interior angle; the shortest side is opposite the smallest angle.

3. Circles:

a. The circumference of a circle is $2\pi r$ or πd, where r is the radius of the circle and d is the diameter.

b. The area of a circle is πr^2, where r is the radius of the circle.

c. A tangent touches a circle at one point; any radius that touches that tangent forms a 90° angle.

4. Rectangles and squares:

a. The perimeter of a rectangle is the sum of the lengths of its sides.

b. The area of a rectangle is length × width.

c. A square is a rectangle whose four sides are all equal in length.

d. Any polygon can be divided into triangles.

f. You must know how to locate points on a grid.

e. The volume of a rectangular solid is length × width × height. The formulas to compute the volume of other three-dimensional figures are supplied in the instructions at the front of every Math section.

5. When you encounter a geometry problem on the SAT, ballpark the answer before trying to work it out.

6. You must never skip an SAT problem that has a drawing with it.

7. You must know the following values:

$$\pi \approx 3$$
$$\sqrt{2} \approx 1.4$$
$$\sqrt{3} \approx 1.7$$

8. You must also be familiar with the size of certain common angles.

9. Most SAT geometry diagrams are drawn to scale. Use your eyes before you use your pencil. Try to eliminate impossible answers.

11. When a diagram is not drawn to scale, redraw it.

12. When no diagram is provided, make your own; when a provided diagram is incomplete, complete it.

13. When information is missing from a diagram, ballpark and plug in.

14. Some extremely difficult SAT geometry problems can be solved quickly and easily through sketching and ballparking, but you will have to stay on your toes. The way to do this is always to ask yourself three questions:

    a. What information have I been given?

    b. What information have I been asked to find?

    c. What is the relationship between these two pieces of information?

13

Grid-Ins:
Cracking the System

WHAT IS A GRID-IN?

One of the Math sections on your SAT will contain a group of ten problems without multiple-choice answers. ETS calls these problems "Student-Produced Responses." We call them *grid-ins*, because you have to mark your answers on a grid printed on your answer sheet. The grid looks like this:

Despite their format, grid-ins are just like other math questions on the SAT, and many of the techniques that you've learned so far still apply. You can still use Plugging In and other great techniques, such as the Ratio Box and the Average Pie. You can still use the order of difficulty and your knowledge of Joe Bloggs to avoid making obvious mistakes on hard questions. Your calculator will still help you out on many problems as well. So grid-ins are nothing to be scared of. In fact, many grid-in questions are simply regular SAT multiple-choice math problems with the answer choices lopped off. The only difference is that you have to arrive at your answer from scratch, rather than choose it from among five possibilities.

You will need to be extra careful when answering grid-in questions, however, because the grid format increases the likelihood of careless errors. It is vitally important that you understand how the grid-in format works before you take the test. In particular, you'll need to memorize ETS's rules about which kinds of answers count and which don't. The instructions may look complicated, but we've boiled them down to a few rules for you to memorize and practice.

Take a look at the grid again. Because of the way it's arranged, ETS can only use certain types of problems for grid-ins. For example, you'll never see variables (letters) in your answer (although there can be variables in the question), because the grid can only accommodate numbers. This is good for you because no matter how good you are at algebra, you're probably better at arithmetic.

Also, this means that your calculator will be useful on several questions. As always, be careful to set up the problem on paper before you carefully punch the numbers into your calculator. Since you have to write in the answer yourself on the grid, you have to be more careful than ever to avoid careless mistakes.

Grid-ins are scored somewhat differently than multiple-choice questions on the SAT. On multiple-choice questions, you lose a fraction of a raw score point for every incorrect answer. This deducted fraction is commonly referred to as a "guessing penalty." We explained earlier in the book why there is really no guessing penalty on SAT multiple-choice questions. For different reasons, there is no guessing penalty for grid-ins, either. Why? Because *nothing* is deducted for an incorrect answer on a grid-in. An incorrect answer on one of these questions is no worse for your score than a question left blank. And, by the same token, a blank is just as costly as an error. Therefore, you *should be very aggressive in answering these questions*. Don't leave a question blank just because you're worried

Order of Difficulty:
Grid-Ins

11–13 Easy
14–17 Medium
18–20 Difficult

that the answer you've found may not be correct. ETS's scoring computers treat incorrect answers and blanks exactly the same. If you have arrived at an answer, you have a shot at earning points, and if you have a shot at earning points, you should take it.

That doesn't mean that you should guess blindly. Your chance of helping your score with a blind guess on a grid-in is very, very small. You would be better off spending your time either working on problems that you know you can answer or checking your work on problems you have already finished.

THE INSTRUCTIONS

Here are the instructions for the Grid-In sections as they will appear on your SAT:

Directions: For Student-Produced Response questions 9-18, use the grids at the bottom of the answer sheet page on which you have answered questions 1-8.

Each of the remaining 10 questions requires you to solve the problem and enter your answer by marking the circles in the special grid, as shown in the examples below. You may use any available space for scratchwork.

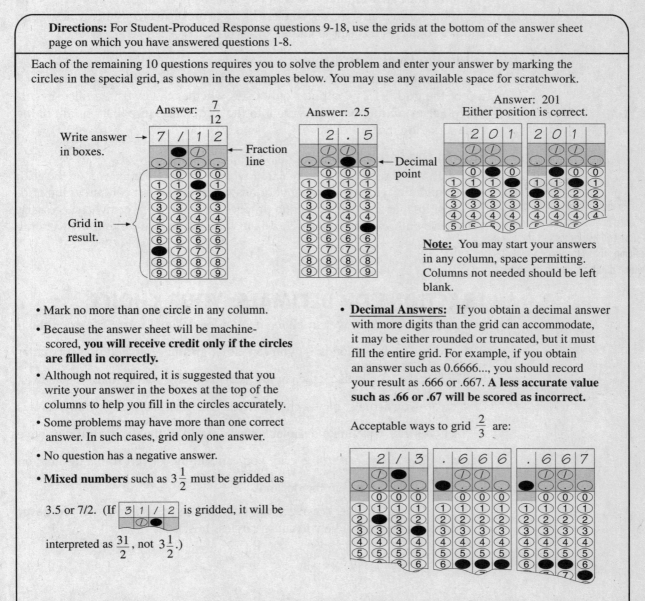

- Mark no more than one circle in any column.

- Because the answer sheet will be machine-scored, **you will receive credit only if the circles are filled in correctly.**

- Although not required, it is suggested that you write your answer in the boxes at the top of the columns to help you fill in the circles accurately.

- Some problems may have more than one correct answer. In such cases, grid only one answer.

- No question has a negative answer.

- **Mixed numbers** such as $3\frac{1}{2}$ must be gridded as

  3.5 or 7/2. (If $\boxed{3\ 1\ /\ 2}$ is gridded, it will be

  interpreted as $\frac{31}{2}$, not $3\frac{1}{2}$.)

- **Decimal Answers:** If you obtain a decimal answer with more digits than the grid can accommodate, it may be either rounded or truncated, but it must fill the entire grid. For example, if you obtain an answer such as 0.6666..., you should record your result as .666 or .667. **A less accurate value such as .66 or .67 will be scored as incorrect.**

Acceptable ways to grid $\frac{2}{3}$ are:

WHAT THE INSTRUCTIONS MEAN

Of all the instructions on the SAT, these are the most important to understand thoroughly before you take the test. Pity the unprepared student who takes the SAT cold and spends ten minutes of potential point-scoring time reading and puzzling over ETS's confusing instructions. We've translated these unnecessarily complicated instructions into a few important rules. Make sure you know them all well.

Fill In the Boxes

Watch Out

Negatives, π, and % cannot be gridded in!

Always write your answer in the boxes at the top of the grid before you darken the ovals below. Your written answers won't affect the scoring of your test; if you write the correct answer in the boxes and grid in the wrong ovals, you won't get credit for your answer (and you won't be able to appeal to ETS). However, writing in the answers first makes you less likely to make an error when you grid in, and it also makes it easier to check your work.

Fill In the Ovals Correctly

As we just pointed out, you receive no credit for writing in the answer at the top of the grid. ETS's computer only cares whether the ovals are filled in correctly. For every number you write into the grid, make sure that you fill in the corresponding oval.

Stay to the Left

Keep Left

No matter how many digits are in your answer, always start gridding in the left-most column. That way, you'll avoid omitting digits and losing points.

Although you'll receive credit no matter where you put your answer on the grid, you should always begin writing your answer in the far left column of the grid. This ensures that you will have enough space for longer answers when necessary. You'll also cut down on careless errors if you always grid in your answers the same way.

FRACTIONS OR DECIMALS: YOUR CHOICE

You can grid in an answer in either fraction or decimal form. For example, if your answer to a question is $\frac{1}{2}$, you can either grid in $\frac{1}{2}$ or .5. It doesn't matter to ETS because $\frac{1}{2}$ equals .5; the computer will credit either form of the answer. That means you actually have a choice. If you like fractions, grid in your answers in fraction form. If you like decimals, you can grid in the decimal. If you have a fraction that doesn't fit in the grid, you can simply convert it to a decimal on your calculator and grid in the decimal.

Here's the bottom line: When gridding in fractions or decimals, use whichever form is easier and least likely to cause careless mistakes.

DECIMAL PLACES AND ROUNDING

When you have a decimal answer of a value less than 1, such as .45 or .678, many teachers ask you to write a zero before the decimal point (for example, 0.45 or 0.678). On grid-in questions, however, ETS doesn't want you to worry about the zero. In fact, there is no 0 in the first column of the grid. If your answer is a decimal less than 1, just write the decimal point in the first column of the grid and then continue from there.

You should also notice that if you put the decimal point in the first column of the grid, you only have three places left to write in numbers. But what if your decimal is longer than three places, such as .87689? In these cases, ETS will give you credit if you round off the decimal so that it fits in the grid. But you'll *also* get credit, however, if you just enter as much of the decimal as will fit.

For example, if you had to grid in .87689, you could just write .876 (which is all that will fit) and then stop. Remember, you only need to grid in whatever is necessary to receive credit for your answer. Don't bother with extra unnecessary steps. You don't have to round off decimals, so don't bother.

If you have a long or repeating decimal, however, be sure to fill up all the spaces in the grid. If your decimal is .666666, you *must* grid in .666. Just gridding in .6 or .66 is not good enough.

Lop

Why do extra work for ETS? After all, they won't give you extra points. If your decimal doesn't fit in the grid, lop off the extra digits and grid in what does fit.

REDUCING FRACTIONS

If you decide to grid in a fraction, ETS doesn't care if you reduce the fraction or not. For example, if your answer to a problem is $\frac{4}{6}$, ETS will give you credit if you grid in $\frac{4}{6}$ or reduce it to $\frac{2}{3}$. So if you have to grid in a fraction, and the fraction fits in the grid, don't bother reducing it. Why give yourself more work (and another chance to make a careless error)?

The only time you might have to reduce a fraction is if it doesn't fit in the grid. If your answer to a question is $\frac{15}{25}$, it won't fit in the grid. You have two options: Either reduce the fraction to $\frac{3}{5}$ and grid that in, or use your calculator to convert the fraction to .6. Choose whichever process makes you the most comfortable.

Relax

If your answer is a fraction and it fits in the grid (fraction bar included), don't reduce it. Why bother? ETS won't give you an extra point. However, if your fraction doesn't fit, reduce it or turn it into a decimal on your calculator.

MIXED NUMBERS

ETS's scoring machine does not recognize mixed numbers. If you try to grid in $2\frac{1}{2}$ by writing "2 1/2," the computer will read this number as $\frac{21}{2}$. You have to convert mixed numbers to fractions or decimals before you grid them in. To grid in $2\frac{1}{2}$, either convert it to $\frac{5}{2}$ or its decimal equivalent, which is 2.5. If you have to convert a mixed number in order to grid it in, be very careful not to change its value accidentally.

Don't Mix

Never grid in a mixed number. Change it into a top-heavy fraction or its decimal equivalent.

DON'T WORRY

The vast majority of grid-in answers will not be difficult to enter in the grid. ETS won't try to trick you by purposely writing questions that are confusing to grid in. Just pay attention to these guidelines and watch out for careless errors.

GRIDDING IN: A TEST DRIVE

To get a feel for this format, let's work through two examples. As you will see, grid-in problems are just regular SAT math problems.

10. If $a + 2 = 6$ and $b + 3 = 21$, what is the value of $\frac{b}{a}$?

Here's How to Crack It

You need to solve the first equation for a and the second equation for b. Start with the first equation, and solve for a. By subtracting 2 from both sides of the equation, you should see that $a = 4$.

Now move to the second equation, and solve for b. By subtracting 3 from both sides of the second equation, you should see that $b = 18$.

The question asked you to find the value of $\frac{b}{a}$. That's easy. The value of b is 18, and the value of a is 4. Therefore, the value of $\frac{b}{a}$ is $\frac{18}{4}$.

That's an ugly-looking fraction. How in the world do you grid it in? Ask yourself: "Does $\frac{18}{4}$ fit?" Yes! Grid in $\frac{18}{4}$.

Your math teacher wouldn't like it, but ETS's computer will. You shouldn't waste time reducing $\frac{18}{4}$ to a prettier fraction or converting it to a decimal. Spend that time on another problem instead. The fewer steps you take, the less likely you will be to make a careless mistake.

Here's another example. This one is quite a bit harder.

GRID-INS

9 10 11   12 13 14 **15** 16 17 18
EASY   MEDIUM   HARD

15. Forty percent of the members of the sixth-grade class wore white socks. Twenty percent wore black socks. If twenty-five percent of the remaining students wore gray socks, what percent of the sixth-grade class wore socks that were not white, black, or gray? (Disregard the % when gridding your answer.)

Here's How to Crack It

The problem doesn't tell you how many students are in the class, so you can plug in any number you like. This is a percentage problem, so the easiest number to plug in is 100. Forty percent of 100 is 40; that means 40 students wore white socks. Twenty percent of 100 is 20. That means that 20 students wore black socks.

Your next piece of information says that 25 percent of the remaining students wore gray socks. How many students remain? Forty, because 60 students wore either white or black socks, and 100 − 60 = 40. Therefore, 25 percent of these 40—10 students—wore gray socks.

How many students are left? 30. Therefore, the percentage of students not wearing white, black, or gray socks is 30 out of 100, or 30 percent. Grid it in, and remember to forget about the percent sign.

ORDER OF DIFFICULTY

Like all other questions on the Math SAT, grid-in problems are arranged in order of increasing difficulty. In each group of ten, the first third is easy, the second third is medium, and the final third is difficult. As always, the order of difficulty will be your guide to how much faith you can place in your hunches.

Guessing is highly unlikely to help you on grid-in questions. For that reason, you must not waste time on questions that are too hard for you to solve. Only students shooting for 700 or above should consider attempting all ten grid-in questions.

Keep in mind, of course, that many of the math techniques that you've learned are still very effective on grid-in questions. Plugging In worked very well on question number 15 on the previous page.

Here's another difficult grid-in question that you can answer effectively by using a technique you've learned before:

GRID-INS		
9 10 11	12 13 14 15	16 17 **18**
EASY	MEDIUM	HARD

18. Grow-Up potting soil is made from only peat moss and compost in a ratio of 3 pounds of peat moss to 5 pounds of compost. If a bag of Grow-Up potting soil contains 12 pounds of potting soil, how many pounds of peat moss does it contain?

Here's How to Crack It

To solve this problem, set up a Ratio Box (the Ratio Box is explained in detail on pages 173–174).

	Peat Moss	Compost	Whole
Ratio (parts)	3	5	8
Multiply By	1.5	1.5	1.5
Actual Number	1.5	1.5	12 (lbs)

What do you multiply by 8 to get 12? If you don't know, divide 12 by 8 on your calculator. The answer is 1.5. Write 1.5 in each of the boxes on the *multiply by* row of your Ratio Box.

	Peat Moss	Compost	Whole
Ratio (parts)	3	5	8
Multiply By	1.5	1.5	1.5
Actual Number			12 (lbs)

The problem asks you how many pounds of peat moss are in a bag. To find out, multiply the numbers in the Peat Moss column. That is, multiply 3 × 1.5, and you get 4.5. ETS's answer is 4.5.

	Peat Moss	Compost	Whole
Ratio (parts)	3	5	8
Multiply By	1.5	1.5	1.5
Actual Number	4.5 (lbs)	7.5 (lbs)	12 (lbs)

Grid it in like this:

JOE BLOGGS AND GRID-IN QUESTIONS

On grid-in questions, you obviously can't use the Joe Bloggs principle to eliminate tempting but incorrect answer choices, since there aren't any choices to choose from. But you can—and must—use your knowledge of Joe Bloggs to double-check your work and keep yourself from making careless mistakes or falling into traps.

The basic idea still holds true: Easy questions have easy answers, and hard questions have hard answers. On hard questions, you must be extremely suspicious of answers that come to you easily or through simple calculations.

Unfortunately, your knowledge of Joe Bloggs alone will never lead you all the way to ETS's answers, the way it sometimes does on multiple-choice questions. In order to earn points on grid-in questions, you're going to have to find the real answers, and you're going to have to be extremely careful when you enter your answers on your answer sheet. But Joe Bloggs may help you find the correct path

Say No to Joe

If it takes you four seconds to answer any grid-in question from 18 to 20, you've probably goofed. Check your work. Hard questions have hard answers.

to ETS's answer. On a hard problem, you may be torn between two different approaches, one easy and one hard. Which should you pursue? The harder one. Joe will take the easy path and, as always on hard questions, it will lead him to the wrong answer.

More Than One

Some grid-in questions have several possible correct answers. None is more correct than any other, so grid in the first one you find and move on.

RANGE OF ANSWERS

Some grid-in problems will have many possible correct answers. It won't matter which correct answer you choose, as long as the one you choose really is correct. Here's an example:

GRID-INS									
9	10	11	**⑫**	13	14	15	16	17	18
EASY			MEDIUM				HARD		

12. What is one possible value of x such that

$$\frac{1}{4} < x < \frac{1}{3}?$$

Here's How to Crack It

Joe Bloggs has trouble imagining how anything could squeeze between $\frac{1}{4}$ and $\frac{1}{3}$, but you know there are lots and lots of numbers in there. Any one of them will satisfy ETS.

The numbers in this problem are both fractions, but your answer doesn't have to be. The easiest approach is to forget about math-class solutions and head straight for your calculator (or your mental calculator). Convert $\frac{1}{4}$ to a decimal by dividing 1 by 4, which gives you .25. Now convert $\frac{1}{3}$ to a decimal by dividing 1 by 3, which gives you .333. All you need to answer the question is any number that falls between those two decimals. How about .26? Or .3? Or .331? Your answer merely has to be bigger than .25 and smaller than .333. Pick one, grid it in, and move on.

Drill 1

Don't lose points to carelessness. Practice by gridding the following numbers in the sample grids below. Answers can be found on page 340.

1. 1.5

2. 5.60

3. 81

4. $\dfrac{1}{3}$

5. $\dfrac{8}{11}$

6. 0.33333

7. $4\dfrac{2}{5}$

8. x, such that $6 < x < 7$

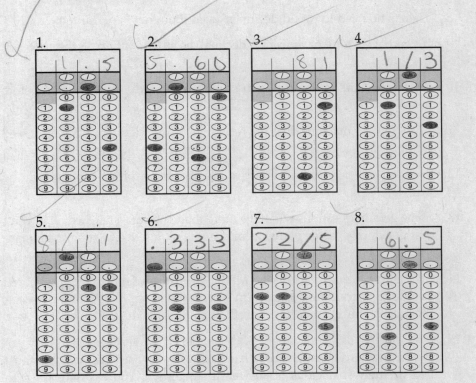

Ungriddable

Some things just won't go in the grid:

- variables
- pi (π)
- negative numbers
- square roots

If they show up in your answer, you've goofed. Redo the problem or skip it.

GRID-INS SUMMARY

1. One of the Math sections on your SAT will contain a group of ten problems without multiple-choice answers. ETS calls these problems "Student-Produced Responses." We call them *grid-ins*, because you have to mark your answers on a grid printed on your answer sheet.

2. Despite their format, grid-ins are really just like other math questions on the SAT, and many of the same techniques that you have learned still apply.

3. The grid format increases the likelihood of careless errors. Know the instructions and check your work carefully.

4. There is no guessing penalty for grid-ins, so you should always grid in your answer, even if you're not sure that it's correct. Blind guessing, however, is very unlikely to improve your score.

5. Always write the numbers in the boxes at the top of the grid before you (carefully) fill in the corresponding ovals.

6. Grid in your answer as far to the left as possible.

7. If the answer to a grid-in question contains a fraction or a decimal, you can grid in the answer in either form. When gridding in fractions or decimals, use whichever form is easier and least likely to cause careless mistakes.

8. There's no need to round decimals, even though it is permitted.

9. If you have a long or repeating decimal, be sure to fill up all the spaces in the grid.

10. If a fraction fits in the grid, you don't have to reduce the fraction before gridding it in.

11. ETS's scoring machine does not recognize mixed numbers. Convert mixed numbers to fractions or decimals before gridding them in.

12. The vast majority of grid-in answers will not be difficult to enter in the grid.

13. Some grid-in questions will have more than one correct answer. It doesn't matter which answer you grid in, as long as it's one of the possible answers.

14. Like all other questions on the Math SAT, grid-in problems are arranged in order of increasing difficulty. In each group of ten, the first third is easy, the second third is medium, and the final third is difficult.

15. On Grid-Ins, as on all other SAT sections, easy questions have easy answers, and hard questions have hard answers. On hard grid-ins, you must be extremely suspicious of answers that come to you easily or through simple calculations.

16. And remember, negatives, π, and % cannot be gridded in.

Putting It All Together

PUTTING IT ALL TOGETHER...

Here's your chance to combine everything you learned in the math chapters and give yourself some extra drills before the practice tests. Remember to practice the techniques we've taught you, even if you could arrive at the answer in a different way, to improve your problem recognition skills (knowing what technique to use on what type of problem).

The problem numbers represent where you would see them on the actual SAT. The difficulty meters have been removed, so you can practice figuring out the difficulty on your own, but keep in mind ALL numbers of multiple-choice questions are based on a 25-minute section. (By the way, the answers and explanations are located after the quiz.)

Good luck!

13. If $a > b$ and $a^2 - 2ab + b^2 = 169$, what is the value of $a - b$?

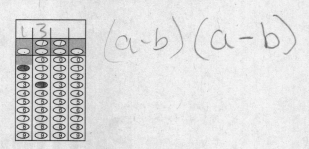

$(a-b)(a-b)$

15. If a is 63% and c is $\dfrac{3}{8}$, which of the following is the closest equivalent of the ratio of a to c?

(A) 0.006

(B) 0.236

(C) 0.381

(D) 0.595

(E) 1.680

$\dfrac{.63}{.375}$

$4\sqrt{x}+2 = 8y^2 - 24y$

$\sqrt{x+2} = 2y^2 - 6y$

$X+2 = 4y^4 - 3y^2 - 2$

11. If $\dfrac{4\sqrt{x+2}}{y-3} = 8y$, what is x in terms of y?

(A) $2y^2 - 12y - 2$

(B) $4y^4 - 24y^3 + 36y^2 - 2$

(C) $4y^4 - 12y^3 - 36y^2$

(D) $4y^4 - 36y^2 - 2$

(E) $4y^4 - 48y^2 - 2$

18. There are 5 cyclists in a race. If the first-place finisher receives a gold medal, the second-place finisher receives a silver medal, and the third-place finisher receives a bronze medal, how many different permutations are possible for the medal winners?

(A) 5

(B) 12

(C) 20

(D) 50

(E) 60

12. If $a + 2b = 10$, and $b - a = 2$, what is the value of b?

(A) 10

(B) 8

(C) 6

(D) 4

(E) 2

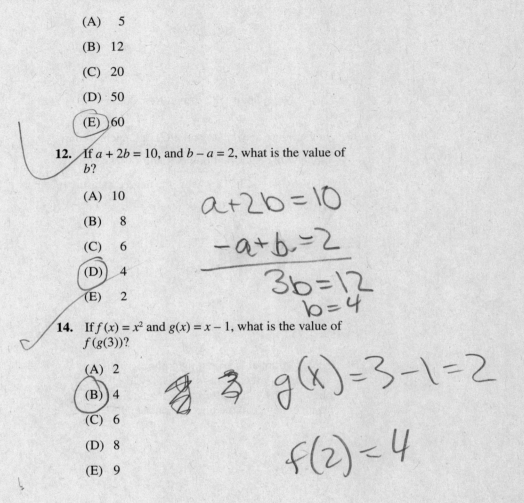

$$a + 2b = 10$$
$$-a + b = 2$$
$$\overline{\qquad\qquad}$$
$$3b = 12$$
$$b = 4$$

14. If $f(x) = x^2$ and $g(x) = x - 1$, what is the value of $f(g(3))$?

(A) 2

(B) 4

(C) 6

(D) 8

(E) 9

$$g(x) = 3 - 1 = 2$$

$$f(2) = 4$$

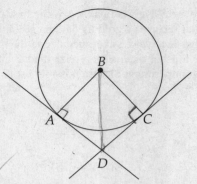

Note: Figure not drawn to scale.

17. In the figure above, *DA* and *DC* are tangent to the circle with center *B* at points *A* and *C*, respectively. If $\angle ABC = \frac{2}{7} \angle ADC$, what is the degree measure of $\angle ADC$?

(A) 40

(B) 51

(C) 129

(D) 140

(E) 154

[handwritten: $\angle ABC = \frac{2}{7} \angle ADC$]

[handwritten: $\angle ABC + \angle ADC = 180$]

10. A photographer is arranging 5 photographs in a row from left to right for a display. If all 5 photographs will be used, how many different arrangements can the photographer make?

(A) 5

(B) 24

(C) 25

(D) 120

(E) 390,625

13. At Ernie's Fruit Stand, 3 apples and 5 cherries cost $1.25. 15 apples and 100 cherries cost $9.25. What is the cost of 6 apples and 35 cherries?

(A) $3.25

(B) $3.50

(C) $3.62

(D) $4.00

(E) $5.25

[handwritten: .35]

[handwritten: $5.25 = 15a$]

[handwritten: $3a + 5c = 1.25$]

[handwritten: $15a + 100c = 9.25$]

[handwritten: $3a + 20c = 1.85$]

[handwritten: $15c = .6$]

[handwritten: $c = .04$]

18. According to local safety regulations, no transit bus may carry more than 66 people in it at one time. Right now, there are 42 people on a particular transit bus. At the next stop, n people enter the bus, but no one exits. If the total number of people on that transit bus is not over the limit, in terms of n, how many people are on the bus?

(A) $n + 42 \le 66$

(B) $n + 42 \ge 66$

(C) $n - 42 \le 66$

(D) $n - 42 \ge 66$

(E) $n \ge 66 - 42$

$n + 42 \le 66$

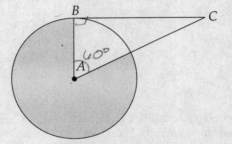

Note: Figure not drawn to scale.

18. The circle above with center A has an area of 21. BC is tangent to the circle with center A at point B. If $AC = 2AB$, what is the area of the shaded region?

14. If $f(x) = |x| + 1$ and $g(x) = x - 3$, what is the value of $f(g(1))$?

(A) −2

(B) −1

(C) 1

(D) 2

(E) 3

[handwritten: −2]

15. If $f(x) = \sqrt{x+1}$ for all values of $x \geq 0$, and $f(x) = x^2 + 2$ for all values of $x < 0$, what is the sum of $f(-3)$ and $f(8)$?

(A) 5

(B) 11

(C) 14

(D) 68

(E) 77

[handwritten: $f(-3) = (-3)^2 + 2 = 11$]
[handwritten: $f(8) = \sqrt{8+1} = 3$]

12. Two lines, a and b, which never intersect, are both tangent to circle C. If the smallest distance between any point on a and any point on b is 4 less than triple that distance, what is the area of circle C?

(A) $\dfrac{\pi}{4}$

(B) π

(C) 2π

(D) 4π

(E) 9π

[handwritten: $\frac{1}{2} = 12$; $1 = 2$; $\sqrt{2} = $; $2 = 4$; $3 = 6$; $d = 3d - 4$; $4 \neq 12 - 4?$; $1 = 3 - 4$]

16. If $f(x) = \dfrac{x-6}{x}$ for all even values of x, and $f(x) = x + 3$ for all odd values of x, what is the value of $f(5) - f(10)$?

(A) $-13\dfrac{1}{5}$

(B) -5

(C) $\dfrac{2}{5}$

(D) $3\dfrac{1}{10}$

(E) $7\dfrac{3}{5}$

[handwritten: $\frac{10-6}{10} = \frac{4}{10} = \frac{2}{5}$; $8 - \frac{2}{5}$; $\frac{16}{5} = \frac{2}{5} = \frac{14}{5}$]

17. Let $f(a, b) = a^2 - b^2$. If $f(5, d) = 9$, what is the positive value of d?

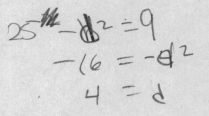

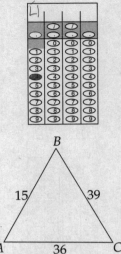

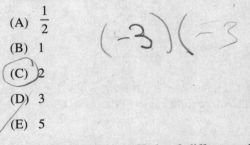

13. What is the measure, in degrees, of the largest angle in the above triangle?

10. If the product of $x^2 - 6x + 5$ and $2x^2 - 7x + 3$ is 0, then x could equal any of the following numbers EXCEPT

(A) $\dfrac{1}{2}$

(B) 1

(C) 2

(D) 3

(E) 5

$(-3)(-3$

13. Jon is making omelets. He has 3 different spices, 4 different vegetables, and 2 different types of eggs. If he will use one spice, one vegetable, and one type of egg, how many combinations of these ingredients can he make?

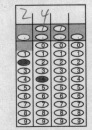

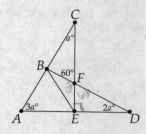

17. In the figure above, *AC*, *CE*, and *BD* intersect at the points shown above. What is the value of *a*?

18. If $f(x) = 2x - 1$, what is the value of $f(f(f(f(5))))$?

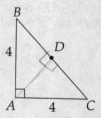

6 3

$f(f(f(9)))$
$f(f(17))$
$f(32)$
63

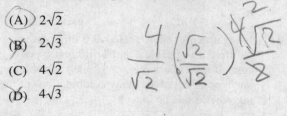

8. In the figure above, *AB* = *BC* = 4 and ∠*BAC* and ∠*ADC* are right angles. What is *AD*?

(A) $2\sqrt{2}$

(B) $2\sqrt{3}$

(C) $4\sqrt{2}$

(D) $4\sqrt{3}$

(E) 8

$$\frac{4}{\sqrt{2}}\left(\frac{\sqrt{2}}{\sqrt{2}}\right)\frac{4\sqrt{2}}{8}$$

12. If the perimeter of a square is 28, what is the length of the diagonal of the square?

(A) $2\sqrt{14}$

(B) $7\sqrt{2}$

(C) $7\sqrt{3}$

(D) 14

(E) $28\sqrt{2}$

20. Carlos and Katherine are estimating acceleration by rolling a ball from rest down a ramp. At 1 second, the ball is moving at 5 meters per second (m/s); at 2 seconds, the ball is moving at 10 m/s; at 3 seconds, the ball is moving at 15 m/s; and at 4 seconds, it is moving at 20 m/s. When graphed on an *xy*-plane, which equation best describes the ball's estimated acceleration where *y* expresses speed and *x* expresses time?

(A) $y = 5x + 5$

(B) $y = 25x$

(C) $y = -5x + 5$

(D) $y = 5x$

(E) $y = (4x + 1)^2 + 5$

17. Which of the following is a factor of $3x^3 - 11x^2 - 42x$?

(A) $x - 7$

(B) x

(C) $x + 6$

(D) $3x - 6$

(E) $3x^2 - 11x$

20. If $x \geq 10$, then which of the following is equivalent to $\dfrac{2x^2 - 7x - 15}{2x^3 + 13x^2 + 15x}$?

(A) $\dfrac{1}{30}$

(B) $\dfrac{x-5}{x+5}$

(C) $\dfrac{-15}{2x^3 + 11x^2 + 22x}$

(D) $\dfrac{2x-3}{2x+5x}$

(E) $\dfrac{x-5}{x^2+5x}$

ANSWERS AND EXPLANATIONS TO PUTTING IT ALL TOGETHER...

13. **13** Use the common quadratic: $(x - y)^2 = x^2 - 2xy - y^2$. So, $a^2 - 2ab + b^2 = (a - b)^2$. That means $(a - b)^2 = 169$. Take the square root of both sides to find $a - b = 13$ or -13; but don't forget $a > b$ and $a - b > 0$, so $a - b = 13$.

15. **E** First, convert a and c to decimals. 63% is $63 \div 100 = 0.63$ and $\frac{3}{8}$ is $3 \div 8 = 0.375$. The ratio of a to c is $\frac{a}{c}$. So, $\frac{0.63}{0.375} = 1.68$. To save time, you can ballpark the answer, since $a > c$ and E is the only choice greater than 1.

11. **B** It's hard to find numbers that work for x and y in the equation, so solve it algebraically. First, multiply both sides by $y - 3$ to get $4\sqrt{x+2} = 8y^2 - 24y$. Divide both sides by 4 to get $\sqrt{x+2} = 2y^2 - 6y$. Square both sides to get $x + 2 = (2y^2 - 6y)(2y^2 - 6y)$. FOIL it out to get $x + 2 = 4y^4 - 24y^3 + 36y^2$. Finally, subtract 2 from both sides to get $x = 4y^4 - 24y^3 + 36y^2 - 2$.

18. **E** There are 5 cyclists that could be first. Then, once you use one for the first spot, there are 4 that could be second, then 3 that could be third and that is all. Remember, who cares about fourth or fifth place, since they're not getting a medal. So, there are $5 \times 4 \times 3 = 60$ places in which the cyclists finish.

12. **D** Rewrite the second equation as $-a + b = 2$. Then, add the two equations together. This yields $3b = 12$. Divide by 3 to get $b = 4$. Alternatively, you could plug in the answers for the value of b to find the values of a and b that work in both equations. Plugging in choice D, if $b = 4$, then $a + 2(4) = 10$; so, $a = 2$. Plug these values into the second equation: Does $4 - 2 = 2$? Yes, so D is correct.

14. **B** First, find $g(3)$ by plugging 3 in for x in $g(x) = x - 1$. So, $g(3) = (3) - 1 = 2$. Next, find $f(2)$ by plugging 2 in for x in $f(x) = x^2$. So, $(2)^2 = 4$. That means $f(g(3)) = 4$.

17. **D** The angles in quadrilateral $ABCD$ (or any other quadrilateral) must add up to $360°$. Since A and C are tangent points, we know that $\angle BAD = \angle BCD = 90°$, so we get $\angle ABC + \angle ADC = 180°$. From the question, $\angle ABC = \frac{2}{7} \angle ADC$. We can substitute and solve: $\frac{2}{7}\angle ADC + \angle ADC = 180°$, so $\frac{9}{7}\angle ADC = 180°$, so $\angle ADC = 140°$.

10. **D**   There are 5 pictures that could be first. Then, once you use one for the first spot, there are 4 that could be second, then 3 that could be third, then 2 that could be fourth, then 1 that could be fifth. So, there are $5 \times 4 \times 3 \times 2 \times 1 = 120$ ways to arrange the photographs.

13. **B**   Rewrite these statements as equations, where a = the price of an apple and c = the price of a cherry: $3a + 5c = 1.25$ and $15a + 100c = 9.25$. Add the equations together to get $18a + 105c = 10.50$, then divide everything by 3 to get $6a + 35c = 3.50$.

18. **A**   If n represents the number of people that are added to the number of people already on the bus (42), you know that the new total on the bus is $n + 42$. Since that number is not *over the limit* of 66, but *could be equal to* the limit, you know that $n + 42 \leq 66$.

18. **17.5 or $\frac{35}{2}$**   The trick is to recognize that ABC is a 30-60-90 right triangle.

$\angle ABC$ must equal 90° since a tangent line must be perpendicular to the radius of a circle drawn to the point of tangency. Only a 30-60-90 has a hypotenuse (AC) equal to double the length of one of the sides (AB). (You can also use the Pythagorean theorem to show this.) This means that $\angle BAC = 60°$, so the shaded region has a central angle measure of $360° - 60° = 300°$. To get the area, use the proportion $\dfrac{Central\ Angle}{360} = \dfrac{Sector\ Area}{Circle\ Area}$, or $\dfrac{300}{360} = \dfrac{s}{21}$. Reduce, cross-multiply, and solve to get $s = 17.5$.

14. **E**   First, find $g(1)$ by plugging in 1 for x in $g(x) = x - 3$. So, $g(1) = (1) - 3 = -2$. Next, find $f(-2)$ by plugging in -2 for x in $f(x) = |x| + 1$. So, $f(-2) = |-2| + 1 = 2 + 1 = 3$. (The bar marks are absolute value, which is the distance from zero on a number line.)

15. **C**   Because -3 is less than 0, find $f(-3)$ by plugging in -3 for x in $f(x) = x^2 + 2$. So, $(-3)^2 + 2 = 9 + 2 = 11$. Because 8 is greater than 0, find $f(8)$ by plugging in 8 for x in $f(x) = \sqrt{x+1}$. So, $f(8) = \sqrt{8+1} = \sqrt{9} = 3$. *Sum* means to add. So, $11 + 3 = 14$.

12. **B**   Since a and b are parallel, and are both tangent to the circle, the distance between a and b is equal to the diameter of circle C. If we let d equal the distance between a and b, we get the equation $d = 3d - 4$, which solves to $d = 2$. Since the diameter of circle C is 2, the radius is 1, and its area = $\pi(1)^2 = \pi$.

16. **E** Because 5 is odd, plug in 5 for x in $f(x) = x + 3$. So, $f(5) = 5 + 3 = 8$. Because 10 is even, plug in 10 for x in $f(10) = \dfrac{10-6}{10} = \dfrac{4}{10} = \dfrac{2}{5}$. So, $f(5) - f(10) = 8 - \dfrac{2}{5} = 7\dfrac{3}{5}$.

17. **4** Plug 5 and d into the equation: $f(5, d) = 9$. So, $(5)^2 - (d)^2 = 9$. So, $25 - d^2 = 9$. Subtract 25 from both sides, then multiply by negative 1 to find $d^2 = 16$. So, $d = \pm 4$. The question asks for the positive value of d. So, $d = 4$.

13. **90** $15^2 + 36^2 = 39^2$. Since this triangle works in the Pythagorean theorem, it is a right triangle, meaning it has a 90-degree angle. (You can also recognize that the sides are in a ratio of 5-12-13.) Since the three angles in any triangle add up to 180 degrees, the right angle must be the largest angle.

10. **C** Factor $x^2 - 6x + 5$ into $(x - 5)(x - 1)$. Factor $2x^2 - 7x + 3$ into $(2x - 1)(x - 3)$. So if their product is equal to zero, that means $(x - 5)(x - 1)(2x - 1)(x - 3) = 0$, or $x = 5, 1, \dfrac{1}{2}$, or 3. Eliminate A, B, D, and E. Alternatively, you can plug the answer choices into the equations and multiply, but that will take a long time.

13. **24** For problems in which you choose one item each from different sources, multiply the number of items in each of the sources together. So, Jon has $3 \times 4 \times 2 = 24$ ways to make omelets.

17. **20** The sum of the angles in triangle ABD must be 180. So, $3a + 2a + \angle ABD = 180$. Thus, $\angle ABD = 180 - 5a$. The sum of the angles in triangle BCF must be 180. So, $a + 60 + \angle CBF = 180$. Thus, $\angle CBF = 120 - a$. Because $\overline{AC}$ is a line segment $\angle ABD + \angle CBF = 180$. Plug in the angles in terms of a: $(180 - 5a) + (120 - a) = 180$. Combine like terms to find $300 - 6a = 180$. Subtract 300 to find $-6a = -120$. Divide by -6 to find $a = 20$.

18. **65** You'll have to plug in for the function four times. First, find $f(5) = 2(5) - 1 = 9$. Second, find $f(9) = 2(9) - 1 = 17$. Third, find $f(17) = 2(17) - 1 = 33$. Finally, find $f(33) = 2(33) - 1 = 65$.

8. **A** Because angles that are opposite equal sides are equal, $\angle ABC = \angle BCA = 45$. Because $\angle ADC$ is 90 and $\angle BCA = 45$, triangle ADC is a 45:45:90 triangle, with sides in the ratio of $x : x : x\sqrt{2}$. The side across from the 90-degree-side is 4, so $x\sqrt{2} = 4$. Divide by $\sqrt{2}$ to find that $x = \dfrac{4}{\sqrt{2}} = \dfrac{4}{\sqrt{2}} \times \dfrac{\sqrt{2}}{\sqrt{2}} = \dfrac{4\sqrt{2}}{2} = 2\sqrt{2}$.

12. **B**   The perimeter of a square is $4s$. So, $28 = 4s$. Divide by 4 to find

$s = 7$. The diagonal of a square divides the square into two

45:45:90 triangles, with sides in the ratio of $x:x:x\sqrt{2}$. If the side is 7,

the diagonal is $7\sqrt{2}$.

20. **D**   Draw a line through or close to the points given: (0, 0), (1, 4),
(2, 10), (3, 16) (4, 19). Then use POE. The line is linear, not
quadratic, so you can eliminate E. It is also clear that the line
begins at the origin, so the y-intercept will be 0. This will eliminate
A and C. A slope of 25 is far too big—ballpark—so we can
eliminate B, leaving D.

17. **B**   Since every term in $3x^3 - 11x^2 - 42x$ has an x, you can factor out an
x to get $x(3x^2 - 11x - 42)$. The answer is B. Do not waste your time
factoring the rest of it.

20. **E**   Factor the top and bottom of $\dfrac{2x^2 - 7x - 15}{2x^3 + 13x^2 + 15x}$ to get

$\dfrac{(2x+3)(x-5)}{(2x+3)(x)(x+5)}$. Since $x \geq 10$, x cannot equal $-\dfrac{3}{2}$, so we can

cancel the $(2x + 3)$ terms to get $\dfrac{x-5}{(x)(x+5)}$ or $\dfrac{x-5}{x^2+5x}$.

PART ◆ IV

How to Crack the Writing Section

Introduction to Grammar

CAN YOU REALLY TEST WRITING ON A STANDARDIZED TEST?

ETS thinks so, but we would beg to differ. What the SAT calls a writing test is really a test of some grammar rules and your ability to crank out an essay in 25 minutes. But those two skills don't really indicate anything about your writing ability. All this section tests is your ability to conform to what essay graders at the SAT consider "good" writing. Based on these standards, William Shakespeare, Ernest Hemingway, and e.e. cummings would all be considered bad writers.

How Can That Be?

Once again, it's all about the "best" answer. In the real world, no one writes an essay in 25 minutes, and many acclaimed writers have a fairly loose conception of grammar. But the SAT is not like the real world, as by now you've surely realized. All we can do is suppress our anger and try to do the best we can on the SAT.

Joe Bloggs and the Writing Section

Like the critical reading questions, the questions in the Writing section do not follow a noticeable order of difficulty. However, knowing how Joe approaches questions in this section can still help us achieve a better score.

Joe's biggest mistake on the grammar questions is basing his answers on what sounds right. This approach, unfortunately, is just about the worst way to go about answering the questions. Most people do not speak in a grammatically correct way. Consider the following conversation:

> Boy (answering the phone): Hello? Who's there?
>
> Girl: It's me.
>
> Boy: Oh hey, where are you at?
>
> Girl: Me and my friends are headed to the movie theater. You coming?
>
> Boy: Cool. I'll be there.

Now listen to the same conversation, edited for grammatical correctness:

> Boy: Hello? Who's there?
>
> Girl: It is I.
>
> Boy: Oh, hey. At what location are you?
>
> Girl: My friends and I are headed to the movie theater. Would you like to join us?
>
> Boy: Indeed. I shall be there.

Chances are you don't talk like this, so it sounds strange to your ear. But that doesn't mean it's wrong. Joe thinks that awkward or weird-sounding sentences or phrases must be wrong. ETS uses this tendency to set traps. Look at the following sentence:

The <u>inconsistencies in</u> the witness's testimony
　　　　　A

<u>notwithstanding</u>, the jury had no choice but to
　　　B

conclude that the suspect <u>was not guilty</u> of the
　　　　　　　　　　　　　　C

charges <u>leveled</u> against him. <u>No error</u>
　　　　　D　　　　　　　　E

ANALYSIS

Joe reads this sentence and something just *sounds* wrong to him. He can't exactly put his finger on it, but he knows that he's supposed to find an error. So Joe decides that something must be wrong with B because he would never use a phrase such as *notwithstanding*. Once again, poor Joe has played right into ETS's devious little hands. ETS hopes that you select answers based on how you would speak.

In this case, the sentence is actually fine as written. Now, you may have noticed that or you might have fallen for a Joe Bloggs's answer. In any case, the questions in the Writing section can be some of the most frustrating on the test. You can't always be sure of the best answer, but make sure you get rid of any answers you know to be wrong.

THE IMPORTANCE OF POE

Process of Elimination is super important on the Writing section. On many questions, you won't be 100-percent certain of the best answer. Even so, you can still eliminate as many wrong answers as you can and then take a guess. Be aggressive!

16
Grammar

WHAT'S IN THE WRITING SECTION?

You will see three types of multiple-choice questions in the Grammar sections: error identifications (a.k.a. Error ID), improving sentences (where you're asked to make a sentence sound better), and improving paragraphs (where you fix errors in a poorly written passage).

Now, before you get worried about all of the grammar rules you've forgotten (or never managed to learn), relax: You have seen this section before. It's simply the PSAT's Writing Skills section, with a new name but the same old attitude. As on the PSAT, ETS is only checking a few, select rules of grammar. Regardless of whether you remember these rules from the PSAT, we will be going over each of the ones you'll need.

The essay is not as bad as it sounds, either. The College Board will present either a statement of opinion (roughly a paragraph long) made by a notable person, or two statements from different people. Then you'll write a two-page essay (approximately) arguing how you feel about the statement(s), and why. Heck, ETS is even kind enough to give you a few options to start approaching the topic.

How to Ace the Writing Section

- Review and learn the rules of grammar, SAT-style.

- Memorize your plan of attack for each type of question.

- Know which questions to do right away and which to skip until the end.

- Understand what the essay graders want from you.

QUESTION STRATEGY

Every question type on the SAT can be cracked, and Grammar section questions are no exception. While reviewing the basic grammar you need, you will also learn how to crack error ID and improving sentences questions. After you solidify your approach to these question types, you'll learn how to crack improving paragraphs questions by employing the grammar and skills you've already mastered. Of course, you need to practice this stuff to really make it work. After working through the drills in this chapter, be sure to take a full-length practice test.

To Do or Not To Do

The Writing section is not arranged in order of difficulty; therefore, to do well on these questions, you need to determine when a problem is hard and should be skipped. What makes a question hard? It either contains grammar that you don't know, or it's long and time-consuming. As a general rule, you will approach the section in this order: Do error IDs first, since they're quick and POE works well on these; do improving sentences questions next, but plan to skip ones in which the entire sentence is underlined; do improving paragraphs questions last because they require dealing with an entire passage for only five questions.

Before we begin reviewing ETS's grammar, let's take a peek at the first two question types you'll see on the Writing section.

Error ID

<u>This</u> is an <u>example</u> of an error ID
  A   B
question <u>that</u> <u>has</u> no error. <u>No error</u>
      C D   E

An error ID question gives you a sentence that has four words or phrases underlined, each with a corresponding letter underneath. At the end of each sentence will be "No error"—choice E. There are some important things you need to know about error IDs:

- There is never more than one error per sentence.

- If there is an error, it's always underlined.

- Approximately 20 percent of all error ID questions are correct as written, so don't be afraid to pick choice E.

- Error IDs are short, and you should usually be able to eliminate at least one answer choice, so guess on all error ID questions.

- Do error ID questions first.

Improving Sentences

This is an example of an improving sentences question <u>that does not contain</u> an error.

(A) that does not contain
(B) that has not been containing
(C) which has not been contain
(D) which is not being with
(E) about which there is nothing to indicate it
      being with

Improving sentences questions give you a sentence, part or all of which is underlined. The underlined part may or may not contain a grammatical error. There are some important things you need to know about improving sentences questions:

- Answer choice A is a reprint of the underlined section. Therefore, if you decide that the sentence contains no error, choose answer choice A.

- Approximately 20 percent of all improving sentences questions are correct as written, so don't be afraid to pick choice A.

- If you decide the underlined portion of the sentence contains an error, eliminate choice A. Also, eliminate any other choice that does not fix the error.

- If you are unsure whether the sentence contains an error, look to your answer choices for a clue (more on this later).

- KISS: Keep It Short and Sweet. Concise answers are preferable.

GRAMMAR? UGH!

To do well on the Writing section, you need to remember some basic grammar rules. Now, don't get worked up about being tested on grammar. SAT grammar is not difficult, nor is it extensive. In fact, the Writing section really only tests five basic grammatical concepts:

1. verbs
2. nouns
3. pronouns
4. prepositions
5. other little things

These are the five areas in which a sentence can "go wrong." They will function as a checklist for you—every time you read a sentence, you will look at these five areas to find the error. If you don't find one after checking these five things, then there probably isn't one.

Everything Is Just Ruined

Remember, only the underlined portion can have an error. Don't try to fix things that aren't underlined.

NO ERROR?

As we've mentioned, 20 percent of error ID questions and improving sentences questions contain no error. If you've used your checklist and can't find a mistake, chances are there isn't one. Don't be afraid to pick "No error"—E on error ID and A on improving sentences questions.

We will use error ID questions to illustrate the first four areas of grammar. Before we get going on the grammar stuff, let's learn how to crack an error ID question.

CRACKING ERROR IDs

As we mentioned, an error ID question is a short sentence that has four words or phrases underlined and lettered. Your job is to determine if any one of those four underlined segments contains an error. If it does, you are to blacken the corresponding oval on your answer sheet. If not, you are to choose E "No error."

Let's look at an example of an error ID to learn how to beat these questions:

Jose told the school counselor <u>his plan</u>: he <u>will</u>
                                    A   B

attend college, major <u>in criminal justice</u>, and
                                      C

<u>to become</u> a lawyer. <u>No error</u>
     D   E

THE APPROACH

To solve an error ID, you need to look at the sentence one piece at a time. As you read through the sentence, pause after each underlined segment and ask, "Is there anything wrong yet?" Run through the first four categories of your grammar checklist. Verb problem? Noun problem? Pronoun problem? Preposition problem? If these four areas check out, cross off the segment (it's not your answer) and move on.

Look at the first segment of this sentence: *Jose told the school counselor his plan…* Is there a problem with the phrase *his plan*? No. Put a slash through answer choice A. Next segment: *he will….* Any problem with this verb? No, it's in the future tense and it's Jose's plan we're talking about, so everything is fine. Cross it off.

Continuing on: *major in criminal justice….* No problem here—cross off C. Keep going: *and to become a lawyer.* Wait a minute—something doesn't sound right. *To become* is a verb. Notice in this example, there is a series of activities (verbs) *attend*, *major*, *to become*. When in a series, all the verbs need to have the same form. Therefore *to become* should be *become*. The answer is D.

By the way, you have just learned the first verb rule: When a series of activities is described in a sentence, make sure all the verbs are expressed the same way—make sure they are *parallel*.

TRIM THE FAT

Often an error ID will contain extraneous phrases that distract from the meat of the sentence and cause you to miss an error. How can you avoid getting waylaid by distracting phrases? Trim the fat. As you work through a sentence, cross off anything that is not essential to the sentence: prepositional phrases, phrases offset by commas, etc. Crossing out the distracting phrases puts the important parts of a sentence, the subject and verb for example, together and prevents you from making careless errors.

Let's look at another example:

Math, <u>developed</u> over 2,000 years ago,
   A

<u>have been</u> a favorite <u>of</u> teachers and school children
  B   C

<u>alike</u> for generations. <u>No error</u>
 D   E

Here's How to Crack It

First, trim the fat. What's the subject of the sentence? *Math*. Once you see that there is no problem with choice A, *developed*, you can cross off the stuff between the commas—it's there to distract you. What's the verb? *Have been*. "*Math* have been?" Don't think so. *Math* is singular, so it needs a singular verb. The answer is B.

BE AGGRESSIVE

Error IDs are typically short and uncomplicated. Be aggressive as you go through these sentences. Read the sentence quickly once, keeping your checklist in mind. If you spot a problem, jump to it—you don't need to labor over the whole sentence if your eye is drawn to a problem right away.

DO I HAVE TO READ THE WHOLE THING?

Once you've found the error, do you need to read the rest of the sentence? Well, if you're sure of the error you've found, a quick read will be easy and reassuring. If you are not so sure, you will need to read the rest of the sentence to be sure you haven't missed anything. Since error IDs are short and sweet, take a quick second to read them through.

GUESSING

There are three reasons why you should always guess on an error ID question:

1. **You can always eliminate at least one answer choice.** If you read a sentence that sounds wrong, you can immediately eliminate answer choice E, even if you are not sure which underlined segment is the culprit.

2. **The odds are with you.** Only one of the four underlined parts of the sentence is wrong, if any at all. You're bound to be able to determine that a few of the segments are correct even if your grammar's not great.

3. **You don't have to fix the error in the sentence; you only have to identify it.** Therefore, guessing is easy. Once you've narrowed it down, take a guess and move on.

As we review the first four areas of grammar, you will work through a bunch of error ID questions. This will give you a feel for how they work and how easy it is to guess aggressively.

Now that you know how to approach error IDs, let's work on reviewing ETS's grammar rules.

VERBS

A verb is an action word. It tells what the subject of the sentence is doing. You've already seen two ways in which a verb can "go wrong." There are a total of three things about a verb to check out:

1. Does it **agree** with its subject?

2. Is it **parallel** in structure to the other verbs in the sentence?

3. Is it in the proper **tense**?

Do They Agree?

The rule regarding subject-verb agreement is simple: singular with singular, plural with plural. If you are given a singular subject (*he, she, it*), then your verb must also be singular (*is, has, was*). (In case you don't remember, the subject of the sentence is the noun that the verb modifies—the person or thing that is *doing* the action.)

Easy enough, except, as you have already seen, ETS has a way of putting lots of stuff between the subject and the verb to make you forget whether your subject was singular or plural. Remember *Math* from the last example? Look at another:

<blockquote>
The answers <u>given by</u> the commission <u>appears</u> to
           A   B
contradict the <u>earlier</u> testimony of <u>its</u> members.
             C   D
<u>No error</u>
    E
</blockquote>

Here's How to Crack It

At first glance, this sentence may appear fine. But let's pull it apart. What is the sentence about? The *answers*—a plural subject. If the subject is plural, then the verb must be plural, too. *Appears* is the verb modifying *answers*, but it is a singular verb—no can do. The answer is B.

Why did the sentence sound okay at first? Because of the stuff stuck between *answers* and *appears*. The phrase *given by the commission* places a singular noun right before the verb. Get rid of the extraneous stuff (i.e., trim the fat) and the error becomes obvious.

Knowing When It's Singlular

Sometimes you may not know if a noun is singular or plural, making it tough to determine whether its verb should be singular or plural. Of course you know nouns like *he* and *cat* are singular, but what about *family* or *everybody*? The following is a list of "tricky" nouns—technically called collective nouns. They are nouns that typically describe a group of people but are considered singular and thus need a singular verb:

The family *is*

The jury *is*

The group *is*

The team *is*

The audience *is*

The congregation *is*

The United States (or any other country) *is*

The following pronouns also take singular verbs:

Either *is*

Neither *is*

None *is*

Each *is*

Anyone *is*

No one *is*

Everyone *is*

And or Or

Subjects joined by *and* are plural: Bill and Pat *were* going to the show. However, nouns joined by *or* can be singular or plural—if the last noun given is singular, then it takes a singular verb; if the last noun given is plural, it takes a plural verb.

John Keats and Percy Bysshe Shelley, <u>each of whom</u>
                                       A   B

is an accomplished <u>Romantic poet,</u> <u>is</u> still well-known today.
                          C   D

<u>No error</u>
   E

Here's How to Crack It

Once again ETS is trying to trip you up by separating the subject from the verb. You know what to do—trim the fat! What's the subject? *John Keats and Percy Bysshe Shelley*. We know the subject is plural because of the *and*. Cross off the stuff between commas and you have *John Keats and Percy Bysshe Shelley . . . is*. Can we use the singular verb *is* with our plural subject? No way—the answer is D.

Are They Parallel?

The next thing you need to check out about a verb is whether it and the other verbs in the sentence are parallel. In the first example used in this chapter, Jose was going to *attend, major,* and *to become.* The last verb, *to become,* is not written in the same form as the other verbs in the series. In other words, it's not parallel. The sentence should read, *Jose will attend college, major in criminal justice, and become a lawyer.*

Try another example:

As <u>a new member</u> of the secret society, George <u>was</u>
    A   B

<u>required</u> to shine the senior members' shoes, to
   C

carry their books, and <u>never revealing</u> the identities
                                 D

of the other members. <u>No error</u>
                           E

Here's How to Crack It

If an error ID contains an underlined verb that is part of a series of activities, isolate the verbs to see if they are parallel. In this sentence, George is required *to shine, to carry,* and *revealing.* What's the problem? He should be required *to shine, to carry,* and *to reveal.* The answer is D.

Are You Tense?

As you know, verbs come in different tenses—for example, *is* is present tense, while *was* is past tense. You've probably heard of other tenses like "past perfect." Well, first of all, don't worry about identifying the kind of tense used in a sentence—you will never be asked to identify verb tense, only to make sure that the tense is consistent throughout a sentence.

For the most part, verb tense should not change within a sentence. Look at the following example:

In Colonial times, children often <u>do not attend</u> high
A   B

school, <u>knowing that</u> they were needed <u>to help with</u>
               C   D

the family business. <u>No error</u>
                      E

Here's How to Crack It

Our subject? *Children.* Our verb? *Attend*—which would be fine if the sentence hadn't started out with *In Colonial times....* Is the sentence talking about children attending (or not attending) school right now? No, it's talking about Colonial times. The verb should be *attended*—the answer is B. If you missed that clue, you should still compare the other verbs in the sentence—*were needed* is in the past tense, and since it's not underlined, we know the other verbs in the sentence should match it.

NOUNS

The only thing you really have to check for with nouns is agreement. Agreement is a big thing for most grammarians, ETS included. Verbs must agree with their subjects, nouns must agree with other nouns, and pronouns must agree with the nouns they represent. When you read an error ID, if you come across an underlined noun, check to see if it refers to or is associated with any other nouns in the sentence. If so, make sure they match in number.

For example:

Some animals, <u>such as</u> the hedgehog, appear <u>quite</u>
              A   B
timid but <u>they can become</u> fierce enemies when
                     C
they perceive a threat to their <u>baby</u>. <u>No error</u>
                                  D   E

Here's How to Crack It

Take it one piece at a time. … *such as the hedgehog…* sounds good. Cross off A. Continuing on, *appear quite timid….* No problem that we can see. Cross it off. Going on, … *but they can become fierce enemies…* checks out. Remember, the subject is *some animals*, not *the hedgehog*. So cross off C.

The last part of the sentence reads… *when they perceive a threat to their baby. Their* is okay; we're referring to a bunch of animals. But what about *baby*? Since we are discussing *some animals*, which is plural, we need to make sure *baby* is plural as well—in other words it should read the *babies* of *some animals*. The answer is D.

PRONOUNS

As with verbs, there are three things you need to check when you have pronouns:

1. Do they **agree**?

2. Are they **ambiguous**?

3. Do they use the right **case**?

I Agree

As you know, a pronoun is a little word that is inserted to represent a noun (*he*, *she*, *it*, *they*, etc.). As with everything else, pronouns must agree with their nouns: The pronoun that replaces a singular noun must also be singular, and the pronoun that replaces a plural noun must be plural. If different pronouns are used to refer to the same subject or one pronoun is used to replace another, the pronouns must also agree.

This may seem obvious, but it is also the most commonly violated rule in ordinary speech. How often have you heard people say, *Everyone must hand in their application before leaving*. Remember from our list of singular pronouns that *everyone* is singular? But *their* is plural. This sentence is incorrect.

To spot a pronoun agreement error, look for pronouns that show up later in a sentence. If you see a pronoun underlined, find the noun or pronoun it is replacing and make sure the two agree. Let's look at an example:

Pronouns

Subject → Verb
  Singular → Singular
  Plural → Plural

Everyone <u>in the department</u> <u>who worked with</u>
            A   B

Heather personally congratulated her

<u>on her promotion</u> and told her how much <u>they</u>
      C   D

enjoyed her company. <u>No error</u>
                      E

Here's How to Crack It

Is there an underlined pronoun late in this sentence? There sure is: *they*. Let's trim the fat to check this sentence:

Everyone… who worked… congratulated her… and told her… they enjoyed…
Everyone is singular, but *they* is plural, so it cannot replace *everyone*.
The answer is D.

To Whom Do You Refer?

When a pronoun appears in a sentence, it should be infinitely clear which noun it replaces. For example:

"After looking over the color samples, Mary agreed with Martha that her porch should be painted green."

Whose porch is being painted green? Mary's or Martha's? This sentence would be unacceptable to ETS because it is not perfectly clear to whom the word *her* in the sentence is referring. This is pronoun ambiguity, and it is unacceptable on the SAT.

If you see a pronoun late in a sentence, check to see if it clearly refers to a noun. Be especially wary if the early part of the sentence contains two singular or two plural nouns. Try the following example:

Whatcha Talkin' About, Willis?

A pronoun replaces a noun, but you always have to be clear which noun it replaces. It's not enough for you to guess. In ETS's world, you have to know for sure. If not, that's the error.

The drummer <u>told</u> the guitar player that <u>he</u> was an
             A   B

integral part <u>of the band</u> and could not easily
                    C

<u>be replaced</u>. <u>No error</u>
     D   E

Here's How to Crack It

Let's take it apart a piece at a time. *The drummer told*... Do a quick tense scan of the sentence. Is it past tense? Yes. Cross off A and go on.

Let's trim the fat to check the next answer choice:

The drummer told the guitar player... *that he was an integral part*...

Who was an integral part? It is not clear whether the pronoun *he* is referring to the drummer or the guitar player. The answer is B.

CASE? WHAT CASE?

Pronouns come in two "flavors," known as cases: subjective or objective. The subject, as you know, is the person or thing performing the action in the sentence. The object is the person or thing *receiving* the action. Think of it this way: An object just sits there. It doesn't *do* anything; rather, things are done to it. The subject, by contrast, does something.

When it comes to pronouns, subjects and objects are represented by different pronouns. For example, *I* is a subjective pronoun, as in *I did it*, while *me* is an objective pronoun, as in *it happened to me*. Most of the time, you will know if the wrong pronoun case (as it's called) is used because the sentence will sound funny. However, this is another area that is often butchered in our spoken language. When in doubt, trim the fat to figure out whether the pronoun is the subject (performing the action) or the object (receiving the action).

SUBJECT PRONOUNS

Singular	Plural
I	We
You	You
He	They
She	They
It	They
Who	Who

OBJECT PRONOUNS

Singular	Plural
Me	Us
You	You
Him	Them
Her	Them
It	Them
Whom	Whom

Try the following example:

The safety check <u>of the new vehicle</u>, including an
                        A

<u>inspection of</u> the brakes and wheel alignment,
        B

<u>was performed by</u> the mechanic and <u>him</u>. <u>No error</u>
        C   D   E

Here's How to Crack It

Read through the sentence, checking each underlined segment. *The safety check of the new vehicle....* No problem here—cross off A and move on. Next segment: *... an inspection of....* Again, it seems fine. Cross it out and keep going.

To check the next two, do a little cutting: *The safety check... was performed by the mechanic and him. Performed by* is fine. What about *him*? Get rid of *the mechanic* to check: *The... the safety check... was performed by... him. Him* is an objective pronoun and, in this sentence, is used correctly. *He performed* would need the subjective pronoun; *performed by him* is the correct use of the objective pronoun. The answer is E, no error.

I OR *ME*?

Are you frequently being corrected on the *I* versus *me* thing? If so, you're not alone. In the example we just did, if you were to replace *him* with either *I* or *me*, which would it be? You would use *me* since you need an objective pronoun. It is often difficult to tell which case to use when the pronoun is coupled with another noun or pronoun. If you are having trouble deciding which case to use, remember to trim the fat: In this case, remove the other person (*the mechanic* in the example we just did).

Which One Is Correct?

The book belongs to Jerry and I.

The book belongs to Jerry and me.

If you're not sure, take Jerry out of the picture:

The book belongs to _____.

Me, of course. It's much easier to tell which is correct if the extraneous stuff is removed. Here's a tricky one:

Clare is more creative than me.

Clare is more creative than I.

Be careful. This may look as though the pronoun is an object, but actually the sentence is written in an incomplete form. What you are really saying in this sentence is *Clare is more creative than I <u>am</u>*. The *am* is understood. When in doubt, say the sentence aloud, adding on the *am* to see whether it is hiding at the end of the sentence.

DON'T BE PASSIVE

One final note about subjects and objects: ETS prefers sentences written in the active voice to the passive voice. If a sentence is written in the active voice, the subject of the sentence is doing something. If a sentence is written in the passive voice, the main player becomes an object and things happen to him.

Which of the following is written in the active voice?

She took the SAT.

The SAT was taken by her.

She took the SAT is active because *she* is the subject of the sentence and *she* is doing something. *The SAT was taken by her* is passive because *her* is now the object of *by*, not the subject of the sentence. This will be important to know when attacking improving sentences questions.

PREPOSITIONS

Remember prepositions? *About, above, across, around, along*....You use prepositions all the time to add information to a sentence. Using different prepositions can change the meaning of a sentence. For example:

I am standing *by* you.

I am standing *for* you.

I am standing *near* you.

I am standing *under* you.

DRILL 1

In the English language, certain words must be paired with certain prepositions. These pairs of words are called *idioms*. There are really no rules to idioms, so you need to just use your ear and memorize ones that are tricky. Here is a list of some common idioms you may come across. Fill in the blanks with the missing prepositions (some may have more than one possibility). Answers can be found on page 341.

1. I am *indebted* ___to___ you.

2. I am *resentful* ___of___ you.

3. I am *delighted* ___for___ you.

4. I am *jealous* ___of___ you.

5. I am *worried* ___about___ you.

6. I am *astounded* ___by___ you.

7. The women had a *dispute* ___over___ politics.

8. You have a *responsibility* _to_ take care of your pet.

9. My friends are not so *different* _from_ your friends.

Try an error ID example:

<u>After</u> seeing Andy <u>fall into</u> the crocodile pit, his
  A   B

girlfriend <u>admitted that</u> she was <u>worried for</u> him.
         C   D

<u>No error</u>
  E

Here's How to Crack It

Let's pull it apart: *After seeing Andy fall into...* Both of these seem okay so let's move on. Next phrase: *his girlfriend admitted that...* No problem there. How about the next part, *worried for him*. You may have heard people say this, but it's wrong. The preposition that should accompany *worry* is *about*. The answer is D.

ERROR ID AND YOUR GRAMMAR CHECKLIST

Let's do a quick review. On error ID questions, have your grammar checklist ready (keep it in your head, or jot it on your test booklet). It should look like this:

1. Is there an underlined **verb**? If so,
   (a) does it **agree** with its subject?
   (b) is it **parallel** in structure to the other verbs in the sentence?
   (c) is it in the proper **tense**?

2. Is there an underlined **noun**? If so,
   (a) does it **agree** in number with any other noun to which it refers?

3. Is there an underlined **pronoun**? If so,
   (a) does it **agree** with the noun/pronoun it represents?
   (b) can you tell to which noun it refers or is it **ambiguous**?
   (c) does it use the right **case** (subjective or objective)?

4. Is there an underlined **preposition**? If so,
   (a) is it the **right one**?

When you approach error ID questions, remember to:

- read them with your checklist in mind

- cross off underlined stuff that is right

- trim the fat

- not be afraid to pick E, "No error"

- guess if you don't know the answer

DRILL 2

Use the following drill to solidify your error ID strategy. Answers can be found on page 341.

1. <u>Although many</u> young children would <u>like to</u> have
      A   B

   a pet, most find <u>it</u> difficult to be <u>responsible to</u>
                 C   (D)

   another living creature at such a tender age.

   <u>No error</u>
      E

2. I <u>told</u> my English teacher that <u>the best part</u> of the
    A   B

   novel was <u>where</u> the antagonist finally realized the
          (C)   *when*

   error of <u>his ways</u>. <u>No error</u>
        (D)   E

3. <u>It</u> was only last month <u>that</u> the hockey playoffs
   A   B

   <u>finally ended</u>, but the new season <u>has started</u> today.
      C   (D)

   <u>No error</u>
      E

4. The postman <u>assured</u> <u>his customers</u> that neither
           A   B

   sleet nor snow <u>were</u> the <u>cause of</u> the delay in their
            (C)   D

   mail delivery. <u>No error</u>
           E

5. Sports journalists <u>have debated</u> whether it is a
               A

   <u>more strenuous</u> task to box for <u>ten rounds</u> or
      B   C

   <u>running a marathon</u>. <u>No error</u>
      (D)   E

6. Regular exercise and a healthy diet <u>will</u> not only
                        A

   <u>increase</u> a person's energy level <u>but also</u> <u>improving</u>
      B   C   (D)

   physical fitness. <u>No error</u>
            E

IMPROVING SENTENCES

So far we have been concentrating on error ID questions while reviewing grammar. The good news is that Improving Sentences questions test a lot of the same grammar. Let's look at a sample question to see how to crack these questions.

Although Senator Fritz and Senator Pierce have both proposed plans to reduce the deficit, <u>only one of the two are viable</u>.

(A) only one of the two are viable
(B) only one of the two is viable
(C) only one of the two plans are viable
(D) only one of the two plans is viable
(E) one only of the two plans has been viable

Here's How to Crack It

There are two ways to go about cracking an improving sentences question. The preferable way is for you to identify the error as you read the underlined part of the sentence. How will you do that, you ask? By using your handy-dandy grammar checklist, of course. Let's try it on this example. The underlined portion of the sentence says *only one of the two are viable*. Let's run through your list. Is there an underlined verb? Yes— *are*. Does it agree with its subject? What is its subject? If we trim the fat (in this case, the prepositional phrase *of the two*) we can easily see the subject is *one*. Is it correct to say *one are*? Of course not.

So you've identified the problem. However, improving sentences questions require you to go further than just identifying the error—they also require you to fix the error, thus "improving" the sentence. To do this, you will use your old friend: Process of Elimination. First, we know that answer choice A is simply a repeat of the underlined portion; therefore, once you've identified an error, cross off answer choice A.

Next, scan the rest of the answer choices and cross off any answer choices that don't fix the problem you've identified. In our example, we know the verb *are* is wrong. What answer choice can we get rid of? Answer choice C.

So far, we have eliminated answer choices A and C. Let's look at the remaining choices to see how they fix the error we found. Answer choice B changes *are* to *is*, a singular verb. That works. Answer choice D does the same thing. Both of these choices are possible. Answer choice E changes the verb to *has been*. A quick glance at the sentence tells us that this is in the wrong tense—we need present tense. Cross off answer choice E.

Okay, down to two. The last thing to check is the difference between the two choices that fixed the original problem. Sometimes the underlined portion of the sentence contains a secondary error that also needs to be fixed. Other times, an answer may fix the original problem, but introduce a new error. In this example, the difference between B and D is that B uses the vague language *only one of the two is viable* while D clarifies *only one of the two plans is viable*. We know that ETS hates to be ambiguous, and B does not make it as clear that the sentence is referring to one of the two plans as opposed to one of the two senators. Therefore, our answer is D.

Can You Say Time-Consuming?

Wow—that took a while! As you can see, improving sentences questions are a bit more work than error IDs. That's why you want to do all the error ID questions before you attempt the improving sentences questions. Also, you may, on occasion, find it necessary to skip a question, especially one where the whole sentence is underlined. As a general rule, if you can spot the error, you should do the question, since POE is on your side. If you can't spot the error immediately, try the back-up plan, but be ready to back out if you are spending too much time on the question.

BACK-UP PLAN?

What's the back-up plan? Let's say you couldn't tell if there was an error in the example we just did. You thought it might be okay, but you weren't sure. How could you check? By scanning your answer choices. Your answer choices can tip you off to the error contained in a sentence by revealing what is being fixed in each choice. In the example we just did, a quick scan of the answer choices reveals that the verb is being altered:

>   (A) . . . are . . .
>   (B) . . . is . . .
>   (C) . . . are . . .
>   (D) . . . is . . .
>   (E) . . . has been . . .

Once you pick up on the error being tested, you can try to figure out which form is correct. Let's try another example, using our back-up plan to illustrate how it works:

> When students are told they will be tested on a
> subject, <u>you tend to be more anxious and find it
> harder to retain the information</u>.
>
> (A) you tend to be more anxious and find it harder
>   to retain the information
> (B) students being more anxious find it harder to
>   retain the information
> (C) they tend to be more anxious and find it harder
>   to retain information that will be tested
> (D) they tend to be more anxious and find it harder
>   to retain the information
> (E) you tend towards anxiety and a failure to
>   retain information

Here's How to Crack It

When you first read this sentence, you may feel that something is wrong, but may not be able to pinpoint what it is. No problem—let your answer choices do the work for you. A quick scan of the answer choices reveals a possible pronoun problem:

>   (A) you . . .
>   (B) students . . .
>   (C) they . . .
>   (D) they . . .
>   (E) you . . .

Now that you know what to check, let's trim the fat:

When students are told they will be tested… you…

Is *you* the right pronoun to represent *students*? No. Cross off A and any other answer that doesn't fix the *you*. That leaves us with B, C, and D. If you have no idea how the rest of the sentence should read, you've still given yourself great odds of "guessing" this question correctly. But let's forge ahead.

Answer choice B doesn't make any sense upon closer inspection. Cross it off. Now you're down to two. Which answer choice is more clear and less awkward? Answer choice D:

> *When students are told they will be tested… they tend to be more anxious and find it harder to retain the information.*

OTHER LITTLE THINGS

We mentioned back at the beginning of this chapter that your grammar checklist should include a number 5: "other little things." In addition to testing the four main areas we've already reviewed, other little grammar things will be tested on the improving sentences questions. Let's look at some of these little grammar tidbits so you are ready for them when they turn up.

If everything else checks out, the sentence may be testing other little things like:

- faulty comparisons
- misplaced modifiers
- adjectives/adverbs
- diction

CAN YOU COMPARE?

There are several little things ETS tries to trip you up with when it comes to comparing. These things are not difficult, but are notoriously misused in spoken English, so you will need to make a note of them. First, when comparing two things, make sure that what you are comparing can be compared. Sound like double-talk? Look at the following sentence:

> Larry goes shopping at Foodtown because the prices are better than Shoprite.

Sound okay? Well, sorry—it's wrong. As written, this sentence says that the prices at Foodtown are better than Shoprite—the entire store. What Larry means is the prices at Foodtown are better than the *prices* at Shoprite. You can only compare like things (prices to prices, not prices to stores).

While we're on the subject of Foodtown, how many of you have seen this sign?

> Express Checkout: Ten items or less.

Unfortunately, supermarkets across America are making a blatant grammatical error when they post this sign. When items can be counted, you must use the word *fewer*. If something cannot be counted, you would use the word *less*. For example:

> If you eat *fewer* french fries, you can use *less* ketchup.

Other similar words include *many* (can be counted) versus *much* (cannot be counted):

> *Many* hands make *much* less work.

Another pair to watch out for is *number* (can be counted) versus *amount* (cannot be counted):

> The same *number* of CDs played different *amounts* of music.

Two's Company; Three or More Is . . .?

Finally, the English language uses different comparison words when comparing two things than when comparing more than two things. The following examples will jog your memory:

- **more** (for two things) vs. **most** (for more than two)
  Given Alex and Dave as possible dates, Alex is the *more* appealing one.
  In fact, of all the guys I know, Alex is the *most* attractive.

- **less** (for two things) vs. **least** (for more than two)
  I am *less* likely to be chosen than you are.
  I am the *least* likely person to be chosen from the department.

- **better** (for two things) vs. **best** (for more than two)
  Taking a cab is *better* than hitchhiking.
  My Princeton Review teacher is the *best* teacher I have ever had.

- **between** (for two things) vs. **among** (for more than two)
  Just *between* you and me, I never liked her anyway.
  Among all the people here, no one likes her.

Try this one:

> Suzie was excited because her fantasy baseball team <u>was far better than Justin</u>.
>
> (A) was far better than Justin
> (B) did far better as Justin
> (C) was far better than Justin's team
> (D) did seem superior to Justin
> (E) was far better than the team of Justin

Here's How to Crack It

What is being compared in this sentence? Susie is comparing her team with Justin. Can she do that? No! She really wants to compare her team with Justin's team.

Since you have identified an error, immediately cross off A. Next, cross off any other answer choice that doesn't fix the error. That gets rid of B and D. Now compare our remaining choices. While E technically fixes our comparison problem, it introduces a new error (*than* is incorrect) and is awkwardly worded. ETS's answer is C.

MISPLACED MODIFIERS

A modifier is a descriptive word or phrase inserted in a sentence to add dimension to the thing it modifies. For example:

> *Because he could talk*, Mr. Ed was a unique horse.

Because he could talk is the modifying phrase in this sentence. It describes a characteristic of Mr. Ed. Generally speaking, a modifying phrase should be right next to the thing it modifies. If it's not, the meaning of the sentence may change. For example:

> Every time he goes to the bathroom outside, John praises his
> new puppy for being so good.

Who's going to the bathroom outside? In this sentence, it's John! There are laws against that! The descriptive phrase *every time he goes to the bathroom outside* needs to be near *puppy* in order for the sentence to say what it means.

When you are attacking improving sentences questions, watch out for sentences that begin with a descriptive phrase followed by a comma. If you see one, make sure the thing that comes after the comma is the person or thing being modified.

Try the following example:

> Clearly one of the most distinctive and impressive
> skylines in the country, New York City is a
> breathtaking sight to behold.
>
> (A) Clearly one of the most distinctive and
>   impressive skylines in the country
> (B) Being one of the most distinctive and
>   impressive skylines in the country
> (C) Possessing one of the most distinctive and
>   impressive skylines in the country
> (D) Its skyline may be the most distinctive and
>   impressive in the country
> (E) More distinctive and impressive in its skyline
>   than any other place in the country

Here's How to Crack It

Is New York City a type of skyline? No, so cross off A. We need an answer that will make the opening phrase modify *New York City*. Answer choice B is still modifying *skyline*, so cross it off. All three other choices fix the problem, but C does it the best. D makes the sentence ungrammatical, and E incorrectly uses *more*, which should be used only to compare. The answer is C.

ADJECTIVES/ADVERBS

Misplaced modifiers aren't the only descriptive errors ETS test writers throw at you. Another way they try to trip you up is by using adjectives where they should use adverbs and vice versa. Remember that an *adjective* modifies a noun, while an *adverb* modifies verbs, adverbs, and adjectives. The adverb is the one that usually has -*ly* on the end. In the following sentence, circle the adverbs and underline the adjectives:

> The stealthy thief, desperately hoping to evade the persistent police, ran quickly into the dank, dark alley after brazenly stealing the stunningly exquisite jewels.

First, let's list the adjectives along with the nouns they modify: *stealthy* thief, *persistent* police, *dank* alley, *dark* alley, *exquisite* jewels. Now for the adverbs with the words they modify: *desperately* hoping (verb), ran (verb) *quickly*, *brazenly* stealing (verb), *stunningly* exquisite (adjective).

Now try the following improving sentences example:

> A bacterium may not reproduce for months, but a sudden influx of heat, moisture, or food <u>can cause its growth rate to increase tremendous</u>.
>
> (A) can cause its growth rate to increase tremendous
> (B) can tremendously increase its growth rate
> (C) increase the tremendous growth rate of it
> (D) increases its growth rate in a tremendous way
> (E) tremendously causes the growth rate to increase

Here's How to Crack It

Hopefully you identified the error as soon as you read the sentence. What should the last word in the sentence be? *Tremendously.* Cross off A, and also D, since it doesn't fix the error and changes the meaning of the sentence. C is way out there, so cross it off, too. In E, the placement of the *tremendously* is awkward and slightly changes the meaning of the sentence. ETS's answer is B.

DICTION

Finally, ETS may occasionally slip in a diction error just to keep you on your toes. Diction means choice of words. Diction errors are tough to spot because the incorrect word often looks a lot like the word that should have been used.

DRILL 3

Here's a list of some potential diction traps. Indicate the difference between the words in each pair. Answers can be found on page 341.

1. Imminent _about to happen_
and Eminent _well known_ ?

2. Proscribe _forbid_
and Prescribe _order (doctor)_ ?

3. Intelligent _smart_
and Intelligible _can be deciphered_ ?

4. Incredible _amazing_
and Incredulous _disbelieving_ ?

5. Irritated _annoyed_
and Aggravated _made worse_ ?

6. Stationary _staying still_
and Stationery _paper_ ?

7. Illicit _illegal_
and Elicit _bring forth_ ?

DRILL 4

Before we move on to improving paragraphs questions, try putting together what you've learned. Do the following Error ID and Improving Sentences questions using your grammar checklist. Remember to trim the fat and use POE. On Improving Sentences questions, do not hesitate to check out the answer choices for a clue to help you spot the error. You may wish to jot down your grammar checklist before you begin. Answers can be found on page 342.

1. After the electricity <u>went</u> out, Dora stumbled <u>blind</u>
             A   (B)

   <u>about</u> her apartment <u>searching for</u> a candle.
    C   D

   <u>No error</u>
     E

2. <u>Heeding the advice</u> of <u>their</u> wise instructor,
        A   B

   Rasheed and Ben <u>each brought</u> a pencil and a
                   C

   calculator <u>to the test</u>. <u>No error</u>
         D   (E)

3. None <u>of the fish</u> in the aquarium <u>is</u> native to this
        A   B

part of the world, <u>having instead</u> been imported
                          C

<u>from overseas</u>. <u>No error</u>
    D   E

4. Since we <u>are</u> brothers, I don't think we
            A

<u>should allow</u> petty disagreements to come
      B

<u>between</u> you and <u>I</u>. <u>No error</u>
    C   D   E

5. Psychologists <u>have found that</u> it is difficult to think
                 A

<u>clear</u> when in a pressure situation, <u>especially</u> when
 B   C

<u>under</u> a time limit. <u>No error</u>
  D   E

6. <u>After</u> all of the day's chores <u>was completed</u> the
   A   B

family <u>sat down</u> to a <u>splendid</u> dinner. <u>No error</u>
        C   D   E

7. Critics often debate whether the role of art is
<u>one that is simply aesthetic or if it should be
instructional</u>.

(A) one that is simply aesthetic or if it should be
     instructional

(B) simply one that is aesthetic or being
     instructional

(C) one that is simply aesthetic or if it should have
     instruction as well

(D) simply an aesthetic one or an instructional one

(E) aesthetic or should it be instructional

8. The civil engineers who designed the city's
streets in the 1800's could <u>never have foreseen the
sprawling metropolis that the town would have
soon become</u>.

(A) never have foreseen the sprawling metropolis
     that the town would have soon become

(B) never have foreseen that the small town would
     soon become a sprawling metropolis

(C) have not foreseen the small town turning into
     a sprawling metropolis

(D) not have foreseen the sprawling metropolis
     that the small town became

(E) have never foreseen the small town being such
     a sprawling metropolis

9. The director felt that the actress was perfect for <u>the part, since he wanted her to</u> research the character first.

    (A) the part, since he wanted her to
    (B) the part, however the director wanted the actress to
    (C) the part, but he wanted her to
    (D) the part, only after she had to
    (E) the part, but wanting her to

10. <u>Cable television, which strikes some television watchers as a modern convenience, actually debuted in the 1940's, it was only used in rural areas at first.</u>

    (A) Cable television, which strikes some television watchers as a modern convenience, actually debuted in the 1940's, it was only used in rural areas at first.
    (B) Only used in rural areas at first, cable television, which strikes some television watchers as a modern convenience, actually debuted in the 1940's.
    (C) To be used only in rural areas, and striking some television watchers as a modern convenience, cable television actually debuted in the 1940's.
    (D) Debuting in 1940's, it was only used in rural areas at first and strikes some television watchers as a modern convenience is cable television.
    (E) Cable television was only used in rural areas at first, striking some television watchers as a modern convenience and actually debuting in the 1940's.

11. Jade is commonly found in two colors, <u>either green or the color is white, which is the more precious of the two</u>.

    (A) either green or the color is white, which is the more precious of the two
    (B) either green or white, although white jade is more precious than green jade
    (C) the color is either green or the color is white, with white being the more precious
    (D) with green or white as the color and white the most precious of the two
    (E) those colors are green and white, which is the more precious

12. The term "mach" does not refer to the speed of an aircraft or vehicle; <u>rather they are the ratio of the speed of sound to the speed of the craft.</u>

(A) rather they are the ratio of the speed of sound to the speed of the craft

(B) they are the ratio of the speed of sound to the speed of the craft rather

(C) instead it is the ratio of the speed of sound to the speed of the craft

(D) rather they are referring to the ratio of the speed of sound and the craft

(E) instead, it refers to the ratio of the speed of sound to the speed of the craft

IMPROVING PARAGRAPHS

Red Pencil Fever

There are probably more errors in the passage than you'll be asked to correct. Who cares? Only worry about the ones for which you'll get points—the ones in the questions.

After you do all of the error ID and improving sentences questions, you'll be left with six improving paragraphs questions. Luckily, these questions come last in the section. They are not particularly difficult, but they are more time-consuming than the other two question types.

The six improving paragraphs questions require you to make corrections to a replica "first draft" of a student's essay. You will be given a "rough draft" comprised of approximately three paragraphs. Each paragraph contains numbered sentences. Your job is to "edit" the rough draft to make it better.

Here is a sample passage:

(1) I'm not sure exactly how I turned out to be a hockey fan. (2) My father was always a big football fan, my mom loves baseball. (3) And my brothers and sisters don't like hockey, either. (4) In any case, I've loved hockey for as long as I can remember.

(5) But despite my love of hockey, I wasn't really that good at playing it. (6) Part of the problem is my skating, as in I'm not very good at it. (7) I didn't even learn to skate until I was twelve. (8) Most hockey players have been skating for their entire lives. (9) *Still,* I wanted to play and I asked my father to have me enrolled in a hockey camp. (10) He did and I went to it, not knowing what to expect. (11) On the first day of the camp, I barely knew how to put my equipment on. (12) Although the other kids were all about my age, they seemed to know so much more and be better players. (13) The first day on ice I was intimidated because they were all so good. (14) I thought that I didn't belong, but I love hockey so much that I wanted to stay. (15) I wanted badly to be able to play the sport that I loved.

(16) And it was worth it. (17) After I got more comfortable with my skills, I became confident. (18) The coaches at the camp really helped me a lot. (19) They told me exactly what I needed to do to be better. (20) Now, I've been playing hockey for three years and while I'm not the best player on the ice, I'm certainly one of the most passionate.

Now, before you get out your red pencil and jump in, there are a few more things you need to know. Your passage may consist of 15 to 20 or more sentences, each potentially containing some kind of error. However, you will only be asked a handful of questions. Don't spend time fixing errors for which there are no questions.

GO TO THE QUESTIONS

Instead of wasting a lot of time reading the rough draft, go directly to the questions. There are far more errors in the passage than you'll ever be asked about—reading the passage first will simply waste your time and confuse you.

Also, for many of the questions, the sentences you need to fix are reprinted right under the question, so you won't necessarily need to go back to the paragraph to answer a question.

There are three basic types of questions that you will be asked:

1. **Revision questions:** These questions ask you to revise sentences or parts of sentences in much the same way as Improving Sentences questions do.

2. **Combination questions:** These questions ask you to combine two or more sentences to improve the quality and/or flow of the paragraph.

3. **Content questions:** These questions ask you about passage content, typically by asking you to insert a sentence before or after a paragraph.

REVISION QUESTIONS

As we mentioned, these questions are very similar to improving sentences questions. Therefore, you can follow the same basic approach. One warning: *There is normally no such thing as "No error" on improving paragraphs questions. Do not assume that A is merely a repeat of the given sentence.*

Even though the sentence you are revising is provided for you, you may still need to go back to the passage to gain some context when trying to fix a sentence. Before going back, however, use POE. If you have spotted an error in the given sentence, cross off answers that don't fix it. Also, cross off answer choices that contain obvious errors. After doing some POE, go back and read a few sentences before and after the given sentence. This should be enough context for you to determine the best edit.

Try the following revision question—refer back to the sample passage when needed.

In context, which is the best way to revise sentence 6 (reproduced below)?

Part of the problem is my skating, as in I'm not very good at it.

(A) One of my problems was my limited skating ability.

(B) Not skating well was a big problem of mine.

(C) A problem was that my skating needed to be better than it was.

(D) Of my problems, I would say that my bad skating was the biggest.

(E) Skating, I'm not very good at it, was part of my problems.

Here's How to Crack It

The correct revision will be concise and unambiguous. It will also flow well. We can get rid of choices B, D, and E before going back to the passage. Choice B is as clunky as the given sentence; choices D and E are awkwardly written.

After doing some elimination, go back and read, beginning with line 5. The author states that he wasn't good at playing. Why not? Apparently the problem is his skating. Answer A is the best choice. When you read this segment, the word *next* should be jumping into your brain. Sentence 6 seems out of place until you realize that it is a new thought, the next step. ETS's answer is A.

COMBINATION QUESTIONS

Combination questions are revision questions with a twist: You are working with two sentences instead of one. The sentences are almost always reprinted for you under the question and you can usually answer these questions without going back to the passage at all. As with revision questions, do what you can first, then go back to the passage if necessary.

To combine sentences you will need to work with conjunctions. If the sentences are flowing in the same direction, look for an answer with words like *and*, *since*, *as well as*, etc. If the sentences seem to be flowing in opposite directions, look for trigger words in the answer choices such as *however*, *but*, *on the contrary*, etc.

Try the following without going back to the passage:

> Which of the following represents the most effective way to combine sentences 18 and 19 (reproduced below)?
>
> *The coaches at the camp really helped me a lot. They told me exactly what I needed to do to be better.*
>
> (A) The coaches who helped me a lot told me exactly what I needed to do be better.
>
> (B) Those coaches at the camp who told me exactly what I needed to do to be better were the ones who helped me the most.
>
> (C) Helping me a lot was the coaches, telling me exactly what I needed to do.
>
> (D) By telling me exactly what was needed to be done by me the coaches helped me a lot.
>
> (E) The coaches at the camp really helped me by telling me exactly what I needed to do to get better.

Here's How to Crack It

First, the sentences are moving in the same direction. Your job is to find a clear, concise way to combine them. A and B are out because they are poorly worded. Choice C contains an agreement error, and D is passive. The best answer is E.

Try another:

> Which of the following represents the best revision of sentences 7 and 8 (reproduced below)?
>
> *I didn't even learn to skate until I was twelve. Most hockey players have been skating for their entire lives.*
>
> (A) I didn't even learn to skate until I was twelve, even though most hockey players have been skating for their entire lives.
>
> (B) I didn't even learn to skate until was twelve, compared with most hockey players have been skating for their entire lives.
>
> (C) I learned to skate when I was twelve; most hockey players have been skating for their entire lives.
>
> (D) Although most hockey players have been skating for their entire lives, I didn't even learn to skate until I was twelve.
>
> (E) Skating, which most hockey players have been doing their entire lives, I didn't learn how until I was twelve.

Here's How to Crack It

First, check the flow of the sentence. It appears as if the sentences are going in opposite directions. Get rid of A and C, which don't change the direction. Answer choice B compares the two ideas, but doesn't establish a contrast. E is horribly awkward, so ditch it. The best answer is D.

Trigger Happy

Make sure when you combine two sentences that they're combined with the right trigger: same-direction or change-direction.

Content Questions

ETS will occasionally ask you a question regarding the content of the passage. These questions may ask:

1. Which sentence should immediately follow or precede the passage?

2. Which sentence should be inserted into the passage?

3. What is the best description of the passage as a whole?

If you are asked the third question, you will need to skim the whole passage. However, you will more likely be asked one of the first two questions. To answer these, you will need to read the relevant paragraph.

Try this example using the sample passage from earlier in this section:

> Which of the following sentences, if added after sentence 4, would best serve to link the first paragraph to the second paragraph?
>
> (A) I found it quite odd that I ended up loving hockey.
> (B) I wanted to be more than just a passionate hockey fan, though.
> (C) My brothers loved baseball, while my sisters were bigger fans of football.
> (D) Perhaps it was my uncle, a big hockey fan, who helped me to love the game.
> (E) Actually, hockey is not a very popular sport in the United States.

Here's How to Crack It

To solve this question, you need to read the first paragraph and the first sentence of the second paragraph quickly. At the end of the first paragraph, he states his love for the game. The next paragraph talks about playing the sport. Find the answer that connects these two ideas.

A, C, and D are out because they focus on the "problems" theme from the first paragraph instead of making a transition to the second paragraph. E is not implied anywhere in the passage. The answer is B.

Time Is of the Essence

Now, keep in mind that this is the end of a 30-minute section at the end of a 3-hour plus test. Chances are you won't have the time or the gumption to do all the improving paragraphs questions. Therefore, reorder the six improving paragraphs questions so you are doing the shorter, easier questions first. Then, if you have the time and the inclination, do the longer questions.

The shorter, easier questions are the combination questions and the revision questions that reprint the sentences you need to edit. Do anything that doesn't require you to go back to the passage. Then do questions that require you to go back to specific areas of the passage. Finally, do the ones that require some reading.

DRILL 5

Try the following improving paragraphs drill to practice what you have learned. Answers can be found on page 342.

(1) Many people dismiss comic books as just something for kids. (2) But comic books, sometimes they are called graphic novels, have had an important place in our culture. (3) You may be surprised to find out that comic books, in one form or another, has a beginning in 19th century Europe. (4) In the United States, the golden age of comics is generally thought to be in the 1930's. (5) Those years saw the birth of two of the most popular characters of all time. (6) Superman was introduced in 1938 and Batman then follows in 1939. (7) The attraction of these two characters, to both adult and children readers alike, elevates the comic book in the public consciousness.

(8) Today, comic books are a major industry. (9) They are able to generate millions and millions of dollars in licensing and movies, as well as toys and other collectibles. (10) Even old favorites like Batman and Superman, now seventy years old, keep coming out new comics. (11) No longer just for kids, the stories of graphic novels are increasingly complex. (12) Now, you can even take a class on the writing of comic books at your local college. (13) You can't say that comics are just for kids anymore.

1. In context, what is the best version of sentence 2, reproduced below?

   But comic books, sometimes they are called graphic novels, have had an important place in our culture.

   (A) (As it is now)
   (B) But comic books, also called graphic novels, have had an important place in our culture.
   (C) But comic books, which are also called graphic novels, have an important place in our culture.
   (D) Comic books, sometimes being called graphic novels, had an important place in our culture.
   (E) Comic books, or graphic novels as they are called, are important to our culture.

2. Which of the following would be the best subject for a paragraph immediately preceding this essay?

   (A) A discussion of popular children's toys
   (B) An overview of 19th century European culture
   (C) A critical perspective on the writing style of graphic novels
   (D) An examination of the toy and game industry
   (E) An analysis of the appeal of comic books to youngsters

3. The author wishes to divide the first paragraph into two shorter paragraphs. The most appropriate place to begin a new paragraph would be

   (A) between sentences 1 and 2
   (B) between sentences 2 and 3
   (C) between sentences 3 and 4
   (D) between sentences 4 and 5
   (E) between sentences 5 and 6

4. In sentence 3, the word *you* could best be replaced with which of the following?

   (A) Young people
   (B) They
   (C) Europeans
   (D) Comic book fans
   (E) Comic book detractors

5. Which word could best replace *birth* in sentence 5?

   (A) resurgence
   (B) production
   (C) beginning
   (D) creation
   (E) addition

6. Which would be the best way to revise and combine the underlined portions of sentences 8 and 9 (reproduced below)?

   Today, comic books are a major industry. They are able to generate millions and millions of dollars in licensing and movies, as well as toys and other collectibles.

   (A) a major industry, generating
   (B) a major industry, which has generated
   (C) a major industry, ably generating
   (D) a major industry, being responsible for generating
   (E) a major industry, one that has been generating

FINAL WORDS OF WISDOM

As with all the sections of the SAT, you are rewarded for answering the question. Don't be afraid to do some POE and guess. You will almost always be able to eliminate some answer choices, so allow your partial knowledge to earn you credit on the test.

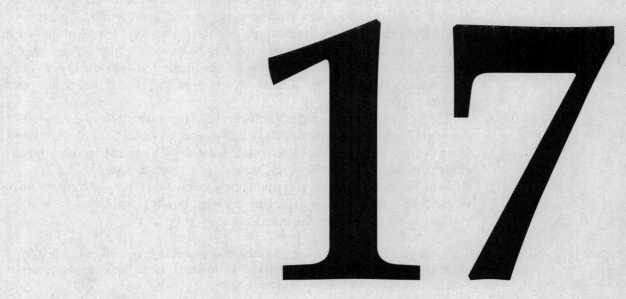

17
Essay

Now we've finally arrived at the last part of your SAT prep, which is the first part of your SAT—the essay. The Writing section is not about writing a great essay that would bring a tear to your Language Arts teacher's eyes or be published in a literary journal. For that kind of writing to be worth the trouble, there would have to be someone carefully reading and evaluating your essay. Don't worry: With readers spending only a minute or two on each essay, that won't really happen on the SAT.

ETS says the essay is graded "holistically." That means essay readers look at the overall impression that the essay makes and give you a score accordingly. In an average of two minutes per essay, what sort of impression can you, as a student, make? Well, with the right approach, a very good one.

In this section we'll give you some tips about what you *should* concentrate on for the SAT essay, and how to pick up the most points possible.

First let's read through the instructions:

The essay gives you an opportunity to show how effectively you can develop and express ideas. You should, therefore, take care to develop your point of view, present your ideas logically and clearly, and use language precisely.

Your essay must be written on the lines provided on your answer sheet—you will receive no other paper on which to write. You will have enough space if you write on every line, avoid wide margins, and keep your handwriting to a reasonable size. Remember that people who are not familiar with your handwriting will read what you write. Try to write or print so that what you are writing is legible to those readers.

You have twenty-five minutes to write an essay on the topic assigned below. DO NOT WRITE ON ANOTHER TOPIC. AN OFF-TOPIC ESSAY WILL RECEIVE A SCORE OF ZERO.

Think carefully about the issue presented in the following excerpt and the assignment below.

Existentialist Jean Paul Sartre believed in personal freedom, holding that man is free to "write the script" for his own life: he can blame no one else if his life is a "poor performance." On the other hand, William Blake and others in the Romantic movement felt that the expectations and restraints of society severely limit a person: they believed that schooling, organized religion, and other social institutions imprison a person's mind and spirit.

Assignment: What is your opinion of the claim that there is no such thing as free choice; to some degree, we are always bound by the rules of society? Plan and write an essay in which you develop your point of view on this issue. Support your position with reasoning and examples taken from your reading, studies, experience, or observations.

DO NOT WRITE YOUR ESSAY IN YOUR TEST BOOK. You will receive credit only for what you write on your answer sheet.

So What Does This Really Mean?

You'll notice the instructions tell you to "think carefully about the issue being presented," and "plan and write an essay in which you develop your point of view on this issue." How much time to you have for all of this planning, developing, AND writing? Twenty-five minutes. That means ETS is not expecting a polished work on par with Hemingway; in fact, your essay will be graded as if it were your rough draft (which it is). So you should really take a couple of minutes to figure out your view and to jot down a few examples before you begin writing—*neatly*. While handwriting isn't supposed to count against you, since the essay will be graded holistically, illegible handwriting can leave a bad impression.

Imagine the sheer number of essays that ETS has to grade once the SAT is administered. Think about the timeline the SAT readers are working against—not to mention, each essay has to be read by two *different* people. So if they can't read the essay… let's just say, they aren't going to be very happy. If you're worried that your handwriting is worse than your doctor's, then try writing bigger and, in extreme circumstances of messiness, in capital letters—your essay may not be pretty, but it will be legible.

The point? Write neatly and you're already on the grader's good side. The larger point? Your essay score will be a function as much of form as of content (more about that below).

What Are the Essays About?

You will read a quotation or short passage that states one or more opinions on some generic topic and you will then write an essay discussing your position or viewpoint on that opinion.

How Are the Essays Scored?

Two people will read your essay, and each will give it a score on a scale of 1–6 (6 being the highest). These two scores are added together and multiplied by a mysterious conversion factor that translates the raw score so it equals about 30 percent of your overall writing score. It's added to the raw score from your multiple-choice Grammar section, and then this total raw score is converted to the familiar 200–800 scale. If, by some chance, the readers differ by more than one point (and this is very rare) a third "master" reader will be called in to score the essay.

The essay, which is graded by two people, is scored on a scale of 1–6 (low to high).

What ETS Says Is Graded

ETS publications tell you that readers are encouraged to look at what has been done well, rather than what hasn't been done. According to ETS the highest score of 6 is reserved for an essay that "effectively and insightfully addresses the writing task"; "is well-organized and fully developed, using clearly appropriate examples to support ideas"; and "displays consistent facility in the use of language, demonstrating variety in sentence structure and range of vocabulary," though it may have "occasional errors." Even an essay with a score of 6 does NOT have to be perfect. As long as your essay is well organized with fully developed ideas, you can make a couple of errors and still get a 6. On the other hand, a

The essay score is converted from the 1-to-6 scale to a 0-to-200 scale.

low score of 1 goes to essays with "very poor organization," "very thin development," and "usage and syntactical errors so severe that meaning is somewhat obscured." (Visit **www.collegeboard.com** to read the entire set of essay-scoring guidelines.)

What's Really Graded

Think about your high school English teacher and how long he or she takes to get writing assignments back to you. Days? Weeks sometimes? Well imagine if your teacher had to grade ten times as many essays in one-tenth the time. Suddenly the time he or she might have to look at your essay is shortened to a few minutes. The ETS reader (who is most likely a high school or college English teacher in real life) is in exactly that crazy situation—he or she may be reading 100 or 200 essays in one sitting. Careful scrutiny under these circumstances is simply not possible. As a result, there are very few things the reader will really have time to look for, and we're going to tell you all about them.

WHAT DOES THIS MEAN FOR YOUR ESSAY?

It means "don't sweat the small stuff," but do sweat the structure and develop your thesis. It means that one or two misspellings probably won't break your score, but not having a good topic and argument for each paragraph will. So a missing apostrophe is not a cause for alarm. On the other hand you'll want to make sure what you write is relevant and that you start with a strong topic sentence and conclusion. Our techniques will help you write a clear, concise essay that will earn you a solid score. To ace this section, grab the reader's attention right from the start and finish strong.

So What's the Most Critical Thing?

Remember, what you're creating is a good impression. Although we're not advocating carelessness, little mistakes are not a big deal in the graders' eyes. In fact, if you checked out what ETS considers to be the paradigms of a great essay and a bad essay, it becomes overwhelmingly clear that one thing is valued more than any other:

Length

For the Writing section, a good essay is a long one.

You see, holistically, a long essay screams, "I have something to say; I have thought it out; I am relating it fully to you." You get around 50 lines to fill. Plan on using most of them. By the way, you cannot use more space then you are given. But don't add fluff just to lengthen an essay, and don't repeat yourself. Add another example or expand upon a previous one to add length. While you should never restate your topic over and over again—nothing drives a grader more insane—it's not a bad idea to refer to it.

It's All in the Details

There are a few other things to think about when you are writing your essay. Some of these may seem like mere details, but if you pay attention to these issues as you write, your essay will stand out from the pack.

Organization

Essays receiving the highest score will be those that use the classic introduction-body-conclusion form that most students learn in their early years of high school. That is, the essay should begin with an introductory paragraph that sets up what the writer is going to argue. The body should be made up of one to three paragraphs that fully develop reasons why you, the writer, are taking your position, with relevant examples supporting each reason. The conclusion should sum up what's in the body of the essay, and paraphrase the thesis or tell how your viewpoint applies to the topic. Nothing says "I'm organized and I know how to structure an essay" better than that.

Indent, indent, indent

Make sure your indentations are clear—indent a full half inch. Skipping a line between paragraphs is not a bad idea, but don't make it obvious that you're trying to lengthen your essay and certainly DO NOT double-space the entire essay. A good rule of thumb is, if you have naturally big handwriting, don't skip a line.

Cite examples from history and literature

Can you imagine how much an English teacher will love you if you actually start talking about *Romeo and Juliet* to explain the sorrow of love lost, instead of your boyfriend or girlfriend? This can mean big points. Make sure, if you do cite any literary examples, to underline them if they're longer works, such as novels; or if they're shorter works, like lyric poems, to put them in quotes. You should get some literary examples ready before the test begins so you won't have to sweat them the day of the exam. The more generic, the better; it will make it easier for you to apply them to the given topic. Most importantly, make sure your examples are relevant to the topic, otherwise you're inviting trouble.

One last thing: Personal examples are not bad as long as they are well-developed and relate completely to your chosen viewpoint. But be careful, because most personal examples end up only loosely relating to your point.

A few big words are nice

Don't go crazy here. A few well-placed words, especially in the introduction or conclusion, will sure look dandy. Words like *advocate, hypothetically, inevitable, allusion, objective, subjective*. Use the Hit Parade list included in this book. Also, if you have a copy of The Princeton Review's *Word Smart*, check it out. There are some beautiful big words in there. Do not, however, use words that you are not comfortable with. Short words are better than misused words. Transitional words and phrases that show your intentions to the reader are also good: *thus, however, in conclusion, etc.*

Simple is better than complex

Please don't let all this "long is better" stuff mislead you. Even though you'll be going for a longer essay, long, convoluted sentences should be avoided. There's nothing like a little convolution to make an overworked English teacher cry.

You want to compose a long essay, but you don't want to use wordy, convoluted sentences.

Stay relevant

Be sure that your essay answers the question(s) asked in the assignment. The big focus for this new essay is to fully develop your ideas so your views are clear. If your essay goes off topic, you will receive a score of 0. That's as bad as it gets.

Complete all of your sentences and paragraphs

If you leave off in the middle of the sentence or leave it ambiguous, the grader is left to wonder what you were trying to say (not good). By having complete paragraphs with a beginning and closing sentence, the essay looks polished, your thoughts look developed, and you look organized. So if you see that you have only a few minutes and you are in your second body paragraph, finish your thought and write that conclusion. Try parenthetical inserts—they are really just paired dashes used in place of parentheses—to impress your reader with your knowledge of punctuation. Also, don't be afraid to throw in a semicolon; it will certainly impress the graders.

If you love writing, all this may seem like the wrong way to focus your attention. But our purpose is to help you raise your SAT score, and it will help to know what the College Board readers are really looking for. Don't forget, this essay is about getting your point across in the best rough draft possible.

Ready for some practice?

SOME SAMPLE ESSAYS

Let's take a look at a couple of sample essays written on the following topic:

> The Romantic movement in poetry was characterized by the importance placed on feelings and emotions. Excessive analysis or thinking was considered a hindrance to experiencing true emotion. For a true Romantic, it mattered not whether the emotion felt was positive or negative; all that mattered was the experience of feeling itself.

Assignment: What is your view of the claim that feelings or emotions are more valuable than thinking or analysis? Plan and write an essay in which you develop your point of view on this issue. Support your position with reasoning and examples taken from your reading, studies, experience, or observations.

Give yourself two minutes to read each essay. Take a second to jot down the good and bad points of each. Think about what you didn't notice and what you noticed right away.

Essay Number One

I agree with the sentiment that it is better to experience love than not to experience it at all. A life filled with love is most certainly better than a life without love. You cannot always worry about whether or not you will lose the love you work hard for.

In all aspects of life, whether it is sports, personal relationships, or study, you should work hard to be the best. You should always strive for "love" and not be concerned about losing. As in sports, when it is better to try really hard and get a home run sometimes than to only be mediocre and get a single.

In personal relationships as well, you can't be afraid of losing your love. Just having had a wonderful experience, whether in personal relationships, or outside of them is worth the pain of loss.

Analysis

How was the essay presented?

_____

Any literary allusions?

_____

Overall, "holistic" impression?

_____

Your score (on a scale of 1–6) _____

This essay would probably have received a score of 6 out of 12 (with each reader awarding 3 points out of a possible 6). It was competent, but not really well presented. It could have used better examples of why the author agreed with the topic. It's not very long, and therefore, in the mind of the grader, not very well developed.

Essay Number Two

I definitely agree that it is better to have loved and lost than not to experience feeling at all. What would life be worth living if you have no love at all in it?

I may be young, but even in family relationships, it is better to have them, even if they are painful, than to be without a family. I am sure that the same is true as you go through life. It is better to try to have relationships, even if they do not last than to have no relationships. This is why it is most certainly better to love than not to love.

Analysis

How was the essay presented?

_____

Any literary allusions?

_____

Overall, "holistic" impression?

_____

Your score (on a scale of 1–6) _____

This essay would probably have received a score of 4 (each reader giving the essay a score of 2). The author's ideas were not very well developed. The sentences are long and rambling. There are no solid examples to back up the ideas. It's also much too SHORT!

Essay Number Three

I most certainly agree with the position of the Romantics that a life with love, even if that love is eventually lost, is far superior to never experiencing love. Both history and literature are filled with examples of characters who strove for great passion, without fear of experiencing the more difficult emotions. These are the people who achieve the greatest heights. The results, often loss and pain, are certainly outweighed by the greatness experienced along the way. Certainly, love, whether of life, country, or another, is worth fighting for and worth the pain that so often accompanies it.

Shakespeare's Romeo and Juliet is probably the greatest example of this idea. The passion felt by Romeo and Juliet, despite the obstacles laid out before them, made it clear that their love was more important than the inevitable fate that awaited them—death. I have no doubt that these two would have verified that a love like theirs, no matter how brief and tragic, was great. It was certainly greater than suffering a long life without a passionate love.

In history as well, we can certainly see many who believed that love of country, no matter what the consequence, was a far greater good than to have no allegiance. The great patriot Nathan Hale held his head high at his execution and proclaimed, "I only regret that I have but one life to give for my country." Had the great leaders of our revolution cared more about being safe, then about love of their ideals and of their country, we would never have won independence from English tyranny. It was men like Nathan Hale, who were willing to lose everything in the struggle for their great love—the love of country, who were responsible for the greatness of our country.

It is without a doubt that a life of love and passion is a better life than one bereft of those emotions. History, literature and life itself bear witness to that idea every day.

Analysis

How was the essay presented?

_____

Any literary allusions?

_____

Overall, "holistic" impression?

_____

Your score (on a scale of 1–6) _____

This essay would probably have received a perfect score of 12 (a score of 6 from each grader). It's well presented and well written. Its main idea is supported by examples from literature and history. It's also nice and long. You may notice that there were a couple of minor errors (*then* instead of *than* near the end). But these don't really matter. As a whole, it is an impressive, thoughtful essay. A small error won't detract from the overall impression.

ESSAY DRILL

For each of the following quotations, think of three examples, either pro or con, or both, that you could use in an essay.

> The Romantic movement in poetry was characterized by the importance placed on feelings and emotions. Excessive analysis or thinking was considered a hindrance to experiencing true emotion. For a true Romantic, it mattered not whether the emotion felt was positive or negative; all that mattered was the experience of feeling itself.

Assignment: What is your view of the claim that feelings or emotions are more valuable than thinking or analysis? Plan and write an essay in which you develop your point of view on this issue. Support your position with reasoning and examples taken from your reading, studies, experience, or observations.

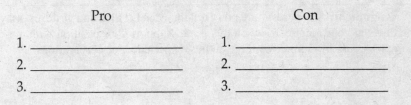

Pro   Con

1. _____   1. _____

2. _____   2. _____

3. _____   3. _____

Winston Churchill once stated that "The inherent vice of capitalism is the unequal sharing of blessings." In many pre-capitalistic societies, there is no concept of "ownership," and all members of the society share resources equally. Capitalism tends to bring out the selfish nature of people.

Assignment: Does capitalism make people more selfish? Plan and write an essay in which you develop your point of view on this issue. Support your position with reasoning and examples taken from your reading, studies, experience, or observations.

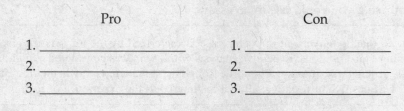

An old saying goes, "If at first you don't succeed, try, try again." History is full of examples of determined individuals who never gave up in pursuit of their goals. But persistence alone is not sufficient for success.

Assignment: What is your view of the claim that persistence alone is not sufficient for success? Plan and write an essay in which you develop your point of view on this issue. Support your position with reasoning and examples taken from your reading, studies, experience, or observations.

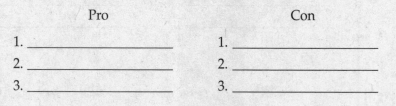

John F. Kennedy claimed that "the highest appreciation is not to utter words, but to live by them." However, some people believe that words have the power to change not just behavior, but people.

Assignment: Are words more powerful than deeds? Plan and write an essay in which you develop your point of view on this issue. Support your position with reasoning and examples taken from your reading, studies, experience, or observations.

	Pro	Con
1.	_____	_____
2.	_____	_____
3.	_____	_____

What is the price of liberty? This question is often asked in civics and political science classes across the country. An examination of history might lead one to conclude that liberty is not a natural human right—slavery, tyranny, and oppression are as old as humanity. Many of the world's great freedom fighters believed that the cost of liberty should be no less than the ultimate cost: one's life.

Assignment: Do you believe that one should sacrifice life for liberty? Plan and write an essay in which you develop your point of view on this issue. Support your position with reasoning and examples taken from your reading, studies, experience, or observations.

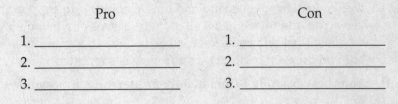

The more we study history, the more likely we are to acquire what is known as a "historical perspective"—the ability to view current accomplishments, failures, and situations in context of what has come before. Using this perspective, it appears that oftentimes, history does indeed repeat itself.

Assignment: Do you believe that history repeats itself? Plan and write an essay in which you develop your point of view on this issue. Support your position with reasoning and examples taken from your reading, studies, experience, or observations.

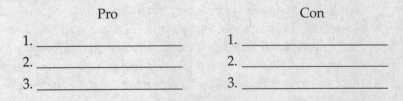

MAKE AN OUTLINE

When you have thought of your examples, make a quick outline and write it in the margin of the section where the question is. This will help you to stay on track. It will also keep you indenting!

If you don't know where to start with an outline, don't worry. Luckily for you, the outline you will use will be pretty standard. It will look like this:

I. State your viewpoint

This opening should only take you a few sentences. Clearly state your position in the beginning of the essay so the grader will know where you stand and how you intend to support that view. You don't have to list all of your reasons of why you hold the view (that will come later in each of your body paragraphs), but you do want to hint that your view is supported.

II. Your best example—from history or literature, if possible

Relate your example back to your viewpoint and develop it as a supporting theme. For example, if you're using *Romeo and Juliet* to prove your view that people in love tend do crazy things, then don't just write that they died for each other. Instead discuss how they chose death over a life without the other and explain how that was crazy. Didn't Juliet stop to think that there were more fish in the sea? How crazy! See what we mean? Show it, don't just tell it. Of course, you want to be a little more comprehensive in your explanation. For example:

Take a look at Shakespeare's play, Romeo and Juliet. It's a great example of the craziness that inevitably comes with love. Romeo, upon finding a highly sedated Juliet, decides that life simply is not worth living without his true love; so he takes some poison and kills himself. This was certainly romantic, but nonetheless crazy. After all, he had only known Juliet for two weeks and he decided that death was better than not being married to his 2 week old girlfriend. Once Romeo dies, Juliet awakes to find him dead right beside her. Being in love, she does almost the same crazy thing: she stabs herself with Romeo's dagger. Had she considered her possibilities before stabbing herself, she could have realized there may be another love for her out there. Perhaps these actions can be viewed as sweet and romantic, but they are undeniably crazy.

III. **Your second example—from history, literature, or personal experience**

Same stuff as before. It's completely fine to use a personal example so long as you fully develop how your experience relates to your thesis and formed your viewpoint. Just don't make the essay grader your therapist: Stick to the topic and don't go on long tangents. Going off topic is fine to give a little background, but DO NOT make it the longest part of your paragraph. Also, try to stick to lessons you learned from people who have influenced your life, for better or for worse, like your big brother, grandmother, best friend, or favorite teacher.

IV. **(Optional) Your third example—from history, literature, or personal experience**

Again, it's like one of the previous two paragraphs.

V. **Warm, concise concluding statement**

Don't take up too much time coming up with a grandiose conclusion. ETS graders are told not to penalize you if your essay is missing a conclusion, but take that with a grain of salt. If you never fully developed your viewpoint, the lack of a conclusion makes your essay look like a second grader's first attempt at "fun with a pencil." So even a simple sentence wrapping up your view is a great idea. Do not introduce a new idea; your job here is to sum up what you've said and answer the question, "Why do you see it this way?"

OUTLINE DRILL

Choose four of the examples given in the last drill and practice writing an outline. When you enter your examples, make sure they are ones about which you know some facts. If you mention a war, make sure you know which countries were allies, for example.

Writing the outline should only take a few minutes. Don't spend more than three minutes gathering your examples and writing your outline. More than that and you're running into precious writing time.

> Your essay should have an introduction, three supporting paragraphs, and a conclusion.

Essay A

    I. _____

    II. _____

    III. _____

    IV. _____

    V. _____

Essay B

    I. _____

    II. _____

    III. _____

    IV. _____

    V. _____

Essay C

    I. _____

    II. _____

    III. _____

    IV. _____

    V. _____

Essay D

    I. _____

    II. _____

    III. _____

    IV. _____

    V. _____

SAMPLE ESSAY

Give yourself 25 minutes and see how you do on this essay topic. Go through the checklist at the end.

The hedonists were a group of philosophers who held that the point of existence was to seek out pleasure. They believed that a good life could be achieved by the pursuit of the good things in life. If one allows that pleasure can be sought out, then one must also consider that pain and grief can be sought out as well. Perhaps people who are constantly enduring struggle in their lives do so because they seek it out. It could be that the greatest pain we encounter is caused by none other than ourselves.

Assignment: What is your view of the claim that the greatest pain we encounter is that which we cause ourselves? Plan and write an essay in which you develop your point of view on this issue. Support your position with reasoning and examples taken from your reading, studies, experience, or observations.

_____

_____

_____

_____

_____

_____

_____

_____

_____

_____

_____

_____

_____

_____

_____

_____

CHECKLIST

- Historical or literary references?

- Most of the space used?

- Neat, with few cross-outs?

- Indented?

- Four or five paragraphs?

If you've covered all the items on the checklist, then you've written a strong New SAT Writing section essay.

SOME VARIATIONS ON A THEME

Some prompts will present you with two quotes to consider. These quotes will usually express opposing opinions or contrast with each other in some way. In any case, your assignment is much the same. Choose a point of view (you can agree with one quote or the other, or take a different perspective on the subject), think of some good examples, write an outline, fill up the space with your neatly written, indented, five paragraph essay. No problem!

Take a look at the following prompt and give it a shot.

Prudence shall be our guiding principle. When faced with a conflict, or a divergent path in the course of life, we shall always make caution our ally. Recklessness and rash action lead not to fruitfulness, but only to regret at the haste of our decisions.

Oftentimes, people ask me how I have been so successful in business. "Everything you touch turns to gold," they say. "What's your secret?" they wonder. When I reflect on my decisions, I realize that the key to my success is nothing more than simple opportunism. When I saw an opening, I jumped at it. While everyone else was standing still, agonizing over the correct course of action, I went in feet first, with no hesitation. That is the key to my success.

CEO Dennis Walker

Assignment: Consider the statement above. What do you believe is the secret of success? Plan and write an essay in which you develop your point of view on this issue. Support your position with reasoning and examples taken from your reading, studies, experience, or observations.

CHECKLIST

- Broad, important themes?
- Most of the space used?
- Neat, with few cross-outs?
- Indented?
- Four or five paragraphs?

FINE TUNING

You now know all you need to know to write a great essay. Here are a few minor points that may help you get that extra point:

- Good pencil work. Yes, you have to write in pencil, so make sure your words can be read—they shouldn't be too faint or overly erased.

- Don't go outside the margins. It makes the essay look sloppy.

- Throw in some important names and dates, if you can think of any appropriate ones.

- Vary your sentence structure. Avoid using all short sentences; a bit of complicated sentence structure is good, as long as you know what you're doing.

- Don't offend your reader! Don't make any extreme statements—political or otherwise.

PART ◆ **V**

Taking the New SAT

The SAT Is a Week Away. What Should You Do?

First of all, you should practice the techniques we've taught you on lots of practice tests. If you don't own any, go buy a copy of *11 Practice Tests for the New SAT & PSAT* at your local bookstore or through **www.randomhouse.com**.

Take and score the three practice tests at the back of this book, as well as the practice tests on our website (see "Online Tools" at the beginning of the book for information on how to log on). The more full-length SATs you practice, the better.

Get a copy of a full-length SAT from your guidance counselor.

More Practice SATs

If you want to get your hands on more SATs, in addition to the practice tests published in *11 Practice Tests for the New SAT & PSAT*, you may be able to obtain copies of recent tests that have been released through ETS's Question and Answer Service. These tests, when available, can be ordered from the College Board through its headquarters:

The College Board
45 Columbus Avenue
New York, NY 10023
212-713-8000

Getting Psyched

The SAT is a big deal, but you don't want to let it scare you. Sometimes students get so nervous about doing well that they freeze up on the test and ruin their scores. The best thing to do is to think of the SAT as a game. It's a game you can get good at, and beating the test can be fun. When you go into the test center, just think about all those poor slobs who don't know how to eyeball geometry diagrams.

The best way to keep from getting nervous is to build confidence in yourself and in your ability to remember and use our techniques. When you take practice tests, time yourself exactly as you will be timed on the real SAT. Develop a sense of how long 25 minutes is and how much time you can afford to spend on cracking difficult problems. If you know ahead of time what to expect, you won't be as nervous.

Of course, taking a real SAT is much more nerve-racking than taking a practice test. Prepare yourself ahead of time for the fact that 25 minutes will seem to go by a lot faster on a real SAT than it did on your practice tests.

It's all right to be nervous; the point of being prepared is to keep from panicking.

SHOULD YOU SLEEP FOR 36 HOURS?

Some guidance counselors tell their students to get a lot of sleep the night before the SAT. This probably isn't a good idea. If you aren't used to sleeping twelve hours a night, doing so will just make you groggy for the test. The same goes for going out all night: Tired people are not good test takers.

A much better idea is to get up early each morning for the entire week before the test and do your homework before school. This will get your brain accustomed to functioning at that hour of the morning. You want to be sharp at test time.

Before you go to sleep the night before the test, spend an hour or so reviewing the Hit Parade. This will make the list fresh in your mind in the morning. You might also practice estimating some angles and looking for direct solutions on a few real SAT math problems. You don't want to exhaust yourself, but it will help to brush up.

FURTHERMORE

Here are a few pointers for test day and beyond:

1. Eat a good breakfast before the test—your brain needs energy.

2. Work out a few SAT problems on the morning of the test to help dust off any cobwebs in your head and get you started thinking analytically.

3. Arrive at the test center early.

4. You must bring acceptable identification to the test center on the day of the test. According to ETS, acceptable identification must include: "(1) a photograph or a written physical description (2) your name, and (3) your signature." Acceptable forms of ID include: your driver's license, a school ID with a photo, or a valid passport. If you don't have an official piece of ID with your signature and your photo, you can have your school make an ID for you. Just have your guidance counselor type up a physical description of you on school stationery, which both you and your guidance counselor then have to sign. Complete instructions for making such an ID are contained in ETS's *Registration Bulletin*. According to ETS, the following forms of ID are *unacceptable*: a birth certificate, a credit card, or a Social Security card.

   Make sure you read all of the rules in the *Registration Bulletin*, because conflicts with ETS are just not worth the headache. Your only concern on the day of the test should be beating the SAT. To avoid hassles and unnecessary stress, make *absolutely certain* that you take your admissions ticket and your ID with you on the day of the test.

#1: Eat Breakfast
You'll work better on a satisfied stomach.

#2: Try Some Problems
Get your mind moving.

#3: Show Up Early
Leave time for traffic.

#4: Bring ID
A driver's license, a passport, or a school photo ID will do.

#5: Bring Equipment

No. 2 pencils (at least 12), a watch, and a calculator.

5. The only outside materials you are allowed to use on the test are No. 2 pencils (take a dozen, all sharp), a wristwatch (an absolute necessity), and a calculator. Digital watches are best, but if it has a beeper, make sure you turn it off. Proctors will confiscate pocket dictionaries, word lists, portable computers, and the like. Proctors have occasionally also confiscated stopwatches and travel clocks. Technically, you should be permitted to use these, but you can never tell with some proctors. Take a watch and avoid the hassles.

#6: Bring Fruit or Other Energy Food

Grapes or oranges can give you an energy boost if you need it.

6. Some proctors allow students to bring food into the test room; others don't. Take some fruit (especially bananas) with you and see what happens. If you don't flaunt them, they probably won't be confiscated. Save them until your break and eat outside the test room, as discreetly as possible.

#7: Your Desk...

should be comfortable and suited to your needs.

7. You are going to be sitting in the same place for more than three hours, so make sure your desk isn't broken or unusually uncomfortable. If you are left-handed, ask for a left-handed desk. (The center may not have one, but it won't hurt to ask.) If the sun is in your eyes, ask to move. If the room is too dark, ask someone to turn on the lights. Don't hesitate to speak up. Some proctors just don't know what they're doing.

#8: Your Test...

should be printed legibly in your booklet.

8. Make sure your booklet is complete. Booklets sometimes contain printing errors that make some pages impossible to read. One year more than ten thousand students had to retake the SAT because of a printing error in their booklets. Also, check your answer sheet to make sure it isn't flawed.

#9: Breaks

You will probably get several—take advantage of them!

9. You will probably get a five-minute break after the second section of the test. Ask for it if your proctor doesn't give it to you. You should be allowed to go to the bathroom at this time. You should also be allowed to take breaks after section four and section six. The breaks are a very good idea. Be sure to get up, move around, and clear your head.

#10: Cancel with Care

Don't cancel your scores just because you feel icky. Think it over carefully, and NEVER cancel on the same day as the test. Make sure you have a really good reason, like you fainted. Remember, you can always retake the test.

10. ETS allows you to cancel your SAT scores. Unfortunately, you can't cancel only your Math, your Writing, or your Critical Reading—it's all or nothing. You will also have to cancel them before you know what your scores are. You can cancel scores at the test center by asking your proctor for a "Request to Cancel Test Scores" form. You must complete this form and hand it in before you leave the test center. If you decide to cancel your scores after you leave, you can do so by contacting ETS by cable, overnight delivery, or e-mail (sat@ets.org). The address is in the *Registration Bulletin*, or you can call ETS at 609-771-7600 to find out where to send your score cancellation request.

We recommend that you not cancel your scores unless you know you made so many errors or left out so many questions that your score will be unacceptably low. Don't cancel your scores on test day just because you have a bad feeling—even the best test takers feel a little shaky after the SAT. You've got five days to think it over.

11. Make sure you darken all your responses before the test is over. At the same time, erase any extraneous marks on the answer sheet. **A stray mark in the margin of your answer sheet can result in correct responses being marked as wrong.**

12. Don't assume that your test was scored correctly. Send away for ETS's Question and Answer Service whenever it is offered. It costs money, but it's worth it. You'll get back copies of your answer sheet, a test booklet, and an answer key. Check your answers against the key and complain if you think your test has been scored incorrectly. (Don't throw away the test booklet you receive from the Question and Answer Service. If you're planning to take the SAT again, save it for practice. If you're not, give it to your guidance counselor or school library.)

13. You deserve to take your SAT under good conditions. If you feel that your test was not administered properly (the high school band was practicing outside the window, or your proctor hovered over your shoulder during the test), call us immediately at 800-333-0369 and we'll tell you what you can do about it.

#11: Bubble with Care

A stray mark can hurt your score.

#12: Keep Tabs on ETS

Get a copy of your SAT, your answer sheet, and an answer key. Make sure your score is accurate.

#13: We're Here for You

The Princeton Review is proud to advise students who have been mistreated by ETS.

PART ◆ VI

Answer Key
to Drills

CHAPTER 4

DRILLS 1 AND 2
Pages 44–45

1. **C** The blank is concerned with what _Citizen Kane_ was (past tense). The only thing that we know about the past is that _theaters refused to show it_. Since it was not played in theaters, it could not have made any money, therefore C.

6. **B** The buildings are _threatened_, so we need a negative word. Eliminate A, D, and E. The clue is _increasing rents_, so (B) is the best choice.

7. **B** Lots of triggers in this one. First, _but_ tells us that we are looking for a contrast between the first blank and _technically slick_, therefore we want a word like _unsophisticated_ or _simplistic_. Eliminate A, C, and D. The sentence also states that the films should be filled with _poignancy_, the best opposite of which is _vacuous_.

DRILL 3
Page 50

8. **B**

8. **A**   Good second guesses: E, B

DRILL 4
Pages 50–51

2. **A**

5. **C**

6. **D**

7. **D**

CHAPTER 5

DRILL 1
Page 75

    1. C

    2. D

    3. E

    4. B

    5. A

    6. C

    7. B

    8. D

    9. D

  10. C

  11. B

  12. E

  13. C

CHAPTER 6

DRILL 1
Page 93

  14. B

  15. A

  16. A

  17. C

  18. D

  19. E

  20. E

  21. A

  22. C

  23. D

  24. E

  25. D

CHAPTER 10

DRILL 1
Page 165

1. 109
2. 38
3. −3
4. 10
5. 15

DRILL 2
Page 166

1. $6(57+13) = 6 \times 70 = 420$
2. $51(48 + 50 + 52) = 51(150) = 7,650$
3. $ab + ac - ad$
4. $x(y - z)$
5. $c(ab + xy)$

DRILL 3
Page 169

1. $\dfrac{25}{3}$
2. $\dfrac{17}{7}$
3. $\dfrac{49}{9}$
4. $\dfrac{5}{2}$
5. $\dfrac{20}{3}$

Drill 4

Page 171

1. 3

2. $\dfrac{31}{5}$

3. $-1\dfrac{4}{15}$ or $-\dfrac{19}{15}$

4. $\dfrac{1}{15}$

5. $\dfrac{6}{7}$

6. $\dfrac{2}{25}$

7. $\dfrac{4}{9}$

Drill 5

Page 172

1. 0.3741
2. 1,457.7
3. 186
4. −2.89

Drill 6

Page 179

	Fraction	Decimal	Percent
1.	$\dfrac{1}{2}$	0.5	50
2.	$\dfrac{3}{1}$	3.0	300
3.	$\dfrac{1}{200}$	0.005	0.5
4.	$\dfrac{1}{3}$	$0.333\overline{3}$	$33\dfrac{1}{3}$

CHAPTER 12

DRILL 1
Page 236

1. 0.4
2. a little bit more than 5
3. 2.8
4. a little bit less than 1
5. a little bit more than 4
6. ∠YXZ = about 30°

   ∠XYZ = about 120°

   ∠YZX = about 30°

   YZ is about 16

   XZ is about 30 (a little less than 32!)

(None of these angle measurements is exact, but remember, you don't have to be exact when you ballpark. Even a very rough estimation will enable you to eliminate one or two answer choices.)

CHAPTER 13

DRILL 1
Page 255

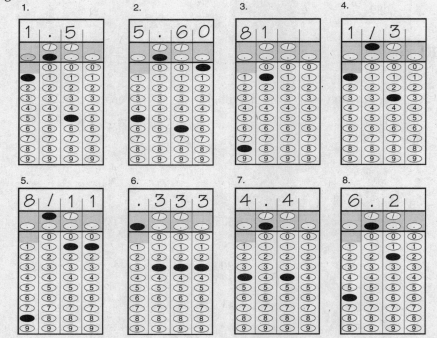

CHAPTER 16

DRILL 1
Page 290

1. to
2. of, for
3. by, for
4. of
5. about
6. by
7. over
8. to
9. from

DRILL 2
Page 292

1. D
2. C
3. D
4. C
5. D
6. D

DRILL 3
Page 299

1. About to happen *versus* prominent or distinguished
2. Forbid, condemn *versus* set down, order (as in medication)
3. Smart *versus* able to be understood
4. Unbelievable *versus* skeptical
5. Annoyed *versus* made worse
6. Fixed, not moving *versus* letter paper
7. Unlawful *versus* draw out

DRILL 4

Pages 299–302

1. B
2. E
3. E
4. D
5. B
6. B
7. D
8. B
9. C
10. B
11. B
12. E

DRILL 5

Pages 307–308

1. C
2. E
3. C
4. E
5. D
6. A

PART ◆ VII

The Princeton Review
New SAT Practice Tests
and Explanations

The best way to learn our techniques for cracking the SAT is to practice them. The following practice tests will give you a chance to do that. The additional practice tests on our website (see "Online Tools" at the beginning of the book for information on how to log on) will provide even more practice.

These practice tests were designed to be as much like a real SAT as possible. The tests in this book contain three Critical Reading sections, three Math sections, three Writing sections (one 25-minute Grammar/Writing Skills section, one 10-minute Grammar/Writing Skills section, and one Essay section), and one experimental section. Our online tests are identical but do not have an experimental section. Our questions test the same concepts that are tested on real SATs.

Since one of the sections on the tests in this book is experimental, none of the questions in it counts toward your final score. The actual SAT will have an experimental section—verbal or math—that ETS now euphemistically terms an "equating section."

Keep Working

It is difficult for most people to tell if a section is experimental, so you should treat all of the sections as real sections.

When you take a practice test, you should try to take it under conditions that are as much like real testing conditions as possible. Take it in a room where you won't be disturbed, and have someone else time you. (It's too easy if you time yourself.) You can give yourself a brief break halfway through, but don't stop for longer than five minutes or so. To put yourself in a proper frame of mind, you might take it on a weekend morning. One more thing: Don't use scrap paper; you will not have any when you take the real SAT.

After taking our tests, you'll have a very good idea of what taking the real SAT will be like. In fact, we've found that students' scores on The Princeton Review's practice tests correspond very closely to the scores they earn on real SATs.

The answers to the questions on the tests in this book and a scoring guide can be found beginning on page 396. The answer sheets are in the back of the book.

If you have any questions about the practice test, the SAT, ETS, or The Princeton Review, give us a call, toll-free, at 1-800-2Review.

The following practice tests were written by the authors of this book and are not actual SATs. The directions and format were used by permission of the Educational Testing Service. This permission does not constitute review or endorsement by the Educational Testing Service or the College Board of this publication as a whole or of any sample questions or testing information it may contain.

Practice Test 1

ESSAY
Time — 25 minutes

Turn to Section 1 of your answer sheet to write your ESSAY.

The essay gives you an opportunity to show how effectively you can develop and express ideas. You should, therefore, take care to develop your point of view, present your ideas logically and clearly, and use language precisely.

Your essay must be written on the lines provided on your answer sheet—you will receive no other paper on which to write. You will have enough space if you write on every line, avoid wide margins, and keep your handwriting to a reasonable size. Remember that people who are not familiar with your handwriting will read what you write. Try to write or print so that what you are writing is legible to those readers.

You have twenty-five minutes to write an essay on the topic assigned below. DO NOT WRITE ON ANOTHER TOPIC. AN OFF-TOPIC ESSAY WILL RECEIVE A SCORE OF ZERO.

Think carefully about the issue presented in the following excerpt and the assignment below.

"No great man lives in vain. The history of the world is but the biography of great men."

Thomas Carlyle, "The Hero as Divinity," (1841)

"In historic events, the so-called great men are labels giving names to events, and like labels they have but the smallest connection with the event itself."

Leo Tolstoy, *War and Peace*, Book 9, Chapter 1

Assignment: What is your view of the claim that history is made not only by the actions of great leaders, but also by the daily contributions of average people? Plan and write an essay in which you develop your point of view on this issue. Support your position with reasoning and examples taken from your reading, studies, experience, or observations.

DO NOT WRITE YOUR ESSAY IN YOUR TEST BOOK. You will receive credit only for what you write on your answer sheet.

BEGIN WRITING YOUR ESSAY IN SECTION 1 OF THE ANSWER SHEET.

If you finish before time is called, you may check your work on this section only. Do not turn to any other section in the test.

SECTION 2

Time — 25 minutes

20 Questions

Turn to Section 2 of your answer sheet to answer the questions in this section.

Directions: For this section, solve each problem and decide which is the best of the choices given. Fill in the corresponding circle on the answer sheet. You may use any available space for scratchwork.

Notes

1. The use of a calculator is permitted.

2. All numbers used are real numbers.

3. Figures that accompany problems in this test are intended to provide information useful in solving the problems. They are drawn as accurately as possible EXCEPT when it is stated in a specific problem that the figure is not drawn to scale. All figures lie in a plane unless otherwise indicated.

4. Unless otherwise specified, the domain of any function f is assumed to be the set of all real numbers x for which $f(x)$ is a real number.

Reference Information

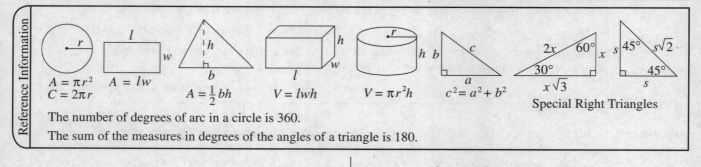

$A = \pi r^2$
$C = 2\pi r$

$A = lw$

$A = \frac{1}{2}bh$

$V = lwh$

$V = \pi r^2 h$

$c^2 = a^2 + b^2$

Special Right Triangles

The number of degrees of arc in a circle is 360.

The sum of the measures in degrees of the angles of a triangle is 180.

1. Andrea subscribed to four publications that cost $12.90, $16.00, $18.00, and $21.90 per year, respectively. If she made an initial payment of one-half of the total yearly subscription cost, and paid the rest in four equal monthly payments, how much was each of the four monthly payments?

   (A) $8.60
   (B) $9.20
   (C) $9.45
   (D) $17.20
   (E) $34.40

2. If $\dfrac{2x}{x^2+1} = \dfrac{2}{x+2}$, what is the value of x ?

   (A) $-\dfrac{1}{4}$

   (B) $\dfrac{1}{4}$

   (C) $\dfrac{1}{2}$

   (D) 0

   (E) 2

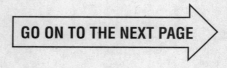

GO ON TO THE NEXT PAGE

3. A survey of Town X found a mean of 3.2 persons per household and a mean of 1.2 televisions per household. If 48,000 people live in Town X, how many televisions are in Town X ?

(A) 15,000
(B) 16,000
(C) 18,000
(D) 40,000
(E) 57,600

If I do not have any flour, I am not able to make cookies.

4. If the statement above is true, which of the following statements must be true?

(A) If I did not make cookies, I must not have had flour.
(B) If I made cookies, I must have had flour.
(C) If I have flour, I must be able to make cookies.
(D) If I was able to make cookies, I must not have had any flour.
(E) If I am not able to make cookies, I must not have any flour.

5. For all integers $n \neq 1$, let $f(n) = \dfrac{n+1}{n-1}$. Which of the following has the greatest value?

(A) $f(0)$
(B) $f(2)$ 3
(C) $f(3)$ 2
(D) $f(4)$
(E) $f(5)$ 1.5

6. If $9b = 81$, then $\sqrt{b} \cdot \sqrt[3]{3b} =$

(A) 9
(B) 27
(C) 81
(D) 243
(E) 729

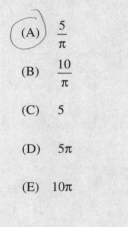

3·3

9

7. What is the diameter of a circle with circumference 5 ?

(A) $\dfrac{5}{\pi}$

(B) $\dfrac{10}{\pi}$

(C) 5

(D) 5π

(E) 10π

8. If the product of $(1 + 2)$, $(2 + 3)$, and $(3 + 4)$ is equal to one-half the sum of 20 and x, what is the value of x ?

(A) 10
(B) 85
(C) 105
(D) 190
(E) 1,210

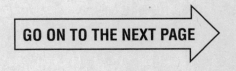

GO ON TO THE NEXT PAGE

9. If $\sqrt{x} = 2^2$, then $x =$

    (A) 1
    (B) 2
    (C) 4
    (D) 8
    (E) 16

4

MERCHANDISE SALES		
Type	Amount of Sales	Percent of Total Sales
Shoes	$12,000	15%
Coats	$20,000	25%
Shirts	$x	40%
Pants	$y	20%

10. According to the table above, $x + y =$

    (A) $32,000
    (B) $48,000
    (C) $60,000
    (D) $68,000
    (E) $80,000

$$\frac{32000}{40\ 1000} = \frac{x t}{100} \quad x = 80,000$$

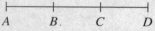

A   B.   C   D

Note: Figure not drawn to scale.

11. If $AB > CD$, which of the following must be true?

    I. $AB > BC$
    II. $AC > BD$
    III. $AC > CD$

    (A) I only
    (B) II only
    (C) III only
    (D) II and III only
    (E) I, II, and III

12. If $f(x) = \left| \left(|x| - 3 \right) \right|$, what is the value of $f(1)$?

    (A) −2
    (B) −1
    (C) 1
    (D) 2
    (E) 3

1 −3

2

13. A researcher found that the number of bacteria in a certain sample doubles every hour. If there were 6 bacteria in the sample at the start of the experiment, how many bacteria were there after 9 hours?

    (A) 54
    (B) 512
    (C) 1,536
    (D) 3,072
    (E) 6,144

14. If $f(x) = x^2 + 2$, which of the following could be a value of $f(x)$?

    (A) −2
    (B) −1
    (C) 0
    (D) 1
    (E) 2

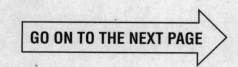

GO ON TO THE NEXT PAGE

15. How many numbers from 1 to 200 inclusive are equal to the cube of an integer?

(A) One   27
(B) Two   64
(C) Three 8
(D) Four
(E) Five

16. If the perimeter of rectangle *ABCD* is equal to *p*,

and $x = \frac{2}{3}y$, what is the value of *y* in terms of *p* ?

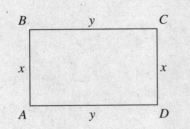

(A) $\dfrac{p}{10}$

(B) $\dfrac{3p}{10}$

(C) $\dfrac{p}{3}$

(D) $\dfrac{2p}{5}$

(E) $\dfrac{3p}{5}$

17. A basketball team had a ratio of wins to losses of 3:1. After the team won six games in a row, its ratio of wins to losses became 5:1. How many games had the team won <u>before</u> winning six games in a row?

(A) 3
(B) 6
(C) 9   3:1
(D) 15
(E) 24

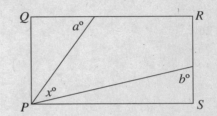

18. In rectangle *PQRS* above, what is *a* + *b* in terms of *x* ?

(A) $90 + x$
(B) $90 - x$
(C) $180 + x$
(D) $270 - x$
(E) $360 - x$

GO ON TO THE NEXT PAGE

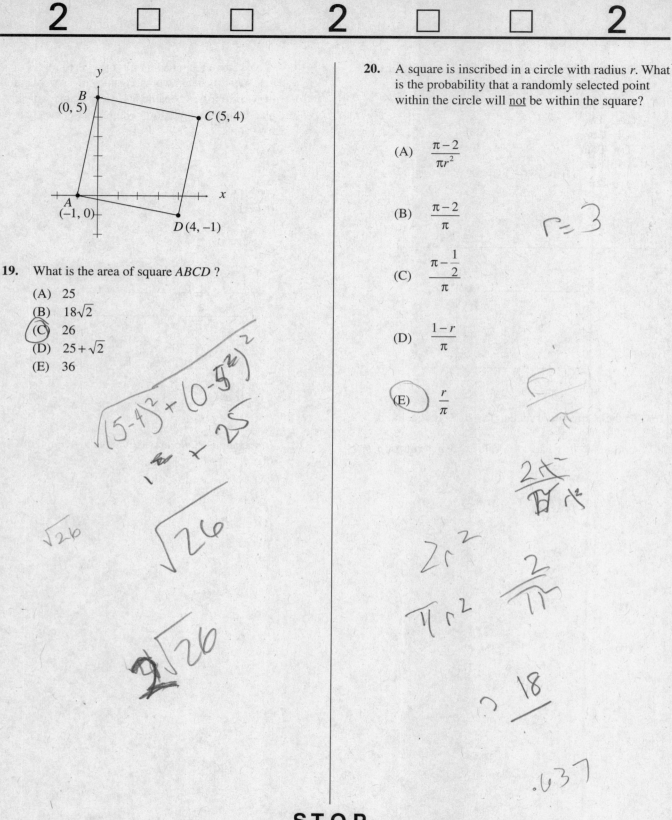

19. What is the area of square *ABCD* ?

(A) 25
(B) $18\sqrt{2}$
(C) 26
(D) $25 + \sqrt{2}$
(E) 36

$\sqrt{(5-4)^2 + (0-5)^2}$

$1 + 25$

$\sqrt{26}$ $\sqrt{26}$

$2\sqrt{26}$

20. A square is inscribed in a circle with radius *r*. What is the probability that a randomly selected point within the circle will <u>not</u> be within the square?

(A) $\dfrac{\pi - 2}{\pi r^2}$

(B) $\dfrac{\pi - 2}{\pi}$

(C) $\dfrac{\pi - \frac{1}{2}}{\pi}$

(D) $\dfrac{1 - r}{\pi}$

(E) $\dfrac{r}{\pi}$

$r = 3$

$\dfrac{6}{\pi}$

$\dfrac{2r^2}{\pi r^2}$

$2r^2$

πr^2 $\dfrac{2}{\pi}$

$\dfrac{18}{}$

$.637$

STOP

If you finish before time is called, you may check your work on this section only.
Do not turn to any other section in the test.

NO TEST MATERIAL ON THIS PAGE.

SECTION 3
Time — 25 minutes
24 Questions

Turn to Section 3 of your answer sheet to answer the questions in this section.

Directions: For each question in this section, select the best answer from among the choices given and fill in the corresponding circle on the answer sheet.

Each sentence below has one or two blanks, each blank indicating that something has been omitted. Beneath the sentence are five words or sets of words labeled A through E. Choose the word or set of words that, when inserted in the sentence, best fits the meaning of the sentence as a whole.

Example:

Hoping to ------- the dispute, negotiators proposed a compromise that they felt would be ------- to both labor and management.

(A) enforce . . useful
(B) end . . divisive
(C) overcome . . unattractive
(D) extend . . satisfactory
(E) resolve . . acceptable

Ⓐ Ⓑ Ⓒ Ⓓ ●

1. To prevent household fires, all flammable liquids, oily rags, and other ------- materials should be properly disposed of.
   (A) combustible   (B) unctuous   (C) restricted
   (D) diluted   (E) extinguishable

2. Mark was intent on maintaining his status as first in his class; because even the smallest mistakes infuriated him, he reviewed all his papers ------- before submitting them to his teacher.
   (A) explicitly   (B) hastily   (C) honestly
   (D) unconsciously   (E) meticulously

3. Because Jenkins neither ------- nor defends either side in the labor dispute, both parties admire his journalistic -------.
   (A) criticizes . . vitality
   (B) attacks . . neutrality
   (C) confronts . . aptitude
   (D) dismisses . . flair
   (E) protects . . integrity

4. It is ironic that the ------- insights of the great thinkers are voiced so often that they have become mere -------.
   (A) original . . clichés
   (B) banal . . beliefs
   (C) dubious . . habits
   (D) philosophical . . questions
   (E) abstract . . assessments

5. Some anthropologists claim that a few apes have been taught to communicate using rudimentary sign language, but skeptics argue that the apes are only ------- their trainers.
   (A) emulating   (B) condoning   (C) instructing
   (D) acknowledging   (E) belaboring

6. Most people imagine organ fugues to be ------- and -------, due to their technical difficulty and challenging counterpoint.
   (A) diminutive . . uplifting
   (B) harmonious . . petrifying
   (C) daunting . . esoteric
   (D) melodious . . enchanting
   (E) inscrutable . . classical

7. Since many disadvantaged individuals view their situations as ------- as well as intolerable, their attitudes can best be described as -------.
   (A) squalid . . obscure
   (B) unpleasant . . bellicose
   (C) acute . . sanguine
   (D) inalterable . . resigned
   (E) political . . perplexed

8. Only when one actually visits the ancient ruins of marvelous bygone civilizations does one truly appreciate the sad ------- of human greatness.
   (A) perspicacity   (B) magnitude   (C) artistry
   (D) transience   (E) quiescence

GO ON TO THE NEXT PAGE

The passages below are followed by questions based on their content. Answer the questions on the basis of what is <u>stated</u> or <u>implied</u> in the passage and in any introductory material that may be provided.

Questions 9-10 are based on the following passage.

Many of the techniques recommended to relieve writer's block actually involve writing. Exercises such as brainstorming and clustering are meant to loosen up
Line the writer and unstop pent-up creativity. But what if the
5 root of the problem were neurological? Recent research on the antipodal condition of hypergraphia has shown that the overwhelming desire to write is a side effect of temporal lobe epilepsy. Located in the area near the ear on both sides of the brain, the temporal lobes control
10 hearing, speech, and memory—all crucial to the task of communicating. Writer's block is usually accompanied by depression, which is said to mimic frontal lobe impairment.

9.   The question posed by the author in lines 4-5 serves to

(A) criticize traditional therapies for writer's block
(B) reflect on the information provided earlier in the passage
(C) transition into a new perspective on treating writer's block
(D) introduce more information on neurological disorders
(E) highlight the contrast between the two problems

10.   The author's primary purpose in the passage is to

(A) compare two problems faced by writers
(B) present a possible cause of writer's block
(C) provide detailed information about the temporal lobe
(D) question current therapeutic techniques for writing problems
(E) describe the side effects of epilepsy

Questions 11-12 are based on the following passage.

Paris is a circular city divided into 20 sectors called *arrondissements*, which spiral out from the center of the city. Romans inhabited the islands that make up
Line the heart of Paris in the first century A.D. and built a
5 wall to protect their territory. New walls were built in concentric circles as the city expanded, the sites of which were transformed into some of today's streets. The first twelve *arrondissements* were laid out by 1795 and the surrounding suburban areas were annexed in 1860 to add
10 eight more.

11.   The tone and content of the passage is most appropriate for which of the following?

(A) An urban planning proposal
(B) A traveler's guidebook
(C) A satire magazine
(D) An art history textbook
(E) A book of Roman history

12.   According to the passage, which of the following has most influenced the layout of Paris?

(A) The decreasing population of the city
(B) The ritual importance of the spiral symbol
(C) A need for defense
(D) Roman experiments in solid geometry
(E) The desire to improve upon Roman architectural styles

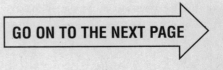
GO ON TO THE NEXT PAGE

Questions 13-24 are based on the following passage.

The following passage is an excerpt from nineteenth-cen-
tury British explorer David Livingston's memoirs of his
journeys to Africa.

The Expedition left England on the 10th of March,
1858, in Her Majesty's Colonial Steamer "Pearl,"
commanded by Captain Duncan; and, after enjoying the
Line   generous hospitality of our friends at Cape Town, with the
5   obliging attentions of Sir George Grey, and receiving on
board Mr. Francis Skead, R.N., as surveyor, we reached
the East Coast in the following May.

Our first object was to explore the Zambesi, its
mouths and tributaries, with a view to their being used
10   as highways for commerce and Christianity to pass into
the vast interior of Africa. When we came within five or
six miles of the land, the yellowish-green tinge of the sea
in soundings was suddenly succeeded by muddy water
with wrack, as of a river in flood. The two colours did
15   not intermingle, but the line of contact was as sharply
defined as when the ocean meets the land. It was observed
that under the wrack—consisting of reeds, sticks, and
leaves—and even under floating cuttlefish bones and
Portuguese "men-of-war" (Physalia), numbers of small
20   fish screen themselves from the eyes of birds of prey, and
from the rays of the torrid sun.

The Zambesi pours its waters into the ocean by four
mouths, namely, the Milambe, which is the most westerly,
the Kongone, the Luabo, and the Timbwe (or Muselo).
25   After the examination of three branches by the able and
energetic surveyor, Francis Skead, R.N., the Kongone was
found to be the best entrance. The immense amount of
sand brought down by the Zambesi has in the course of
ages formed a sort of promontory, against which the long
30   swell of the Indian Ocean, beating during the prevailing
winds, has formed bars, which, acting against the waters
of the delta, may have led to their exit sideways. The
Kongone is one of those lateral branches, and safest,
inasmuch as the bar has nearly two fathoms on it at
35   low water, and the rise at spring tides is from twelve
to fourteen feet. The bar is narrow, the passage nearly
straight, and, were it buoyed and a beacon placed on Pearl
Island, would always be safe to a steamer. When the wind
is from the east or north, the bar is smooth; if from the
40   south and south-east, it has a heavy break on it, and is
not to be attempted in boats. A strong current setting to
the east when the tide is flowing, and to the west when
ebbing, may drag a boat or ship into the breakers. If one
is doubtful of his longitude and runs east, he will soon
45   see the land at Timbwe disappear away to the north; and
coming west again, he can easily make out East Luabo
from its great size; and Kongone follows several miles

west. East Luabo has a good but long bar, and not to be
attempted unless the wind be north-east or east. It has
50   sometimes been called "Barra Catrina," and was used
in the embarkations of slaves. This may have been the
"River of Good Signs," of Vasco de Gama, as the mouth
is more easily seen from the seaward than any other; but
the absence of the pillar dedicated by that navigator to
55   "St. Raphael," leaves the matter in doubt. No Portuguese
live within eighty miles of any mouth of the Zambesi.

The Kongone is five miles east of the Milambe, or
western branch, and seven miles west from East Luabo,
which again is five miles from the Timbwe. We saw but
60   few natives, and these, by escaping from their canoes
into the mangrove thickets the moment they caught sight
of us, gave unmistakeable indications that they did not
have a very favourable opinion of white men. They were
probably fugitives from Portuguese slavery. In the grassy
65   glades buffaloes, wart-hogs, and three kinds of antelope
were abundant, and the latter easily obtained. A few
hours' hunting usually provided venison enough for a
score of men for several days.

13. The passage provides the most information about
which aspect of Livingston's journey?

(A) The people he met
(B) The colors of the surrounding environment
(C) The time he spent in Africa
(D) The river system on which he traveled
(E) The type of food available

14. According to the passage, Livingston explored the
Zambesi primarily in order to

(A) map the course of the river and its tributaries
(B) attempt to make contact with the Portuguese
settlers that live along it
(C) find a safe route along the coast of Africa
(D) determine whether the waterway could be
used for trade
(E) be the first to survey a new land

15. As used in the passage, the word "torrid" (line 21)
most nearly means

(A) pleasant
(B) dangerous
(C) hurried
(D) hidden
(E) scorching

GO ON TO THE NEXT PAGE

16. It may be inferred from the discussion of the bar in the Kongone river that

(A) under certain wind conditions, a ship traveling over the bar would most likely pass safely

(B) a beacon will soon be built on Pearl Island to help guide ships over the bar

(C) if the wind comes from the east or south, the bar in the Kongone river will be smooth

(D) of all the rivers in Africa, the Kongone is the best way of reaching the interior of Africa

(E) ships should not attempt to travel the Kongone unless the wind is from the northeast

17. According to the passage, a strong current on the Kongone

(A) may, depending on the tide, increase the danger to a boat traveling along the river

(B) will make the river impassable to most ships

(C) increases the water level from two fathoms to twelve to fourteen feet

(D) led de Gama to name the river the "Barra Catrina"

(E) caused an immense amount of sand to form a promontory in the river

18. The author most likely mentions Vasco de Gama (line 52) in order to

(A) indicate that other explorers have already charted the course of the river

(B) refer to a previous navigator that Livingston admires

(C) demonstrate a possible connection between Livingston's expedition and that of a another navigator

(D) explain why no Portuguese live within eighty miles of the river

(E) reveal why there is pillar dedicated to St. Raphael at the mouth of the river

19. The tone of the passage may best be described as

(A) disinterested

(B) enthusiastic

(C) passionate

(D) personally revealing

(E) objective

20. The mention of the natives in the final paragraph suggests that

(A) most of the inhabitants of Africa do not have a favorable view of Livingston

(B) the people Livingston encountered had little interest in making contact with him

(C) there were not many people living along the rivers that Livingston explored

(D) the Portuguese had enslaved a great many of the native inhabitants of Africa

(E) the native inhabitants were upset by the arrival of Livingston

21. The primary function of the first paragraph is to

(A) give the reader a glimpse into Livingston's private life

(B) establish Livingston's personal characteristics and skills as an explorer

(C) provide a brief prelude to the later details in the passage

(D) emphasize the lackadaisical nature of Livingston and his companions

(E) explain why Livingston was in Africa

22. The passage lists which of the following as a factor in Livingston's designation as Kongone as the "best" entrance to the Zambesi for boat travel?

(A) The ease with which a boat can travel on the river, regardless of the current or the wind direction

(B) The abundant food, including antelope and buffalo, that can be found along the banks of the river

(C) The lack of native inhabitants living near the river

(D) The presence of prominent land features that make it easy for a navigator to find the Kongone

(E) The beacon placed on Pearl Island

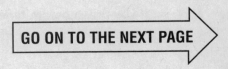

GO ON TO THE NEXT PAGE

23. Based on the passage, which of the following may be properly inferred about the Kongone?

    (A) The waters of the Kongone are home to a large variety of cuttlefish and small fish.
    (B) The water levels in the Kongone change significantly with the seasons.
    (C) The Kongone is the most westerly of the four mouths of the Zambesi.
    (D) The Kongone has the smoothest bar of any of the mouths of the Zambesi.
    (E) The Kongone was often used by the Portuguese for the disembarkation of slaves.

24. The passage states that East Luabo offers which advantage to navigators?

    (A) Of the tributaries of the Zambesi, it is the most prominent to a viewer approaching from the sea.
    (B) No Portuguese live within eighty miles of East Luabo.
    (C) Its bar is safe to boaters under most conditions.
    (D) East Luabo is more familiar to European navigators than the other mouths of the Zambesi.
    (E) It is the only tributary of the Zambesi that had previously been charted.

STOP

If you finish before time is called, you may check your work on this section only.
Do not turn to any other section in the test.

NO TEST MATERIAL ON THIS PAGE.

SECTION 4

Time — 25 minutes

20 Questions

Turn to Section 4 of your answer sheet to answer the questions in this section.

Directions: This section contains two types of questions. You have 25 minutes to complete both types. For questions 1-8, solve each problem and decide which is the best of the choices given. Fill in the corresponding circle on the answer sheet. You may use any available space for scratchwork.

Notes

1. The use of a calculator is permitted.

2. All numbers used are real numbers.

3. Figures that accompany problems in this test are intended to provide information useful in solving the problems. They are drawn as accurately as possible EXCEPT when it is stated in a specific problem that the figure is not drawn to scale. All figures lie in a plane unless other wise indicated.

4. Unless otherwise specified, the domain of any function f is assumed to be the set of all real numbers x for which $f(x)$ is a real number.

Reference Information

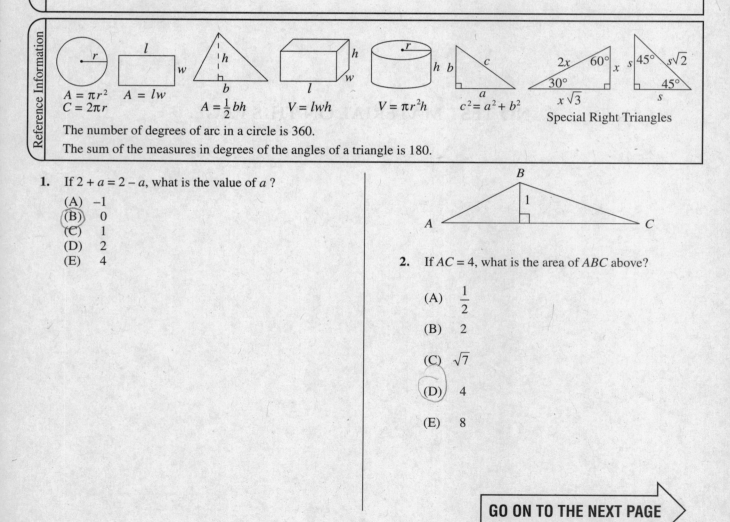

$A = \pi r^2$
$C = 2\pi r$

$A = lw$

$A = \frac{1}{2}bh$

$V = lwh$

$V = \pi r^2 h$

$c^2 = a^2 + b^2$

Special Right Triangles

The number of degrees of arc in a circle is 360.

The sum of the measures in degrees of the angles of a triangle is 180.

1. If $2 + a = 2 - a$, what is the value of a ?

(A) −1
(B) 0
(C) 1
(D) 2
(E) 4

2. If $AC = 4$, what is the area of ABC above?

(A) $\dfrac{1}{2}$

(B) 2

(C) $\sqrt{7}$

(D) 4

(E) 8

GO ON TO THE NEXT PAGE

3. In the figure above, the perimeter of square A is $\frac{2}{3}$ the perimeter of square B, and the perimeter of square B is $\frac{2}{3}$ the perimeter of square C. If the area of square A is 16, what is the area of square C?

   (A) 24
   (B) 36
   (C) 64
   (D) 72
   (E) 81

$16 = \frac{2}{3} \, 6$

4. A bakery uses a special flour mixture that contains corn, wheat, and rye in the ratio of 3:5:2. If a bag of the mixture contains 5 pounds of rye, how many pounds of wheat does it contain?

   (A) 2
   (B) 5
   (C) 7.5
   (D) 10
   (E) 12.5

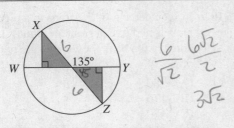

$\frac{5}{x} = \frac{2}{5}$ $\frac{8}{5}$

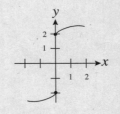

5. If $\overline{WY}$ and $\overline{XZ}$ are diameters with lengths of 12, what is the area of the shaded region?

   (A) 36
   (B) 30
   (C) 18
   (D) 12
   (E) 9

$\frac{6}{\sqrt{2}}$ $\frac{6\sqrt{2}}{2}$ $3\sqrt{2}$

6. If the function f is defined for $-2 \le x \le 2$, then which of the following could be the graph of $f(x)$?

   (A)
   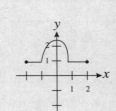

   (B)
   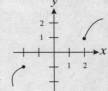

   (C)
   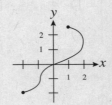

   (D)
   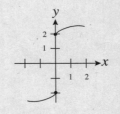

   (E)
   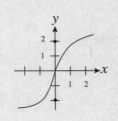

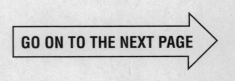
GO ON TO THE NEXT PAGE

Temperature in °F	Number of Customers
10	4
20	9
30	37
40	66
50	100

7. A coffee shop noticed that the outside temperature affected the number of customers who came to the shop that day, as shown in the table above. Which of the following graphs best represents the relationship between the outside temperature and the number of customers, as indicated by the table?

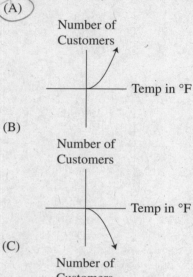

(A)

Number of Customers

Temp in °F

(B)

Number of Customers

Temp in °F

(C)

Number of Customers

Temp in °F

(D)

Number of Customers

Temp in °F

(E)

Number of Customers

Temp in °F

8. If c is positive, what percent of $3c$ is 9 ?

(A) $\dfrac{c}{100}\%$

(B) $\dfrac{c}{3}\%$

(C) $\dfrac{9}{c}\%$

(D) 3%

(E) $\dfrac{300}{c}\%$

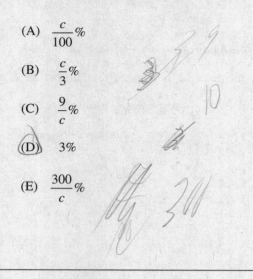

9. $\dfrac{900}{10} + \dfrac{90}{100} + \dfrac{9}{1000} =$

(A) 90.09
(B) 90.099
(C) 90.909
(D) 99.09
(E) 999

10. Fifteen percent of the coins in a piggy bank are nickels and five percent are dimes. If there are 220 coins in the bank, how many are <u>not</u> nickels or dimes?

(A) 80
(B) 176
(C) 180
(D) 187
(E) 200

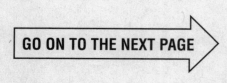

GO ON TO THE NEXT PAGE

11. At the beginning of 1999, the population of Rockville was 204,000 and the population of Springfield was 216,000. If the population of each city increased by exactly 20% in 1999, how many more people lived in Springfield than in Rockville at the end of 1999?

    (A) 2,400
    (B) 10,000
    (C) 12,000
    (D) 14,400
    (E) 43,200

    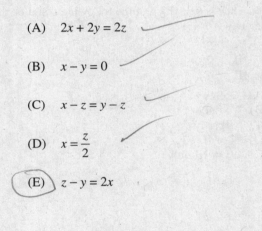

12. If $x + y = z$ and $x = y$, then all of the following are true EXCEPT

    (A) $2x + 2y = 2z$

    (B) $x - y = 0$

    (C) $x - z = y - z$

    (D) $x = \dfrac{z}{2}$

    (E) $z - y = 2x$

13. In a list of seven integers, 13 is the lowest member, 37 is the highest member, the mean is 23, the median is 24, and the mode is 18. If the numbers 8 and 43 are then included in the list, which of the following will change?

    I.   The mean
    II. The median
    III. The mode

    (A) I only
    (B) I and II only
    (C) I and III only
    (D) II and III only
    (E) I, II, and III

    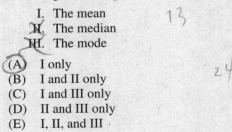

14. If $|x| \neq 0$, which of the following statements must be true?

    (A) x is positive.

    (B) $2x$ is positive.

    (C) $\dfrac{1}{x}$ is positive.

    (D) x^2 is positive.

    (E) x^3 is positive.

15. Rock climbing routes are rated on a numbered scale with the highest number representing the most difficult route. Sally tried a range of shoe sizes on each of several routes of varying difficulty and found that when she wore smaller shoes, she could climb routes of greater difficulty. If D represents the difficulty rating of a route Sally successfully climbed and s represents the size of the shoes she wore on such a route, then which of the following could express D as a function of s ?

    (A) $D(s) = s^2$

    (B) $D(s) = \sqrt{s}$

    (C) $D(s) = 4s$

    (D) $D(s) = s - 3.5$

    (E) $D(s) = \dfrac{45}{s}$

    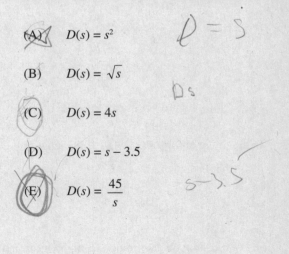

GO ON TO THE NEXT PAGE

16. If $a^2b = 12^2$, and b is an odd integer, then a could be divisible by all of the following EXCEPT

    (A)   3
    (B)   4
    (C)   6
    (D)   9
    (E)   12

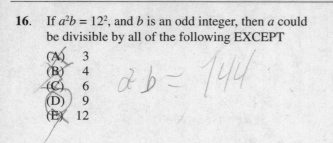

$ab = 144$

17. Which of the following must be true?

    I.   The sum of two consecutive integers is odd.
    II. The sum of three consecutive integers is even.
    III. The sum of three consecutive integers is a multiple of 3.

    (A)   I only
    (B)   II only
    (C)   I and II only
    (D)   I and III only
    (E)   I, II, and III

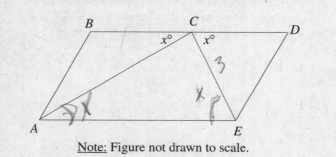

Note: Figure not drawn to scale.

18. In the figure above, $\overline{BD} \parallel \overline{AE}$. If the length of $\overline{CE}$ is 3, what is the length of $\overline{AC}$?

    (A)   3
    (B)   4
    (C)   5
    (D) $3\sqrt{3}$
    (E)   It cannot be determined from the information given.

19. If $(a - 5)(b + 5) < 0$, then which of the following must be true?

    I. $a < 5$
    II. $b > -5$
    III. $b \neq -5$

    (A)   None of the above
    (B)   I only
    (C)   III only
    (D)   II and III only
    (E)   I, II, and III

20. The value of the nth term of a sequence is given by the expression $a^{3n} - 3$. If the second term of the sequence is 61, which of the following could be the value of a?

    I. -2
    II. 2
    III. 4

    (A)   I only
    (B)   II only
    (C)   III only
    (D)   I or II only
    (E)   II or III only

n^{th}

a^{3n-3}

$a^{3n} - 3 = 61$

$a^{3n} = 64$

$4^6 = 64$

STOP

If you finish before time is called, you may check your work on this section only.
Do not turn to any other section in the test.

NO TEST MATERIAL ON THIS PAGE.

SECTION 5
Time — 25 minutes
35 Questions

Turn to Section 5 of your answer sheet to answer the questions in this section.

Directions: For each question in this section, select the best answer from among the choices given and fill in the corresponding circle on the answer sheet.

The following sentences test correctness and effectiveness of expression. Part of each sentence or the entire sentence is underlined; beneath each sentence are five ways of phrasing the underlined material. Choice A repeats the original phrasing; the other four choices are different. If you think the original phrasing produces a better sentence than any of the alternatives, select choice A; if not, select one of the other choices.

In making your selection, follow the requirements of standard written English; that is, pay attention to grammar, choice of words, sentence construction, and punctuation. Your selection should result in the most effective sentence—clear and precise, without awkwardness or ambiguity.

EXAMPLE:

Laura Ingalls Wilder published her first book <u>and she was sixty-five years old then</u>.
(A) and she was sixty-five years old then
(B) when she was sixty-five
(C) at age sixty-five years old
(D) upon the reaching of sixty-five years
(E) at the time when she was sixty-five

Ⓐ ● Ⓒ Ⓓ Ⓔ

1. Laura Southworth, a children's author who is beginning to attract the notice of critics and librarians alike, wrote and illustrated her first story *Tika* <u>and she was only seven years old then</u>.

(A) and she was only seven years old then
(B) at age seven years old only
(C) when she was only seven years old
(D) upon the reaching of only seven years
(E) at the time when she was only seven

2. Many building technologies <u>are changing</u> significantly in the last two thousand years, but today's concrete is still similar to the concrete of Roman times.

(A) are changing
(B) have changed
(C) had changed
(D) are going to change
(E) change

3. The video class that meets on Thursdays <u>makes use of the innovative software MAYA, which enables students to design and build</u> a virtual stage set, a home, or even a city in three dimensions.

(A) makes use of the innovative software MAYA, which enables students to design and build
(B) using the innovative software MAYA and enabling students to design and build
(C) besides making use of the innovative software MAYA, enables students to design and build
(D) because it makes use of the innovative software MAYA, it enables students to design and build
(E) not only making use of the innovative software MAYA, but also enabling students in the design and building of

4. The ancient belief <u>of all matter being in continuous motion</u> seems borne out by modern discoveries about atomic structure.

(A) of all matter being in continuous motion
(B) is that all matter is in continuous motion
(C) which is that all matter is in continuous motion
(D) that all matter is in continuous motion
(E) of all matter that is in continuous motion

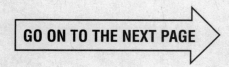

GO ON TO THE NEXT PAGE

5. If Marcel Proust's memory <u>had not been felicitously stirred by the taste of a madeleine</u>, he might never have been moved to write *Remembrance of Things Past*.

   (A) had not been felicitously stirred by the taste of a madeleine
   (B) had not been stirred by means of the felicitous taste of a madeleine
   (C) were not to be felicitously stirred by the taste of a madeleine
   (D) were not to be stirred by the taste of a felicitous madeleine
   (E) should not be stirred by the felicitous taste of a madeleine

6. The game hadn't ended yet, but Sarin <u>knows that his chances of winning are slipping away by the second and he needs a miracle</u>.

   (A) knows that his chances of winning are slipping away by the second and he needs a miracle
   (B) knew that he had no chance of winning and in a second he would need a miracle
   (C) knows that winning is a long shot and that he needs a miracle
   (D) knew that his chances to win were slipping away by the second and a miracle is what he needed
   (E) knew that his chances of winning were slipping away by the second and he needed a miracle

7. When preparing to write a research paper, you should gather information from books, periodicals, and the Internet, <u>and your documenting of sources should be carefully done</u>.

   (A) and your documenting of sources should be carefully done
   (B) and document your sources carefully
   (C) and you should document your careful sources
   (D) because your sources need to be documented carefully
   (E) yet you need to carefully document your sources

8. Because it has rich limestone similar to <u>the Rhine Valley</u>, Pennsylvania's Lehigh Valley attracted many German settlers who had brought traditional farming methods with them from home.

   (A) the Rhine Valley
   (B) the Rhine Valley did
   (C) it has the Rhine Valley
   (D) the Rhine Valleys
   (E) that of the Rhine Valley

9. Catherine II of Russia died at <u>67, and her reputation still surviving as one of the forward-looking, enlightened monarchs of Europe</u>.

   (A) 67, and her reputation still surviving as one of the forward-looking, enlightened monarchs of Europe
   (B) 67, however her reputation is surviving as one of the forward-looking, enlightened monarchs of Europe
   (C) 67, her reputation as one of the forward-looking, enlightened monarchs of Europe still surviving
   (D) 67; her reputation as one of the forward-looking, enlightened monarchs of Europe still survives
   (E) 67; and her reputation as being one of the more forward-looking, enlightened monarchs of Europe will always survive

10. <u>You may not realize that it is still possible to pick one's own fruit from an orchard</u>; the supermarket is not the only place where fruit is available today.

    (A) You may not realize that it is still possible to pick one's own fruit from an orchard
    (B) One may not realize that it is still possible to pick your own fruit from an orchard
    (C) Picking your own fruit from the orchard
    (D) Although many don't realize it, picking fruit from the orchard is still an option
    (E) Picking your own fruit from the orchard can be a possibility

11. The Bauhaus school of design, craft, and architecture held many theories in common with the De Stijl movement; <u>however, it instigated a paradigm shift in design</u>.

    (A) however, it instigated a paradigm shift in design
    (B) however, they instigated a paradigm shift in design
    (C) however, the Bauhaus school instigated a paradigm shift in design
    (D) and the Bauhaus school instigated a paradigm shift in design
    (E) and a paradigm shift was instigated by the Bauhaus school

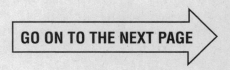

GO ON TO THE NEXT PAGE

The following sentences test your ability to recognize grammar and usage errors. Each sentence contains either a single error or no error at all. No sentence contains more than one error. The error, if there is one, is underlined and lettered. If the sentence contains an error, select the one underlined part that must be changed to make the sentence correct. If the sentence is correct, select choice E. In choosing answers, follow the requirements of standard written English.

EXAMPLE:

The other delegates and him immediately
A   B   C
accepted the resolution drafted by the
                        D
neutral states. No error
                E

Ⓐ ● Ⓒ Ⓓ Ⓔ

12. Two of Charles Dickens' most famous characters,
                              A
    Oliver Twist and David Copperfield, were

    an orphan who fell upon hard luck as children,
    B   C
    but found happiness later in life. No error
    D   E

13. A number of horticultural arts, including bonsai
      A   B
    and ikebana, began in Japan. No error
                 C   D   E

14. When my sister and me visited the eulogized city
                        A   B
    of Troy, we noticed it was much smaller than the
                                             C
    epic tales had suggested. No error
         D   E

15. Complete exhausted from a hard day at work,
    A   B
    Evelyn fell asleep on the bus and,

    when she finally awoke, found that she had missed
         C   D
    her stop. No error
              E

16. There is many benefits to biking; it is both a rigor-
          A   B
    ous form of exercise and an environmentally
        C
    sustainable, conscious mode of transportation.
    D
    No error
    E

17. Despite having had no formal training, Jackie was
             A
    nonetheless able to master the piano by listening
    B
    to recordings, reading instructional books, and
    C
    she practiced on her own. No error
    D   E

18. Of all the jingoists in the country, that politician,
                        A   B
    known for fanatical patriotism, appears to be the
                                    C
    more dangerous. No error
    D   E

19. Many scholars consider Ulysses James Joyce's
                    A
    greatest work; however, many readers find
    B   C
    Dubliners more accessible. No error
             D   E

20. Dentists agree that brushing your teeth three times
            A   B
    a day promote good dental health and a
          C
    more attractive smile. No error
    D   E

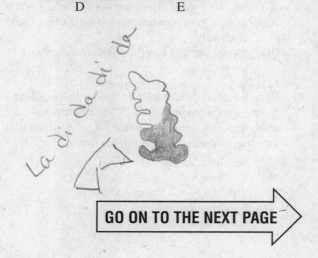

GO ON TO THE NEXT PAGE

21. Two current television trends, the home improve-

ment show craze and the "hot rod" automobile fad,

<u>seem</u> to show a <u>dissatisfaction with</u> our domestic
  A   B

spaces and <u>indicating</u> a desire for
           C

<u>something riskier</u> and more exciting. <u>No error</u>
    D   E

22. <u>Before</u> handing <u>in her</u> assignment, Michelle
    A   B

<u>checked</u> all of her sources twice; her greatest fear
  C

<u>being</u> receiving any grade lower than a B. <u>No error</u>
  D   E

23. Species of monkeys <u>living among</u> a variety of
                    A

creatures in the rainforest come <u>in contact with</u>
                                  B

predators and prey alike as <u>it swings</u> <u>through</u> the
                         C   D

trees. <u>No error</u>
      E

24. The pitch of the note that a stringed <u>instrument</u>
                                A

<u>makes</u> depends on the length, weight, and tension
  B

of the string: <u>highest</u> notes <u>are produced by</u> shorter,
             C   D

lighter, or tighter strings. <u>No error</u>
                   E

25. When his daughter asked him <u>hundreds of questions</u>
                           A

about the blue whale model <u>suspended</u> in the Ameri-
                        B

can Museum of Natural History, the father <u>exercised</u>
                              C

<u>patients</u> and answered every query. <u>No error</u>
  D   E

26. I <u>choose</u> to carry my necessities in my pockets, <u>and</u>
    A   B

most other women <u>prefer</u> <u>to use</u> purses. <u>No error</u>
              C   D   E

27. Saif knew that the other <u>applicants</u> weren't
                    A

<u>as good as him</u>, so he wasn't surprised when the
  B   C

company <u>offered him</u> the lucrative position. <u>No error</u>
       D   E

28. Noelle and Natalie argued <u>at great length</u> about the
                      A

<u>authenticity</u> of the painting; <u>finally</u> Noelle decided
  B   C

that <u>she</u> was right. <u>No error</u>
    D   E

29. <u>Not</u> everyone <u>would agree</u> that Lawrence Olivier's
  A   B

performance in *Henry V* <u>was</u> superior
                   C

<u>to Kenneth Branagh</u>. <u>No error</u>
  D   E

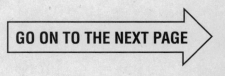

GO ON TO THE NEXT PAGE

Directions: The following passage is an early draft of an essay. Some parts of the passage need to be rewritten.

Read the passage and select the best answers for the questions that follow. Some questions are about particular sentences or parts of sentences and ask you to improve sentence structure or word choice. Other questions ask you to consider organization and development. In choosing answers, follow the requirements of standard written English.

Questions 30-35 are based on the following passage.

(1) Many laws seem to be created for the purpose of protecting people from themselves. (2) Some examples are age limits for off-road vehicles, seatbelt requirements for cars, and wearing a helmet when riding a motorcycle. (3) Opponents of these laws feel that their rights are being restricted. (4) If it doesn't hurt anyone else, why should there be a law? (5) But if they become injured, it can raise insurance rates for everyone.

(6) In another context, consider people putting aside money for their retirement. (7) Suppose they work for a fast-growing company, the hot new stock pick. (8) Many employees invest heavily in the stock. (9) The stock price plummets, their savings disappear.

(10) Laws preventing people from having too much company stock in their retirement accounts could protect them from financial disaster. (11) It isn't easy to find the proper balance between individual rights and the common good. (12) Some people will think that the new law goes too far. (13) Others complaining that it doesn't go far enough. (14) If it is too much, we can stand up and fight it. (15) Although we may not agree with every law, some minor inconveniences are part of living in our society.

30. Which of the following is the best revision of the underlined portion of sentence 1 (reproduced below)?

Many laws seem to be created for the purpose of protecting people from themselves.

(A) (as it is now)
(B) in order to protect people
(C) as a result of protecting people
(D) so that people will have protection
(E) that let people be protected

31. What is the best way to deal with sentence 6?
(A) Replace "another context" with "a similar vein."
(B) Replace the word "context" with "way."
(C) Insert the words "you could" before "consider."
(D) Delete the word "another."
(E) Omit the entire sentence.

32. In which of the following ways could sentences 8 and 9 (reproduced below) best be written?

Many employees invest heavily in the stock. The stock price plummets, their savings disappear.

(A) (As they are now)
(B) Employees can invest heavily in the stock; then the stock price plummets, their savings will disappear.
(C) After the employees invest heavily in the stock, the plummeting stock price causes their savings to disappear.
(D) When employees invest heavily in the stock, it is then that the stock price can plummet and their savings disappear.
(E) If employees invest heavily in the stock and the stock price plummets, their savings will disappear.

33. What should be done with sentence 10?
(A) Insert "On the other hand" at the beginning.
(B) Switch it with sentence 7.
(C) Move it to the end of the second paragraph.
(D) Change "their" to "his."
(E) Change "accounts" to "account."

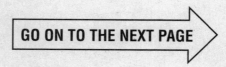
GO ON TO THE NEXT PAGE

34. Which of the following most effectively revises the underlined portions of sentences 12 and 13 (reproduced below) in order to combine the sentences?

Some people will think that the new law goes too far. Others complaining that it doesn't go far enough.

(A) far: some others complaining
(B) far, others complain
(C) far; others are complaining
(D) far; others have complained
(E) far, while others will complain

35. Which of the following sentences could best be deleted without detracting from the flow of the passage?

(A) Sentence 3
(B) Sentence 7
(C) Sentence 11
(D) Sentence 14
(E) Sentence 15

STOP

If you finish before time is called, you may check your work on this section only.
Do not turn to any other section in the test.

SECTION 6

Time — 25 minutes

18 Questions

Turn to Section 6 of your answer sheet to answer the questions in this section.

Directions: This section contains two types of questions. You have 25 minutes to complete both types. For questions 1-8, solve each problem and decide which is the best of the choices given. Fill in the corresponding oval on the answer sheet. You may use any available space for scatchwork.

Notes

1. The use of a calculator is permitted.

2. All numbers used are real numbers.

3. Figures that accompany problems in this test are intended to provide information useful in solving the problems. They are drawn as accurately as possible EXCEPT when it is stated in a specific problem that the figure is not drawn to scale. All figures lie in a plane unless otherwise indicated.

4. Unless otherwise specified, the domain of any function f is assumed to be the set of all real numbers x for which $f(x)$ is a real number.

Reference Information

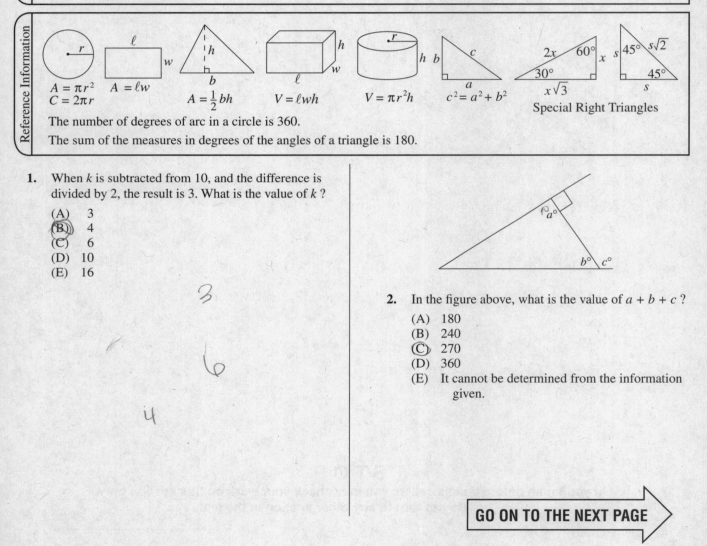

$A = \pi r^2$
$C = 2\pi r$

$A = \ell w$

$A = \frac{1}{2} bh$

$V = \ell w h$

$V = \pi r^2 h$

$c^2 = a^2 + b^2$

Special Right Triangles

The number of degrees of arc in a circle is 360.

The sum of the measures in degrees of the angles of a triangle is 180.

1. When k is subtracted from 10, and the difference is divided by 2, the result is 3. What is the value of k ?

    (A)   3
    (B)   4
    (C)   6
    (D)   10
    (E)   16

2. In the figure above, what is the value of $a + b + c$?

    (A)   180
    (B)   240
    (C)   270
    (D)   360
    (E)   It cannot be determined from the information given.

GO ON TO THE NEXT PAGE

3. Steve ran a 12-mile race at an average speed of 8 miles per hour. If Adam ran the same race at an average speed of 6 miles per hour, how many minutes longer than Steve did Adam take to complete the race than did Steve?

(A)   9
(B)   12
(C)   16
(D)   24
(E)   30

4. Which of the following is equivalent to $\frac{4a}{3} \cdot 6a$?

(A) $\frac{8a^2}{3}$

(B) $\frac{10a^2}{3}$

(C) $\frac{24a}{3}$

(D) $8a^2$

(E) $24a^2$

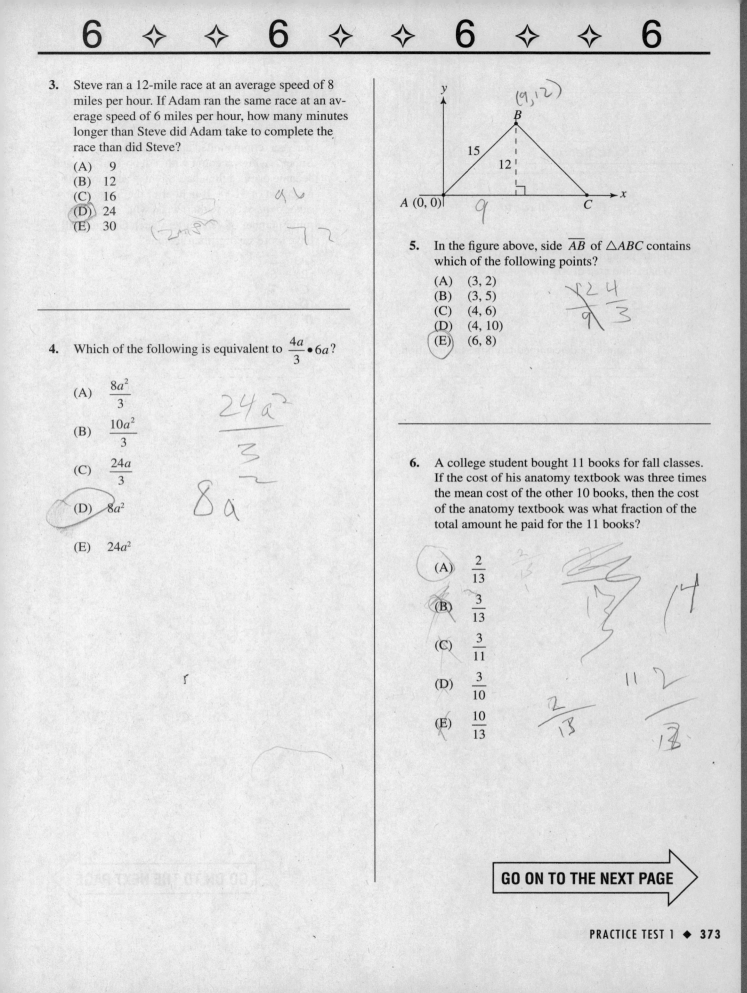

5. In the figure above, side $\overline{AB}$ of $\triangle ABC$ contains which of the following points?

(A)   (3, 2)
(B)   (3, 5)
(C)   (4, 6)
(D)   (4, 10)
(E)   (6, 8)

6. A college student bought 11 books for fall classes. If the cost of his anatomy textbook was three times the mean cost of the other 10 books, then the cost of the anatomy textbook was what fraction of the total amount he paid for the 11 books?

(A) $\frac{2}{13}$

(B) $\frac{3}{13}$

(C) $\frac{3}{11}$

(D) $\frac{3}{10}$

(E) $\frac{10}{13}$

GO ON TO THE NEXT PAGE

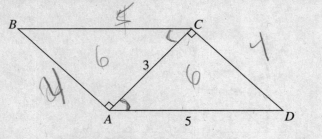

Note: Figure not drawn to scale.

7. In parallelogram *ABCD* above, *AC* = 3 and *AD* = 5.
   What is the area of *ABCD* ?

   (A) 12
   (B) 15
   (C) 18
   (D) 20
   (E) It cannot be determined from the information
        given.

8. A bank offers two types of savings accounts. The
   "Standard Savings" account pays interest at a rate
   of 5% per year compounded annually. The "Super
   Savings" account pays interest at a rate of 8%
   per year, compounded annually. Graham opens a
   Super Savings account with a deposit of $80 and
   Jeannie opens a Standard Savings account with
   a deposit of $100. If neither of them makes any
   other deposits or withdrawals, what is the minimum number of years after which Graham will
   have more savings than Jeannie?

   (A) 5
   (B) 6
   (C) 7
   (D) 8
   (E) 10

GO ON TO THE NEXT PAGE

Directions: For Student-Produced Response questions 9-18, use the grids at the bottom of the answer sheet page on which you have answered questions 1-8.

Each of the remaining 10 questions requires you to solve the problem and enter your answer by marking the circles in the special grid, as shown in the examples below. You may use any available space for scratchwork.

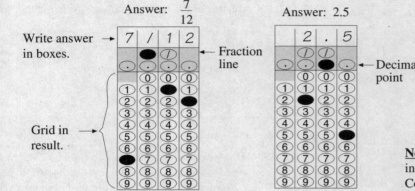

Answer: $\frac{7}{12}$

Write answer in boxes.

Fraction line

Grid in result.

Answer: 2.5

Decimal point

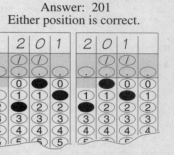

Answer: 201
Either position is correct.

Note: You may start your answers in any column, space permitting. Columns not needed should be left blank.

• Mark no more than one circle in any column.

• Because the answer sheet will be machine-scored, **you will receive credit only if the circles are filled in correctly.**

• Although not required, it is suggested that you write your answer in the boxes at the top of the columns to help you fill in the circles accurately.

• Some problems may have more than one correct answer. In such cases, grid only one answer.

• No question has a negative answer.

• **Mixed numbers** such as $3\frac{1}{2}$ must be gridded as

  3.5 or 7/2. (If ⬛ is gridded, it will be

  interpreted as $\frac{31}{2}$, not $3\frac{1}{2}$.)

• **Decimal Answers:** If you obtain a decimal answer with more digits than the grid can accommodate, it may be either rounded or truncated, but it must fill the entire grid. For example, if you obtain an answer such as 0.6666..., you should record your result as .666 or .667. **A less accurate value such as .66 or .67 will be scored as incorrect.**

Acceptable ways to grid $\frac{2}{3}$ are:

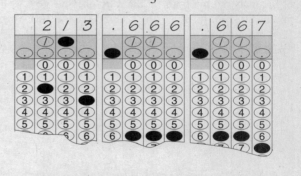

9. If $\dfrac{x + 2x + 3x}{2} = 6$, what is the value of x?

10. When n is divided by 5, the remainder is 4. When n is divided by 4, the remainder is 3. If $0 < n < 100$, what is one possible value of n?

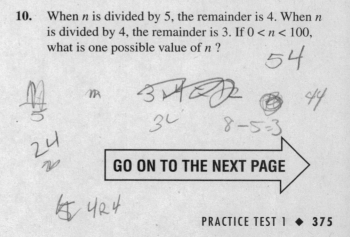

GO ON TO THE NEXT PAGE

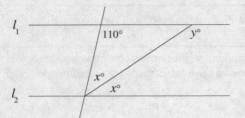

11. If l_1 is parallel to l_2 in the figure above, what is the value of y ?

12. If $x^2 = 16$ and $y^2 = 4$, what is the greatest possible value of $(x - y)^2$?

$$(-4 - 2)^2 \qquad 36$$

13. There are 250 students in 10th grade at Northgate High School. All 10th graders must take French or Spanish, but not both. If the ratio of males to females in 10th grade is 2 to 3, and 80 of the 100 French students are male, how many females take Spanish?

100   150   5

40   80

130

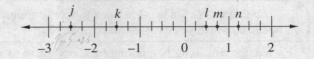

14. On the number line above, j, k, l, m, and n are coordinates of the indicated points. What is the value of $\dfrac{jk}{lmn}$?

$$3.75 \quad \frac{-5}{.46\,2.5} \quad \frac{-10}{5} = \frac{-2}{1}$$

15. Hanna is arranging tools in a toolbox. She has one hammer, one wrench, one screwdriver, one tape measure, and one staple gun to place in 5 empty spots in her toolbox. If all of the tools will be placed in a spot, one tool in each spot, and the hammer and screwdriver only fit in the first 2 spots, how many different ways can she arrange the tools in the spots?

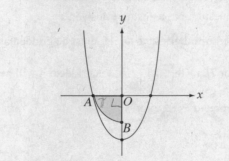

16. In the figure above, AB is the arc of a circle with center O. Point A lies on the graph of $y = x^2 - b$, where b is a constant. If the area of sector AOB is π, then what is the value of b ?

$$S = r\theta$$
$$\pi = r\theta$$
$$\frac{\pi}{90} = \theta$$

GO ON TO THE NEXT PAGE ⟩

17. $AB \perp BD$, and $\overline{AB}$ and $\overline{CD}$ bisect each other at point X. If $AB = 8$ and $CD = 10$, what is the length of $\overline{BD}$?

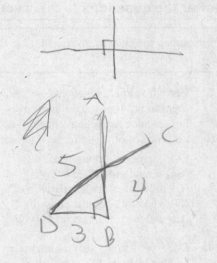

18. A researcher found that the amount of sleep that she allowed her mice to get was inversely proportional to the number of errors the mice made, on average, in a maze test. If mice that got 2 hours of sleep made 3 errors in the maze test, how many errors, on average, do mice with 5 hours of sleep make?

$(2)(3)$

$\dfrac{2}{3}$ $\dfrac{5}{X}$

STOP
If you finish before time is called, you may check your work on this section only.
Do not turn to any other section in the test.

SECTION 7

Time — 25 minutes

24 Questions

Turn to Section 7 of your answer sheet to answer the questions in this section.

Directions: For each question in this section, select the best answer from among the choices given and fill in the corresponding circle on the answer sheet.

Each sentence below has one or two blanks, each blank indicating that something has been omitted. Beneath the sentence are five words or sets of words labeled A through E. Choose the word or set of words that, when inserted in the sentence, best fits the meaning of the sentence as a whole.

Example:

Hoping to ------- the dispute, negotiators proposed a compromise that they felt would be ------- to both labor and management.

(A) enforce . . useful
(B) end . . divisive
(C) overcome . . unattractive
(D) extend . . satisfactory
(E) resolve . . acceptable

Ⓐ Ⓑ Ⓒ Ⓓ ●

---

1. If it is true that morality cannot exist without religion, then does not the erosion of religion herald the ------- of morality?

    (A) regulation   (B) basis   (C) belief
    (D) collapse   (E) value

2. Shaken by two decades of virtual anarchy, the majority of people were ready to buy ------- at any price.

    (A) stability   (B) emancipation   (C) prosperity
    (D) liberty   (E) enfranchisement

3. Certain animal behaviors, such as mating rituals, seem to be -------, and therefore ------- external factors such as climate changes, food supply, or the presence of other animals of the same species.

    (A) learned . . immune to
    (B) innate . . unaffected by
    (C) intricate . . beleaguered by
    (D) specific . . confused with
    (E) memorized . . controlled by

4. The stoic former general led his civilian life as he had his military life, with simplicity and ------- dignity.

    (A) benevolent   (B) informal   (C) austere
    (D) aggressive   (E) succinct

5. Although bound to uphold the law, a judge is free to use his discretion to ------- the cruel severity of some criminal penalties.

    (A) mitigate   (B) understand   (C) condone
    (D) provoke   (E) enforce

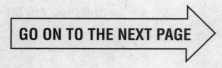

GO ON TO THE NEXT PAGE

The passages below are followed by questions based on their content; questions following a pair of related passages may also be based on the relationship between the paired passages. Answer the questions on the basis of what is <u>stated</u> or <u>implied</u> in the passage and in any introductory material that may be provided.

Questions 6-9 are based on the following passages.

Passage 1

Geological Evolutionary Theory, the idea of scientifically dating Earth, is a relatively recent concept. Seventeenth-century scientists began to use geological
Line evidence to bolster the idea that Earth evolved over time.
5 In the eighteenth century, British scientist James Hutton posited his Theory of Uniformity. According to this theory, processes that changed the Earth in the past are still at work today. In the nineteenth century, Charles Darwin expanded the idea of geological evolution to
10 include biological evolution. Combining Hutton and Darwin's theories, scientists then used fossil evidence to begin dating the Earth. Compared to other geological sciences, Geological Evolutionary Theory is still relatively new, and many of its fundamental assumptions
15 are constantly challenged.

Passage 2

Geological Evolutionary Theory is based on a simple assumption: older rock strata came first and hence, should lie underneath younger rock strata. While distinct layers or "strata" of rock of varying ages are a commonly
20 observed phenomenon, the order of the layers does not necessarily correlate to the presumed age of the rocks themselves. The Heart Mountain Thrust in Wyoming is one such thorn in the side of evolutionary geologists. At Heart Mountain, 50 separate blocks of Paleozoic strata
25 are resting horizontally on top of Eocene beds which are supposed to be 250 million years younger. Numerous theories for this seeming anomaly have been put forth; however, none has yet emerged as an intuitive truth.

6. It can be inferred from Passage 1 that

(A) theories of the earth's age evolved from the work of more than one scientist
(B) there is general agreement on theories of geological evolution
(C) geologists used biological evolution to disprove the Theory of Uniformity
(D) geology is a new, and therefore inexact, science
(E) attempts to scientifically date the earth began with Hutton's work

7. Passage 1 is unlike Passage 2 in that Passage 1

(A) attempts to prove a theory while Passage 2 attempts to disprove it
(B) places a theory in time while Passage 2 offers an example to contradict it
(C) proves a new geological theory while Passage 2 offers a counterexample
(D) contradicts an existing theory while Passage 2 proves one
(E) criticizes a popular theory while Passage 2 defends it

8. Which of the following statements about Geological Evolutional Theory is supported by both passages?

(A) Geological Evolutionary Theory has not yet been proven to be true.
(B) Geological Evolutionary Theory cannot yet explain the placement of Paleozoic strata.
(C) Geological Evolutionary Theory is not yet old enough to be true.
(D) Geological Evolutionary Theory is a commonly observed phenomenon.
(E) Geological Evolutionary Theory is not as old as the Theory of Uniformity.

9. Passage 2 is best described as

(A) a confirmation of a firmly established theory
(B) an exception to a generally accepted truth
(C) an itemization of the flaws of newly established theory
(D) a discussion of an intuitively plausible hypothesis
(E) a potential exception to an observable theory

GO ON TO THE NEXT PAGE

Questions 10-15 are based on the following passage.

The following passage is an excerpt from a book by novelist Gregor von Rezzori.

Skushno is a Russian word that is difficult to translate. It means more than dreary boredom; a spiritual void that sucks you in like a vague but intensely urgent longing.
Line When I was thirteen, at a phase that educators used to call
5 "the awkward age," my parents were at their wits' end. We lived in the Bukovina, today an almost astronomically remote province in southeastern Europe. The story I am telling seems as distant—not only in space but also in time—as if I'd merely dreamed it. Yet it begins as a very
10 ordinary story.

I had been expelled by a *consilium abeundi*—an advisory board with authority to expel unworthy students—from the schools of the then kingdom of Rumania, whose subjects we had become upon the
15 collapse of the Austro-Hungarian Empire after the first great war. An attempt to harmonize the imbalances in my character by means of strict discipline at a boarding school in Styria (my people still regarded Austria as our cultural homeland) nearly led to the same ignominious
20 end, and only my pseudo-voluntary departure from the institution in the nick of time prevented my final ostracism from the privileged ranks of those for whom the path to higher education was open. Again in the jargon of those assigned the responsible task of raising
25 children to become "useful members of society," I was a "virtually hopeless case." My parents, blind to how the contradictions within me had grown out of the highly charged difference between their own natures, agreed with the schoolmasters; the mix of neurotic sensitivity
30 and a tendency to violence, alert perception and inability to learn, tender need for support and lack of adjustability, would only develop into something criminal.

One of the trivial aphorisms my generation owes to Wilhelm Busch's *Pious Helene* is the homily "Once your
35 reputation's done / You can live a life of fun." But this optimistic notion results more from wishful thinking than from practical experience. In my case, had anyone asked me about my state of mind, I would have sighed and answered, "*Skushno!*" Even though rebellious thoughts
40 occasionally surged within me, I dragged myself, or rather I let myself be dragged, listlessly through my bleak existence in the snail's pace of days. Nor was I ever free of a sense of guilt, for my feeling guilty was not entirely foisted upon me by others; there were deep reasons I
45 could not explain to myself; had I been able to do so, my life would have been much easier.

10. It can be inferred from the passage that the author's parents were

(A) frustrated by the author's performance in school
(B) oblivious to the author's inability to do well in school
(C) wealthy, making them insensitive to the needs of the poor
(D) schoolmasters who believed in the strict disciplining of youth
(E) living in Russia while their son lived in Bukovina

11. Lines 16-23 are used by the author to demonstrate that

(A) the author posed an imminent danger to others
(B) the schools that the author attended were too difficult
(C) the tactics used to make the author more obedient were failing
(D) the author was often criticized by both his schoolmasters and classmates
(E) the author's academic career was nearing an end

12. In lines 18-19, the author implies that Styria

(A) belongs to his people
(B) is in Austria
(C) does not belong to Austria
(D) is not a lenient boarding school
(E) belongs to Hungary rather than Austria

13. The word "ignominious" in line 19 means

(A) dangerous
(B) harsh
(C) unappreciated
(D) disreputable
(E) discriminating

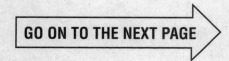

GO ON TO THE NEXT PAGE

14. The passage as a whole suggests that the author felt
    (A) happy because he was separated from his parents
    (B) upset because he was unable to maintain good friendships
    (C) melancholy and unsettled in his environment
    (D) suicidal and desperate because of his living in Russia
    (E) hopeful because he'd soon be out of school

15. The passage indicates that the author regarded the aphorism mentioned in the last paragraph with
    (A) relief because it showed him that he would eventually feel better
    (B) dissatisfaction because he found it unrealistic
    (C) contempt because he saw it working for others
    (D) bemusement because of his immunity to it
    (E) sorrow because his faith in it nearly killed him

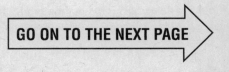

GO ON TO THE NEXT PAGE

Questions 16-24 are based on the following passage.

The following passage, published in 1986, is from a book written by a zoologist.

The domestic cat is a contradiction. No other animal has developed such an intimate relationship with humanity, while at the same time demanding and getting
Line such independent movement and action. The cat manages
5 to remain a tame animal because of the sequence of its upbringing. By living both with other cats (its mother and littermates) and with humans (the family that has adopted it) during its infancy and kittenhood, the cat becomes attached to and considers that it belongs to both species. It
10 is like a child that grows up in a foreign country and, as a consequence, becomes bilingual. The young cat becomes bimental. It may be a cat physically, but mentally it is both feline and human. Once it is fully adult, however, most of its responses are feline ones, and it has only one
15 major reaction to its human owners. It treats them as pseudoparents. The reason is that they took over from the real mother at a sensitive stage of the kitten's development and went on giving it milk, solid food, and comfort as it grew up.
20   This is rather different from the kind of bond that develops between human and dog. The dog sees its human owners as pseudoparents, as does the cat. On that score the process of attachment is similar. But the dog has an additional link. Canine society is group-organized; feline
25 society is not. Dogs live in packs with tightly controlled status relationships among the individuals. There are top dogs, middle dogs, and bottom dogs, and under natural circumstances they move around together, keeping tabs on one another the whole time. So the adult pet dog
30 sees its human family both as pseudoparents and as the dominant members of the pack, hence the dog's renowned reputation for obedience and its celebrated capacity for loyalty. Cats do have a complex social organization, but they never hunt in packs. In the wild, most of their day is
35 spent in solitary stalking. Going for a walk with a human, therefore, has no appeal for them. And as for "coming to heel" and learning to "sit" and "stay," they are simply not interested. Such maneuvers have no meaning for them.
   So the moment a cat manages to persuade a human
40 being to open a door (that most hated of human inventions), it is off and away without a backward glance. As it crosses the threshold, the cat becomes transformed. The kitten-of-human brain is switched off and the wildcat brain is clicked on. The dog, in such a situation,
45 may look back to see if its human packmate is following to join in the fun of exploring, but not the cat. The cat's mind has floated off into another, totally feline world, where strange, bipedal* primates have no place.

Because of this difference between domestic cats
50 and domestic dogs, cat-lovers tend to be rather different from dog-lovers. As a rule, cat-lovers have a stronger personality bias toward working alone, independent of the larger group. Artists like cats; soldiers like dogs. The much-lauded "group loyalty" phenomenon is alien to
55 both cats and cat-lovers. If you are a company person, a member of the gang, or a person picked for the squad, the chances are that at home there is no cat curled up in front of the fire. The ambitious Yuppie, the aspiring politician, the professional athlete, these are not typical cat-owners.
60 It is hard to picture football players with cats in their laps—much easier to envisage them taking their dogs for walks.
   Those who have studied cat-owners and dog-owners as two distinct groups report that there is also a gender
65 bias. The majority of cat lovers are female. This bias is not surprising in view of the division of labor evident in the development of human societies. Prehistoric males became specialized as group-hunters, while the females concentrated on food-gathering and childbearing. This
70 difference contributed to a human male "pack mentality" that is far less marked in females. Wolves, the wild ancestors of domestic dogs, also became pack-hunters, so the modern dog has much more in common with the human male than with the human female.
75   The argument will always go on—feline self-sufficiency and individualism versus canine camaraderie and good-fellowship. But it is important to stress that in making a valid point I have caricatured the two positions. In reality there are many people who enjoy equally the
80 company of both cats and dogs. And all of us, or nearly all of us, have both feline and canine elements in our personalities. We have moods when we want to be alone and thoughtful, and other times we wish to be in the center of a crowded, noisy room.

*bipedal: walking on two feet

16.   The primary purpose of the passage is to
   (A) show the enmity that exists between cats and dogs
   (B) advocate dogs as making better pets than cats
   (C) distinguish the different characteristics of dogs and cats
   (D) show the inferiority of dogs because of their dependent nature
   (E) emphasize the role that human society plays in the personalities of domestic pets

17. In line 16, the word "pseudoparents" means

(A) part-time parents who are only partially involved with their young

(B) individuals who act as parents of adults

(C) parents who neglect their young

(D) parents who have both the characteristics of humans and their pets

(E) adoptive parents who aren't related to their young

18. The passage as a whole does all of the following EXCEPT

(A) use a statistic

(B) make parenthetical statements

(C) quote a knowledgeable individual

(D) restate an argument

(E) make a generalization

19. According to the passage, the domestic cat can be described as

(A) a biped because it possesses the characteristics of animals with two feet

(B) a pseudopet because it can't really be tamed and will always retain its wild habits

(C) a contradiction because although it lives comfortably with humans, it refuses to be dominated by them

(D) untamed because it preserves its independence

(E) dominant because although it plays the part of a pet, it acquires obedience from humans

20. The author suggests that an important difference between dogs and cats is that, unlike dogs, cats

(A) do not have complex social organizations

(B) obey mainly because of their obedient nature

(C) have a more creative nature

(D) do not regard their owners as the leader of their social group

(E) are not skilled hunters

21. It can be inferred from lines 20-38 that the social structure of dogs is

(A) flexible

(B) hierarchical

(C) abstract

(D) male-dominated

(E) somewhat exclusive

22. The "ambitious Yuppie" mentioned in line 58 is an example of a person

(A) who lacks the ability to be self-sufficient

(B) who seeks group-oriented status

(C) who is a stereotypical pet-owner

(D) who has a weak personality

(E) who cares little for cat lovers

23. The fifth paragraph (lines 63-74) indicates that human females

(A) prefer the society of cats less than that of dogs

(B) developed independent roles that didn't require group behavior

(C) had to gather food because they were not strong enough to hunt

(D) are not good owners for the modern dog

(E) were negatively affected by the division of labor of human societies

24. The author uses lines 75-78 ("The argument… positions.") to

(A) show that the argument stated in the passage is ultimately futile and thus not worth continuing

(B) disclaim contradictions that are stated in the passage

(C) qualify the generalizations used to make the author's point

(D) ensure that the reader doesn't underestimate the crux of the passage

(E) highlight a difference between individualism and dependency

STOP

If you finish before time is called, you may check your work on this section only.
Do not turn to any other section in the test.

SECTION 8

Time — 20 minutes

16 Questions

Turn to Section 8 of your answer sheet to answer the questions in this section.

Directions: For this section, solve each problem and decide which is the best of the choices given. Fill in the corresponding oval on the answer sheet. You may use any available space for scatchwork.

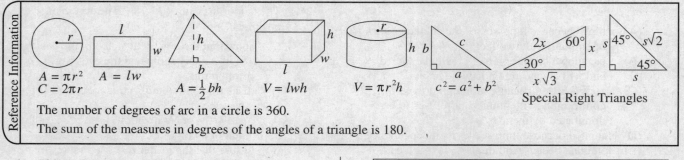

Reference Information

$A = \pi r^2$
$C = 2\pi r$

$A = lw$

$A = \frac{1}{2}bh$

$V = lwh$

$V = \pi r^2 h$

$c^2 = a^2 + b^2$

Special Right Triangles

The number of degrees of arc in a circle is 360.

The sum of the measures in degrees of the angles of a triangle is 180.

1. If $3x - 5 = 4$, what is the value of $9x - 15$?

(A) 3
(B) 4
(C) 9
(D) 12
(E) 15

$$3x = 9$$
$$x = 3$$

Price of Buttons in Store X	
Color	**Price**
Black	$2 per 5 buttons
Blue	$2 per 6 buttons
Brown	$3 per 8 buttons
Orange	$4 per 12 buttons
Red	$4 per 7 buttons

2. In Store X, which color costs the most per button?

(A) Black
(B) Blue
(C) Brown
(D) Orange
(E) Red

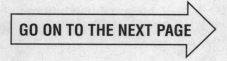
GO ON TO THE NEXT PAGE

3. In the *xy*-coordinate plane, which of the following ordered pairs is a point on the line $y = 2x - 6$?

(A) (6, 7)
(B) (7, 7)
(C) (7, 8)
(D) (8, 7)
(E) (8, 8)

4. For which of the following values of *x* is $\dfrac{x^2}{x^3}$ the least?

(A) 1
(B) −1
(C) −2
(D) −3
(E) −4

$$\frac{x^2}{x^3}$$

$$\frac{16}{-64} \qquad \frac{9}{-27}$$

5. If $(a + b)^2 = 49$, and $ab = 10$, which of the following represents the value of *b* in terms of *a* ?

(A) $\dfrac{\sqrt{29}}{a}$

(B) $\sqrt{29 - a^2}$

(C) $\sqrt{39 - a}$

(D) $\sqrt[a]{\dfrac{49}{10}}$

(E) $a^2\sqrt{49}$

$$a + b = 7$$
$$ab = 10$$

6. If the area of square *ABFE* = 25, and the area of *BCF* = 10, what is the length of $\overline{DE}$?

(A) 7
(B) 8
(C) 9
(D) 10
(E) 14

$5\sqrt{2}$

45°

7. If $x + 2y = 20$, $y + 2z = 9$, and $2x + z = 22$, what is the value of $x + y + z$?

(A) 10
(B) 12
(C) 17
(D) 22
(E) 51

$$y = 9 - 2z$$

$$x + 9 - 2z = 20$$
$$2x - 4z = 22$$
$$x - 2z = 11$$
$$2x + z = 22$$
$$-5z = 0$$

GO ON TO THE NEXT PAGE

8. If the sum of two numbers is 10, and one of these numbers is equal to the sum of 6 and twice the other number, what is the value of the larger number minus the smaller number?

(A) 2

(B) $5\frac{1}{4}$

(C) 6

(D) $7\frac{1}{3}$

(E) $8\frac{1}{2}$

[handwritten:]
$x + y = 10$
$x = 6 + 2y$

$x - 2y = 6$
$x + y = 10$
_____
$-3y = -4$
$y = \frac{4}{3}$

9. If $f(x) = \dfrac{x+2}{x+1}$, what is the range of $f(x)$?

(A) All real numbers greater than 0
(B) All real numbers greater than 1
(C) All real numbers except 0
(D) All real numbers except 1
(E) All real numbers

10. If the average measure of two angles in a parallelogram is $y°$, what is the average degree measure of the other two angles?

(A) $180 - y$

[handwritten: $2y°$]

(B) $180 - \dfrac{y}{2}$

(C) $360 - 2y$ *[circled]*

(D) $360 + y$

(E) y

11. If $m > 0$ and $b > 0$, which of the following could be a graph of $y = mx^2 + b$?

(A) *[crossed out]*

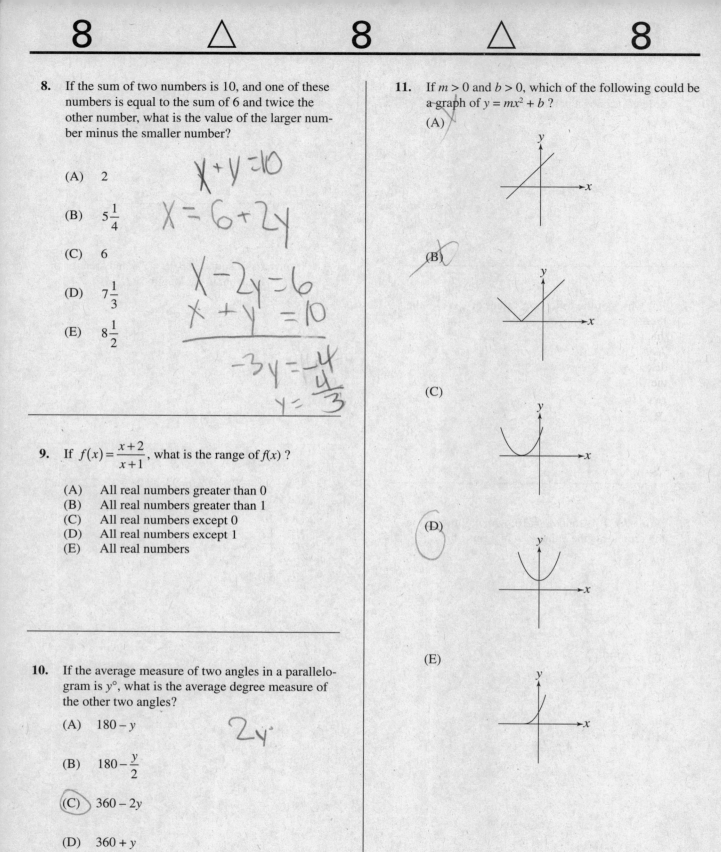

(B) *[circled]*

(C)

(D) *[circled]*

(E)

GO ON TO THE NEXT PAGE

12. S is the set of all positive numbers n such that $n < 100$ and $\sqrt{n}$ is an integer. What is the median value of the members of set S ?

(A) 5
(B) 5.5
(C) 25
(D) 50
(E) 99

13. Point K lies outside the circle with center C such that $CK = 26$. $\overline{JK}$ is tangent to the circle at point J, and the distance from J to K is 2 less than the distance from K to C. What is the circumference of the circle?

(A) 10π
(B) 15π
(C) 20π
(D) 22π
(E) 24π

14. On a map, 1 centimeter represents 6 kilometers. A square on the map with a perimeter of 16 centimeters represents a region with what area?

(A) 64 square kilometers
(B) 96 square kilometers
(C) 256 square kilometers
(D) 576 square kilometers
(E) 8,216 square kilometers

15. If 0.1% of m is equal to 10% of n, then m is what percent of $10n$?

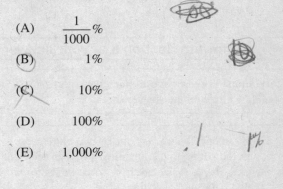

(A) $\dfrac{1}{1000}\%$

(B) 1%

(C) 10%

(D) 100%

(E) 1,000%

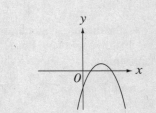

16. The graph of $y = g(x)$ is shown in the figure above. If $g(x) = ax^2 + bx + c$ for constants a, b, and c, and if $abc \neq 0$, then which of the following must be true?

(A) $b > 0$
(B) $c > 0$
(C) $ab < 0$
(D) $bc > 0$
(E) $ac < 0$

STOP

If you finish before time is called, you may check your work on this section only.
Do not turn to any other section in the test.

SECTION 9
Time — 20 minutes
19 Questions

Turn to Section 9 of your answer sheet to answer the questions in this section.

Directions: For each question in this section, select the best answer from among the choices given and fill in the corresponding circle on the answer sheet.

Each sentence below has one or two blanks, each blank indicating that something has been omitted. Beneath the sentence are five words or sets of words labeled A through E. Choose the word or set of words that, when inserted in the sentence, best fits the meaning of the sentence as a whole.

Example:

Hoping to ------- the dispute, negotiators proposed a compromise that they felt would be ------- to both labor and management.

(A) enforce . . useful
(B) end . . divisive
(C) overcome . . unattractive
(D) extend . . satisfactory
(E) resolve . . acceptable

Ⓐ Ⓑ Ⓒ Ⓓ ●

1. Max's grandmother seems -------; she is frequently observed behaving in an unconventional manner.
    (A) ordinary (B) eccentric (C) chronological
        (D) sociable   (E) industrious

2. The antibiotic ointment was so effective on the infection in Molly's swollen finger that after only one application, the finger was no longer -------.
    (A) compressed (B) deflated (C) distended
        (D) fractured   (E) disintegrated

3. Professor Cooligan told his class that since the Industrial Revolution, the global warming trend has been -------; human disregard for the environment precipitated many of the alterations in the earth's climate zones.
    (A) inevitable (B) malevolent (C) reciprocal
        (D) stagnant   (E) guileless

4. After just one hour of study, Tyler unrealistically expected a ------- rise in his test scores, and was reluctant to work longer hours for steady, ------- score improvements.
    (A) repetitive . . swift
    (B) sudden . . interminable
    (C) trivial . . gradual
    (D) steep . . incremental
    (E) significant . . rapid

5. When participating in a yoga class, Katarina attains a ------- state; the soothing music and soft lighting invoke a serenity that is otherwise lacking in her frenzied existence.
    (A) euphonious   (B) perspicuous   (C) placid
       (D) prolific   (E) supple

6. Dr. Schwartz's lecture on art, while detailed and scholarly, focused ------- on the pre-modern; some students may have appreciated his specialized knowledge, but those with more ------- interests may have been disappointed.
    (A) literally . . medieval
    (B) completely . . antediluvian
    (C) prodigiously . . germane
    (D) voluminously . . creative
    (E) utterly . . eclectic

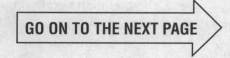
GO ON TO THE NEXT PAGE

The passages below are followed by questions based on their content; questions following a pair of related passages may also be based on the relationship between the paired passages. Answer the questions on the basis of what is <u>stated</u> or <u>implied</u> in the passage and in any introductory material that may be provided.

Questions 7-19 are based on the following passages.

The two passages below discuss the causes of deviant behavior and strategies for deterring it. The first passage is taken from a discussion of the classical perspective on deviance, while Passage 2 recounts a more recent interpretation of behavior.

Passage 1

Early attempts to understand what caused deviant behavior in society always centered on supernatural causes. People were criminals, it was assumed, because
Line of some otherworldly influence, a demonic presence that
5 tempted and manipulated otherwise good individuals into performing antisocial actions. But the arrival of the Enlightenment in Europe marked the end of this so-called demonic perspective and ushered in a new conception of the roots of deviant behavior, a viewpoint that came to be
10 called the classical perspective.

The Enlightenment brought numerous changes to European culture. Foremost among them was an increased reliance on human rationality. Philosophers moved away from theologically centered debates and
15 focused on such intellectual exercises as empiricism and the limits of human reason. Thus, it is no coincidence that the classical perspective on deviance describes criminal behavior not as the result of some supernatural entity but as the fruit of human rationality. Classicists
20 maintain that a person chooses deviant behavior based on an intellectual "risk/reward" evaluation. The classicists start from the assumption that each individual wishes to maximize pleasure and minimize pain. Deviance occurs when an individual decides that the reward to be gained
25 from an action outweighs the potential risk associated with the behavior. Thus, a person who decides to rob a bank has determined that the potential profits from the heist are worth the risk of incarceration.

Not surprisingly, adherents of the classical perspective
30 advocate punishment as the best deterrent to deviant behavior. In order to prevent individuals from engaging in criminal activities, the risk associated with each activity must outstrip the reward. One classicist, Cesare Beccaria, even went so far as to maintain that
35 a precise, mathematical system could be devised that would calculate the exact type of punishment necessary. However, arbitrary, excessive, or tyrannical punishments are not encouraged by the classical perspective. Because each deviant act arises from a rational calculation of
40 pleasure versus pain, the appropriate punishment must merely exceed the expected pleasure in order to serve as a deterrent.

Passage 2

Just as people are able to influence and change society, society affects the behavior of its charges. It would be
45 remiss to ascribe the emergence of deviant behavior solely to the perpetrator of that behavior. No individual exists in a vacuum; in order to understand the actions of an individual one must examine the society that produces the individual. Only by gaining an understanding of the
50 relationship between individual and society can we begin to understand the causes of social deviance.

One way to begin to understand the existence of deviance is to imagine a "perfect" society. In this perfect society, each member shares common values and
55 internalizes the norms of the group. In such a setting, each person is at peace because his or her relationship to the society at large is in harmony. Furthermore, since each individual's goals and values are shared by the rest of the community, each participant in this perfect society
60 feels actualized and secure, content that the needs of the individual are also the needs of the whole. Surely, deviant behavior would have no role in this utopia. The entire society would be coordinated by the predominance of shared mores, and each member's behavior would be
65 bound by these common values. Unfortunately, perfect societies do not exist in the real world.

Consider now a realistic model of society. Change is constant; immigration brings new members to the society, urbanization uproots families, and technological advances
70 offer new and different ways of living. Harmony and organization are not the norm. Instead, disorganization reigns supreme. With society in a state of flux, it is impossible for individuals to remain in harmony with the community, and it is this discord that breeds social
75 deviance. Lacking the coordination of an overarching social consensus, individuals replace it with dissention. While in time particular changes in society might bring about new social norms, and thus new models of consensus, new changes will inevitably occur, giving rise
80 to a new cycle of deviant behavior.

It follows, then, that in order to control deviant behavior, one must first look to stabilize the society that engenders it. When disorganization is replaced with organization and disparate values are supplanted by
85 shared norms, deviant behavior will be eliminated.

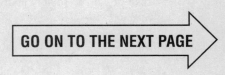
GO ON TO THE NEXT PAGE

7. The arrival of the Enlightenment in Europe shifted philosophers' focus from

    (A) superstition to spirituality
    (B) demons to angels
    (C) criminals to law-abiding citizens
    (D) classicists to modernists
    (E) theology to intellectualism

8. According to the classical perspective, deviant behavior is the result of

    (A) a criminal act
    (B) a demonic presence
    (C) a rational decision based on intellectual evaluation
    (D) a concept developed by philosophers
    (E) rationale that minimizes pleasure and maximizes pain

9. Classicists did not encourage harsh, despotic punishments because

    (A) risks must outstrip potential profits from a heist
    (B) punishment can be meted out precisely and mathematically
    (C) the demonic, otherworldly influence on actions will prevail
    (D) the appropriate punishment must merely exceed the pain
    (E) deviant acts arise from a reasoned assessment of pleasure versus pain

10. In line 45 of Passage 2, "ascribe" most nearly means

    (A) reveal
    (B) attribute
    (C) describe
    (D) distinguish
    (E) explain

11. In lines 46-47 of Passage 2, "no individual exists… vacuum" suggests that

    (A) society plays a key role in determining an individual's behavior
    (B) an individual is accountable to those around him
    (C) there is no relationship between individual behavior and society
    (D) an individual can have a major impact on society
    (E) without organized society, individuals would cease to exist

12. The author of Passage 2 uses the example of a "perfect" society to suggest that

    (A) common values are necessary for a successful society
    (B) it is a reflection of today's world
    (C) society is obsessed with perfection
    (D) people will never be happy in an imperfect society
    (E) deviant behavior would not exist in such a society

13. In line 83, "engenders" most nearly means

    (A) sexualizes
    (B) publicizes
    (C) enables
    (D) advocates
    (E) causes

14. In Passage 2, the author describes the realistic model of society in a tone that is

    (A) nostalgic for the calmer days of society
    (B) objectively summarizing a realistic society
    (C) critical of disorganization in society
    (D) reproachful of companies that promote technological growth
    (E) approving of individuals who dissent from society

15. When change is constant, which of the following is LEAST likely to result, according to the author of the second passage?

    (A) Immigration augments a society.
    (B) Organization and harmony become the rule.
    (C) Technological advancement spurs innovations.
    (D) Disorganization reigns supreme.
    (E) Social fluctuation is the norm.

16. Both passages support which generalization about deviant behavior?

    (A) Acts of deviance are ultimately the decision of the individual.
    (B) Society is the main cause of deviant behavior.
    (C) Deviant behavior can only be eliminated through severe punishment.
    (D) Societal adjustments are the only way to eradicate deviance.
    (E) The arrival of the Enlightenment in Europe promoted social deviance.

GO ON TO THE NEXT PAGE

17. Which aspect of deviant behavior seems to matter a great deal in Passage 1, but not in Passage 2?

    (A) The influence of demons on criminals
    (B) The intellectual evaluation made by an individual
    (C) The methods for calculating punishment
    (D) The effects society has on the individual
    (E) The act of robbing a bank

18. The passages differ in tone in that Passage 1 is

    (A) enthusiastic while Passage 2 is cautious
    (B) indignant while Passage 2 is nostalgic
    (C) matter-of-fact while Passage 2 is sarcastic
    (D) objective while Passage 2 is critical
    (E) sensationalistic while Passage 2 is understated

19. Which statement best describes a significant difference between the two interpretations of how deviant behavior is propagated?

    (A) Passage 1 emphasizes the individual's role; Passage 2 emphasizes society's role.
    (B) Passage 1 explains the history of deviance; Passage 2 emphasizes the modern perspective.
    (C) Passage 1 discusses the demonic perspective; Passage 2 discusses the role of disorganization.
    (D) Each passage presents several reasons for deviant behavior.
    (E) Each passage discusses society's role in deviant behavior.

STOP

If you finish before time is called, you may check your work on this section only.
Do not turn to any other section in the test.

SECTION 10

Time — 10 minutes

14 Questions

Turn to Section 10 of your answer sheet to answer the questions in this section.

Directions: For each question in this section, select the best answer from among the choices given and fill in the corresponding circle on the answer sheet.

The following sentences test correctness and effectiveness of expression. Part of each sentence or the entire sentence is underlined; beneath each sentence are five ways of phrasing the underlined material. Choice A repeats the original phrasing; the other four choices are different. If you think the original phrasing produces a better sentence than any of the alternatives, select choice A; if not, select one of the other choices.

In making your selection, follow the requirements of standard written English; that is, pay attention to grammar, choice of words, sentence construction, and punctuation. Your selection should result in the most effective sentence—clear and precise, without awkwardness or ambiguity.

EXAMPLE:

Laura Ingalls Wilder published her first book and she was sixty-five years old then.
(A) and she was sixty-five years old then
(B) when she was sixty-five
(C) at age sixty-five years old
(D) upon the reaching of sixty-five years
(E) at the time when she was sixty-five

Ⓐ ● Ⓒ Ⓓ Ⓔ

1. Weather vanes range in style from the practical to the fanciful, but in the end <u>its purpose is still the same</u>: to point out the direction of the wind.

    (A) its purpose is still the same
    (B) their purpose being same
    (C) the purpose is the same for every one of them
    (D) they all share the same purpose
    (E) the purpose is the same for all of them

2. The horrors of war and the experiences of a woman serving in the Woman's Royal Navy Service during <u>the second World War, which are stirringly chronicled</u> in Edith Pargeter's novel *She Goes to War*.

    (A) the second World War, which are stirringly chronicled
    (B) the second World War are stirringly chronicled
    (C) a stirring chronicle of the second World War
    (D) the second World War, that appear in a stirring chronicle
    (E) a chronicle of the second World War that stirs the emotions

3. The commercial airliner flew too close to the military base, an act that the army viewed <u>as</u> a violation of its air space.

    (A) as
    (B) as if it was
    (C) to be
    (D) that it was
    (E) for

4. <u>Arvo Pärt is an Estonian composer, he is noted for his ethereal, unusual harmonies, and he</u> will direct the symphony concert tonight.

    (A) Arvo Pärt is an Estonian composer, he is noted for his ethereal, unusual harmonies, and he
    (B) Arvo Pärt is an Estonian composer noted for his ethereal, unusual harmonies, he
    (C) Arvo Pärt, an Estonian composer, and because he is noted for his ethereal, unusual harmonies, he
    (D) Although Arvo Pärt is an Estonian composer, he is noted for his ethereal, unusual harmonies, and he
    (E) Arvo Pärt, an Estonian composer noted for his ethereal, unusual harmonies,

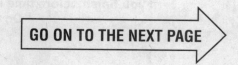

GO ON TO THE NEXT PAGE

5. The lawyer for the plaintiff in the civil court case responded to the emotional appeals of the <u>defendant she produced</u> actual physical evidence of the defendant's culpability.

   (A) defendant she produced
   (B) defendant with the production of
   (C) defendant, produced
   (D) defendant; and produced
   (E) defendant by producing

6. Sandeep could only objectively judge the results of the experiment after he realized that he <u>could depend on expertise different from his own</u>.

   (A) could depend on expertise different from his own
   (B) can depend on expertise different from his own
   (C) could depend on expertise different from his expertise
   (D) can depend on expertise different from his expertise
   (E) would have the ability to depend on expertise different from his own

7. Dr. Kornstein's colleagues considered him not only a great surgeon but also <u>being an inspiring teacher of</u> innovative surgical techniques.

   (A) being an inspiring teacher of
   (B) having inspired the teaching of
   (C) with inspiration teaching
   (D) he was inspiring in his teaching of
   (E) an inspiring teacher of

8. Many employees chose to switch to the new company insurance plan <u>for the reasons that their monthly payments would be reduced</u>.

   (A) for the reasons that their monthly payments would be reduced
   (B) because their monthly payments would be reduced
   (C) because of their reductions in monthly payments
   (D) because its monthly payments were to be reduced
   (E) for the reason that they reduced their monthly payment

9. <u>In spite of an appearance of no specific expression on its face, a squirrel</u> sometimes plays clever games with anyone trying to view it, scrambling to the opposite side of a tree to elude a would-be observer.

   (A) In spite of an appearance of no specific expression on its face, a squirrel
   (B) Despite the fact of an appearance of no specific expression on its face, a squirrel
   (C) Although the expression on the face of the squirrel is not specific in appearance, it
   (D) Although a squirrel appears to have no specific expression on its face, it
   (E) Although the face of a squirrel has no specific expression, it

10. Learning from recent field tests, <u>the efficiency of the engine on which they would base next year's trucks was significantly increased by the designers</u>.

    (A) the efficiency of the engine on which they would base next year's trucks was significantly increased by the designers
    (B) the designers based next year's truck engine on a significant increase in efficiency
    (C) the designers significantly increased the efficiency of the engine on which they would base next year's trucks
    (D) their efficiency was significant in designing the engine as a basis for next year's trucks
    (E) the engine on which the designers would base next year's trucks was significantly increased in efficiency

11. The crash of the Mars Climate Orbiter was caused by a lack of training among the members of the navigation team and <u>failing to use metric units</u> in the coding of the software.

    (A) failing to use metric units
    (B) a failure to use metric units
    (C) by people which failed to use metric units
    (D) because of the failure to use metric units
    (E) because people failed to use metric units

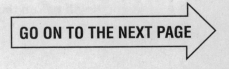

GO ON TO THE NEXT PAGE

12. <u>Rory and I, starting to clear the snow away from the front door</u>, we still have hours of work ahead of us.

(A) Rory and I, starting to clear the snow away from the front door

(B) Rory and I, starting to clear the snow away from the front door, however

(C) Rory and I have started to clear the snow away from the front door, and

(D) Even though starting from the front door to clear the snow away, Rory and I

(E) Even though Rory and I have started to clear the snow away from the front door

13. While rhododendron and cherry blossoms are both bright in color, <u>the main difference being the size of the tree that grows them</u>.

(A) the main difference being the size of the tree that grows them

(B) the main difference is that they grow on two trees that are different

(C) the two grow on trees of different sizes

(D) the main difference being they grow on different-size trees

(E) and the trees they grow on are different in size

14. Better known for *The Foreigner*, <u>other works of Larry Shue, such as *The Nerd*,</u> were of equal quality even though they were less famous.

(A) other works of Larry Shue, such as *The Nerd*,

(B) other works by Larry Shue, such as *The Nerd*,

(C) Larry Shue also created other works, such as *The Nerd*, that

(D) Larry Shue's other works, like *The Nerd*,

(E) Larry Shue wrote other stories, like *The Nerd*, that

STOP

If you finish before time is called, you may check your work on this section only.
Do not turn to any other section in the test.

NO TEST MATERIAL ON THIS PAGE.

PRACTICE TEST 1: ANSWER KEY

Section 2 Math	Section 3 Reading	Section 4 Math (Exp)	Section 5 Writing	Section 6 Math	Section 7 Reading	Section 8 Math	Section 9 Reading	Section 10 Writing
1. A	1. A	1. B	1. C	1. B	1. D	1. D	1. B	1. D
2. C	2. E	2. B	2. B	2. C	2. A	2. E	2. C	2. B
3. C	3. B	3. E	3. A	3. E	3. B	3. C	3. A	3. A
4. B	4. A	4. E	4. D	4. D	4. C	4. B	4. D	4. E
5. B	5. A	5. C	5. A	5. E	5. A	5. B	5. C	5. E
6. A	6. C	6. A	6. E	6. B	6. A	6. C	6. E	6. A
7. A	7. D	7. A	7. B	7. A	7. B	7. C	7. E	7. E
8. D	8. D	8. E	8. E	8. D	8. A	8. D	8. C	8. B
9. E	9. C	9. C	9. D	9 2	9. E	9. D	9. E	9. D
10. B	10. B	10. B	10. D	10. 19,	10. A	10. A	10. D	10. C
11. D	11. B	11. D	11. C	39,	11. C	11. D	11. A	11. B
12. D	12. C	12. E	12. B	59,	12. B	12. C	12. E	12. E
13. D	13. D	13. A	13. E	79,	13. D	13. C	13. E	13. C
14. E	14. D	14. D	14. A	99	14. C	14. D	14. C	14. C
15. E	15. E	15. E	15. A	11. 145	15. B	15. E	15. B	
16. B	16. A	16. D	16. A	12. 36	16. C	16. D	16. A	
17. C	17. A	17. D	17. D	13. 130	17. E		17. B	
18. A	18. C	18. A	18. D	14. 8	18. C		18. D	
19. C	19. E	19. C	19. E	15. 12	19. C		19. A	
20. B	20. B	20. D	20. C	16. 4	20. D			
	21. C		21. C	17. 3	21. B			
	22. D		22. D	18. $\frac{6}{5}$	22. B			
	23. B		23. C	or	23. B			
	24. A		24. C	1.2	24. C			
			25. D					
			26. B					
			27. C					
			28. D					
			29. D					
			30. B					
			31. A					
			32. E					
			33. C					
			34. E					
			35. D					

SAT SCORING WORKSHEET

For directions on how to score your SAT practice test, see pages 5–7. Section 4 is an unscored, experimental section.

SAT Writing Section

Total Writing Multiple-Choice Questions Correct from Sections 5 and 10: | 43 |

Total Writing Multiple-Choice Questions Incorrect
from Sections 4 and 10: ___6___ ÷ 4 = | 1.5 |

5

Grammar Raw Score: | 41.5 | —— | 71 – 75 |

Grammar Scaled Subscore!

Compare the Grammar Raw Score to the Writing Multiple-Choice Subscore Conversion Table on the next page to find the Grammar Scaled Subscore.

+

Your Essay Score (2–12): _____ × 2 = | |

Writing Raw Score: | |

> Compare Raw Score to SAT Score Conversion Table on the next page to find the Writing Scaled Score.

Writing Scaled Score!

| |

SAT Critical Reading Section

Total Critical Reading Questions Correct from Sections 3, 7, and 9: | 57 |

—

Total Critical Reading Questions Incorrect from Sections 3, 7, and 9:
___10___ ÷ 4 = | 2.5 |

Critical Reading Raw Score: | 54.5 |

> Compare Raw Score to SAT Score Conversion Table on the next page to find the Critical Reading Scaled Score.

Critical Reading Scaled Score!

| 660 – 700 |

SAT Math Section

Total Math Grid-In Questions Correct from Section 6: | 6 |

+

Total Math Multiple-Choice Questions Correct from Sections 2, 6, and 8: | 29 |

—

Total Math Multiple-Choice Questions Incorrect from Sections 2, 6, and 8:
___8___ ÷ 4 = | 2 |

Don't include wrong answers from grid-ins!

Math Raw Score: | 33 |

> Compare Raw Score to SAT Score Conversion Table on the next page to find the Math Scaled Score.

Math Scaled Score!

| |

SAT SCORE CONVERSION TABLE

Raw Score	Writing Scaled Score	Reading Scaled Score	Math Scaled Score	Raw Score	Writing Scaled Score	Reading Scaled Score	Math Scaled Score	Raw Score	Writing Scaled Score	Reading Scaled Score	Math Scaled Score
73	800			47	590–630	600–640	680–720	21	400–440	420–460	460–500
72	790–800			46	590–630	590–630	670–710	20	390–430	410–450	450–490
71	780–800			45	580–620	580–620	660–700	19	380–420	400–440	450–490
70	770–800			44	570–610	580–620	650–690	18	370–410	400–440	440–480
69	770–800			43	570–610	570–610	640–680	17	370–410	390–430	430–470
68	760–800			42	560–600	570–610	630–670	16	360–400	380–420	420–460
67	760–800	800		41	560–600	560–600	620–660	15	350–390	380–420	420–460
66	760–800	770–800		40	550–590	550–590	620–660	14	340–380	370–410	410–450
65	750–790	750–790		39	540–580	550–590	610–650	13	330–370	360–400	400–440
64	740–780	740–780		38	530–570	540–580	600–640	12	320–360	350–390	400–440
63	730–750	740–780		37	530–570	530–570	590–630	11	320–360	350–390	390–430
62	720–760	730–770		36	520–560	530–570	590–630	10	310–350	340–380	380–420
61	710–750	720–760		35	510–550	520–560	580–620	9	300–340	330–370	370–410
60	700–740	710–750		34	500–540	510–550	570–610	8	290–330	310–350	360–400
59	690–730	700–740		33	490–530	500–540	560–600	7	280–320	300–340	350–390
58	680–720	690–730		32	480–520	500–540	560–600	6	270–310	300–340	340–380
57	680–720	680–720		31	470–510	490–530	540–580	5	260–300	290–330	330–370
56	670–710	670–710		30	470–510	480–520	530–570	4	240–280	280–320	320–360
55	660–720	670–710		29	460–500	470–510	520–560	3	230–270	270–310	310–350
54	650–690	660–700	800	28	450–490	470–510	510–550	2	230–270	260–300	290–330
53	640–680	650–690	780–800	27	440–480	460–500	510–550	1	220–260	230–270	270–310
52	630–670	640–680	750–790	26	430–470	450–490	500–540	0	210–250	200–240	240–280
51	630–670	630–670	740–780	25	420–460	450–490	490–530	–1	200–240	200–230	220–260
50	620–660	620–660	730–770	24	410–450	440–480	480–520	–2	200–230	200–220	210–250
49	610–650	610–650	710–750	23	410–450	430–470	480–520	–3	200–220	200–210	200–240
48	600–640	600–640	700–740	22	400–440	420–460	470–510				

WRITING MULTIPLE-CHOICE SUBSCORE CONVERSION TABLE

Grammar Raw Score	Grammar Scaled Subscore	Grammar Raw Score	Grammar Scaled Subscore	Grammar Raw Score	Grammar Scaled Subscore	Grammar Raw Score	Grammar Scaled Subscore	Grammar Raw Score	Grammar Scaled Subscore	Grammar Raw Score	Grammar Scaled Subscore
49	79–80	40	70–74	31	61–65	22	52–56	13	43–47	4	33–37
48	78–80	39	69–73	30	60–64	21	52–56	12	42–46	3	31–35
47	78–80	38	68–72	29	59–63	20	51–55	11	41–45	2	28–32
46	77–80	37	67–71	28	58–62	19	50–54	10	40–44	1	26–30
45	76–80	36	66–70	27	57–61	18	49–53	9	39–43	0	23–27
44	75–79	35	65–69	26	56–60	17	48–52	8	37–41	–1	22–26
43	73–77	34	64–68	25	55–59	16	47–51	7	36–40	–2	21–25
42	72–76	33	63–67	24	54–58	15	46–50	6	35–39	–3	20–24
41	71–75	32	62–66	23	53–57	14	45–49	5	34–38		

19

Answers and Explanations for Practice Test 1

SECTION 2

1. **A** Answer this question in bite-sized pieces. The first step is to use your calculator to compute the sum of the subscriptions: $68.80. The down payment was half that amount, leaving $34.40 to be paid in 4 installments of $8.60 each. If you answered (D) or (E), you may have misread the question.

2. **C** Try plugging in the answers. Starting with C, put $\frac{1}{2}$ in for x:

$$\frac{2\left(\frac{1}{2}\right)}{\left(\frac{1}{2}\right)^2 + 1} = \frac{2}{\frac{1}{2}+2}$$

$$\frac{1}{1\frac{1}{4}} = \frac{2}{2\frac{1}{2}}$$

Cross-multiply: $2\frac{1}{2} = 2\left(1\frac{1}{4}\right) = 2\frac{1}{2}$. So (C) is correct. Another way would be to cross-multiply first to get $2x^2 + 4x = 2x^2 + 2$. Subtract $2x^2$ from both sides to get $2 = 4x$. Divide by 4 to get $x = \frac{1}{2}$.

3. **C** This is an excellent time to turn on your calculator. Since 48,000 people live in Town X and each household has 3.2 people, you can determine the number of households: $48,000 \div 3.2 = 15,000$. And since each household has 1.2 televisions, you can now determine the number of televisions: $15,000 \times 1.2 = 18,000$.

4. **B** From the statement, you know that flour is necessary to make the cookies. You don't know that flour is the only thing necessary to make the cookies. For example, you may also need sugar and eggs. You cannot conclude (A) or (E), because there may be other reasons for not making the cookies (maybe you didn't feel like it, or maybe you were out of sugar). (C) is not necessarily true because there may be other things necessary besides flour. (D) contradicts the original statement.(B) must be true because you couldn't have made the cookies without the flour.

5. **B** If you selected (E), you impulsively grabbed at the Joe Bloggs answer. On this question, the safest way—as usual—is to try choices rather than to reason algebraically. Plugging in the choices for n, you get the following results:

(A) $\quad f(0) = \dfrac{0+1}{0-1} = -1$

(B) $\quad f(2) = \dfrac{2+1}{2-1} = 3$

(C) $\quad f(3) = \dfrac{3+1}{3-1} = 2$

(D) $\quad f(4) = \dfrac{4+1}{4-1} = \dfrac{5}{3}$

(E) $\quad f(5) = \dfrac{5+1}{5-1} = \dfrac{3}{2}$

Now you can easily see that (B) yields the greatest value.

6. **A** First solve for b. If $9b = 81$, then b must equal 9. Insert 9 for b into $\sqrt{b} \cdot \sqrt[3]{3b}$:
$$\sqrt{9} \cdot \sqrt[3]{3 \cdot 9} = 3 \cdot \sqrt[3]{27} = 3 \cdot 3 = 9$$

7. **A** The formula for the circumference of a circle is $C = 2\pi r$ or $C = d\pi$. (If you forget the formula, you can look it up at the beginning of the section.) The circumference of the circle is 5, so $5 = \pi d$. Now, just solve for d, which equals $\dfrac{5}{\pi}$.

8. **D** If you got this question wrong, you either misread it or forgot the correct order of operations. Remember to do parentheses first. Translating the information to an equation, you'd get the following:

$$(1+2)(2+3)(3+4) = \frac{1}{2}(20+x)$$
$$3 \times 5 \times 7 = \frac{1}{2}(20+x)$$
$$105 = \frac{1}{2}(20+x)$$
$$210 = 20 + x$$
$$190 = x$$

SECTION 2

9. E Approach the problem in bite-size pieces. $\sqrt{x} = 2^2$ so $\sqrt{x} = 4$. Square both sides to get $x = 16$.

10. B We're solving for shirts and pants, which constitute 60% of total sales. Since shoes ($12,000) account for 15%, shirts and pants would be four times that amount, or $48,000. Another way to solve this is to find out the total value of sales and find 60% of that. If $20,000 represents 25% (or $\frac{1}{4}$) of sales, then the total must be $80,000. Using translation, you'll find that $\frac{60}{100} \times \$80,000 = \$48,000$.

11. D You should have noticed several things about this question. First, the figure was not drawn to scale. So a good first step would be to redraw the figure to comply with the condition ($\overline{AB} > \overline{CD}$). Second, the question asks which of the following *must* be true. *Must* is an important word—if it were *which of the following could be true,* you'd change your analysis completely. So, redrawing the figure, you'd get something like this:

In this figure, $\overline{AB}$ is clearly larger than $\overline{CD}$. Since plugging in numbers makes the distance more concrete, you might have made $AB = 3$ and $CD = 2$, for example. Since you don't know the length of BD, however, you'd have to leave it alone. Now, let's check the conditions. Option I: Well, this could be true, but it doesn't have to be. So, option I is out. This allows you to eliminate (A) and (E). Option II: Since you let $AB = 3$ and $CD = 2$, $AC = 3 + BC$ while $BD = BC + 2$. No matter what BC is, $AC > BD$. Option II is true. This allows you to eliminate (C), which does not include Option II. We still need to check one more. Option III: Since $AB > CD$, and $AC > AB$, then $AC > CD$. Option III is true; therefore, (D) is the answer.

12. D Absolute value, a number's distance from zero on a number line, is always expressed as a positive number. Cross out (A) and (B) since both are negative. Solve the function with $x = 1$: $f(1) = \left| \left| 1 \right| - 3 \right| = 2$.

13. D This geometric sequence can be expressed as 6×2^x, where x is the number of hours. So, after 9 hours, there will be $6 \times 2^9 = 6 \times 512 = 3,072$. Alternatively, you could just work out the problem each hour by doubling. So, after the 1st hour, there are $6 \times 2 = 12$. Then, after the 2nd hour, there are $12 \times 2 = 24$, etc., until you get to the 9th hour.

14. E Because any value squared must be 0 or positive, the least possible value for x^2 is 0. This means the least possible value of $x^2 + 2$ is 2. So, (A), (B), (C), and (D) are not possible values for $f(x)$. Only E is a possible value because when $x = 0$, $f(x) = 2$.

15. E Once again, the way *not* to solve an SAT question is to reason algebraically. Instead, use your calculator to start cubing integers and stop when you find an integer cubed that is greater than 200. 1^3, 2^3, 3^3, 4^3, and 5^3 are all less than 200. 6^3 is 216, so that's too large. Thus there are 5 numbers.

16. B Plug in! Since the values you choose for x and y must satisfy the equation, let x equal 6 and y equal 9. The perimeter p would then equal $6 + 6 + 9 + 9$, or 30. The target is y, which is equal to 9. Plugging 30 in for p in each of the choices, you'd get (B) as the answer. Although some of you might have answered this question correctly by using algebra, doing so might have caused you to make a mistake without realizing it. Trust us. Plugging in is always the safer method for this type of problem. The Joe Bloggs choice, by the way, was (C).

17. **C** And yet again, the slow way to solve a word problem like this is to set up equations. Letting *w* and *l* represent the number of wins and losses, respectively, the slow method of setting up equations would yield the following:

$$\frac{w}{l} = \frac{3}{1}$$

$$\frac{w+6}{l} = \frac{5}{1}$$

Then you'd have to substitute $\frac{3}{1}$ for $\frac{w}{l}$ in the second equation and solve for *l* and then go back to solve for *w*.

We can also plug in the answer choices, starting in the middle, (C), and see which one works:

	Before		After	
	Wins	Losses	Wins	Losses
(A)	3			
(B)	6			
(C)	9	3 (3:1)	15	3 (5:1)
(D)	15			
(E)	24			

Bingo! We found the answer on the first try! If (C) didn't work, you'd move up or down depending on whether the result was too small or too big.

18. **A** This is a great opportunity to plug in. Make up a value for *x*—let's say 40. Then name the two other angles created by the lines that meet at vertex *P*— let's call the one to the left of *x* (within the same triangle as the angle labeled *a*°) angle *y* and the one to the right of *x* (within the same triangle as the angle labeled *b*°) angle *z*. Now make up values for these two angles so the sum of *x*, *y*, and *z* is 90. Let's say that $y = 30$ and $z = 20$. Since both of these triangles are right triangles, $a = 180 - 90 - 30 = 60$, and $b = 180 - 90 - 20 = 70$. Thus $a + b = 130$, which becomes our target. Only (A) yields this answer.

19. **C** First a little error avoidance: Since 5 is one of the numbers you see, 5^2, or 25 is not going to be the answer. It's a Joe Bloggs answer. So, eliminate (A). Next, let's estimate the area before you try to solve directly. The length of the square's side is a little more than 5, so the area is going to be a little more than 5^2 or 25. (E) is too large, so before solving the problem, you've eliminated (A) and (E). If you couldn't calculate the area exactly, you could guess from among the remaining choices. To determine the area, let's begin by assigning the variable *s* to indicate the length of the square's sides. The area is given by the formula: $A = s^2$. Notice the triangle formed by side $\overline{AB}$ and the *x*- and *y*-axes. The base of that triangle is 1 and the height is 5, so you can use the Pythagorean theorem to find the length of side $\overline{AB}$ or *s*:

$$1^2 + 5^2 = s$$

$$26 = s$$

$$s = \sqrt{26}$$

$$s^2 = 26$$

20. **B** Probability is the chance of something happening. In this case, to find the probability, find the area that is in the circle but not the square, divided by the area of the circle (which represents all possibilities). Plug in for the radius of the circle. Let's say $r = 5$. So, the area of the circle is $\pi \times 5^2 = 25\pi$. The area that is in the circle but not the square is the area of the circle minus the area of the square. Find the area of the square. The diagonal of the square is equal to the diameter of the circle: $2 \times 5 = 10$. The diameter creates a $45°$-$45°$-$90°$ triangle from the square. So, the side of the square is $\dfrac{10}{\sqrt{2}}$. That means the area of the square is $\left(\dfrac{10}{\sqrt{2}}\right)^2 = \dfrac{100}{2} = 50$. Therefore, the area within the circle but not the square is $25\pi - 50$. That means the probability is $\dfrac{25\pi - 50}{25\pi} \approx 3.63$. This is the target. Only (B) matches. After you've plugged in and realized that the probablity is $\dfrac{(25\pi - 50)}{25\pi}$, you can also solve algebraically:

$\dfrac{25\pi - 50}{25\pi} = \dfrac{25(\pi - 2)}{25\pi} = \dfrac{\pi - 2}{\pi}$. Another even more complicated approach would be to call the area of the circle πr^2, the diameter $2r$, and the area of the square $\left(\dfrac{2r}{\sqrt{2}}\right)^2 = \dfrac{4r^2}{2} = 2r^2$. The probability would be $\dfrac{\pi r^2 - 2r^2}{\pi r^2}$. This is simplified: $\dfrac{r^2(\pi - 2)}{\pi r^2} = \dfrac{\pi - 2}{\pi}$. It's much more confusing when you don't plug in numbers!

SECTION 3

1. **A** The clues *to prevent household fires* and *flammable liquids* make *flammable* a good word to recycle for the blank. (A) comes closest to this meaning. (B), (C), and (D) are unrelated. (E) means the opposite of the word needed.

2. **E** The semicolon is a same-direction trigger. Because Mark hates mistakes, he will review his papers "carefully." We can immediately eliminate (B), (C), and (D). (E) means "very carefully." If you weren't sure what (A) meant, you had to guess. Give yourself a pat on the back if you guessed rather than leaving the question blank. Even though you got the question wrong, you did the right thing. And in the long run, that's how your score goes up.

3. **B** The clue for the first blank is *defends* and the trigger word is *nor*. A good word to use for the first blank will be one that is the opposite of *defends*, such as "disagrees with." This eliminates (D) and (E). Now look at the second blank. According to the first part of the sentence, Jenkins doesn't do anything positive or negative, so a good word for the blank is "neutrality." This eliminates (A) and (C).

4. **A** *Great thinkers* must have "great" *insights*, so the first blank is a positive word. The clues here are *voiced so often* and *mere,* which indicate something trivial or unimportant. Things that are voiced can often be called "repetitions," or some related negative word. The word *ironic* also suggests that the first and second blanks contrast in meaning. The only choice that has a positive word followed by a negative word is (A). Remember to use POE to avoid words you don't know. Since *beliefs* is not negative, you can eliminate (B), even if you do not know what *banal* means.

5. **A** The clue is *been taught to communicate*, and the trigger word *but* indicates that the *skeptics* doubt this. So the skeptics must be arguing that the apes have *not really been taught*; they may be "mimicking" (aping!) their trainers. (A) is the best choice. Even if you don't know what (A), (B), or (E) means, you should be able to use POE on (C) and (D), and then guess.

6. **C** The clue is *technical difficulty and challenging counterpoint*, so good words for the blanks are "difficult" and "complex," which agree with each other. This eliminates (B) and (D), as both contain answers which disagree with each other. You can eliminate (A) because *diminutive* means small. Although *inscrutable* in (E) means "difficult to understand," the word *classical* does not mean "difficult" or "complex."

7. **D** The first and second blanks are both somewhat negative words. (E) is the only bad guess, since it doesn't make much sense to view a situation as *political* and be *perplexed* by it. (A), (B), (C), and (D) are all good guesses because at least one of the words is somewhat negative. Guessing one of these choices would have been better than leaving the question blank. If you look closely, you'll notice that the trigger *since* tells you that the two blanks must be similar to each other. Eliminate (A), as there is no evidence for how *obscure* or "little known" their situations are. (B) is close, but *bellicose* means "prone to fighting," which is not supported by sentence. Eliminate (C), as *sanguine* means "confident and positive," which does not agree with *acute* and is not negative.

8. **D** The clues in this sentence are *ancient ruins of marvelous bygone civilizations* and *sad*. What is sad about looking at the ruins of ancient civilizations? Seeing that, you can gather that human greatness doesn't last. This idea is reinforced by the time trigger—if an ETS sentence completion compares past and present, it is usually to show a change. Therefore, you can put *doesn't last* in the blank, and the best match is *transience*.

SECTION 3

9. C After the second sentence, the passage shifts into information about *hypergraphia* and also suggests that if the cause of writer's block is found to be *neurological*, then different treatment techniques might be appropriate. Therefore, we need an answer referring to a shift in meaning. (A) is not supported by the passage, which is not critical. (B) is too vague and doesn't really refer to anything, and (D) is too broad. (E) refers to two problems, although only one, *writer's block*, is mentioned in the passage.

10. B After a discussion of treatments for writer's block in the first half of the passage, the second half of the passage develops the idea that writer's block may have a *neurological* cause after the first half gives a brief introduction to current treatments. (A) is incorrect because no comparison takes place. (C) is incorrect because some information is provided, but it is not detailed. (D) is incorrect since the passage doesn't question *current techniques*. (E) is incorrect because only one side effect of *temporal lobe epilepsy* is mentioned.

11. B (B) is correct, because the passage gives interesting historical information about a city like a travel guide does. (A) is incorrect, because the information given about the *arrondissements* is not detailed enough for a proposal, nor is the author recommending that other cities follow Paris' example. There is no evidence of *satire*, making (C) incorrect. The passage does not mention connections to art or Roman history, making both (D) and (E) incorrect.

12. C The passage states that *Paris was protected by a wall. New walls were built* that became the site of today's streets. The protective walls determined the shape of the city. (A) is incorrect, because an increase in population required expansion of the city's walls. There is no evidence for (B) or (D). Although the passage mentions Romans, there is no reference to improving upon their architecture, making (E) incorrect.

13. D (D) is the best answer. A majority of the passage discusses the Zambesi river and its tributaries. Very little information is given on people, making (A) wrong. (B) is incorrect; color is mentioned in line 12 ("yellowish-green tinge") but not again. No mention is made of (C). (E) is mentioned only in the last line.

14. D The best choice is (D). In lines 8–11, the passage states that Livingston explored the Zambesis and its tributaries in order to find if they could be used *for commerce*. (A) is not the primary reason for the expedition. Although refugees from Portuguese slavery are mentioned in passing at the end of the passage, contacting Portuguese settlers, (B), is not mentioned at all in the passage. (C) is incorrect because it is not known if the way is safe or not. (E) is incorrect, because it is not stated that Livingston was the first to survey the land.

15. E The fish *screen* themselves from the *rays* of the *sun*—thus, (E) is the best answer. (A) is too positive; fish would not *screen themselves* from a *pleasant* sun. (B) is not supported by the passage. (C) is one definition of *torrid*, but it doesn't fit in this context. (D) does not refer to the sun but rather to the fish.

16. A The passage states that the Kongone is the "safest" branch for travel, due to the straight course and the depth of the water. The passage states that boats should not attempt the bar when the wind is from the south and south east though. Thus, (A) is the best answer. (B) cannot be inferred since it is unknown if and when the beacon would be built. (C) is deceptive; the passage states that if the wind is from the *east or north* the bar would be smooth. (D) is too extreme; of the three rivers that Livingston explored, the Kongone is the best route. But that is not the same as being the best of all rivers in Africa. (E) is a misstating of the passage. East Luabo should not attempted unless the wind is from the northeast, not the Kongone.

17. **A** Although the Kongone is mentioned throughout the third paragraph, the passage describes the effects of the current in lines 41–43. (B) is too strong. The change of water level is not attributed to the current, eliminating (C). (D) is not supported by the passage. (E) refers not to the Kongone, but refers instead to the situation on the Zambesi.

18. **C** Livingston indicates that the river he is charting may be the river described by de Gama. (A) is incorrect, because Livingston isn't certain that the river is same one that de Gama referred to. (B) is not supported by the passage. (D) doesn't make any sense; mentioning de Gama does not explain the lack of Portuguese settlers. (E) is wrong; there is no pillar at the river. (C) is the best answer.

19. **E** (E) is the best answer; the passage presents factual information in an objective tone. (A) is incorrect; an author is not disinterested in his or her subject. (B) and (C) are too strong. (D) is wrong, as little personal information about Livingston is revealed.

20. **B** Lines 59–63 indicate that the natives had no interest in making contact with Livingston. (A) is extreme. No information is given about *most* of the inhabitants of Africa. (C) is not supported by the passage. Although Livingston saw few people, many people might have lived there. (D) is beyond the information given in the passage. (E) is incorrect because while the natives are not interested in making contact with Livingston, the passage never states they are *upset*.

21. **C** (C) is the best choice. The first paragraph gives some details about the beginnings of the journey, which is later described in greater detail. (A) is not correct because Livingston's private life is not described. (B) is wrong because no mention is made of characteristics or skills. (D) is incorrect; Livingston and his companions are not *lackadaisical*. (E) is wrong, because it doesn't actually explain why he was in Africa.

22. **D** In lines 57–59, the author describes how one can locate the Kongone by using Tiwambe and East Laubo. (A) is incorrect, because the current and wind can make it more difficult to travel on the Kongone. (B) is mentioned in the passage, but is not given as a reason that Livingston decided that the river was the "best" course for a boat. (C) is also not stated as a contributing factor. (E) is wrong; there is no beacon on Pearl Island.

23. **B** Line 34 states that the water level of the Kongone is at *two fathoms* at low water, but during the spring rises by 12 to 14 feet. The *cuttlefish* referred to in (A) are not clearly part of the Kongone; they are mentioned as being observed when Livingston was still offshore. (C) is incorrect; the passage clearly states that the Milambe is the most westerly. (D) is wrong because the bar of the Kongone is not contrasted with the bars of the other tributaries. (E) refers to East Luabo, not to the Kongone.

24. **A** (A) is the best choice, because lines 46–48 state that the East Luabo is the most easy to spot. (B) is mentioned, but not as reason that East Luabo is favorable to navigators. (C) is contradicted by the passage, as the river is only safe when the wind is east or northeast. (D) is beyond the information given in the passage since no mention is given of *European navigators*. (E) is also not supported. The passage makes it clear that Livingston is not certain whether East Luabo is the same as the river described by de Gama.

SECTION 4

1. B This simple equation should present you with little difficulty, but beware: It is on precisely such questions that your guard might come down and you can become careless! Plugging in the answer choices is safest. Only (B) works:

$$2 + (0) = 2 - (0)$$
$$2 = 2$$

2. B As the directions at the beginning of every math section remind us, the area of a triangle is given by this formula: $A = \frac{1}{2}bh$. Since the base is 4 and the height is 1, the area is 2. $A = \frac{1}{2} \times 4 \times 1 = 2$.

3. E If the area of square A is 16, the length of each side is 4, and the perimeter is 16. You are told that this is $\frac{2}{3}$ of B's perimeter, which you can calculate:

$$\frac{2}{3}x = 16$$
$$x = 16 \times \frac{3}{2} = 24$$

Now that you know the perimeter of B, you can calculate the perimeter of C:

$$\frac{2}{3}x = 24$$
$$x = 24 \times \frac{3}{2} = 36$$

If the perimeter of (C) is 36, each side is 9, and the area of (C) is 9^2, or 81. If you chose (B), you need to read the question more carefully.

4. E According to the ratios given, you know that the mixture contains more wheat than rye; there must be more than 5 pounds of wheat. So let's eliminate (A) and (B). Use the Ratio Box.

Corn	Wheat	Rye	Total
3	5	2	10
2.5	2.5	2.5	2.5
7.5	12.5	5	25

Since there is a total of 5 pounds of rye, the multiplier is 2.5. This allows you to solve for 12.5 pounds for the wheat.

5. C Since 135° is one of the middle angles of the circle, the triangles must each have a 45° angle, and are therefore both identical 45°-45°-90° triangles. Remember (or check the front page of the test) that the ratio of the sides in such a triangle is $x : x : \sqrt{2}x$. You know that the diameter of the circle is 12, so the hypotenuse (which is equal to the radius of the circle) of each triangle is 6. Since 6 is the long side, the other side of each triangle must be $\frac{6}{\sqrt{2}}$. Now you can find the area of one of the triangles and double it. The area of a triangle is $\frac{1}{2}bh$, and both the base and height are equal to $\frac{6}{\sqrt{2}}$. So $\frac{1}{2} \times \frac{6}{\sqrt{2}} \times \frac{6}{\sqrt{2}} = \frac{36}{4} = 9$. You have found the area for one of the triangles, so double it to get 18, or (C). Another way to solve this is to use the side of your answer sheet as a ruler and ballpark. Since $XZ = 12$, the hypotenuse of each triangle is 6. Now mark off the length of 6 with your homemade ruler and compare that to a side of one of the triangles. You can guesstimate that the side is about 4. Using that approximation, calculate that since the base and height of both triangles is 4, the area of each triangle is $\frac{1}{2} \times 4 \times 4 = 8$. The area of both triangles together is 16, which is closest to 18, or (C). Remember, ETS wants you to do complicated geometry, but all you care about is finding the answer.

6. A The question tells you that the function is defined for values of x between −2 and 2; that is, you are told the domain of the function. This means you're looking for a graph that extends horizontally from −2 to 2 (including values everywhere in that interval), but no further. Only the graph in (A) fits this description. (C) is out because it is not a graph of a function; there is more than one y-value for some of the x-values. (E) seems to keep going past −2 and 2. Eliminate (B) and (D), too, since the graph of a function must be continuous.

7. **A** Try roughly plotting the data points, and then look at your graph. Find the answer that best fits your graph. Alternatively, notice that the number of customers increases as the temperature increases. The line of best fit will go up as you follow the graph from left to right, so eliminate (B), (D), and (E). Notice that the number of customers does not increase by the same number for each 10-degree temperature increase. This is an exponential increase, not a linear increase. So, the graph will be curved. Eliminate (C). Only (A) fits the data in the chart.

8. **E** Plug in 6 for c. The question is now asking what percent of 18 is 9. The answer would be 50. Whichever choice gives you 50 when 6 is plugged in for (C) is the answer. Therefore (E) is the answer. Remember, plugging in good numbers will make your life much easier!

9. **C** If you missed this question, you should review decimal place values.

$$\frac{900}{10} = 90$$

$$\frac{90}{100} = .9$$

$$\frac{9}{1000} = 0.009$$

$$90 + 0.9 + 0.009 = 90.909$$

Remember, you can use your calculator to help you solve this problem.

10. **B** Since 20% of the coins are either nickels or dimes, 80% are neither. 80% of 220 equals 176. Use your calculator or write it out and solve:

$$\frac{8}{10} \times 220 = 176$$

11. **D** Take out your calculator:

$$216,000 + 20\% \text{ of } 216,000 = 259,200$$
$$204,000 + 20\% \text{ of } 204,000 = 244,800$$
$$259,200 - 244,800 = 14,400$$

Another route to the answer is to take the difference immediately ($216,000 - 204,000 = 12,000$) and then increase that by 20%.

Watch out for partial answers. (E) is 20% of Springfield's population, and (A) is the difference between 20% of Springfield's population and 20% of Rockville's population.

12. **E** With algebraic answer choices, you should plug in numbers. Let's let $x = y = 2$, which makes $z = 4$. Plugging these values into the choices, you'd get the following:

(A) $2(2) + 2(2) = 2(4)$ [Yes]

(B) $2 - 2 = 0$ [Yes]

(C) $2 - 4 = 2 - 4$ [Yes]

(D) $2 = \frac{4}{2}$ [Yes]

(E) $4 - 2 = 2(2)$ [No]

The correct answer is (E). Don't forget the EXCEPT!

13. **A** Do NOT try to figure out the seven numbers in the original list! The median is the middle number in a list of numbers. Since 8 is lower than every other number, and 43 is higher, they won't change the value of the median. This means that option II is wrong, so you can eliminate (B), (D), and (E). Since (A) and (C) both include I, you know it must be true without even checking it. Let's focus on option III. The mode is the number repeated most often. Since 8 and 43 weren't in the original list, they can't change the mode. Eliminate (C) and pick (A).

14. **D** There are variables in the answer choices, and the question asks you what *must be* true. This indicates that you will need to plug in values for x, possibly more than once. Try both –2 and 3. Only (D) remains true for both. Remember that the square of any nonzero number, either positive or negative, is always positive.

15. **E** The relationship is the smaller the shoes, the greater the difficulty. This is an inverse relationship. So, look for an inverse function. Only (E) is an inverse function. If you weren't sure, try plugging in 8 and 10 for the s. The function should yield a greater D for 8 than it does for 10. Only (E) has a $D(8) > D(10)$.

16. **D** Note first that this is an EXCEPT question. Now, since $a^2b = 12^2$, and b is an odd integer, let's see what you can come up with. Let's make b equal 1, so you get the following: $a^2 \times 1 = 12^2 = 144$, so $a = 12$. If a equals 12, it is divisible by 1, 2, 3, 4, 6, and 12. The only choice that remains is (D).

17. **D** Note before you begin that the question asks for what *must* be true. Let's start with the first option:

I. Try some consecutive integers.

$2 + 3 = 5$

$3 + 4 = 7$

Option I must be true because consecutive integers will always be even + odd which is always odd. Eliminate (B). Let's check the second option:

II. $2 + 3 + 4 = 9$

Option II is false. Eliminate (C) and (E). You still need to check option III:

$2 + 3 + 4 = 9$

$3 + 4 + 5 = 12$

$4 + 5 + 6 = 15$

Option III must be true. Eliminate (A).

18. **A** Keep in mind that this figure is not drawn to scale. Since $\overline{BD} \parallel \overline{AE}$, you know that the following angles are equal: $\angle DCE, \angle CEA, \angle BCA, \angle CAE$ Since $\triangle ACE$ has two equal angles, it is isosceles and the sides opposite those angles are also equal. Therefore, $CE = AC = 3$.

19. **C** Plug in numbers. If $a = 10$ and $b = -10$, the equation works. So you can eliminate any answer choices that have I or II: eliminate (B), (D), and (E). If $b = -5$, then the left side of the equation always equals 0, so the equation never works. So III must be true: Eliminate (A).

20. **D** Since 61 is the value of the *second* term in the sequence, plug in 2 for n: $a^{3(2)} - 3 = 61$. Therefore, $a^6 = 64$, and a must be equal to ± 2. Make certain you read carefully; III would work if 61 were the value of the *first* term.

SECTION 5

1. **C** All versions of the underlined phrase except (C) are wordy or awkward.

2. **B** If something has been happening for the last two thousand years, it shouldn't be discussed in the present or future tense. Eliminate (A), (D), and (E) for that error. *Building technologies* continue to change, so it would be better to use *have changed* rather than *had changed*. *Had changed* implies that the technologies will no longer change.

3. **A** The sentence is correct as it is written. (B) and (E) rewrite the verbs in *–ing* form, not the first choice for a clear sentence. (C) eliminates the cause-and-effect relationship present in the original. (D) adds the word *it*, which makes the sentence a run-on.

4. **D** (D) uses the correct idiom, *belief that*. Both (A) and (E) use an incorrect idiom, *belief of*. In (B), the first *is* is unnecessary and makes the sentence awkward. (C) adds another unnecessary word, *which*.

5. **A** There is no error in the sentence as it is written.

6. **E** The beginning of the sentence is in the past tense, so get rid of anything that uses present tense in the underlined portion: (A) and (C). (B) changes the meaning by using *second* in a different context. (D) changes the wording to *a miracle is what he needed*, which isn't parallel with the rest of the sentence.

7. **B** As written, (A) contains nonparallel structure. (C) misplaces the word *careful*; (D) mistakenly implies a cause-and-effect relationship; and (E) uses the word *yet*, implying a contradiction which does not exist, and splits the infinitive *to document*. Only (B) correctly uses the parallel structure *you should gather...and document*, without adding other errors.

8. **E** The sentence should compare the soil of Pennsylvania with the soil of the Rhine. Only (E) does so correctly: the phrase *that of* helps draw the proper comparison. Each of the other choices creates a faulty comparison.

9. **D** An *-ing* form of a verb cannot be the main verb of a sentence, as in (A) and (C). Also, to avoid a misplaced modifier, the phrase *as one of the forward-looking, enlightened monarchs of Europe* should follow the word *reputation* as it does in (D). (B) adds the word *however*, which is unnecessary, and (E) says *always,* which changes the meaning.

10. **D** Watch out for switches from the pronoun *you* to the pronoun *one*. Stick with one or the other. Both (A) and (B) switch between the two. (C) isn't a complete sentence, and (E) is awkward and somewhat changes the meaning.

11. **C** This sentence contains the ambiguous pronoun *it,* leaving the reader unsure which design movement *instigated* the paradigm shift. Eliminate (A) and (B) for this error. Both (D) and (E) use *and* instead of *however*. Since the second half of the sentence shows a difference between the two schools of design, and the first half shows a similarity, *however* is better, so eliminate (D) and (E).

12. **B** Plural nouns must refer to plural nouns. There are two *characters* so they cannot be *an orphan*; they would be *orphans*.

13. **E** There is no error in the sentence as it is written.

14. **A** This sentence confuses subject with object. Since the speaker is the subject, *me* should be changed to *I*.

15. **A** An adverb, "completely," is needed to modify the verb *exhausted*.

16. **A** To correct the error in subject-verb agreement, change *is* to "are" because *benefits* is plural.

17. **D** (D) creates an error in verb parallelism. The verbs in the list, *listening* and *reading,* do not agree with *she practiced.* It should be "practicing."

18. **D** This sentence misuses an incorrect comparison modifier. Since more than two *jingoists* are mentioned (*all*), change *more* to the superlative "most."

19. **E** There is no error in the sentence as it is written.

20. **C** The verbal phrase *brushing your teeth* acts as a singular noun (you could replace this phrase with "it"), which requires the singular verb "promotes."

21. **C** In this sentence, the *trends* discussed *seem* to do two things: *show* and *indicating*. The verbs need to be parallel in form but are not. (C) should read "indicate" instead.

22. **D** The semicolon indicates that both clauses must be independent, so *being* creates a fragment. The correct form should be "was."

23. **C** In (C), *it* is a singular pronoun, which doesn't agree with the plural subject *species*. The sentence should read "they swing."

24. **C** This adjective should be in comparative form ("higher") to parallel *shorter, lighter, or tighter.*

25. **D** This is a diction error; *patients* are people receiving medical treatment. Replace *patients* with "patience," which means "tolerance."

26. **B** This sentence uses the wrong conjunction. Since the sentence contrasts two unlike things, replace *and* with but for greater logic and clarity.

27. **C** The sentence should read: "Saif knew that the other applicants weren't as good as he"; using *him* isn't correct. Some may even write the sentence as: "Saif knew that the other applicants weren't as good as he was"; however, the verb *was* isn't necessary.

28. **D** *She* is ambiguous in this sentence; it could refer either to Natalie or to Noelle. It should read "Natalie."

29. **D** In (D), *Branagh* sets up a faulty comparison. *Olivier's* performance should be compared to *Branagh's* performance, not to *Branagh* himself. It should read "to Kenneth Branagh's."

30. **B** Although there are no big errors in the original version, it is longer and less straightforward than (B). (C) and (E) change the meaning of the sentence, and (D) is as awkward as the original.

31. **A** (B) and (C) introduce a casual tone that doesn't flow with the rest of the passage. Deleting the word *another,* as (D) suggests, and deleting the entire sentence, as (E) suggests, would confuse the meaning and flow of the sentence and passage. (A) is best because it creates a transition between two examples that both support the author's main point.

32. **E** Only (E) retains the correct meaning of the sentence while using correct grammar. The original version, as given in (A), uses a run-on sentence. (B) does not fix this original error just by adding a semicolon. Both (C) and (D) suggest that the employees will invest in the stock, the stock will plummet, and their savings will disappear. You need to retain the original meaning—that this is a possibility and not a definite occurrence.

33. **C** The first paragraph discusses one side of an issue: protective legislation may limit freedom and be unnecessary. The second paragraph shows the other side of the debate: some laws may be helpful. The third paragraph concludes that a compromise is best. Thus, sentence 10 should be the concluding sentence of the second paragraph, making (C) the best answer. (B) would upset the chronology of the second paragraph. (A) improperly creates a contrast with the preceding ideas. (D) destroys the agreement between *their* and *people*. Similarly, (E)'s lack of noun agreement illogically implies that the employees all share one retirement account.

34. **E** Only (E) correctly uses the parallel construction *some people will think...others will complain.*

35. **D** With omission questions, read the sentence with the sentences immediately before and after it, then read those two sentences without the sentence in question. You are looking for a sentence with a piece of information that is not relevant to the passage. Sentences 3, 7, 11, and 15 are all necessary parts of the passage; therefore you can eliminate them and choose (D).

SECTION 6

1. **B** The best way to approach this problem is to plug in the answers. Start with (C). When 6 is subtracted from 10, the result is 4. Divide 4 by 2 to see if it equals 3. It does not, so (C) can't be correct. Since our answer was too small, you need to subtract a smaller number from 10. Try (B). When 4 is subtracted from 10, the result is 6. Divide by 2 to get 3; this is correct.

2. **C** The number of degrees in a line is 180. Therefore, $b + c = 180$. And since $a + 90 = 180$, $a = 90$. So $a + b + c = 270$. Note that (E) is the Joe Bloggs choice—"it cannot be determined" is rarely the correct answer.

3. **E** Use the formula for distance: *distance = rate × time.*

   Steve runs 12 miles at 8 miles per hour, which means that he runs for $1\frac{1}{2}$ hours (or 1.5 if you're using your calculator). Adam runs the same 12 miles at 6 miles per hour, which means that he runs for 2 hours. Adam takes half an hour longer to complete the race, and half an hour is 30 minutes.

4. **D** Since there are variables in the answers, try Plugging In! If $a = 2$, then $\frac{4a}{3} \times 6a = \frac{8 \times 12}{3} = 32$. Plug $a = 2$ into the answers to find that only (D) is 32. Another option is to rewrite the problem as $\frac{4a}{3} \times \frac{6a}{1}$. Reduce before you multiply by dividing the denominator of the first term and the numerator of the second term by 3 to get $\frac{4a}{1} \times \frac{2a}{1} = 8a^2$.

5. **E** To solve this problem, you need to figure out the ratio between the *x* and *y* values on line segment $\overline{AB}$. Looking at the figure, $\overline{AB}$ is the hypotenuse of a right triangle with a side of 12. You can see this is a multiple of one of ETS's favorite right triangles: 3:4:5. This is a 9:12:15 triangle, and the coordinates of point *B* are (9,12). All the points on line segment $\overline{AB}$ are in a ratio of 9:12. Only (E) has a similar ratio.

6. **B** Since you aren't given the cost of any book, you can plug in our own values. Let's say that the average cost of the textbooks, excluding the anatomy textbook, is $10. You can make all the books cost $10 each to make the problem easier. The anatomy textbook would cost $30. The total cost of all the textbooks would be $130. The anatomy textbook would be $\frac{\$30}{\$130} = \frac{3}{13}$ of the total cost.

7. **A** The trick is to notice that this parallelogram is actually made of two equal triangles. By finding the area of the triangles, you can find the area of the parallelogram. The triangles are both right triangles, and the two sides given in the figure follow the 3:4:5 pattern. If you look at $\triangle ACD$ with $\overline{AC}$ as the base, the base is 3 and the height is 4. Now use the formula for area of a triangle:

$$A = \frac{1}{2} \times 3 \times 4 = 6$$

   That means the parallelogram is $2 \times 6 = 12$.

   Also, if you estimate the area, the base is 5 and the height is less than 3, so the area is less than 15. The only answer less than 15 is (A)!

8. **D** Plug in the answer choices. You need to find the smallest value *n* such that the value of the Super Savings account is greater than the value of the Standard Savings account, or $80 \times 1.08^n > 100 \times 1.05^n$. Start in the middle with (C). After 7 years, you get $137.11 > 140.71$, which is not true. Eliminate 7 and any smaller number—(A) and (B). At 8 years, you get $148.07 > 147.75$, which is true. Since you are looking for the smallest value, eliminate (E).

9.   **2**
Just simplify and solve for *x*:

$$\frac{x + 2x + 3x}{2} = 6$$

$$\frac{6x}{2} = 6$$

$$6x = 12$$

$$x = 2$$

Remember that the first grid-in question returns the difficulty meter to easy!

10.   **19, 39, 59, 79, or 99**
The simplest way to solve this problem would be to find values of *n* that satisfy the first condition, and then to check which of those also satisfies the second condition. So, let's find some numbers that leave a remainder of 4 when divided by 5: {9, 14, 19, 24, 29}.

That should be enough. Now let's check which of these leaves a remainder of 3 when divided by 4:

$$9 \div 4 = 2\ R1$$
$$14 \div 4 = 3\ R2$$
$$19 \div 4 = 4\ R3$$

19 is one acceptable response.

11.   **145**
Since the two lines are parallel, $110 + 2x = 180$. Solving this equation for *x*, you get $x = 35$. Looking at the triangle, the missing angle (*m*) can be found by solving the equation $110 + x + m = 180$. Since $x = 35$, $m = 35$. If $m + y = 180$ and $m = 35$, $y = 145$.

12.   **36**
If $x^2 = 16$ then $x = \pm 4$. If $y^2 = 4$ then $y = \pm 2$. To maximize $(x - y)^2$, you need to maximize the difference. The greatest difference is $(-4) - 2 = -6$ or $4 - (-2) = 6$, and both 6^2 and $(-6)^2$ equal 36.

13.   **130**
First use a Ratio Box to find the number of males and females. If the ratio is 2 to 3, the total ratio is 5. The actual is 250, so the multiplier is 50. That means there are $50 \times 2 = 100$ males and $50 \times 3 = 150$ females. Set up a group grid (the bolded numbers are information from the problem):

	Males	Females	Total
French	**80**	20	**100**
Spanish	20	130	150
Total	100	150	**250**

You find that 20 females must be taking French and since there 150 females total, 130 must be taking Spanish.

14.   **8**
In the diagram, you can assume that the shorter ticks are evenly spaced, so each one must be 0.25 units long. Plugging the coordinates of the points into the given expression gives you

$$\frac{jk}{lmn} = \frac{(-2.5)(-1.5)}{(0.5)(0.75)(1.25)} = 8$$

. As you can see, canceling works well: the two negatives cancel each other out, and two of the numbers in the numerator are double the size of two of the numbers in the denominator. This leaves you with

$$\frac{jk}{lmn} = \frac{(2)(2)}{(0.5)} = 8$$

. You can also just plug the whole thing into your calculator, but make sure you use enough parentheses: you need to enclose the entire numerator in parentheses, and then the entire denominator in parentheses.

15. **12**

Start with the most restricted spots. There are 2 tools that can go in the first spot. Once you put 1 there, only 1 tool can go in the second spot. Once you've used these 2 tools, there are only 3 that can go in the third spot, then 2 in the fourth spot and 1 in the fifth spot. So, there are $2 \times 1 \times 3 \times 2 \times 1 = 12$ ways to arrange the tools.

16. **4**

This question looks tough, so work it one step at a time, and start with what you know. Sector *AOB* is a quarter-circle (it covers an angle of 90 out of 360 degrees), so multiplying its area (π) by 4 gives you the area of the whole circle (4π). Plugging this into the equation for the area of a circle, $A = \pi r^2$, gives you $4\pi = \pi r^2$, and the radius must be a positive value, so $r = 2$. This means that the coordinates of point *A* must be $(-2, 0)$. Since *A* is on both the circle and the parabola, you can plug its *x*- and *y*-coordinates into the given equation of the parabola, $y = x^2 - b$. This becomes $0 = (-2)^2 - b$, so $b = 4$.

17. **3**

The first step is to draw a diagram:

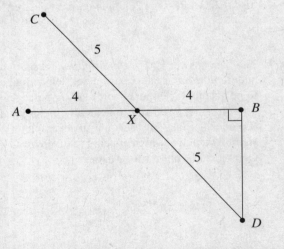

You should notice that *BD* is part of one of ETS's favorite right triangles: a 3:4:5 triangle. So *BD* = 3.

18. $\dfrac{6}{5}$ **or 1.2**

Inversely proportional means $x_1 y_1 = x_2 y_2$ where *x* represents hours of sleep and *y* represents the number of errors: (2 hours)(3 errors) = (5 hours)(*y* hours).

$6 = 5y$

$y = \dfrac{6}{5}$

SECTION 7

1. **D** Since *morality* is being linked with *religion*, you need a word along the lines of "erosion"; *collapse* is the only choice that fits.

2. **A** The clue in this sentence is *anarchy*, which means lack of order. If people have been shaken by the lack of order, they must be ready to buy *order* at any price. (A) comes closest to this meaning.

3. **B** You may have had trouble coming up with your own words on this question. This is because there is a relationship between the blanks. The phrase *external factors* is a clue. On the one hand, if animal behaviors are inherited, they would be relatively unaffected by external factors. On the other hand, if the animal behaviors are learned, they would be affected by external factors. (B) is the only one to preserve this relationship.

4. **C** We know the general's civilian life is simple, dignified, and *stoic*. The only blank that fits is (C); (B) and (D) miss the clues. (A) and (E), if you weren't sure what they mean, are good guesses, but incorrect.

5. **A** The clue is *cruel severity of some criminal penalties*. A judge (at least one that ETS likes) would probably want to avoid or to lessen *the cruel severity of some criminal penalties*. (B) and (D) miss the point completely. If you know what *condone* means, it also misses the point; if not, it's not a bad guess. (E) is a Joe Bloggs trap that contradicts the clue.

6. **A** *Hutton* and *Darwin* are used as examples of different scientists who contributed to geology. (B) is incorrect because the last sentence states that controversy surrounds many geologic theories are *constantly challenged*. (C) is incorrect because biological evolution expanded upon, rather than disproved, the Theory of Uniformity. (D) is too negative an answer; though the science may be relatively new, it is not *inexact*. (E) is incorrect, because the passage mentions *seventeenth-century* attempts to date the earth.

7. **B** The best answer is (B). Passage 1 does not attempt to *prove*, *contradict*, or *criticize* a theory. Therefore (A), (C), (D), and (E) can all be eliminated.

8. **A** Both passages refer to Geological Evolution as a theory, which implies that it has not yet been proven to be a fact. (B) and (D) are mentioned only in Passage 2 whereas (D) and (E) are mentioned or implied only in Passage 1. (C) is not correct because the age of the theory is not discussed in Passage 2. (A) is the best answer.

9. **E** The best answer is (E). *Confirmation*, *exception*, and *itemization* are too extreme or demanding to be accomplished in a short reading passage. Therefore, (A), (B) and (C) can all be eliminated. (D) does not take into account the example of Heart Mountain, which appears to disprove Geological Evolutionary Theory.

SECTION 7

10. A The lead words in this question are *the author's parents*. You learn about the author's parents in line 5: *my parents were at their wits' end*. The author mentions his parents again in lines 26–29: *My parents...agreed with the schoolmasters.* (A) paraphrases the answer well (*frustrated*). (B) is incorrect because the author's parents clearly knew that he had a problem. How could they be oblivious to the fact that he was expelled from several schools? (C) has nothing to do with the passage. You might be able to infer that the author's parents were wealthy because they sent him to a boarding school, but you cannot know their attitude toward the poor from the passage. (D) confuses several unconnected ideas mentioned in the passage. There is nothing in the passage to suggest that the author's parents were schoolmasters. The first paragraph states that the author's family lived together *in Bukovina*, so (E) is incorrect.

11. C According to lines 16–20, *An attempt to harmonize the imbalances in my character by means of strict discipline at a boarding school... nearly led to the same ignominious end.* Even if you don't know what ignominious means, it should still be clear that the attempt to straighten out the author had the same result as it did before—it didn't work. This idea is paraphrased in (C), which says that *the tactics were failing.* (A) is extreme. Perhaps the author was a bit unstable, but there is nothing in the passage that suggests the author was *a danger to others.* Remember, if an answer choice is half bad, it's all bad. (B) is a trap. Maybe the author did poorly in school partly because the schools were too difficult. Or maybe not. The passage tells you nothing about the difficulty of the schools. All you know is that the author was having a really hard time. (D) is another trap. You have no way of knowing from the passage how well the author got along with his peers. In (E), you know that his academic career is in bad shape, but does that mean he'll never finish school?

12. B The best answer is (B). You are told that the author's people were once subjects of the Austro-Hungarian Empire. In a parenthetical aside he tells you that they still regard Austria as their cultural homeland. This is attached to the sentence in which you are told that he was sent to school in Styria, presumably a place in Austria.

13. D Go back to the passage, find the word *ignominious*, and cross it out. Then read the sentence and come up with your own word. According to lines 21–22, the author just barely escaped *final ostracism from the privileged ranks.* If he was about to get thrown out of the privileged ranks, the word that best describes that situation is *disgraceful* or something strongly negative. The other answers are incorrect because they don't accurately describe the author's situation as it is described in the passage.

14. C This is a general question, so you only need to know the main idea of the passage. You know that the author was not happy in the passage, because he says he felt *skushno*, a word that means *more than dreary boredom.* You can get rid of (A) and (E) because they're positive. (D) is too extreme; it is highly unlikely ETS would ever suggest that someone was suicidal. (B) is incorrect because the passage never says that the author had trouble with his friends.

15. B Your first clue to the author's attitude toward the aphorism is that he calls it *trivial*. After he quotes the aphorism, the author says, *this optimistic notion results more from wishful thinking than from practical experience.* The author clearly has a very negative opinion of it. (B) gives a perfect paraphrase of *wishful thinking* by saying that the author found the aphorism *unrealistic.* You can get rid of (A) it is positive. (D) can be eliminated because the author wasn't confused (*bemused*), and you can eliminate (E) because it refers to his *faith in it*; the author clearly has no faith in the aphorism. (C) is incorrect because the author doesn't say anything about the aphorism working for others.

16. **C** This is a general question, so you only need to know the main idea of the passage. In simple terms, the passage talks about the difference between cats and dogs. This is exactly what choice (C) says. Notice that the author presents both sides of the issue and doesn't advocate one animal over the other. That's why (B) and (D) are wrong. (A) is way too extreme. If you don't know what *enmity* means, look it up and you'll see. (E) only covers one section of the passage, not the primary purpose of the passage as a whole.

17. **E** According to the passage, the cat treats its human owners as *pseudoparents* because they took over from the real mother at a sensitive stage of the kitten's development. That means the human owners are obviously not the kitten's real parents, but rather like adoptive parents that took over from the kitten's real mother. (E) says exactly that. (A) is wrong because *pseudo-* doesn't mean part-time. Human owners can be full-time parents to a cat, but that doesn't make them the cat's real parents. (B) misses the mark be cause the passage is talking about the parents of cats, not the parents of adults. (C) is wrong because the passage doesn't say anything about neglect. (D) makes no sense. How can someone have the characteristics of both humans and cats?

18. **C** This is a general question, but it is also an EXCEPT question, so do it last. The only way to answer this question is to search through the passage for each of the answer choices. Remember, you're looking for the answer choice that is not there. The passage uses a statistic in lines 63–65, makes a parenthetical statement in lines 40–41, restates an argument in lines 75–77, and makes generalizations throughout the passage. (C) is the only one left.

19. **C** The lead words in this question are *the domestic cat*, which should lead you to the first paragraph. According to lines 11–13, *the young cat becomes bimental. It may be a cat physically, but mentally it is both feline and human*. To be both feline and human is definitely a contradiction. Common sense kills (A) because cats don't have two feet. (B) and (D) are incorrect because domestic cats are tame by definition. Otherwise, they would be wild. (E) doesn't make any sense. Do cats dominate humans? No way!

20. **D** The lead words in this question are *difference between dogs and cats*, which should lead you right to the beginning of the second paragraph. According to lines 21–33, the adult *pet dog sees its human family as both pseudoparents* and *dominant members of the pack*. On the other hand, cats *never hunt in packs*, and most of their day is spent in *solitary stalking*. So while dogs see their owners as leaders of the pack, cats do not, because they're solitary. This is paraphrased in (D). (A) directly contradicts the passage. According to lines 33–34, *cats do have a complex social organization*. Read carefully. (B) has it backward. Dogs are obedient, not cats. (C) comes out of nowhere. Where does it say that cats are creative? (E) also contradicts the passage. According to lines 34–35, cats spend most of their time in solitary stalking, which means they're probably good hunters.

21. **B** According to the lines 25–27, *dogs live in packs with tightly controlled status relationships among the individuals. There are top dogs, middle dogs, and bottom dogs….* This describes a social structure that is *hierarchical*. (If you don't know what hierarchical means, look it up!) The other answers are incorrect because none of them accurately describes the social structure in the lines quoted above. There is nothing abstract (C) or flexible (A) about tightly controlled status relationships, nor is there any mention of male domination in the passage. And exclusivity (E) is certainly not the issue.

22. **B** According to the passage, an *ambitious Yuppie* is an example of someone who is *not a typical cat owner*. Since *cat-owners are solitary* people, this means the *ambitious Yuppie must be a group oriented person*. Accordingly, (B) is the answer. (A) and (D) are insulting to Yuppies, and ETS wants to avoid controversy. (C) might be tempting, but ETS likes to avoid stereotypes. (E) is not mentioned in the passage.

23. **B** You can immediately eliminate (C) and (D) because ETS would never say anything negative or overly stereotypical about women. According to the fifth paragraph, the differences between the roles of prehistoric men and women *contributed to a human male "pack mentality" that is far less marked in females*. This idea is paraphrased in (B). (A) is the opposite of what is said in the passage, and (E) is not supported.

24. **C** To answer this question, you have to know what *caricature* means. A caricature is an exaggerated drawing, so the author is saying that he exaggerated in the passage. He is thus qualifying some of the generalizations he has made in the passage. (A) is too extreme. ETS would never suggest that the author of one of its passages made a futile argument. (B) misses the point of these lines, which refer to generalizations, not contradictions. (D) goes in the wrong direction. In the lines cited in the question, the author admits that he exaggerated in order to make his point, so he's trying to ensure that readers don't overestimate what he said in the passage. (E) sounds like psychobabble; it also has nothing to do with what the author is saying at the end of the passage.

1. **D** Use the first equation to solve for $3x$: $3x - 5 = 4$, so $x = 3$. Plug in 3 for x:

$$9x - 15 = 27 - 15 = 12$$

2. **E** This is an excellent calculator question. Here are the costs per unit for each color:

$$\text{Black} = \frac{\$2.00}{5} = \$.40 \text{ per button}$$

$$\text{Blue} = \frac{\$2.00}{6} = .33 \text{ per button}$$

$$\text{Brown} = \frac{\$3.00}{8} = .375 \text{ per button}$$

$$\text{Orange} = \frac{\$4.00}{12} = .33 \text{ per button}$$

$$\text{Red} = \frac{\$4.00}{7} = .57 \text{ per button}$$

The red buttons are the most expensive.

3. **C** Plug the answers into the equation starting with (C). The (x, y) point is $(7, 8)$, so plug in 7 for x and 8 for y. Since $8 = 2(7) - 6$, (C) is the correct answer.

4. **B** Before you reach for your calculator, reduce the expression.

$$\frac{x^2}{x^3} = \frac{x \cdot x}{x \cdot x \cdot x} = x^{-1}$$

Then simply try each choice; -1 (B) has the least value. If you selected (E), you didn't work out each choice.

5. **B** One way to solve this problem is to plug in. First, simplify $(a + b)^2 = 49$ by taking the square root of both sides to find $a + b = 7$. Now, brainstorm some values for a and b that make $a + b = 7$ and $ab = 10$: let's say a is 2 and b is 5. So, find the answer that yields 5 when you plug in $a = 2$. Only (B) works. The second, more complicated, way is to FOIL out $(a + b)^2 = 49$ to get $a^2 + 2ab + b^2 = 49$. Plug in 10 for ab to get $a^2 + 2(10) + b^2 = 49$. That means, $a^2 + 20 + b^2 = 49$. Subtract 20 from both sides to get $a^2 + b^2 = 29$. Subtract a^2 from both sides to get $b^2 = 29 - a^2$. Take the square root of both sides to find $b = \sqrt{29 - a^2}$.

6. **C** First, you can estimate. Since square $ABFE$ has an area of 25, EF equals 5 and EC looks to be a little less than twice EF, or in the 7–9 range. Thus, since $CE = ED$ because they are the legs of a 45°-45°-90° triangle, you can eliminate (D) and (E). You also know that the area of $\triangle BCF$ is 10, and that its base (BF) is 5. Using the formula for area, you can calculate FC, the height of the triangle: $10 = \left(\frac{1}{2}\right)(5) \times (h)$, $h = 4$. So $5(FE) + 4(FC) = 9$, which is the length of $\overline{CE}$ and $\overline{DE}$.

7. **C** Stack all three equations and add them together to get $3x + 3y + 3z = 51$. Factor out a 3 to get $3(x + y + z) = 51$. Divide both sides by 3 to get $x + y + z = 17$.

8. **D** Translate into algebra. *The sum of two numbers is 10* means $x + y = 10$. Next, *one number is equal to the sum of 6 and twice the other number* means $x = 6 + 2y$. Rearrange the second equation into $x - 2y = 6$. Subtract the second equation from the first to find $3y = 4$. Divide by 3 to find $y = \frac{4}{3}$. Plug that into the first equation to get $x + \frac{4}{3} = 10$. So, $x = 8\frac{2}{3}$. *The larger number minus the smaller number* is $8\frac{2}{3} - 1\frac{1}{3} = 7\frac{1}{3}$.

9. **D** The easiest way to solve this is to graph it on a graphing calculator. You will notice that it is both positive and negative, but both sides are asymptotic at $y = 1$. Without graphing, you can easily plug in numbers. Plugging in 2 for x yields a result of 0: eliminate (A), (B), and (C). Now check to see what the difference is between (D) and (E). Since (D) doesn't allow 1, try it out! For $\frac{x + 2}{x + 1}$ to equal 1, that would mean that $x + 2 = x + 1$, for which there are no solutions. Eliminate (E).

10. A Let's begin by drawing a parallelogram and plugging in a number for y, say 50 and calling the other two angles x:

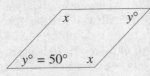

Since there are 360° in a quadrilateral, you know that $2x + 100° = 360°$, which means $x = 130°$. So, you're looking for the choice that gives you 130 when $y = 50$. You simply plug 50 into all of the answer choices to find that (A) is the only one that works.

11. D This is a parabola, because one of the two variables is squared. Eliminate (A), (B), and (E) which are not parabolic graphs. Because the smallest possible value of mx^2 is 0, the smallest possible value of $mx^2 + b$ is b, so all of the curve must be above the x-axis. Only (D) works.

12. C First, you need to compute all possible values of n:

$\sqrt{n}$	n
1	1
2	4
3	9
4	16
5	25
6	36
7	49
8	64
9	81

Now, be careful! The median value for $\sqrt{n}$ is 5, but the median value for n is 25.

13. C

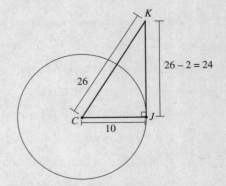

Draw a picture! Look at triangle CJK. $\angle CJK$ is 90 because the radius of a circle is always perpendicular to a line tangent to that circle. Use the Pythagorean theorem, $(CJ)^2 + 24^2 = 26^2$, or your knowledge of right triangles (this is a multiple of a 5:12:13 triangle) to get $CJ = 10$, which represents the radius of the circle. So the circumference of the circle $= 2\pi \times 10$ or 20π.

14. D This is a tricky question. Let's draw a picture:

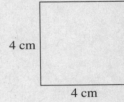

Since 1 centimeter equals 6 kilometers, 4 centimeters equals 24 kilometers:

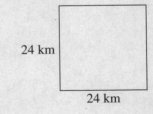

The area of this region is 24^2 or 576. In case you were wondering, (B) is the Joe Bloggs answer because $16 \times 6 = 96$.

15. **E** Plug in values for m and n and use translation to solve this percent problem. You're working with a small percent, so plug in a big number for m. Let's say $m = 2{,}000$. 0.1% of 2,000 = $\dfrac{0.1}{100} \times \dfrac{2{,}000}{1} = 2$. Therefore, 10% of n is 2; rewrite this as $\dfrac{10}{100} \times n = 2$. Solving for n, you get $n = 20$. Now translate the rest of the problem: m is what percent of $10n$ can be written as $2{,}000 = \dfrac{x}{100} \times 10 \times 20$. Solving for x, you get $x = 1{,}000$, so the answer is 1,000%.

16. **D** The parabola points downwards, so a is negative. The y-intercept of the parabola is negative, so c is negative. Now you can eliminate (B) and (E) (multiplying two negatives gives you a positive). The value of b tells you whether the vertex of the parabola is to the right of the y-axis (b is negative) or to the left of the y-axis (b is positive). So for this parabola, b is negative, and you can eliminate (A) and (C).

SECTION 9

1. B The best choice is (B). The clue is *unconventional*, which tells you that "out of the ordinary" is a good phrase for the blank. *Eccentric*, (B), is closest in meaning. Even if you are not sure what (B) means, you can eliminate (A) as it is opposite from the meaning of the blank. (C) has to do with the order of events in time, not with a person's behavior; (D), *friendly*, and (E), *hardworking*, have nothing to do with behaving in an unusual manner.

2. C We can recycle the clue *swollen* into the blank, and immediately eliminate (A) and (B), which have the opposite connotation. (D) and (E) do not mean *swollen*, so only (C), *distended*, is left, making (C) the best answer.

3. A The best answer is (A). The idea of human carelessness causing changes tells you that the blank should mean "bound to happen." You can eliminate (B) and (E) because "wishing evil" and "being honest" are human attributes. (C), "equally shared," and (D), "sluggish," do not mean "bound to happen," so you are left with (A), *inevitable*.

4. D The clue *unrealistically* tells you that Tyler expected to improve his score greatly right away, so you can save (B), (D), and (E), all of which could describe a great rise in his score. Thus you can eliminate (A), *repeating*, and (C), *unimportant*. Looking at the finalists, since the second blank should mean "slow and steady," you can cross out (B), *endless*, and (E), *fast*. You are left with (D), which is the best answer.

5. C The clue is *invoke a serenity that is otherwise lacking in her frenzied existence.* A good word for the blank is "relaxed." Only (C) agrees with our word. If you guessed (A) because the root *eu–* means "good" as in *euphoria*, don't feel bad. That was a smart guess, and smart guesses mean more points overall.

6. E The clue for the second blank is *appreciated his specialized knowledge*, and the trigger word is *but*, which tells you that the second part of the sentence must mean the opposite of the clue. If some students didn't appreciate the specialized knowledge, then the *disappointed* students had "non-specialized" interests. The only word in the answer choices that means "non-specialized" is *eclectic*. The other word in (E) also makes sense because it fits the clue. You know that the professor *has specialized knowledge*, so if his lecture focused *utterly* on something, then it was very specialized.

7. E (E) is correct because Passage 1 states in the beginning of the second paragraph that philosophers shifted from theology to *intellectual exercises*. (A) is incorrect given the information in the passage. (B) is not supported, because there is not mention of angels anywhere in the passage, (C) is not supported because there is no mention of law-abiding citizens. (D) is a trap answer because the mention of *classicists* may make this look like an attractive answer choice.

8. C (C) is the credited choice because of lines 16–19 in Passage 1. (A) is incorrect because deviant behavior <u>is</u> a criminal act, not the result of one. (B) is incorrect because that would be *according to the demonic perspective*. (D) is not supported in the passage and (E) is incorrect because deviant behavior is the result of rationale that maximizes pleasure and minimizes pain, not the opposite.

9. E (E) is a close paraphrase of lines 39–40 in Passage 1, *each deviant act arises from a rational calculation of pleasure versus pain.* Every other answer choice contains expressions found in the passage, but not as a cause for avoiding arbitrary, tyrannical punishment. (B) might seem like an attractive choice, but the belief that punishment could be *meted out precisely and mathematically* is not cited as a reason for avoiding overly severe punishment.

10. **B** (A), (C), and (E) are incorrect because the author is not revealing, describing, or explaining the emergence of deviant behavior to the individual. The author says that it is wrong to attribute the behavior solely to the individual; (D) does not reflect this meaning, but (B) does.

11. **A** (A) is the credited choice because of the phrase that follows the semicolon: *society produces the individual.* (B) is not in the passage. (C) is the opposite of what is said in the passage. (D) is a stretch from line 1 and does not answer the question. (E) is extreme.

12. **E** The author states in line 62 *deviant behavior would have no role in this utopia.* (A) is too broad; while the author does place emphasis on having an organized society, the point of doing so was to show how the relationship between the individual and society produces deviant behavior. (B) is the opposite of what is stated by the passage, as it says that the utopia does not exist. (C) and (D) are extreme.

13. **E** (A) is a trap answer, because it relates gender to sexuality. (B) and (D) do not make sense. (C) means "allows." Between (C) and (E), though, (E) is the better answer, because the disorganization in society is causing the deviance (lines 71–75).

14. **C** While ETS tends to be middle-of-the-road, the author's emphatic description of society's disorganization gives the third paragraph a distinctly critical tone. (A) is not mentioned in passage, as there is no indication that the calmer, utopian days ever existed. In (B), the third paragraph is not objective. (D) is not mentioned in passage. (E) is wrong because the author does not approve of the deviance.

15. **B** With constant change, there cannot be harmony and organization. (A), (C), (D), and (E) can all result from change, but remember that the question asks which is the <u>least</u> likely to occur.

16. **A** According to both the third paragraph of Passage 2 and the main discussion in Passage 1, deviance is a choice made by an individual. (B) is not supported, since both authors discuss the individual causes of deviance. (C) is wrong because severe punishment is never advocated. (D) is true for 2 but not for 1. (E) is wrong because it contradicts information in Passage 1. The Enlightenment did not cause deviance; it only viewed it differently.

17. **B** Rationality is a central focus of Passage 1, but is not mentioned in 2. (A) is not important in either. (C) is not the focus of 1 and is not mentioned at all in 2. (D) is important in the second passage, not the first. (E) is mentioned in the first, but as an act of deviant behavior, not an aspect of it, and even so, it does not matter a great deal to the passage.

18. **D** Passage 1 is presented very factually, while 2 has a note of criticism in describing the disorganization of society. (A) is not true of either passage. (B) is wrong because Passage 1 is not indignant. (C) is wrong because Passage 2 is not sarcastic. (E) is not true of either passage.

19. **A** Passage 1 discusses the intellectual evaluation made by the individual, and Passage 2 discusses how deviance would not increase if it weren't for disharmony in society. (B) and (C) do not answer to the propagation aspect of the question because neither answer has any effect on how or why deviance is increased. (D) and (E) do not describe any difference between the interpretations.

SECTION 10

1. **D** *Weather vanes* is plural, so it's important to use a plural pronoun later in the sentence: get rid of (A). (B) unnecessarily uses the word *being*, so eliminate it. Only (D) matches the sentence structure of the beginning of the sentence: *weather vanes* comes first, so in the second half *they* comes first.

2. **B** This sentence is a fragment. By eliminating the word *which,* the sentence becomes complete. In (B) the sentence says correctly, *horrors...and experiences...are...chronicled.* In (C), (D), and (E), the verb is missing, so these versions of the sentence are also fragments.

3. **A** There is no error in this sentence as it is written.

4. **E** As written, (A) includes several words that make the sentence unnecessarily wordy. Because (E) omits the words *is, he is,* and *and he,* this version of the sentence becomes streamlined and correct. (B) is a run-on. (C) and (D) add *because* and *although,* changing the meaning of the sentence.

5. **E** Only (E) uses the correct idiom *responded...by.* In addition, the original sentence is a run-on. (B) is needlessly wordy. (C) and (D) both create fragments: (C) needs a conjunction in order to be correct; in (D), the phrase that follows the semicolon lacks a grammatical subject.

6. **A** The original sentence is concise and uses the past tense required by *could* and *after* in the non-underlined portion. (B) and (D) use the present tense. (C) and (E) are wordy and redundant.

7. **E** The construction *not only...but also* achieves parallelism in (E), since the noun *an inspiring teacher* matches *a great surgeon* in form. (A) unnecessarily uses the word *being.* (B), (C), and (D) violate parallelism.

8. **B** (A) is unnecessarily wordy. (E) is wordy and contains a noun agreement error; employees have monthly payments. (C) changes the meaning of the sentence, suggesting that they switched plans after their payments were reduced, which is not correct. (D) also changes the meaning, suggesting that the new plan's payments were being reduced from a higher price point to a lower one.

9. **D** Choices (A) and (B) are wordy and unidiomatic. (C) and (E) warp the intended meaning by (among other things) implying that *the expression* (C) or *the face* (E) *plays games.* Only (D) correctly and concisely expresses the idea that *the squirrel... plays games.*

10. **C** Only *the designers* can logically be modified by the phrase *learning from recent tests,* so eliminate (A), (D), and (E). (B) changes the intended meaning, illogically saying that an *engine* can be based on an increase in efficiency.

11. **B** Parallelism requires a noun such as *a failure* to follow *a lack of training,* making (B) the only possible answer. Also, *which* in (C) is inappropriate, because you must use the pronoun *who* when referring to people. (C) also changes the intended meaning by implying that the *people,* rather than *a failure,* caused the crash. *Because,* in choices (D) and (E), is redundant with *caused by* in the non-underlined portion of the sentence.

12. **E** Because the pronoun *we* is not underlined and therefore must remain in the sentence, beginning the sentence with *Rory and I* will make it a run-on. Kill (A), (B), and (C). (D) ends with *Rory and I,* making the *we* which follows it unnecessary and incorrect. (E) provides a properly constructed subordinate clause and is correct.

13. **C** Always watch out for unnecessary use of the word *being*. It shows up incorrectly in both (A) and (D), so eliminate both of those. The sentence should set up an opposite, since it starts with a way in which the two are similar, and ends with a way in which the two are different. (E) uses *and*, which doesn't accomplish this. Between (B) and (C), (B) uses both *while* and *but* and is therefore redundant.

14. **C** Watch out for misplaced modifiers. The phrase *better known for* The Foreigner should describe *Larry Shue*, but in (A), (B), and (D) the phrase incorrectly describes something else. (E) incorrectly uses the word *like* instead of *such as*. *Like* should be used to compare two nouns; *such as* should be used to give an example.

20

Practice Test 2

ESSAY
Time — 25 minutes

The essay gives you an opportunity to show how effectively you can develop and express ideas. You should, therefore, take care to develop your point of view, present your ideas logically and clearly, and use language precisely.

Your essay must be written on the lines provided on your answer sheet—you will receive no other paper on which to write. You will have enough space if you write on every line, avoid wide margins, and keep your handwriting to a reasonable size. Remember that people who are not familiar with your handwriting will read what you write. Try to write or print so that what you are writing is legible to those readers.

You have twenty-five minutes to write an essay on the topic assigned below. DO NOT WRITE ON ANOTHER TOPIC. AN OFF-TOPIC ESSAY WILL RECEIVE A SCORE OF ZERO.

Think carefully about the issue presented in the following excerpt and the assignment below.

> Psychologist Carl Jung said, "The more critical reason dominates, the more impoverished life becomes…. [When reason is overvalued,] the individual is pauperized." He felt that relying more on facts and rationality than on imagination and theory detracts from the quality of a person's intellectual life.

Assignment: What is your view of the claim that knowing facts isn't as important as understanding ideas and concepts? Plan and write an essay in which you develop your point of view on this issue. Support your position with reasoning and examples taken from your reading, studies, experience, or observations.

DO NOT WRITE YOUR ESSAY IN YOUR TEST BOOK. You will receive credit only for what you write on your answer sheet.

BEGIN WRITING YOUR ESSAY IN SECTION 1 OF THE ANSWER SHEET.

If you finish before time is called, you may check your work on this section only. Do not turn to any other section in the test.

SECTION 2
Time — 25 minutes
24 Questions

Turn to Section 2 of your answer sheet to answer the questions in this section.

Directions: For each question in this section, select the best answer from among the choices given and fill in the corresponding circle on the answer sheet.

Each sentence below has one or two blanks, each blank indicating that something has been omitted. Beneath the sentence are five words or sets of words labeled A through E. Choose the word or set of words that, when inserted in the sentence, best fits the meaning of the sentence as a whole.

Example:

Hoping to ------- the dispute, negotiators proposed a compromise that they felt would be ------- to both labor and management.

(A) enforce . . useful
(B) end . . divisive
(C) overcome . . unattractive
(D) extend . . satisfactory
(E) resolve . . acceptable

Ⓐ Ⓑ Ⓒ Ⓓ ●

---

1. Nuclear power plants are some of the largest producers of ------- wastes, with each plant producing barrels of radioactive material that must be stored in special protective containers.

(A) biodegradable   (B) artificial
    (C) reasonable   (D) durable   (E) noxious

2. The scientific community was ------- when a living specimen of the coelacanth, thought to be no longer -------, was discovered by deep-sea fishermen.

(A) perplexed . . common
(B) overjoyed . . dangerous
(C) unconcerned . . local
(D) astounded . . extant
(E) dismayed . . alive

3. After the governor's third trip overseas, voters complained that he was paying too little attention to ------- affairs.

(A) intellectual   (B) extraneous
    (C) specialized   (D) aesthetic   (E) domestic

4. The Roman Emperor Claudius was viewed with ------- by generations of historians until newly discovered evidence showed him to be ------- administrator.

(A) suspicion . . a deficient
(B) reluctance . . an inept
(C) antagonism . . an eager
(D) indignation . . an incompetent
(E) disdain . . a capable

5. Communities in primitive areas where natural ------- is scarce must be resourceful in order to secure adequate nutrition.

(A) development   (B) competition   (C) sustenance
    (D) augmentation   (E) intervention

6. Morgan's interest was focused on ------- the division between theory and empiricism; she was convinced that a ------- of philosophy and applied science was possible and necessary.

(A) eradicating . . synthesis
(B) maintaining . . restoration
(C) crossing . . stabilization
(D) overlooking . . duplicity
(E) refuting . . delineation

7. His style is best described as -------: his signature vivid colors and mixture of bold patterns, combined with his dramatic bearing, always make him the center of attention.

(A) vehement   (B) imperious   (C) modest
    (D) flamboyant   (E) stoic

8. Although at times Nikolai could be disagreeable and even -------, more often than not he was the most ------- person you could hope to meet.

(A) contentious . . complaisant
(B) disgruntled . . befuddled
(C) contradictory . . disconcerted
(D) misguided . . solicitous
(E) curmudgeonly . . didactic

GO ON TO THE NEXT PAGE

The passages below are followed by questions based on their content. Answer the questions on the basis of what is stated or implied in the passage and in any introductory material that may be provided.

Questions 9-10 are based on the following passage.

Though today Zora Neale Hurston is best known as an author, many readers overlook Hurston's contributions as an anthropologist. Drawn by the Harlem Renaissance,
Line Hurston crafted both fiction and nonfiction that
5 deconstructed the African-American experience. Hurston also worked with noted anthropologist Franz Boas to debunk the claims of racist scientists. Her desire to disprove these eugenicists' claims led her to measure the skulls of African-Americans on the streets of New York.
10 Her cultural studies of Eatonville, Florida, still remain some of the richest anthropological writing about the African-American South.

9.   The term "deconstructed" in line 5 implies that Hurston

  (A) participated fully in the Harlem Renaissance
  (B) engaged in scientific experiments
  (C) made a deliberate study of African-American life
  (D) cut herself off from Harlem to write about it objectively
  (E) attempted to bring about sweeping changes to African-American communities

10. The passage LEAST supports which of the following statements about Zora Neale Hurston?

  (A) She was influenced by the blossoming of the arts in Harlem.
  (B) She was a widely acclaimed social anthropologist.
  (C) She attempted to measure the cranial capacity of African Americans.
  (D) She investigated the culture of a Southern town.
  (E) She was an author highly skilled in several genres.

Questions 11-12 are based on the following passage.

Many modern naval vessels are equipped with a sophisticated new sonar system called SURTASS LFA. Environmentalists argue that the intensity of the sound
Line bursts emitted by the system, measured at 215 decibels,
5 poses a serious threat to marine wildlife. (In contrast, a rock concert reaching only 150 decibels is considered a health risk to humans.) They claim that the alarming number of whale carcasses found on beaches near areas where vessels use SURTASS LFA are evidence of its
10 impact. Proponents of SURTASS LFA argue that no causal link between the use of the system and these whale deaths has been established, and contend that the system is safe.

11. The purpose of this passage is primarily to

  (A) demonstrate that the claims of environmentalists are unfounded
  (B) argue against further use of SURTASS LFA
  (C) outline a controversy regarding the use of a new technology
  (D) emphasize the danger humans pose to wildlife
  (E) summarize the arguments of environmentalists who oppose SURTASS LFA

12. The example of the rock concert

  (A) compares the way humans and whales are affected by sound
  (B) bolsters the author's overall argument in favor of banning SURTASS LFA
  (C) refutes environmentalists' claims about sonar's dangers
  (D) provides a context from which to judge the intensity of SURTASS LFA emissions
  (E) has nothing to do with the rest of the passage

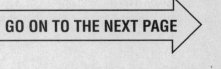
GO ON TO THE NEXT PAGE

Questions 13-24 are based on the following passage.

The following passage was excerpted from a book called The Extraordinary Origins of Everyday Things, *which was published in 1987.*

Because early man viewed illness as divine punishment and healing as purification, medicine and religion were inextricably linked for centuries. This notion is apparent in the origin of our word "pharmacy,"
5 which comes from the Greek *pharmakon*, meaning "purification through purging."

By 3500 B.C., the Sumerians in the Tigris-Euphrates Valley had developed virtually all of our modern methods of administering drugs. They used gargles, inhalations,
10 pills, lotions, ointments, and plasters. The first drug catalog, or pharmacopoeia, was written at that time by an unknown Sumerian physician. Preserved in cuneiform script on a single clay tablet are the names of dozens of drugs to treat ailments that still afflict us today.

15 The Egyptians added to the ancient medicine chest. The Ebers Papyrus, a scroll dating from 1900 B.C. and named after the German egyptologist George Ebers, reveals the trial-and-error know-how acquired by early Egyptian physicians. To relieve indigestion, a chew of
20 peppermint leaves and carbonates (known today as antacids) was prescribed, and to numb the pain of tooth extraction, Egyptian doctors temporarily stupefied a patient with ethyl alcohol.

The scroll also provides a rare glimpse into the
25 hierarchy of ancient drug preparation. The "chief of the preparers of drugs" was the equivalent of a head pharmacist, who supervised the "collectors of drugs," field workers who gathered essential minerals and herbs. The "preparers' aides" (technicians) dried and pulverized
30 ingredients, which were blended according to certain formulas by the "preparers." And the "conservator of drugs" oversaw the storehouse where local and imported mineral, herb, and animal-organ ingredients were kept.

By the seventh century B.C., the Greeks had adopted a
35 sophisticated mind-body view of medicine. They believed that a physician must pursue the diagnosis and treatment of the physical (body) causes of disease within a scientific framework, as well as cure the supernatural (mind) components involved. Thus, the early Greek physician
40 emphasized something of a holistic approach to health, even if the suspected "mental" causes of disease were not recognized as stress and depression but interpreted as curses from displeased deities.

The modern era of pharmacology began in the
45 sixteenth century, ushered in by the first major discoveries in chemistry. The understanding of how chemicals interact to produce certain effects within the body would eventually remove much of the guesswork and magic from medicine.

50 Drugs had been launched on a scientific course, but centuries would pass before superstition was displaced by scientific fact. One major reason was that physicians, unaware of the existence of disease-causing pathogens such as bacteria and viruses, continued to dream up
55 imaginary causative evils. And though new chemical compounds emerged, their effectiveness in treating disease was still based largely on trial and error.

Many standard, common drugs in the medicine chest developed in this trial-and-error environment. Such is the
60 complexity of disease and human biochemistry that even today, despite enormous strides in medical science, many of the latest sophisticated additions to our medicine chest shelves were accidental finds.

13. The author cites the literal definition of the Greek word *pharmakon* in lines 5-6 in order to

(A) show that ancient civilizations had an advanced form of medical science
(B) point out that many of the beliefs of ancient civilizations are still held today
(C) illustrate that early man thought recovery from illness was linked to internal cleansing
(D) stress the mental and physical causes of disease
(E) emphasize the primitive nature of Greek medical science

14. It was possible to identify a number of early Sumerian drugs because

(A) traces of these drugs were discovered during archaeological excavations
(B) the ancient Egyptians later adopted the same medications
(C) Sumerian religious texts explained many drug-making techniques
(D) a pharmacopoeia in Europe contained detailed recipes for ancient drugs
(E) a list of drugs and preparations was compiled by an ancient Sumerian

GO ON TO THE NEXT PAGE

15. The passage suggests that which of the following is a similarity between ancient Sumerian drugs and modern drugs?

(A) Ancient Sumerian drugs were made of the same chemicals as modern drugs.
(B) Like modern drugs, ancient Sumerian drugs were used for both mental and physical disorders.
(C) The different ways patients could take ancient Sumerian drugs are similar to the ways modern drugs are taken.
(D) Both ancient Sumerian drugs and modern drugs are products of sophisticated chemical research.
(E) Hierarchically organized groups of laborers are responsible for the preparation of both ancient Sumerian and modern drugs.

16. According to the passage, the seventh-century Greeks' view of medicine differed from that of the Sumerians in that the Greeks

(A) discovered more advanced chemical applications of drugs
(B) acknowledged both the mental and physical roots of illness
(C) attributed disease to psychological, rather than physical, causes
(D) established a rigid hierarchy for the preparation of drugs
(E) developed most of the precursors of modern drugs

17. The "hierarchy" referred to in line 25 is an example of

(A) a superstitious practice
(B) the relative severity of ancient diseases
(C) the role of physicians in Egyptian society
(D) a complex division of labor
(E) a recipe for ancient drugs

18. In the final paragraph, the author makes which of the following observations about scientific discovery?

(A) Human biochemistry is such a complex science that important discoveries are uncommon.
(B) Chance events have led to the discovery of many modern drugs.
(C) Many cures for common diseases have yet to be discovered.
(D) Trial and error is the best avenue to scientific discovery.
(E) Most of the important discoveries made in the scientific community have been inadvertent.

19. Which of the following is NOT cited in the passage as a characteristic of ancient Egyptian medicine?

(A) Anesthesia
(B) Ointments
(C) Ingredients derived from animals
(D) Use of trial-and-error
(E) A workplace hierarchy

20. It can be inferred from the passage that some drugs commonly used in 1987

(A) were not created intentionally
(B) caused the very diseases that they were designed to combat
(C) were meant to treat imaginary causative evils
(D) were created in the sixteenth century
(E) are now known to be ineffective

21. Which of the following documents from seventh-century Greece, if discovered, would most support the author's characterization of ancient Greek medicine?

(A) A sophisticated formula for an antacid
(B) A scientific paper theorizing that stress causes disease
(C) A doctor's prescription that urges the patient to pray to Asclepius, the Greek god of healing
(D) An essay that details the ancient Egyptian influence upon Greek medicine
(E) A book in which the word "pharmacology" was used repeatedly

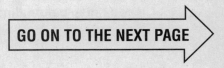
GO ON TO THE NEXT PAGE

22. The passage implies that

(A) ancient Greek medicine was superior to ancient Egyptian medicine
(B) some maladies have supernatural causes
(C) a modern head pharmacist is analogous to an ancient Egyptian conservator of drugs
(D) most ailments that afflicted the ancient Sumerians still afflict modern human beings
(E) the ancient Egyptians made no major discoveries in the field of chemistry

23. In line 40, the word "holistic" most nearly means

(A) psychological
(B) modern
(C) physiological
(D) comprehensive
(E) homeopathic

24. The passage indicates that advances in medical science during the modern era of pharmacology may have been delayed by

(A) the lack of a clear understanding of the origins of disease
(B) primitive surgical methods
(C) a shortage of chemical treatments for disease
(D) an inaccuracy in pharmaceutical preparation
(E) an overemphasis on the psychological causes of disease

STOP
If you finish before time is called, you may check your work on this section only.
Do not turn to any other section in the test.

NO TEST MATERIAL ON THIS PAGE.

SECTION 3
Time — 25 minutes
20 Questions

Turn to Section 3 of your answer sheet to answer the questions in this section.

Directions: For this section, solve each problem and decide which is the best of the choices given. Fill in the corresponding oval on the answer sheet. You may use any available space for scratchwork.

Notes

1. The use of a calculator is permitted.

2. All numbers used are real numbers.

3. Figures that accompany problems in this test are intended to provide information useful in solving the problems. They are drawn as accurately as possible EXCEPT when it is stated in a specific problem that the figure is not drawn to scale. All figures lie in a plane unless otherwise indicated.

4. Unless otherwise specified, the domain of any function f is assumed to be the set of all real numbers x for which $f(x)$ is a real number.

Reference Information

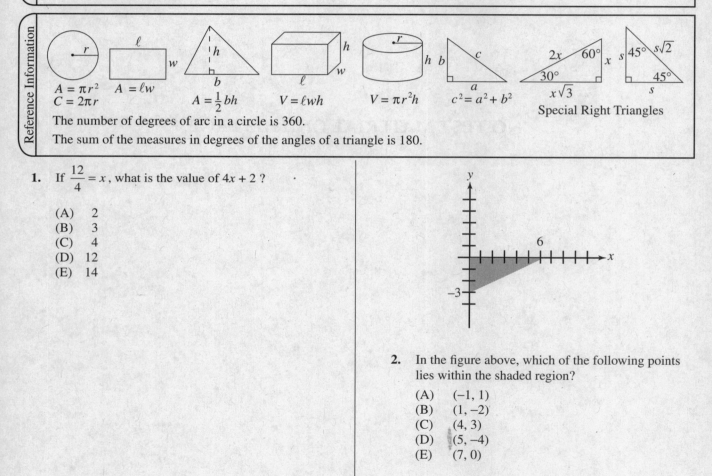

$A = \pi r^2$
$C = 2\pi r$

$A = \ell w$

$A = \frac{1}{2} bh$

$V = \ell wh$

$V = \pi r^2 h$

$c^2 = a^2 + b^2$

Special Right Triangles

The number of degrees of arc in a circle is 360.

The sum of the measures in degrees of the angles of a triangle is 180.

1. If $\dfrac{12}{4} = x$, what is the value of $4x + 2$?

(A) 2
(B) 3
(C) 4
(D) 12
(E) 14

2. In the figure above, which of the following points lies within the shaded region?

(A) $(-1, 1)$
(B) $(1, -2)$
(C) $(4, 3)$
(D) $(5, -4)$
(E) $(7, 0)$

GO ON TO THE NEXT PAGE

3. Six cups of flour are required to make a batch of cookies. How many cups of flour are required to make enough cookies to fill 12 cookie jars, if each cookie jar holds 1.5 batches?

(A) 108
(B) 90
(C) 81
(D) 78
(E) 72

4. If n is an even integer, which of the following must be an odd integer?

(A) $3n - 2$

(B) $3(n + 1)$

(C) $n - 2$

(D) $\dfrac{n}{3}$

(E) n^2

5. In the coordinate plane, what is the midpoint of the line segment with endpoints at (3, 4) and (0, 0) ?

(A) (1.5, 2)
(B) (5, 0)
(C) (2.5, 0)
(D) (3.5, 3.5)
(E) (1.75, 1.75)

6. $x\sqrt{4} - x\sqrt{9} =$

(A) $-5x$
(B) $-x\sqrt{5}$
(C) $-x$
(D) x
(E) $3x$

	Number Sold	Average Weight per Parrot (in pounds)
Red Parrots	5	2
Blue Parrots	4	3

7. The chart above shows the number of red and blue parrots Toby sold in May and the average weight of each type of bird sold. If Toby sold no other parrots, what was the average (arithmetic mean) weight, in pounds, of the parrots that Toby sold in May?

(A) 2

(B) $2\dfrac{4}{9}$

(C) $2\dfrac{1}{2}$

(D) 5

(E) 9

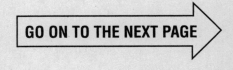
GO ON TO THE NEXT PAGE

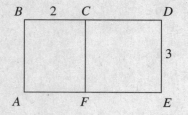

8. In the figure above, the perimeter of square *FCDE* is how much smaller than the perimeter of rectangle *ABDE*?

(A) 2
(B) 3
(C) 4
(D) 7
(E) 16

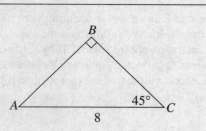

9. In △*ABC* above, if *AC* = 8, what is the length of $\overline{BC}$?

(A) $8\sqrt{2}$
(B) 8
(C) 6
(D) $4\sqrt{2}$
(E) $3\sqrt{2}$

10. If $\dfrac{\sqrt{x}}{2} = 2\sqrt{2}$, what is the value of *x*?

(A) 4
(B) 16
(C) $16\sqrt{2}$
(D) 32
(E) 64

11. If *b* equals 40% of *a*, then in terms of *b*, 40% of 4*a* is equal to which of the following?

(A) $\dfrac{b}{40}$

(B) $\dfrac{b}{4}$

(C) *b*

(D) 4*b*

(E) 16*b*

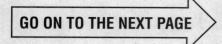
GO ON TO THE NEXT PAGE

Questions 12-13 refer to the following definition.

For all real numbers x, let $f(x) = 2x^2 + 4$.

12. What is the value of $f(4)$?
   (A) 16
   (B) 18
   (C) 20
   (D) 36
   (E) 72

13. Which of the following is equal to $f(3) + f(5)$?
   (A) $f(4)$
   (B) $f(6)$
   (C) $f(8)$
   (D) $f(10)$
   (E) $f(15)$

14. If the circle with center O has a diameter of 9, then what is the area of the circle with center O ?

   (A) 81π

   (B) $\dfrac{9}{2}\pi$

   (C) $\dfrac{81}{4}\pi$

   (D) 18π

   (E) 9π

15. The graph of which of the following equations is parallel to the line with equation $y = -3x - 6$?

   (A) $x - 3y = 3$

   (B) $x - \dfrac{1}{3}y = 2$

   (C) $x + \dfrac{1}{6}y = 4$

   (D) $x + \dfrac{1}{3}y = 5$

   (E) $x + 3y = 6$

16. How many solutions exist to the equation $|x| = |2x - 1|$?
   (A) 0
   (B) 1
   (C) 2
   (D) 3
   (E) 4

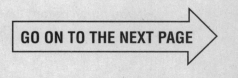
GO ON TO THE NEXT PAGE

17. There are k gallons of gasoline available to fill a tank. After d gallons have been pumped, in terms of k and d, what percent of the gasoline has been pumped?

(A) $\dfrac{100d}{k}\%$

(B) $\dfrac{k}{100d}\%$

(C) $\dfrac{100k}{d}\%$

(D) $\dfrac{k}{100(k-d)}\%$

(E) $\dfrac{100(k-d)}{k}\%$

18. Ray and Jane live 150 miles apart. Each drives toward the other's house along a straight road connecting the two, Ray at a constant rate of 30 miles per hour and Jane at a constant rate of 50 miles per hour. If Ray and Jane leave their houses at the same time, how many miles are they from Ray's house when they meet?

(A) 40

(B) $51\dfrac{1}{2}$

(C) $56\dfrac{1}{4}$

(D) 75

(E) $93\dfrac{1}{4}$

19. A bag contains 4 red hammers, 10 blue hammers, and 6 yellow hammers. If three hammers are removed from the bag at random and no hammer is returned to the bag after removal, what is the probability that all three hammers will be blue?

(A) $\dfrac{1}{2}$

(B) $\dfrac{1}{8}$

(C) $\dfrac{3}{20}$

(D) $\dfrac{2}{19}$

(E) $\dfrac{3}{18}$

20. If x is an integer, which of the following could be x^3?

(A) 2.7×10^{11}
(B) 2.7×10^{12}
(C) 2.7×10^{13}
(D) 2.7×10^{14}
(E) 2.7×10^{15}

STOP

If you finish before time is called, you may check your work on this section only.
Do not turn to any other section in the test.

NO TEST MATERIAL ON THIS PAGE.

SECTION 4
Time — 25 minutes
24 Questions

Turn to Section 4 of your answer sheet to answer the questions in this section.

Directions: For each question in this section, select the best answer from among the choices given and fill in the corresponding circle on the answer sheet.

Each sentence below has one or two blanks, each blank indicating that something has been omitted. Beneath the sentence are five words or sets of words labeled A through E. Choose the word or set of words that, when inserted in the sentence, best fits the meaning of the sentence as a whole.

Example:

Hoping to ------- the dispute, negotiators proposed a compromise that they felt would be ------- to both labor and management.

(A) enforce . . useful
(B) end . . divisive
(C) overcome . . unattractive
(D) extend . . satisfactory
(E) resolve . . acceptable

Ⓐ Ⓑ Ⓒ Ⓓ ●

1. Plants that grow in the desert or on high rocky ledges can survive long periods of ------- because they hoard water in their leaves, stems, and root systems.

    (A) darkness   (B) inactivity   (C) dormancy
       (D) warmth   (E) aridity

2. Thanks to his eloquence and logic, Liam spoke ------- and made it difficult for even his most bitter opponents to ------- his opinions.

    (A) monotonously . . clash with
    (B) charmingly . . yield to
    (C) tediously . . contend with
    (D) abhorrently . . concede to
    (E) cogently . . disagree with

3. Some subatomic particles, ------- only through their effects on other bodies, have been compared to outer planets whose ------- was first deduced from eccentricities in other planets' orbits.

    (A) feasible . . irregularity
    (B) palpable . . creation
    (C) perceptible . . fallacy
    (D) discernable . . existence
    (E) verifiable . . proximity

4. Miranda, in her desire to foster -------, often felt compelled to ------- readily to others in tense situations.

    (A) cooperation . . object
    (B) fortitude . . defer
    (C) dissension . . surrender
    (D) harmony . . acquiesce
    (E) discourse . . appeal

5. Although detractors labeled Margaret Thatcher's policies -------, she asserted that her ideas ultimately helped bring about a period of prosperity in the United Kingdom.

    (A) premature   (B) autocratic   (C) regressive
       (D) ingenious   (E) seditious

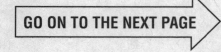

GO ON TO THE NEXT PAGE

The passages below are followed by questions based on their content; questions following a pair of related passages may also be based on the relationship between the paired passages. Answer the questions on the basis of what is <u>stated</u> or <u>implied</u> in the passage and in any introductory material that may be provided.

Questions 6-9 are based on the following passages.

Passage 1

The War of 1812 between the U.S. and England is one of the least-known in American history. Ironically, this war cemented America's independence in Europe's
Line eyes. Although lacking a clear winner, it proved to the
5 Old World that the U.S. could hold its own against the mighty British navy, then in the heyday of its impressive power. The war was fought for several reasons: the U.S. declaration of war was ostensibly in response to British actions against American goods and sailors. Also, many
10 Americans had their eyes on the rich Spanish territory of Florida and the vast land of Canada.

Passage 2

Curiously, one of the most important battles of the War of 1812 actually took place after the war was over. For three years, The United States and Britain were
15 locked in a stalemate, with neither side emerging as a clear victor. While the Americans forced the British into Canada and defeated them at the Battle of the Thames, the British succeeded in burning Washington. Less than three weeks after signing the Treaty of Ghent on
20 December 24, 1814, General Andrew Jackson defeated the British in a decisive battle at New Orleans, a victory that contributed greatly to the development of American confidence and nationalism.

6. According to the passage, which of the following contributed to the U.S.'s decision to declare war on England in 1812?

    I. Expansionist tendencies among United States citizens and leaders
    II. British actions taken against U.S. interests
    III. A desire to show U.S. independence from England

(A) I only
(B) II only
(C) I and II
(D) I and III
(E) I, II, and III

7. Both passages support which of the following statements about the War of 1812?

(A) Neither side was able to score a decisive victory in the war.
(B) The war was important not just for the results of the battles but for its effect on the American psyche.
(C) It is likely that the U.S. would have won the war if it had continued on.
(D) The war was the most significant international engagement of the nineteenth century.
(E) The war was justified due to British injustices against the U.S.

8. The authors of both passages would likely agree that

(A) from a military standpoint, neither the United States nor Britain could claim to have won the War of 1812
(B) the War of 1812 had a much greater impact on American citizens than it did on British citizens
(C) the British forces would most likely have won the War of 1812 if they had not lost the Battle of the Thames
(D) Andrew Jackson's victory at New Orleans was the most important battle of the War of 1812
(E) The War of 1812 is not well known among people in the United States and Britain

9. In Passage 2, the author most likely considers Andrew Jackson's victory the "most important" battle because

(A) it proved to the British that the American army was a force to be reckoned with
(B) the American forces had not won a battle since the burning of Washington
(C) without Jackson's victory, the British would have been less willing to sign a peace treaty
(D) it was the only battle in which the American forces had been able to defeat the British
(E) the victory at New Orleans carried a great symbolic value to the people of America

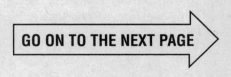

GO ON TO THE NEXT PAGE

Questions 10-15 are based on the following passage.

A parable is a symbolic story that, like a fable, teaches a moral lesson. The parable below was written by the Czech author Franz Kafka and was published in 1935.

Poseidon sat at his desk, doing figures. The administration of all the waters gave him endless work. He could have had assistants, as many as he wanted—and
Line he did have very many—but since he took his job very
5 seriously, he would in the end go over all the figures and calculations himself, and thus his assistants were of little help to him. It cannot be said that he enjoyed his work; he did it only because it had been assigned to him; in fact, he had already filed petitions for—as he put it—more
10 cheerful work, but every time the offer of something different was made to him it would turn out that nothing suited him quite as well as his present position. And anyhow, it was quite difficult to find something different for him. After all, it was impossible to assign him to
15 a particular sea; aside from the fact that even then the work with figures would not become less but only more petty, the great Poseidon could in any case only occupy an executive position. And when a job away from the water was offered to him he would get sick at the very
20 prospect; his divine breathing would become troubled, and his brazen chest would begin to tremble. Besides, his complaints were not really taken seriously; when one of the mighty is vexatious, the appearance of an effort must be made to placate him, even when the case is most
25 hopeless. In actuality, a shift of posts was unthinkable for Poseidon—he had been appointed God of the Sea in the beginning, and that he had to remain.
What irritated him most—and it was this that was chiefly responsible for his dissatisfaction with his job—
30 was to hear of the conceptions formed about him: how he was always riding about through the tides with his trident when all the while he sat here in the depths of the world-ocean, doing figures uninterruptedly, with now and then a trip to Jupiter as the only break in the monotony—a trip,
35 moreover, from which he usually returned in a rage. Thus he had hardly seen the sea—had seen it fleetingly in the course of hurried ascents to Olympus, and he had never actually traveled around it. He was in the habit of saying that what he was waiting for was the fall of the world;
40 then, probably, a quiet moment would yet be granted in which, just before the end and after having checked the last row of figures, he would be able to make a quick little tour.
Poseidon became bored with the sea. He let fall his
45 trident. Silently he sat on the rocky coast and a gull, dazed by his presence, described wavering circles around his head.

10. It can be inferred from the author's description of Poseidon's routine (lines 35-38) that

(A) Poseidon prefers performing his duties to visiting Jupiter
(B) Poseidon is too busy to familiarize himself with his kingdom
(C) Poseidon requires silence for the performance of his duties
(D) if the world falls, Poseidon will no longer be able to travel
(E) Poseidon's dissatisfaction with his job detracts from his efficiency

11. According to the passage, Poseidon's dissatisfaction with his job primarily stems from

(A) the constant travel that is required of him
(B) the lack of seriousness with which his complaints are received
(C) the constantly changing nature of his duties
(D) others' mistaken notions of his routine
(E) his assistants' inability to perform simple bookkeeping tasks

12. The author of the passage portrays the god Poseidon as

(A) a dissatisfied bureaucrat
(B) a powerful deity
(C) a disgruntled vagabond
(D) a capable accountant
(E) a ruthless tyrant

13. Poseidon is unable to change occupations for all of the following reasons EXCEPT

(A) his appointment as God of the Sea is inherently unchangeable
(B) he has fallen into disfavor with the gods on Mount Olympus
(C) he cannot imagine a life away from the water
(D) nothing else suits him as well as his present position
(E) his job must be appropriate to his elevated status

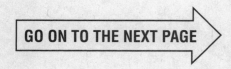

GO ON TO THE NEXT PAGE

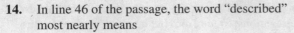

14. In line 46 of the passage, the word "described" most nearly means

(A) soared
(B) conveyed
(C) imagined
(D) followed
(E) traced

15. Which of the following statements best characterizes the moral lesson that the parable is meant to impart?

(A) It is better to be an assistant than an executive.
(B) A bad job can be hazardous to one's health.
(C) Power can be a source of unhappiness.
(D) All careers inevitably lead to boredom.
(E) A job is not meant to be a source of amusement.

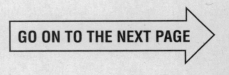

GO ON TO THE NEXT PAGE

Questions 16-24 are based on the following passage.

The role of women has historically been different in different cultures. The following passage presents an analysis of women in Frankish society by Suzanne Fonay Wemple.

Although the laws and customs in lands under
Frankish domination emphasized the biological function
and sexual nature of women, they did not deprive women
Line of opportunities to find personal fulfillment in a variety
5 of roles. Frankish women could sublimate their sexual
drives and motherly instincts in ways not available
to women in ancient societies. Their labor, moreover,
was not as exploited as it had been in primitive tribal
societies. Queens had access to power not only through
10 their husbands but also through churchmen and secular
officials whom they patronized. As widows, acting as
regents for their sons, they could exercise political power
directly. The wives of magnates issued donations jointly
with their husbands, founded monasteries, endowed
15 churches, cultivated interfamilial ties, transmitted clan
ideology to their children, supervised the household, and
administered the family's estates when their husbands
were away. Whether they contracted a formal union
or entered into a quasi-marriage, their children could
20 inherit. As widows, they acted as guardians of their minor
children, arranged their marriages, and in the absence of
sons, wielded economic power as well. In the dependent
classes, women shared their husbands' work, produced
textiles and articles of clothing both for their family's and
25 the lords' use, and were instrumental in bringing about
the merger of the free and slave elements in society.

For those who wished to free their bodies, souls, and
brains from male domination and devote their lives to
the service of God, Christianity provided an alternative
30 way of life. Although, in relation to the total population,
women in religious life remained a small minority
even in the seventh and eighth centuries, when many
female communities were founded, their roles, social
functions, and cultural contributions have an importance
35 for the history of women that outweighs their numbers.
This alternative way of life was available not only to
the unmarried but also to widows. Monasteries served
as places of refuge for married women as well. The
rich and the poor, at least until the late eighth century,
40 were accepted as members. Women from all walks of
life, as well as relatives, friends, and dependents of the

foundresses and abbesses, were invited to join the new
congregations. Freed from the need to compete for the
attention of men, women in these communities sustained
45 each other in spiritual, intellectual, scholarly, artistic,
and charitable pursuits. Writings by early medieval nuns
reveal that female ideals and modes of conduct were
upheld as the way to salvation and as models of sanctity
in the monasteries led by women. By facilitating the
50 escape of women from the male-dominated society to
congregations where they could give expression to their
own emotions, ascetic ideals, and spiritual strivings,
Christianity became a liberating force in the lives of
women. Historians have often overlooked these positive
55 effects and concentrated instead on the misogynistic
sentiments perpetuated by the male hierarchy.

16. The passage suggests that women under Frankish
law were

(A) confined to narrow social roles
(B) cut off from religious communities
(C) exploited as slaves and servants
(D) defined in physical or biological terms
(E) valued but essentially powerless

17. It can be inferred from the passage that marriage in
Frankish society

(A) was the only means of exchanging wealth
(B) could be entered into formally or informally
(C) always raised women to positions of greater
influence
(D) held greater importance than in primitive
societies
(E) was generally arranged by the bride's mother

18. The word "instrumental" as used in line 25 most
nearly means

(A) profitable
(B) skilled
(C) harmonious
(D) resistant
(E) vital

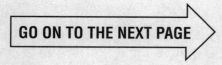

GO ON TO THE NEXT PAGE

19. The passage suggests which of the following about women in religious life?

    (A) Only unmarried women could participate in the religious lifestyle.
    (B) Many women turned to the religious life to escape difficulties with their husbands.
    (C) Writing by these women became the model for life in a monastery.
    (D) The impact on society they had was not proportionate to the actual number of women engaged in religious life.
    (E) Women in religious lifestyles were able to overcome the misogynistic tendencies of the male hierarchy.

20. The passage attributes women's ability to engage in "spiritual, intellectual, scholarly, artistic, and charitable pursuits" (lines 45–46) to

    (A) the monastic lifestyle present in religious communities
    (B) their freedom from the traditional duties ascribed to women
    (C) the homogeneous nature of the religious communities
    (D) the overthrow of the male dominated social hierarchy
    (E) the sense of salvation the women experienced upon joining a religious community

21. The status of women in Frankish society can best be described as

    (A) accorded different rights and responsibilities based on their social class and marital status
    (B) able to exercise political power by acting in place of their sons
    (C) having their marriages arranged for them by a widow
    (D) necessary in order to bring about the peaceful merger of slaves and freemen
    (E) free to divorce their husbands in order to enter into religious life

22. The primary purpose of the passage is to

    (A) settle a dispute regarding the importance of religious communities in Frankish societies
    (B) evaluate the position of women in Frankish society relative to that of women in other societies
    (C) argue that Frankish women had more rights than women in any other society
    (D) provide new evidence in the field of women's history
    (E) detail the different roles and lifestyles of women of varying social position in Frankish society

23. The passage implies that Frankish women outside religious communities

    (A) felt obliged to compete for male attention
    (B) were not inclined to religious feeling
    (C) had greatly diminished economic power
    (D) did not contribute to Frankish culture
    (E) relied on males for emotional support

24. According to the passage, Christianity facilitated the "escape of women from the male-dominated society" (line 50) by doing all of the following EXCEPT

    (A) permitting women self-expression
    (B) providing refuge for widows
    (C) putting pressure on women to study
    (D) removing male social pressures
    (E) diversifying women's social roles

STOP

**If you finish before time is called, you may check your work on this section only.
Do not turn to any other section in the test.**

SECTION 5

Time — 25 minutes

18 Questions

Turn to Section 5 of your answer sheet to answer the questions in this section.

Directions: This section contains two types of questions. You have 25 minutes to complete both types. For questions 1-20, solve each problem and decide which is the best of the choices given. Fill in the corresponding oval on the answer sheet. You may use any available space for scatchwork.

Notes

1. The use of a calculator is permitted.

2. All numbers used are real numbers.

3. Figures that accompany problems in this test are intended to provide information useful in solving the problems. They are drawn as accurately as possible EXCEPT when it is stated in a specific problem that the figure is not drawn to scale. All figures lie in a plane unless otherwise indicated.

4. Unless otherwise specified, the domain of any function f is assumed to be the set of all real numbers x for which $f(x)$ is a real number.

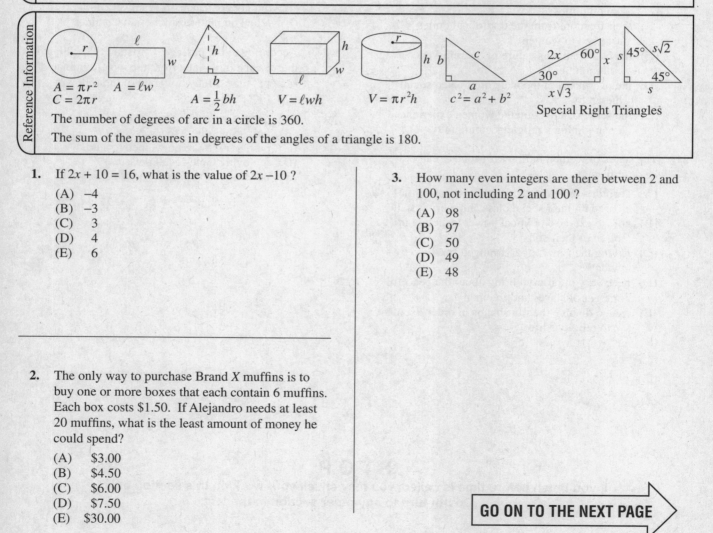

Reference Information

$A = \pi r^2$
$C = 2\pi r$

$A = \ell w$

$A = \frac{1}{2}bh$

$V = \ell w h$

$V = \pi r^2 h$

$c^2 = a^2 + b^2$

Special Right Triangles

The number of degrees of arc in a circle is 360.

The sum of the measures in degrees of the angles of a triangle is 180.

---

1. If $2x + 10 = 16$, what is the value of $2x - 10$?

(A) −4
(B) −3
(C) 3
(D) 4
(E) 6

2. The only way to purchase Brand X muffins is to buy one or more boxes that each contain 6 muffins. Each box costs $1.50. If Alejandro needs at least 20 muffins, what is the least amount of money he could spend?

(A) $3.00
(B) $4.50
(C) $6.00
(D) $7.50
(E) $30.00

3. How many even integers are there between 2 and 100, not including 2 and 100 ?

(A) 98
(B) 97
(C) 50
(D) 49
(E) 48

GO ON TO THE NEXT PAGE

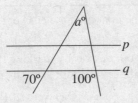

4. In the figure above, line p is parallel to line q. What is the value of a ?

(A) 10
(B) 30
(C) 35
(D) 40
(E) 70

5. If $f(3) = 6$ and $f(4) = 13$, then which of the following could be $f(x)$?

(A) $x + 3$
(B) $2x$
(C) $3x + 1$
(D) $x^2 - 2$
(E) $x^2 - 3$

6. In $\triangle ABC$, $\overline{AB} \cong \overline{BC}$ and $\overline{AB} \perp \overline{BC}$. If $AC = 10$, what is the area of the triangle?

(A) $10\sqrt{2}$
(B) 25
(C) 50
(D) $50\sqrt{2}$
(E) 100

7. In 1998, Andrei had a collection of 48 baseball caps. Since then, he has given away 13 caps, purchased 17 new caps, and traded 6 of his caps to Pierre for 8 of Pierre's caps. Since 1998, what has been the net percent increase in Andrei's collection?

(A) 6%

(B) $12\frac{1}{2}\%$

(C) $16\frac{2}{3}\%$

(D) 25%

(E) $28\frac{1}{2}\%$

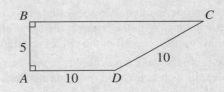

8. What is the area of quadrilateral $ABCD$ in the figure above?

(A) 50
(B) $50 + 12.5\sqrt{2}$
(C) 70
(D) $50 + 12.5\sqrt{3}$
(E) 75

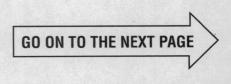
GO ON TO THE NEXT PAGE

Directions: For Student-Produced Response questions 9-18, use the grids at the bottom of the answer sheet page on which you have answered questions 1-8.

Each of the remaining 10 questions requires you to solve the problem and enter your answer by marking the circles in the special grid, as shown in the examples below. You may use any available space for scratchwork.

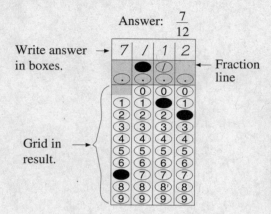

Answer: $\frac{7}{12}$

Write answer in boxes. → | 7 | / | 1 | 2 |

Fraction line ←

Grid in result. →

Answer: 2.5

Decimal point ←

Answer: 201
Either position is correct.

Note: You may start your answers in any column, space permitting. Columns not needed should be left blank.

- Mark no more than one circle in any column.

- Because the answer sheet will be machine-scored, **you will receive credit only if the circles are filled in correctly.**

- Although not required, it is suggested that you write your answer in the boxes at the top of the columns to help you fill in the circles accurately.

- Some problems may have more than one correct answer. In such cases, grid only one answer.

- No question has a negative answer.

- **Mixed numbers** such as $3\frac{1}{2}$ must be gridded as

  3.5 or 7/2. (If | 3 | 1 | / | 2 | is gridded, it will be

  interpreted as $\frac{31}{2}$, not $3\frac{1}{2}$.)

- **Decimal Answers:** If you obtain a decimal answer with more digits than the grid can accommodate, it may be either rounded or truncated, but it must fill the entire grid. For example, if you obtain an answer such as 0.6666..., you should record your result as .666 or .667. **A less accurate value such as .66 or .67 will be scored as incorrect.**

Acceptable ways to grid $\frac{2}{3}$ are:

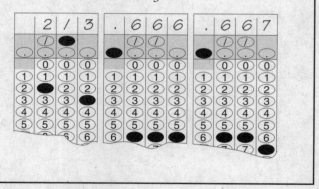

9. A certain clothing store sells only T-shirts, sweat-shirts, and turtlenecks. On Wednesday, the store sells T-shirts, sweatshirts, and turtlenecks in a ratio of 2 to 3 to 5. If the store sells 30 sweatshirts on that day, what is the total number of garments that the store sells on Wednesday?

10. A rectangular box has a height of 4.5 inches and a base with an area of 18 square inches. What is the volume of the rectangular box in cubic inches?

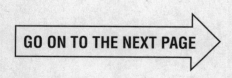

GO ON TO THE NEXT PAGE

11. If $5x - 4 = x - 1$, what is the value of x ?

12. If $a^b = 4$, and $3b = 2$, what is the value of a ?

13. If b is a prime number such that $3b > 10 > \frac{5}{6}b$, what is one possible value of b ?

14. The Tyler Jackson Dance Company plans to perform a piece that requires 2 dancers. If there are 7 dancers in the company, how many possible pairs of dancers could perform the piece?

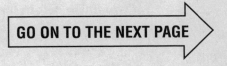

GO ON TO THE NEXT PAGE

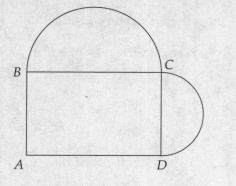

SPICE PRICES OF DISTRIBUTOR D

Spice	Price per pound
cinnamon	$8.00
nutmeg	$9.00
ginger	$7.00
cloves	$10.00

15. In the figure above, if semicircular arc *BC* has length 6π and semicircular arc *CD* has length 4π, what is the area of rectangle *ABCD* ?

17. The owner of a spice store buys 3 pounds each of cinnamon, nutmeg, ginger, and cloves from distributor D. She then sells all of the spices at $2.00 per ounce. What is her total dollar profit (1 pound = 16 ounces)? (Disregard the $ sign when gridding your answer.)

16. $f(x) = x^2 - 5$. If $f(6) - f(4) = f(y)$, what is the absolute value of y ?

18. Points *E*, *F*, *G*, and *H* lie on a line in that order. If $EG = \dfrac{5}{3}EF$ and $HF = 5FG$, then what is $\dfrac{EF}{HG}$?

STOP
If you finish before time is called, you may check your work on this section only.
Do not turn to any other section in the test.

NO TEST MATERIAL ON THIS PAGE.

SECTION 6
Time — 25 minutes
18 Questions

Turn to Section 6 of your answer sheet to answer the questions in this section.

Directions: This section contains two types of questions. You have 25 minutes to complete both types. For questions 1-8, solve each problem and decide which is the best of the choices given. Fill in the corresponding oval on the answer sheet. You may use any available space for scratchwork.

Notes

1. The use of a calculator is permitted.

2. All numbers used are real numbers.

3. Figures that accompany problems in this test are intended to provide information useful in solving the problems. They are drawn as accurately as possible EXCEPT when it is stated in a specific problem that the figure is not drawn to scale. All figures lie in a plane unless otherwise indicated.

4. Unless otherwise specified, the domain of any function f is assumed to be the set of all real numbers x for which $f(x)$ is a real number.

Reference Information

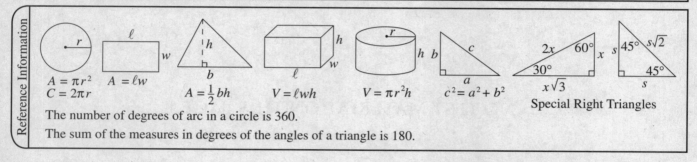

$A = \pi r^2$
$C = 2\pi r$

$A = \ell w$

$A = \frac{1}{2}bh$

$V = \ell wh$

$V = \pi r^2 h$

$c^2 = a^2 + b^2$

Special Right Triangles

The number of degrees of arc in a circle is 360.
The sum of the measures in degrees of the angles of a triangle is 180.

1. If $x + 6 > 0$ and $1 - 2x > -1$, then x could equal each of the following EXCEPT

(A) -6

(B) -4

(C) -2

(D) 0

(E) $\frac{1}{2}$

2. Elsa has a pitcher containing x ounces of root beer. If she pours y ounces of root beer into each of z glasses, how many ounces of root beer will remain in the pitcher?

(A) $\dfrac{x}{y} + z$

(B) $xy - z$

(C) $\dfrac{x}{yz}$

(D) $x - yz$

(E) $\dfrac{x}{y} - z$

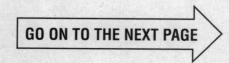

GO ON TO THE NEXT PAGE

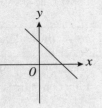

3. Which of the following could be the equation of the line represented in the graph above?

(A) $y = 2x + 4$
(B) $y = 2x - 4$
(C) $y = -2x - 1$
(D) $y = -2x - 4$
(E) $y = -2x + 4$

4. If $x = 8^{\frac{4}{3}}$, what is the value of x ?

(A) $4\frac{3}{4}$

(B) 6

(C) $10\frac{2}{3}$

(D) 12

(E) 16

5. If $x = y + 1$ and $y \geq 1$, then which of the following is equal to $x^2 - y^2$?

(A) $(x - y)^2$
(B) $x^2 - y - 1$
(C) $x + y$
(D) $x^2 - 1$
(E) $y^2 + 1$

6. Triangle ABC has a perimeter of 10, and the lengths of its sides are all integers. If a is the length of side $\overline{BC}$, what is the difference between the largest and smallest possible values of a ?

(A) 1
(B) 2
(C) 3
(D) 4
(E) 7

7. What is the greatest number of regions into which an equilateral triangle can be divided using exactly three straight lines?

(A) 4
(B) 6
(C) 7
(D) 8
(E) 9

8. If $a = 4b + 26$, and b is a positive integer, then a could be divisible by all of the following EXCEPT

(A) 2
(B) 4
(C) 5
(D) 6
(E) 7

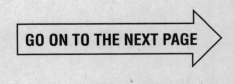

GO ON TO THE NEXT PAGE

Directions: For Student-Produced Response questions 9-18, use the grids at the bottom of the answer sheet page on which you have answered questions 1-8.

Each of the remaining 10 questions requires you to solve the problem and enter your answer by marking the circles in the special grid, as shown in the examples below. You may use any available space for scratchwork.

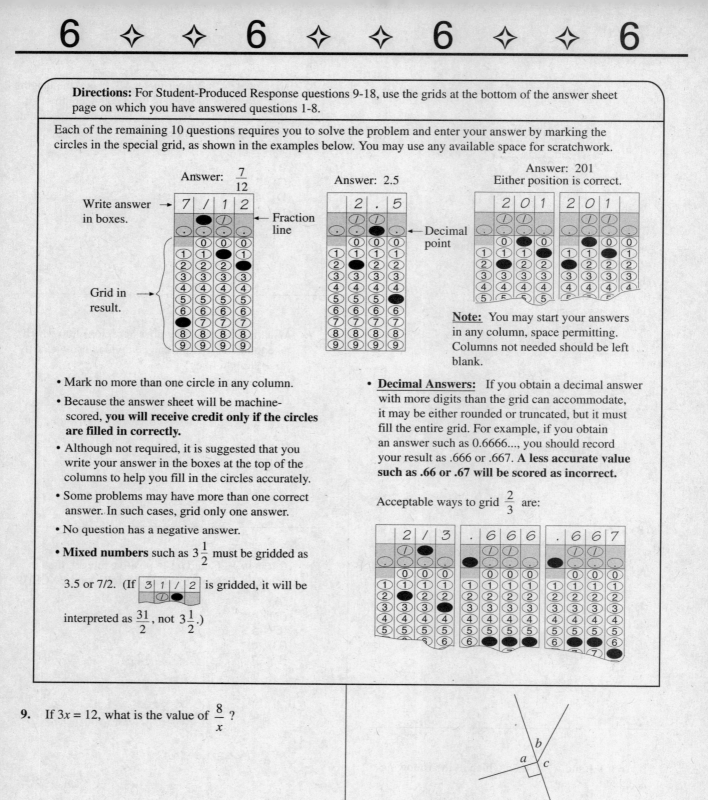

Answer: $\frac{7}{12}$

Write answer in boxes.

Fraction line

Grid in result.

Answer: 2.5

Decimal point

Answer: 201
Either position is correct.

Note: You may start your answers in any column, space permitting. Columns not needed should be left blank.

- Mark no more than one circle in any column.

- Because the answer sheet will be machine-scored, **you will receive credit only if the circles are filled in correctly.**

- Although not required, it is suggested that you write your answer in the boxes at the top of the columns to help you fill in the circles accurately.

- Some problems may have more than one correct answer. In such cases, grid only one answer.

- No question has a negative answer.

- **Mixed numbers** such as $3\frac{1}{2}$ must be gridded as

  3.5 or 7/2. (If [3 1 / 2] is gridded, it will be

  interpreted as $\frac{31}{2}$, not $3\frac{1}{2}$.)

- **Decimal Answers:** If you obtain a decimal answer with more digits than the grid can accommodate, it may be either rounded or truncated, but it must fill the entire grid. For example, if you obtain an answer such as 0.6666..., you should record your result as .666 or .667. **A less accurate value such as .66 or .67 will be scored as incorrect.**

Acceptable ways to grid $\frac{2}{3}$ are:

9. If $3x = 12$, what is the value of $\frac{8}{x}$?

10. In the figure above, what is the value of $a + b + c$?

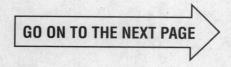

GO ON TO THE NEXT PAGE

11. Y is a point on $\overline{XZ}$ such that $XY = \dfrac{1}{2}XZ$. If the length of $\overline{YZ}$ is $4a + 6$, and the length of $\overline{XZ}$ is 68, what is the value of a ?

12. If $4x + 2y = 24$ and $\dfrac{7y}{2x} = 7$, what is the value of x ?

13. If $\dfrac{x^2 + x - 6}{x^2 - 8x + 12} = 4$, what is the value of x ?

14. Twenty bottles contain a total of 8 liters of apple juice. If each bottle contains the same amount of apple juice, how many liters of juice are in each bottle?

15. What is the sum of the positive even factors of 12 ?

16. If the domain of $f(x) = \dfrac{1}{2^x} - 7$ is all integers, what is a two-digit positive integer that is in the range of $f(x)$?

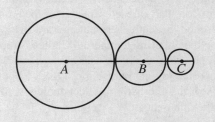

17. In the figure above, the radius of the circle with center A is twice the radius of the circle with center B and four times the radius of the circle with center C. If the sum of the areas of the three circles is 84π, what is the length of $\overline{AC}$?

18. One-fifth of the cars in a parking lot are blue and $\dfrac{1}{2}$ of the blue cars are convertibles. If $\dfrac{1}{4}$ of the convertibles in the parking lot are blue, then what percent of the cars in the lot are neither blue nor convertibles? (Disregard the percent sign when gridding your answer.)

STOP
If you finish before time is called, you may check your work on this section only.
Do not turn to any other section in the test.

SECTION 7

Time — 25 minutes
35 Questions

Turn to Section 7 of your answer sheet to answer the questions in this section.

Directions: For each question in this section, select the best answer from among the choices given and fill in the corresponding circle on the answer sheet.

The following sentences test correctness and effectiveness of expression. Part of each sentence or the entire sentence is underlined; beneath each sentence are five ways of phrasing the underlined material. Choice A repeats the original phrasing; the other four choices are different. If you think the original phrasing produces a better sentence than any of the alternatives, select choice A; if not, select one of the other choices.

In making your selection, follow the requirements of standard written English; that is, pay attention to grammar, choice of words, sentence construction, and punctuation. Your selection should result in the most effective sentence—clear and precise, without awkwardness or ambiguity.

EXAMPLE:

Laura Ingalls Wilder published her first book and she was sixty-five years old then.
(A) and she was sixty-five years old then
(B) when she was sixty-five
(C) at age sixty-five years old
(D) upon the reaching of sixty-five years
(E) at the time when she was sixty-five

Ⓐ ● Ⓒ Ⓓ Ⓔ

1. Rotary phones, once the height of technology, are now so obsolete and rare as to be unknown to younger generations.

    (A) are now so obsolete and rare as to be unknown to younger generations
    (B) are now so obsolete and rare and unknown to younger generations
    (C) are now unknown to younger generations stemming from their obsoleteness and rareness
    (D) now are obsolete and rare, which means that younger generations are unaware of it
    (E) now are unknown and younger generations think they are obsolete and rare

2. The hearings of the McCarthy era often cast doubt on the integrity of those brought to trial as well as anyone that had a relation to them, however distant.

    (A) that had a relation to them, however distant
    (B) with relationships to them, even distantly
    (C) related to them, however distantly
    (D) with a relationship to the defendants, however distantly
    (E) related to them, however distant

3. When you look at a sixteenth-century painting of the *Annunciation* by Lorenzetti or Giotto, one may notice certain sartorial or architectural details outlined in gold leaf.

    (A) one may notice
    (B) people may notice
    (C) you may notice
    (D) one may be noticing
    (E) one's thoughts are

4. Fats nicknamed "trans fats" cling to body cells for 57 days, and this is not true of unsaturated fats such as olive and canola oils, which nourish the body without damaging the cells.

    (A) and this is not true of unsaturated fats such as olive and canola oils, which nourish
    (B) not true of unsaturated fats such as olive and canola oils, which nourish
    (C) as opposed to unsaturated fats such as olive and canola oils, nourishing
    (D) unsaturated fats such as olive and canola oils nourish
    (E) but unsaturated fats such as olive and canola oils nourish

GO ON TO THE NEXT PAGE ⟶

5. Knoll, <u>known for their Scandinavian designs</u>, sells the Barcelona chair that the architect Mies van der Rohe designed in the style of his own building in Barcelona.

   (A) known for their Scandinavian designs
   (B) known for its Scandinavian designs
   (C) designing the Scandinavian furniture that it's known for
   (D) though they're known for Scandinavian designs
   (E) known to be Scandinavian designers

6. Towing companies face harsh new restrictions that detail where they can operate, which vehicles are off limits, and when they can begin; <u>because of new legislation is why</u>.

   (A) because of new legislation is why
   (B) new legislation being the reason
   (C) with new legislation as the reason
   (D) these restrictions are the result of new legislation
   (E) all of those restrictions come from new legislation recently passed

7. The increase in hours they are required to work in an understaffed, unsupportive situation <u>have angered the nurses at West Branch Rest Home and threatened a walkout</u>.

   (A) have angered the nurses at West Branch Rest Home and threatened a walkout
   (B) has angered the nurses at West Branch Rest Home and caused them to threaten a walkout
   (C) have angered the nurses at West Branch Rest Home, and a walkout is threatened
   (D) has angered the nurses at West Branch Rest Home, which caused a threat to have a walkout
   (E) has angered the nurses at West Branch Rest Home to have a walkout

8. Galleons, <u>a sailing ship from the seventeenth century, were known for their</u> large size, however they were unable to sail into the wind because of the design of their sails.

   (A) a sailing ship from the seventeenth century, were known for their
   (B) a sailing ship from the seventeenth century, was known for its
   (C) a seventeenth-century sailing ship, was known for its
   (D) seventeenth-century sailing ships, was known for its
   (E) seventeenth-century sailing ships, were known for their

9. Just an hour after Evan and Ken reached the skate park, <u>he fell and broke his wrist in two places</u>.

   (A) he fell and broke his wrist in two places
   (B) his wrist broke when he fell in two places
   (C) his wrist being broke in two places as a result of falling
   (D) Evan fell and broke his wrist in two places
   (E) Evan was falling and breaking two bones in his wrist

10. The Advanced Acting course requires <u>neither a final exam or project other than the performance of</u> a major role in the spring play.

   (A) neither a final exam or project other than the performance of
   (B) no final exam and assigns no project, but does expect each student to perform
   (C) no other final exam or project excepting for the performing by students of
   (D) no other final exam nor assigns any project other than to be performing
   (E) neither a final exam or a major project other than performing

11. Many <u>regard Sappho as</u> the writer who originated the tradition of expressing tormented love in Western poetry.

   (A) regard Sappho as
   (B) regard Sappho to be
   (C) regard Sappho to have been
   (D) consider that Sappho is
   (E) consider Sappho as being

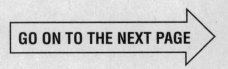
GO ON TO THE NEXT PAGE

The following sentences test your ability to recognize grammar and usage errors. Each sentence contains either a single error or no error at all. No sentence contains more than one error. The error, if there is one, is underlined and lettered. If the sentence contains an error, select the one underlined part that must be changed to make the sentence correct. If the sentence is correct, select choice E. In choosing answers, follow the requirements of standard written English.

EXAMPLE:

The other delegates and him immediately
  A   B   C

accepted the resolution drafted by the
                    D

neutral states. No error
        E

Ⓐ ● Ⓒ Ⓓ Ⓔ

12. The object of the game of chess is to put the other
    A   B

player's king in a vulnerable position, so that you
         C

can eventually capture them. No error
         D   E

13. In the author's latest novel, the hero traveled to
                   A
Montana where she finds a mysteriously deserted
            B
house and, through a series of misunderstandings,
        C
becomes embroiled in an international smuggling
      D
ring. No error
     E

14. Many biographers had claimed that Samuel Lang-
  A   B
horne Clemens changed his name to Mark Twain
         C
to echo the riverboat captain's call ascertaining the

safe navigation depth of the Mississippi River.
     D
No error
  E

15. After having read numerous diet books, Charles
    A
decided that the simplest plan would be the best:
    B
eat fewer calories and exercise more. No error
      C   D   E

16. Instead of using pencils and paper to record their
    A   B
work, students in frontier schools rather used
            C
pieces of chalk and a slate for their daily lessons.
            D
No error
  E

17. When learning how to paint, one should comply to
                 A
the teacher's instruction; with more experience, the
         B
burgeoning painter can experiment with technique.
  C   D
No error
  E

18. Not having traveled abroad before, John was both
    A   B   C
apprehensive and excited about his upcoming trip
         D
to the Galápagos Islands. No error
        E

19. The field of consumer electronics have never been
             A
fixed; DVDs have replaced VHS tapes, just as CDs
            B
replaced cassette tapes in the past. No error
  C   D   E

20. One should use parchment paper while baking
    A   B
cookies because the cookies won't stick to this
      C
lining and you won't have to scrub the pan.
      D
No error
  E

GO ON TO THE NEXT PAGE

21. Salma and Raiza <u>may be</u> identical twins, <u>but</u> Salma
                  A   B

is <u>the more</u> athletic and Raiza <u>the most</u> studious.
    C   D

<u>No error</u>
   E

22. Forest fires, long <u>thought to be</u> a detriment to the
                     A

environment, <u>are</u> now understood <u>not only</u> to be
             B   C

unavoidable but also to be <u>a boon</u> to the forests.
                     D

<u>No error</u>
   E

23. Superbowl commercials <u>perfectly</u> target <u>their</u>
                     A   B

demographics because the advertisers regularly

<u>spent</u> exorbitant amounts of time and money
   C

<u>designing</u> the ads. <u>No error</u>
   D   E

24. Although many people <u>scoff at</u> superstitions, <u>they</u>
                   A   B

usually have some of their own, <u>from</u> retrieving
                     C

only for face-up pennies from the sidewalk to

<u>selecting</u> lucky numbers for the lottery. <u>No error</u>
   D   E

25. <u>Returning</u> to school in September, Linnea told us
     A

in <u>minute</u> detail how she <u>had rode</u> her bike from
     B   C

our town in coastal New Jersey to Eugene, Oregon,

<u>entirely</u> on her own. <u>No error</u>
   D   E

26. The sculptor Rodin <u>often departed</u> from traditional
                  A

styles in his creations; unlike <u>other sculptors</u>, his
                     B

creations <u>made obvious</u> the materials from which
       C

they were <u>built</u>. <u>No error</u>
       D   E

27. Jane, who is <u>known for</u> her diligence, smugly re-
           A

minded Jason that if he <u>would have planned</u> ahead
                     B

instead of <u>procrastinating</u>, he would not <u>have had</u> to
         C   D

write his entire research paper in just one weekend.

<u>No error</u>
   E

28. Some words in the English <u>language has</u> several
                     A

meanings which are unrelated <u>except through</u> their
                     B

origins: *testudinate*, for example, <u>can mean either</u>
                     C

curved and vault-shaped, or extremely slow

moving, since the word <u>derives from</u> the Latin
               D

word for *turtle*. <u>No error</u>
           E

29. The woman <u>whom</u> the board picked <u>to design</u> the
          A   B

new building is a <u>renowned</u> architect and
             C

<u>has received</u> many awards. <u>No error</u>
   D   E

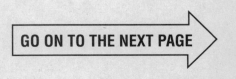

GO ON TO THE NEXT PAGE

Directions: The following passage is an early draft of an essay. Some parts of the passage need to be rewritten.

Read the passage and select the best answers for the questions that follow. Some questions are about particular sentences or parts of sentences and ask you to improve sentence structure or word choice. Other questions ask you to consider organization and development. In choosing answers, follow the requirements of standard written English.

Questions 30-35 are based on the following passage.

(1) When I agreed to stage-manage my school's production of *Guys and Dolls*, I really had no idea of what a stage manager actually did. (2) Still, I decided that it would be an interesting experience, and a way to get involved with theater, since I am definitely not an actor. (3) Besides, if there were already a director, a choreographer, and sets and lights to be built and run by technicians, how much could there be left for a stage manager to do? (4) I figured that I would spend a lot of time watching rehearsal and doodling into my script.

(5) My illusions were shattered by the first rehearsal. (6) I discovered that it was my responsibility to make sure that all of the actors were present, had scripts, and gave me their schedules before they left the room. (7) It became a nightmare. (8) I found that it was virtually impossible to get all twenty-five cast members together for a group scene, especially since actors kept calling me with emergency orthodontist appointments, and last-minute family gatherings. (9) When the actor who was playing Sky was sick one day and had to miss rehearsal, I had to walk through his part myself. (10) It was probably the first time in the history of American theater that Sky Masterson was ever wearing a miniskirt and leggings.

(11) I sat to the side of the stage, with my script open on a music stand in front of me. (12) "Standby, cue 1," I whispered into my headset. (13) "Cue 1: go." The lights came up, the show began, and I knew that it had all been worthwhile.

30. Which of the following words or phrases is unnecessary in sentence 1?

(A) production of
(B) actually did
(C) agreed to
(D) When
(E) really

31. In context, which version of the underlined part of sentence 3 (reproduced below) is the best?

Besides, if there were already a director, a choreographer, <u>and sets and lights to be built and run by technicians</u>, how much could there be left for a stage manager to do?

(A) (as it is now)
(B) and sets, lights, and technicians
(C) and the building and running of sets and lights by technicians
(D) and technicians to build the sets and run the lights
(E) and technicians who would run the lights and be building the sets

32. In context, the best version of the underlined portion of sentence 10 (reproduced below) is which of the following?

It was probably the first time in the history of American theater that Sky Masterson <u>was ever wearing</u> a miniskirt and leggings.

(A) (as it is now)
(B) had ever worn
(C) could have worn
(D) would ever be wearing
(E) had ever before worn

33. Which of the following sentences, if added at the beginning of the final paragraph, would provide the best transition?

(A) Luckily, the actor soon regained his health.
(B) We rehearsed for five weeks.
(C) Finally, it was opening night.
(D) Everyone was filled with nervous excitement.
(E) I communicated with the light and sound operators through a headset.

GO ON TO THE NEXT PAGE

34. The writer's story would be most improved if a paragraph were included on which of the following topics?

  (A) The author's other extracurricular activities
  (B) The author's responsibilities during different phases of rehearsal
  (C) The historical background of *Guys and Dolls*
  (D) The audition process
  (E) The plays produced in previous years

35. In context, which is the best version of the underlined portion of sentence 11 (reproduced below)?

I sat to the side of the stage, with my script open on a music stand in front of me.

  (A) (as it is now)
  (B) stage, my script being open
  (C) stage, my script having been opened
  (D) stage. With my script opened
  (E) stage. My script open

STOP

If you finish before time is called, you may check your work on this section only.
Do not turn to any other section in the test.

SECTION 8

Time — 20 minutes

16 Questions

Turn to Section 8 of your answer sheet to answer the questions in this section.

Directions: For this section, solve each problem and decide which is the best of the choices given. Fill in the corresponding oval on the answer sheet. You may use any available space for scratchwork.

Notes

1. The use of a calculator is permitted.

2. All numbers used are real numbers.

3. Figures that accompany problems in this test are intended to provide information useful in solving the problems. They are drawn as accurately as possible EXCEPT when it is stated in a specific problem that the figure is not drawn to scale. All figures lie in a plane unless otherwise indicated.

4. Unless otherwise specified, the domain of any function f is assumed to be the set of all real numbers x for which $f(x)$ is a real number.

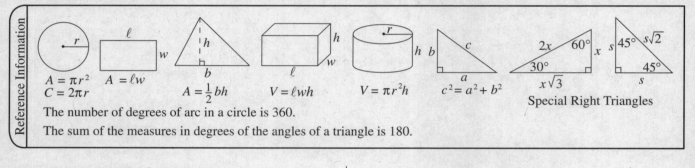

Reference Information

$A = \pi r^2$
$C = 2\pi r$

$A = \ell w$

$A = \frac{1}{2} bh$

$V = \ell wh$

$V = \pi r^2 h$

$c^2 = a^2 + b^2$

Special Right Triangles

The number of degrees of arc in a circle is 360.

The sum of the measures in degrees of the angles of a triangle is 180.

1. If $6 - y = 2y - 6$, what is the value of y ?

(A) 0
(B) 2
(C) 4
(D) 6
(E) 12

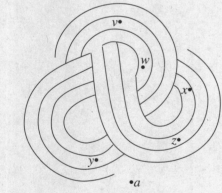

2. Which of the following points can be connected to point a by a continuous path without crossing any line or curve in the figure above?

(A) v
(B) w
(C) x
(D) y
(E) z

GO ON TO THE NEXT PAGE

Computer Production		
	Morning Shift	Afternoon Shift
Monday	200	375
Tuesday	245	330
Wednesday	255	340
Thursday	250	315
Friday	225	360

3. Computer production at a factory occurs during two shifts, as shown in the chart above. If computers are only produced during the morning and afternoon shifts, on which pair of days is the greatest total number of computers produced?

(A) Monday and Thursday
(B) Tuesday and Thursday
(C) Tuesday and Wednesday
(D) Tuesday and Friday
(E) Monday and Friday

4. If a rectangular swimming pool has a volume of 16,500 cubic feet, a uniform depth of 10 feet, and a length of 75 feet, what is the width of the pool, in feet?

(A)   22
(B)   26
(C)   32
(D)   110
(E) 1,650

5. Cindy has a collection of 80 records. If 40% of her records are jazz records, and the rest are blues records, how many blues records does she have?

(A) 32
(B) 40
(C) 42
(D) 48
(E) 50

6. A science class has a ratio of girls to boys of 4 to 3. If the class has a total of 35 students, how many more girls are there than boys?

(A) 20
(B) 15
(C)   7
(D)   5
(E)   1

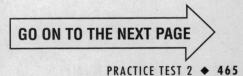

GO ON TO THE NEXT PAGE

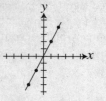

7. The graph above shows $y = 2x$. Which of the following graphs represents $y = |2x|$?

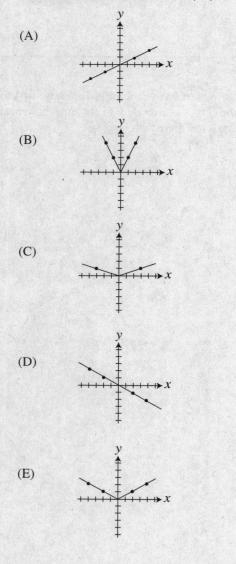

(A)

(B)

(C)

(D)

(E)

8. The length of a certain rectangle is twice the width. If the area of the rectangle is 128, what is the length of the rectangle?

(A)   4

(B)   8

(C) 16

(D) $21\frac{1}{3}$

(E) $42\frac{2}{3}$

9. Which of the following is equivalent to $5^5 \times 2^2 \times 10^{10}$?

(A) $5^3 \times 10^{12}$
(B) $5^2 \times 10^{15}$
(C) 10^{15}
(D) 100^{17}
(E) 100^{100}

10. For positive integer x, 10 percent of x percent of 1,000 is equal to which of the following?

(A) x
(B) $10x$
(C) $100x$
(D) $1,000x$
(E) $10,000x$

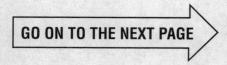

GO ON TO THE NEXT PAGE

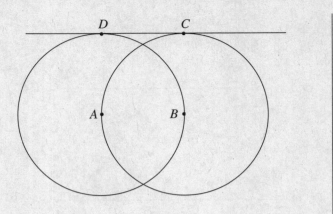

11. In the figure above, A and B are the centers of two circles of identical circumference. $\overleftrightarrow{CD}$ is tangent to both circles and parallel to $\overleftrightarrow{AB}$ (not shown). If r is the radius of the circle with center A, what is the area of quadrilateral $ABCD$ (not shown) in terms of r?

(A) $4r^2$
(B) $4r$
(C) $2r^2$
(D) $2r$
(E) r^2

12. Nails are sold in 8-ounce and 20-ounce boxes. If 50 boxes of nails were sold and the total weight of the nails sold was less than 600 ounces, what is the greatest possible number of 20-ounce boxes that could have been sold?

(A) 34
(B) 33
(C) 25
(D) 17
(E) 16

13. If $c = \dfrac{1}{x} + \dfrac{1}{y}$ and $x > y > 0$, then which of the following is equal to $\dfrac{1}{c}$?

(A) $x + y$

(B) $x - y$

(C) $\dfrac{x+y}{xy}$

(D) $\dfrac{xy}{x+y}$

(E) $\dfrac{1}{x} + \dfrac{1}{y}$

14. In the xy-plane, which of the following is a point of intersection between the graphs of $y = x + 2$ and $y = x^2 + x - 2$?

(A) $(0, -2)$
(B) $(0, 2)$
(C) $(1, 0)$
(D) $(2, 4)$
(E) $(3, 5)$

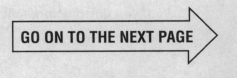

GO ON TO THE NEXT PAGE

15. If $f(g(a)) = 6$, $f(x) = \dfrac{x}{2} + 2$, and $g(x) = \left| x^2 - 10 \right|$,

which of the following is a possible value of a ?

(A) $\sqrt{2}$
(B) $\sqrt{3}$
(C) 2
(D) 6
(E) 18

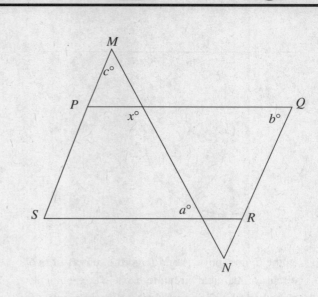

16. If $PQRS$ is a parallelogram, then which of the following must be equal to x ?

(A) $180 - b$
(B) $180 - c$
(C) $a + b$
(D) $a + c$
(E) $b + c$

STOP
If you finish before time is called, you may check your work on this section only.
Do not turn to any other section in the test.

NO TEST MATERIAL ON THIS PAGE.

SECTION 9

Time — 20 minutes

19 Questions

Turn to Section 9 of your answer sheet to answer the questions in this section.

Directions: For each question in this section, select the best answer from among the choices given and fill in the corresponding circle on the answer sheet.

Each sentence below has one or two blanks, each blank indicating that something has been omitted. Beneath the sentence are five words or sets of words labeled A through E. Choose the word or set of words that, when inserted in the sentence, best fits the meaning of the sentence as a whole.

Example:

Hoping to ------- the dispute, negotiators proposed a compromise that they felt would be ------- to both labor and management.

(A) enforce . . useful
(B) end . . divisive
(C) overcome . . unattractive
(D) extend . . satisfactory
(E) resolve . . acceptable

Ⓐ Ⓑ Ⓒ Ⓓ ●

---

1. The success of the school's Book Club is owed to the club's policy that the novels selected, authored by a ------- group, cover a broad array of subject matters and range of historical eras.

    (A) scholarly   (B) meritorious   (C) diverse
        (D) erudite   (E) sophisticated

2. The apparent ------- with which professional skiers descend the slopes is deceptive; this activity requires ------- effort and intense concentration.

    (A) trepidation . . conscious
    (B) motivation . . resolute
    (C) nonchalance . . strenuous
    (D) consideration . . unpredictable
    (E) insouciance . . minimal

3. The children in the parade wore a range of costumes, some dressing in classic ghost or witch costumes, some as civic figures such as firefighters or police officers, and others as famous singers and other ------- of popular culture.

    (A) monikers   (B) diplomats   (C) icons
        (D) pariahs   (E) dupes

4. Mr. Planka's explanations were unnecessarily -------, incorporating entirely too many layers of trivial information that his students did not need.

    (A) winsome   (B) terse   (C) convoluted
        (D) fallacious   (E) deafening

5. Reflecting upon her vacation, Cecilia felt that it was both ------- and -------; she enjoyed visiting New York, but did not like all the traveling required to get there.

    (A) arduous . . distressing
    (B) realistic . . dramatic
    (C) relaxing . . peaceful
    (D) restful . . wearisome
    (E) traditional . . con sistent

6. Despite appearing stylistically -------, Pablo Picasso's paintings exhibit artistic ------- on multiple levels.

    (A) superficial . . inaccuracy
    (B) excessive . . abundance
    (C) precise . . elegance
    (D) unsophisticated . . complexity
    (E) imaginative . . creativity

GO ON TO THE NEXT PAGE

The passages below are followed by questions based on their content; questions following a pair of related passages may also be based on the relationship between the paired passages. Answer the questions on the basis of what is <u>stated</u> or <u>implied</u> in the passage and in any introductory material that may be provided.

Questions 7-19 are based on the following passages.

The discipline of physics has seen a number of changes in the last 100 years. The following passages discuss two of those changes.

Passage 1

It is mandatory to preface any discussion of atoms by paying homage to Democritus, an Ionian philosopher of the fifth century B.C., the earliest known proponent of
Line an atomic theory. Though Democritus's ideas were in
5 many ways strikingly modern and were promulgated by his more celebrated successor Epicurus, his theory never gained wide acceptance in Greek thought. It had largely been forgotten by the time of the late Renaissance rebirth of science. While the dramatic rise of the atomic theory
10 over the last century and a half seems to have vindicated Democritus, only the Greek name atom ("indivisible") remains to establish his claim as the father of the theory.

Nonetheless, Democritus's thinking contained the seed of the idea that has dominated twentieth-century
15 physical thought. He was one of the first to perceive that nature on a sufficiently small scale might be qualitatively different in a striking way from the world of our ordinary experience. And he was the first to voice the hope, today almost an obsession, that underlying all the complex
20 richness, texture, and variety of our everyday life might be a level of reality of stark simplicity, with the turmoil we perceive representing only the nearly infinite arrangements of a smaller number of constituents.

Today, the notion that simplicity is to be found by
25 searching nature on a smaller level is embedded in physical thought to the point that few physicists can imagine any other approach.

Democritus's ideas were popular among the philosophically sophisticated founders of modern physics.
30 Galileo, Newton, and most of their contemporaries were atomists, but their beliefs were based more on intuition than on concrete evidence. Moreover, the invention of calculus had eliminated the difficulties with continuity that had in part motivated the Greek atomists, so the
35 theory received little attention in the century following Newton's work. Still, the atomic theory remained a popular speculation among physicists, because it offered the hope that all the properties of matter might ultimately be explained in terms of the motion of the atoms
40 themselves.

It remained for the chemists of the early nineteenth century to find the first solid empirical support for atomism. Without stretching the point too far, it is fair to say that in 1800 the atomic theory was something
45 physicists believed but couldn't prove, while the chemists were proving it but didn't believe it.

Passage 2

The discovery that the universe is expanding was one of the great intellectual revelations of the twentieth century. With hindsight, it is easy to wonder why no one
50 had thought of it before. Newton, and others, should have realized that a static universe would soon start to contract under the influence of gravity. But suppose instead the universe is expanding. If it were expanding fairly slowly, the force of gravity would cause it eventually to stop
55 expanding and then to start contracting. However, if it were expanding at more than a certain critical rate, gravity would never be strong enough to stop it, and the universe would continue to expand forever. This is a bit like what happens when one fires a rocket upward
60 from the surface of the earth. If it has a fairly low speed, gravity will eventually stop the rocket and it will start falling back. On the other hand, if the rocket has more than a certain critical speed (about seven miles per second), gravity will not be strong enough to pull it back,
65 so it will keep going away from the earth forever. This behavior of the universe could have been predicted from Newton's theory of gravity at any time in the nineteenth, the eighteenth, or even the late seventeenth centuries. Yet so strong was the belief in a static universe that it
70 persisted into the early twentieth century. Even Einstein, when he formulated the general theory of relativity in 1915, was so sure that the universe had to be static that he modified his theory to make this possible, introducing a so-called cosmological constant into his equations.
75 Einstein introduced a new "antigravity" force, which, unlike other forces, did not come from any particular source, but was built into the very fabric of space-time. He claimed that space-time had an inbuilt tendency to expand, and this could be made to balance exactly the
80 attraction of all the matter in the universe, so that a static universe would result.

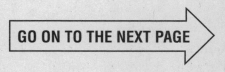

GO ON TO THE NEXT PAGE

7. In line 5, the word "promulgated" most nearly means
   - (A) plagiarized
   - (B) dismissed
   - (C) protected
   - (D) obscured
   - (E) promoted

8. From the information presented in Passage 1, which of the following can be properly inferred about Democritus?
   - (A) Although his view was initially met with skepticism, Democritus was among the first to advocate an atomic theory.
   - (B) Although he was more known for his work in politics, Democritus also made important scientific discoveries.
   - (C) His ideas were incompatible with those of Galileo and Newton.
   - (D) Democritus was unduly credited with being the father of Greek atomism.
   - (E) Democritus was more known for his discovery of calculus than for his theory of atomism.

9. The "obsession" that the author describes in line 19 can best be described as
   - (A) Democritus' desire to see his ideas accepted by the scientific community
   - (B) physicists' search for Democritus' original writings on atoms
   - (C) the author's own search for the principles underlying matter
   - (D) modern scientists' quest for a simple unifying property of everyday matter
   - (E) early nineteenth-century chemists' search for the first solid evidence of atomism

10. The third paragraph of Passage 1 is used by the author to
    - (A) express dismay at the narrow-mindedness of early scientists
    - (B) highlight the ironic acceptance of a once spurned theory
    - (C) convey wonder for the inexplicableness of this obsession
    - (D) transition into a discussion of the usefulness of atomic theory
    - (E) show how modern physicists are unwilling to explore alternatives to atomic theory

11. The last paragraph of Passage 1 suggests that
    - (A) it was only after the physicists proved the existence of atoms that the chemists believed their claims
    - (B) chemistry was the first scientific field to take atomic theory seriously
    - (C) atomic theory did not strictly fall within the domain of any one scientific discipline
    - (D) while physicists first proved the theory, it was chemists who made the most practical use of atoms
    - (E) the recognition of chemistry and physics as separate disciplines is arbitrary and detrimental to the pursuit of knowledge

12. Which of the following can be inferred from Passage 2 about the expanding universe?
    - (A) It was incompatible with accepted nineteenth-century beliefs.
    - (B) Newton discovered it during his work with gravity.
    - (C) Most scientists believe that the idea is no longer tenable.
    - (D) The existence of gravity makes it impossible for the universe to expand.
    - (E) The expanding universe theory cannot be proven.

13. The author of Passage 2 mentions Newton in order to
    - (A) point out the ignorance of many physicists
    - (B) give one example of a proponent of the expanding universe theory
    - (C) illustrate the point that the expanding universe theory could have been discovered earlier
    - (D) provide evidence that the universe is not expanding
    - (E) show the consequences of a scientist's disregard for a new theory

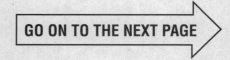

GO ON TO THE NEXT PAGE

14. The author's reference to a rocket (lines 58-65) serves to illustrate

(A) the implications of an expanding universe
(B) the forces governing the universe's gradual expansion
(C) the similarity of the energy released by the universe and that released by rockets
(D) the way in which gravity prevents the universe from expanding
(E) the theory of a static universe

15. In Passage 2, the author's description of Einstein's general theory of relativity serves to

(A) bolster the author's theory that the universe is expanding
(B) show that scientists were reluctant to abandon the theory of a static universe
(C) indicate the creativity that Einstein brought to his work
(D) question the validity of the theory of the expanding universe
(E) underscore Einstein's reliance on Newtonian physics

16. The term "cosmological constant" (line 74) refers to

(A) a mathematical constant employed by Einstein to bring his theories in line with the idea of a static universe
(B) an equation used by Einstein to debunk Newton's ideas about universal expansion
(C) a theory developed by opponents of Einstein's general theory of relativity
(D) the mathematical model that was used to disprove Newtonian physics
(E) the theory that the mass of all matter in the universe must remain the same

17. In the last line of Passage 2, the word "static" most nearly means

(A) charged
(B) conflicting
(C) particulate
(D) unchanging
(E) dynamic

18. The authors of both passages would most probably agree with which of the following statements?

(A) Democritus and Newton both struggled to see their theories accepted by others.
(B) Neither Democritus nor Newton received credit for his theory.
(C) Newton, Einstein, and Democritus are all responsible in part for setting back modern physics.
(D) The atomic model of matter and the theory of the expanding universe cannot both be correct.
(E) Scientists may adopt particular theories in spite of weak or contradictory evidence.

19. Based on the information in both passages, a difference between atomism and the expanding universe theory is

(A) the idea of atomism can be traced to the ancient Greeks, while the model of the expanding universe is a relatively recent theory
(B) atomism is easier to understand and explore than the static universe theory
(C) atomism was developed for political reasons, while the static universe theory is purely scientific
(D) the theory of atomism has been thoroughly proven, while the static universe theory is now thought to be incorrect
(E) the static universe theory is more adaptable to modern science than is the atomistic theory

STOP
If you finish before time is called, you may check your work on this section only.
Do not turn to any other section in the test.

SECTION 10
Time — 10 minutes
14 Questions

Turn to Section 10 of your answer sheet to answer the questions in this section.

Directions: For each question in this section, select the best answer from among the choices given and fill in the corresponding circle on the answer sheet.

The following sentences test correctness and effectiveness of expression. Part of each sentence or the entire sentence is underlined; beneath each sentence are five ways of phrasing the underlined material. Choice A repeats the original phrasing; the other four choices are different. If you think the original phrasing produces a better sentence than any of the alternatives, select choice A; if not, select one of the other choices.

In making your selection, follow the requirements of standard written English; that is, pay attention to grammar, choice of words, sentence construction, and punctuation. Your selection should result in the most effective sentence—clear and precise, without awkwardness or ambiguity.

EXAMPLE:

Laura Ingalls Wilder published her first book and she was sixty-five years old then.
(A) and she was sixty-five years old then
(B) when she was sixty-five
(C) at age sixty-five years old
(D) upon the reaching of sixty-five years
(E) at the time when she was sixty-five

Ⓐ ● Ⓒ Ⓓ Ⓔ

1. Of the top investment firms, only the few that have complied with SEC guidelines should be trusted by investors looking for a good place to build capital.

   (A) Of the top investment firms, only the few that have complied with SEC guidelines
   (B) Of the top investment firms, only a few, those which have compliance with SEC guidelines,
   (C) Only a few of the top investment firms, because of complying with SEC guidelines
   (D) Only a few of the top investment firms, in which the SEC guidelines were complied by,
   (E) Only a few of the top investment firms complied with SEC guidelines,

2. The audience, though still trying to appreciate the modern theater production, are getting restless and won't be able to sit still for much longer.

   (A) production, are getting restless and won't be able to
   (B) production is getting restless and aren't able to
   (C) production, are getting restless and they won't be able to
   (D) production is getting restless and they won't be able to
   (E) production, is getting restless and won't be able to

3. Antique furniture can be worth a great deal of money, but so many fakes abound that it can be difficult to distinguish valuable and worthless pieces.

   (A) valuable and worthless pieces
   (B) valuable to worthless pieces
   (C) between valuable and worthless pieces
   (D) between valuable from worthless pieces
   (E) valuable pieces from those that are worthless pieces

GO ON TO THE NEXT PAGE

4. Unlike the Asian people that we now think of as Japanese, <u>the first settlements in the Japanese Archipelago were established by Caucasians called the Ainu.</u>

    (A) the first settlements in the Japanese Archipelago were established by Caucasians called the Ainu
    (B) the settling of the Japanese Archipelago was first done by the Ainu, who were Caucasians
    (C) the Ainu, who established the first settlements in the Japanese Archipelago, were Caucasians
    (D) the Ainu, as Caucasians, were the first to establish settlements in the Japanese Archipelago
    (E) settling the Japanese Archipelago was first done by Caucasians called the Ainu

5. A Mongol emperor associated with ancient Chinese <u>splendor, the tiny Japanese fleet nevertheless managed to defeat Kublai Khan's huge, nearly invincible army</u>.

    (A) splendor, the tiny Japanese fleet nevertheless managed to defeat Kublai Khan's huge, nearly invincible army
    (B) splendor, the tiny Japanese fleet nevertheless being the first to defeat Kublai Khan's huge nearly invincible army
    (C) splendor, Kublai Khan's army was nevertheless defeated by the tiny, nearly invincible Japanese fleet
    (D) splendor, Kublai Khan commanded a nearly invincible army that was nevertheless defeated by the tiny Japanese fleet
    (E) splendor, the tiny, nearly invincible fleet of the Japanese nevertheless managing to defeat the huge army commanded by Kublai Khan

6. In 1666, the Great Fire of London, though it destroyed over 14,000 buildings and left 100,000 people <u>homeless, actually ended</u> the bubonic plague outbreak by incinerating the rats that carried the disease.

    (A) homeless, actually ended
    (B) homeless, actually ending
    (C) homeless, actually it had ended
    (D) homeless; actually ended
    (E) homeless, and it ended

7. Though all of Dawn's Siamese kittens are descended from the same four progenitors, <u>each kitten has its own distinct personality</u>.

    (A) each kitten has its own distinct personality
    (B) each kitten has their own distinct personalities
    (C) with each one there having distinct personalities
    (D) which each has its own distinct personality
    (E) each kitten is having a distinct personality of their own

8. Jenna was very self-assured about the upcoming audition, <u>this</u> confidence gave her the ability to continue performing her scene even after she forgot several lines.

    (A) this
    (B) and this
    (C) however, her
    (D) that
    (E) because her

9. One of the deciding factors in Edward III's retreat from France in 1390 was a freak electrical <u>hailstorm; killing</u> scores of his horses and armored knights.

    (A) hailstorm; killing
    (B) hailstorm and it killed
    (C) hailstorm, and killing
    (D) hailstorm, being the death of
    (E) hailstorm that killed

10. The effects of the poliomyelitis that author Kyra Stanley contracted as a young child <u>had been evident</u> in her early stories.

    (A) had been evident
    (B) being evident
    (C) was evident
    (D) were evident
    (E) and she was evident

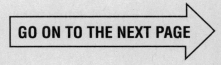

GO ON TO THE NEXT PAGE

11. During his semester of student teaching, the observation of several students copying from each other's papers without consequence gave Mr. Peters the impression that the school had no effective policy against cheating.

(A) the observation of several students copying from each other's papers without consequence gave Mr. Peters

(B) Mr. Peters observed several students copying from each other's papers without consequence; he formed

(C) observing several students copying from each other's papers without consequence gave Mr. Peters

(D) Mr. Peters, observing several students copying from each other's papers without consequence and forming

(E) the observation by Mr. Peters of several students copying from each other's papers without consequence gave him

12. When Jacques Lacan was developing his psychoanalytical theories, ideas from Freud, Heidigger, and even the structural linguists were used, but also original concepts were added by him.

(A) ideas from Freud, Heidigger, and even the structural linguists were used, but also original concepts were added by him

(B) ideas from Freud, Heidigger, and even the structural linguists were used, as well as original concepts were added by him

(C) he used not only ideas from Freud, Heidigger, and even the structural linguists, but also his original concepts

(D) he used not only ideas from Freud, Heidigger, and even the structural linguists and added original concepts, too

(E) ideas from Freud, Heidigger, the structural linguists, and original concepts were added by him

13. The nutrition guideline called the "Food Pyramid" has not been as effective in fighting obesity and heart disease as experts had anticipated; as a result, reduced levels of carbohydrate intake will be recommended by them.

(A) reduced levels of carbohydrate intake will be recommended by them

(B) experts now recommend eating fewer carbohydrates

(C) had recommended reduced levels of carbohydrate intake

(D) the recommendations for reduced carbohydrate intake will be made by them

(E) will be recommending reduced levels of carbohydrate intake

14. In contrast to them in New York and other American cities, Belgium's streets are not littered with fast food containers and discarded papers; however, pedestrians do need to watch out for dog droppings.

(A) In contrast to them in New York and other American cities, Belgium's streets

(B) Belgium's streets, in contrast to them in New York and other American cities,

(C) Belgium's streets, when in contrast to those in New York and other American cities,

(D) Belgium's streets, in contrast to those in New York and other American cities,

(E) Belgium's streets contrast to New York and American cities, they

STOP
If you finish before time is called, you may check your work on this section only.
Do not turn to any other section in the test.

NO TEST MATERIAL ON THIS PAGE.

PRACTICE TEST 2: ANSWER KEY

Section 2 Reading	Section 3 Math	Section 4 Reading	Section 5 Math (Exp)	Section 6 Math	Section 7 Writing	Section 8 Math	Section 9 Reading	Section 10 Writing
1. E	1. E	1. E	1. A	1. A	1. A	1. C	1. C	1. A
2. D	2. B	2. E	2. C	2. D	2. C	2. B	2. C	2. E
3. E	3. A	3. D	3. E	3. E	3. C	3. C	3. C	3. C
4. E	4. B	4. D	4. B	4. E	4. E	4. A	4. C	4. C
5. C	5. A	5. C	5. E	5. C	5. B	5. D	5. D	5. D
6. A	6. C	6. C	6. B	6. B	6. D	6. D	6. D	6. A
7. D	7. B	7. B	7. B	7. C	7. B	7. B	7. E	7. A
8. A	8. C	8. A	8. D	8. B	8. E	8. C	8. A	8. B
9. C	9. D	9. E	9. 100	9. 2	9. D	9. A	9. D	9. E
10. B	10. D	10. B	10. 81	10. 270	10. B	10. A	10. B	10. D
11. C	11. D	11. D	11. .75	11. 7	11. A	11. E	11. C	11. B
12. D	12. D	12. A	or	12. 3	12. D	12. E	12. A	12. C
13. C	13. B	13. B	$\frac{3}{4}$	13. 9	13. A	13. D	13. C	13. B
14. E	14. C	14. E	12. 8	14. .4	14. B	14. D	14. B	14. D
15. C	15. D	15. C	13. 5, 7,	or	15. E	15. A	15. B	
16. B	16. C	16. D	or 11	$\frac{2}{5}$	16. C	16. E	16. A	
17. D	17. A	17. B	14. 21	15. 24	17. A		17. D	
18. B	18. C	18. E	15. 96	16. 25	18. E		18. E	
19. B	19. D	19. D	16. 5	or	19. A		19. A	
20. A	20. C	20. C	17. 282	57	20. D			
21. C		21. A	18. .375	17. 18	21. D			
22. E		22. E	or	18. 50	22. E			
23. D		23. A	$\frac{3}{8}$		23. C			
24. A		24. C			24. E			
					25. C			
					26. B			
					27. B			
					28. A			
					29. E			
					30. E			
					31. D			
					32. B			
					33. C			
					34. B			
					35. A			

SAT SCORING WORKSHEET

For directions on how to score your SAT practice test, see pages 5–7. Section 4 is an unscored, experimental section.

SAT WRITING SECTION

Total Writing Multiple-Choice Questions Correct from Sections 5 and 10: ▢

−

Total Writing Multiple-Choice Questions Incorrect from Sections 4 and 10: _____ ÷ 4 = ▢

Grammar Raw Score: ▢

Grammar Scaled Subscore! ▢

Compare the Grammar Raw Score to the Writing Multiple-Choice Subscore Conversion Table on the next page to find the Grammar Scaled Subscore.

+

Your Essay Score (2–12): _____ × 2 = ▢

Writing Raw Score: ▢

Compare Raw Score to SAT Score Conversion Table on the next page to find the Writing Scaled Score.

Writing Scaled Score! ▢

SAT CRITICAL READING SECTION

Total Critical Reading Questions Correct from Sections 3, 7, and 9: ▢

−

Total Critical Reading Questions Incorrect from Sections 3, 7, and 9: _____ ÷ 4 =

Critical Reading Raw Score: ▢

Compare Raw Score to SAT Score Conversion Table on the next page to find the Critical Reading Scaled Score.

Critical Reading Scaled Score! ▢

SAT MATH SECTION

Total Math Grid-In Questions Correct from Section 6: ▢

+

Total Math Multiple-Choice Questions Correct from Sections 2, 6, and 8: ▢

−

Total Math Multiple-Choice Questions Incorrect from Sections 2, 6, and 8: _____ ÷ 4 = ▢

Don't include wrong answers from grid-ins!

Math Raw Score: ▢

Compare Raw Score to SAT Score Conversion Table on the next page to find the Math Scaled Score.

Math Scaled Score! ▢

SAT SCORE CONVERSION TABLE

Raw Score	Writing Scaled Score	Reading Scaled Score	Math Scaled Score	Raw Score	Writing Scaled Score	Reading Scaled Score	Math Scaled Score	Raw Score	Writing Scaled Score	Reading Scaled Score	Math Scaled Score
73	800			47	590–630	600–640	680–720	21	400–440	420–460	460–500
72	790–800			46	590–630	590–630	670–710	20	390–430	410–450	450–490
71	780–800			45	580–620	580–620	660–700	19	380–420	400–440	450–490
70	770–800			44	570–610	580–620	650–690	18	370–410	400–440	440–480
69	770–800			43	570–610	570–610	640–680	17	370–410	390–430	430–470
68	760–800			42	560–600	570–610	630–670	16	360–400	380–420	420–460
67	760–800	800		41	560–600	560–600	620–660	15	350–390	380–420	420–460
66	760–800	770–800		40	550–590	550–590	620–660	14	340–380	370–410	410–450
65	750–790	750–790		39	540–580	550–590	610–650	13	330–370	360–400	400–440
64	740–780	740–780		38	530–570	540–580	600–640	12	320–360	350–390	400–440
63	730–750	740–780		37	530–570	530–570	590–630	11	320–360	350–390	390–430
62	720–760	730–770		36	520–560	530–570	590–630	10	310–350	340–380	380–420
61	710–750	720–760		35	510–550	520–560	580–620	9	300–340	330–370	370–410
60	700–740	710–750		34	500–540	510–550	570–610	8	290–330	310–350	360–400
59	690–730	700–740		33	490–530	500–540	560–600	7	280–320	300–340	350–390
58	680–720	690–730		32	480–520	500–540	560–600	6	270–310	300–340	340–380
57	680–720	680–720		31	470–510	490–530	540–580	5	260–300	290–330	330–370
56	670–710	670–710		30	470–510	480–520	530–570	4	240–280	280–320	320–360
55	660–720	670–710		29	460–500	470–510	520–560	3	230–270	270–310	310–350
54	650–690	660–700	800	28	450–490	470–510	510–550	2	230–270	260–300	290–330
53	640–680	650–690	780–800	27	440–480	460–500	510–550	1	220–260	230–270	270–310
52	630–670	640–680	750–790	26	430–470	450–490	500–540	0	210–250	200–240	240–280
51	630–670	630–670	740–780	25	420–460	450–490	490–530	–1	200–240	200–230	220–260
50	620–660	620–660	730–770	24	410–450	440–480	480–520	–2	200–230	200–220	210–250
49	610–650	610–650	710–750	23	410–450	430–470	480–520	–3	200–220	200–210	200–240
48	600–640	600–640	700–740	22	400–440	420–460	470–510				

WRITING MULTIPLE-CHOICE SUBSCORE CONVERSION TABLE

Grammar Raw Score	Grammar Scaled Subscore	Grammar Raw Score	Grammar Scaled Subscore	Grammar Raw Score	Grammar Scaled Subscore	Grammar Raw Score	Grammar Scaled Subscore	Grammar Raw Score	Grammar Scaled Subscore	Grammar Raw Score	Grammar Scaled Subscore
49	79–80	40	70–74	31	61–65	22	52–56	13	43–47	4	33–37
48	78–80	39	69–73	30	60–64	21	52–56	12	42–46	3	31–35
47	78–80	38	68–72	29	59–63	20	51–55	11	41–45	2	28–32
46	77–80	37	67–71	28	58–62	19	50–54	10	40–44	1	26–30
45	76–80	36	66–70	27	57–61	18	49–53	9	39–43	0	23–27
44	75–79	35	65–69	26	56–60	17	48–52	8	37–41	–1	22–26
43	73–77	34	64–68	25	55–59	16	47–51	7	36–40	–2	21–25
42	72–76	33	63–67	24	54–58	15	46–50	6	35–39	–3	20–24
41	71–75	32	62–66	23	53–57	14	45–49	5	34–38		

21

Answers and Explanations for Practice Test 2

1. **E** The blank in this sentence is a word that describes the wastes produced by nuclear power plants. What do you know about the wastes? The wastes are *radioactive materials that have to be stored in protective containers*, which means they must be dangerous, so "dangerous" would be a good word for the blank. (E), *noxious*, is the best match for dangerous.

2. **D** Let's start with the second blank. The clues for this blank are *living specimen* and *thought to be no longer*. If a *living specimen* was found, and it affects the *scientific community*, then the creature must have been thought to be no longer *living*—a good word for the second blank. Only (D) and (E) have second blank words that match *living*. For the first blank, a word that means "surprised" is needed, because you'd certainly be surprised if something you thought was dead turned out to be alive. There is nothing in the sentence to indicate disappointment, so (E), *dismayed,* can be eliminated. *Astounded* comes closest to the meaning of surprised.

3. **E** The clues here are *third trip overseas* and *voters complained*. Why would the voters complain about the governor taking a lot of trips abroad? If he's always away in a foreign country, then he probably isn't paying a lot of attention to the affairs of his own country. So you can put "his own country" in the blank. Looking to the answer choices, *domestic* is the best match; it means the opposite of foreign.

4. **E** For this question you need to figure out the relationship between the blanks. Claudius *was viewed* one way by *generations of historians*, until *newly discovered evidence* changed everyone's mind. So the words in the blanks must be somewhat opposite in meaning. You can get rid of (A), (B), and (D) because the words aren't opposites. In (C) and (E), the first word is negative and the second is positive, so they are both possibilities. To narrow it down, let's look at the second blank, which describes Claudius's ability as an administrator. Would it make sense to call him an *eager* administrator? Not really, so get rid of (C).

5. **C** The clues in this sentence are *scarce* and *nutrition*. In these primitive areas, something is scarce, so they have to be *resourceful* in order to find nutrition. What is scarce? It must be *nutrition*; that's why they have to be resourceful in order to find it. So you can recycle the clue and put *nutrition* in the blank. Looking at the answer choices, *sustenance* is the best match for nutrition.

6. **A** Let's start with the first blank. The first clue in the sentence is *division between*. Morgan wants to do something with the *division between theory and empiricism*. In the second part of the sentence, you learn that she thinks doing something with philosophy and applied science is possible and necessary. If doing something with both things together is possible and necessary, then she must be against the division, so the word in the first blank must mean "against." Eliminate (B) and (C). Since Morgan is against the division, she must be convinced that a combination is possible and necessary, so you can put "combination" in the second blank. Eliminate (D) and (E), neither of which contains a second word meaning "combination."

7. **D** The colon is a same-direction trigger telling you that the clue for the blank is *vivid colors and mixture of bold patterns* and *center of attention*. A good word to use for the blank is "showy." *Flamboyant* comes closest in meaning to "showy."

8. **A** Let's start with the second blank. The clue in this sentence is *disagreeable*, and the trigger word for the second blank is *although*, which means that the word in the second blank is the opposite of *disagreeable*. Therefore you can put "agreeable" in the second blank. Looking at the answer choices, the only word that matches "agreeable" is *complaisant*, and *contentious* is close in meaning to *disagreeable.*

9. C Hurston consciously wrote about the lives of African Americans. In (A), although Hurston did participate in the Harlem Renaissance, the term *deconstructed* refers to her writing, not her participation. (B) is too literal: Hurston's writing is not about actual scientific experimentation. (D) is incorrect because there is no evidence that Hurston was *cut off* from Harlem. Finally, (E) is too extreme; there's no support for Hurston trying to make *sweeping changes.*

10. B This is the only statement that is not implied or stated in the passage: Although she was indeed an anthropologist, *widely acclaimed* is too extreme and makes this statement inaccurate. All the other choices are supported by information in the passage and therefore are the incorrect answers.

11. C (C) is correct, because it says that the author merely relates the arguments of both sides without adding his own opinion. This also explains why (A) and (B) are incorrect. (D) is too broad and not discussed in the passage, and (E) is only partially correct. While the passage does touch upon some arguments of opponents to SURTASS LFA, he also discusses the views of *proponents,* and thus this is not the author's main point.

12. D (D) is correct because the example demonstrates how harmful sounds at 150 decibels can be, and this allows the reader to appreciate how dangerous sounds at 215 decibels would be. (A) is incorrect because the author is comparing different sound levels, not humans and whales. (B) and (C) are both incorrect because the author neither supports nor attacks either side in the argument. (E) is unsupported by the text.

13. C According to the first paragraph, *early man viewed ... healing as purification,* and this notion is apparent in the *origin of our word for "pharmacy."* The passage then gives the meaning of the Greek word *pharmakon,* which is *purification through purging.* Therefore, the literal definition is cited in order to give an example of how early man thought of healing as purging, or internal cleansing, as is paraphrased in (C). Remember, the answer to most specific questions will be an exact paraphrase of what the passage says. Choice (A) doesn't make any sense. Did ancient civilization have an advanced form of medical science? No way. Don't forget to use your common sense. (B) doesn't answer the question, and it is irrelevant. You're talking about ancient medicine, not ancient beliefs in general. (D) is wrong because the passage doesn't say anything in the first paragraph about the mental and physical causes of diseases. This is mentioned much later in the passage. Make sure you're reading in the right place. (E) is too extreme, and it actually contradicts the passage. In lines 34–35, the passage says that *the Greeks had adopted a sophisticated mind-body view of medicine,* so they were certainly not primitive.

14. E The lead words in this question are *early Sumerian drugs,* which should lead you back to the second paragraph. According to lines 10–14, *the first drug catalog, or pharmacopoeia, was written...by an unknown Sumerian physician. Preserved in cuneiform script on a single clay tablet are the names of dozens of drugs to treat ailments that still afflict us today.* So it was possible to identify a number of early Sumerian drugs because somebody back then wrote them all down, which is exactly what (E) says. (A) is wrong because the passage doesn't say anything at all about traces of the drugs being found in archeological excavations. If it's not in the passage, then it's not ETS's answer. (B) is wrong because the passage says in line 15 that the Egyptians added to the ancient knowledge of medicine. The passage doesn't say that they used the same medications as the Sumerians. (C) is wrong because the passage doesn't say anything at all about Sumerian religious texts. (D) is way off the topic. The passage is about ancient civilizations, not about Europe. Modern Europe didn't even exist back then. Read the answer choices carefully.

SECTION 2

15. C This question asks about Sumerian drugs again, so you need to go back to the second paragraph. This time the question is looking for a similarity between Sumerian drugs and modern drugs. According to lines 7–9, *the Sumerians in the Tigris-Euphrates Valley had developed virtually all of our modern methods of administering drugs*. So the similarity between Sumerian and modern drugs is in the methods of administering drugs, which is paraphrased in (C) as the delivery of drugs. Remember, the answer to most specific questions will be an exact paraphrase of what the passage says. (A) is wrong because the passage says that the Sumerians had the same methods of administering drugs, not that they used the same chemicals. Besides, it doesn't make any sense to say that an ancient civilization had the same chemicals that you do now. They didn't have penicillin, or anything like that, did they? Don't forget about common sense. (B) is wrong because the passage doesn't talk about mental and physical disorders until much later in the passage. Use the lead words to make sure you are reading in the right place. (D) doesn't make any sense at all. Were ancient Sumerian drugs the products of sophisticated chemical research? No way! Use common sense. (E) is wrong because a hierarchy of drug producers was part of Egyptian society, not Sumerian society.

16. B The lead words in this question are *the seventh-century Greeks*, which should lead you to the fifth paragraph. The question asks how the view of medicine differed between the Greeks and the Sumerians. According to lines 34–35, *By the seventh century B.C., the Greeks had adopted a sophisticated mind-body view of medicine*. If this view were newly adopted by the Greeks, it must have been different from what the Sumerians thought. So the difference is that the Greeks had a mind-body view. Mind-body is paraphrased in (B) as the mental and physical roots of illness. (A) is wrong because the passage doesn't say anything about advanced chemical applications. Read carefully. (C) contradicts the passage. The Greeks believed that it was necessary to treat the mind and the body. That is the point of the fifth paragraph. Go back and read it again. (E) is wrong because the word *most* makes it an extreme answer. The Greeks didn't develop *most* of the precursors of modern drugs. What about the Egyptians and the Sumerians?

17. D For this question, you should read before and after the word *hierarchy* to give yourself some context. In the fourth paragraph, the passage talks about the *hierarchy of ancient drug preparation*. In lines 24–33, the passage describes the different people involved in the process of making drugs, including the *chief of the preparers of drugs*, the *collectors of drugs*, the *preparers*, the *preparers' aides*, and the *conservator of drugs*. With all these different jobs, the *hierarchy* must be an example of a *division of labor*. (A) is wrong because the fourth paragraph doesn't say anything about superstitious practices. (B) is wrong because the passage doesn't say anything about the severity of ancient diseases. (C) is close, but the fourth paragraph is about the people who *made drugs* in ancient Egypt, not the doctors who administered the drugs. (E) is also wrong because the fourth paragraph is about the people who made the drugs, not the recipes for the drugs them selves. Read carefully.

18. **B** To answer this question, you just need to read the final paragraph and find out what the passage says about *scientific discovery*. According to the last paragraph, *many of the latest sophisticated additions to our medicine chest shelves were accidental finds.* In other words, many modern drugs were discovered by accident. (B) paraphrases the idea of *accidental finds* as *chance events*. (A) doesn't make any sense. Are discoveries in biochemistry *uncommon*? Most biochemists would probably disagree. Don't forget to use common sense. (C) may actually be true, but the passage doesn't mention it, so it can't be ETS's answer. Remember, ETS's answers come right out of the passage. You don't need any outside knowledge. (D) is wrong because the word *best* makes this a *must* answer. How do you know that trial and error is the *best* way to make scientific discoveries? The passage never says that it's the best way. (E) is wrong because it is also a *must* answer. Is it really true that *most* of the important scientific discoveries have been accidents? Besides, you're only talking about *drugs* here!

19. **B** The best answer is (B). Ointments are mentioned in the passage as a characteristic of *Sumerian,* not Egyptian, medicine (line 12). Each of the other answer choices is cited as a characteristic of Egyptian medicine: anesthesia (lines 21–23, in which ethyl alcohol is used to *numb the pain of tooth extraction*), ingredients derived from animals (line 33), use of trial-and-error (line 18), and a workplace hierarchy (lines 24–33).

20. **A** According to lines 59–63 of the passage, many drugs common in 1987 *were accidental finds;* this supports (A). (B) is not only a bit wacky, but also unsupported by the passage. (C) and (D) use deceptive language—they quote directly from the passage, but they don't answer the question. Neither choice refers to drugs used in 1987. (D) is especially tricky, because the *modern era of pharmacology* (line 44) began in the sixteenth century, which does *not* necessarily mean that any modern *drugs* were created then. (E) may well be true, but this idea is not discussed in the passage and therefore it is not correct.

21. **C** The best answer is (C). Seventh-century Greek medicine is discussed in the fifth paragraph. The author contends that the seventh-century Greeks had a *mind-body view of medicine* (line 35) in which mental maladies were *interpreted as curses from displeased deities* (lines 42–43). Evidence that a seventh-century Greek doctor's prescription urged a patient to pray to a Greek deity, would support this contention. (A) is incorrect because in the passage, the author discusses the Egyptian, not Greek, use of antacids. In the fifth paragraph, the author states that *the suspected 'mental' causes of disease were not (emphasis added) recognized as stress* (lines 41–42), so (B) is incorrect. There is no discussion in the passage of the Egyptian influence on Greek medicine, or of Greek use of the term "pharmacology," so choices (D) and (E) are incorrect as well. Note that most of the incorrect answer choices for this question contain a word or phrase that is used in the passage (e.g., *sophisticated*). Remember that the use of a word or phrase from the passage in an answer choice does not ensure that the choice is correct. In fact, such an inclusion is often a trap! The right answer often contains a paraphrase of material in the passage, instead of the exact wording.

22. **E** The best answer is (E). The language in (E) can be characterized as extreme, but that language is supported by the passage. In lines 44–46, the author states that the first major discoveries in chemistry occurred in the sixteenth century. This statement supports choice (E), because the ancient Egyptians lived long before the sixteenth century. (A) is an extreme statement that is not supported by the passage. (B) is tricky—the author states that throughout history, many people have *believed* that diseases can have supernatural causes, but nowhere does the author state that this belief is in fact true. (C) is wrong because, according to the passage, a modern head pharmacist is analogous to the Egyptian *chief of preparers of drugs* (lines 25–27), not to the conservator of drugs. (D) would be correct if you substituted the word "some" for *most*. As written, however, it is an extreme answer choice that is unsupported by the passage.

23. **D** Go back to the passage, find the word *holistic*, and cross it out. Then read the sentence and come up with your own word. The paragraph is talking about how the Greeks had a *mind-body view of medicine*, meaning they believed it was important to treat the mind as well as the body. Since they believed in treating the whole person, that means they emphasized an approach to health that included everything. So you use "included everything" in place of *holistic*. The best match in the answer choices is *comprehensive*. (A) and (C) are wrong because *holistic* doesn't just describe the psychological perspective or just the physiological perspective, but both together. (B) gets the time frame wrong. The Greeks were ancient, not modern. (E) is a trap answer, since it is a type of medicine.

24. **A** The lead words in this sentence are *modern era of pharmacology*, which should lead you to the sixth paragraph. This paragraph talks about how the modern era of pharmacology began, but the question asks what delayed advances in medical science during the modern era. So you need to keep reading into the next paragraph to find the answer: *physicians, unaware of the existence of disease-causing pathogens such as bacteria and viruses, continued to dream up imaginary causative evils*. So the problem was that doctors didn't really know what caused diseases, and that is exactly what (A) says. The other answer choices are wrong because none of them is mentioned anywhere in the passage. Go back and read the second to last paragraph carefully.

SECTION 3

1. **E** If you divide 12 by 4, you'll see that $x = 3$. When you plug $x = 3$ into the term, you'll see that $4(3) + 2 = 12 + 2 = 14$.

2. **B** The shaded region lies in the quadrant where x is positive and y is negative. Given this, you can get rid of (A), (C), and (E). If you plot answers (B) and (D), you'll find that $(1, -2)$ is inside the shaded region, while $(5, -4)$ is not.

3. **A** You need to take this question one step at a time. First, figure out how many batches there are in 12 jars of cookies. If one jar holds 1.5 batches, then 12 jars will hold 12×1.5, or 18 batches. Now you need to figure out how much flour is needed for 18 batches. If you need 6 cups of flour for 1 batch, then for 18 batches you will need 18×6, or 108 cups.

4. **B** There are variables in the answers, so this is a plug-in question. If $n = 2$, then answer choice (B) is the only answer choice that gives you an odd integer: $3(n + 1) = 3(2 + 1) = 3(3) = 9$.

5. **A** Use the midpoint formula $\left(\dfrac{x_1 + x_2}{2}, \dfrac{y_1 + y_2}{2} \right)$: take the average of the x-coordinates of the two points to get the x coordinate of the midpoint, and do the same for the y-coordinates. The midpoint between $(3, 4)$ and $(0, 0)$ is therefore $\left(\dfrac{3 + 0}{2}, \dfrac{4 + 0}{2} \right) =$ $(1.5, 2)$.

6. **C** This question is much easier if you work out the square roots first. You know that $4 = 2$ and $9 = 3$, so you can rewrite the question like this: $2x - 3x = -x$.

7. **B** Use average pies:

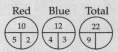

In the first pie you have the number of red parrots sold, which is 5, and the average weight, which is 2. That gives you a total weight of 10 pounds. In the second pie you have the number of blue parrots, which is 4, and the average weight, which is 3. That gives you a total weight of 12. To find the average weight of all the parrots, you need to find the total weight of all the parrots. This is simply the total of the red plus the total of the blue. In the last pie you have the total number of parrots, which is 9, and the total weight of all the parrots, which is 22. This gives you an average weight of $\dfrac{22}{9} = 2\dfrac{4}{9}$.

8. **C** Remember that the perimeter is the sum of all the sides. *FCDE* is a square, so all the sides are equal. Since $\overline{DE} = 3$, each side of the square is 3, so you know that $\overline{CD}$, $\overline{CF}$, and $\overline{EF}$ are all 3. *ABDE* is a rectangle, which means that the opposite sides are equal. $\overline{BC} = 2$, so $\overline{AF} = 2$ also. Along the same lines $\overline{DE}$ equals 3, so that means the opposite side, $\overline{AB}$, also equals 3. Add up all the sides of *ABDE* to find the perimeter: $2 + 2 + 3 + 3 + 3 + 3 = 16$. To find out how much smaller the perimeter of *FCDE* is, just subtract: $16 - 12 = 4$.

9. D The sides of a 45°-45°-90° triangle have a special pattern, which you can find in the gray box at the beginning of every Math section. Each leg of a 45°-45°-90° triangle is equal to the hypotenuse divided by $\sqrt{2}$. Since the hypotenuse in triangle ABC is 8, $\overline{BC}$ must be equal to $\dfrac{8}{\sqrt{2}}$. You can't have a square root on the bottom of a fraction; so multiply the top and the bottom by $\sqrt{2}$. That gives you $\dfrac{8\sqrt{2}}{2} = 4\sqrt{2}$. Meanwhile, you can use Ballparking to eliminate (A) and (B). Since the hypotenuse of a right triangle is always the longest of the three sides, $\overline{BC}$ must be less than 8.

10. D Multiply both sides by 2 to get $\sqrt{x} = 4\sqrt{2}$. Square both sides to get $x = 16 \times 2$. Therefore, $x = 32$. You could also have plugged in the answer choices. For (D), put 32 in for x and ask, does $\dfrac{\sqrt{32}}{2} = 2\sqrt{2}$? Then does $\sqrt{32} = 4\sqrt{2}$? Square both sides to find that it does, so (D) is correct.

11. D If there are variables in the answer choices you should…Plug In! First, cross out that phrase *in terms of b*, because you don't need it. Next, let's plug in a number for a. This is a percent question, so let $a = 100$. Since b is 40% of a, that means $b = 40$. If $a = 100$, then $4a = 400$. Use your calculator to find 40% of 400, which is 160. That's your target answer. When $b = 40$, (D) gives you 160.

12. D According to the function, $f(x) = 2x^2 + 4$. To find the value of $f(4)$, just substitute 4 for x: $f(4) = 2(4)^2 + 4 = 32 + 4 = 36$.

13. B To find the value of $f(3) + f(5)$, find the values of $f(3)$ and $f(5)$ separately: $f(3) = 2(3)^2 + 4 = 22$ and $f(5) = 2(5)^2 + 4 = 54$. So $f(3) + f(5) = 76$. You already know that $f(4) = 36$ from question 15, so you can cross out (A). (C) is the Joe Bloggs answer because Joe simply adds 3 and 5, and it can't be that easy. If you ballpark (D) and (E), putting 10 or 15 in the function will give you a number bigger than 100, and you're looking for 76, so (D) and (E) are too big. That means the answer is (B) by POE.

14. C The formula for the area of a circle is πr^2, so you need to find the radius, r, of the circle. You know that the diameter is 9, and the radius is half of the diameter, so the radius is $\dfrac{9}{2}$. Since there are fractions in the answer choices, you might as well keep the radius as a fraction. Now you replace r with $\dfrac{9}{2}$ in the formula for area of a circle: $A = \pi\left(\dfrac{9}{2}\right)^2 = \dfrac{81}{4}\pi$.

15. D Lines that are parallel have the same slope. In the form $y = mx + b$, m is the slope. So, the slope is -3. Find the line that has a slope of -3 when you rewrite it in the form $y = mx + b$. Only (D) works when you rewrite it: subtract x from both sides to get $\dfrac{1}{3}y = 5 - x$, then multiply both sides by 3 to get $y = 5 - 3x$ or $y = -3x + 5$.

16. **C** $|x| = |2x - 1|$ means that either $x = 2x - 1$ or $-x = 2x - 1$. The solutions to these equations are 1 and $\frac{1}{3}$, respectively. However, you only need to recognize that the equation has two different solutions to establish that the answer is (C).

17. **A** Variables in the answer choices? Plug in! This is a percent question, so make $k = 100$ and $d = 40$. If 40 out of the 100 gallons have been pumped, that equals 40%. So 40% is your target answer. When you plug $k = 100$ and $d = 40$ into the answers, only (A) gives you 40. Plugging in turns a hard question into a much easier question.

18. **C** For this question you need to know the distance formula: $d = r \times t$. There are two good ways to solve this question. One is plugging in the answer choices. The question asks how far Ray and Jane will be from Ray's house when they meet. Start with (C): If they are $56\frac{1}{4}$ miles away from Ray's house, and Ray traveled from home at 30 miles per hour, then you can figure out the time he traveled using the $d = r \times t$ formula (and your calculator): $56\frac{1}{4} = 30 \times t$, $t = 1\frac{7}{8}$. In this case Ray has traveled for $1\frac{7}{8}$ hours. If Jane has traveled $93\frac{3}{4}$ miles and Ray has traveled $56\frac{1}{4}$ miles, then they have traveled a total of 150 miles when they meet. Bingo! You're done. An even easier way is to think about how fast Ray and Jane are traveling put together. You can simply add the rates. Together they are traveling at 80 miles per hour. Therefore you can figure out the time by setting 150 miles $= 80 \times t$. The time is $1\frac{7}{8}$ hours. To find how far Ray has traveled, use the formula one last time: $d = 30 \times 1\frac{7}{8} = 56\frac{1}{4}$.

19. **D** To figure out probability, you need to work with fractions; the total number of possible outcomes goes on the bottom, and the number of desired outcomes goes on the top. To figure out the probability of selecting three blue hammers, you need to figure out the probability of getting a blue hammer each time a hammer is selected. The first time, there are a total of 20 hammers and 10 of them are blue, so the probability of getting a blue hammer is $\frac{10}{20} = \frac{1}{2}$. When the second hammer is selected, there are only 19 hammers left, and only 9 of them are blue. So the probability of getting a blue hammer the second time is $\frac{9}{19}$. When the third hammer is selected, there are a total of 18 hammers left and 8 are blue, so the probability of getting a blue hammer on the third try is $\frac{8}{18} = \frac{4}{9}$. To find the probability of selecting three blue hammers, you need to multiply the three separate probabilities: $\frac{1}{2} \times \frac{9}{19} \times \frac{4}{9} = \frac{2}{19}$. By the way, (A) and (C) are Joe Bloggs answers because he doesn't consider how the probability changes with each event.

20. **C** The question asks which of the answer choices could be x^3. If x is an integer, then the cube root of one of the answer choices should be an integer. You should be able to find the cube root on most scientific calculators. Here, the answer is (C). $2.7 \times 10^{13} = 27 \times 10^{12}$. The cube root of 27 is 3 and the cube root of 10^{12} is 10^4. One easy way to do cube roots on a calculator is to raise the number to the power of $\frac{1}{3}$.

SECTION 4

1. **E** The clue in this sentence is *they hoard water in their leaves*. If the plants are hoarding water, they must be doing it to survive long periods without water. So you can put "without water" in the blank, in which case the best match is *aridity*.

2. **E** The clue for this sentence is *eloquence and logic*. If Liam is eloquent and logical, he must speak "very well"; therefore, you can eliminate (A), (C), and (D) because they're negative. Liam's eloquence and logic probably made it difficult for his *most bitter opponents* to contradict his opinions. The best match for "contradict" is *disagree with*, in (E). It also makes sense that Liam's eloquence and logic made him speak *cogently*.

3. **D** The clue in this sentence is *first deduced from eccentricities in other planets' orbits*. If subatomic particles are being compared to the outer planets, then these particles must have been deduced through their effects on other particles. If you put "deducible" (recycle the clues!) in the first blank, you can get rid of (A). What was deduced about the outer planets and subatomic particles? That they existed. So you can put "existence" in the second blank, which means (D) must be the answer. Notice that it would not make sense to talk about the outer planets' *proximity*, or their *creation;* they are not close by and you really can't deduce creation.

4. **D** The clues in this sentence are *foster* and *in tense situations*. Since *foster* is a positive word, meaning to care for or nurture, a good phrase for the first blank must be positive; you can get rid of (C) because *dissension* is a negative word and (E) because *discourse* is neither positive nor negative. If Miranda wants to foster something good, then in tense situations she is probably compelled to give in to others. You can use "give in" for the second blank, which means you can eliminate (A). Between (B) and (D), you can eliminate (B) because *fortitude* doesn't make any sense in the first blank. Remember, it's often easier to figure out which answer is wrong than to figure out which one is right.

5. **C** The clue in this sentence is *helped bring about a period of prosperity in the United Kingdom*, and the trigger word is *although*, which means the blank must be the opposite of *helped*. If you put "harmful" in the, blank, the best match is *regressive*.

6. **C** I and II are both true. The author tells you that the war was fought for several reasons. The reasons that are mentioned are a desire for Florida and Canada on the part of the U.S.—i.e., *expansionist tendencies*—and as a response to *British actions taken against the U.S.* Statement III is mentioned as an unexpected result of the war, which means it couldn't have been a reason for starting the war.

7. **B** (B) is the best answer. Passage 1 states that the war was in effect a second War of Independence. Passage 2 states that American confidence and nationalism increased after the war. (A) is wrong because Passage 2 mentions battles that each side won. The passage does not give you any information to support (C). (D) may be true, but neither passage speaks about other international conflicts. (E) is more closely related to Passage 1 than Passage 2.

8. **A** In the first passage, the author says the war lacked a *clear winner*. Passage 2 says that there was no *clear victor*. (B), while perhaps true, is incorrect because the impact on British citizens is not mentioned in the passages. (C) can't be supported anywhere in Passage 2. (D) is more relevant to Passage 2 than Passage 1. (E) is incorrect because the second passage doesn't mention how well known the war is in either the United States or Britain. (A) is the best answer.

9. **E** (E) is the best choice. Passage 2 states that although the war was over, Jackson's victory contributed greatly to American confidence and nationalism. (A) contains information from Passage 1 and so is incorrect. (B) is not clearly supported by Passage 2 since no other battles are mentioned. (C) is incorrect because Jackson's victory took place after the treaty was signed. (D) is directly contradicted by the passage which says that the Americans defeated the British at the battle of the Thames.

10. **B** In lines 35–38, the passage says, *Thus he had hardly seen the sea—had seen it only fleetingly... and he had never actually traveled around it.* If you read further, you also learn that Poseidon was waiting for the fall of the world so he would have a quiet moment to make a quick little tour of the sea. From that you can infer that Poseidon is too busy to see his own kingdom. (A) gets it backward. The passage says that Poseidon's trips to visit Jupiter are the only break in the monotony of his job, so if anything, he prefers the trips to his duties, not the other way around. (C) is wrong because the passage doesn't say anything about Poseidon needing silence. (D) contradicts the passage. Poseidon is waiting for the fall of the world so that he can finally get out and make a quick little tour of his domain, which he has never had a chance to see. (E) is wrong because the passage doesn't say anything to suggest that Poseidon is inefficient.

11. **D** The lead word for this question is *dissatisfaction*, so you should go back to the passage and find where it mentions Poseidon's dissatisfaction. Lines 28–31 describe what is chiefly responsible for his dissatisfaction. He does not like to hear the conceptions formed about him: how he *was always riding about through the tides with his trident.* According to the passage, Poseidon doesn't actually get out much at all, so people have the *wrong idea about what he actually does.* This is exactly what (D) says. (A) contradicts the passage. Poseidon was so irritated by the false idea people had that he was always riding around with his trident. (B) is a trap. The question asks what is primarily responsible for Poseidon's dissatisfaction. Although something similar to (B) is mentioned earlier in the passage, it's not chiefly responsible for his dissatisfaction (line 29). Use the lead words to make sure you are reading in the right place. (C) contradicts the passage. Poseidon does the exact same thing every day. That's why he's so bored and unhappy. (E) is incorrect because the passage says that Poseidon actually did most of the bookkeeping tasks himself, leaving little for his assistants to do (lines 5–7).

12. **A** This is a general question, so you only need to know the main idea of the passage. The passage portrays Poseidon as *someone who sits around working out figures* all day and doesn't go out much. Poseidon is also clearly *unhappy* (as you learned in questions 15 and 17), so he is best described as a *dissatisfied bureaucrat.* The other answer choices are wrong because they don't fit the main idea of the passage. Poseidon may be a deity, but the passage doesn't characterize him as being *powerful.* Poseidon is definitely not a *vagabond,* and he's definitely not a *tyrant.* (D) is half-wrong, which means that it's all wrong. Although the description of Poseidon's duties make him sound like an *accountant,* the passage focuses on his unhappiness, not his capabilities as an accountant.

13. **B** This is an EXCEPT question, so you should definitely save it for last. You need to know why Poseidon is unable to change his job, so you need to go back to the passage and find where that is discussed. Remember, you're looking for the reason that is not mentioned, so you can eliminate answer choices that are mentioned. The passage mentions (A) in lines 26–27: *he had been appointed God of the Sea in the beginning, and that he had to remain.* (C) is in lines 18–20: *when a job away from the water was offered to him he would get sick at the very prospect.* (D) is in lines 11–12 (*nothing suited him quite as well as his present position*), and (E) is in lines 17–18 (*Poseidon could in any case only occupy an executive position*). Therefore (B) must be the answer.

14. **E** The best answer is (E). This is a vocab in context (VIC) question, so you should work it like a sentence completion. Go back to the passage, cross out the word *described*, and fill in your own word based on the context of the passage. In this case, a good word to put in the blank is "formed." The only answer choice that is close to "formed" is *traced*, in (E). (A) is tempting, because it seems to describe something that a gull would do, but it does not make sense in context. (Is it possible to *soar* circles? Nope.) (B) is also tempting, because it refers to a more common meaning of the word *described*, but that is not the meaning that is used in the passage. Remember: when a VIC question asks you about a commonly known word, such as *described*, the primary meaning of the word is almost always a trap. Eliminate it! (C) is wrong, because the gull was not *imagining* circles. (This passage is not about the inner lives of animals!) There is no evidence in the passage to support choice (D), which does not match up with "formed."

15. **C** The main idea of the passage is that Poseidon's power, in the form of his job as *God of the Sea*, caused him to be unhappy. Choice (C) matches this idea best. (A) is never implied by the passage. (B) is incorrect because Poseidon's sickness results from a job *offer,* not from a job itself. (D) and (E) are extreme answer choices unsupported by the passage.

16. **D** The lead words in this question are *Frankish law*, which should lead you to the beginning of the passage. According to lines 1–3, *the laws and customs in lands under Frankish domination emphasized the biological function and sexual nature of women....* These lines are perfectly paraphrased in (D), which says that women were *defined in physical or biological terms*. (A) contradicts the passage. Frankish society did not deprive women of opportunities to find personal fulfillment in a variety of roles (lines 3–5). (B) completely contradicts the second half of the passage, which is all about women in religious communities. Always keep in mind the main idea of the passage. (C) contradicts lines 8–9, which tell you that Frankish society did not exploit women's labor. (E) is wrong because lines 9–26 say that women had access to power in several different ways.

17. **B** The lead word in this question is *marriage*, which should lead to lines 18–19. According to these lines, in Frankish society people either *contracted a formal union or entered into a quasi-marriage*. (B) paraphrases this sentence by saying that marriage could be entered into formally or informally. (A) is wrong because the word *only* makes this a must answer, and not likely to be right. Besides, does it make sense to say that marriage *was the only means of exchanging wealth*? (C) implies that marriage *always* raised women to positions of power, which is definitely not the case. (D) is wrong because there is no comparison made in the passage between marriage in primitive society and marriage within Frankish society. Read carefully. (E) is wrong because the passage doesn't say anything about arranged marriages.

18. **E** Go back to the passage, find the word *instrumental*, and cross it out. Then read the sentence and come up with your own word. According to the passage, women *were instrumental in bringing about the merger of the free and slave elements in society* (lines 25–26); therefore, they were *vital* to the process. (C) is a trap answer since it refers to the word *instrument* and because instruments remind you of harmony. The other choices are wrong because they don't make any sense in context.

19. **D** (D) is supported by lines 33–35. (A) is contradicted by the passage, which states that widows were also able to participate. (B) is incorrect. The passage states that monasteries were a refuge for married women, but doesn't say that *many* women sought refuge. (C) is not stated. The writings of medieval nuns are mentioned, but not as a model for "*life in a monastery.*" (E) is beyond the information in the passage.

20. **C** (C) is the best answer. Once the women were *freed from the need to compete for the attention of men* (lines 43–44), they were able to engage in the pursuits mentioned in line 45. (A) and (B) may be true, but are not explicitly stated in the passage as reasons. (D) is not stated in the passage. (E) is beyond the information provided.

21. **A** Lines 9–26 detail the different rights and roles of queens, the wives of magnates, and the wives of members of the working classes. (B), (C), and (D) are wrong because they do not answer the question. They all refer to specific classes of women, not *women in Frankish society*. (E) is never mentioned. (A) is the best answer.

22. **E** Based on the blurb and the passage, (E) is the best answer. The passage lists the role of women in Frankish society, giving information on the Queen, the working class, and the religious population. (A) can be eliminated because there is no dispute in the passage. (B) cannot be correct because no other societies are mentioned. (C) is too extreme and, additionally, no other societies are presented. (D) is incorrect because there is no indication that the passage provides new information.

23. **A** The only answer choice that comes from something stated in the passage is (A). According to lines 43–46, women outside the communities must have had to compete for the attention of men. (B) doesn't make any sense. How can it be true that women outside the religious community were not inclined to any religious feeling at all? Just because they weren't nuns doesn't mean they weren't religious. (C) is wrong because it makes no sense to say that women outside the religious community had less economic power. If anything, the opposite would be true. (D) is too extreme and offensive. ETS would never say that women outside religious communities did not contribute to Frankish culture. (E) is wrong because ETS would never suggest that women had to rely on men for emotional support. Besides, the passage never says that. Read carefully.

24. **C** This is an EXCEPT question, so you should definitely save it for last. ETS is asking how Christianity allowed women to escape from male-dominated society, so you have to go back to the passage and find where that is discussed. Remember, you are looking for the answer choice that is not mentioned. (A) is mentioned in line 51; (B) is mentioned in lines 37–38; (D) is mentioned in lines 43–46; (E) is mentioned in lines 27–30. That leaves (C).

SECTION 5

1. **A** Subtract 10 from both sides to find $2x = 6$, then substitute 6 for $2x$. $6 - 10 = -4$. You could also solve for x, and then plug that into the expression. If $2x = 6$, then $x = 3$. So, $2(3) -10 = 6 - 10 = -4$.

2. **C** If he bought 3 boxes of muffins at $4.50, he would have $3 \times 6 = 18$ muffins. That's not enough muffins. So, he needs to buy 4 boxes of muffins. Each box costs $1.50; so, the cost is $4 \times \$1.50 = \$6.00$.

3. **E** From 1 to 100, there are 50 even integers. If you don't include 2 and 100, then there are only 48.

4. **B** Fill in the angles of the small triangle. Using Fred's theorem, the lower left angle is 70° and the lower right angle is 80°. Since the angles in a triangle must add up to 180°, $a = 180 - 70 - 80 = 30$.

5. **E** Plug 3 into each answer choice, and try to get 6. Eliminate (C) and (D). Now plug 4 into each remaining answer choice, and try to get 13. Eliminate (A) and (B).

6. **B** This is a right triangle with two equal sides, so it is a 45°-45°-90° triangle. $\overline{AC}$ must be the hypotenuse, so the legs are each $\dfrac{10}{\sqrt{2}}$. The legs are also the height and base of the triangle. $A = \dfrac{1}{2}bh$, so $A = \dfrac{1}{2} \times \dfrac{10}{\sqrt{2}} \times \dfrac{10}{\sqrt{2}} = \dfrac{100}{2 \times 2} = 25$.

7. **B** This question has several steps, so don't try to do it all at once. Take it one step at a time. Andrei starts out with 48 baseball caps. In the first step, Andrei gives away 13 caps, so he has 35 left. In the next step, he buys 17 new caps, so now he has 52. Then Andrei gives Pierre 6 caps (46 left) and gets 8 caps in return. In the end, Andrei has 54 baseball caps, which is 6 more caps than he had originally. The percent increase is $\dfrac{change}{original} \times 100 = \dfrac{6}{48} \times 100 = \dfrac{100}{8} = 12.5$. You can also change $\dfrac{6}{48}$ to a percent by typing it into your calculator and multiplying by 100.

8. **D** Draw a line straight up from D in order to divide the shape into a rectangle and a triangle. The area of a 5-by-10 rectangle is 50. To get the area of the triangle, find the length of the base; you already know the height is 5. Use the Pythagorean theorem, or to save time, recognize that this is a 30°-60°-90° triangle because the hypotenuse is twice as long as the shortest side. The base is therefore $5\sqrt{3}$. The area of the triangle is therefore $\dfrac{1}{2} \times 5 \times 5\sqrt{3} = 12.5\sqrt{3}$. The total area of $ABCD$ is therefore $50 + 12.5\sqrt{3}$.

9. 100

Use a Ratio Box:

T-shirts	Sweatshirts	Turtlenecks	Total
2	3	5	10
10	10	10	10
20	30	50	100

You only need to work out the *total* column to figure out the total number of garments that the store sold, which is 100.

10. 81

The formula for the volume of a box is length × width × height. But the question gives you the area of the base of the crate, so you already know that length × width = 18. The volume of the crate, then, is simply the area of the base times the height: $18 \times 4.5 = 81$.

11. .75 or $\frac{3}{4}$

All you have to do is solve for x:

$$5x - 4 = x - 1$$
$$5x = x + 3$$
$$4x = 3$$
$$x = \frac{3}{4} \text{ or } .75$$

12. 8

Using $3b = 2$, solve for b by dividing both sides by 3 to get $b = \frac{2}{3}$. That means $a^{\frac{2}{3}} = 4$. Fractional exponents tell you to use the denominator as the root and use the numerator as a regular exponent. So, $\sqrt[3]{a^2} = 4$. First, cube both sides to find $a^2 = 4^3 = 64$. Next, take the square root of both sides to find $a = 8$.

13. 5, 7, or 11

First, think of a prime number that will make $3b$ greater than 10. How about 5? To see if that fits the other side of the inequality, you need to find the value of $\frac{5}{6} \times 5 = \frac{25}{6}$ which is less than 10, so 5 is one possible value of b. Remember, you only need to find *one* possible value of b.

14. 21

Let's say you have seven dancers: A, B, C, D, E, F, and G. How many different ways can you pair them up? This is a combination question, because A and B is the same pair as B and A, and you don't want to count them twice. Start by finding the number of possible *permutations*: $7 \times 6 = 42$. Finally, divide this number by $2 \times 1 = 2$ (we're looking to fill 2 positions) to eliminate redundant combinations. There are 21 possible combinations.

15. 96

You know that arc BC is a semicircle, which means it's half a circle. So the circumference of the entire circle would be $6\pi \times 2 = 12\pi$. Therefore, the diameter of that circle is 12. Since $\overline{BC}$ is also a side of the rectangle you know that the length of rectangle $ABCD$ is 12. You can also use the same method to find the width. If the length of semicircle CD is 4π, then the circumference of the entire circle would be 8π and the diameter is 8. Since $\overline{CD}$ is the width of the rectangle, you can find the area: length × width = $12 \times 8 = 96$.

16. **5**

$f(6) = 6^2 - 5 = 31$. $f(4) = 4^2 - 5 = 11$. So $f(6) - f(4) = 20$. You then find y such that $y^2 - 5 = 20$. $y^2 = 25$, so $y = 5$ or -5, and the absolute value of $y = 5$.

17. **282**

This is a hard question, so you have to stay on your toes. If the owner buys 3 pounds of each spice, that means she pays the following amounts for each spice:

cinnamon: $\$8 \times 3 = \$24$
nutmeg: $\$9 \times 3 = \$27$
ginger: $\$7 \times 3 = \$21$
cloves: $\$10 \times 3 = \$30$

So she pays a total of $24 + 27 + 21 + 30$, or 102 dollars for 12 pounds of spices. She then sells the spices per *ounce*, so you have to figure out first how many ounces of spices she has. If 1 pound is 16 ounces, then 12 pounds is 12×16, or 192 ounces. She sells all the spices at 2 dollars per ounce, so she makes $192 \times \$2$, or \$384. To figure out her profit, subtract the amount she paid for the spices from the amount she made selling them: $384 - 102 = 282$.

18. **.375 or** $\dfrac{3}{8}$

Since the question doesn't give you a figure, you should draw one. Then plug in some values.

If $EG = \dfrac{5}{3} EF$, then you can make $EF = 3$ and $EG = 5$. That means FG must be 2. If $HF = 5FG$, then $HF = 5(2) = 10$. If $HF = 10$ and $FG = 2$, then $HG = 8$. So $\dfrac{EF}{FG} = \dfrac{3}{8}$ or .375.

SECTION 6

1. **A** The question is essentially asking which of the answers cannot be a value of x. So just try each answer one at a time by plugging the number into each of the two inequalities in the question, and see which one doesn't fit. If $x = -6$, is $-6 + 6 > 0$? No, because zero is not greater than zero. So -6 is the exception.

2. **D** Whenever there are variables in the answers, you should always plug in. Let's say $x = 20$, which means there are 20 ounces of root beer in the pitcher. Next, let's make $y = 3$ and $z = 4$. That means Elsa pours 3 ounces into each of 4 glasses, so she pours a total of 12 ounces. The question asks how much root beer remains in the pitcher, so your target answer is $20 - 12$, or 8. Go to the answer choices and plug in $x = 20$, $y = 3$, and $z = 4$. In answer choice (D), $x - yz = 20 - (3)(4) = 20 - 12 = 8$.

3. **E** Remember that the equation of a line is $y = mx + b$, where m is the slope and b is the y-intercept. POE! The line in the graph has negative slope, so you can eliminate (A) and (B), and it has a positive y-intercept, so you can eliminate (C) and (D).

4. **E** You can plug in this exponent on your calculator as a fraction, or remember that $8^{\frac{4}{3}} = \sqrt[3]{8^4}$, and then use the calculator.

5. **C** Whenever there are variables in the answer choices, you should plug in. Since $x = y + 1$ and $y \geq 1$, you can make $x = 5$ and $y = 4$. In that case, $x^2 - y^2 = 25 - 16 = 9$, so 9 is your target answer. When you plug $x = 5$ and $y = 4$ into the answer choices, only (C) gives you 9. Plugging In turns a hard question into a much easier question.

6. **B** The "Third Side Rule" states that any side must be less than the sum of the other two sides, and greater than the difference between the other two sides. In other words, if the sides are a, b, and c, $|b - c| < a < b + c$. Find the smallest possible value of a. If $a = 1$, then $b + c = 9$. For example, $b = 4$ and $c = 5$. This is illegal, as $|b - c| = a$. If $a = 2$, then $b = 4$ and $c = 4$, so 2 is okay. The largest a can be is 4, because if $a = 5$, then $a = b + c$ and you have violated the Third Side Rule. Thus, the difference between the largest possible value of a and the smallest possible value of a is $4 - 2 = 2$.

7. **C** The Joe Bloggs answer is (E) because Joe simply chooses the greatest number. If you draw three straight intersecting lines through the center of the triangle, you get six regions, so you know that you can have at least six. Therefore, you can eliminate (A). But that was too easy. That means the answer must be 7 or 8. If you don't have time, you can guess between (C) and (D). Here's how you can actually get seven regions:

8. **B** To find out what numbers a could be divisible by, you need to try different values of b. If $b = 1$, then $a = 4(1) + 26 = 30$. In this case, a is divisible by 2, 5, and 6, so you can cross out (A), (C), and (D). If $b = 4$, then $a = 42$, which is divisible by 7, so cross out (E). That only leaves (B), which must be the answer.

9. **2** First, solve for x. Divide both sides of the equation by 3, and you get $x = 4$. Then divide 8 by 4, which gives you 2.

10. **270**

The trick here is that ETS is not asking for the value of a, b, or c. It just wants to know what they add up to. ETS is only testing the Rule of 360. All the angles in the figure make up a circle, so they all add up to 360. The right angle is 90 degrees, so $90 + a + b + c = 360$. Therefore $a + b + c = 270$.

11. **7**

It would definitely help to draw out this question:

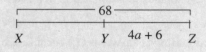

$XY = \frac{1}{2}XZ$, that means Y is the midpoint of $\overline{XZ}$. So $XY = YZ$, and therefore $YZ = \frac{1}{2}XZ$. If $YZ = 4a + 6$ and $XZ = 68$, then $4a + 6 = \frac{1}{2}(68)$. Now just solve for a:

$$4a + 6 = \frac{1}{2}(68)$$
$$4a + 6 = 34$$
$$4a = 28$$
$$a = 7$$

12. **3**

You can solve this question using simultaneous equations because you have two equations with two variables. First, you need to rearrange the equations a bit: $4x + 2y = 24$ divided by 2 on both sides becomes $2x + y = 12$. $\frac{7y}{2x} = 7$, multiplied by $2x$ on both sides, becomes $7y = 14x$. This, divided by 7 on both sides, becomes $y = 2x$, which can be manipulated into $2x - y = 0$. Now you can add the equations:

$$2x + y = 12$$
$$+ \ 2x - y = 0$$
$$\overline{ 4x = 12}$$

So $x = 3$.

13. **9**

Factor the numerator and the denominator into: $\frac{(x-2)(x+3)}{(x-2)(x-6)} = 4$. The $(x - 2)$ cancels out of the top and bottom to leave $\frac{(x+3)}{(x-6)} = 4$. Multiply both sides by $(x - 6)$ to get $x + 3 = 4x - 24$. Subtract x from both sides: $3 = 3x - 24$. Add 24 to both sides: $27 = 3x$. Divide by 3 to get $x = 9$.

14. **.4 or $\frac{2}{5}$**

You can solve this question by setting up a proportion. There are 8 liters in 20 bottles of juice, and you need to find out how many liters are in one bottle. Here's what the proportion looks like: $\frac{8}{20} = \frac{x}{1}$. Solve for x, and your answer is $\frac{2}{5}$ or 0.4.

15. **24**

For this question you need your math vocabulary. First, list all the factors of 12: 1, 2, 3, 4, 6, 12. Make sure you don't miss any factors. Now add up the even factors: $2 + 4 + 6 + 12 = 24$.

16. **25 or 57**

Remember that range represents the possible y values. The trick is to use negative integers for x. $\frac{1}{2^{-5}} - 7 = 2^5 - 7 = 25$. $\frac{1}{2^{-6}} - 7 = 2^6 - 7 = 57$.

17. **18**

To answer this question you have to set up an equation. If the radius of C is r, then the radius of B is $2r$ and the radius of A is $4r$. The formula for the area of a circle is πr^2. Since 84π is the sum of the areas of the circles, this is your equation:

$$\pi r^2 + \pi(2r)^2 + \pi(4r)^2 = 84\pi$$
$$r^2 + 4r^2 + 16r^2 = 84$$
$$21r^2 = 84$$
$$r^2 = 4$$
$$r = 2$$

If $r = 2$, then the radius of C is 2, the radius of B is 4, and the radius of A is 8. $\overline{AC}$ consists of the radius of A, the diameter of B, and the radius of C, so $AC = 8 + 4 + 4 + 2 = 18$.

18. **50**

You don't know how many cars are in the parking lot, so you can plug in a number. Let's say there are 40 cars in the parking lot. Now read through the question; if $\frac{1}{5}$ of the cars are blue, there are 8 blue cars. If $\frac{1}{2}$ of the blue cars are convertibles, there are 4 blue convertibles. If $\frac{1}{4}$ of all the convertibles are blue, and there are 4 blue convertibles, that means there are 16 convertibles all together. The question asks what percent of the cars are neither blue nor convertibles. At this point, the question becomes a group question, and you have a formula for solving such questions:

total = group 1 + group 2 − both + neither. In this question, the total is 40 cars, group 1 is the 8 blue cars, and group 2 is the 16 convertibles. You also know that 4 cars are both blue and convertibles. Now just plug those values into the formula:

$40 = 16 + 8 - 4 + n$. Then solve for n, which equals 20. So 20 out of the total 40 cars are neither blue nor convertibles: $\frac{20}{40} = \frac{1}{2} = 50\%$.

SECTION 7

1. **A** Take care of the answers one by one for this sentence. (B) is not a complete sentence. (C) uses an ambiguous pronoun *their*, (D) uses the ambiguous pronoun *it*, and (E) changes the meaning by suggesting rotary phones are unknown in general.

2. **C** (C) correctly modifies the verb *related* with the adverb *distantly*. (A) is incorrect because in general, *anyone* is a "who" and not a "that." In (B) and (D), to modify *relationships* (a noun) you need *distant* (an adjective) and not *distantly* (an adverb). In (E), to modify *related* (a verb) you need *distantly* (an adverb) and not *distant* (an adjective).

3. **C** The pronoun *you* refers to the person viewing the paintings, and so the next pronoun which refers to that person should also be *you* rather than *people*, as in (B) or *one*, as in (A), (D), and (E).

4. **E** In the original sentence (A), *and* does not imply the contrast between the two types of fat; you need the conjunction *but,* which is used in (E). (B) and (D), each missing a conjunction, are run-on sentences. (C) uses the *-ing* form of the verb, which is not the first choice for a clear sentence.

5. **B** *Knoll* isn't clearly singular or plural, so look for its verb: *sells*. Since *sells* is singular, so too is *Knoll* (neither is underlined). Eliminate (A), (D), and (E) since all are plural. Between (B) and (C), (B) is much more concise and clear.

6. **D** Since there is a semicolon in this sentence, there should be a complete sentence on each side of it. Eliminate (C) since it is not a complete sentence. (B) unnecessarily uses the word *being*, so eliminate it. (E) uses the word *those*, but since it is referring to something in the same sentence it should have been *these*. Between (A) and (D), (A) is redundant, using both *because* and *is why*.

7. **B** A singular noun needs a singular verb (*Increase... has*), so this eliminates choices (A) and (C). In (D), the word *which* follows the name of the rest home, implying that the home caused the nurses to threaten. In (E), *angered the nurses...to have a walkout* sounds awkward and makes little sense.

8. **E** *Galleons* is plural, so eliminate anything that tries to describe them singularly: (A), (B), and (C). (D) also uses the singular pronoun *its*, and so should be eliminated.

9. **D** In both (A) and the original sentence, the pronoun *he* is unclear in its reference: it could mean either Evan or Ken. Only (D) and (E) correct this error, but (E) needlessly uses the *-ing* form of the verbs.

10. **B** The error in the original and (A) uses the incorrect construction *neither...or*. (E) put the final verb in the awkward *-ing* form. (C) and (D) unnecessarily add the word *other*. (B) uses the correct parallel structure: *requires...assigns...does expect*.

11. **A** There is no error in this sentence as written. The idiom, *regard...as,* is the proper construction.

12. **D** The pronoun in (D) disagrees with the noun it replaces; *king* is singular, *them* is plural.

13. **A** *Traveled* is in the wrong tense. The rest of the sentence describes the plot in the present tense, so it should read *travels*.

14. **B** The verb should be *claim* or *have claimed*. There is no reason to use the past perfect, as there is no action occuring after it to warrant this tense.

15. **E** There is no error in the sentence as it is written.

16. **C** The word *rather* is unnecessary in this sentence. If *rather* is omitted, the sentence is concise and clear.

17. **A** This sentence has an idiom error; *comply to* should be *comply with*.

18. **E** There is no error in the sentence as it is written.

19. **A** The subject *field* is singular and the verb *have* is plural. Watch out for prepositional phrases that follow nouns: *of consumer electronics* is only a description of *field*. It is the *field* that *has never been fixed*, not *consumer electronics*.

20. **D** The pronouns shift from *one* to *you*. Correct this error by making both words *one* or *you*.

21. **D** When comparing two people, you must always use the comparative form *the more* rather than the superlative form *the most*, which is only used with three or more things.

22. **E** There is no error in the sentence as it is written.

23. **C** To correct the verb-tense problem in this sentence, change *spent* to *spend* since *target* is in the present tense.

24. **E** There is no error in the sentence as it is written.

25. **C** This sentence contains an error in verb tense: (C) should say *had ridden*. The simple past tense, *rode*, is always used without a helping verb (*has, had, is, was,* for example).

26. **B** You cannot compare *other sculptors* to Rodin's *creations*. It should be: unlike other sculptors' creations, or unlike those of other sculptors.

27. **B** When making a contrary-to-fact statement (Jason did not, in fact, plan ahead), never use a *would* in an *if* clause. Thus, if he *had planned,...he would not have had to write*, etc.

28. **A** The subject is *words*, which is plural, so the verb needs to be plural, as well. Trim the fat—cross out the inessential words, such as prepositional phrases—to find the basics of the sentence: *words...have...meanings*.

29. **E** There is no error in the sentence as it is written.

30. **E** If you try to remove the words *production of* in (A) and *actually did* in (B), you will see that the sentences make no sense without these words. Likewise, if you remove *agreed to* in (C), the sentence loses an important verb. Removing *when* in (D) creates a run-on sentence. (E) is the only available choice.

31. **D** The sentence uses a list of items and all items in that list should be parallel. Only (D) does this correctly. (B) changes the meaning. (C) is in the passive voice, and (E) is awkward with the use of *be building*.

32. **B** The tense *was ever wearing* is used incorrectly in the original sentence. In (C), the use of *could* makes no sense in context. Likewise, in (D), the uses of *would ever be* makes no sense and is awkward. (E) is also awkward and makes no sense.

33. **C** The last paragraph talks of the opening night, and only (C) uses a transition word, *finally,* and introduces the topic of the paragraph.

34. **B** With addition questions, always stick to the main topic. Only (B) does so by discussing the author's responsibilities during the rehearsal. This goes well with the discussion of the production and opening night. In (A), the author's other activities are not applicable to a passage about a theater production. (C) is too broad as this is a personal account of a production. Likewise, (D) and (E) are too broad.

35. **A** The sentence is acceptable as it is now, and therefore (A) is the best choice. (B) and (C) are inferior because the words *being* and *having* are rarely the verb forms found in the best version of the sentence. (D) and (E) each create a sentence that lacks a verb.

SECTION 8

1. **C** To solve for y, begin by adding y to both sides of the equation, which gives you $6 = 3y - 6$. Then add 6 to both sides, which gives you $12 = 3y$. Now divide both sides by 3, and you find that $y = 4$. You can also plug in the answer choices for any question that asks you to solve for a variable: $6 - 4 = 2(4) - 6$.

2. **B** This is what is called a visual perception problem. It's like a maze. Just put your pencil on a and see which other letter you can connect to a without crossing any lines. The only letter you can reach directly is w, all the way in the middle.

3. **C** This is a perfect calculator question. Just add the morning shift and the afternoon shift for each day and see which total is the greatest. The total for both Tuesday and Wednesday (the greatest) is $575 + 595 = 1170$.

4. **A** For this question, you need to know that volume equals *length* $\times$ *width* $\times$ *height*. You know that the volume is 16,500, the depth, or height, is 10, and the length is 75. Just put those numbers in the formula: $16,500 = 75 \times w \times 10$. Use your calculator to solve for w, which equals 22.

5. **D** The idea of *the rest* in this question can save you from doing unnecessary arithmetic. If 40% of the records are jazz, then *the rest*, or 60%, are blues. Since there are 80 records, just use your calculator to find 60% of 80, which is 48.

6. **D** Use a Ratio Box:

Girls	Boys	Total
4	3	7
5	5	5
20	15	**35**

There are 20 girls and 15 boys, so there are 5 more girls than boys.

7. **B** Try plugging in some values for x and see if the graphs include that point. If $x = 0$, then $y = 0$, so, $(0, 0)$ should be a point on the graph. Unfortunately this doesn't eliminate anything. If $x = 1$, then $y = 2$, so, $(1, 2)$ should be a point on the graph. Eliminate (A), (C), (D) and (E).

8. **C** Plug in the answers starting with (C). If the length is 16, the width is half of that. $16 \div 2 = 8$. Area is length $\times$ width. So, does $128 = 16 \times 8$? Yes, so (C) is correct. Alternatively, write an equation. The equation is area = $w \times 2w$. So, $128 = 2w^2$. Divide by 2 to get $64 = w^2$. Take the square root of both sides to find $w = 8$. The length is twice this width, so length = $2 \times 8 = 16$, so the answer is (C).

9. **A** First, notice that the answer choices have mostly a base of 10. So, your goal is to make as many sets of 10 as possible. 10 is 2×5. So, rewrite $5^5 \times 2^2 \times 10^{10}$ as $5 \times 5 \times 5 \times 5 \times 5 \times 2 \times 2 \times 10^{10}$. Rearrange to make sets of 5×2: $(5 \times 2) \times (5 \times 2) \times 5 \times 5 \times 5 \times (10)^{10}$. So, $10 \times 10 \times 5 \times 5 \times 5 \times (10)^{10}$. Rearrange to get the 10s together: $5 \times 5 \times 5 \times 10 \times 10 \times (10)^{10}$. So, $5 \times 5 \times 5 \times (10)^{12}$. Rewrite the 5's using an exponent to get $5^3 \times 10^{12}$.

10. **A** Once again, plug in: Let's say $x = 50$. Now you can translate the question:

$$\frac{10}{100} \times \frac{50}{100} \times 1000 =$$

If you work this out on your calculator, you should get 50 as your target answer. If $x = 50$, the only answer that works is (A).

11. E Because A is the center of one circle and B is a point on the circumference, $\overline{AB}$ is r. $\overline{AD}$ and $\overline{BC}$ are also r. Whenever a line is tangent to a circle, the radius drawn to the point of tangency is perpendicular to the line. So, $\overline{AD}$ and $\overline{BC}$ are perpendicular to $\overline{CD}$. That means $ABCD$ is a square. Plug in for the radius, say $r = 6$. The area of a square is the square of a side, so the area is 36. Plug 6 into the answer choices to see which agrees with 36. Only (E) is 36!

12. E This is a perfect question for PITA (Plugging In the Answers). The question asks for the greatest possible number of 20-ounce boxes. Start with (C). If there are twenty-five 20-ounce boxes, then there are twenty-five 8-ounce boxes because a total of 50 boxes were purchased. In this case, the twenty-five 20-ounce boxes weigh 500 ounces, and the twenty-five 8-ounce boxes weigh 200 ounces; the total is 700 ounces. This is too big because the question says the total weight was less than 600. If (C) is too big, (A) and (B) must also be too big; eliminate all three. If you try (D), the total weight is 604 ounces, which is still too big. So the answer must be (E).

13. D Here's yet another chance to plug in because of the variables in the answer choices. In this case, you have several variables. You should start by plugging in values for x and y, and then work out c. Since $x > y > 0$, let's say $x = 6$ and $y = 3$. Therefore, $c = \frac{1}{6} + \frac{1}{3}$, which equals $\frac{1}{2}$. The question asks for the value of $\frac{1}{c}$, which is the reciprocal of $\frac{1}{2}$, or 2. This is your target answer. If you plug $x = 6$ and $y = 3$ into all of the answer choices, you'll find that only (D) equals 2.

14. D Test the answer choices. The first number in each pair represents x, and the second number represents y. The ordered pair should work in both functions. Try (C) in the first equation: Does $0 = (1) + 2$? No. So, (C) is not the answer. Try (D) in the first equation: Does $4 = (2) + 2$? Yes. So, try (D) in the second equation: Does $4 = (2)^2 + 2 - 2$? Yes. Because (D) works in both equations, it is the correct answer.

15. A This a great opportunity to Plug In The Answers! Start with (C), and plug into $g(x)$ first: $|2^2 - 10| = 6$. Now plug that value into $f(x)$: $\frac{6}{2} + 2 = 5$. Cross out (C). Now the tough decision is whether or not a bigger or smaller value of a is needed. If you aren't sure which way to go, then just try another answer. For instance, plug (D) into $g(x)$: $|6^2 - 10| = 26$. Now into $f(x)$: $\frac{26}{2} + 2 = 15$. You got a lot farther away from the answer, and using (D) resulted in a number much too big! Cross out (E) as well, and try one of the first two answers. Plug (A) into $g(x)$: $\left|\sqrt{2}^2 - 10\right| = 8$. Now into $f(x)$: $\frac{8}{2} + 2 = 6$! (A) is the correct answer.

16. E There are variables in the answer choices, so Plug In. However, you can't plug in a value for all the variables at once because you must follow the rules of geometry. (Makes sense, right? It's the last question in the section.) Let's start by saying $a = 70$ and $b = 60$. Since $PQRS$ is a parallelogram, angle Q must equal angle S, so angle S also equals 60. If you look at the big triangle that contains a and c, you already know that two of the angles are 60 and 70, so the third angle, c, must be 50. You know that PQ and SR are parallel and, using Fred's theorem, you can see that x is a big angle and a is a small angle. So $a + x = 180$. Since $a = 70$, that means $x = 110$. Therefore, your target answer is 110. Plug your values for a, b, and c into the answers and you'll find that (E) equals 110.

SECTION 9

1. **C** In this sentence, the clue is *cover a broad array of subject matters and range of historical eras*. A good word or phrase to use for the blanks would be "varied" or "all different." *Diverse* comes closest to this meaning. Remember to use word roots to help you eliminate answers. *Meritorious* shares the same root as merit, and merit means something of worth. So *meritorious* probably means something similar and does not match our word for the blank.

2. **C** The clues in this sentence are *apparent* and *deceptive*. Professional skiers descend the slopes with apparent "ease," but this apparent ease is deceptive. Therefore, it must actually be difficult to ski well. The best way to complete the second part of the sentence is to say that skiing *requires great effort and intense concentration*. So you can put "great" in the second blank. That gets rid of (E). Then you have "ease" in the first blank, and the best match among the remaining answers is *nonchalance*.

3. **C** The missing word here needs to describe the role of *famous singers* in *popular culture*. Therefore "famous people" would fit well here. (C) is the best choice, since an *icon* is an idol or person who is the object of great attention.

4. **C** The clues here are *unnecessarily*, *trivial information*, and *did not need*. A good word for the blank is "wordy." (A) is incorrect as *winsome* means "charming." (B) is incorrect as *terse* means "concise." (E) is incorrect as *deafening* means "loud." (D) is incorrect as *fallacious* means "wrong." So the best answer is (C), which means "complicated."

5. **D** The blanks here are related to each other, but the clues tell you in what manner. The clues *enjoyed visiting New York* and *did not like all the traveling* indicate that Cecilia had two contradictory feelings— one good, one bad. Look for a contradictory relationship between the blanks. (A) and (C) include two similar words. Cross them off. (B) and (E) have answers that are not really related at all. Only (D) includes two answers that are contradictory, involving both rest and work.

6. **D** In this sentence, putting a word in one blank affects the word in the other blank, so the relationship between the blanks should be determined first. The trigger *despite* suggests that the two blanks have an opposite relationship. (A), (B), (C), and (E) can be eliminated because the words in those choices do not comply with the trigger, thus (D) is the best answer.

7. **E** Go back to the passage, find the word *promulgated*, and cross it out. Then read the sentence and come up with your own word. The first part of the sentence is saying something very positive about Democritus's ideas, so you need a positive word. That means you can eliminate (A), (B), and (D). It doesn't make sense to say that Democritus's ideas were protected, so you can cross out (C). (E) is the only choice left.

8. **A** The best way to find the answer to this question is to use POE. (B) says that Democritus was known for his work in politics, but this is not mentioned anywhere in the passage. (C) says that his ideas were incompatible with those of Galileo and Newton, which contradicts lines 30–32. (D) says that Democritus was unduly credited, but the passage is all about giving him proper credit. (E) says that Democritus was known for his discovery of calculus, which is not said anywhere in the passage, and it also happens to be completely false. That leaves only (A).

9. **D** The obsession referred to in Passage 1 (lines 18–23) is *the search for a level of stark simplicity underlying all the complex richness, texture, and variety of our everyday life*. This idea is paraphrased perfectly in (D), which says that scientists are on a *quest for a simple unifying property of everyday matter*. The passage is talking about something that is today almost an obsession, so (A) and (E) are wrong because they are not about modern science. (B) and (C) are wrong because they aren't mentioned anywhere in the passage. If it's not in the passage, then it's not the right answer.

10. **B** For this question you need to understand the main idea of Passage 1; Democritus's ideas were way ahead of his time. The first passage states *his theory never gained wide acceptance in Greek thought*. The third paragraph tells you that now his ideas are so *embedded in physical thought to the point where few physicists can imagine any other approach*. You know that Democritus's ideas were once not accepted but now they are, making (B) a good answer. You can also use POE on this question. (A) is wrong because the word *dismay* is extreme and the author never says that the early scientists were *narrow-minded*. You can get rid of (C) because the author does not tell you he is surprised or confused by the modern acceptance of Democritus's ideas. Eliminate (D), since the passage does not go on to talk about the uses of atomic theory. (E) is close, but not close enough. The author does not say that they are unwilling to explore other theories, but rather that they cannot even think of them.

11. **C** This is an inference question, since it uses the word *suggests*, which tells you that the author did not directly state the right answer but gave you enough information to draw a conclusion. On inference questions, look for an answer that you can definitely say is right. (C) is supported by the paragraph, since you know that both chemists and physicists dealt with it and its implications. There is no support in the passage for (A), (B), (D), or (E).

12. **A** According to the first sentence of Passage 2, *the discovery that the universe is expanding was one of the great intellectual revelations of the twentieth century*. (B) is wrong because it says that Newton *should have realized*, not that he did. (C) isn't right because the idea was discovered, and is still accepted, by modern physicists. You can eliminate (D) because it's too extreme and contradicts the passage. (E) is also too extreme. That leaves only (A).

13. **C** Go back to Passage 2 and find where Newton is mentioned. According to lines 49–52, *With hindsight, it is easy to wonder why no one thought of it before. Newton, and others, should have realized that a static universe would soon start to contract under the influence of gravity.* So the passage uses Newton as an example of a scientist who might have come up with the idea of an expanding universe before it was actually discovered in the twentieth century. This idea is paraphrased in (C). (A) is wrong because ETS would never suggest that many physicists are ignorant. Remember, ETS has great respect for scientists. Newton wasn't a proponent of the expanding-universe theory, so you can discount (B). (D) contradicts the main idea of the passage. According to the author, the universe is expanding. Go back and read the first sentence of the passage. (E) is wrong because Newton didn't disregard the expanding-universe theory. There was no such theory back then!

14. B According to lines 55–60, *if the universe was expanding at more than a certain critical rate, gravity would never be strong enough to stop it…This is a bit like what happens when one fires a rocket upward from the surface of the earth.* So the rocket is being used as an example of how the force of gravity applies to the idea of an expanding universe. (B) paraphrases this nicely. (A) is wrong because the rocket example is not an implication of the expanding universe. The rocket is simply an example used to illustrate the implications of gravity on the expanding-universe theory. (C) makes no sense. Is the energy released by a rocket similar to the energy released by an entire universe? No way! (D) and (E) contradict the main idea of the author, that the universe is expanding.

15. B The lead words for this question are *Einstein's general theory of relativity*, which should lead you back to lines 70–73. According to these lines, *Even Einstein, when he formulated the general theory of relativity in 1915, was so sure that the universe had to be static that he modified his theory to make this possible.* So the passage is showing you that, among modern scientists, even Einstein wanted to maintain the idea that the universe is static. He even changed his famous theory of relativity to make this possible. This idea is perfectly paraphrased in (B). (A) is wrong because the expanding-universe theory is not the author's theory. (C) is incorrect because the passage says nothing about Einstein's creativity. The point is that Einstein disagreed with the expanding-universe theory. (D) is wrong because the passage never suggests that the expanding-universe theory may not be valid. Just because Einstein didn't agree with the theory doesn't mean it's wrong. (E) strays too far from the main idea. Remember, the passage is about the expanding-universe theory, not about Einstein's relation to Newton.

16. A According to lines 70–81, Einstein wanted so much to maintain the idea of the static universe that he *modified his theory of relativity to make this possible.* The change he made was to introduce the so-called cosmological constant. That is exactly what (A) says. (B) is wrong because Newton didn't have any ideas about the expanding-universe theory. The theory didn't exist back in Newton's time! (C) is off the mark because the cosmological constant is part of Einstein's theory of relativity, not an idea developed by his opponents. Read more carefully. You can't pick (D), either, because Newtonian physics has never been disproved, and this is not suggested anywhere in the passage. Remember, the passage is about the expanding-universe theory. Don't forget the main idea. (E) is incorrect because the passage is not about the mass of all matter. Again, everything in the passage relates to the expanding-universe theory.

17. D Go back to Passage 2, find the word *static*, and cross it out. Then read the sentence and come up with your own word. According to the passage, Einstein and many other modern scientists were against the idea of an expanding universe. That means they must have believed in a universe that wasn't expanding. So you can put "not expanding" in place of static. The best match for "not expanding" in the answer choices is *unchanging*. The other answers are wrong because they don't make any sense in context.

18. **E** Since this question involves both passages, you should definitely do it last. The easiest way to answer this question is to use POE. (A) is only about Passage 1, so you can eliminate it. Newton certainly received credit for his theories, so you can eliminate (B). (C) is wrong because the passages discuss the contribution of the three scientists mentioned, so you can eliminate it. Between (D) and (E), (E) is better because it's a *may* answer, and ETS likes wishy-washy answers.

19. **A** According to the passages, Democritus, an ancient Greek scientist, first came up with the theory of atomism while the expanding-universe theory was first put forth in the twentieth century. That is one clear difference between the two theories, and it also happens to be exactly what (A) says. (B) is wrong because the passages never suggest that atomism is easier to understand than the static universe theory. The comparison is never made. (C) is way off base. There is no mention of politics anywhere in either passage. (D) is too extreme. The passage never says that the theory of atomism had been proven. Remember, it's just a theory. (E) contradicts the main idea of the passage. Modern science has rejected the static universe theory in favor of the expanding-universe theory.

SECTION 10

1. **A** Always check the answer choices to determine if any works with the part of the sentence that is not underlined. (B) is wordy and choppy due to all the phrases that are set off by commas. The phrase *because of complying* in (C) would be stronger if it was *because they comply*. (D) uses *complied by*, which is not the correct idiom. (E) is a run-on. (A) is the strongest choice.

2. **E** Collective nouns, such as *audience*, are singular, so make sure to use singular pronouns and verbs with them. (A) and (C) use *are*—a plural verb. (D) uses the plural *they*. (B) contains a plural verb, *aren't*.

3. **C** There are two idioms at work in this sentence and the answer choices: *distinguish...from* and *between...and*. (A), (B), and (D) all use the idioms incorrectly. (E) is wordier than (C) and fails to maintain parallelism in comparing the two things.

4. **C** As written, the sentence creates a faulty comparison. It states that something is *unlike the Asian people*. Only another people can be contrasted with the Asian people. But this sentence says that the *settlements* were unlike the Asian people, so (A) is incorrect. (B) and (E) have this error as well. (D) fixes the faulty comparison by placing *the Ainu* right after the comma, but *as Caucasians* makes no sense here.

5. **D** An introductory phrase (in this case, *A Mongol emperor associated with ancient Chinese splendor*) must directly precede the noun to which it refers. Only (D) does this by placing Kublai Khan's name right after the comma. (C) is deceptive because it uses his name as a modifier: the noun is actually *army*. In the other three answer choices, the noun is *fleet*, which is not what the introductory phrase is referring to.

6. **A** The sentence is correct as it stands. (B) turns the sentence into a fragment. (C) unnecessarily changes the verb tense by adding *had*. (D) incorrectly changes the comma to a semicolon, which is used only when the word group on each side of it expresses a complete thought. In this case, the phrase following the semicolon is missing a subject. In (E), *and it* is redundant. Therefore, (A) is the best answer.

7. **A** This sentence is correct as it stands. The word *each* is singular, and is therefore correctly referred to by the pronoun *its*. In (B) and (E), the word *their* is plural and therefore incorrect. (C) says each kitten has personalities (plural), and (D) unnecessarily adds the word *which*. Thus, (A) is the best answer.

8. **B** (B) is the best answer. The clause which precedes the comma and the one after the comma can stand as complete sentences, and must therefore be separated by a period, a semicolon, or a comma followed by a conjunction. (B) correctly uses this last option. Both (A) and (D) create comma splices, while (C) and (E) add unnecessary words which change the meaning of the sentence.

9. **E** (E) correctly uses the word *that* to introduce a description of what the storm did. The semicolon is incorrect in (A) because the words following it are missing a subject and therefore express an incomplete thought. In (B), *and it* is an unnecessary addition. Answers containing *-ing* verbs, such as (C) and (D), are rarely the best choice, leaving (E) as the best answer.

10. **D** The best choice is (D). The subject is *effects*, so the verb must be plural (*were*). (A) uses the past perfect for no reason; the simple past tense (D) is sufficient here. The verb in (C) is singular and so does not agree with the subject. The word *being* (B) makes the sentence a fragment. (E) uses the wrong pronoun, thereby changing the meaning of the second part of the sentence.

11. **B** (B) is the best answer. *Mr. Peters* has to follow the comma, since the opening modifier describes him, not *the observation*, as in (A) and (E), or the act of *observing*, as in (C). Choice (D) doesn't actually contain a main verb.

12. **C** The best answer is (C). (A), (B), and (E) are passive. (C) also correctly uses the construction *not only...but also*, while (D) incorrectly says *not only...and...too*.

13. **B** The original sentence, (A), and the sentence in (D) are written in the passive voice. In (C), the verb is in the past tense but needs to be in the future. (E) uses the future progressive tense, which unnecessarily adds –*ing*. Only (B) is clearly worded.

14. **D** The pronoun *them* is incorrect in the original, (A), and in (B). The pronoun *those* should refer to the streets in Belgium: this appears in both (C) and (D), although (C) unnecessarily adds the word *when*. (E) is a comma splice, a form of run-on sentence.

22

Practice Test 3

ESSAY
Time — 25 minutes

Turn to Section 1 of your answer sheet to write your ESSAY.

The essay gives you an opportunity to show how effectively you can develop and express ideas. You should, therefore, take care to develop your point of view, present your ideas logically and clearly, and use language precisely.

Your essay must be written on the lines provided on your answer sheet—you will receive no other paper on which to write. You will have enough space if you write on every line, avoid wide margins, and keep your handwriting to a reasonable size. Remember that people who are not familiar with your handwriting will read what you write. Try to write or print so that what you are writing is legible to those readers.

You have twenty-five minutes to write an essay on the topic assigned below. DO NOT WRITE ON ANOTHER TOPIC. AN OFF-TOPIC ESSAY WILL RECEIVE A SCORE OF ZERO.

Think carefully about the issue presented in the following excerpt and the assignment below.

> America's founders thought deeply and debated at length whether to accept, question, or reject Great Britain's authority over the colonies. In the Declaration of Independence they wrote, "when a long train of abuses…evinces a design to reduce them under absolute despotism, it is their right, it is their duty, to throw off such government."

Assignment: What is your view of the claim that questioning authority makes a society stronger, not weaker? Plan and write an essay in which you develop your point of view on this issue. Support your position with reasoning and examples taken from your reading, studies, experience, or observations.

DO NOT WRITE YOUR ESSAY IN YOUR TEST BOOK. You will receive credit only for what you write on your answer sheet.

BEGIN WRITING YOUR ESSAY IN SECTION 1 OF THE ANSWER SHEET.

**If you finish before time is called, you may check your work on this section only.
Do not turn to any other section in the test.**

SECTION 2

Time — 25 minutes

20 Questions

Turn to Section 2 of your answer sheet to answer the questions in this section.

Directions: For this section, solve each problem and decide which is the best of the choices given. Fill in the corresponding oval on the answer sheet. You may use any available space for scratchwork.

Notes

1. The use of a calculator is permitted.

2. All numbers used are real numbers.

3. Figures that accompany problems in this test are intended to provide information useful in solving the problems. They are drawn as accurately as possible EXCEPT when it is stated in a specific problem that the figure is not drawn to scale. All figures lie in a plane unless otherwise indicated.

4. Unless otherwise specified, the domain of any function f is assumed to be the set of all real numbers x for which $f(x)$ is a real number.

Reference Information

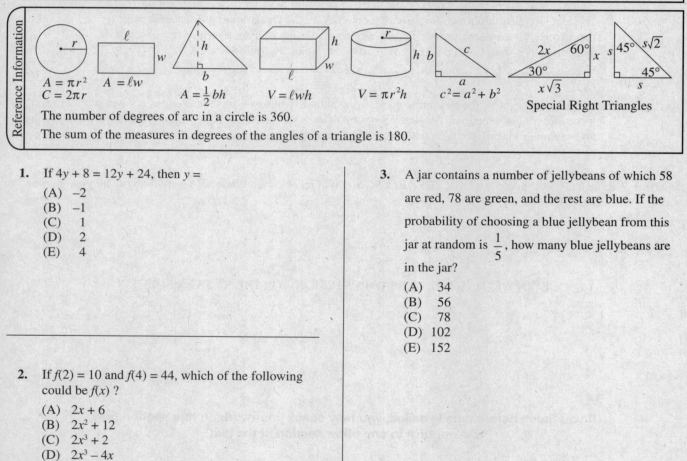

$A = \pi r^2$
$C = 2\pi r$

$A = \ell w$

$A = \frac{1}{2}bh$

$V = \ell wh$

$V = \pi r^2 h$

$c^2 = a^2 + b^2$

Special Right Triangles

The number of degrees of arc in a circle is 360.

The sum of the measures in degrees of the angles of a triangle is 180.

---

1. If $4y + 8 = 12y + 24$, then $y =$

    (A) −2
    (B) −1
    (C) 1
    (D) 2
    (E) 4

2. If $f(2) = 10$ and $f(4) = 44$, which of the following could be $f(x)$?

    (A) $2x + 6$
    (B) $2x^2 + 12$
    (C) $2x^3 + 2$
    (D) $2x^3 - 4x$
    (E) $3x^2 - x$

3. A jar contains a number of jellybeans of which 58 are red, 78 are green, and the rest are blue. If the probability of choosing a blue jellybean from this jar at random is $\frac{1}{5}$, how many blue jellybeans are in the jar?

    (A) 34
    (B) 56
    (C) 78
    (D) 102
    (E) 152

GO ON TO THE NEXT PAGE

4. If the nth term in a sequence is 3×2^n, what is the 10th term in the sequence?

(A)   60
(B) 1,024
(C) 1,536
(D) 3,072
(E) 6,144

5. If 3 more than x is 2 more than y, what is x in terms of y ?

(A) $y - 5$
(B) $y - 1$
(C) $y + 1$
(D) $y + 5$
(E) $y + 6$

6. $ABCD$ is a quadrilateral such that $AB = BC$, $AD = \dfrac{1}{2}CD$, $AD = \dfrac{1}{4}AB$. If $BC = 12$, what is the perimeter of $ABCD$?

(A) 44
(B) 42
(C) 40
(D) 36
(E) 33

7. If $a, b, c,$ and d are consecutive multiples of 5, where $a < b < c < d$, what is the value of $(a - c)(d - b)$?

(A) −100
(B)   −25
(C)   0
(D)   50
(E)   100

8. Which of the following is equivalent to $-9 \le 3b + 3 \le 18$?

(A) $-4 \le b \le 5$
(B) $-4 \le b \le 6$
(C) $-3 \le b \le 5$
(D) $3 \le b \le 5$
(E) $4 \le b \le 6$

9. A store sells boxes of 6 light bulbs for $30 each, and boxes of 12 light bulbs for $48 each. The price per bulb is what percent less when purchased in a box of 12 than in a box of 6 ?

(A) 80%
(B) 75%
(C) 50%
(D) 25%
(E) 20%

10. What is the domain of $g(x) = \sqrt{x^2 + 9}$?

(A) $x > -9$
(B) $x > -3$
(C) $|x| < 3$
(D) $|x| > 3$
(E) All real numbers

GO ON TO THE NEXT PAGE

Questions 11-12 refer to the following table, which shows the amount of rain that fell during a 30-day period in 1998.

Rainfall	
Rainfall (in inches)	Number of Days
0	17
1	5
2	3
3	3
4	2

11. What is the mode of the amount of rainfall, in inches, over these 30 days?

(A) 0
(B) 1
(C) 2
(D) 3
(E) 4

12. If 200 inches of rainfall were expected to fall during all of 1998, what percent of the expected yearly rainfall was reached during this 30-day period?

(A) 56%
(B) 42%
(C) 28%
(D) 14%
(E) 7%

13. Line l contains points (3, 2) and (4, 5). If line m is perpendicular to line l, then which of the following could be the equation of line m ?

(A) $y = -\dfrac{1}{5}x + 3$

(B) $y = -\dfrac{1}{3}x + 5$

(C) $y = -3x + 5$

(D) $y = 5x + \dfrac{1}{3}$

(E) $y = \dfrac{1}{3}x + 5$

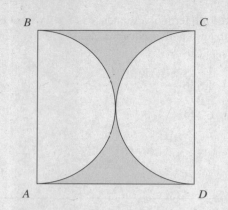

14. In the figure above, $ABCD$ is a square with sides of length 2. The square contains two semicircles with diameters $\overline{AB}$ and $\overline{CD}$. What is the sum of the areas of the two shaded regions?

(A) $2 - \dfrac{\pi}{2}$

(B) $2 - \pi$

(C) $4 - \pi$

(D) $4 - 2\pi$

(E) $4 - \dfrac{\pi}{4}$

15. Jennifer ran from her house to school at an average speed of 6 miles per hour and returned along the same route at an average speed of 4 miles per hour. If the total time it took her to run to the school and back was one hour, how many minutes did it take her to run from her house to school?

(A) 16
(B) 18
(C) 20
(D) 22
(E) 24

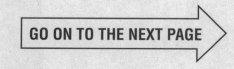
GO ON TO THE NEXT PAGE

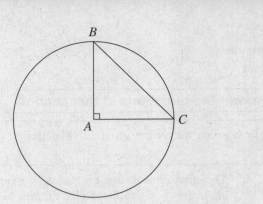

16. In the figure above, $\overline{AC}$ and $\overline{AB}$ are radii of the circle with center A. If $\triangle ABC$ has area 18, what is the circumference of the circle?

(A) 6π
(B) 9π
(C) 12π
(D) 18π
(E) 36π

17. If a circle has an area that is half its circumference, what is its radius?

(A) $\dfrac{1}{2}$

(B) 1

(C) 4

(D) π

(E) 2π

18. If Marta is assigned to Project A, then the project will be completed on time. Which of the following can be concluded?

(A) If Project A is completed on time, then Marta must have been assigned to Project A.
(B) If Marta was assigned to Project B, then Project A will not be completed on time.
(C) If Project A is not completed late, then no one other than Marta was assigned to Project A.
(D) If Marta is not assigned to Project A, then Project A will be completed late.
(E) If the project is completed one week late, then Marta was not assigned to Project A.

19. The lengths of two sides of a triangle are 5 and 7. If the length of the third side is an integer, what is the least possible perimeter of the triangle?

(A) 12
(B) 13
(C) 14
(D) 15
(E) 17

20. If $x^2 - x = 12$ and $y^2 - y = 12$, what is the greatest possible value of $x - y$?

(A) 0
(B) 4
(C) 7
(D) 12
(E) 24

STOP
If you finish before time is called, you may check your work on this section only.
Do not turn to any other section in the test.

SECTION 3
Time — 25 minutes
24 Questions

Turn to Section 3 of your answer sheet to answer the questions in this section.

Directions: For each question in this section, select the best answer from among the choices given and fill in the corresponding circle on the answer sheet.

Each sentence below has one or two blanks, each blank indicating that something has been omitted. Beneath the sentence are five words or sets of words labeled A through E. Choose the word or set of words that, when inserted in the sentence, best fits the meaning of the sentence as a whole.

Example:

Hoping to ------- the dispute, negotiators proposed a compromise that they felt would be ------- to both labor and management.

(A) enforce . . useful
(B) end . . divisive
(C) overcome . . unattractive
(D) extend . . satisfactory
(E) resolve . . acceptable   Ⓐ Ⓑ Ⓒ Ⓓ ●

---

1. While Sarah may have been rather quiet, she was by no means a -------, for she often spent evenings with other people and considered that time to be quite -------.

    (A) recluse . . enjoyable
    (B) conservative . . worthless
    (C) reformer . . irritating
    (D) barbarian . . confusing
    (E) critic . . demanding

2. One of the serious ------- of meteorology is that natural weather patterns cannot be ------- in the laboratory for investigation.

    (A) successes . . achieved
    (B) complexities . . broadened
    (C) premises . . accredited
    (D) limitations . . recreated
    (E) advantages . . analyzed

3. The playwright ------- realism and fantasy in her work so well that the audience is never sure whether the characters' experiences are ------- or imaginary.

    (A) integrates . . actual
    (B) mingles . . congenial
    (C) combines . . apparent
    (D) delineates . . indistinct
    (E) exposes . . verifiable

4. The improvements made on the new automobile are largely -------; although the exterior has been changed, the engine has remained unchanged.

    (A) mechanical   (B) superficial   (C) economical
    (D) redundant   (E) expensive

5. Some educators view television as an entirely ------- presence in society, virtually disregarding the idea that television has the potential to be -------.

    (A) pernicious . . understood
    (B) auxiliary . . discontinued
    (C) deleterious . . beneficial
    (D) cohesive . . informative
    (E) stabilizing . . veiled

6. Zora Neale Hurston's talent at convincing her readers to believe in the world as she describes it in her novels is due to her ability to create extremely ------- characters.

    (A) unsavory   (B) demonstrative   (C) ambiguous
    (D) unilateral   (E) credible

7. It is often said that seventeenth-century literature is ------- to today's readers, especially when compared with more recent works, which introduce fewer problems of -------.

    (A) significant . . interpretation
    (B) impractical . . tradition
    (C) inscrutable . . comprehension
    (D) opaque . . contemplation
    (E) instructional . . agreement

8. Drew was a ------- boss, one who gave generous holiday bonuses and often overlooked minor lapses in judgment.

    (A) miserly   (B) supercilious   (C) disingenuous
    (D) munificent   (E) gregarious

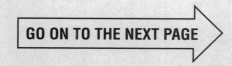
GO ON TO THE NEXT PAGE

The passages below are followed by questions based on their content. Answer the questions on the basis of what is stated or implied in the passage and in any introductory material that may be provided.

Questions 9-10 are based on the following passage.

The theory that a meteor struck the Earth 65 million years ago, blanketing the earth in dust and killing the dinosaurs, has recently been challenged. A layer of
Line iridium has been identified in sites worldwide and linked
5 with this event. Scientists concluded that the meteor that caused a large crater in Mexico also wiped out the dinosaurs. New evidence suggests otherwise. Current researchers note that many fossils that contain glass globules from the meteor were deposited immediately
10 after impact, but are separated by a layer of shale and limestone from the iridium. Recent estimates that the shale and limestone would take 300,000 years to form suggest, instead, a second, later iridium-laden meteor.

9. The structure of the passage could best be described in what way?

(A) A theory is explained in depth and supported by additional information.

(B) A theory is explained and discredited based on inaccurate data.

(C) A theory is explained, a flaw is exposed, and another theory espoused.

(D) A theory is explained and its many flaws are exposed.

(E) A theory is explained and the proponents of that theory are then criticized.

10. The primary purpose of the passage is to

(A) estimate the time when the dinosaurs became extinct

(B) systematically debunk alternatives to the current theory explaining dinosaurs' extinction

(C) note the contents of meteors, particularly iridium and glass globules

(D) explain conclusively what caused the extinction of the dinosaurs

(E) propose a possible cause of the extinction of the dinosaurs

Questions 11-12 are based on the following passage.

The author of the Pledge of Allegiance was not an American political icon such as Thomas Jefferson or Benjamin Franklin, but rather an employee of *Youth's*
Line *Companion* magazine named Francis Bellamy. Written
5 in 1892, the Pledge was part of a larger program to commemorate the arrival of Christopher Columbus in the Americas, thereby inspiring allegiance in a country recuperating from the horrors of civil war. Later revisions added the words "under God" as a reaction to "godless"
10 communism. In historical perspective, then, the Pledge of Allegiance assumes a surprisingly fluid meaning considering it has been recited for more than one hundred years.

11. The author of the passage mentions Thomas Jefferson and Benjamin Franklin in order to

(A) suggest authors who might have written a better Pledge of Allegiance

(B) emphasize the relative obscurity of the author of the Pledge of Allegiance

(C) provide more information about the origin of the Pledge of Allegiance

(D) commemorate their contributions to American political writings

(E) imply that they inspired Francis Bellamy to write the Pledge of Allegiance

12. It can be most reasonably inferred from the passage that

(A) the Pledge of Allegiance unified Americans after the Civil War

(B) the Pledge of Allegiance has not retained the original phrasing as written by Francis Bellamy

(C) Francis Bellamy would have supported the addition of "under God" to the Pledge of Allegiance

(D) the phrase "under God" sparked great controversy about reciting the Pledge of Allegiance

(E) an earlier version of the Pledge of Allegiance referred to the arrival of Christopher Columbus

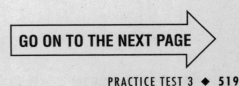
GO ON TO THE NEXT PAGE

Questions 13-24 are based on the following passage.

In this excerpt from the book The Brain *written in 1984, Dr. Richard M. Restak discusses two different schools of thought in brain research: those who believe there is a strong relationship between the brain and the mind, and those who do not. By citing various neuroscientists, Restak conveys the struggle many scientists have with the issue.*

Two years before his death at age eighty-four, neurosurgeon Wilder Penfield was writing his final book, *The Mystery of the Mind*. During moments away from his
Line desk, Penfield continued to ponder the theme of his book:
5 the relationship of mind, brain, and science.

One weekend while at his farm outside of Montreal, Penfield began painting on a huge rock. On one side, he painted a Greek word for "spirit" along with a solid line connecting it to an Aesculapian torch, which represented
10 science. The line continued around the rock to the other side, where he drew an outline of a human head with a brain drawn inside, which contained, at its center, a question mark. At this point, Penfield was satisfied: brain studies, if properly conducted, would lead inevitably to an
15 understanding of the mind.

But as Penfield progressed with his book, he became less certain that the study of the brain, a field in which he had done pioneering work earlier in his career, would ever lead to an understanding of the mind. Finally, six months
20 before he died, he reached a conclusion.

Donning six sweaters to protect himself from the harsh Canadian wind, Penfield returned to the rock and, with shaking hands, converted the solid line connecting the spirit and brain into an interrupted one. This
25 alteration expressed, in a form for all to see, Penfield's doubts that an understanding of the brain would ever lead to an explanation of the mind.

Among neuroscientists, Penfield is not alone in undergoing, later in life, a change in belief about the
30 relationship of the mind to the brain. Sir John Eccles, a Nobel Prize winner, has teamed up in recent years with Karl Popper. Together they have written *The Self and Its Brain*, an updated plea for dualism: the belief that the mind and the brain are distinct entities. Brain
35 researcher Karl Pribram is currently collaborating with physicist David Bohm in an attempt to integrate mind and consciousness with ideas drawn from quantum physics. Together they are searching for a model capable of integrating matter and consciousness into a holistic
40 worldview.

Why should these brain researchers have a change of heart late in their careers about the adequacy of our present knowledge of the brain to provide an "explanation" for mind and consciousness? What compels
45 them toward a mystical bent?

Interest and enthusiasm regarding the brain can't be the only explanations why neuroscientists are susceptible to a mystical bent, since only a small number of them end up waxing philosophical. But the nature of their
50 research and the kinds of questions asked undoubtedly contribute to later "conversions." Penfield's work involved neurosurgical explorations into the temporal lobes. In response to Penfield's electrical probe, his patients reported familiar feelings and vivid memories.
55 In essence, these patients reported experiences that did not correspond to actual events in the operating theater, but rather were the result of direct stimulation of neural tissues. Does this mean that our conscious experience can be understood solely in terms of electrical impulses?

60 Researchers like Wilder Penfield and Roger Sperry are examples of brain researchers who have become disillusioned with claims that the mind can "be explained" in terms of brain functioning. They have revolted against what another neuroscientist calls the
65 "Peter Pan school of neuroscience" with its "bloodless dance of action potentials" and its "hurrying to and fro of molecules."

Common to all these brain scientists is a willingness to adapt innovative attitudes as well as pursue
70 unorthodox lines of inquiry. They have also been open to transcendental influences. Eccles, for instance, had a "sudden overwhelming experience" at age eighteen that aroused an intense interest in the mind-brain problem. He attributes his choice of career in the neurosciences to this
75 experience.

Brain researchers with a "mystical bent" have also been comfortable sharing their findings and ideas with specialists in other fields. Penfield's book, *The Mystery of the Mind*, was encouraged by Charles Hendle,
80 professor of philosophy at Yale. It was a much-needed encouragement, since the other neuroscientists to whom Penfield had shown his early draft discouraged him from proceeding with the project. To them, Penfield's speculative leap from neurophysiologist to philosopher
85 was "unscientific." At Hendle's urging, Penfield proceeded to detail "how I came to take seriously, even to believe, that the consciousness of man, the mind, is something not to be reduced to brain mechanisms."

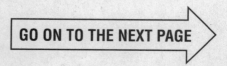

13. The "solid line" painted by Penfield (line 8) represents

(A) Penfield's desire to link art and science within one discipline
(B) Penfield's reluctance to make any connections between the mind and the brain
(C) Penfield's conclusion that experiments had proven the link between the brain and the mind
(D) an example of Penfield's mental confusion
(E) Penfield's confidence that the mind would eventually be understood through study of the brain

14. It can be inferred from the passage that Pribram and Bohm decided to collaborate because

(A) they felt that a holistic world view could explain quantum physics
(B) they felt that consciousness might better be understood by unorthodox avenues of inquiry
(C) they wanted to expand on the findings of Eccles and Popper
(D) new findings in the field of quantum physics had convinced them that there is no relationship between matter and consciousness
(E) Penfield's book contained factual errors that they felt they must correct

15. The word "bent" in line 45 most nearly means

(A) inclination
(B) distortion
(C) determination
(D) talent
(E) revelation

16. It can be inferred that skeptics believe that advocates of the "Peter Pan school of neuroscience"

(A) succeed in creating a definitive technique for neurosurgeons to follow
(B) fail to take brain study seriously as a field of endeavor
(C) misunderstand the importance of brain waves in the study of the mind
(D) rely too much on the physiological to explain the workings of the mind
(E) believe that abstract aspects of the mind cannot be explained scientifically

17. The main distinction between orthodox and unorthodox neuroscientists is that

(A) the former believe in enlarging the pool of research topics, while the latter tend to stay within their own field
(B) the latter seek out alternative sources for research, while the former only regard those with a mystical bent as worthy
(C) the former encourage "unscientific" research, while the latter concern themselves primarily with mystical phenomena
(D) the latter regard the former with contempt, while the former consider the latter to be colleagues
(E) the former tend to ignore research that is not based in science, while the latter support exploration that calls on various sources

18. In line 49, "waxing" most nearly means

(A) shining
(B) waning
(C) becoming
(D) increasing
(E) sealing

19. Penfield's doubts about the validity of the brain-mind connection were tangibly represented by

(A) an Aesculapian torch
(B) a broken line
(C) a Greek word
(D) a large painted rock
(E) a solid line

20. Which of the following statements is NOT supported by the information in the passage?

(A) Speculation about the mind-brain connection extends across disciplines.
(B) Some brain scientists are not unwilling to try avant-garde approaches.
(C) It is not unusual for brain researchers to have a late-in-life change of heart.
(D) Penfield expressed deep doubts about the correctness of his early conclusions.
(E) Properly executed brain studies lead to a full understanding of the mind.

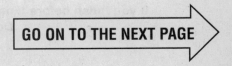
GO ON TO THE NEXT PAGE

21. According to the passage, during neurosurgical exploration, Penfield's patients

    (A) behaved like victims of brain traumas
    (B) asked their doctor probing questions
    (C) followed their impulses while under sedation
    (D) perceived events that had never happened
    (E) clearly recalled things unrelated to their surroundings

22. The author mentions Eccles and Popper (lines 30 and 32) in order to

    (A) prove definitively that neuroscience is incapable of explaining the mind
    (B) give examples of other neuroscientists who altered their convictions about the brain-mind link
    (C) indicate that only through teamwork can dualism be fully explained
    (D) contrast their beliefs about the relation between the brain and the mind with those of Penfield
    (E) present concrete evidence that the brain and the mind are distinct entities

23. An orthodox neuroscientist is most likely of the opinion that

    (A) consciousness can be understood in terms of electrical impulses
    (B) the Greeks were correct about the relation of the spirit to scientific inquiry
    (C) mysticism and philosophy are useful disciplines for scientists
    (D) transcendentalist concepts are influential in brain research
    (E) quantum physics has great potential in the study of consciousness

24. Which of the following statements is NOT supported by information in the passage?

    (A) Penfield gradually lost the convictions which had earlier satisfied him.
    (B) Pribam and Bohm worked together to investigate the relation of physics to neuroscience.
    (C) There may be more to the workings of the body and the mind than can be explained by science.
    (D) Charles Hendle was Penfield's teacher when the latter was an undergraduate.
    (E) Penfield used the results of brain experiments to try to form a theory of the mind.

STOP
If you finish before time is called, you may check your work on this section only.
Do not turn to any other section in the test.

NO TEST MATERIAL ON THIS PAGE.

SECTION 4

Time — 25 minutes

35 Questions

Turn to Section 4 of your answer sheet to answer the questions in this section.

Directions: For each question in this section, select the best answer from among the choices given and fill in the corresponding circle on the answer sheet.

The following sentences test correctness and effectiveness of expression. Part of each sentence or the entire sentence is underlined; beneath each sentence are five ways of phrasing the underlined material. Choice A repeats the original phrasing; the other four choices are different. If you think the original phrasing produces a better sentence than any of the alternatives, select choice A; if not, select one of the other choices.

In making your selection, follow the requirements of standard written English; that is, pay attention to grammar, choice of words, sentence construction, and punctuation. Your selection should result in the most effective sentence—clear and precise, without awkwardness or ambiguity.

EXAMPLE:

Laura Ingalls Wilder published her first book <u>and she was sixty-five years old then</u>.
(A) and she was sixty-five years old then
(B) when she was sixty-five
(C) at age sixty-five years old
(D) upon the reaching of sixty-five years
(E) at the time when she was sixty-five

Ⓐ ● Ⓒ Ⓓ Ⓔ

---

1. Radio broadcasts once were the most popular form of entertainment; families used to <u>gather around the radio at night for their favorite programs</u>.

   (A) gather around the radio at night for their favorite programs
   (B) gather around to listen to its favorite programs
   (C) gather around the radio at night for they're favorite programs
   (D) gather around to listen to it's favorite programs
   (E) gather around the radio at night for there favorite programs

2. Concluding the final session of the communications class, <u>speak slowly and enunciate clearly while making eye contact was the recommendation Ms. Benton gave her students</u>.

   (A) speak slowly and enunciate clearly while making eye contact was the recommendation Ms. Benton gave her students
   (B) speaking slowly and enunciating clearly while making eye contact were what Ms. Benton told her students to do
   (C) her students were advised by Ms. Benton to speak slowly and enunciate clearly while making eye contact
   (D) speak slowly and enunciate clearly while making eye contact, recommendations made by Ms. Benton, were what her students should do
   (E) Ms. Benton recommended that her students speak slowly and enunciate clearly while making eye contact

3. First President George Washington is credited <u>to breed</u> the first mules in the United States using a jack and a jennet presented to him by the King of Spain in 1786.

   (A) to breed
   (B) since he bred
   (C) by breeding
   (D) with breeding
   (E) having bred

4. Classical composers who influenced the genre of the string quartet range from <u>Haydn's credit for its invention in the eighteenth century, as well as</u> Shostakovich.

   (A) Haydn's credit for its invention in the eighteenth century, as well as
   (B) Haydn, who in the eighteenth century was inventing it, and
   (C) Haydn, who is credited with its invention in the eighteenth century, to
   (D) Haydn's invention in the eighteenth century, for which he received the credit, and
   (E) its invention by Haydn, who received the credit in the eighteenth century, to

GO ON TO THE NEXT PAGE

5. A major cause of stress in school is <u>where seniors must manage not only academic requirements and sports schedules, but also</u> standardized testing and college applications, during the first semester.

(A) where seniors must manage not only academic requirements and sports schedules, but also

(B) seniors need to manage not only academic requirements and sports schedules, but also

(C) where seniors must manage not only academic requirements and sports schedules, and also

(D) when seniors must manage both academic requirements and sports schedules, but also

(E) the management by seniors of not only academic requirements and sports schedules, but also

6. Alaska, the largest state by far with nearly 2.5 times the land area of the next largest <u>state, which has one of the smallest populations</u> with only 650 thousand residents.

(A) state, which has one of the smallest populations

(B) state, that has one of the smallest populations

(C) state and has one of the smallest populations

(D) state, has one of the smallest populations

(E) state, will have one of the smallest populations

7. Stars other than our sun, <u>astronomers have discovered, have</u> planets the size of Jupiter in orbit about them.

(A) astronomers have discovered, have

(B) which, astronomers have discovered, have

(C) having possibly, according to the discovery of many astronomers

(D) there are some astronomers who have discovered that they may have

(E) astronomers are discovering they have

8. <u>She was one of the most famous mystery writers of the century, and Dorothy L. Sayers</u> also built one of her most famous novels around the question of higher education for women in the pre-war era.

(A) She was one of the most famous mystery writers of the century, and Dorothy L. Sayers

(B) One of the most famous mystery writers of the century, Dorothy L. Sayers

(C) Famous mystery writer of the century that she was, Dorothy L. Sayers

(D) Dorothy L. Sayers has been one of the most famous mystery writers of the century, and she

(E) Being one of the most famous mystery writers of the century, Dorothy L. Sayers

9. In addition to having more natural resources, <u>the land area of the United States is significantly larger than most other countries</u>.

(A) the land area of the United States is significantly larger than most other countries

(B) the land area is significantly larger than most other countries for the United States

(C) the United States also has significantly more land area than most other countries

(D) the United states has more land area also than most other significant countries

(E) the land area of other countries is less than that of the United States

10. Some students of literary criticism consider the theories of Blaine <u>to be a huge advance in modern critical thinking and questions</u> the need to study the discounted theories of Rauthe and Wilson.

(A) to be a huge advance in modern critical thinking and questions

(B) as a huge advance in modern critical thinking and question

(C) as being a huge advance in modern critical thinking and questioned

(D) a huge advance in modern critical thinking and question

(E) are a huge advance in modern critical thinking, and questioned

11. Clifton Chenier became known as the "King of Zydeco" because <u>of his spending much of his life in the popularizing of</u> zydeco music.

(A) of his spending much of his life in the popularizing of

(B) he spent much of his life popularizing it,

(C) of his popularization for much of his life of

(D) he spent much of his life in the popularizing of

(E) he spent much of his life popularizing

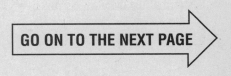
GO ON TO THE NEXT PAGE

The following sentences test your ability to recognize grammar and usage errors. Each sentence contains either a single error or no error at all. No sentence contains more than one error. The error, if there is one, is underlined and lettered. If the sentence contains an error, select the one underlined part that must be changed to make the sentence correct. If the sentence is correct, select choice E. In choosing answers, follow the requirements of standard written English.

EXAMPLE:

The other delegates and him immediately
    A   B   C
accepted the resolution drafted by the
                             D
neutral states. No error
                    E

Ⓐ ● Ⓒ Ⓓ Ⓔ

12. Celestial navigation, the ancient practice of

using heavenly bodies to guide a ship's course, has
  A   B
becoming a dying art since the advent of modern
  C   D
global positioning systems. No error
                              E

13. The artist's repeated use of pale colors and
                    A
amorphous forms, intended to imbue his paintings
                          B
with a sense of ambiguity, only makes the paintings
          C
look weakly. No error
    D   E

14. Excessive sugar intake can lead to addiction,
        A   B   C
obesity, and to diabetes. No error
              D   E

15. During late summer evenings, we would sit on
                          A   B
the porch swing and rock very slow in time to the
                              C
sound of the cicadas. No error
        D   E

16. Popping corn is possible because of the tiny

amount of water present in dried kernels; when the
                  A
kernels are heated, the water expands until it bursts
                              B   C
the seams of the kernels. No error
        D   E

17. The improvements people make in how they eat
                                A
and exercise pay off in that individuals have more
                      B
energy and are happier after becoming
              C
more healthier. No error
    D   E

18. *Fortuitous* means "happening by chance," but since
                                              A
so many have used it to mean "lucky," this
          B
malapropism has been added to dictionaries as a
    C   D
secondary definition. No error
                        E

19. After I realized last summer that no one could
    A   B
see through my mirrored sunglasses, I wear them
              C   D
everywhere. No error
              E

20. During the Triassic period, there was only one huge

land mass, Pangaea, which encompassed all the
                          A
present-day continents; some of the plants and trees
    B
familiar to us today also grew on Pangaea. No error
    C   D   E

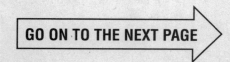
GO ON TO THE NEXT PAGE

21. Many of the students <u>which</u> were chosen for the
                                A

National Student Leadership Conference <u>opted for</u>
                                                B

the U.S. Politics and Policies program; they spent

several days attending Congressional events and

touring the <u>capitol's</u> <u>sights</u>. <u>No error</u>
                C   D   E

22. If you do not enjoy fearless pigeons <u>landing</u> on
                                                A

<u>yourself</u> for food, you <u>should avoid</u> St. Mark's
   B   C

Square <u>in</u> Venice. <u>No error</u>
        D   E

23. Both John and I <u>had been</u> eagerly <u>anticipating</u> the
                        A   B

arrival of the latest model, <u>but after</u> trying it, we
                                C

decided that John liked it more than <u>me</u>. <u>No error</u>
                                        D   E

24. <u>Some</u> people, <u>independent from</u> their approval of
        A   B

citizen participation <u>in government</u>, dislike
                        C

performing jury duty <u>themselves</u>. <u>No error</u>
                        D   E

25. <u>They say</u> comedians <u>face</u> a difficult task: they must
        A   B

challenge and mock the <u>status quo</u> without
                            C

<u>alienating</u> their audiences who represent the status
   D

quo. <u>No error</u>
        E

26. <u>Upon reviewing</u> a map of his property, John real-
        A

ized that he <u>could not build</u> the barn where he had
                B

intended because <u>it belonged</u> to a <u>neighboring</u>
                    C   D

farmer. <u>No error</u>
            E

27. Most art critics <u>agree</u> that <u>of the two</u> painters, Elena
                        A   B

<u>is</u> <u>more</u> skilled at conveying the inner emotions of
C D

her subjects. <u>No error</u>
                E

28. The viewers <u>will have</u> the opportunity to make
                    A

<u>their preference</u> clear, <u>as</u> the station plans
   B   C

<u>to conduct</u> an extensive voter survey. <u>No error</u>
   D   E

29. Around <u>the year 1643</u>, the Florentine Torricelli
                A

<u>invented</u> the barometer, a device <u>that</u> measures the
   B   C

weight of the atmosphere, in order <u>to predict</u> the
                                        D

weather. <u>No error</u>
            E

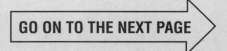

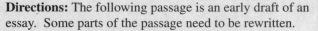

Directions: The following passage is an early draft of an essay. Some parts of the passage need to be rewritten.

Read the passage and select the best answers for the questions that follow. Some questions are about particular sentences or parts of sentences and ask you to improve sentence structure or word choice. Other questions ask you to consider organization and development. In choosing answers, follow the requirements of standard written English.

Questions 30-35 are based on the following passage.

(1) John Graham had been taking pre-law courses at Yale in hopes of becoming a lawyer. (2) In 1980 his career path took a major turn when he decided to be a professional football player. (3) Graham is always enthusiastic about sports, and so his change of path was not a total surprise. (4) When he was growing up in Sayville, New York, he played varsity football in high school.

(5) His father was the Sayville High School football coach. (6) When Graham was playing on the Yale football team, a professional football scout discovered him. (7) Because of this, upon graduating from college, Graham became a part of the New York Jets. (8) After a highly successful football career, he began to receive offers from the major networks for sports commentary jobs. (9) Jobs that relied upon his keen insight and understanding of the workings of football.

(10) Now he is one of the most respected football commentators in the country, frequently compared to Howard Cosell. (11) One might assume that any well-known sports broadcaster would be satisfied enough with his success. (12) A highly compassionate person, Graham cares very much about the assistance he gives to charities that help seriously ill children. (13) Because of the work he has done, he was named "Sportsman of the Year" on two occasions. (14) As an athlete, broadcaster, and philanthropist, John Graham is certainly someone to look up to.

30. In the context of the passage, which of these words would be most logical to insert at the beginning of sentence 2?

(A) Certainly,
(B) Of course,
(C) Furthermore,
(D) However,
(E) Predictably,

31. Which of the following changes is most needed in sentence 3?

(A) Change "Graham" to "He"
(B) Change "is always" to "had always been"
(C) Omit "and so"
(D) Replace "path" with "paths"
(E) Replace "change of" with "changing"

32. Which of the following is the best revision of the underlined portion of sentence 9 (reproduced below)?

Jobs that relied upon his keen insight and understanding of the workings of football.

(A) These jobs relied
(B) Such jobs were relying
(C) Jobs like these ones relied
(D) In them, he relied
(E) These were relying

33. Which of the following would be the best way to combine sentences 11 and 12 (reproduced below)?

One might assume that any well-known sports broadcaster would be satisfied enough with his success. A highly compassionate person, Graham cares very much about the assistance he gives to charities that help seriously ill children.

(A) Like any well-known sport broadcaster satisfied with his success, Graham is a highly compassionate person, assisting charities that help seriously ill children.
(B) A well-known sports broadcaster, Graham assists charities that help seriously ill children, and is a highly compassionate person.
(C) Graham is a highly compassionate person, which means assisting charities that help seriously ill children as well as being a well-known sports broadcaster.
(D) Graham has shown his compassionate nature, assisting charities which help seriously ill children, and is a well-known sports broadcaster.
(E) Not satisfied with his success as a well-known sports broadcaster, Graham has shown his compassionate nature by assisting charities that help seriously ill children.

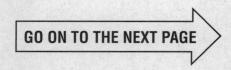

GO ON TO THE NEXT PAGE

34. Which of the following would be the best way to conclude the passage?

(A) (As it is now)
(B) Add the phrase "Of course," at the beginning of sentence 14.
(C) Omit sentence 14.
(D) Place sentence 13 after sentence 14.
(E) Add the sentence "He too had many accomplishments." after sentence 14.

35. In context, which of the following is the best sentence to insert between sentences 11 and 12?

(A) But not for Graham.
(B) Graham became too well-known for his own good.
(C) For Graham, though, success is not enough.
(D) Graham is a great admirer of Howard Cosell.
(E) Graham, having qualities of success and of caring.

STOP

**If you finish before time is called, you may check your work on this section only.
Do not turn to any other section in the test.**

SECTION 5

Time — 25 minutes

18 Questions

Turn to Section 5 of your answer sheet to answer the questions in this section.

Directions: This section contains two types of questions. You have 25 minutes to complete both types. For questions 1-8, solve each problem and decide which is the best of the choices given. Fill in the corresponding oval on the answer sheet. You may use any available space for scatchwork.

Notes

1. The use of a calculator is permitted.

2. All numbers used are real numbers.

3. Figures that accompany problems in this test are intended to provide information useful in solving the problems. They are drawn as accurately as possible EXCEPT when it is stated in a specific problem that the figure is not drawn to scale. All figures lie in a plane unless otherwise indicated.

4. Unless otherwise specified, the domain of any function f is assumed to be the set of all real numbers x for which $f(x)$ is a real number.

Reference Information

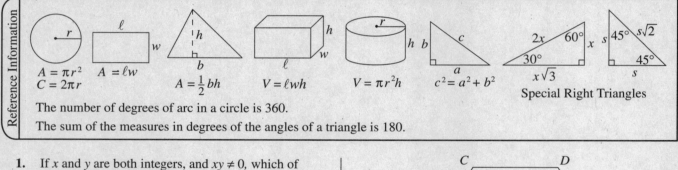

$A = \pi r^2$
$C = 2\pi r$

$A = \ell w$

$A = \frac{1}{2}bh$

$V = \ell wh$

$V = \pi r^2 h$

$c^2 = a^2 + b^2$

Special Right Triangles

The number of degrees of arc in a circle is 360.

The sum of the measures in degrees of the angles of a triangle is 180.

---

1. If x and y are both integers, and $xy \neq 0$, which of the following MUST be true of $|xy|$?

   (A) It is greater than zero.
   (B) It is less than zero.
   (C) It is an even number.
   (D) It is an odd number.
   (E) It is a prime number.

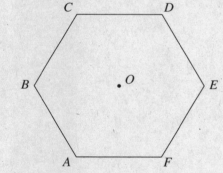

2. O is the center of equilateral hexagon $ABCDEF$, shown above. What is the degree measure of $\angle FOD$ (not shown)?

   (A)   60
   (B)   72
   (C)   110
   (D)   120
   (E)   150

GO ON TO THE NEXT PAGE

3. If $x > 0$ and $\left(3 - \sqrt{x}\right)\left(3 + \sqrt{x}\right) = 7$, what is the value of x ?

(A) 4
(B) 3
(C) 2
(D) 1
(E) 0

4. If one worker can pack 15 boxes every two minutes, and another can pack 15 boxes every three minutes, how many minutes will it take these two workers, working together, to pack 300 boxes?

(A) 10
(B) 12
(C) 15
(D) 24
(E) 30

5. If the remainder when x is divided by 5 equals the remainder when x is divided by 4, then x could be any of the following EXCEPT

(A) 20
(B) 21
(C) 22
(D) 23
(E) 24

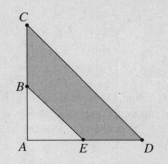

Note: Figure not drawn to scale.

6. B is the midpoint of $\overline{AC}$ and E is the midpoint of $\overline{AD}$. What fraction of $\triangle ACD$ is shaded?

(A) $\dfrac{1}{4}$

(B) $\dfrac{1}{3}$

(C) $\dfrac{1}{2}$

(D) $\dfrac{2}{3}$

(E) $\dfrac{3}{4}$

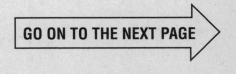

GO ON TO THE NEXT PAGE

$A = \{1, 2, 4, 8\}$

$B = \{1, 3, 6, 8, 9\}$

$C = A \cup B$

$D = A \cap B$

7. Sets A, B, C, and D are shown above. If c and d are chosen at random from sets C and D, respectively, then what is the probability that the product of c and d is odd?

(A) $\dfrac{13}{14}$

(B) $\dfrac{11}{14}$

(C) $\dfrac{1}{2}$

(D) $\dfrac{3}{7}$

(E) $\dfrac{3}{14}$

8. The product of integers x and y is divisible by 36. If x is divisible by 6, which of the following must be true?

I. y is divisible by x.

II. y is divisible by 6.

III. $\dfrac{y}{6}$ is divisible by 6.

(A) None
(B) I only
(C) II only
(D) I and III only
(E) II and III only

GO ON TO THE NEXT PAGE

Directions: For Student-Produced Response questions 9-18, use the grids at the bottom of the answer sheet page on which you have answered questions 1-8.

Each of the remaining 10 questions requires you to solve the problem and enter your answer by marking the circles in the special grid, as shown in the examples below. You may use any available space for scratchwork.

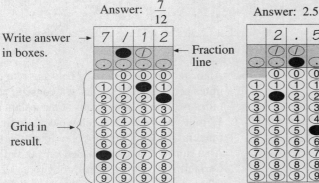

Answer: $\frac{7}{12}$

Write answer in boxes. → Fraction line

Grid in result. →

Answer: 2.5

Decimal point

Answer: 201
Either position is correct.

Note: You may start your answers in any column, space permitting. Columns not needed should be left blank.

- Mark no more than one circle in any column.
- Because the answer sheet will be machine-scored, **you will receive credit only if the circles are filled in correctly.**
- Although not required, it is suggested that you write your answer in the boxes at the top of the columns to help you fill in the circles accurately.
- Some problems may have more than one correct answer. In such cases, grid only one answer.
- No question has a negative answer.
- **Mixed numbers** such as $3\frac{1}{2}$ must be gridded as

  3.5 or 7/2. (If ┌3│1│/│2┐ is gridded, it will be

  interpreted as $\frac{31}{2}$, not $3\frac{1}{2}$.)

- **Decimal Answers:** If you obtain a decimal answer with more digits than the grid can accommodate, it may be either rounded or truncated, but it must fill the entire grid. For example, if you obtain an answer such as 0.6666..., you should record your result as .666 or .667. **A less accurate value such as .66 or .67 will be scored as incorrect.**

Acceptable ways to grid $\frac{2}{3}$ are:

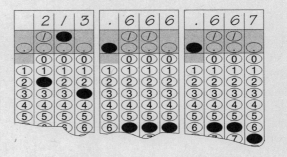

---

9. If $9^{-2} = \left(\frac{1}{3}\right)^{x}$, then $x =$

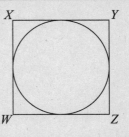

10. In the figure above, a circle is inscribed in square *WXYZ*. If the area of the circle is 400π, what is the area of *WXYZ* ?

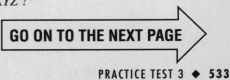

GO ON TO THE NEXT PAGE

11. There were 320 students at a school assembly attended only by juniors and seniors. If there were 60 more juniors than seniors and if there were 30 more female juniors than male juniors, how many male juniors were at the assembly?

12. A rectangle of width 5 has a diagonal of length 13. What is the perimeter of the rectangle?

13. Jeannette's average (arithmetic mean) score for six tests was 92. If the sum of the scores of two of her tests was 188, then what was her average score for the other four tests?

14. If Alexandra pays $56.65 for a table, and this amount includes a tax of 3% on the price of the table, what is the amount, in dollars, that she pays in tax? (Ignore the dollar sign when gridding your answer.)

15. Tiles numbered 1 through 25 are placed in a bag. If one tile is removed at random, what is the probability that the number on the tile is a prime number?

16. Alan and Ben each run at a constant rate of 7.5 miles per hour. Carla runs at a constant rate of 10 miles per hour. Debby runs at a constant rate of 12 miles per hour. In a relay race with these four runners as a team running one right after the other, Alan runs 0.3 miles, then Ben runs 0.3 miles, then Carla runs 0.5 miles, then Debby runs 0.24 miles. What is the team's average speed in miles per hour?

17. If the distance from $(2, 6)$ to $(1, b)$ is a, $a = \left(|-1| + 16\right)^{\frac{1}{2}}$, and $b < a$, what is the value of b ?

18. If $-1 \le a \le 2$ and $-3 \le b \le 2$, what is the greatest possible value of $(a + b)(b - a)$?

STOP

If you finish before time is called, you may check your work on this section only.
Do not turn to any other section in the test.

NO TEST MATERIAL ON THIS PAGE.

SECTION 6
Time — 25 minutes
24 Questions

Turn to Section 6 of your answer sheet to answer the questions in this section.

Directions: For each question in this section, select the best answer from among the choices given and fill in the corresponding circle on the answer sheet.

Each sentence below has one or two blanks, each blank indicating that something has been omitted. Beneath the sentence are five words or sets of words labeled A through E. Choose the word or set of words that, when inserted in the sentence, best fits the meaning of the sentence as a whole.

Example:

Hoping to ------- the dispute, negotiators proposed a compromise that they felt would be ------- to both labor and management.

(A) enforce . . useful
(B) end . . divisive
(C) overcome . . unattractive
(D) extend . . satisfactory
(E) resolve . . acceptable   Ⓐ Ⓑ Ⓒ Ⓓ ⬤

---

1. The fireworks display created so much ------- that the night sky was completely -------, almost as if it were the middle of the day.

    (A) heat . . exploded
    (B) gunpowder . . polluted
    (C) color . . decorated
    (D) refuse . . detonated
    (E) light . . illuminated

2. In speech and in action, she was never haughty or -------; she was always willing to ------- any recommendations, even if she did not agree with them at first.

    (A) arrogant . . deny
    (B) conceited . . consider
    (C) ornery . . oppose
    (D) lenient . . embrace
    (E) accommodating . . ignore

3. Presidents of large companies have traditionally been very -------; they rarely suggest radical new ideas unless all other options have been investigated and found to be impossible.

    (A) inventive   (B) conservative   (C) gentrified
    (D) ingenuous   (E) gratuitous

4. Although it has begun to garner -------, until recently, African drum music was virtually ------- by all but those with the most esoteric tastes.

    (A) acclaim . . overlooked
    (B) respect . . praised
    (C) criticism . . ignored
    (D) recognition . . played
    (E) censure . . disregarded

5. While many health-conscious individuals have stopped eating eggs, dietitians say that in appropriate quantities, eggs can be quite -------.

    (A) injurious   (B) erudite   (C) convenient
    (D) perfunctory   (E) salubrious

GO ON TO THE NEXT PAGE

The passages below are followed by questions based on their content; questions following a pair of related passages may also be based on the relationship between the paired passages. Answer the questions on the basis of what is stated or implied in the passage and in any introductory material that may be provided.

Questions 6-9 are based on the following passages.

Passage 1

The most striking outgrowths of the expansion of the Internet over that past few years have been the numerous legal questions regarding copyright laws and the right to
Line privacy. For many consumers, these two issues create a
5 surprising paradox. Jane Doe wants to freely download music and movies without fear of retribution for violation of copyright laws. Simultaneously, she opposes companies acquiring her personal information to sell to advertisers. Activist groups, whose presence will play
10 a major role in legal decisions, are still considering the issue. In the meantime, Ms. Doe pays for her new CDs with an unusual currency: a list of the sites she frequents each week and an e-mail address with lenient filters.

Passage 2

In the days of the Victorian operetta creators Gilbert
15 and Sullivan, artists learned that "pirates" in American audiences transcribed songs and lyrics during shows and rushed away afterwards to produce cribbed versions of the play. The artists' outrage helped to spark the first American copyright law. However, with the advent of
20 low-tech home recording equipment, new measures needed to be taken. In response to the rapid increase in copyright infringement, Congress has aided copyright holders imposing Draconian punishments to discourage breach of the laws. Today's casual Internet users should
25 take care to avoid getting caught in the crossfire between consumers and copyright owners.

6. The statements about Jane Doe in the third and fourth sentences (lines 5–9)

(A) exacerbate an already controversial issue
(B) argue for more lenient copyright laws
(C) illustrate the contradiction identified in the previous sentence
(D) contradict the paradox explained earlier in the paragraph
(E) apply the theory from the previous sentence to a specific case

7. The content of both passages suggests that Jane Doe and the "pirates" in American audiences would not be averse to

(A) divulging personal details
(B) protecting intellectual property
(C) appealing to the activist groups to support their claims
(D) having open access to other's creative yield
(E) seeking retribution for copyright violations

8. It is implied in both passages that

(A) in earlier times, singers and songwriters were glad to share their works freely
(B) existing copyright laws on intellectual property are not always effectual
(C) civic activist organizations deserve more respect than the law
(D) unusual currency is an equitable exchange for intellectual property
(E) artists and songwriters should be more defensive of their property

9. In the context of the passage, the meaning of "Draconian" (line 23) is closest to

(A) high-tech
(B) dragon-like
(C) illicit
(D) legal
(E) severe

GO ON TO THE NEXT PAGE

Questions 10-15 are based on the following passage.

The following passage is about the art and recreation of Southeastern Indians.

The ceremonies and rituals of the Southeastern Indians seem bizarre, outlandish, even irrational, until viewed against the background of their belief system.
Line When seen in their original context, the ceremonies and
5 rituals of the Southeastern Indians are no more irrational than are our own. We encounter the same sort of problem in understanding the art forms and games of the Southeastern Indians, and likewise we find the solution to be similar. Our best road to understanding the Indians'
10 artistic and recreational forms is to view them as the outward expressions of their belief system.

In some ways the task of understanding the artistic and recreational forms of the Southeastern Indians is more difficult than understanding their ceremonial life.
15 One problem is that the Indians reached their highest artistic development in the late prehistoric and early historic period. De Soto saw architectural forms and artistic creations that surpassed anything witnessed by the Europeans who came after him, and because many of
20 these creations were made of perishable materials, they did not survive. Hence, perhaps the best Southeastern Indian art is irretrievably gone.

A further difficulty in dealing with the artistic and recreational forms of the Southeastern Indians is that
25 all of these are intimately imbedded in other social and cultural institutions. They are neither as self-contained nor as separable from other institutions as are the art forms and games in our own culture. For instance, the Southeastern Indians placed a high value on men who
30 could use words skillfully. Jack and Anna Kilpatrick have discussed the condensed poetry in some of the Cherokee magical formulas, some of them containing a single word, compound in form, which might be likened to tiny imagist poems. Another form of verbal artistry
35 was oratory, the words of a gifted speaker that could move contentious men to reach consensus or the timid and hesitant to go against the enemy. And yet oratory can hardly be separated from the political institutions of the Southeastern Indians.
40 In looking at the art and recreation of the Southeastern Indians, we will often wish that we knew more about underlying social factors. For example, even though we know much about the Southeastern Indian ball game, we do not know the precise nature of the social and
45 political forces that led them to play it with such ferocity. To a lesser extent, we know the basic rules of chunkey, but what we do not understand is why the Indians would sometimes bet the last thing they owned on the outcome

of a game. In general, we sense that the players of these
50 games were motivated by social factors that lie outside the playing field, but we cannot often be specific about what these factors were.

10.   The main purpose of the passage is to

(A) show how bizarre certain Southeastern Indian ceremonies and rituals are

(B) explain the rules of several games played by the Southeastern Indians

(C) describe the difficulties inherent in appreciating the Southeastern Indians' artistic and recreational forms

(D) explore the mysticism of the ceremonies and rituals in the Southeastern Indians' belief system

(E) delineate the difference between the artistic forms of the Southeastern Indians and the Cherokee Indians

11.   Which of the following best describes the "problem" mentioned in line 7?

(A) The belief system of the Southeastern Indians was irrational and therefore impossible to understand.

(B) It is difficult to comprehend the artistic and recreational expression of the Southeastern Indians without understanding their belief system.

(C) A superficial examination of the ceremonies and rituals of the Southeastern Indians makes them appear similar to our own.

(D) Since we have virtually no understanding of the beliefs of the Southeastern Indians, it is unlikely we will ever understand the significance of their art.

(E) Scholars are unwilling to acquaint themselves sufficiently with the artistic and recreational forms of the Southeastern Indians.

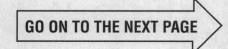
GO ON TO THE NEXT PAGE

12. According to the passage, which of the following was an advantage of skilled oratory?

(A) It was effective in enhancing one's athletic ability.

(B) An orator was responsible for composing the magical formulas used in spiritual rituals.

(C) Orators were usually the most powerful warriors among the Southeastern Indians.

(D) Timid and hesitant speakers could soothe anxious tempers.

(E) A skilled speaker could mend differences between opposing parties.

13. The author mentions the game "chunkey" in line 46 primarily in order to

(A) prove that the Southeastern Indians were more concerned with politics than with organized competition

(B) show how social politics and ferocious violence were interconnected in the lives of the Southeastern Indians

(C) explain how the Southeastern Indians' interest in competition and artistic endeavor was dictated by separate social factors

(D) provide an example of how the Southeastern Indians' competitive nature was motivated by social influences

(E) describe the unusual and ambiguous rules of a little-known competition

14. Our difficulties in understanding the recreational and artistic systems of the Southeastern Indians can be ascribed to which of the following causes?

I. All instances of original Southeastern Indian art are unavailable to us.

II. We do not know to what degree Indian poetic and rhetorical output was political, and to what extent it was artistic.

III. We are unclear about the exact significance of certain forms of Indian recreation.

(A) I

(B) III

(C) I and II

(D) II and III

(E) I, II, and III

15. The author mentions the loss of many of the Indians' artistic and architectural creations as a parallel to

(A) the Indian art seen by later European explorers

(B) our own irrational rituals and ceremonies

(C) poetry expressed by Cherokee magical formulas

(D) contentious men rallying against attackers

(E) the reason the Indians wagered heavily on chunkey

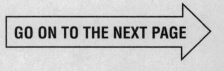

GO ON TO THE NEXT PAGE

Questions 16-24 are based on the following passage.

The following passage discusses the history and some of the characteristics of jazz.

Like the blues, jazz emphasizes individualism. The performer is at the same time the composer, shaping the music into style and form. A traditional melody or
Line harmonic framework may serve as the takeoff point for
5 improvisation, but it is the personality of the player and the way he or she improvises that produce the music. Performances of the same work differ from player to player, for each recreates the music in his or her own individual way. Jazz is learned through oral tradition, as
10 is folk song, and those who would learn to play it do so primarily by listening to others playing jazz.

Although improvisational in nature, jazz nonetheless contains recognizable elements that derive from older musical traditions. The influence of ragtime is represented
15 in jazz by the emphasis on syncopation and the presence of the piano in the ensemble. The influence of the brass band reveals itself in the jazz instrumentation*, in the roles assigned to each instrument, and in the resulting musical texture. In the classic New Orleans band, for
20 example, three instruments are given melodic roles; the cornet typically plays the lead, the clarinet plays a counter melody, and the trombone plays the lower voice of the trio. The other instruments—the drums, banjos, guitars, and basses—function as the rhythm section. Although
25 pianos were added to jazz bands from the beginning, and often a second cornet as well, the instruments remained basically the same as in brass bands. Later, trumpets took the place of cornets and saxophones were added or used in place of clarinets. The addition of saxophones suggests
30 the influence of the syncopated dance orchestra, which used saxophones early in its development.

The brass band emphasized the ensemble sound, as distinguished from solo music, and this tradition, too, passed over into the performances of early jazz bands. In
35 many jazz performances of the early 1920's, for example, all of the instruments played throughout the piece, the cornet always retaining the lead melody. In performances that included solo passages, the other instruments typically gave firm support, particularly the rhythm
40 section. The ensemble sound of the brass band was basically polyphonic in nature, not chordal. As many as two or three clearly defined melodic lines dominated the texture, and frequently the rhythm instruments furnished little counter melodies.

45 The polyphonic texture of the music was a result of "collective improvisation" with each melody player improvising his or her part in such a way that the parts combined into a balanced, integrated whole. The concept of jazz improvisation changed its implications over the
50 years. In this early period, the performer embellished the melody, adding extra tones and altering note values, but in such a manner as to retain the essential shape of the original melody.

The most salient features of jazz derive directly from
55 the blues; its soloists approximate the voice with their instruments, but try to recreate its singing style and blue notes by using scooping, sliding, whining, growling, and falsetto effects. Finally, jazz uses the call-and-response style of the blues, by employing an antiphonal relationship
60 between two solo instruments or between solo and ensemble.

Jazz is created from the synthesis of certain elements in the style of its precursors. Its most striking feature is its exotic sound, which is produced not only by the kinds
65 of instruments used in the orchestra, but also by the manner in which intonation is used. Instead of obtaining exact pitches, the players glide freely from one note to another (or through long series of notes in glissandos) and frequently fluctuate the pitches (i.e., use a wide vibrato).

*Instrumentation refers to the choice of instruments within a musical group.

16. The main purpose of the passage is to show that
    (A) three instrument melodies were not the dominant style of jazz
    (B) the call-and-response style of the blues was highly successful
    (C) blues was a uniquely American form of music with a completely original style
    (D) the New Orleans band was the single greatest influence on the evolution of jazz
    (E) jazz is a complex musical form with a complicated history

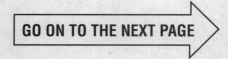
GO ON TO THE NEXT PAGE

17. The author uses the examples of ragtime and brass bands to illustrate

    (A) that jazz is not entirely an original creation
    (B) the diversity of elements that jazz has passed on to other styles
    (C) the origins of certain jazz compositions
    (D) the relative growth in popularity of modern jazz
    (E) the long, illustrious history that led to the creation of jazz

18. The influence of the brass band on jazz performance includes all of the following EXCEPT

    (A) the playing of the lead melody by the cornet
    (B) emphasis on the ensemble sound
    (C) polyphonic music rather than chordal music
    (D) the playing of all the instruments throughout the song
    (E) the complete lack of solo passages

19. One of the "salient features" of jazz (line 54) would be that

    (A) the instruments mimic human voices
    (B) jazz is dominated by singers
    (C) music lovers prefer the blues to jazz
    (D) the music is composed with singers in mind
    (E) every jazz musician is also a jazz singer

20. The word "striking" in line 63 most nearly means

    (A) removing
    (B) pounding
    (C) thoughtful
    (D) remarkable
    (E) believable

21. The exotic sound of jazz is primarily a result of

    (A) the use of syncopated rhythms
    (B) the influences of ragtime and brass bands
    (C) the selection of instruments and the ways in which sounds are manipulated
    (D) the addition of extra tones and the replacement of one note with another
    (E) the first and third beat percussion work

22. According to the passage, the development of jazz was influenced by all of the following EXCEPT

    (A) ragtime bands
    (B) dance orchestras
    (C) brass bands
    (D) folk instrumentation
    (E) blues singing

23. Which of the following statements is NOT supported by the information in the passage?

    (A) Jazz is sometimes considered to be the only original American art form.
    (B) Learning jazz takes place through the ear more so than through the eye.
    (C) Jazz is more contrapuntal than harmonic.
    (D) Jazz compositions do not always observe strict rhythms.
    (E) The clarinet was the precursor to the saxophone in the jazz band.

24. It can be inferred from the passage that

    (A) music composed or performed before the advent of jazz was not polyphonic
    (B) the first known instance of a jazz performance was in 1920
    (C) the classic New Orleans jazz band consisted of three categories of instruments
    (D) a clear and exact sound is characteristic of instruments playing jazz
    (E) a jazz composition may not sound exactly the same from one performance to the next

STOP
If you finish before time is called, you may check your work on this section only.
Do not turn to any other section in the test.

SECTION 7
Time — 25 minutes
24 Questions

Turn to Section 7 of your answer sheet to answer the questions in this section.

Directions: For each question in this section, select the best answer from among the choices given and fill in the corresponding circle on the answer sheet.

Each sentence below has one or two blanks, each blank indicating that something has been omitted. Beneath the sentence are five words or sets of words labeled A through E. Choose the word or set of words that, when inserted in the sentence, best fits the meaning of the sentence as a whole.

Example:

Hoping to ------- the dispute, negotiators proposed a compromise that they felt would be ------- to both labor and management.

(A) enforce . . useful
(B) end . . divisive
(C) overcome . . unattractive
(D) extend . . satisfactory
(E) resolve . . acceptable   Ⓐ Ⓑ Ⓒ Ⓓ ●

1. Their daughter's story that she was robbed of her homework by wandering gypsies was so entirely implausible that the parents believed it to be -------.

    (A) an explanation   (B) an intimidation
      (C) a fabrication   (D) a rationalization
        (E) a confirmation

2. While industry in the late twentieth century believed itself to be ------- in its treatment of laborers, Cesar Chavez made a career of revealing the ------- experienced by farm workers.

    (A) generous . . injustices
    (B) just . . satisfaction
    (C) vindictive . . challenges
    (D) superior . . relationships
    (E) immutable . . consistency

3. The two teams reached an agreement that was -------: they promised to exchange players of comparable talent.

    (A) equitable   (B) variable   (C) hypocritical
      (D) inconvenient   (E) extended

4. Professor Yang's article was unusually -------, but its brevity did not conceal the importance of Yang's discovery.

    (A) intricate   (B) coherent   (C) irrelevant
      (D) terse   (E) ambitious

5. The Black Plague was so ------- that in a few short years it had reduced the population of medieval Europe substantially.

    (A) lenient   (B) susceptible   (C) suppressed
      (D) maudlin   (E) virulent

6. Her promotional tour was ------- by missteps, but the increasing appreciation for her works suggests that the effects of these blunders were -------.

    (A) enervated . . destructive
    (B) avoided . . ancillary
    (C) surrounded . . astute
    (D) beleaguered . . negligible
    (E) besmirched . . indubitable

7. While the ambassador was not ------- about the path that his country was taking, he did not believe that its economic politics would cause a significant amount of -------.

    (A) pragmatic . . affluence
    (B) sanguine . . distress
    (C) impartial . . ambivalence
    (D) despondent . . despair
    (E) agitated . . tumult

8. Lisa was known for her ------- speeches in which she rambled for a long time with frequent repetitions about trivial topics.

    (A) eloquent   (B) hoarse   (C) garrulous
      (D) terse   (E) compelling

GO ON TO THE NEXT PAGE

The passages below are followed by questions based on their content. Answer the questions on the basis of what is stated or implied in the passage and in any introductory material that may be provided.

Questions 9-10 are based on the following passage.

A procedure known as a cochlear implant can allow people who exhibit certain kinds of deafness to detect and interpret sounds. Although the procedure does not
Line restore the natural hearing mechanism, it does permit the
5 interpretation of speech and a high level of interaction with the "hearing world." Despite its possible benefits, the procedure remains controversial. In addition to concerns regarding the risk of surgery to correct a non-fatal disorder, opponents of the procedure cite a moderately
10 high proportion of cases in which the procedure is not effective. Moreover, deaf individuals often value their deafness as an integral part of their identity; cochlear implants may jeopardize that identity.

9. The author's primary purpose is to

(A) argue for the universal implementation of cochlear implants
(B) introduce the cochlear implant procedure and illustrate some of its drawbacks
(C) soundly condemn doctors who perform cochlear implants
(D) admonish those who do not value an individual's unique identity
(E) describe the scientific basis for a certain type of hearing loss

10. Which of the following most accurately describes the purpose of the final three sentences of the passage?

(A) To illustrate important points about the nature of identity
(B) To discuss possible objections to a potentially beneficial procedure
(C) To offer alternatives to a controversial surgery
(D) To provide factual evidence in support of a disputed theory
(E) To question the appropriateness of surgical interventions in non-fatal maladies

Questions 11-12 are based on the following passage.

When Igor Stravinsky's *Le Sacre du Printemps* (The Rite of Spring) premiered in Paris in 1913, the ballet sparked violent riots for over three days. Although the
Line composer blamed the dancers, choreography, and theater's
5 management for causing the melee, contemporary reports suggest that it may have been the composer's use of unconventional harmonies that provoked the crowd. The resulting violence may remind modern audiences of the riots sometimes associated with sporting events. While
10 the public's propensity for rioting seems to have remained constant over the last century, the nature of the events that trigger public violence has certainly changed.

11. Which of the following was NOT mentioned as a possible cause of the riots in 1913?

(A) Theater management
(B) Ballet dancers
(C) Unconventional harmonies used in the ballet
(D) Choreography used in *Le Sacre du Printemps*
(E) Dissatisfied audience members

12. Which of the following can be properly inferred from the information above?

(A) Before 1913, people did not riot over public performances.
(B) No prior rioting event had been as long or as widespread as was the 1913 Paris incident.
(C) Stravinsky had hoped to spark violence in support of the arts.
(D) The catalyst of the modern riot may be different from that of its antecedents.
(E) Violence is never justified, regardless of the provocation.

GO ON TO THE NEXT PAGE

Questions 13-24 are based on the following passage.

The following passage written in 1989 is taken from A Year in Provence *by Peter Mayle. In this excerpt, we follow a family's first exposure to the French district.*

The proprietor of Le Simiane wished us a happy new year and hovered in the doorway as we stood in the narrow street, blinking into the sun.

Line
5   "Not bad, eh?" he said, with a flourish of one velvet-clad arm which took in the village. "One is fortunate to be in Provence."

Yes indeed, we thought, one certainly was. If this was winter, we wouldn't be needing all the foul-weather paraphernalia—boots and coats and inch-thick
10 sweaters—that we had brought over from England. We drove home, warm and well fed, making bets on how soon we could take the first swim of the year, and feeling a smug sympathy for those poor souls in harsher climates who had to suffer real winters.

15   Meanwhile, a thousand miles to the north, the wind that had started in Siberia was picking up speed for the final part of its journey. We had heard stories about the mistral. It drove people, and animals, mad; it was an extenuating circumstance in crimes of violence. It blew
20 for fifteen days on end, uprooting trees, overturning cars, smashing windows, tossing old ladies into the gutter, splintering telegraph poles, moaning through houses like a cold and baleful ghost—every problem in Provence that couldn't be blamed on the politicians was the fault of the
25 *sacre vent*[1] which the Provençeaux spoke about with a kind of masochistic pride.

Typical Gallic exaggeration, we thought. If they had to put up with the gales that come off the English Channel and bend the rain so that it hits you in the face almost
30 horizontally, then they might know what a real wind was like. We listened to their stories and, to humor the tellers, pretended to be impressed.

And so we were poorly prepared when the first mistral of the year came howling down the Rhône valley, turned
35 left, and smacked into the west side of the house with enough force to skim roof tiles into the swimming pool and rip a window that had carelessly been left open off its hinges. The temperature dropped twenty degrees in twenty-four hours. It went to zero, then six below.
40 Readings taken in Marseilles showed a wind speed of 180 kilometers an hour. And then one morning, with the sound of branches snapping, the pipes burst one after the other under the pressure of water that had frozen in them overnight.

45   They hung off the wall, swollen and stopped up with ice, and Monsieur Menicucci studied them with his professional plumber's eye.

"*Oh là là,*" he said. "*Oh là là.*" He turned to his young apprentice, whom he invariably addressed as *jeune*
50 *homme*[2] or *jeune*. "You see what we have here, *jeune*. Naked pipes. No insulation. Côte d'Azur plumbing. In Cannes, in Nice, it would do, but here ..."

He made a clucking sound of disapproval and wagged his finger under *jeune's* nose to underline the difference
55 between the soft winters of the coast and the biting cold in which we were now standing, and pulled his woolen bonnet firmly down over his ears. He was short and compact, built for plumbing, as he would say, because he could squeeze himself into constricted spaces that
60 more ungainly men would find inaccessible. While we waited for *jeune* to set up the blowtorch, Monsieur Menicucci delivered the first of a series of lectures and collected *pensées* which I would listen to with increasing enjoyment throughout the coming year. Today, we had
65 a geophysical dissertation on the increasing severity of Provençal winters.

For three years in a row, winters had been noticeably harder than anyone could remember—cold enough, in fact, to kill ancient olive trees. But why? Monsieur
70 Menicucci gave me a token two seconds to ponder this phenomenon before warming to his thesis, tapping me with a finger from time to time to make sure I was paying attention.

It was clear, he said, that the winds which brought
75 the cold down from Russia were arriving in Provence with greater velocity than before, taking less time to reach their destination and therefore having less time to warm up en route. And the reason for this—Monsieur Menicucci allowed himself a brief but dramatic pause—
80 was a change in the configuration of the earth's crust. *Mais oui*[3]. Somewhere between Siberia and Ménerbes the curvature of the earth had flattened, enabling the wind to take a more direct route south. It was entirely logical. Unfortunately, part two of the lecture ("Why the Earth Is
85 Becoming Flatter") was interrupted by a crack of another burst pipe, and my education was put aside for some virtuoso work with the blowtorch.

1 French for "sacred wind"
2 French for "young man"
3 French for "But, of course"

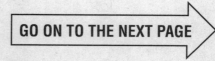

13. The author's comment about the family "making bets on how soon we could take the first swim of the year" (lines 11-12) refers to

(A) the vain desire to partake of the French waters
(B) the longing for real pleasure on an otherwise dull French vacation
(C) the hope that a return to the British shore would cure their homesickness
(D) the faith that the powerful Mistral would soon vanish and allow them to swim happily once again
(E) the anticipation of warm weather that would make it conceivable to swim, despite the season

14. The word "poor" in line 13 most nearly means

(A) humble
(B) unfortunate
(C) inferior
(D) destitute
(E) underprivileged

15. The author describes the mistral as "an extenuating circumstance in crimes of violence" in lines 18-19 in order to

(A) explain the problems attributed to the judicial system
(B) illustrate that the primary cause of problems in Provence is natural disasters beyond human control
(C) explain how the mistral is blamed for damage caused by politicians
(D) emphasize that damage caused by the mistral is negligible compared to that caused by the English gale winds
(E) illustrate the severity of the effects of the mistral on people

16. The word "baleful" in line 23 most nearly means

(A) lonely
(B) ambitious
(C) sprightly
(D) menacing
(E) rambunctious

17. In line 28 the author implies that "the gales that come off the English Channel"

(A) prevent most nautical vessels from reaching their destination
(B) can combine with a Mistral and cause unimaginable havoc across the European countryside
(C) have greater force than their French counterparts
(D) bend the rain into horizontal streams only under certain storm conditions
(E) cause damage only around the English Channel

18. The "clucking sound of disapproval" (line 53) made by Monsieur Menicucci signifies his

(A) belief that the plumbing installation was inappropriate for the climate conditions
(B) disdain for the English visitors
(C) opinion of his assistant's work ethic
(D) preference for the warmer winters of the coast
(E) sense that the plumbing in Cannes and Nice is superior to that in Provence

19. The author implies that Monsieur Menicucci offers the "token two seconds" (line 70)

(A) as an effrontery to the author whose opinion was not regarded with sufficient consideration
(B) in sincere hope that the author might be able to shed some light on the mystery
(C) simply as a courtesy, since Menicucci believes he can provide the definitive theory on the phenomenon's cause
(D) in confusion, momentarily forgetting what he had been discussing
(E) to reveal his own respect for the Mistral's capacity for destruction

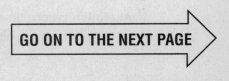

GO ON TO THE NEXT PAGE

20. Which of the following best describes Menicucci's theory about the earth's crust?

(A) The burst pipes were the result of the increased velocity of the mistral.
(B) Siberia is gradually moving closer to Provence.
(C) The presence of wind in most regions is completely determined by the curvature of the earth.
(D) Wind slows down across a flat plain, since it wants to change directions.
(E) A deviation in the earth's shape results in changes in weather patterns.

21. The author's comment *"Mais oui"* suggests the author regards Menicucci as a

(A) highly educated thinker whose theory is provocative
(B) confused character who cannot adequately articulate his ideas
(C) plumber whose grasp of the English language is impressive
(D) slightly pompous comic figure who perceives himself to be overly knowledgeable
(E) deceitful man interested in misleading the author into believing fanciful tales

22. Which of the following can be inferred from the passage?

I. The author's house in Provence had a swimming pool.
II. The author was born in England.
III. The first mistral that the author experienced lasted for fifteen days.

(A) None of the above
(B) I only
(C) III only
(D) I and II only
(E) I, II and III

23. The tone of the passage can best be described as

(A) passionate
(B) exasperated
(C) anecdotal
(D) argumentative
(E) sentimental

24. Which of the following does the passage imply about Cannes?

(A) It is a coastal city.
(B) It shares a border with Nice.
(C) It is a popular tourist destination.
(D) It typically has harsher winters than does Provence.
(E) It is the hometown of Monsieur Menicucci.

STOP
**If you finish before time is called, you may check your work on this section only.
Do not turn to any other section in the test.**

NO TEST MATERIAL ON THIS PAGE.

SECTION 8
Time — 20 minutes
19 Questions

Turn to Section 8 of your answer sheet to answer the questions in this section.

Directions: For each question in this section, select the best answer from among the choices given and fill in the corresponding circle on the answer sheet.

Each sentence below has one or two blanks, each blank indicating that something has been omitted. Beneath the sentence are five words or sets of words labeled A through E. Choose the word or set of words that, when inserted in the sentence, best fits the meaning of the sentence as a whole.

Example:

Hoping to ------- the dispute, negotiators proposed a compromise that they felt would be ------- to both labor and management.

(A) enforce . . useful
(B) end . . divisive
(C) overcome . . unattractive
(D) extend . . satisfactory
(E) resolve . . acceptable

(A) (B) (C) (D) ●

---

1. Upon learning that she had won the grand prize instead of just any prize, her initial joy turned into -------.

   (A) apathy   (B) euphoria   (C) spontaneity
      (D) contention   (E) misery

2. The increased humidity coupled with oppressively high temperatures made us feel ------- at the beach this summer.

   (A) earnest   (B) animated   (C) resilient
      (D) exotic   (E) listless

3. Anthropologists had long assumed that hunter-gatherers moved continually in their search for food; however, recent findings indicate that during the Mesolithic period, such groups were often quite -------.

   (A) prudent   (B) credulous   (C) industrious
      (D) indigent   (E) sedentary

4. Since none of the original doors or windows of the Mayan Indian homes have survived, restoration work on these portions of the buildings has been largely -------.

   (A) exquisite   (B) impertinent   (C) speculative
      (D) decorous   (E) abstract

5. The council was divided into such strong factions that it was almost impossible to garner ------- support to pass the bill.

   (A) biased   (B) strenuous   (C) bureaucratic
      (D) bipartisan   (E) unnecessary

6. The boys expected to be admonished for their mischief, but they were not prepared to be so completely ------- by their parents.

   (A) welcomed   (B) beguiled   (C) esteemed
      (D) nonplussed   (E) castigated

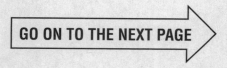

The passages below are followed by questions based on their content; questions following a pair of related passages may also be based on the relationship between the paired passages. Answer the questions on the basis of what is <u>stated</u> or <u>implied</u> in the passage and in any introductory material that may be provided.

Questions 7-19 are based on the following passages.

The following passages deal with the question of air pollution. Passage 1 gives a broad historical overview, and Passage 2 discusses one type of pollutant.

Passage 1

Even before there were people, there were cases of air pollution. Volcanoes erupted, spewing ash and poisonous gases into the atmosphere. There were dust storms. Gases
Line collected over marshes. When people appeared on the
5 scene and began their conquest of nature, they also began to pollute the air. They cleared land, which made possible even larger dust storms. They built cities, and the soot from their hearths and the stench from their waste filled the air. The Roman author Seneca wrote in A.D. 61 of the
10 "stink, soot and heavy air" of the imperial city. In 1257, the Queen of England was forced to move away from the city of Nottingham because the heavy smoke was unendurable.

The Industrial Revolution brought even worse air
15 pollution. Coal was burned to power factories and to heat homes. Soot, smoke, and sulfur dioxide filled the air. The good old days? Not in the factory towns. But there were large rural areas unaffected by air pollution.

With increasing population, the entire world is
20 becoming more urban. It is the huge megalopolises that are most affected by air pollution. But rural areas are not unaffected. In the neighborhoods around smoky factories, there is evidence of increased rates of spontaneous abortion and of poor wool quality in sheep, decreased egg
25 production and high mortality in chickens, and increased food and care required for cattle. The giant Ponderosa pines are dying over a hundred miles from the smog-plagued Los Angeles basin. Orbiting astronauts visually traced drifting blobs of Los Angeles smog as far east
30 as western Colorado. Other astronauts, more than 100 kilometers up, were able to see the plume of smoke from the Four Corners power plant near Farmington, New Mexico. This was the only evidence from that distance that Earth is inhabited.

35 Traffic police in Tokyo have to wear gas masks and take "oxygen breaks"—breathing occasionally from tanks of oxygen. Smog in Athens at times has forced factory closings and traffic restrictions. Acid rain in Canada is spawned by air pollution in the United States,
40 contributing to strained relationships between the two countries. Sydney, Rome, Tehran, Ankara, Mexico City, and most other major cities in the world have had frightening episodes of air pollution.

Passage 2

One of the two major types of smog—consisting of
45 smoke, fog, sulfur dioxide, sulfuric acid, ash, and soot— is called London smog. Indeed, the word smog is thought to have originated in England in 1905 as a contraction of the words "smoke" and "fog."

Probably the most notorious case of smog in history
50 started in London on Thursday, 4 December, 1952. A large cold air mass moved into the valley of the Thames River. A temperature inversion placed a blanket of warm air over the cold air. With nightfall, a dense fog and below-freezing temperatures caused the people of London
55 to heap coal into their small stoves. Millions of these fires burned throughout the night, pouring sulfur dioxide and smoke into the air. The next day, Friday, the people continued to burn coal when the temperature remained below freezing. The factories added their smoke and
60 chemical fumes to the atmosphere.

Saturday was a day of darkness. For twenty miles around London, no light came through the smog. The air was cold and still. And the coal fires continued to burn throughout the weekend. On Monday, 8 December,
65 more than one hundred people died of heart attacks while trying desperately to breathe. The city's hospitals were overflowing with patients with respiratory diseases.

By the time a breeze cleared the air on Tuesday, 9 December, more than 4,000 deaths had been attributed
70 to the smog. This is more people than were ever killed in any single tornado, mine disaster, shipwreck, or airplane crash. This is more people than were killed in the attack on Pearl Harbor in 1941. Air pollution episodes may not be as dramatic as other disasters, but they can be just as
75 deadly.

Soot and ash can be removed by electrostatic precipitators. These devices induce an electric charge on the particles, which then are attracted to oppositely charged plates and deposited. Unfortunately, electrostatic
80 precipitators use large amounts of electricity, and the electrical energy has to come from somewhere. Fly ash

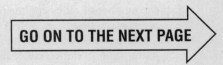
GO ON TO THE NEXT PAGE

removed from the air has to be put on the land or water, although it could be used in some way. Increasingly, fly ash is being used to replace part of the clay in making
85 cement.

The elimination of sulfur dioxide is more difficult. Low-sulfur coal is scarce and expensive. The most plentiful fuel that exists is low-grade, high-sulfur coal. Pilot runs have shown that sulfur can be washed from
90 finely pulverized coal, but the process is expensive. There are also processes for converting dirty coal to clean liquid and gaseous fuels. These processes may hold promise for the future, but they are too expensive to compete economically with other fuels at present. They also waste
95 a part of the coal's energy.

7. Passage 1 implies that air pollution

(A) was originally caused by the Industrial Revolution
(B) affects only urban areas
(C) has natural as well as manmade causes
(D) will never be eliminated through the use of better fuels because they are too expensive
(E) seriously affects the nervous systems of both people and animals

8. The author of Passage 1 uses both the Roman author Seneca and the Queen of England (lines 9-13) as evidence that

(A) civilization has necessarily caused air pollution
(B) air pollution has always existed in cities
(C) urban air pollution is not just a modern problem
(D) humanity disregards its environment
(E) recently, the level of air pollution has risen dramatically

9. According to the author of Passage 1, air pollution problems of today differ from those of the industrial revolution and before in that

(A) remote communities may now feel the effects of air pollution regardless of their proximity to the source of the pollution
(B) today's polluted factory towns were once clean rural communities unaffected by urban air pollution
(C) modern urban areas are no longer more polluted than the suburban and rural communities that surround them
(D) the use of coal as fuel has greatly increased the number of cities and megalopolises that are contributing to the world's air pollutants
(E) modern disasters caused by incidents of extreme air pollution cause far more damage than they did hundreds of years ago

10. The orbiting astronauts are discussed by the author (lines 28-34) in order to

(A) demonstrate the increased urbanization of modern civilization
(B) prove that air pollution is an inevitable consequence of human progress
(C) support the claim that pollution has become the defining characteristic of modern society
(D) provide evidence that pollution is no longer restricted to urban areas
(E) further the argument that large urban areas are most affected by air pollution

11. The last paragraph of Passage 1 suggests that air pollution causes all of the following EXCEPT

(A) difficulties in international relations
(B) otherwise unnecessary closings of businesses
(C) changes in the quality of some water
(D) changes in work habits
(E) high levels of lung disease

12. The author of Passage 2 discusses the 1952 outbreak of London smog in order to

(A) demonstrate that smog has serious effects that are not controllable by human action
(B) point out that air pollution is a major threat to human health only over a long period of time
(C) describe an example of the lethal potential of air pollution
(D) support the claim that air pollution must be controlled
(E) prove that the toxic effects of air pollution are far worse in Europe than in the United States

13. According to Passage 2, London smog can best be described as

(A) a deadly type of air pollution that cannot be completely eliminated
(B) a phenomenon responsible for more deaths than from any other natural cause
(C) a threat to human health that we are often unaware of
(D) a combination of fog conditions and heavy accumulations of smoke from fossil fuel fires
(E) a new, mostly uninvestigated, type of air pollution

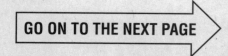
GO ON TO THE NEXT PAGE

14. The statistics cited in lines 68-75 imply that

(A) any effects of a serious air pollution episode cannot be seen until some time after the episode

(B) in the short run, air pollution produces more traumatic health problems than other disasters

(C) most of the fatalities from air pollution do not occur during an air pollution episode

(D) air pollution episodes can be among the most devastating types of disasters

(E) it is impossible to know the total death rate from a given episode of air pollution

15. Passage 2 suggests that electrostatic precipitators work by a process in which

(A) electricity is attracted to particles

(B) charged particles are attracted to plates with the opposite charge

(C) a large amount of electricity ionizes the air

(D) induction acts on charged particles

(E) ash and soot are naturally charged particles

16. The author of Passage 2 believes that the removal of sulfur dioxide from air pollution is difficult because

(A) the technology to remove sulfur dioxide is only currently in development

(B) any successful process utilizes more natural resources than it produces

(C) sulfur is made up of very resilient molecules that cannot be broken down easily

(D) sulfur is a basic compound in all fuels that are currently used

(E) the available methods are costly and involve some waste

17. It can be inferred that the author of Passage 1 would agree with which statement about the cost of pollution control discussed in Passage 2?

(A) Society must be prepared to spend whatever it takes to eliminate all forms of air pollution.

(B) The cost of pollution control is too high to make it economically efficient with current technology.

(C) The more we are concerned with limiting the effects of pollution, the less we will be able to eliminate the sources of pollution.

(D) Dealing with pollution can be a significant challenge for urban populations.

(E) The cost of pollution control is much higher than the cost of changing to better energy sources.

18. Which factor mentioned in Passage 1 most likely contributed to the environmental disaster described in Passage 2?

(A) The Industrial Revolution

(B) Natural sources of air pollution

(C) Land clearing

(D) Heavy smoke from Nottingham

(E) Improper disposal of solid waste

19. Which of the following is NOT a difference that exists between the two passages?

(A) Passage 1 views air pollution as a timeworn problem and gives historical contexts to show its permanence in human society past and present while Passage 2 focuses only on the modern era.

(B) Passage 2 focuses on the effect of air pollution on urban populations while Passage 1 discusses the effect it has had on both urban and rural areas.

(C) Passage 2 uses one historical example to illustrate the dangers of air pollution while Passage 1 uses several historical examples.

(D) Passage 1 recognizes the industrial revolution as a major factor in air pollution while Passage 2 contends that it was no worse than other factors.

(E) Passage 2 provides the reader with possible methods for preventing or treating polluted air while Passage 1 does not.

STOP

If you finish before time is called, you may check your work on this section only.
Do not turn to any other section in the test.

SECTION 9

Time — 20 minutes

16 Questions

> **Turn to Section 9 of your answer sheet to answer the questions in this section.**

Directions: For this section, solve each problem and decide which is the best of the choices given. Fill in the corresponding oval on the answer sheet. You may use any available space for scratchwork.

Notes

1. The use of a calculator is permitted.
2. All numbers used are real numbers.
3. Figures that accompany problems in this test are intended to provide information useful in solving the problems. They are drawn as accurately as possible EXCEPT when it is stated in a specific problem that the figure is not drawn to scale. All figures lie in a plane unless otherwise indicated.
4. Unless otherwise specified, the domain of any function f is assumed to be the set of all real numbers x for which $f(x)$ is a real number.

Reference Information

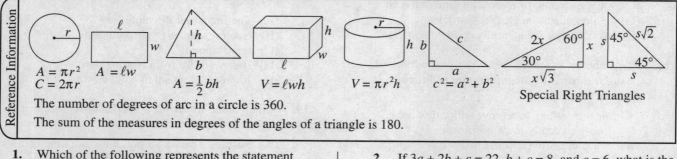

$A = \pi r^2$
$C = 2\pi r$
$A = \ell w$
$A = \frac{1}{2}bh$
$V = \ell wh$
$V = \pi r^2 h$
$c^2 = a^2 + b^2$

Special Right Triangles

The number of degrees of arc in a circle is 360.

The sum of the measures in degrees of the angles of a triangle is 180.

---

1. Which of the following represents the statement "the sum of the squares of x and y is equal to the square root of the difference of x and y"?

   (A) $x^2 + y^2 = \sqrt{x - y}$

   (B) $x^2 - y^2 = \sqrt{x + y}$

   (C) $(x + y)^2 = \sqrt{x} - \sqrt{y}$

   (D) $\sqrt{x + y} = (x - y)^2$

   (E) $\sqrt{x} + \sqrt{y} = x^2 - y^2$

2. If $3a + 2b + c = 22$, $b + c = 8$, and $c = 6$, what is the value of $a + b + c$?

   (A) 4
   (B) 8
   (C) 12
   (D) 18
   (E) 36

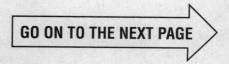

GO ON TO THE NEXT PAGE

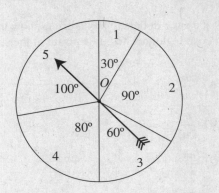

3. In the ABC board game, the circular spinner centered at O shown in the figure above is used to determine how far a player's piece will advance on the board during a given turn. After each spin, the arrow points in a random direction, and the number printed in the region where the arrow points gives the number of spaces a piece will advance. What is the probability that Kim's piece will advance 3 or 4 spaces during her turn?

    (A) $\dfrac{11}{18}$

    (B) $\dfrac{7}{18}$

    (C) $\dfrac{2}{9}$

    (D) $\dfrac{1}{6}$

    (E) $\dfrac{1}{18}$

4. If x and y are integers such that $4x - 8 > 0$ and $4y + 8 < 0$, then which of the following must be true?

    (A) xy is even.
    (B) xy is odd.
    (C) xy is negative.
    (D) xy is positive.
    (E) xy is equal to zero.

5. A rectangle with length 16 and width 6 has an area that is 3 times the area of a triangle with height 8. What is the length of the base of the triangle?

    (A) 4
    (B) 8
    (C) 12
    (D) 16
    (E) 22

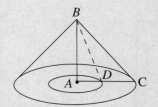

Note: Figure not drawn to scale.

6. A right circular cone is drawn above, with two circles centered at A on its base as shown. AB is the height of the cone, the measure of $\angle ABC$ is $60°$, and $\overline{BC}$ has a length of y. If $\overline{BD}$ bisects $\angle ABC$, which of the following gives the area of the smaller circle in terms of y ?

    (A) $8\pi\sqrt{y}$

    (B) $4\pi\sqrt{y}$

    (C) $y\pi$

    (D) $\dfrac{\pi}{4}y^2$

    (E) $\dfrac{\pi}{12}y^2$

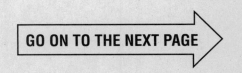

GO ON TO THE NEXT PAGE

7. During the past week, a factory produced 10,000 computer disks, of which 30 were found to be defective. At this rate, if the factory produced 1,000,000 computer disks, approximately how many would be defective?

(A)   3
(B)   30
(C)   300
(D) 3,000
(E) 30,000

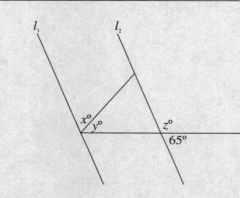

Note: Figure not drawn to scale.

8. In the figure above, lines k and l are tangent to the circle with center O at points A and C, respectively. If $OB = 4$, $OA = AB$, $AB = BC$, and $\overline{OA} \perp \overline{OC}$, then $OA =$

(A) $\sqrt{2}$
(B)   2
(C) $2\sqrt{2}$
(D)   4
(E) $4\sqrt{2}$

9. If it costs z dollars to buy n pizzas, how much will it cost, in dollars, to buy b pizzas at the same rate?

(A) $\dfrac{zb}{n}$

(B) $\dfrac{b}{zn}$

(C) $\dfrac{nb}{z}$

(D) $\dfrac{zn}{b}$

(E) znb

10. In the figure above, if $l_1 \parallel l_2$ and $x = 55$, then $y + z =$

(A) 120
(B) 145
(C) 175
(D) 180
(E) 195

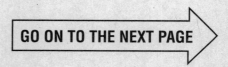

GO ON TO THE NEXT PAGE

P

O   Q   R

Note: Figure not drawn to scale.

11. In the circle above with center O, $OQ = QR$. If the radius of the circle is 8, what is the area of $\triangle OPQ$?

(A) 4
(B) $4\sqrt{3}$
(C) 8
(D) $8\sqrt{3}$
(E) 16

12. Eighty students went on a class trip. If there were fourteen more boys than girls on the trip, how many girls were on the trip?

(A) 26
(B) 33
(C) 40
(D) 47
(E) 66

13. For all x, let $f(x) = (10 - x)^2$. If $p = f(6)$, which of the following is equal to $4p$?

(A) $f(24)$
(B) $f(18)$
(C) $f(12)$
(D) $f(8)$
(E) $f(4)$

14. If b is a positive number not equal to 1, which of the following must also be positive?

(A) $\dfrac{b}{b+1}$

(B) $\dfrac{b+6}{b-3}$

(C) $\dfrac{1}{2b-2}$

(D) $2 - b$

(E) $2b - 1$

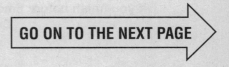
GO ON TO THE NEXT PAGE

Car 1	Blue
Car 2	Not black or green
Car 3	Green
Car 4	Same color as Car 2
Car 5	Black
Car 6	Same color as Car 3
Car 7	Red

15. The information above concerns 7 cars that drove past Janet on Friday. The cars were each one of 4 colors (red, blue, green, black). If $x = 3$, which of the following is true for x ?

(A) x could be the number of green cars.
(B) x must be the number of blue cars.
(C) x must be the number of both blue and red cars.
(D) x must be the number of black cars.
(E) x could be the number of either blue or red cars.

16. Which of the following is equivalent to $1,200 \times 10^3$?

(A) $12,000 \times 10^1$
(B) $120,000 \times 10^2$
(C) 120×10^5
(D) 120×10^4
(E) 12×10^4

STOP
If you finish before time is called, you may check your work on this section only.
Do not turn to any other section in the test.

NO TEST MATERIAL ON THIS PAGE.

SECTION 10

Time — 10 minutes

14 Questions

Turn to Section 10 of your answer sheet to answer the questions in this section.

Directions: For each question in this section, select the best answer from among the choices given and fill in the corresponding circle on the answer sheet.

The following sentences test correctness and effectiveness of expression. Part of each sentence or the entire sentence is underlined; beneath each sentence are five ways of phrasing the underlined material. Choice A repeats the original phrasing; the other four choices are different. If you think the original phrasing produces a better sentence than any of the alternatives, select choice A; if not, select one of the other choices.

In making your selection, follow the requirements of standard written English; that is, pay attention to grammar, choice of words, sentence construction, and punctuation. Your selection should result in the most effective sentence—clear and precise, without awkwardness or ambiguity.

EXAMPLE:

Laura Ingalls Wilder published her first book <u>and she was sixty-five years old then</u>.
(A) and she was sixty-five years old then
(B) when she was sixty-five
(C) at age sixty-five years old
(D) upon the reaching of sixty-five years
(E) at the time when she was sixty-five

Ⓐ ● Ⓒ Ⓓ Ⓔ

1. Theater doesn't allow much extra time, a fact with which Ryan is familiar <u>being as he was</u> in many different productions.

   (A) being as he was
   (B) as he has been
   (C) seeing as how he will be
   (D) being that he was
   (E) because he will be

2. In order to follow the building code for commercial construction, all doors should be <u>at least 3 feet wide</u> <u>and swing outward to allow wheelchair access</u>.

   (A) at least 3 feet wide and swing outward to allow wheelchair access
   (B) at least 3 feet wide and swung outward to allow wheelchair access
   (C) at least 3 feet wide and should be made to swing outward to allow wheelchair access
   (D) at least 3 feet wide or wider and swing outward to allow wheelchair access
   (E) at least 3 feet wide or wider and swung outward to allow wheelchair access

3. *On a Sunday Afternoon on the Island of the Grande Jatte*, <u>a nineteenth-century pointillism masterpiece by Seurat, is one of the better examples</u> of paintings created in this unique style.

   (A) a nineteenth-century pointillism masterpiece by Seurat, is one of the better examples
   (B) Seurat's pointillism masterpiece of the nineteenth-century can be one of the best examples
   (C) a nineteenth-century pointillism masterpiece by Seurat, is to be one of the better examples
   (D) Seurat's pointillism masterpiece, is one of the best examples in the nineteenth century
   (E) a nineteenth-century pointillism masterpiece by Seurat, is one of the best examples

4. American etiquette is different from <u>other countries</u> in that it requires the recipients of compliments to accept them with thanks, rather than turn them aside with protest.

   (A) other countries
   (B) other countries are
   (C) that of another country
   (D) what another country is
   (E) that of other countries

GO ON TO THE NEXT PAGE

5. Dr. Eglise's students were required to do a certain amount of preparation for each <u>class: this being that</u> <u>they had to</u> read an article he gave them and brainstorm ideas for an essay on the same topic.

(A) class: this being that they had to
(B) class, including
(C) class: they had to
(D) class, however having to
(E) class, and they had to not only

6. Renowned for her writing across several subjects and <u>genres, Barbara Kingsolver's poems are</u> <u>impassioned denunciations of</u> violence in Central America.

(A) genres, Barbara Kingsolver's poems are impassioned denunciations of
(B) genres; Barbara Kingsolver wrote poems that are impassioned denunciations of
(C) genres, Barbara Kingsolver writes poems which passionately denounce
(D) genres, the poems of Barbara Kingsolver poems passionately denounce
(E) genres; passionately denouncing is what Barbara Kingsolver's poems do to

7. A satellite of the sun as the moon is of the Earth, a planet usually has a synodic mass, a sidereal <u>period, and they have moons of their own</u>.

(A) period, and they have moons of their own
(B) period, and with moons of their own
(C) period, and it has moons of its own
(D) period, and moons of their own
(E) period, and moons of its own

8. Although the badger has a reputation as a fierce animal, it has a gentler side which is shown in several works of <u>literature, these include</u> *Cold Moons* by Aeron Clement and *Incident at Hawk's Hill* by Allen Eckert.

(A) literature, these include
(B) literature, two of these are
(C) literature, these being
(D) literature, such as
(E) literature, like

9. A majority of the girls in Toria's class wore sandals even on wintry days, <u>however there was a great the</u> <u>effort made by teachers and parents</u> to discourage them from doing so.

(A) however there was a great effort made by teachers and parents
(B) along with great efforts made by the teachers and parents
(C) when even parents and teachers are making the effort
(D) despite great efforts made by teachers and parents
(E) even though great efforts by teachers and parents

10. After polling the parish, the church's roof committee voted to replace the slate tiles with asphalt shingles <u>and they did this to</u> save thousands of dollars.

(A) and they did this to
(B) and so it could
(C) they wanted to
(D) in order that they might
(E) in order to

11. A truck collided with Emma's car and, although she was <u>uninjured, she could hardly stop</u> trembling with fright.

(A) uninjured, she could hardly stop
(B) uninjured; she couldn't hardly stop
(C) uninjured, she couldn't hardly stop
(D) uninjured, since she couldn't stop
(E) uninjured, she could, however, hardly stop

12. Because of the danger of rabies within the state, <u>this is the reason for the ban on transporting skunks</u> <u>and raccoons to open spaces across town lines</u>.

(A) this is the reason for the ban on transporting skunks and raccoons to open spaces across town lines
(B) there is a ban on transporting skunks and raccoons to open spaces across town lines
(C) a ban on skunks and raccoons in open spaces across town lines has been declared
(D) a ban has been declared on skunks and raccoons openly across town lines
(E) it is the reason for the open ban to transport skunks and raccoons to spaces across town lines

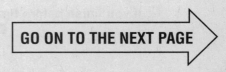
GO ON TO THE NEXT PAGE

13. The population of Las Vegas, the fastest growing city in the United States, <u>has increased by more than three times</u> in the past hundred years.

    (A) has increased by more than three times
    (B) increased by more than three times
    (C) was more than tripled
    (D) has more than tripled
    (E) had more than tripled

14. Several recent studies have indicated that a student's ability <u>to seek help from their teachers predicts</u> college success as well as a standardized test score does.

    (A) to seek help from their teachers predicts
    (B) in seeking help from their teachers and predicting
    (C) to seek help from teachers predicts
    (D) to seek help from his or her teachers always predicts
    (E) to not only seek the help of teachers but also predict

STOP
**If you finish before time is called, you may check your work on this section only.
Do not turn to any other section in the test.**

NO TEST MATERIAL ON THIS PAGE.

PRACTICE TEST 3: ANSWER KEY

Section 2 Math	Section 3 Reading	Section 4 Writing	Section 5 Math	Section 6 Reading	Section 7 Reading (Exp)	Section 8 Reading	Section 9 Math	Section 10 Writing
1. A	1. A	1. A	1. A	1. E	1. C	1. B	1. A	1. B
2. E	2. D	2. E	2. D	2. B	2. A	2. E	2. C	2. A
3. A	3. A	3. D	3. C	3. B	3. A	3. E	3. B	3. E
4. D	4. B	4. C	4. D	4. A	4. D	4. C	4. C	4. E
5. B	5. C	5. B	5. E	5. E	5. E	5. D	5. B	5. C
6. E	6. E	6. D	6. E	6. C	6. D	6. E	6. E	6. C
7. A	7. C	7. A	7. E	7. D	7. B	7. C	7. D	7. E
8. A	8. D	8. B	8. A	8. B	8. C	8. C	8. C	8. D
9. E	9. C	9. C	9. 4	9. E	9. B	9. A	9. A	9. D
10. E	10. E	10. D	10. 1600	10. C	10. B	10. D	10. C	10. E
11. A	11. B	11. E	11. 80	11. B	11. E	11. E	11. D	11. A
12. D	12. B	12. C	12. 34	12. E	12. D	12. C	12. B	12. B
13. B	13. E	13. D	13. 91	13. D	13. E	13. D	13. B	13. D
14. C	14. B	14. D	14. 1.65	14. D	14. B	14. D	14. A	14. C
15. E	15. A	15. C	15. $\frac{9}{25}$ or .36	15. E	15. E	15. B	15. E	
16. C	16. D	16. E	16. 8.93	16. E	16. D	16. E	16. D	
17. B	17. E	17. D	17. 2	17. A	17. C	17. D		
18. E	18. C	18. E	18. 9	18. E	18. A	18. A		
19. D	19. B	19. D		19. A	19. C	19. D		
20. C	20. E	20. E		20. D	20. E			
	21. E	21. A		21. C	21. D			
	22. B	22. B		22. D	22. B			
	23. A	23. D		23. A	23. C			
	24. D	24. B		24. E	24. A			
		25. A						
		26. C						
		27. E						
		28. B						
		29. A						
		30. D						
		31. B						
		32. A						
		33. E						
		34. A						
		35. C						

SAT SCORING WORKSHEET

For directions on how to score your SAT practice test, see pages 5–7. Section 4 is an unscored, experimental section.

SAT WRITING SECTION

Total Writing Multiple-Choice Questions Correct from Sections 5 and 10:

—

Total Writing Multiple-Choice Questions Incorrect from Sections 4 and 10: _____ ÷ 4 =

Grammar Raw Score:

Grammar Scaled Subscore!

Compare the Grammar Raw Score to the Writing Multiple-Choice Subscore Conversion Table on the next page to find the Grammar Scaled Subscore.

+

Your Essay Score (2–12): _____ × 2 =

Writing Raw Score:

Compare Raw Score to SAT Score Conversion Table on the next page to find the Writing Scaled Score.

Writing Scaled Score!

SAT CRITICAL READING SECTION

Total Critical Reading Questions Correct from Sections 3, 7, and 9:

—

Total Critical Reading Questions Incorrect from Sections 3, 7, and 9: _____ ÷ 4 =

Critical Reading Raw Score:

Compare Raw Score to SAT Score Conversion Table on the next page to find the Critical Reading Scaled Score.

Critical Reading Scaled Score!

SAT MATH SECTION

Total Math Grid-In Questions Correct from Section 6:

+

Total Math Multiple-Choice Questions Correct from Sections 2, 6, and 8:

—

Total Math Multiple-Choice Questions Incorrect from Sections 2, 6, and 8: _____ ÷ 4 =

Don't include wrong answers from grid-ins!

Math Raw Score:

Compare Raw Score to SAT Score Conversion Table on the next page to find the Math Scaled Score.

Math Scaled Score!

SAT SCORE CONVERSION TABLE

Raw Score	Writing Scaled Score	Reading Scaled Score	Math Scaled Score	Raw Score	Writing Scaled Score	Reading Scaled Score	Math Scaled Score	Raw Score	Writing Scaled Score	Reading Scaled Score	Math Scaled Score
73	800			47	590–630	600–640	680–720	21	400–440	420–460	460–50
72	790–800			46	590–630	590–630	670–710	20	390–430	410–450	450–49
71	780–800			45	580–620	580–620	660–700	19	380–420	400–440	450–49
70	770–800			44	570–610	580–620	650–690	18	370–410	400–440	440–48
69	770–800			43	570–610	570–610	640–680	17	370–410	390–430	430–47
68	760–800			42	560–600	570–610	630–670	16	360–400	380–420	420–46
67	760–800	800		41	560–6 00	560–600	620–660	15	350–390	380–420	420–46
66	760–800	770–800		40	550–590	550–590	620–660	14	340–380	370–410	410–45
65	750–790	750–790		39	540–580	550–590	610–650	13	330–370	360–400	400–44
64	740–780	740–780		38	530–570	540–580	600–640	12	320–360	350–390	400–44
63	730–750	740–780		37	530–570	530–570	590–630	11	320–360	350–390	390–43
62	720–760	730–770		36	520–560	530–570	590–630	10	310–350	340–380	380–42
61	710–750	720–760		35	510–550	520–560	580–620	9	300–340	330–370	370–41
60	700–740	710–750		34	500–540	510–550	570–610	8	290–330	310–350	360–40
59	690–730	700–740		33	490–530	500–540	560–600	7	280–320	300–340	350–39
58	680–720	690–730		32	480–520	500–540	560–600	6	270–310	300–340	340–38
57	680–720	680–720		31	470–510	490–530	540–580	5	260–300	290–330	330–37
56	670–710	670–710		30	470–510	480–520	530–570	4	240–280	280–320	320–36
55	660–720	670–710		29	460–500	470–510	520–560	3	230–270	270–310	310–35
54	650–690	660–700	800	28	450–490	470–510	510–550	2	230–270	260–300	290–33
53	640–680	650–690	780–800	27	440–480	460–500	510–550	1	220–260	230–270	270–31
52	630–670	640–680	750–790	26	430–470	450–490	500–540	0	210–250	200–240	240–28
51	630–670	630–670	740–780	25	420–460	450–490	490–530	–1	200–240	200–230	220–26
50	620–660	620–660	730–770	24	410–450	440–480	480–520	–2	200–230	200–220	210–25
49	610–650	610–650	710–750	23	410–450	430–470	480–520	–3	200–220	200–210	200–24
48	600–640	600–640	700–740	22	400–440	420–460	470–510				

WRITING MULTIPLE-CHOICE SUBSCORE CONVERSION TABLE

Grammar Raw Score	Grammar Scaled Subscore	Grammar Raw Score	Grammar Scaled Subscore	Grammar Raw Score	Grammar Scaled Subscore	Grammar Raw Score	Grammar Scaled Subscore	Grammar Raw Score	Grammar Scaled Subscore	Grammar Raw Score	Grammar Scaled Subscore
49	79–80	40	70–74	31	61–65	22	52–56	13	43–47	4	33–37
48	78–80	39	69–73	30	60–64	21	52–56	12	42–46	3	31–35
47	78–80	38	68–72	29	59–63	20	51–55	11	41–45	2	28–32
46	77–80	37	67–71	28	58–62	19	50–54	10	40–44	1	26–30
45	76–80	36	66–70	27	57–61	18	49–53	9	39–43	0	23–27
44	75–79	35	65–69	26	56–60	17	48–52	8	37–41	–1	22–26
43	73–77	34	64–68	25	55–59	16	47–51	7	36–40	–2	21–25
42	72–76	33	63–67	24	54–58	15	46–50	6	35–39	–3	20–24
41	71–75	32	62–66	23	53–57	14	45–49	5	34–38		

23

Answers and Explanations for Practice Test 3

1. **A** To solve for y, you should start by moving all the y's to one side of the equation. If you subtract $4y$ from each side, you get $8 = 8y + 24$. Now subtract 24 from each side of the equation, to give you $-16 = 8y$. Finally, you should divide each side by 8, which gives you $-2 = y$.

2. **E** Let's plug $x = 2$ and $x = 4$ into the answer choices, and see which choice makes $f(2) = 10$ and $f(4) = 44$. If you plug 2 into (A), you get 10. (B) gives you 20. (C) gives you 18, and (D) gives you 8. (E) gives you 10; leave it in. Now plug in $x = 4$ into the choices that remain. (A) gives you 14 so eliminate it. (E) gives you 44. Only (E) works for both of our numbers, so it must be the answer.

3. **A** If the probability of picking a blue jellybean is $\frac{1}{5}$, then you know that $\frac{1}{5}$ of the beans in the jar are blue. Let's try plugging in the answers. If there are 78 blue jellybeans, then you would have a total of $58 + 78 + 78 = 214$ beans in the jar. Is 78 equal to $\frac{1}{5}$ of 214? Nope, so (C) cannot be right. Let's try (B). If there are 56 blue jellybeans, then you would have a total of $58 + 78 + 56 = 192$ beans in the jar. Is 56 equal to $\frac{1}{5}$ of 192? Nope. So let's try (A). If there are 34 blue jellybeans, then there will be a total of $58 + 78 + 34 = 170$ jellybeans. Is 34 equal to $\frac{1}{5}$ of 170? Yes, so (A) is our answer.

4. **D** To find the 10th term of 3×2^n, plug 10 in for n: $3 \times 2^{10} = 3 \times 1{,}024 = 3{,}072$.

5. **B** Whenever you see variables in the answer choices, you should plug in. Start by plugging in a number for x. If $x = 10$, then 3 more than x is 13. Now you know that 13 is 2 more than y, so $y = 11$. When you plug in 11 for y in all of the answers, (B) is the only one that gives you the answer $x = 10$, your target answer.

6. **E** Don't assume that the figure $ABCD$ must be a rectangle; it doesn't have to be. All you need to do here is follow the rules: You know that $AB = BC$ and that $BC = 12$, so you now know two of the four sides (sides AB and BC) are equal to 12. You know that AD is going to be one quarter of AB, so AD must be equal to 3. Finally, you know that AD is one half of CD, so CD must be equal to 6. This makes the total perimeter $12 + 12 + 3 + 6$, or 33.

7. **A** Since it is much easier working with numbers than with variables, let's plug in some consecutive multiples of 5. Let's say that $a = 5$, $b = 10$, $c = 15$, and $d = 20$. The question then asks for the value of $(a - c)(d - b)$. Using the numbers you just plugged in, this becomes $(5 - 15)(20 - 10)$, or $(-10)(10)$, which equals -100.

8. **A** Let's take this one step at a time. First, just concentrate on the right side: $3b + 3 \leq 18$. You can simply treat this like an equation: If you subtract 3 from each side, you get $3b \leq 15$. Now you can divide each side by 3 to get $b \geq 5b$. This will allow you to eliminate (B) and (E). Now let's focus on the left side: $-9 \leq 3b + 3$. Again, let's subtract 3 from each side, which gives you $-12 \leq 3b$. By dividing each side by 3, you get $-4 \leq b$. This will eliminate (C) and (D), so our answer must be (A).

9. **E** Let's start by finding the amount per bulb when bought in a pack of 6: If you can buy 6 bulbs for \$30, then each bulb will cost $\$30 \div 6$, or \$5. In a box of 12, each bulb will cost $\$48 \div 12$, or \$4. Now you need to figure out the percentage difference between \$5 and \$4. The formula for percentage difference is $\frac{difference}{original} \times 100$. In this case, a reduction from \$5 to \$4 is a difference of \$1 over an original price of \$5. So the percentage difference is $\frac{1}{5} = 20\%$.

10. **E** When dealing with ranges of values in the answer choices, plug in numbers that appear in some, but not all, of the ranges in the answer choices. This allows you to use POE. For example, if $x = -5$, then $g(-5) = \sqrt{(-5^2) - 9} = \sqrt{25 - 9} = \sqrt{16} = 4$. Since you can plug 5 into the function without any problem, -5 is in the domain of g, so eliminate answers that exclude -5: eliminate (B) and (C). Now plug in -10 for x. -10 works, so eliminate (A), which doesn't include -10. Plugging in $x = 0$ also works, which eliminates (D), leaving you with (E). Another option is to graph the function on a graphing calculator, and look for the values of x that are, and are not, allowed.

11. **A** Remember that the mode is the number that appears most often in a list. The number that appears most often (17 times) in the rainfall chart is 0.

12. **D** If you add up the amount of rainfall accounted for in the chart, you get:

    5 days of 1 inch = 5 total inches of rain
    3 days of 2 inches = 6 total inches of rain
    3 days of 3 inches = 9 total inches of rain
    2 days of 4 inches = 8 total inches of rain

    for a grand total of 28 inches. If you expect 200 inches in a year, what percent of 200 is 28 inches? Translate this into algebra as $\frac{x}{100} \cdot 200 = 28$, and you get $x = 14\%$.

13. **B** First, find the slope of line l by using the slope formula: $\frac{y_1 - y_2}{x_1 - x_2} = \frac{5 - 2}{4 - 3} = \frac{3}{1}$. A line perpendicular to line l must have a slope that is the negative reciprocal of l's slope. So, its slope should be $-\frac{1}{3}$. In the standard line equation $y = mx + b$, m is the slope. Only (B) has a slope of $-\frac{1}{3}$. If you didn't remember the rule about the slope of perpendicular lines, you could have sketched out each of the lines and looked for the answer that looked perpendicular to l.

14. **C** (B) and (D) have negative values, so you can eliminate them right away. Let's start with the area of the whole figure. The square has sides of 2, so its area is 4. Now let's remove the area of the two semicircles (which is the same as the area of one whole circle). These semi-circles have a radius of 1, so the area of one whole circle will be π. So the area of the shaded region will be $4 - \pi$.

15. **E** Let's plug in the answer choices, starting with (C). 20 minutes is $\frac{1}{3}$ of an hour, so (using *rate* × *time = distance*) Jennifer ran $6 \times \frac{1}{3} = 2$ miles to school. If she returned at 4 miles per hour, you can find the time for her return trip using the formula $4 \times t = 2$. Her return time is $\frac{1}{2}$ hour, or 30 minutes. Her total time is supposed to be one hour, but here it's only 50 minutes. Eliminate (A), (B), and (C) because they're too small. Let's skip to (E); that multiple of 6 looks like it will work better with time units than 22. 24 minutes is $\frac{2}{5}$ of an hour, so Jennifer ran $6 \times \frac{2}{5} = 2.4$ miles to school. If she returned at 4 miles per hour, you can find the time for her return trip using $4 \times t = 2.4$. Her return time is $\frac{3}{5}$ of an hour, or 36 minutes. Her total time is indeed one hour, so (E) is the answer.

SECTION 2

16. **C** Since $\overline{AC}$ and $\overline{AB}$ are each radii of the circle, you know they are equal in length. This means that the triangle *ABC* must be isosceles, and the base and the height are equal. What base and height would give the triangle an area of 18? The base and height would each have to equal to 6, since $\frac{1}{2} \times 6 \times 6 = 18$. Since the circumference of the circle is equal to $2\pi r$, the circumference will be equal to 12π.

17. **B** Plugging In the Answers is the easiest way to solve this problem. If the radius is 4, then the area, πr^2 is 16π, and the circumference, $2\pi r$, is 8π. The area using the value in (C) is *twice* the area, not half. In order to make the area smaller, try (B). If the radius is 1, then the area is π and the circumference is 2π. This is what the problem asks for! (B) must be the correct answer.

18. **E** The statement tells you that Marta will get the project completed on time. You don't know if other people could get the project done on time. You cannot conclude (A), (B), (C), or (D) because there could be other people that also get projects completed on time. Also, for (B), Marta could be assigned to Project B and Project A. You can conclude (E): If the project is not on time, then Marta could not have been assigned to it because if Marta were assigned to it, the project would be on time.

19. **D** You know that any two sides of a triangle must add up to be larger than the third side. This means that whatever the third side of the triangle is, its value + 5 must be larger than 7. This means that the third side must be larger than 2. Since the question specifies that the third side has an integer value, the smallest integer larger than 2 is 3. So the third side will measure 3, and the perimeter will be $3 + 5 + 7 = 15$.

20. **C** A good rule of thumb on the SAT is: If it looks like a quadratic equation, try to make it into a quadratic equation. If you try to solve for *x*, the best way is to move 12 to the same side of the equation, and then factor. $x^2 - x - 12 = 0$ will factor as $(x - 4)(x + 3)$. This means that *x* could be 4 or –3. You can factor for *y* in the same way, so *y* could also be 4 or –3. The greatest value for $x - y$ will be if $x = 4$ and $y = -3$, which is a difference of 7.

1. **A** For the second blank, a good clue is *rather quiet* combined with the trigger *while*. This tells you that whatever comes in the second blank must mean that she was the opposite of *rather quiet*; in fact, she must have liked being around people. You can eliminate (B), (C), (D), and (E), leaving only (A).

2. **D** Even if you can't find an exact word for the first blank, you can probably tell that it's going to be a negative word because of the clues *serious* and *natural weather patterns cannot*. This makes it likely that the first blank is discussing a problem with meteorology. This will allow you to eliminate (A), (C), and (E). What might be a problem with meteorology? Probably if natural weather patterns cannot be "studied" or "created" in a lab. This will eliminate (B), and makes (D) our best answer.

3. **A** In this sentence the second blank has a better clue, so you should start there. The clue is *imaginary* and the trigger *or* tells you that the blank is the opposite of *imaginary*. A good word for the blank is *real* or *not imaginary*. You can eliminate (B), (C), and (D). For the first blank, what kind of word would describe what a playwright could do in order to make the audience uncertain? That playwright might combine realism and fantasy. Conversely, if the playwright *exposed realism* and *fantasy,* why would you be unable to tell fantasy from reality? Therefore, eliminate (E); (A) is our best answer.

4. **B** The key to this question is the semicolon; this trigger tells you that whatever follows the semicolon describes the word in the blank. What follows says that the exterior of the car is different but the interior is the same. A good phrase for the blank is "on the surface." (B) is the closest.

5. **C** This sentence may seem to lack a good clue. That is because the clue is the relationship between the two blanks. In this case, *virtually disregarding the idea that* indicates that they need to be opposites; either educators view it as bad while it actually has the power to be good, or educators view it as good while ignoring the fact that it can be bad. Knowing this, you can eliminate any answer pairs whose words are not strongly opposed—choices such as (A), (B), (D), and (E). The only answer that contains two strongly opposed words is (C).

6. **E** In this sentence, the clue is *convincing her readers to believe*. This means that she must be able to create extremely "believable" characters. (E) comes closest to this meaning.

7. **C** From the clue that *more recent works…introduce fewer problems*, you know that the first blank should describe a problem of seventeenth-century literature—a word like "difficult" for readers. This eliminates (A) and (E). For the second blank, you will need to say that the *more recent works* are not difficult for readers. (B) and (D) don't really have anything to do with reading, so our best answer is (C).

8. **D** The clue in this sentence is *who gave generous holiday bonuses and often overlooked minor lapses in judgment*. A word to describe someone like this is *kind* or *generous*. This easily eliminates (A), (B), and (C), which are negative words. *Gregarious* and *munificent* come close as both are positive words, but *gregarious* means social and *munificent* means generous, making (D) the best choice.

9. **C** With questions that ask you about the structure of a passage, try to match the description to the specifics of the passage. For (A), the meteor theory is not explained in depth. How much depth can you have in one paragraph? Remember to watch out for extreme words or answer choices that don't make common sense. Eliminate (A). There is no mention of *inaccurate data,* as mentioned in (B), so you can eliminate it. Only one flaw of the first theory is mentioned in the paragraph, so you need to eliminate (D) because it talks about *many flaws.* The people who support the first theory are barely mentioned and never criticized, so eliminate (E). The structure of the passage is most similar to (C).

SECTION 3

10. E Before answering a main idea question, always state the main idea in your own words. The author's main point is that there is a flaw in the current theory of dinosaur extinction leading to a revised theory. (A) and (C) are too narrow and not about *why* the dinosaurs died out. Eliminate them. (D) is too extreme; you do not know if this *conclusively* explains *what caused the extinction of the dinosaurs.* Eliminate it. You now have two choices, (B) and (E). When you have it down to two, look for what makes one of the answers wrong. The author never says that the original theory is totally wrong, but rather that there is a flaw in it. This makes (B) extreme because it says that the passage thoroughly disproves the current theory. Eliminate (B) and choose (E).

11. B The author introduces Jefferson and Franklin as examples of famous American figures whom you might have thought had written the pledge of allegiance, whereas the Pledge's true author is not well known. (A) is close, but says that Jefferson and Franklin could have written a *better* pledge, and the author never says that. Eliminate it. (C), (D), and (E) are not supported by the passage and were not the point of the sentence that mentions Franklin and Jefferson.

12. B Remember that in an inference question you need to find an answer that is supported by the passage. (B) is supported by the sentence that mentions that there were later revisions that added the words *"under God."* You have no information on (A), (C), or (E), so eliminate them. (D) is true, but is never mentioned in the passage. Don't use outside information to answer the questions on this test.

13. E This is a line reference question, so you should read these lines in context to find the answer. You know from lines 13–15 that Penfield believed *brain studies…would lead inevitably to an understanding of the mind.* The correct answer is a paraphrase of this idea. (E) says exactly this.

14. B Pribram's and Bohm's collaboration is discussed in paragraph 5. Reread the paragraph and then use POE. (A), (C), (D), and (E) may sound tempting but none of them are actually stated. (B) is a nice, general choice, which sums up the scientists' intentions.

15. A For a vocab-in-context question like this one, you should cover the word *bent*, reread the sentence, and put our own word in the blank. In this sentence, you would probably insert a word like *belief* or *inclination.* The word that best fits this idea is (A).

16. D *"Peter Pan school of neuroscience"* is mentioned in paragraph 8. If you read the rest of the paragraph for context, you see that the point of the paragraph is that researchers become disillusioned with claims that the mind can *be explained* in terms of brain functioning. Which choice best paraphrases this idea? (D) does.

17. E Unorthodox research is mentioned at the beginning of paragraph 9. There it states that unorthodox researchers were open to innovative attitudes and transcendental influences. (E) paraphrases this idea.

18. C The best answer is (C). If you replace the word *waxing* with a blank, the sentence says *a small number of them end up ------- philosophical* and "becoming" is the only choice that fits sensibly into the sentence. The other words all relate to the word *waxing*, but do not make sense in this context.

19. B In paragraph four, Dr. Penfield changes *the solid line connecting the spirit and brain into an interrupted one.* (A), (C), and (E) were all painted on the rock mentioned in (D), but did not signify his doubts. Lines 24–27 explain why Penfield's motivation behind changing the line. (B) is the best answer.

SECTION 3

20. **E** The best answer is (E). The wording in this choice is too extreme and thus appropriate for a NOT answer; the passage focuses on scientists who came to believe that brain studies could NOT explain fully the mind's workings. (A) appears in lines 77–78, and in (B), *not unwilling* means willing; the passage focuses on scientists willing to *adopt innovative attitudes as well as pursue unorthodox lines of inquiry*. In (C), the five scientists mentioned in the first half of this article are *brain researchers [who] have a change of heart late in their careers*. (D) appears in lines 25–27.

21. **E** Brain-injured patients such as those in (A) are not mentioned in the passage, nor are the type of questions patients asked Penfield. *Impulses* in the passage refers to electrical impulses applied to parts of the brain, (C), not to actions. Patients reported experiences that were not happening at the time, not ones that had never taken place, (D). The best answer is (E), mentioned in lines 55–56.

22. **B** The best answer is (B), as stated in lines 28–32. The wordings in answer choices (A), *prove definitively*, (C), *fully explained*, and (E), *concrete evidence* are too extreme. (D) is incorrect because these scientists are in agreement, not in contrast, with Penfield.

23. **A** The operative word here is *orthodox*: An orthodox scientist does not believe anything out of the ordinary in his field, and the scientists mentioned in the article did indeed believe that the mind could be understood through study of its physical functioning—until they had a change of heart. Orthodox scientists have not changed their views from the original one (lines 58–59). A Greek word is mentioned in the second paragraph, but not a Greek belief about science, so (B) can be eliminated. (C), (D), and (E) are unorthodox approaches to scientific inquiry, as detailed throughout the paragraph. (A) is the best answer.

24. **D** The best answer is (D). Hendle is mentioned as a professor of philosophy at Yale, but not necessarily as Penfield's former teacher. (A) appears in lines 25–27, (B) in 35–38, (C) throughout the passage, and (E) in lines 51–54.

1. **A** There are no errors in the sentence as it is written. (B), (C), (D), and (E) all introduce pronouns that are incorrect: In (B), *its* is singular but *families* is plural; in (C), *they're* has the wrong meaning; in (D), *it's* has the wrong meaning and is singular; and in (E), *there* isn't even a pronoun.

2. **E** The original sentence is in the passive voice, rarely the best choice. (B), (C), and (D) are also in the passive voice; (B) and (D) are also rewritten awkwardly. (E) is the most streamlined version of the sentence, and avoids having a misplaced modifier.

3. **D** The original sentence contains an idiom error. (D) avoids the unidiomatic phrasing of the original by linking an appropriate prepositional phrase, *with breeding*, to the verb *credited*.

4. **C** Because the subject is *classical composers*, the examples must be the composers themselves; not *Haydn's credit*, but *Haydn*. That eliminates all but (B) and (C). (B) does not use the *from...to* construction that describes a *range* and it changes the meaning by eliminating mention of *credit*.

5. **B** A *cause* cannot be *where*, as in (A) and (C), or *when*, as in (D). (E) is a very awkward passive phrase, *the management by seniors of*.

6. **D** The original sentence would be fine if the word *which* was just taken out, which (D) does. The word *which* makes this sentence a fragment, as does *that* in (B). *And* in (C) simply does not make sense as a sentence. (E) incorrectly uses the future tense; the sentence should be in the present.

7. **A** This sentence is correct as it stands. Adding *which* in (B) makes it a fragment. Both (C) and (D) are wordy, and (E), with the addition of *–ing*, makes little sense.

8. **B** (B) is the clearest, most concise choice. As written in (A), *she was* is redundant. (C) is awkward. (D) changes the verb tense so it no longer agrees with the non-underlined part of the sentence. (E) uses the word *being*, which on the SAT usually indicates unnecessary wordiness.

9. **C** This sentence contains a misplaced modifier: *In addition to having more natural resources* should be describing *the United States*. This eliminates (A), (B), and (E). (C) and (D) both properly place *The United States* directly after the comma, but (D) moves the words *also* and *significantly*, changing the meaning.

10. **D** The original sentence contains a verb agreement error. The word *consider* cannot be followed by *as*. Hence (B) and (C) are incorrect. (E) is also not idiomatic.

11. **E** The original sentence is awkward and wordy, as are (C) and (D). (B) contains an unnecessary and awkward pronoun, *it*. (E) provides the most clear and concise phrasing.

12. **C** (C), which uses the *-ing* form, creates a problem in verb construction. *Has become* is the correct phrasing.

13. **D** *Weakly* is describing the appearance of the paintings, not the painting's sense of vision, and so it should be an adjective (describing a noun), not an adverb. It should read *look weak*.

14. **D** Parallelism is the problem in this sentence. To keep the list parallel, omit *to*.

15. **C** Since *rock* is a verb, the modifying word *slow* should be an adverb. Change *slow* to *slowly*.

16. **E** There is no error in the sentence as it is written.

17. **D** In (D), *more* is redundant; *healthier,* all by itself, is the proper phrasing.

18. **E** There is no error in the sentence as it is written.

19. **D** This is a verb tense error. Since *realized* is in the past tense and the sentence mentions the previous summer, *wear* should be the past tense *wore*.

20. **E** There is no error in the sentence as it is written.

21. **A** The pronoun refers to people, and thus should read, *the students who*; the word *which* is appropriate for anything else except humans.

22. **B** There is a pronoun agreement error here. Since the subject is *you*, change *yourself* to *you*.

23. **D** The pronoun *me* is incorrect, as the sentence indicates that John liked the new model more than the author liked the model, not that John liked the new model more than he liked the author. It should read either *I* or *I did*.

24. **B** This sentence has an idiom error; *independent from* should be *independent of*.

25. **A** To correct this ambiguous pronoun, name the people who make this statement or, if none exist, remove *they say*.

26. **C** In (C), *it* is an ambiguous pronoun; it is unclear whether *it* refers to the *barn,* the *property,* or *where he had intended*.

27. **E** There is no error in this sentence as it is written.

28. **B** Because *viewers* is plural, *preference* should also be plural. It should read *their preferences*.

29. **A** There is no need to state that 1643 is a year. To reduce the redundancy, omit *the year*.

30. **D** The use of the word *however* in (D) best reflects the shift in the meaning of the two sentences. The first sentence discusses Graham's hope of becoming a lawyer and the second sentence shows a change in this plan. None of the other answers emphasizes this transition.

31. **B** The first two sentences make it clear that you are discussing the past. The use of the present tense verb *is* in sentence 3 is therefore incorrect, and needs to be changed to the past tense.

32. **A** The original sentence is a fragment. (A) is short and correctly uses the past tense. (B) incorrectly uses the verb *were relying,* which is not in the simple past tense. (C) is unnecessarily wordy and subtly changes the meaning. (D) also changes the meaning by saying that it is Graham and not the *jobs* that relied on his keen insight. (E) incorrectly uses the verb *were relying.*

33. **E** When combining two sentences, determine how their content should be linked. The first sentence discusses what you would expect of most people, while the second sentence discusses how Graham's behavior differs. Only (E) shows that contrasting relationship between the two sentences.

34. **A** There is no reason to include the phrase *of course* at the beginning of the last sentence, as the passage does not give you a reason to think this is an obvious fact. Eliminate (B). (C) and (D) would make the end of the passage awkward, and (E) does not agree with the author's opinion of Graham's accomplishments as expressed throughout the passage.

35. **C** (C) is the best bridge between the two sentences, linking Graham's success with his compassion. (A) and (E) are fragments; (B) and (D) are not indicated in the passage.

1. **A** If both x and y are integers, it doesn't matter if they are positive or negative, odd or even; when the absolute value of their product is taken, by definition, it will be positive. (None of the other answer choices need *necessarily* be true, although (C), (D), and (E) *could* be.)

2. **D** If you draw the lines from the center of a hexagon to its six vertices, you create 6 equilateral triangles. All the interior angles must add up to 360. $\angle FOD$ comprises 2 of them. The answer is 120, or (D).

3. **C** Let's multiply out what you have in parentheses using FOIL. This gives you $9 + 3\sqrt{x} - 3\sqrt{x} - x$, or $9 - x$. So our equation now reads $9 - x = 7$. This makes $x = 2$.

4. **D** The easiest way to solve this problem is to get to a common rate. You know that one packer packs 15 boxes every 2 minutes, and the other packs 15 boxes every 3 minutes. If you put these in terms of 6-minute intervals, the first packer will pack 45 boxes in 6 minutes, while the other packs 30 every 6 minutes. This means that together they will pack 75 boxes in 6 minutes, 150 boxes in 12 minutes, and 300 boxes in 24 minutes.

5. **E** One of the safest ways to solve this problem is by Plugging In the Answers. While you normally start with (C), you don't want to forget that this is an EXCEPT question, so let's just start with (A) and go straight through to (E). Assume $x = 20$. Is the remainder when 20 is divided by 5 the same as the remainder when 20 is divided by 4? Sure, the remainder is 0 in each case. So you can cross off (A). (This is an EXCEPT question, don't forget!). How about (B)? If $x = 21$, is the remainder the same? Yes, the remainder is 1 when 21 is divided by 4 and when it is divided by 5. How about (C)? If $x = 22$, the remainder is 2 when divided by 4 and when divided by 5. How about (D)? If $x = 23$, then the remainder is 3 when divided by 4 and when divided by 5. If $x = 24$, however, the remainder when 24 is divided by 4 is 0, while the remainder when 24 is divided by 5 is 4. Therefore, (E) is our answer.

6. **E** Plug in numbers for the base and height of triangle ACD. For example, $AC = 10$ and $AD = 8$. The area of ACD is therefore $\frac{1}{2}(10)(8) = 40$. The area of ABE is $\frac{1}{2}(5)(4) = 10$. The area of the shaded region is therefore $40 - 10 = 30$, so the fraction of ACD that is shaded is $\frac{30}{40} = \frac{3}{4}$.

7. **E** First, find the union, (C), and intersection, (D), of sets A and B. (C) = {1, 2, 3, 4, 6, 8, 9}. (D) = {1, 8}. For cd to be odd, both c and d must be odd. The probability that c is odd is $\frac{3}{7}$, and the probability that d is odd is $\frac{1}{2}$. To get the probability that both are odd, you multiply the two probabilities together. Alternatively, list out the 14 pairs of c and d and you'll find 3 of them that multiply to an odd number.

8. **A** Let's try plugging in some numbers for this problem. Let's start by choosing 18 for x and 2 for y. This makes their product 36, which is divisible by 36. You also made sure to pick a value for x that is divisible by 6. Using these numbers, let's look at statements I, II, and III. Are they true? Statement I is not true, since 2 cannot be evenly divided by 18; since statement I is not true, you can eliminate (B) and (D). Now what about statement II? It's also false, so you can cross off (C) and (E). This means our answer must be (A).

9. **4**

    Negative exponents mean to take the reciprocal and raise it to the power. So $9^{-2} = \left(\frac{1}{9}\right)^2 = \frac{1}{81}$. Now find what power of $\frac{1}{3} = \frac{1}{81}$. Since $3^4 = 81$, $\left(\frac{1}{3}\right)^4 = \frac{1}{81}$, and x must be 4.

SECTION 5

10. 1600

If the area of the circle is 400π, then you can figure out its radius. $A = \pi r^2$ so $400 = \pi r^2$, and the radius is 20. The diameter of the circle is twice the radius, or 40. Since this circle is inscribed in the square, you know that the diameter of the circle is equal to one side of the square, so you know that each side is equal to 40. The area of the square is $40 \times 40 = 1,600$.

11. 80

You know that the total number of students is 320. Since you know that there are 60 more juniors than seniors, the easy way to find out how many of each there are is to take half of 320 (which is 160) and then add half of 60 to get the number of juniors, and subtract half of 60 to get the number of seniors. This means that the number of juniors is 190 and the number of seniors is 130. (Their difference is 60 and their sum is 320.) Therefore, there are 190 juniors. Knowing that there are 30 more female juniors than male juniors, you can find the number of male juniors the same way—take half of 190 (which is 95) and subtract half of 30: $95 - 15 = 80$.

12. 34

If a rectangle has a width of 5 and a diagonal of 13, this means that its other side must be 12, since 5:12:13 is a Pythagorean triple. Therefore, the perimeter of the rectangle will be $5 + 12 + 5 + 12 = 34$.

13. 91

Let's begin by using our average pie. If Jeanette's average on 6 tests was 92, then you know that her total score on all six tests must be $92 \times 6 = 552$. Two of those test scores add up to 188; if you remove those two tests, the other four tests must have a sum that adds up to $552 - 188$, or 364. So the average of these four tests will be $364 \div 4$, or 91.

14. 1.65

The best way to approach this problem is to set up an equation. There is some price such that if you add 3% of the price to the price itself, you get $56.65. This means that you can set up an equation: $x + 3\%$ of $x = 56.65$, or $x + 0.03x = 56.65$. Now you can just solve for x, and you get the original price, which was $55. Subtract this from $56.65 to get the tax $1.65.

15. $\frac{9}{25}$ or .36

Probability in this case is the number of prime numbers divided by the total number of possibilities (25 numbers). The prime numbers between 1 and 25 are 2, 3, 5, 7, 11, 13, 17, 19, and 23. So, there are 9 prime numbers. The probability is $\frac{9}{25}$.

16. 8.93

In order to solve this problem, it is important to remember the formula: distance = rate × time.

Here, in order to get the overall average speed, you need to know the total distance and total time. The total distance is found by adding all of the distances given: $0.3 + 0.3 + 0.5 + 0.24 = 1.34$. To find the time for each, rewrite the rate formula as follows: time$= \dfrac{\text{dist.}}{\text{rate}}$, thus time $= \dfrac{0.3}{7.5} = 0.4$ hours for both Alan and Ben. For Carla, time $= \dfrac{0.5}{10} = 0.05$ hours, and for Debby time $= \dfrac{0.24}{12} = 0.02 =$ hours. The total time is $0.4 + 0.4 + 0.05 + 0.02 = 0.15$ hours.

Thus the average rate is $\dfrac{1.34 \text{ miles}}{0.15 \text{ hours}} = 8.93$ miles per hour.

SECTION 5

17. 2

Absolute value is the distance from zero to the number on the number line, or in other words, the positive version of the number. So, $\left(\left|-1\right|+16\right)^{\frac{1}{2}}=\left(17\right)^{\frac{1}{2}}$. A fractional exponent means the denominator is used as a root, so this is $\sqrt{17}$. Next, use the distance formula: distance = $\sqrt{\left(x_1-x_2\right)^2+\left(y_1-y_2\right)^2}$. Thus, $\sqrt{17}=\sqrt{\left(2-1\right)^2+\left(6-b\right)^2}$. Square both sides: $17=(2-1)^2+(6-b)^2$. So, $17=1+(6-b)^2$. Subtract 1 from both sides to get $16=(6-b)^2$. Take the square root of both sides to get $4=6-b$. Subtract 6 from both sides to find $-2=-b$. So, $b=2$.

18. 9

This looks suspiciously like a quadratic equation, and if you multiply it out, its equivalent is b^2-a^2. You want to make this as large as possible, so you want b^2 to be large and a^2 to be small. If $b=-3$, $b^2=9$; if $a=0$, $a^2=0$. So b^2-a^2 can be as large as 9.

SECTION 6

1. E The clue here is *almost as if it were the middle of the day*. This tells you that the second blank must be a word like "lit up" and the first word something like *light*. This makes (E) our best choice.

2. B A good clue for the first blank is *haughty*. You know that the first blank has to be a negative word that goes along with haughty—a word like "stubborn" or "arrogant." This will eliminate (D) and (E). The second blank needs to be an opposing idea, something like "willing to listen." This eliminates (A) and (C), which leaves you with (B).

3. B In this sentence you have a punctuation trigger (the semicolon) that tells you that the word in the blank will mean *rarely suggest radical new ideas*. (B), *conservative*, fits the bill.

4. A The trigger word *although* tells you that the words in the blanks should have opposite meanings. (B), (C), (D), and (E) are all pairs that have similar meanings, so they can be eliminated. This leaves you with (A).

5. E The trigger word *while* combined with *health conscious individuals have stopped eating eggs* means that the word in the blank must be a word that means healthful (or at least not unhealthful). (E) means exactly this.

6. C The statements about Jane Doe demonstrate the author's assertion that *For the average consumer, these two issues* (right to privacy and copyright rules) *create a humorous, even surprising, paradox* (lines 4–5). (C) best summarizes this. (A) is incorrect because no controversy is clearly identified in the passage. (B) is an almost word-for-word paraphrase of the first sentence. However, the statements about Jane Doe demonstrate the paradox (or conflict), not the legal and ethical questions. Be wary of choosing answers that seem to come straight from the passage. The sentences do not contradict the paradox mentioned in the first two sentences, making (D) incorrect. Finally, (E) sounds okay until you look at it closely. First, the previous two sentences provide you with an assertion or statement about the Internet and its users, not a theory. Second, Jane Doe is an example of the average user mentioned in the second sentence, not a real, specific case.

7. D (D) is the best answer. Since "not averse" means willing, you see that in Jane Doe's case, she is willing to download others' creations at no cost, and likewise, the "pirates" of Victorian times "cribbed" what they could of new operettas and produced them on their own without paying the creators. The subjects of (A) and (C) do not appear in both passages. (B) and (E) would impede the copying that Ms. Doe and the pirates did or would like to do.

8. **B** Although copyright laws regarding intellectual property have existed for years, evolving technology makes it possible for individuals to circumvent the protection they offer, so the laws are not always effective or immediately enforceable. (A) says the opposite of what the Gilbert and Sullivan passage says. (C) is not correct because respect for laws and organizations is not mentioned in either passage. (D) cannot work because while the Jane Doe passage says that she pays for her downloads in *unusual currency*, the passage does not imply whether she or the author thinks this is a fair exchange. Neither passage implies that artists should be more self-protective as in (E). The best answer is (B).

9. **E** If you cross out the word *Draconian* and fill in our own word, in the context of the sentence (*imposing ------- punishments*), the blank should mean something like "harsh." *Severe*, (E), is closest to this meaning. There is a similarly-spelled word (*dragonian*) which means "dragon-like," as in (B), but it is not the same as *Draconian*. The concepts in (A), (C), and (D) all appear in the passages, but they are not used to describe punishments. Therefore, (E) is the best answer.

10. **C** From the introductory blurb, you know that the passage is about the *art and recreation of the Southeastern Indians*. (A) is too extreme and slightly offensive. Eliminate it. (B) isn't the main purpose of the passage. (D) doesn't mention art and recreation; eliminate it. For (E), the Cherokee Indians were mentioned only as a detail. This makes our best choice (C).

11. **B** If you read about the problem in context, the passage says that you need to view the art and games as the *outward expressions of their belief system.* That is, you need to understand their beliefs to understand their art and recreation. (B) states this best. (A) is extreme and offensive. The passage never states that the belief system is *impossible to understand*. Eliminate it. (C) and (E) are never mentioned in the passage so you can safely eliminate them. Finally, (D) isn't mentioned and contradicts the passage. You do have some understanding of the beliefs of Southeastern Indians. Eliminate it.

12. **E** Used the lead words *advantage of skilled oratory* to locate the right reference. In lines 35–36 the passage says that the words of a *gifted speaker... could move contentious men to reach consensus.* (E) is a paraphrase of these lines. None of the other answers are supported and (D) twists the reference. It says that *timid,* not skilled, speakers could soothe anxious tempers.

13. **D** In lines 42–45 the author says *even though we know much about the Southeastern Indian ball game, we do not know the precise nature of the social and political forces that led them to play it with such ferocity.* This best supports (D). There is no support for the other four answers.

14. **D** (D) is the best answer. Statement II is true, because the third paragraph discusses the fact that poetry and public speaking were both artistic and political, but you do not know which aspect was more important. Likewise, III is supported in the passage: *we do not know the precise nature of the social and political forces that led them to play...with such ferocity.* Statement I is unsupported because it is too extreme: while the second paragraph says *many of these creations* and *the best Southeastern Indian art* is gone, it does not state that all of it is gone.

15. **E** The important part of the question asks for a parallel instance to *the loss of many of the Indians' artistic and architectural creations*. The final paragraph states that *we do not understand...why the Indians would sometimes bet the last thing they owned on the outcome of a game [of chunkey]*. Both the instances of art and the reasons for the game's importance have been lost in the centuries that have passed since they were central to the Indian culture, and are therefore parallel examples. (A) is incorrect because this art was seen by explorers and is therefore mentioned in contrast, not in parallel; (B) is incorrect because our rituals are not mentioned as being irrational. Poetic magical formulas are mentioned in the passage, but not in relation to our lack of knowledge about them, therefore (C) is wrong. The *contentious men* need to reach consensus, not fight the enemy, thus (D) can be eliminated.

16. **E** From the introductory blurb, you know that this passage is primarily about jazz. This means that (B) and (C) can't be the answer, so eliminate them. (A) is just too narrow to be correct; the passage is not primarily about three instrument melodies. Likewise, the New Orleans band is a detail of the passage, but not the main idea. After crossing off (A) and (D), you are left with (E).

17. **A** The lead words here are *ragtime and brass bands*. You can find these mentioned on the first lines of the second paragraph. There it says that jazz contains...*elements that derive from older musical traditions*. (A) is a paraphrase of this idea.

18. **E** This could be a time-consuming question, so save it for last. From answering the previous question, you know that the answers may be found starting in the second paragraph. You can find support for (A) in line 21, (B) in line 32, (C) in line 41, and (D) in lines 34–37. This means our answer must be (E).

19. **A** Since this question has a line reference, let's go to that line and read it in context. There, the passage says that jazz tries to imitate blues by recreating its singing style. This best supports (A).

20. **D** For a vocab-in-context question, cover the word you're being asked about, reread the sentence, and come up with a word you think fits the blank. You'll probably pick a word like "interesting" or "distinctive." Which choice comes closest to this idea? (D) does.

21. **C** The lead words here are *exotic sound*. You can find these in the beginning of the final paragraph of the passage, which says that the kinds of instruments used and the manner in which intonation is used are characteristic of jazz. The best paraphrase of this idea is (C). (A), (B), (D), and (E) are too specific and do not paraphrase the reference.

22. **D** Since this question will take a lot of time, you should save it for last. You can find evidence in the second paragraph that jazz was heavily influenced by ragtime, brass bands, and dance orchestras. In the next-to-last paragraph you see evidence that it was heavily influenced by blues. This allows you to eliminate (A), (B), (C), and (E), which leaves (D) as our best answer.

23. **A** (A) is the best answer, because while the statement is true, it is mentioned nowhere in the passage. The other answer choices are all supported by the passage. (B) is found in lines 9–11; counterpoint, (C), is mentioned in lines 21–22; syncopation (lack of strict rhythm), (D), is found in line 30; and the clarinet-saxophone connection is mentioned in lines 28–29.

24. **E** Because of the information about improvisation in the fourth paragraph, (E) is the best answer. None of the other answer choices contain statements supported by the passage.

SECTION 7

1. **C** The clue is *entirely implausible*. A good word for the blank might be "falsehood." Only (C) means falsehood.

2. **A** This sentence starts with the trigger *while*. So you know that the two blanks need to be contrasting ideas. The only pair that has a strong opposite relationship is (A).

3. **A** The clue is *exchange players of comparable talent*. Therefore, as the colon is a same-direction trigger, the agreement was "equal." (A) best expresses this meaning.

4. **D** A good clue for this blank is *brevity*—the sentence says that the article's brevity didn't *detract from its importance*, so you know that the article was brief. What is another word for brief? *Terse!*

5. **E** Here you have a great clue: *reduced the population substantially*. So you need a word that means very deadly. The choice that most nearly means this is (E).

6. **D** The clue for the first blank is *by missteps*. Since *missteps* is another word for mistakes you know that the blank must be something like *affected negatively*. (A) and (B) do not match this meaning. Eliminate them. The clues for the second blank are the trigger words *but* and *increasing appreciation*. Therefore you know the *missteps* have not done permanent damage to the author's reputation. A good word for the second blank is *unimportant*. (D) best matches this meaning.

7. **B** Let's look at the relationship between the blanks. You could be looking for a pair of words like "happy" and "harm," or you could be looking for a pair like "sad" and "good." So you're looking for words that are somewhat opposite. Eliminate (A), (C), (D), and (E).

8. **C** (C) is the best answer because the clue is *rambled for a long time with frequent repetitions about trivial topics*. Therefore, words like "rambling" or "boring" would work well in the blank. Since the words in (A), (B), (D), and (E) do not agree with the clue, they can be eliminated.

9. **B** (B) best states the main idea of the passage. (A) and (C) are both too extreme; the passage does not argue for or against the procedure. (D) and (E) are not supported by the passage; neither deaf culture nor the scientific basis for hearing loss are discussed at length in the passage.

10. **B** (B) specifically describes the purpose of all three of the final sentences. (A) and (E) are not correct because they refer to only one sentence of the final three. (C) is incorrect because no alternatives are provided. (D) is not correct because there is no disputed theory to support.

11. **E** Remember to check the passage for each item and not rely on memory. (E) is correct, since it is the only choice not mentioned in the passage as a possible cause of the riots in 1913. All the remaining answers are mentioned in the second sentence.

12. **D** (D) is the best answer because it can be proven with information from the passage. Since you know that both ballet and sporting events have caused riots, (D) must be true. (A) is incorrect because you have no information about the nature of prior riots. (C) and (B) are unsupported by the passage. (E) is a nice thought, but has nothing in the passage to back it up.

13. **E.** Just following these lines the author says that his family felt *a smug sympathy for those poor souls in harsher climates who had to suffer real winters.* This means that he was discussing the warmth of the weather he was used to. (E) is the best paraphrase of this idea.

14. **B** For a vocab-in-context question, you should cover the word in question, reread the line, and put our own word into the blank. In this case, you'd probably use a word like "unhappy." The closest choice is (B).

15. **E** If you read these lines in context, you see that they are followed by a list of problems that the wind causes: *uprooted trees, overturned cars*, and the like. These all illustrate how powerful and destructive the wind is, which best supports (E).

16. **D** Here you have another vocab-in-context question. If you cover up the word *baleful* and try to use our own word in its place, you'd probably choose a word like "scary." Which choice comes closest to this idea? (D) does.

17. **C** In the previous lines, the author discusses how certain people complained about the wind in Provence, and that they would think differently *if they had to put up with the gales that come off the English Channel.* The author is thereby saying that the gales off the English Channel are worse than anything in Provence. This best supports (C).

18. **A** For this question you know from lines 42–44 that Menicucci was concerned that *the pipes burst... under the pressure of water that had frozen in them overnight.* You also know that Menicucci was a plumber (so he would naturally be working on the pipes). This best supports (A).

19. **C** In the first lines of the last paragraph, you find Menicucci clearly expounding on his theory of why the winds were so bitterly cold. He therefore thinks he knows the answer, which allows you to eliminate (B), (D), and (E). (A) is extreme, so you should avoid it as well. This leaves you with (C) as the best choice.

20. **E** This is a tough question, so you should expect to solve it by POE. From the last paragraph you know that Menicucci thinks that the harsher wind was due to a flattening of the curvature of the earth, which enabled the wind to take a more direct route south from Siberia to Provence. Since the pipes have nothing to do with this question, (A) should be crossed off. (B), (C), and (D) look tempting, but if you reread the paragraph, you'll see that Menicucci never said any of these things. (E) sounds just like his theory and is the best answer.

21. **D** Remember that every question will have some support in the passage. Immediately prior to saying *mais oui*, the passage says that Menicucci allowed himself a brief but dramatic pause. This indicates that he was being somewhat theatrical and pompous. This best supports (D).

22. **B** The best answer is (B). You can infer Statement I from the mention of the author's swimming pool in line 36. Because Statement I must be in the correct answer, eliminate (A) and (C). You cannot infer Statement II. You know that the author and his family came to Provence from England, but the author's birthplace is never mentioned in the passage. Eliminate (D) and (E), because they include Statement II. *Voila!* You're done without having to check Statement III. But just for the record—you cannot infer Statement III, either. People tell the author stories about the mistral lasting fifteen days on end (lines 19–20), but the length of the first mistral that the author actually experienced is not mentioned in the passage.

23. **C** This passage is a first-person narrative, told in an informal and humorous manner. An anecdote is a short account of an interesting or humorous incident, so (C) is the best answer. None of the other answer choices fits. (E) is the second best answer, but the author's humor is far too dry to be accurately characterized as sentimental.

24. **A** The best answer is (A). In lines 53–57, the author states that Monsieur Menicucci *wagged his finger under* jeune's *nose to* underline *[emphasis added] the difference between the soft winters of the coast and the biting cold in which you were now standing. Underline*, as used here, means to emphasize, so this sentence is emphasizing the point made in the previous paragraph, which was that pipes without insulation can freeze and burst in Provence, but are far less likely to do so in Cannes or Nice. Thus, it is implied that Cannes and Nice are coastal cities. None of the other answer choices are implied by the passage. (D) is a trap answer, because it says the opposite of what the passage implies.

SECTION 8

1. B (B) is the best answer, because the clue is *she had won the grand prize instead of just any prize.* This suggests that her joy would increase, so a good phrase for the blank is "more joy." None of the other answer choices agrees with the clue; therefore each can be eliminated.

2. E The clue is *increased humidity coupled with oppressively high temperatures*, which describes a rather unpleasant situation. A word with a negative connotation would work well in the blank, like "bad." Since *listless* in (E) means lacking energy, it is the best answer.

3. E Our clue here is *had assumed that the hunter gatherers moved* combined with the trigger *however*. So you need a word in the blank that means the opposite of moving—a word that means staying in one place. The word that best fits this idea is (E).

4. C The clue here is *none of the original doors or windows...survived.* In that case, the restoration is largely guesswork. (C) is the best choice.

5. D The clues and the sentence are *divided into strong factions*, *impossible to garner* and *support to pass the bill*. A good phrase to describe the support that would be needed to pass the bill is "from both sides," and *bipartisan* in (D) means exactly that. Since none of the answer choices agree with the clues, all are incorrect.

6. E The clue in the sentence is *expected to be admonished*. There is also the trigger *but* which indicates a change in idea and the additional clue *completely*. In this case, it introduces the idea that what they expected is not exactly what they got. They got it worse. So a recycled word to fill in is *admonished* or a word that means to harshly scold. (E), *castigated*, means severely criticized. (B), *beguiled,* means deceived or charmed; (C), *esteemed,* means highly regarded; and (D), *nonplussed,* means confused.

7. C According to the first paragraph, some of the causes of pollution included the eruption of volcanoes, dust storms, and marsh gases. In the following lines, the passage states that humans were also responsible for pollution. (C) restates these ideas.

8. C Let's go back to the passage and read the lines in question. They mention ancient cities that had pollution problems. This sounds a lot like either (B) or (C). Both of these are plausible, so you should pick the one that is more general and defendable based on what the passage says. Earlier in the passage, the author tells you that people early on *began to pollute the air*. The passage doesn't say that the air pollution *always existed in cities.* Beware of extreme words; they are often wrong. This makes (C) a better choice than (B).

9. A Using the lead words *air pollution* and *Industrial Revolution,* and knowing that the answer to the last question was found in the first paragraph, you can find the relevant reference. The second paragraph tells you that *The Industrial Revolution brought even worse air pollution* and *there were large rural areas unaffected by air pollution.* In the beginning of the third paragraph, the passage tells you that today *rural areas are not unaffected* (lines 21–22). (A) best summarizes this difference. (B) uses words from the passage but says something the passage didn't. You don't know what the factory towns were before they were factory towns. (C), (D), and (E) are never mentioned and are therefore incorrect.

10. D If you read these lines in context, you find in lines 28–30 that *the astronauts traced drifting blobs of Los Angeles smog as far east as western Colorado.* This means that the smog has spread from a big city to the countryside. This is paraphrased by (D). (B) and (C), while tempting, are much too extreme to be correct.

SECTION 8

11. **E** This is an EXCEPT question, so it's best left for last. The final paragraph of Passage 1 mentions *strained relationships between the U.S. and Canada, factory closings, and acid rain.* This means you can eliminate (A), (B), and (C). The passage also mentions a change in the work habits of traffic police, so (D) can be eliminated. This leaves (E) as our best answer.

12. **C** Remember to look back to the passage for evidence to support your answer. (A) is quite extreme, so you should avoid it. (B) is tempting, but the passage never really talks about the long run. Instead, it only mentions a particular historical event. Lines 69–70 say that *more than 4,000 deaths had been attributed to the smog*, which makes (C) our best answer.

13. **D** The lead words here are *London smog.* You can find London smog described in the first paragraph of Passage 2, where you are told it was a combination of *smoke, fog, sulfur dioxide, sulfuric acid, ash, and soot.* This is best paraphrased by (D).

14. **D** The opening lines of this paragraph say that air pollution has killed *more people than were ever killed in any single tornado.* In other words, air pollution is extremely dangerous and deadly. (D) is a paraphrase of this idea.

15. **B** For a detail question like this one, be sure to look back to find the answer in the passage. Lines 77–79 say that electrostatic precipitators *induce an electric charge on the particles, which are then attracted to oppositely charged plates and deposited.* This makes (B) the best choice.

16. **E** Again, let's look back to the passage. In lines 89–90 you find that the processes to remove sulfur dioxide from air pollution are expensive and waste a part of the coal's energy. (E) says exactly this.

17. **D** This is a difficult question, so save it for last and plan to use POE. (A) and (B) are extreme, so you should avoid them. Neither author discusses eliminating the sources of pollution, so you can also cross off (C). Finally, neither author says that the cost of pollution control is much higher than the cost of changing to better energy sources, so you can eliminate (E) as well. (D) is a nice SAT-type answer, since it's fairly general and hard to argue with.

18. **A** In lines 14–17, the first passage says *The Industrial Revolution brought even worse air pollution...Soot, smoke, and sulfur dioxide filled the air.* This explains why sulfur dioxide and soot created London smog. This makes (A) our answer.

19. **D** Since the passage asks you to choose the one that is NOT a difference and therefore not mentioned in the passages, let's look for what is mentioned and cross them off. Whatever is left must be right. (A) is true; Passage 1 discusses pollution from Seneca's time to today, while Passage 2 talks only of the past one hundred years. Cross it off. (B) is also true since Passage 2 discusses the problem of smog in London, while Passage 1 talks about a range of affected areas. Cross it off. (C) is mentioned as well; Passage 1 brings up Seneca, Queen Elizabeth, and Tokyo while Passage 2 focuses solely on London. (E) is also true, since Passage 2 discusses some methods employed in treating air pollution, while Passage 1 offers no solutions to the problems it discusses.

1. A Take it one phrase at a time. The "sum" means you will add two things. The "squares of x and y" means to square x and square y, or x^2 and y^2. Add these to get $x^2 + y^2$. Cross out any answer that does not have $x^2 + y^2$ as the first part of the equation. Only (A) is left.

2. C If $c = 6$ and $b + c = 8$, then you know that $b = 2$. Since you know that $c = 6$ and $b = 2$, you can solve for a: If $3a + 2b + c = 22$, then $3a + 4 + 6 = 22$, so $3a = 12$, and $a = 4$. Therefore $a + b + c = 4 + 2 + 6$, or 12.

Or try stacking:

$$3a + 2b + c = 22$$
$$b + c = 8$$
$$c = 6$$
$$3a + 3b + 3c = 36$$
$$3(a + b + c) = 36$$
$$a + b + c = 12$$

3. B Since probability = # of outcomes fulfilling the requirements over the total # of outcomes , you need to find the total area of sectors that are labeled 3 and 4 over the total area of the circular spinner. Even though you don't know the area of the circle, you know that this fraction is the same part of the whole as the total degree measure of central angles that enclose 3 and 4 over the total degree measure of the circular spinner, which is the total area of sectors that are labeled 3 and 4 over the total area of the circular spinner. This gives you $\dfrac{60° + 80°}{360°}$, or $\dfrac{140°}{360°} = \dfrac{7}{18}$.

4. C Let's start by figuring out what the values of x and y could be. You know that $4x - 8 > 0$. If you add 8 to each side of the equation, you get $4x > 8$, which means that $x > 2$. So x could be 3, 3.5, 4, or any value larger than 2. Likewise, you know that $4y + 8 < 0$. If you subtract 8 from each side of this equation, you get $4y < -8$, which means that $y < -2$. So y could be -3, -3.5, -4, or any value less than -2. Neither x nor y can be zero, so the product xy cannot be zero. This means you can eliminate (E). And since you don't know whether x and y are odd or even (or even that they are integers) you can also eliminate (A) and (B). You do know, though, that x will always be positive and y will always be negative, so whatever numbers x and y are, you know their product will always be negative.

5. B If a rectangle has length 16 and width 6, then its area will be the length times the width, or 16×6, which equals 96. If this is 3 times the area of a triangle, then the triangle will have an area of 32. If a triangle with area 32 has height of 8, you can use the triangle formula for area of a triangle to find the base: $\dfrac{1}{2} \times base \times height = area$. $32 = \dfrac{1}{2}b \times 8$, so $base \times 4 = 32$. This means that the base is equal to 8.

6. E Plug In! There are two 30°-60°-90° triangles imbedded in this problem, so that is the best way to tackle this. Plug in for y, and go on from there. Be careful! Avoid numbers in the answer choices. If you were to use 18 for y, the height of the cone would be 6. The base of the smaller triangle would be $\dfrac{9}{\sqrt{3}}$. That is also the radius of the circle, so square that number and get 27, and then multiply by π to get the area of the circle, which is 27π. This is the target. Plug your original value into the answer choices. If $y = 18$, the only answer that works out to 27π is (E). Algebraically, the height is $\dfrac{y}{2}$, and the base of the smaller triangle is $\dfrac{y}{2\sqrt{3}}$ (using the 30°-60°-90°). Square that and multiply by π, and you get (E).

SECTION 9

7. **D** You can set up a proportion, or simply notice that 1,000,000 is 10,000 × 100. So if you multiply 30 by 100 you get 3,000.

8. **C** Since lines k and l are tangent to the circle, they form right angles with the radii. Angles OAB, AOC, and OCB in quadrilateral $OABC$ are all 90°, and all four angles must add to 360°, so the remaining angle must also be 90°, which makes $OABC$ a rectangle. Since $\overline{OA}$ and $\overline{OC}$ are radii, they are equal, and you are told that $\overline{OA}$ is the same length as the other two sides. Thus, all four sides are equal. So $OABC$ is actually a square. Draw in $\overline{OB}$ and you'll see that it bisects the square, forming two 45°-45°-90° triangles (see the reference information at the beginning of any math section). So $OB = 4 = s\sqrt{2}$. Solving for s gives you $2\sqrt{2}$, which is the length of each side of the square.

9. **A** This is a great problem for Plugging In. Let's try using $z = 2$, $n = 5$, and $b = 15$. If $2 will buy 5 pizzas, then how much will 15 pizzas cost? Three times the number of pizzas will have three times the cost, so $6. Now you just need to figure out which choice will give you $6. Try calculating each of the answer choices, and you'll find that only (A) equals $6.

10. **C** Since you have parallel lines, let's identify the big and small angles. The small angles measure 65°, so the big angles measure 115°. So $x + y = z = 115$. If you add everything together and substitute $x = 55$, you get $55 + y + z = 230$, so $y + z = 175$.

11. **D** Since $\overline{OP}$ is a radius of the circle, $OP = 8$. Since $\overline{OR}$ is a radius of the circle, $OR = OQ + QR$, and $OQ = QR$, therefore $OQ = 4$. Using the Pythagorean theorem—or recognizing the ratio of sides in a 30°-60°-90° triangle—will give you the value of PQ: $4\sqrt{3}$. Since area $= \frac{1}{2}bh$, the area is $\frac{1}{2} \times 4 \times 4\sqrt{3} = 8\sqrt{3}$.

12. **B** This is a great problem to solve by Plugging In The Answers. Let's start with (C). Could the number of girls on the trip be 40? If there are 14 more boys than girls, then there must be $40 + 14 = 54$ boys. But that makes a total of 94 students; that's too much since there are only 80 students. So you can cross off (C), (D), and (E) because they are all too big. Let's try (B). Could there be 33 girls? In this case there will be $33 + 14 = 47$ boys, and $33 + 47$ equals 80. So (B) is the answer.

13. **B** Let's start by solving for p. You know that $p = f(6)$, which means that it will be equal to $(10 - 6)^2$, or 16. So $4p$ will be equal to $4(16)$, or 64. Now you simply have to figure out which choice gives you 64. $p(18)$ will equal $(10 - 18)^2$, which is 64. So, (B) is the answer.

14. **A** Be sure to read the question carefully; the key here is *must be positive*. Let's try plugging in an easy number for b. If you make $b = 2$, then let's see which of the choices is positive. (A) becomes $\frac{2}{3}$. (B) becomes $\frac{8}{-1}$, so you can eliminate it. (C) becomes $\frac{1}{2}$. (D) becomes 0, so you can eliminate it, and (E) becomes 3. Now let's try making $b = \frac{1}{2}$. In this case, (A) becomes $\frac{1}{3}$. (C) becomes -1, so you eliminate it. (E) becomes 0; eliminate. That leaves you with (A).

15. **E** Car 2 can be blue or red, and car 4 is same color as car 2 (so also blue or red). Since car 1 is blue and car 2 and 4 might both be blue, there could be 3 blue cars. However, since car 7 is red and car 2 and 4 might both be red, there could also be 3 red cars. There could not be 3 cars that are blue and 3 cars that are red. (E) is the best answer.

16. **D** First, rewrite $1,200 \times 10^3$ as 1,200,000. Find the answer that is equal to 1,200,000. (A) is 120,000. (B) is 12,000,000. (C) is 12,000,000. (D) is 1,200,000. (E) is 120,000.

SECTION 10

1. **B** Avoid the word *being* if possible, which eliminates (A) and (D). Also, watch out for verb tense. The non-underlined part of the sentence is in the present tense, so eliminate (C) and (E) since they are both in the future tense.

2. **A** There are no errors in the sentence as it is written. Both (D) and (E) use the phrase *at least 3 feet wide or wider,* which is redundant. (B) incorrectly uses *swung* instead of *swing*, and (C) is unnecessarily wordy.

3. **E** The original sentence, (A), has the comparative adjective *better,* which is incorrect when comparing more than two things. (B) uses *can be,* which changes the meaning of the sentence. (C) uses future tense, which doesn't really make sense. In (D), switching the adjective *nineteenth-century* into a modified noun changes the meaning of the sentence.

4. **E** (E) correctly compares American etiquette with the etiquette of other countries. This answer choice includes the phrase *that of* and thus uses the correct form of comparison. The rest of the choices all have a faulty comparison. (A) and (B) are missing the phrase *that of* and do not correctly establish a comparison. (C) is closer, but you need to compare American etiquette with the etiquette of other countries (plural). In (D), the comparison is not properly drawn. The word *what* doesn't do the job.

5. **C** The problem with the original sentence is that it uses the long-winded and awkward phrase *this being that they had to* instead of a concise one. (B) is very concise, but the phrase *including read an article* is grammatically incorrect. (C), on the other hand, is both concise and grammatically correct, so get rid of (A), since there is a better alternative. (D) and (E) are no less awkward than the original sentence, so eliminate them. (C) is the remaining choice.

6. **C** The best choice is (C). Only a person can be *renowned for her writing,* and thus *Barbara Kingsolver* should follow the comma. However, (A) follows the comma with *Barbara Kingsolver's poems,* while (D) follows it with *the poems of Barbara Kingsolver.* (B) and (E) incorrectly insert a semicolon in place of the comma, turning the initial modifier into a fragment.

7. **E** The best choice is (E). Items in a list need to be parallel in structure. In this case, since the planet is said to have *a...mass* and *a...period,* the third item in this list should be *moons.* Eliminate (A), (B) and (C) for violating this rule. Then eliminate (D) for saying *of their own* even though the sentence is discussing a planet, singular.

8. **D** (A) and (B) both contain comma splices. (C) tries to rephrase the sentence using the word *being,* which is seldom desirable, and also suggests that the works that follow are the only two examples in the history of literature. (D) offers a concise way to introduce examples. (E) is even more concise, but improperly uses the word *like* to introduce examples.

9. **D** The original sentence is awkward, wordy, and incorrectly uses *however* as a substitute for *but* or *though.* (B) uses *along with* to join the two halves of the sentence, failing to signal that there is a conflict between the adults and the girls. In (C), the word *even* is unnecessary. (E) is missing a verb. This leaves (D) as the best answer.

10. **E** (E) is the most concise answer, and since it introduces no grammatical errors, it is correct. (A), (C), and (D) all refer to the singular committee as *they,* while (B) is unnecessarily wordy and awkward compared to (E).

SECTION 10

11. A The best choice is (A). The sentence is correct as it stands. Eliminate (B) and (C) are because, with or without the semicolon, a double negative (*not hardly*) is considered incorrect. The word *since* in (D) is unnecessary: it means "because" here and does not make sense in the sentence. The addition of *however* in (E) is redundant, since the sentence already uses the word *although*.

12. B The original sentence contains the word *because*, so adding *the reason* is redundant; eliminate (A) and (E). (C) and (D) wrongly imply that the ban is on the animals, not on transporting them. This leaves you with (B) as the best answer.

13. D In (D), the present perfect *has tripled* agrees with the present tense of *this century* to indicate a time frame *from one point until now* and is the most concise way of stating this idea. (A) and (B) are wordy. In (C), *was tripled* is passive—when possible, choose the active voice on the SAT. (E) has the incorrect verb tense; *had tripled* is the past perfect while the sentence is discussing something that started in the past, but has not finished.

14. C This sentence's error is in pronoun agreement: *Student* is singular, but *their* is plural in both (A) and (B). (D) corrects this error but adds *always*, which changes the meaning. (E) unnecessarily adds *not only...but also*. In (C), the corrected phrase reads *to seek help from teachers*, eliminating the pronoun and, thus, the error.

Afterword

IS THIS BOOK JUST LIKE YOUR COURSE?

Since the book came out, many students and teachers have asked us, "Is this book just like your course?" The short answer is no.

It isn't easy to raise SAT scores. Our course is more than fifty hours long and requires class participation, quizzes, homework, four practice examinations, and possibly additional tutoring.

We like to think that this book is fun, informative, and well written, but no book can capture the magic of our instructors and course structure. Each Princeton Review instructor has attended a top college and has excelled on the SAT. Moreover, each of our instructors undergoes rigorous training.

While this book contains many of the techniques we teach in our course, some of our techniques are too difficult to include in a book without a trained and experienced Princeton Review teacher to explain and demonstrate them. Moreover, this book is written for the average student. Classes in our course are grouped by ability so that we can gear our techniques to each student's level.

WE'RE FLATTERED, BUT...

Some tutors and schools use this book to run their own "Princeton Review course." While we are flattered, we are also concerned.

It has taken us many years of teaching tens of thousands of students across the country to develop our SAT program, and we're still learning. Many teachers think that our course is simply a collection of techniques that can be taught by anyone. It isn't that easy.

We train each Princeton Review instructor for many hours for every hour he or she will teach class. Each of the instructors is monitored, evaluated, and supervised throughout the course.

Another concern is that many of our techniques conflict with traditional math and English techniques as taught in high school. For example, in the Math section, we tell our students to avoid setting up algebraic equations. Can you imagine your math teacher telling you that? And in the Critical Reading section, we tell our students not to read the passage too carefully. Can you imagine your English teacher telling you that?

While we also teach traditional math and English in our course, some teachers may not completely agree with some of our approaches.

Beware of Princeton Review Clones

We have nothing against people who use our techniques, but we do object to tutors or high schools who claim to "teach The Princeton Review method." If you want to find out whether your teacher has been trained by The Princeton Review or whether you're taking an official Princeton Review course, call us toll-free at 1-800-2REVIEW.

If You'd Like More Information

Princeton Review sites are in hundreds of cities around the country. For the office nearest you, call 1-800-2REVIEW.

ABOUT THE AUTHORS

Adam Robinson was born in 1955, and lives in New York City.

John Katzman was born in 1959. He graduated from Princeton University in 1980. After working briefly on Wall Street, he founded The Princeton Review in 1981. Having begun with nineteen high school students in his parents' apartment, Katzman now oversees courses that prepare millions of high school and college students annually for tests, including the SAT, GRE, GMAT, and LSAT. He lives in New York City.

SAT Practice Test System Software

ABOUT THE SOFTWARE

The Practice Test System on the CD-ROM was designed to be as much like a real SAT as possible. However, since at this time the real test can only be taken using pencil and paper, we also recommend practicing with written tests (such as those included in your *Cracking the New SAT* book and The Princeton Review's *11 Practice Tests for the New SAT & PSAT*).

Of course we know you got the book with the CD inside so you could benefit from its obvious advantages like offline testing and easy review of answer explanations, so you definitely want to use it!

Don't forget to have scratch paper handy. Since all the information will be on your computer screen, it'll be important to have a place to write things down.

Although the software does have a feature that lets you suspend the test in the middle and finish it later, we recommend trying to take an entire test in one sitting. We also advise making good use of the review features—look at the explanations for questions you missed, and see what types of problems you are having the most trouble with.

SYSTEM REQUIREMENTS

WINDOWS™	MACINTOSH®
600-MHz or higher Pentium-based processor	600-MHz or faster G3 processor
Windows 98, 2000, ME, XP only (does not include NT)	Macintosh OS 9.0.1 or higher (including all versions of OS 10)
32 MB RAM (64 MB RAM recommended)	32 MB RAM (64 MB RAM recommended)
40 MB hard disk space	40 MB hard disk space
800 x 600-pixel monitor (capable of displaying at least thousands of colors)	800 x 600-pixel monitor (capable of displaying at least thousands of colors)
Keyboard	Keyboard
Mouse	Mouse
8X or faster CD-ROM drive	8X or faster CD-ROM drive
Internet connection recommended, but not required for basic use	Internet connection recommended, but not required for basic use

INSTALLATION AND START-UP

IMPORTANT: Your Practice Test System software will expire one year after the first use. During that year, the software's **Update** feature will automatically check for newer versions. You may manually check for updates by launching the Updater for your test type and following the instructions. If you have access to the Internet, you should log on to your Internet Service Provider before you launch. This will enable the Update software to operate and download any updates that may be available. Since the test is subject to change, we recommend using the "update" feature so you can be sure to have the latest version of the software available.

WINDOWS

Make sure that no other applications are running before installing the software.

1. Insert the CD in your CD-ROM drive. The CD will automatically launch the Setup program. If not, open the CD under My Computer and double-click on SAT Installer.exe. **Note:** You will need to have your book handy for the setup process!

2. Follow the instructions in the installer.

3. At the end of the setup, you may select the option to run the Practice Test System software after exiting the setup.

To run the Practice Test System software any time after you have installed it, select it from The Princeton Review folder in the Start menu.

MACINTOSH

1. Insert the CD in your CD-ROM drive.

2. Double-click the SAT Practice Test Installer icon. **Note:** You will need to have your book handy for the setup process!

3. Follow the onscreen instructions until installation is complete.

USING SAT PRACTICE TESTS

LOGGING IN

You will be prompted to create an account before using the Practice Test System software for the first time, and you'll need to sign in each time you use it. The log-in information enables the program to distinguish your history and answer choices from those of anyone else who may also be using the Practice Test System on the same computer.

If you have already registered at PrincetonReview.com, simply enter the same username and password to access your Practice Test System. (This requires Internet access.) If you have forgotten your username or password, you can retrieve it from the Forgot Password button or through PrincetonReview.com.

If you do not have an account with PrincetonReview.com, then you will need to create a new username just for the Practice Test System. When you create your account, you will also be asked to enter some additional information that will let you retrieve your password later if you forget it.

If you want more detailed score reports, you'll want to upload your tests from the Practice Test System to the website. To do this, you need to register online. Go to PrincetonReview.com/cracking and sign up for the online tools that go along with your book. Then update your Practice Test System information so you can successfully upload your tests.

Be sure to have your book handy before you take your first test, since you will be prompted to enter a code from the book in order to use the program.

The Main Menu

Each time you launch the Practice Test System, you will begin with the main menu screen. Any **Completed** or **Suspended** tests will be marked as such. From the main menu screen, you can either **Take a Test**—one of four SAT practice exercises—or you can **Review a Test** you've already taken. You can also exit the software by clicking **Quit** on the lower left-hand corner.

Taking a Test

To start a test, select one from the list and click **Start Test**. You will be asked to type in a word from your copy of the book, and then you will then go directly to the first question of your selected test. If you need to review the functions of any of the buttons on your screen, simply click them. Also, you can click the **?** button at the bottom of any active screen to access the Help section.

To select an answer, click on the oval next to the answer or the answer itself. You can change an answer as many times as you want by clicking on a new selection.

Section 2   Question ID: 21413

Time Remaining: 0:24:24   Question 3 of 25

Most chefs are not likely to use very spicy habañero chiles unless they know how to roast them to make their flavor more --------.

- ○ flavorless
- ○ practical
- ○ appalling
- ○ palatable
- ○ spicy

| Quit Test | Skip Section | Review Section | Mark | Reset | ? | ◀ | ▶ |

THE TOOLBAR

Once you begin your practice session, you will see various buttons on the screen. These buttons are **Quit Test**, **Skip Section**, **Review Section**, **Mark**, **Reset**, **? (Help)**, **◀ (Left Arrow)**, and **▶ (Right Arrow)**. These buttons allow you to navigate through your tests.

Quit Test   Clicking **Quit Test** will give you the following warning:

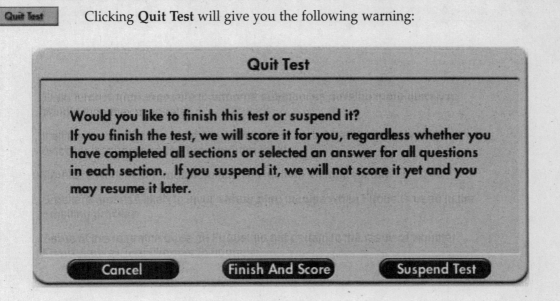

If you click **Finish and Score**, the test will end, regardless of whether you have completed all sections or selected an answer for all questions in each section.

If you click **Suspend Test**, you may resume your test later.

If you choose **Cancel**, you will return to the test.

Skip Section   Clicking **Skip Section** will allow you to move to the next section.

However, you will not be able to return to the section you are leaving, nor will you be able to make any changes to your answers in this section before scoring.

Clicking **Mark** will flag the question on the screen to remind you that it requires further attention.

Time Remaining: 0:22:12   Question 3 of 25

Most chefs are not likely to use very spicy habañero chiles unless they know how to roast them to make their flavor more -------.

○   flavorless

○   practical

○   appalling

○   palatable

○   spicy

| Quit Test | Skip Section | Review Section | Mark | Reset | ? | ◀ | ▶ |

Marking a question is not the same as answering it, and has no effect on your score. Unmark a question by clicking the **Mark** button a second time. Unmarking a question does not erase your answer.

Review Section Clicking **Review Section** will allow you to see a chart of every question in the section.

Question Number	Answered	Marked
1	X	
2	X	
3	X	X
4	X	
5	X	
6	X	
7	X	
8	X	
9	X	
10	X	
11	X	
12	X	
13	X	
14	X	
15	X	
16	X	
17	X	
18	X	
19	X	
20	X	

Cancel   Show Question

The chart lets you see which questions you have answered and which you have not. Any question that you marked earlier using the **Mark** tool will be checked. To return to one of these questions, select it with the mouse and click **Show Question**.

To return to the place in the test where you were when you clicked **Review Section**, click on **Cancel**.

 Clicking **Reset** clears your answer to a question, if you want to erase your answer before moving on to the next question.

Clicking **? (Help)** reviews directions, lists the tools, and explains their functions.

Left Arrow will take you to the preceding question.

Right Arrow will take you to the very next question in that section, or, if you are on the last question in a section, it will bring you to the first question in the next section. Once you click the **Right Arrow** on the last question in a section, all of the answers you selected in that section will be recorded as your choices. Once you click the **Right Arrow** on the last question of the last section, your entire test will be recorded.

To Uninstall

Windows

1. Select Control Panel from your Start Menu.

2. Click on "Add/Remove Programs."

3. Locate the test that you want to uninstall.

4. Click on the Add/Remove option.

Macintosh

1. Select the Practice Test System folder from your hard drive.

2. Click and drag to the Trash. (Please note that this will uninstall the Practice Test System for all users.)

If you have any questions, please e-mail our Technical Support Center at:
techsupport.online@mail.review.com.

The Princeton Review

Diagnostic Test Form

1 Your Name:

(Print)

_____
Last   First   M.I.

Signature: _____   Date ___/___/___

Home Address: _____
Number and Street   City   State   Zip Code

E-Mail: _____   School: _____   Class: _____
(Print)

2 YOUR NAME

Last Name
(First 4 Letters)

| | | | | FIRST INIT | MID INIT |

Ⓐ Ⓑ Ⓒ Ⓓ Ⓔ Ⓕ Ⓖ Ⓗ Ⓘ Ⓙ Ⓚ Ⓛ Ⓜ Ⓝ Ⓞ Ⓟ Ⓠ Ⓡ Ⓢ Ⓣ Ⓤ Ⓥ Ⓦ Ⓧ Ⓨ Ⓩ

3 PHONE NUMBER

Ⓞ Ⓞ Ⓞ Ⓞ Ⓞ Ⓞ Ⓞ
① ① ① ① ① ① ①
② ② ② ② ② ② ②
③ ③ ③ ③ ③ ③ ③
④ ④ ④ ④ ④ ④ ④
⑤ ⑤ ⑤ ⑤ ⑤ ⑤ ⑤
⑥ ⑥ ⑥ ⑥ ⑥ ⑥ ⑥
⑦ ⑦ ⑦ ⑦ ⑦ ⑦ ⑦
⑧ ⑧ ⑧ ⑧ ⑧ ⑧ ⑧
⑨ ⑨ ⑨ ⑨ ⑨ ⑨ ⑨

4 DATE OF BIRTH

MONTH	DAY		YEAR
○ JAN			
○ FEB			
○ MAR	⓪	⓪	⓪
○ APR	①	①	①
○ MAY	②	②	②
○ JUN	③	③	③
○ JUL		④	④
○ AUG		⑤	⑤
○ SEP		⑥	⑥
○ OCT		⑦	⑦
○ NOV		⑧	⑧
○ DEC		⑨	⑨

5 SEX

○ MALE
○ FEMALE

IMPORTANT: Fill in items 6 and 7 exactly as shown on the preceding page.

6 TEST FORM
(Copy from back of test book)

7 TEST CODE

Ⓞ Ⓞ Ⓞ Ⓞ
① ① ① ①
② ② ② ②
③ ③ ③ ③
④ ④ ④ ④
⑤ ⑤ ⑤ ⑤
⑥ ⑥ ⑥ ⑥
⑦ ⑦ ⑦ ⑦
⑧ ⑧ ⑧ ⑧
⑨ ⑨ ⑨ ⑨

8 OTHER

1 Ⓐ Ⓑ Ⓒ Ⓓ Ⓔ
2 Ⓐ Ⓑ Ⓒ Ⓓ Ⓔ
3 Ⓐ Ⓑ Ⓒ Ⓓ Ⓔ

PLEASE DO NOT WRITE IN THIS AREA

SERIAL #

THIS PAGE INTENTIONALLY LEFT BLANK

The Princeton Review
Diagnostic Test Form

ESSAY

SECTION

1

Begin your essay on this page. If you need more space, continue on the next page. Do not write outside of the essay box.

Continue on the opposite side if necessary.

PLEASE DO NOT WRITE IN THIS AREA

SERIAL #

Start with number 1 for each new section. If a section has fewer questions than answer spaces, leave the extra answer spaces blank. Be sure to erase any errors or stray marks completely.

SECTION 2

1 Ⓐ Ⓑ Ⓒ Ⓓ Ⓔ	11 Ⓐ Ⓑ Ⓒ Ⓓ Ⓔ	21 Ⓐ Ⓑ Ⓒ Ⓓ Ⓔ	31 Ⓐ Ⓑ Ⓒ Ⓓ Ⓔ
2 Ⓐ Ⓑ Ⓒ Ⓓ Ⓔ	12 Ⓐ Ⓑ Ⓒ Ⓓ Ⓔ	22 Ⓐ Ⓑ Ⓒ Ⓓ Ⓔ	32 Ⓐ Ⓑ Ⓒ Ⓓ Ⓔ
3 Ⓐ Ⓑ Ⓒ Ⓓ Ⓔ	13 Ⓐ Ⓑ Ⓒ Ⓓ Ⓔ	23 Ⓐ Ⓑ Ⓒ Ⓓ Ⓔ	33 Ⓐ Ⓑ Ⓒ Ⓓ Ⓔ
4 Ⓐ Ⓑ Ⓒ Ⓓ Ⓔ	14 Ⓐ Ⓑ Ⓒ Ⓓ Ⓔ	24 Ⓐ Ⓑ Ⓒ Ⓓ Ⓔ	34 Ⓐ Ⓑ Ⓒ Ⓓ Ⓔ
5 Ⓐ Ⓑ Ⓒ Ⓓ Ⓔ	15 Ⓐ Ⓑ Ⓒ Ⓓ Ⓔ	25 Ⓐ Ⓑ Ⓒ Ⓓ Ⓔ	35 Ⓐ Ⓑ Ⓒ Ⓓ Ⓔ
6 Ⓐ Ⓑ Ⓒ Ⓓ Ⓔ	16 Ⓐ Ⓑ Ⓒ Ⓓ Ⓔ	26 Ⓐ Ⓑ Ⓒ Ⓓ Ⓔ	36 Ⓐ Ⓑ Ⓒ Ⓓ Ⓔ
7 Ⓐ Ⓑ Ⓒ Ⓓ Ⓔ	17 Ⓐ Ⓑ Ⓒ Ⓓ Ⓔ	27 Ⓐ Ⓑ Ⓒ Ⓓ Ⓔ	37 Ⓐ Ⓑ Ⓒ Ⓓ Ⓔ
8 Ⓐ Ⓑ Ⓒ Ⓓ Ⓔ	18 Ⓐ Ⓑ Ⓒ Ⓓ Ⓔ	28 Ⓐ Ⓑ Ⓒ Ⓓ Ⓔ	38 Ⓐ Ⓑ Ⓒ Ⓓ Ⓔ
9 Ⓐ Ⓑ Ⓒ Ⓓ Ⓔ	19 Ⓐ Ⓑ Ⓒ Ⓓ Ⓔ	29 Ⓐ Ⓑ Ⓒ Ⓓ Ⓔ	39 Ⓐ Ⓑ Ⓒ Ⓓ Ⓔ
10 Ⓐ Ⓑ Ⓒ Ⓓ Ⓔ	20 Ⓐ Ⓑ Ⓒ Ⓓ Ⓔ	30 Ⓐ Ⓑ Ⓒ Ⓓ Ⓔ	40 Ⓐ Ⓑ Ⓒ Ⓓ Ⓔ

SECTION 3

1 Ⓐ Ⓑ Ⓒ Ⓓ Ⓔ	11 Ⓐ Ⓑ Ⓒ Ⓓ Ⓔ	21 Ⓐ Ⓑ Ⓒ Ⓓ Ⓔ	31 Ⓐ Ⓑ Ⓒ Ⓓ Ⓔ
2 Ⓐ Ⓑ Ⓒ Ⓓ Ⓔ	12 Ⓐ Ⓑ Ⓒ Ⓓ Ⓔ	22 Ⓐ Ⓑ Ⓒ Ⓓ Ⓔ	32 Ⓐ Ⓑ Ⓒ Ⓓ Ⓔ
3 Ⓐ Ⓑ Ⓒ Ⓓ Ⓔ	13 Ⓐ Ⓑ Ⓒ Ⓓ Ⓔ	23 Ⓐ Ⓑ Ⓒ Ⓓ Ⓔ	33 Ⓐ Ⓑ Ⓒ Ⓓ Ⓔ
4 Ⓐ Ⓑ Ⓒ Ⓓ Ⓔ	14 Ⓐ Ⓑ Ⓒ Ⓓ Ⓔ	24 Ⓐ Ⓑ Ⓒ Ⓓ Ⓔ	34 Ⓐ Ⓑ Ⓒ Ⓓ Ⓔ
5 Ⓐ Ⓑ Ⓒ Ⓓ Ⓔ	15 Ⓐ Ⓑ Ⓒ Ⓓ Ⓔ	25 Ⓐ Ⓑ Ⓒ Ⓓ Ⓔ	35 Ⓐ Ⓑ Ⓒ Ⓓ Ⓔ
6 Ⓐ Ⓑ Ⓒ Ⓓ Ⓔ	16 Ⓐ Ⓑ Ⓒ Ⓓ Ⓔ	26 Ⓐ Ⓑ Ⓒ Ⓓ Ⓔ	36 Ⓐ Ⓑ Ⓒ Ⓓ Ⓔ
7 Ⓐ Ⓑ Ⓒ Ⓓ Ⓔ	17 Ⓐ Ⓑ Ⓒ Ⓓ Ⓔ	27 Ⓐ Ⓑ Ⓒ Ⓓ Ⓔ	37 Ⓐ Ⓑ Ⓒ Ⓓ Ⓔ
8 Ⓐ Ⓑ Ⓒ Ⓓ Ⓔ	18 Ⓐ Ⓑ Ⓒ Ⓓ Ⓔ	28 Ⓐ Ⓑ Ⓒ Ⓓ Ⓔ	38 Ⓐ Ⓑ Ⓒ Ⓓ Ⓔ
9 Ⓐ Ⓑ Ⓒ Ⓓ Ⓔ	19 Ⓐ Ⓑ Ⓒ Ⓓ Ⓔ	29 Ⓐ Ⓑ Ⓒ Ⓓ Ⓔ	39 Ⓐ Ⓑ Ⓒ Ⓓ Ⓔ
10 Ⓐ Ⓑ Ⓒ Ⓓ Ⓔ	20 Ⓐ Ⓑ Ⓒ Ⓓ Ⓔ	30 Ⓐ Ⓑ Ⓒ Ⓓ Ⓔ	40 Ⓐ Ⓑ Ⓒ Ⓓ Ⓔ

CAUTION

Use the answer spaces in the grids below for Section 2 or Section 3 only if you are told to do so in your test book.

Student-Produced Responses

ONLY ANSWERS ENTERED IN THE OVALS IN EACH GRID WILL BE SCORED. YOU WILL NOT RECEIVE CREDIT FOR ANYTHING WRITTEN IN THE BOXES ABOVE THE OVALS.

9 / ⊙ 0 1 2 3 4 5 6 7 8 9
10 / ⊙ 0 1 2 3 4 5 6 7 8 9
11 / ⊙ 0 1 2 3 4 5 6 7 8 9
12 / ⊙ 0 1 2 3 4 5 6 7 8 9
13 / ⊙ 0 1 2 3 4 5 6 7 8 9

14 / ⊙ 0 1 2 3 4 5 6 7 8 9
15 / ⊙ 0 1 2 3 4 5 6 7 8 9
16 / ⊙ 0 1 2 3 4 5 6 7 8 9
17 / ⊙ 0 1 2 3 4 5 6 7 8 9
18 / ⊙ 0 1 2 3 4 5 6 7 8 9

Start with number 1 for each new section. If a section has fewer questions than answer spaces, leave the extra answer spaces blank. Be sure to erase any errors or stray marks completely.

SECTION 4

1 (A) (B) (C) (D) (E) 11 (A) (B) (C) (D) (E) 21 (A) (B) (C) (D) (E) 31 (A) (B) (C) (D) (E)
2 (A) (B) (C) (D) (E) 12 (A) (B) (C) (D) (E) 22 (A) (B) (C) (D) (E) 32 (A) (B) (C) (D) (E)
3 (A) (B) (C) (D) (E) 13 (A) (B) (C) (D) (E) 23 (A) (B) (C) (D) (E) 33 (A) (B) (C) (D) (E)
4 (A) (B) (C) (D) (E) 14 (A) (B) (C) (D) (E) 24 (A) (B) (C) (D) (E) 34 (A) (B) (C) (D) (E)
5 (A) (B) (C) (D) (E) 15 (A) (B) (C) (D) (E) 25 (A) (B) (C) (D) (E) 35 (A) (B) (C) (D) (E)
6 (A) (B) (C) (D) (E) 16 (A) (B) (C) (D) (E) 26 (A) (B) (C) (D) (E) 36 (A) (B) (C) (D) (E)
7 (A) (B) (C) (D) (E) 17 (A) (B) (C) (D) (E) 27 (A) (B) (C) (D) (E) 37 (A) (B) (C) (D) (E)
8 (A) (B) (C) (D) (E) 18 (A) (B) (C) (D) (E) 28 (A) (B) (C) (D) (E) 38 (A) (B) (C) (D) (E)
9 (A) (B) (C) (D) (E) 19 (A) (B) (C) (D) (E) 29 (A) (B) (C) (D) (E) 39 (A) (B) (C) (D) (E)
10 (A) (B) (C) (D) (E) 20 (A) (B) (C) (D) (E) 30 (A) (B) (C) (D) (E) 40 (A) (B) (C) (D) (E)

SECTION 5

1 (A) (B) (C) (D) (E) 11 (A) (B) (C) (D) (E) 21 (A) (B) (C) (D) (E) 31 (A) (B) (C) (D) (E)
2 (A) (B) (C) (D) (E) 12 (A) (B) (C) (D) (E) 22 (A) (B) (C) (D) (E) 32 (A) (B) (C) (D) (E)
3 (A) (B) (C) (D) (E) 13 (A) (B) (C) (D) (E) 23 (A) (B) (C) (D) (E) 33 (A) (B) (C) (D) (E)
4 (A) (B) (C) (D) (E) 14 (A) (B) (C) (D) (E) 24 (A) (B) (C) (D) (E) 34 (A) (B) (C) (D) (E)
5 (A) (B) (C) (D) (E) 15 (A) (B) (C) (D) (E) 25 (A) (B) (C) (D) (E) 35 (A) (B) (C) (D) (E)
6 (A) (B) (C) (D) (E) 16 (A) (B) (C) (D) (E) 26 (A) (B) (C) (D) (E) 36 (A) (B) (C) (D) (E)
7 (A) (B) (C) (D) (E) 17 (A) (B) (C) (D) (E) 27 (A) (B) (C) (D) (E) 37 (A) (B) (C) (D) (E)
8 (A) (B) (C) (D) (E) 18 (A) (B) (C) (D) (E) 28 (A) (B) (C) (D) (E) 38 (A) (B) (C) (D) (E)
9 (A) (B) (C) (D) (E) 19 (A) (B) (C) (D) (E) 29 (A) (B) (C) (D) (E) 39 (A) (B) (C) (D) (E)
10 (A) (B) (C) (D) (E) 20 (A) (B) (C) (D) (E) 30 (A) (B) (C) (D) (E) 40 (A) (B) (C) (D) (E)

CAUTION Use the answer spaces in the grids below for Section 4 or Section 5 only if you are told to do so in your test book.

Student-Produced Responses

ONLY ANSWERS ENTERED IN THE OVALS IN EACH GRID WILL BE SCORED. YOU WILL NOT RECEIVE CREDIT FOR ANYTHING WRITTEN IN THE BOXES ABOVE THE OVALS.

9   10   11   12   13

14   15   16   17   18

PLEASE DO NOT WRITE IN THIS AREA

SERIAL #

Start with number 1 for each new section. If a section has fewer questions than answer spaces, leave the extra answer spaces blank. Be sure to erase any errors or stray marks completely.

SECTION 6

1 Ⓐ Ⓑ Ⓒ Ⓓ Ⓔ   11 Ⓐ Ⓑ Ⓒ Ⓓ Ⓔ   21 Ⓐ Ⓑ Ⓒ Ⓓ Ⓔ   31 Ⓐ Ⓑ Ⓒ Ⓓ Ⓔ
2 Ⓐ Ⓑ Ⓒ Ⓓ Ⓔ   12 Ⓐ Ⓑ Ⓒ Ⓓ Ⓔ   22 Ⓐ Ⓑ Ⓒ Ⓓ Ⓔ   32 Ⓐ Ⓑ Ⓒ Ⓓ Ⓔ
3 Ⓐ Ⓑ Ⓒ Ⓓ Ⓔ   13 Ⓐ Ⓑ Ⓒ Ⓓ Ⓔ   23 Ⓐ Ⓑ Ⓒ Ⓓ Ⓔ   33 Ⓐ Ⓑ Ⓒ Ⓓ Ⓔ
4 Ⓐ Ⓑ Ⓒ Ⓓ Ⓔ   14 Ⓐ Ⓑ Ⓒ Ⓓ Ⓔ   24 Ⓐ Ⓑ Ⓒ Ⓓ Ⓔ   34 Ⓐ Ⓑ Ⓒ Ⓓ Ⓔ
5 Ⓐ Ⓑ Ⓒ Ⓓ Ⓔ   15 Ⓐ Ⓑ Ⓒ Ⓓ Ⓔ   25 Ⓐ Ⓑ Ⓒ Ⓓ Ⓔ   35 Ⓐ Ⓑ Ⓒ Ⓓ Ⓔ
6 Ⓐ Ⓑ Ⓒ Ⓓ Ⓔ   16 Ⓐ Ⓑ Ⓒ Ⓓ Ⓔ   26 Ⓐ Ⓑ Ⓒ Ⓓ Ⓔ   36 Ⓐ Ⓑ Ⓒ Ⓓ Ⓔ
7 Ⓐ Ⓑ Ⓒ Ⓓ Ⓔ   17 Ⓐ Ⓑ Ⓒ Ⓓ Ⓔ   27 Ⓐ Ⓑ Ⓒ Ⓓ Ⓔ   37 Ⓐ Ⓑ Ⓒ Ⓓ Ⓔ
8 Ⓐ Ⓑ Ⓒ Ⓓ Ⓔ   18 Ⓐ Ⓑ Ⓒ Ⓓ Ⓔ   28 Ⓐ Ⓑ Ⓒ Ⓓ Ⓔ   38 Ⓐ Ⓑ Ⓒ Ⓓ Ⓔ
9 Ⓐ Ⓑ Ⓒ Ⓓ Ⓔ   19 Ⓐ Ⓑ Ⓒ Ⓓ Ⓔ   29 Ⓐ Ⓑ Ⓒ Ⓓ Ⓔ   39 Ⓐ Ⓑ Ⓒ Ⓓ Ⓔ
10 Ⓐ Ⓑ Ⓒ Ⓓ Ⓔ   20 Ⓐ Ⓑ Ⓒ Ⓓ Ⓔ   30 Ⓐ Ⓑ Ⓒ Ⓓ Ⓔ   40 Ⓐ Ⓑ Ⓒ Ⓓ Ⓔ

SECTION 7

1 Ⓐ Ⓑ Ⓒ Ⓓ Ⓔ   11 Ⓐ Ⓑ Ⓒ Ⓓ Ⓔ   21 Ⓐ Ⓑ Ⓒ Ⓓ Ⓔ   31 Ⓐ Ⓑ Ⓒ Ⓓ Ⓔ
2 Ⓐ Ⓑ Ⓒ Ⓓ Ⓔ   12 Ⓐ Ⓑ Ⓒ Ⓓ Ⓔ   22 Ⓐ Ⓑ Ⓒ Ⓓ Ⓔ   32 Ⓐ Ⓑ Ⓒ Ⓓ Ⓔ
3 Ⓐ Ⓑ Ⓒ Ⓓ Ⓔ   13 Ⓐ Ⓑ Ⓒ Ⓓ Ⓔ   23 Ⓐ Ⓑ Ⓒ Ⓓ Ⓔ   33 Ⓐ Ⓑ Ⓒ Ⓓ Ⓔ
4 Ⓐ Ⓑ Ⓒ Ⓓ Ⓔ   14 Ⓐ Ⓑ Ⓒ Ⓓ Ⓔ   24 Ⓐ Ⓑ Ⓒ Ⓓ Ⓔ   34 Ⓐ Ⓑ Ⓒ Ⓓ Ⓔ
5 Ⓐ Ⓑ Ⓒ Ⓓ Ⓔ   15 Ⓐ Ⓑ Ⓒ Ⓓ Ⓔ   25 Ⓐ Ⓑ Ⓒ Ⓓ Ⓔ   35 Ⓐ Ⓑ Ⓒ Ⓓ Ⓔ
6 Ⓐ Ⓑ Ⓒ Ⓓ Ⓔ   16 Ⓐ Ⓑ Ⓒ Ⓓ Ⓔ   26 Ⓐ Ⓑ Ⓒ Ⓓ Ⓔ   36 Ⓐ Ⓑ Ⓒ Ⓓ Ⓔ
7 Ⓐ Ⓑ Ⓒ Ⓓ Ⓔ   17 Ⓐ Ⓑ Ⓒ Ⓓ Ⓔ   27 Ⓐ Ⓑ Ⓒ Ⓓ Ⓔ   37 Ⓐ Ⓑ Ⓒ Ⓓ Ⓔ
8 Ⓐ Ⓑ Ⓒ Ⓓ Ⓔ   18 Ⓐ Ⓑ Ⓒ Ⓓ Ⓔ   28 Ⓐ Ⓑ Ⓒ Ⓓ Ⓔ   38 Ⓐ Ⓑ Ⓒ Ⓓ Ⓔ
9 Ⓐ Ⓑ Ⓒ Ⓓ Ⓔ   19 Ⓐ Ⓑ Ⓒ Ⓓ Ⓔ   29 Ⓐ Ⓑ Ⓒ Ⓓ Ⓔ   39 Ⓐ Ⓑ Ⓒ Ⓓ Ⓔ
10 Ⓐ Ⓑ Ⓒ Ⓓ Ⓔ   20 Ⓐ Ⓑ Ⓒ Ⓓ Ⓔ   30 Ⓐ Ⓑ Ⓒ Ⓓ Ⓔ   40 Ⓐ Ⓑ Ⓒ Ⓓ Ⓔ

CAUTION Use the answer spaces in the grids below for Section 6 or Section 7 only if you are told to do so in your test book.

Student-Produced Responses

ONLY ANSWERS ENTERED IN THE OVALS IN EACH GRID WILL BE SCORED. YOU WILL NOT RECEIVE CREDIT FOR ANYTHING WRITTEN IN THE BOXES ABOVE THE OVALS.

Grid-in answer spaces numbered 9, 10, 11, 12, 13, 14, 15, 16, 17, 18, each with fraction-bar and decimal-point ovals and digit ovals 0 through 9.

Start with number 1 for each new section. If a section has fewer questions than answer spaces, leave the extra answer spaces blank. Be sure to erase any errors or stray marks completely.

SECTION 8

1	Ⓐ Ⓑ Ⓒ Ⓓ Ⓔ	11	Ⓐ Ⓑ Ⓒ Ⓓ Ⓔ	21	Ⓐ Ⓑ Ⓒ Ⓓ Ⓔ	31	Ⓐ Ⓑ Ⓒ Ⓓ Ⓔ
2	Ⓐ Ⓑ Ⓒ Ⓓ Ⓔ	12	Ⓐ Ⓑ Ⓒ Ⓓ Ⓔ	22	Ⓐ Ⓑ Ⓒ Ⓓ Ⓔ	32	Ⓐ Ⓑ Ⓒ Ⓓ Ⓔ
3	Ⓐ Ⓑ Ⓒ Ⓓ Ⓔ	13	Ⓐ Ⓑ Ⓒ Ⓓ Ⓔ	23	Ⓐ Ⓑ Ⓒ Ⓓ Ⓔ	33	Ⓐ Ⓑ Ⓒ Ⓓ Ⓔ
4	Ⓐ Ⓑ Ⓒ Ⓓ Ⓔ	14	Ⓐ Ⓑ Ⓒ Ⓓ Ⓔ	24	Ⓐ Ⓑ Ⓒ Ⓓ Ⓔ	34	Ⓐ Ⓑ Ⓒ Ⓓ Ⓔ
5	Ⓐ Ⓑ Ⓒ Ⓓ Ⓔ	15	Ⓐ Ⓑ Ⓒ Ⓓ Ⓔ	25	Ⓐ Ⓑ Ⓒ Ⓓ Ⓔ	35	Ⓐ Ⓑ Ⓒ Ⓓ Ⓔ
6	Ⓐ Ⓑ Ⓒ Ⓓ Ⓔ	16	Ⓐ Ⓑ Ⓒ Ⓓ Ⓔ	26	Ⓐ Ⓑ Ⓒ Ⓓ Ⓔ	36	Ⓐ Ⓑ Ⓒ Ⓓ Ⓔ
7	Ⓐ Ⓑ Ⓒ Ⓓ Ⓔ	17	Ⓐ Ⓑ Ⓒ Ⓓ Ⓔ	27	Ⓐ Ⓑ Ⓒ Ⓓ Ⓔ	37	Ⓐ Ⓑ Ⓒ Ⓓ Ⓔ
8	Ⓐ Ⓑ Ⓒ Ⓓ Ⓔ	18	Ⓐ Ⓑ Ⓒ Ⓓ Ⓔ	28	Ⓐ Ⓑ Ⓒ Ⓓ Ⓔ	38	Ⓐ Ⓑ Ⓒ Ⓓ Ⓔ
9	Ⓐ Ⓑ Ⓒ Ⓓ Ⓔ	19	Ⓐ Ⓑ Ⓒ Ⓓ Ⓔ	29	Ⓐ Ⓑ Ⓒ Ⓓ Ⓔ	39	Ⓐ Ⓑ Ⓒ Ⓓ Ⓔ
10	Ⓐ Ⓑ Ⓒ Ⓓ Ⓔ	20	Ⓐ Ⓑ Ⓒ Ⓓ Ⓔ	30	Ⓐ Ⓑ Ⓒ Ⓓ Ⓔ	40	Ⓐ Ⓑ Ⓒ Ⓓ Ⓔ

SECTION 9

1	Ⓐ Ⓑ Ⓒ Ⓓ Ⓔ	11	Ⓐ Ⓑ Ⓒ Ⓓ Ⓔ	21	Ⓐ Ⓑ Ⓒ Ⓓ Ⓔ	31	Ⓐ Ⓑ Ⓒ Ⓓ Ⓔ
2	Ⓐ Ⓑ Ⓒ Ⓓ Ⓔ	12	Ⓐ Ⓑ Ⓒ Ⓓ Ⓔ	22	Ⓐ Ⓑ Ⓒ Ⓓ Ⓔ	32	Ⓐ Ⓑ Ⓒ Ⓓ Ⓔ
3	Ⓐ Ⓑ Ⓒ Ⓓ Ⓔ	13	Ⓐ Ⓑ Ⓒ Ⓓ Ⓔ	23	Ⓐ Ⓑ Ⓒ Ⓓ Ⓔ	33	Ⓐ Ⓑ Ⓒ Ⓓ Ⓔ
4	Ⓐ Ⓑ Ⓒ Ⓓ Ⓔ	14	Ⓐ Ⓑ Ⓒ Ⓓ Ⓔ	24	Ⓐ Ⓑ Ⓒ Ⓓ Ⓔ	34	Ⓐ Ⓑ Ⓒ Ⓓ Ⓔ
5	Ⓐ Ⓑ Ⓒ Ⓓ Ⓔ	15	Ⓐ Ⓑ Ⓒ Ⓓ Ⓔ	25	Ⓐ Ⓑ Ⓒ Ⓓ Ⓔ	35	Ⓐ Ⓑ Ⓒ Ⓓ Ⓔ
6	Ⓐ Ⓑ Ⓒ Ⓓ Ⓔ	16	Ⓐ Ⓑ Ⓒ Ⓓ Ⓔ	26	Ⓐ Ⓑ Ⓒ Ⓓ Ⓔ	36	Ⓐ Ⓑ Ⓒ Ⓓ Ⓔ
7	Ⓐ Ⓑ Ⓒ Ⓓ Ⓔ	17	Ⓐ Ⓑ Ⓒ Ⓓ Ⓔ	27	Ⓐ Ⓑ Ⓒ Ⓓ Ⓔ	37	Ⓐ Ⓑ Ⓒ Ⓓ Ⓔ
8	Ⓐ Ⓑ Ⓒ Ⓓ Ⓔ	18	Ⓐ Ⓑ Ⓒ Ⓓ Ⓔ	28	Ⓐ Ⓑ Ⓒ Ⓓ Ⓔ	38	Ⓐ Ⓑ Ⓒ Ⓓ Ⓔ
9	Ⓐ Ⓑ Ⓒ Ⓓ Ⓔ	19	Ⓐ Ⓑ Ⓒ Ⓓ Ⓔ	29	Ⓐ Ⓑ Ⓒ Ⓓ Ⓔ	39	Ⓐ Ⓑ Ⓒ Ⓓ Ⓔ
10	Ⓐ Ⓑ Ⓒ Ⓓ Ⓔ	20	Ⓐ Ⓑ Ⓒ Ⓓ Ⓔ	30	Ⓐ Ⓑ Ⓒ Ⓓ Ⓔ	40	Ⓐ Ⓑ Ⓒ Ⓓ Ⓔ

SECTION 10

1	Ⓐ Ⓑ Ⓒ Ⓓ Ⓔ	11	Ⓐ Ⓑ Ⓒ Ⓓ Ⓔ	21	Ⓐ Ⓑ Ⓒ Ⓓ Ⓔ	31	Ⓐ Ⓑ Ⓒ Ⓓ Ⓔ
2	Ⓐ Ⓑ Ⓒ Ⓓ Ⓔ	12	Ⓐ Ⓑ Ⓒ Ⓓ Ⓔ	22	Ⓐ Ⓑ Ⓒ Ⓓ Ⓔ	32	Ⓐ Ⓑ Ⓒ Ⓓ Ⓔ
3	Ⓐ Ⓑ Ⓒ Ⓓ Ⓔ	13	Ⓐ Ⓑ Ⓒ Ⓓ Ⓔ	23	Ⓐ Ⓑ Ⓒ Ⓓ Ⓔ	33	Ⓐ Ⓑ Ⓒ Ⓓ Ⓔ
4	Ⓐ Ⓑ Ⓒ Ⓓ Ⓔ	14	Ⓐ Ⓑ Ⓒ Ⓓ Ⓔ	24	Ⓐ Ⓑ Ⓒ Ⓓ Ⓔ	34	Ⓐ Ⓑ Ⓒ Ⓓ Ⓔ
5	Ⓐ Ⓑ Ⓒ Ⓓ Ⓔ	15	Ⓐ Ⓑ Ⓒ Ⓓ Ⓔ	25	Ⓐ Ⓑ Ⓒ Ⓓ Ⓔ	35	Ⓐ Ⓑ Ⓒ Ⓓ Ⓔ
6	Ⓐ Ⓑ Ⓒ Ⓓ Ⓔ	16	Ⓐ Ⓑ Ⓒ Ⓓ Ⓔ	26	Ⓐ Ⓑ Ⓒ Ⓓ Ⓔ	36	Ⓐ Ⓑ Ⓒ Ⓓ Ⓔ
7	Ⓐ Ⓑ Ⓒ Ⓓ Ⓔ	17	Ⓐ Ⓑ Ⓒ Ⓓ Ⓔ	27	Ⓐ Ⓑ Ⓒ Ⓓ Ⓔ	37	Ⓐ Ⓑ Ⓒ Ⓓ Ⓔ
8	Ⓐ Ⓑ Ⓒ Ⓓ Ⓔ	18	Ⓐ Ⓑ Ⓒ Ⓓ Ⓔ	28	Ⓐ Ⓑ Ⓒ Ⓓ Ⓔ	38	Ⓐ Ⓑ Ⓒ Ⓓ Ⓔ
9	Ⓐ Ⓑ Ⓒ Ⓓ Ⓔ	19	Ⓐ Ⓑ Ⓒ Ⓓ Ⓔ	29	Ⓐ Ⓑ Ⓒ Ⓓ Ⓔ	39	Ⓐ Ⓑ Ⓒ Ⓓ Ⓔ
10	Ⓐ Ⓑ Ⓒ Ⓓ Ⓔ	20	Ⓐ Ⓑ Ⓒ Ⓓ Ⓔ	30	Ⓐ Ⓑ Ⓒ Ⓓ Ⓔ	40	Ⓐ Ⓑ Ⓒ Ⓓ Ⓔ

Diagnostic Test Form

Use a No. 2 pencil only. Be sure each mark is dark and completely fills the intended oval. Completely erase any errors or stray marks.

1 Your Name:
(Print)

_____ | _____ | _____
Last | First | M.I.

Signature: _____ Date ___/___/___

Home Address: _____
Number and Street | City | State | Zip Code

E-Mail: _____ School: _____ Class: _____
(Print)

2 YOUR NAME
Last Name (First 4 Letters) | FIRST INIT | MID INIT

(bubble grid A–Z with symbols)

3 PHONE NUMBER

(bubble grid 0–9, seven columns)

4 DATE OF BIRTH

MONTH	DAY		YEAR
JAN			
FEB			
MAR	⓪	⓪	⓪
APR	①	①	①
MAY	②	②	②
JUN	③	③	③
JUL		④	④
AUG		⑤	⑤	⑤
SEP		⑥	⑥
OCT		⑦	⑦
NOV		⑧	⑧
DEC		⑨	⑨

5 SEX
◯ MALE
◯ FEMALE

IMPORTANT: Fill in items 6 and 7 exactly as shown on the preceding page.

6 TEST FORM
(Copy from back of test book)

7 TEST CODE

(bubble grid 0–9, four columns)

8 OTHER

1 Ⓐ Ⓑ Ⓒ Ⓓ Ⓔ
2 Ⓐ Ⓑ Ⓒ Ⓓ Ⓔ
3 Ⓐ Ⓑ Ⓒ Ⓓ Ⓔ

OpScan iNSIGHT™ forms by Pearson NCS EM-253760-3:654321   Printed in U.S.A.

SERIAL #

THIS PAGE INTENTIONALLY LEFT BLANK

Begin your essay on this page. If you need more space, continue on the next page. Do not write outside of the essay box.

Continue on the opposite side if necessary.

Start with number 1 for each new section. If a section has fewer questions than answer spaces, leave the extra answer spaces blank. Be sure to erase any errors or stray marks completely.

SECTION 2

1 Ⓐ Ⓑ Ⓒ Ⓓ Ⓔ	11 Ⓐ Ⓑ Ⓒ Ⓓ Ⓔ	21 Ⓐ Ⓑ Ⓒ Ⓓ Ⓔ	31 Ⓐ Ⓑ Ⓒ Ⓓ Ⓔ
2 Ⓐ Ⓑ Ⓒ Ⓓ Ⓔ	12 Ⓐ Ⓑ Ⓒ Ⓓ Ⓔ	22 Ⓐ Ⓑ Ⓒ Ⓓ Ⓔ	32 Ⓐ Ⓑ Ⓒ Ⓓ Ⓔ
3 Ⓐ Ⓑ Ⓒ Ⓓ Ⓔ	13 Ⓐ Ⓑ Ⓒ Ⓓ Ⓔ	23 Ⓐ Ⓑ Ⓒ Ⓓ Ⓔ	33 Ⓐ Ⓑ Ⓒ Ⓓ Ⓔ
4 Ⓐ Ⓑ Ⓒ Ⓓ Ⓔ	14 Ⓐ Ⓑ Ⓒ Ⓓ Ⓔ	24 Ⓐ Ⓑ Ⓒ Ⓓ Ⓔ	34 Ⓐ Ⓑ Ⓒ Ⓓ Ⓔ
5 Ⓐ Ⓑ Ⓒ Ⓓ Ⓔ	15 Ⓐ Ⓑ Ⓒ Ⓓ Ⓔ	25 Ⓐ Ⓑ Ⓒ Ⓓ Ⓔ	35 Ⓐ Ⓑ Ⓒ Ⓓ Ⓔ
6 Ⓐ Ⓑ Ⓒ Ⓓ Ⓔ	16 Ⓐ Ⓑ Ⓒ Ⓓ Ⓔ	26 Ⓐ Ⓑ Ⓒ Ⓓ Ⓔ	36 Ⓐ Ⓑ Ⓒ Ⓓ Ⓔ
7 Ⓐ Ⓑ Ⓒ Ⓓ Ⓔ	17 Ⓐ Ⓑ Ⓒ Ⓓ Ⓔ	27 Ⓐ Ⓑ Ⓒ Ⓓ Ⓔ	37 Ⓐ Ⓑ Ⓒ Ⓓ Ⓔ
8 Ⓐ Ⓑ Ⓒ Ⓓ Ⓔ	18 Ⓐ Ⓑ Ⓒ Ⓓ Ⓔ	28 Ⓐ Ⓑ Ⓒ Ⓓ Ⓔ	38 Ⓐ Ⓑ Ⓒ Ⓓ Ⓔ
9 Ⓐ Ⓑ Ⓒ Ⓓ Ⓔ	19 Ⓐ Ⓑ Ⓒ Ⓓ Ⓔ	29 Ⓐ Ⓑ Ⓒ Ⓓ Ⓔ	39 Ⓐ Ⓑ Ⓒ Ⓓ Ⓔ
10 Ⓐ Ⓑ Ⓒ Ⓓ Ⓔ	20 Ⓐ Ⓑ Ⓒ Ⓓ Ⓔ	30 Ⓐ Ⓑ Ⓒ Ⓓ Ⓔ	40 Ⓐ Ⓑ Ⓒ Ⓓ Ⓔ

SECTION 3

1 Ⓐ Ⓑ Ⓒ Ⓓ Ⓔ	11 Ⓐ Ⓑ Ⓒ Ⓓ Ⓔ	21 Ⓐ Ⓑ Ⓒ Ⓓ Ⓔ	31 Ⓐ Ⓑ Ⓒ Ⓓ Ⓔ
2 Ⓐ Ⓑ Ⓒ Ⓓ Ⓔ	12 Ⓐ Ⓑ Ⓒ Ⓓ Ⓔ	22 Ⓐ Ⓑ Ⓒ Ⓓ Ⓔ	32 Ⓐ Ⓑ Ⓒ Ⓓ Ⓔ
3 Ⓐ Ⓑ Ⓒ Ⓓ Ⓔ	13 Ⓐ Ⓑ Ⓒ Ⓓ Ⓔ	23 Ⓐ Ⓑ Ⓒ Ⓓ Ⓔ	33 Ⓐ Ⓑ Ⓒ Ⓓ Ⓔ
4 Ⓐ Ⓑ Ⓒ Ⓓ Ⓔ	14 Ⓐ Ⓑ Ⓒ Ⓓ Ⓔ	24 Ⓐ Ⓑ Ⓒ Ⓓ Ⓔ	34 Ⓐ Ⓑ Ⓒ Ⓓ Ⓔ
5 Ⓐ Ⓑ Ⓒ Ⓓ Ⓔ	15 Ⓐ Ⓑ Ⓒ Ⓓ Ⓔ	25 Ⓐ Ⓑ Ⓒ Ⓓ Ⓔ	35 Ⓐ Ⓑ Ⓒ Ⓓ Ⓔ
6 Ⓐ Ⓑ Ⓒ Ⓓ Ⓔ	16 Ⓐ Ⓑ Ⓒ Ⓓ Ⓔ	26 Ⓐ Ⓑ Ⓒ Ⓓ Ⓔ	36 Ⓐ Ⓑ Ⓒ Ⓓ Ⓔ
7 Ⓐ Ⓑ Ⓒ Ⓓ Ⓔ	17 Ⓐ Ⓑ Ⓒ Ⓓ Ⓔ	27 Ⓐ Ⓑ Ⓒ Ⓓ Ⓔ	37 Ⓐ Ⓑ Ⓒ Ⓓ Ⓔ
8 Ⓐ Ⓑ Ⓒ Ⓓ Ⓔ	18 Ⓐ Ⓑ Ⓒ Ⓓ Ⓔ	28 Ⓐ Ⓑ Ⓒ Ⓓ Ⓔ	38 Ⓐ Ⓑ Ⓒ Ⓓ Ⓔ
9 Ⓐ Ⓑ Ⓒ Ⓓ Ⓔ	19 Ⓐ Ⓑ Ⓒ Ⓓ Ⓔ	29 Ⓐ Ⓑ Ⓒ Ⓓ Ⓔ	39 Ⓐ Ⓑ Ⓒ Ⓓ Ⓔ
10 Ⓐ Ⓑ Ⓒ Ⓓ Ⓔ	20 Ⓐ Ⓑ Ⓒ Ⓓ Ⓔ	30 Ⓐ Ⓑ Ⓒ Ⓓ Ⓔ	40 Ⓐ Ⓑ Ⓒ Ⓓ Ⓔ

CAUTION Use the answer spaces in the grids below for Section 2 or Section 3 only if you are told to do so in your test book.

Student-Produced Responses

ONLY ANSWERS ENTERED IN THE OVALS IN EACH GRID WILL BE SCORED. YOU WILL NOT RECEIVE CREDIT FOR ANYTHING WRITTEN IN THE BOXES ABOVE THE OVALS.

Grids numbered 9, 10, 11, 12, 13 (top row) and 14, 15, 16, 17, 18 (bottom row), each with four columns of bubbles containing fraction bars (⁄), decimal points (·), and digits 0–9.

Start with number 1 for each new section. If a section has fewer questions than answer spaces, leave the extra answer spaces blank. Be sure to erase any errors or stray marks completely.

SECTION 4

1 Ⓐ Ⓑ Ⓒ Ⓓ Ⓔ	11 Ⓐ Ⓑ Ⓒ Ⓓ Ⓔ	21 Ⓐ Ⓑ Ⓒ Ⓓ Ⓔ	31 Ⓐ Ⓑ Ⓒ Ⓓ Ⓔ
2 Ⓐ Ⓑ Ⓒ Ⓓ Ⓔ	12 Ⓐ Ⓑ Ⓒ Ⓓ Ⓔ	22 Ⓐ Ⓑ Ⓒ Ⓓ Ⓔ	32 Ⓐ Ⓑ Ⓒ Ⓓ Ⓔ
3 Ⓐ Ⓑ Ⓒ Ⓓ Ⓔ	13 Ⓐ Ⓑ Ⓒ Ⓓ Ⓔ	23 Ⓐ Ⓑ Ⓒ Ⓓ Ⓔ	33 Ⓐ Ⓑ Ⓒ Ⓓ Ⓔ
4 Ⓐ Ⓑ Ⓒ Ⓓ Ⓔ	14 Ⓐ Ⓑ Ⓒ Ⓓ Ⓔ	24 Ⓐ Ⓑ Ⓒ Ⓓ Ⓔ	34 Ⓐ Ⓑ Ⓒ Ⓓ Ⓔ
5 Ⓐ Ⓑ Ⓒ Ⓓ Ⓔ	15 Ⓐ Ⓑ Ⓒ Ⓓ Ⓔ	25 Ⓐ Ⓑ Ⓒ Ⓓ Ⓔ	35 Ⓐ Ⓑ Ⓒ Ⓓ Ⓔ
6 Ⓐ Ⓑ Ⓒ Ⓓ Ⓔ	16 Ⓐ Ⓑ Ⓒ Ⓓ Ⓔ	26 Ⓐ Ⓑ Ⓒ Ⓓ Ⓔ	36 Ⓐ Ⓑ Ⓒ Ⓓ Ⓔ
7 Ⓐ Ⓑ Ⓒ Ⓓ Ⓔ	17 Ⓐ Ⓑ Ⓒ Ⓓ Ⓔ	27 Ⓐ Ⓑ Ⓒ Ⓓ Ⓔ	37 Ⓐ Ⓑ Ⓒ Ⓓ Ⓔ
8 Ⓐ Ⓑ Ⓒ Ⓓ Ⓔ	18 Ⓐ Ⓑ Ⓒ Ⓓ Ⓔ	28 Ⓐ Ⓑ Ⓒ Ⓓ Ⓔ	38 Ⓐ Ⓑ Ⓒ Ⓓ Ⓔ
9 Ⓐ Ⓑ Ⓒ Ⓓ Ⓔ	19 Ⓐ Ⓑ Ⓒ Ⓓ Ⓔ	29 Ⓐ Ⓑ Ⓒ Ⓓ Ⓔ	39 Ⓐ Ⓑ Ⓒ Ⓓ Ⓔ
10 Ⓐ Ⓑ Ⓒ Ⓓ Ⓔ	20 Ⓐ Ⓑ Ⓒ Ⓓ Ⓔ	30 Ⓐ Ⓑ Ⓒ Ⓓ Ⓔ	40 Ⓐ Ⓑ Ⓒ Ⓓ Ⓔ

SECTION 5

1 Ⓐ Ⓑ Ⓒ Ⓓ Ⓔ	11 Ⓐ Ⓑ Ⓒ Ⓓ Ⓔ	21 Ⓐ Ⓑ Ⓒ Ⓓ Ⓔ	31 Ⓐ Ⓑ Ⓒ Ⓓ Ⓔ
2 Ⓐ Ⓑ Ⓒ Ⓓ Ⓔ	12 Ⓐ Ⓑ Ⓒ Ⓓ Ⓔ	22 Ⓐ Ⓑ Ⓒ Ⓓ Ⓔ	32 Ⓐ Ⓑ Ⓒ Ⓓ Ⓔ
3 Ⓐ Ⓑ Ⓒ Ⓓ Ⓔ	13 Ⓐ Ⓑ Ⓒ Ⓓ Ⓔ	23 Ⓐ Ⓑ Ⓒ Ⓓ Ⓔ	33 Ⓐ Ⓑ Ⓒ Ⓓ Ⓔ
4 Ⓐ Ⓑ Ⓒ Ⓓ Ⓔ	14 Ⓐ Ⓑ Ⓒ Ⓓ Ⓔ	24 Ⓐ Ⓑ Ⓒ Ⓓ Ⓔ	34 Ⓐ Ⓑ Ⓒ Ⓓ Ⓔ
5 Ⓐ Ⓑ Ⓒ Ⓓ Ⓔ	15 Ⓐ Ⓑ Ⓒ Ⓓ Ⓔ	25 Ⓐ Ⓑ Ⓒ Ⓓ Ⓔ	35 Ⓐ Ⓑ Ⓒ Ⓓ Ⓔ
6 Ⓐ Ⓑ Ⓒ Ⓓ Ⓔ	16 Ⓐ Ⓑ Ⓒ Ⓓ Ⓔ	26 Ⓐ Ⓑ Ⓒ Ⓓ Ⓔ	36 Ⓐ Ⓑ Ⓒ Ⓓ Ⓔ
7 Ⓐ Ⓑ Ⓒ Ⓓ Ⓔ	17 Ⓐ Ⓑ Ⓒ Ⓓ Ⓔ	27 Ⓐ Ⓑ Ⓒ Ⓓ Ⓔ	37 Ⓐ Ⓑ Ⓒ Ⓓ Ⓔ
8 Ⓐ Ⓑ Ⓒ Ⓓ Ⓔ	18 Ⓐ Ⓑ Ⓒ Ⓓ Ⓔ	28 Ⓐ Ⓑ Ⓒ Ⓓ Ⓔ	38 Ⓐ Ⓑ Ⓒ Ⓓ Ⓔ
9 Ⓐ Ⓑ Ⓒ Ⓓ Ⓔ	19 Ⓐ Ⓑ Ⓒ Ⓓ Ⓔ	29 Ⓐ Ⓑ Ⓒ Ⓓ Ⓔ	39 Ⓐ Ⓑ Ⓒ Ⓓ Ⓔ
10 Ⓐ Ⓑ Ⓒ Ⓓ Ⓔ	20 Ⓐ Ⓑ Ⓒ Ⓓ Ⓔ	30 Ⓐ Ⓑ Ⓒ Ⓓ Ⓔ	40 Ⓐ Ⓑ Ⓒ Ⓓ Ⓔ

CAUTION Use the answer spaces in the grids below for Section 4 or Section 5 only if you are told to do so in your test book.

Student-Produced Responses ONLY ANSWERS ENTERED IN THE OVALS IN EACH GRID WILL BE SCORED. YOU WILL NOT RECEIVE CREDIT FOR ANYTHING WRITTEN IN THE BOXES ABOVE THE OVALS.

Grids 9, 10, 11, 12, 13 (each with fraction bar, decimal point, and digits 0–9)

Grids 14, 15, 16, 17, 18 (each with fraction bar, decimal point, and digits 0–9)

PLEASE DO NOT WRITE IN THIS AREA

SERIAL #

Start with number 1 for each new section. If a section has fewer questions than answer spaces, leave the extra answer spaces blank. Be sure to erase any errors or stray marks completely.

SECTION 6

1 Ⓐ Ⓑ Ⓒ Ⓓ Ⓔ	11 Ⓐ Ⓑ Ⓒ Ⓓ Ⓔ	21 Ⓐ Ⓑ Ⓒ Ⓓ Ⓔ	31 Ⓐ Ⓑ Ⓒ Ⓓ Ⓔ
2 Ⓐ Ⓑ Ⓒ Ⓓ Ⓔ	12 Ⓐ Ⓑ Ⓒ Ⓓ Ⓔ	22 Ⓐ Ⓑ Ⓒ Ⓓ Ⓔ	32 Ⓐ Ⓑ Ⓒ Ⓓ Ⓔ
3 Ⓐ Ⓑ Ⓒ Ⓓ Ⓔ	13 Ⓐ Ⓑ Ⓒ Ⓓ Ⓔ	23 Ⓐ Ⓑ Ⓒ Ⓓ Ⓔ	33 Ⓐ Ⓑ Ⓒ Ⓓ Ⓔ
4 Ⓐ Ⓑ Ⓒ Ⓓ Ⓔ	14 Ⓐ Ⓑ Ⓒ Ⓓ Ⓔ	24 Ⓐ Ⓑ Ⓒ Ⓓ Ⓔ	34 Ⓐ Ⓑ Ⓒ Ⓓ Ⓔ
5 Ⓐ Ⓑ Ⓒ Ⓓ Ⓔ	15 Ⓐ Ⓑ Ⓒ Ⓓ Ⓔ	25 Ⓐ Ⓑ Ⓒ Ⓓ Ⓔ	35 Ⓐ Ⓑ Ⓒ Ⓓ Ⓔ
6 Ⓐ Ⓑ Ⓒ Ⓓ Ⓔ	16 Ⓐ Ⓑ Ⓒ Ⓓ Ⓔ	26 Ⓐ Ⓑ Ⓒ Ⓓ Ⓔ	36 Ⓐ Ⓑ Ⓒ Ⓓ Ⓔ
7 Ⓐ Ⓑ Ⓒ Ⓓ Ⓔ	17 Ⓐ Ⓑ Ⓒ Ⓓ Ⓔ	27 Ⓐ Ⓑ Ⓒ Ⓓ Ⓔ	37 Ⓐ Ⓑ Ⓒ Ⓓ Ⓔ
8 Ⓐ Ⓑ Ⓒ Ⓓ Ⓔ	18 Ⓐ Ⓑ Ⓒ Ⓓ Ⓔ	28 Ⓐ Ⓑ Ⓒ Ⓓ Ⓔ	38 Ⓐ Ⓑ Ⓒ Ⓓ Ⓔ
9 Ⓐ Ⓑ Ⓒ Ⓓ Ⓔ	19 Ⓐ Ⓑ Ⓒ Ⓓ Ⓔ	29 Ⓐ Ⓑ Ⓒ Ⓓ Ⓔ	39 Ⓐ Ⓑ Ⓒ Ⓓ Ⓔ
10 Ⓐ Ⓑ Ⓒ Ⓓ Ⓔ	20 Ⓐ Ⓑ Ⓒ Ⓓ Ⓔ	30 Ⓐ Ⓑ Ⓒ Ⓓ Ⓔ	40 Ⓐ Ⓑ Ⓒ Ⓓ Ⓔ

SECTION 7

1 Ⓐ Ⓑ Ⓒ Ⓓ Ⓔ	11 Ⓐ Ⓑ Ⓒ Ⓓ Ⓔ	21 Ⓐ Ⓑ Ⓒ Ⓓ Ⓔ	31 Ⓐ Ⓑ Ⓒ Ⓓ Ⓔ
2 Ⓐ Ⓑ Ⓒ Ⓓ Ⓔ	12 Ⓐ Ⓑ Ⓒ Ⓓ Ⓔ	22 Ⓐ Ⓑ Ⓒ Ⓓ Ⓔ	32 Ⓐ Ⓑ Ⓒ Ⓓ Ⓔ
3 Ⓐ Ⓑ Ⓒ Ⓓ Ⓔ	13 Ⓐ Ⓑ Ⓒ Ⓓ Ⓔ	23 Ⓐ Ⓑ Ⓒ Ⓓ Ⓔ	33 Ⓐ Ⓑ Ⓒ Ⓓ Ⓔ
4 Ⓐ Ⓑ Ⓒ Ⓓ Ⓔ	14 Ⓐ Ⓑ Ⓒ Ⓓ Ⓔ	24 Ⓐ Ⓑ Ⓒ Ⓓ Ⓔ	34 Ⓐ Ⓑ Ⓒ Ⓓ Ⓔ
5 Ⓐ Ⓑ Ⓒ Ⓓ Ⓔ	15 Ⓐ Ⓑ Ⓒ Ⓓ Ⓔ	25 Ⓐ Ⓑ Ⓒ Ⓓ Ⓔ	35 Ⓐ Ⓑ Ⓒ Ⓓ Ⓔ
6 Ⓐ Ⓑ Ⓒ Ⓓ Ⓔ	16 Ⓐ Ⓑ Ⓒ Ⓓ Ⓔ	26 Ⓐ Ⓑ Ⓒ Ⓓ Ⓔ	36 Ⓐ Ⓑ Ⓒ Ⓓ Ⓔ
7 Ⓐ Ⓑ Ⓒ Ⓓ Ⓔ	17 Ⓐ Ⓑ Ⓒ Ⓓ Ⓔ	27 Ⓐ Ⓑ Ⓒ Ⓓ Ⓔ	37 Ⓐ Ⓑ Ⓒ Ⓓ Ⓔ
8 Ⓐ Ⓑ Ⓒ Ⓓ Ⓔ	18 Ⓐ Ⓑ Ⓒ Ⓓ Ⓔ	28 Ⓐ Ⓑ Ⓒ Ⓓ Ⓔ	38 Ⓐ Ⓑ Ⓒ Ⓓ Ⓔ
9 Ⓐ Ⓑ Ⓒ Ⓓ Ⓔ	19 Ⓐ Ⓑ Ⓒ Ⓓ Ⓔ	29 Ⓐ Ⓑ Ⓒ Ⓓ Ⓔ	39 Ⓐ Ⓑ Ⓒ Ⓓ Ⓔ
10 Ⓐ Ⓑ Ⓒ Ⓓ Ⓔ	20 Ⓐ Ⓑ Ⓒ Ⓓ Ⓔ	30 Ⓐ Ⓑ Ⓒ Ⓓ Ⓔ	40 Ⓐ Ⓑ Ⓒ Ⓓ Ⓔ

CAUTION

Use the answer spaces in the grids below for Section 6 or Section 7 only if you are told to do so in your test book.

Student-Produced Responses

ONLY ANSWERS ENTERED IN THE OVALS IN EACH GRID WILL BE SCORED. YOU WILL NOT RECEIVE CREDIT FOR ANYTHING WRITTEN IN THE BOXES ABOVE THE OVALS.

Grids 9, 10, 11, 12, 13 — each a student-produced response grid with fraction bars (/), decimal points (·), and digits 0–9.

Grids 14, 15, 16, 17, 18 — each a student-produced response grid with fraction bars (/), decimal points (·), and digits 0–9.

Start with number 1 for each new section. If a section has fewer questions than answer spaces, leave the extra answer spaces blank. Be sure to erase any errors or stray marks completely.

SECTION 8

1 Ⓐ Ⓑ Ⓒ Ⓓ Ⓔ	11 Ⓐ Ⓑ Ⓒ Ⓓ Ⓔ	21 Ⓐ Ⓑ Ⓒ Ⓓ Ⓔ	31 Ⓐ Ⓑ Ⓒ Ⓓ Ⓔ
2 Ⓐ Ⓑ Ⓒ Ⓓ Ⓔ	12 Ⓐ Ⓑ Ⓒ Ⓓ Ⓔ	22 Ⓐ Ⓑ Ⓒ Ⓓ Ⓔ	32 Ⓐ Ⓑ Ⓒ Ⓓ Ⓔ
3 Ⓐ Ⓑ Ⓒ Ⓓ Ⓔ	13 Ⓐ Ⓑ Ⓒ Ⓓ Ⓔ	23 Ⓐ Ⓑ Ⓒ Ⓓ Ⓔ	33 Ⓐ Ⓑ Ⓒ Ⓓ Ⓔ
4 Ⓐ Ⓑ Ⓒ Ⓓ Ⓔ	14 Ⓐ Ⓑ Ⓒ Ⓓ Ⓔ	24 Ⓐ Ⓑ Ⓒ Ⓓ Ⓔ	34 Ⓐ Ⓑ Ⓒ Ⓓ Ⓔ
5 Ⓐ Ⓑ Ⓒ Ⓓ Ⓔ	15 Ⓐ Ⓑ Ⓒ Ⓓ Ⓔ	25 Ⓐ Ⓑ Ⓒ Ⓓ Ⓔ	35 Ⓐ Ⓑ Ⓒ Ⓓ Ⓔ
6 Ⓐ Ⓑ Ⓒ Ⓓ Ⓔ	16 Ⓐ Ⓑ Ⓒ Ⓓ Ⓔ	26 Ⓐ Ⓑ Ⓒ Ⓓ Ⓔ	36 Ⓐ Ⓑ Ⓒ Ⓓ Ⓔ
7 Ⓐ Ⓑ Ⓒ Ⓓ Ⓔ	17 Ⓐ Ⓑ Ⓒ Ⓓ Ⓔ	27 Ⓐ Ⓑ Ⓒ Ⓓ Ⓔ	37 Ⓐ Ⓑ Ⓒ Ⓓ Ⓔ
8 Ⓐ Ⓑ Ⓒ Ⓓ Ⓔ	18 Ⓐ Ⓑ Ⓒ Ⓓ Ⓔ	28 Ⓐ Ⓑ Ⓒ Ⓓ Ⓔ	38 Ⓐ Ⓑ Ⓒ Ⓓ Ⓔ
9 Ⓐ Ⓑ Ⓒ Ⓓ Ⓔ	19 Ⓐ Ⓑ Ⓒ Ⓓ Ⓔ	29 Ⓐ Ⓑ Ⓒ Ⓓ Ⓔ	39 Ⓐ Ⓑ Ⓒ Ⓓ Ⓔ
10 Ⓐ Ⓑ Ⓒ Ⓓ Ⓔ	20 Ⓐ Ⓑ Ⓒ Ⓓ Ⓔ	30 Ⓐ Ⓑ Ⓒ Ⓓ Ⓔ	40 Ⓐ Ⓑ Ⓒ Ⓓ Ⓔ

SECTION 9

1 Ⓐ Ⓑ Ⓒ Ⓓ Ⓔ	11 Ⓐ Ⓑ Ⓒ Ⓓ Ⓔ	21 Ⓐ Ⓑ Ⓒ Ⓓ Ⓔ	31 Ⓐ Ⓑ Ⓒ Ⓓ Ⓔ
2 Ⓐ Ⓑ Ⓒ Ⓓ Ⓔ	12 Ⓐ Ⓑ Ⓒ Ⓓ Ⓔ	22 Ⓐ Ⓑ Ⓒ Ⓓ Ⓔ	32 Ⓐ Ⓑ Ⓒ Ⓓ Ⓔ
3 Ⓐ Ⓑ Ⓒ Ⓓ Ⓔ	13 Ⓐ Ⓑ Ⓒ Ⓓ Ⓔ	23 Ⓐ Ⓑ Ⓒ Ⓓ Ⓔ	33 Ⓐ Ⓑ Ⓒ Ⓓ Ⓔ
4 Ⓐ Ⓑ Ⓒ Ⓓ Ⓔ	14 Ⓐ Ⓑ Ⓒ Ⓓ Ⓔ	24 Ⓐ Ⓑ Ⓒ Ⓓ Ⓔ	34 Ⓐ Ⓑ Ⓒ Ⓓ Ⓔ
5 Ⓐ Ⓑ Ⓒ Ⓓ Ⓔ	15 Ⓐ Ⓑ Ⓒ Ⓓ Ⓔ	25 Ⓐ Ⓑ Ⓒ Ⓓ Ⓔ	35 Ⓐ Ⓑ Ⓒ Ⓓ Ⓔ
6 Ⓐ Ⓑ Ⓒ Ⓓ Ⓔ	16 Ⓐ Ⓑ Ⓒ Ⓓ Ⓔ	26 Ⓐ Ⓑ Ⓒ Ⓓ Ⓔ	36 Ⓐ Ⓑ Ⓒ Ⓓ Ⓔ
7 Ⓐ Ⓑ Ⓒ Ⓓ Ⓔ	17 Ⓐ Ⓑ Ⓒ Ⓓ Ⓔ	27 Ⓐ Ⓑ Ⓒ Ⓓ Ⓔ	37 Ⓐ Ⓑ Ⓒ Ⓓ Ⓔ
8 Ⓐ Ⓑ Ⓒ Ⓓ Ⓔ	18 Ⓐ Ⓑ Ⓒ Ⓓ Ⓔ	28 Ⓐ Ⓑ Ⓒ Ⓓ Ⓔ	38 Ⓐ Ⓑ Ⓒ Ⓓ Ⓔ
9 Ⓐ Ⓑ Ⓒ Ⓓ Ⓔ	19 Ⓐ Ⓑ Ⓒ Ⓓ Ⓔ	29 Ⓐ Ⓑ Ⓒ Ⓓ Ⓔ	39 Ⓐ Ⓑ Ⓒ Ⓓ Ⓔ
10 Ⓐ Ⓑ Ⓒ Ⓓ Ⓔ	20 Ⓐ Ⓑ Ⓒ Ⓓ Ⓔ	30 Ⓐ Ⓑ Ⓒ Ⓓ Ⓔ	40 Ⓐ Ⓑ Ⓒ Ⓓ Ⓔ

SECTION 10

1 Ⓐ Ⓑ Ⓒ Ⓓ Ⓔ	11 Ⓐ Ⓑ Ⓒ Ⓓ Ⓔ	21 Ⓐ Ⓑ Ⓒ Ⓓ Ⓔ	31 Ⓐ Ⓑ Ⓒ Ⓓ Ⓔ
2 Ⓐ Ⓑ Ⓒ Ⓓ Ⓔ	12 Ⓐ Ⓑ Ⓒ Ⓓ Ⓔ	22 Ⓐ Ⓑ Ⓒ Ⓓ Ⓔ	32 Ⓐ Ⓑ Ⓒ Ⓓ Ⓔ
3 Ⓐ Ⓑ Ⓒ Ⓓ Ⓔ	13 Ⓐ Ⓑ Ⓒ Ⓓ Ⓔ	23 Ⓐ Ⓑ Ⓒ Ⓓ Ⓔ	33 Ⓐ Ⓑ Ⓒ Ⓓ Ⓔ
4 Ⓐ Ⓑ Ⓒ Ⓓ Ⓔ	14 Ⓐ Ⓑ Ⓒ Ⓓ Ⓔ	24 Ⓐ Ⓑ Ⓒ Ⓓ Ⓔ	34 Ⓐ Ⓑ Ⓒ Ⓓ Ⓔ
5 Ⓐ Ⓑ Ⓒ Ⓓ Ⓔ	15 Ⓐ Ⓑ Ⓒ Ⓓ Ⓔ	25 Ⓐ Ⓑ Ⓒ Ⓓ Ⓔ	35 Ⓐ Ⓑ Ⓒ Ⓓ Ⓔ
6 Ⓐ Ⓑ Ⓒ Ⓓ Ⓔ	16 Ⓐ Ⓑ Ⓒ Ⓓ Ⓔ	26 Ⓐ Ⓑ Ⓒ Ⓓ Ⓔ	36 Ⓐ Ⓑ Ⓒ Ⓓ Ⓔ
7 Ⓐ Ⓑ Ⓒ Ⓓ Ⓔ	17 Ⓐ Ⓑ Ⓒ Ⓓ Ⓔ	27 Ⓐ Ⓑ Ⓒ Ⓓ Ⓔ	37 Ⓐ Ⓑ Ⓒ Ⓓ Ⓔ
8 Ⓐ Ⓑ Ⓒ Ⓓ Ⓔ	18 Ⓐ Ⓑ Ⓒ Ⓓ Ⓔ	28 Ⓐ Ⓑ Ⓒ Ⓓ Ⓔ	38 Ⓐ Ⓑ Ⓒ Ⓓ Ⓔ
9 Ⓐ Ⓑ Ⓒ Ⓓ Ⓔ	19 Ⓐ Ⓑ Ⓒ Ⓓ Ⓔ	29 Ⓐ Ⓑ Ⓒ Ⓓ Ⓔ	39 Ⓐ Ⓑ Ⓒ Ⓓ Ⓔ
10 Ⓐ Ⓑ Ⓒ Ⓓ Ⓔ	20 Ⓐ Ⓑ Ⓒ Ⓓ Ⓔ	30 Ⓐ Ⓑ Ⓒ Ⓓ Ⓔ	40 Ⓐ Ⓑ Ⓒ Ⓓ Ⓔ

The Princeton Review

Diagnostic Test Form

Use a No. 2 pencil only. Be sure each mark is dark and completely fills the intended oval. Completely erase any errors or stray marks.

1 Your Name:
(Print)

Last _____ First _____ M.I. _____

Signature: _____ Date __/__/__

Home Address: _____
Number and Street _____ City _____ State _____ Zip Code

E-Mail: _____ School: _____ Class: _____
(Print)

2 YOUR NAME
Last Name (First 4 Letters)

FIRST INIT | MID INIT

(A B C D E F G H I J K L M N O P Q R S T U V W X Y Z ovals for each letter position)

3 PHONE NUMBER

(0 1 2 3 4 5 6 7 8 9 ovals across columns)

4 DATE OF BIRTH

MONTH	DAY		YEAR
JAN			
FEB			
MAR	0	0	0
APR	1	1	1
MAY	2	2	2
JUN	3	3	3
JUL		4	4
AUG		5	5	5
SEP		6	6	6
OCT		7	7	7
NOV		8	8	8
DEC		9	9	9

5 SEX
○ MALE
○ FEMALE

IMPORTANT: Fill in items 6 and 7 exactly as shown on the preceding page.

6 TEST FORM
(Copy from back of test book)

7 TEST CODE

(0 1 2 3 4 5 6 7 8 9 ovals across four columns)

8 OTHER
1 A B C D E
2 A B C D E
3 A B C D E

pScan iNSIGHT™ forms by Pearson NCS EM-253760-3:654321   Printed in U.S.A.

PLEASE DO NOT WRITE IN THIS AREA

SERIAL #

THIS PAGE INTENTIONALLY LEFT BLANK

The Princeton Review
Diagnostic Test Form

ESSAY

Begin your essay on this page. If you need more space, continue on the next page. Do not write outside of the essay box.

Continue on the opposite side if necessary.

SERIAL #

Start with number 1 for each new section. If a section has fewer questions than answer spaces, leave the extra answer spaces blank. Be sure to erase any errors or stray marks completely.

SECTION 2

1 (A)(B)(C)(D)(E)	11 (A)(B)(C)(D)(E)	21 (A)(B)(C)(D)(E)	31 (A)(B)(C)(D)(E)
2 (A)(B)(C)(D)(E)	12 (A)(B)(C)(D)(E)	22 (A)(B)(C)(D)(E)	32 (A)(B)(C)(D)(E)
3 (A)(B)(C)(D)(E)	13 (A)(B)(C)(D)(E)	23 (A)(B)(C)(D)(E)	33 (A)(B)(C)(D)(E)
4 (A)(B)(C)(D)(E)	14 (A)(B)(C)(D)(E)	24 (A)(B)(C)(D)(E)	34 (A)(B)(C)(D)(E)
5 (A)(B)(C)(D)(E)	15 (A)(B)(C)(D)(E)	25 (A)(B)(C)(D)(E)	35 (A)(B)(C)(D)(E)
6 (A)(B)(C)(D)(E)	16 (A)(B)(C)(D)(E)	26 (A)(B)(C)(D)(E)	36 (A)(B)(C)(D)(E)
7 (A)(B)(C)(D)(E)	17 (A)(B)(C)(D)(E)	27 (A)(B)(C)(D)(E)	37 (A)(B)(C)(D)(E)
8 (A)(B)(C)(D)(E)	18 (A)(B)(C)(D)(E)	28 (A)(B)(C)(D)(E)	38 (A)(B)(C)(D)(E)
9 (A)(B)(C)(D)(E)	19 (A)(B)(C)(D)(E)	29 (A)(B)(C)(D)(E)	39 (A)(B)(C)(D)(E)
10 (A)(B)(C)(D)(E)	20 (A)(B)(C)(D)(E)	30 (A)(B)(C)(D)(E)	40 (A)(B)(C)(D)(E)

SECTION 3

1 (A)(B)(C)(D)(E)	11 (A)(B)(C)(D)(E)	21 (A)(B)(C)(D)(E)	31 (A)(B)(C)(D)(E)
2 (A)(B)(C)(D)(E)	12 (A)(B)(C)(D)(E)	22 (A)(B)(C)(D)(E)	32 (A)(B)(C)(D)(E)
3 (A)(B)(C)(D)(E)	13 (A)(B)(C)(D)(E)	23 (A)(B)(C)(D)(E)	33 (A)(B)(C)(D)(E)
4 (A)(B)(C)(D)(E)	14 (A)(B)(C)(D)(E)	24 (A)(B)(C)(D)(E)	34 (A)(B)(C)(D)(E)
5 (A)(B)(C)(D)(E)	15 (A)(B)(C)(D)(E)	25 (A)(B)(C)(D)(E)	35 (A)(B)(C)(D)(E)
6 (A)(B)(C)(D)(E)	16 (A)(B)(C)(D)(E)	26 (A)(B)(C)(D)(E)	36 (A)(B)(C)(D)(E)
7 (A)(B)(C)(D)(E)	17 (A)(B)(C)(D)(E)	27 (A)(B)(C)(D)(E)	37 (A)(B)(C)(D)(E)
8 (A)(B)(C)(D)(E)	18 (A)(B)(C)(D)(E)	28 (A)(B)(C)(D)(E)	38 (A)(B)(C)(D)(E)
9 (A)(B)(C)(D)(E)	19 (A)(B)(C)(D)(E)	29 (A)(B)(C)(D)(E)	39 (A)(B)(C)(D)(E)
10 (A)(B)(C)(D)(E)	20 (A)(B)(C)(D)(E)	30 (A)(B)(C)(D)(E)	40 (A)(B)(C)(D)(E)

CAUTION Use the answer spaces in the grids below for Section 2 or Section 3 only if you are told to do so in your test book.

Student-Produced Responses

ONLY ANSWERS ENTERED IN THE OVALS IN EACH GRID WILL BE SCORED. YOU WILL NOT RECEIVE CREDIT FOR ANYTHING WRITTEN IN THE BOXES ABOVE THE OVALS.

Grids numbered 9, 10, 11, 12, 13, 14, 15, 16, 17, 18 — each a Student-Produced Response bubble grid.

Start with number 1 for each new section. If a section has fewer questions than answer spaces, leave the extra answer spaces blank. Be sure to erase any errors or stray marks completely.

SECTION 4

1 (A)(B)(C)(D)(E)	11 (A)(B)(C)(D)(E)	21 (A)(B)(C)(D)(E)	31 (A)(B)(C)(D)(E)
2 (A)(B)(C)(D)(E)	12 (A)(B)(C)(D)(E)	22 (A)(B)(C)(D)(E)	32 (A)(B)(C)(D)(E)
3 (A)(B)(C)(D)(E)	13 (A)(B)(C)(D)(E)	23 (A)(B)(C)(D)(E)	33 (A)(B)(C)(D)(E)
4 (A)(B)(C)(D)(E)	14 (A)(B)(C)(D)(E)	24 (A)(B)(C)(D)(E)	34 (A)(B)(C)(D)(E)
5 (A)(B)(C)(D)(E)	15 (A)(B)(C)(D)(E)	25 (A)(B)(C)(D)(E)	35 (A)(B)(C)(D)(E)
6 (A)(B)(C)(D)(E)	16 (A)(B)(C)(D)(E)	26 (A)(B)(C)(D)(E)	36 (A)(B)(C)(D)(E)
7 (A)(B)(C)(D)(E)	17 (A)(B)(C)(D)(E)	27 (A)(B)(C)(D)(E)	37 (A)(B)(C)(D)(E)
8 (A)(B)(C)(D)(E)	18 (A)(B)(C)(D)(E)	28 (A)(B)(C)(D)(E)	38 (A)(B)(C)(D)(E)
9 (A)(B)(C)(D)(E)	19 (A)(B)(C)(D)(E)	29 (A)(B)(C)(D)(E)	39 (A)(B)(C)(D)(E)
10 (A)(B)(C)(D)(E)	20 (A)(B)(C)(D)(E)	30 (A)(B)(C)(D)(E)	40 (A)(B)(C)(D)(E)

SECTION 5

1 (A)(B)(C)(D)(E)	11 (A)(B)(C)(D)(E)	21 (A)(B)(C)(D)(E)	31 (A)(B)(C)(D)(E)
2 (A)(B)(C)(D)(E)	12 (A)(B)(C)(D)(E)	22 (A)(B)(C)(D)(E)	32 (A)(B)(C)(D)(E)
3 (A)(B)(C)(D)(E)	13 (A)(B)(C)(D)(E)	23 (A)(B)(C)(D)(E)	33 (A)(B)(C)(D)(E)
4 (A)(B)(C)(D)(E)	14 (A)(B)(C)(D)(E)	24 (A)(B)(C)(D)(E)	34 (A)(B)(C)(D)(E)
5 (A)(B)(C)(D)(E)	15 (A)(B)(C)(D)(E)	25 (A)(B)(C)(D)(E)	35 (A)(B)(C)(D)(E)
6 (A)(B)(C)(D)(E)	16 (A)(B)(C)(D)(E)	26 (A)(B)(C)(D)(E)	36 (A)(B)(C)(D)(E)
7 (A)(B)(C)(D)(E)	17 (A)(B)(C)(D)(E)	27 (A)(B)(C)(D)(E)	37 (A)(B)(C)(D)(E)
8 (A)(B)(C)(D)(E)	18 (A)(B)(C)(D)(E)	28 (A)(B)(C)(D)(E)	38 (A)(B)(C)(D)(E)
9 (A)(B)(C)(D)(E)	19 (A)(B)(C)(D)(E)	29 (A)(B)(C)(D)(E)	39 (A)(B)(C)(D)(E)
10 (A)(B)(C)(D)(E)	20 (A)(B)(C)(D)(E)	30 (A)(B)(C)(D)(E)	40 (A)(B)(C)(D)(E)

CAUTION Use the answer spaces in the grids below for Section 4 or Section 5 only if you are told to do so in your test book.

Student-Produced Responses ONLY ANSWERS ENTERED IN THE OVALS IN EACH GRID WILL BE SCORED. YOU WILL NOT RECEIVE CREDIT FOR ANYTHING WRITTEN IN THE BOXES ABOVE THE OVALS.

9   10   11   12   13

14   15   16   17   18

PLEASE DO NOT WRITE IN THIS AREA

SERIAL #

Start with number 1 for each new section. If a section has fewer questions than answer spaces, leave the extra answer spaces blank. Be sure to erase any errors or stray marks completely.

SECTION 6

1 A B C D E	11 A B C D E	21 A B C D E	31 A B C D E
2 A B C D E	12 A B C D E	22 A B C D E	32 A B C D E
3 A B C D E	13 A B C D E	23 A B C D E	33 A B C D E
4 A B C D E	14 A B C D E	24 A B C D E	34 A B C D E
5 A B C D E	15 A B C D E	25 A B C D E	35 A B C D E
6 A B C D E	16 A B C D E	26 A B C D E	36 A B C D E
7 A B C D E	17 A B C D E	27 A B C D E	37 A B C D E
8 A B C D E	18 A B C D E	28 A B C D E	38 A B C D E
9 A B C D E	19 A B C D E	29 A B C D E	39 A B C D E
10 A B C D E	20 A B C D E	30 A B C D E	40 A B C D E

SECTION 7

1 A B C D E	11 A B C D E	21 A B C D E	31 A B C D E
2 A B C D E	12 A B C D E	22 A B C D E	32 A B C D E
3 A B C D E	13 A B C D E	23 A B C D E	33 A B C D E
4 A B C D E	14 A B C D E	24 A B C D E	34 A B C D E
5 A B C D E	15 A B C D E	25 A B C D E	35 A B C D E
6 A B C D E	16 A B C D E	26 A B C D E	36 A B C D E
7 A B C D E	17 A B C D E	27 A B C D E	37 A B C D E
8 A B C D E	18 A B C D E	28 A B C D E	38 A B C D E
9 A B C D E	19 A B C D E	29 A B C D E	39 A B C D E
10 A B C D E	20 A B C D E	30 A B C D E	40 A B C D E

CAUTION Use the answer spaces in the grids below for Section 6 or Section 7 only if you are told to do so in your test book.

Student-Produced Responses ONLY ANSWERS ENTERED IN THE OVALS IN EACH GRID WILL BE SCORED. YOU WILL NOT RECEIVE CREDIT FOR ANYTHING WRITTEN IN THE BOXES ABOVE THE OVALS.

9, 10, 11, 12, 13, 14, 15, 16, 17, 18 — grid-in answer boxes with ovals numbered 0–9 and fraction/decimal markers.

Start with number 1 for each new section. If a section has fewer questions than answer spaces, leave the extra answer spaces blank. Be sure to erase any errors or stray marks completely.

SECTION 8

1	Ⓐ Ⓑ Ⓒ Ⓓ Ⓔ	11	Ⓐ Ⓑ Ⓒ Ⓓ Ⓔ	21	Ⓐ Ⓑ Ⓒ Ⓓ Ⓔ	31	Ⓐ Ⓑ Ⓒ Ⓓ Ⓔ
2	Ⓐ Ⓑ Ⓒ Ⓓ Ⓔ	12	Ⓐ Ⓑ Ⓒ Ⓓ Ⓔ	22	Ⓐ Ⓑ Ⓒ Ⓓ Ⓔ	32	Ⓐ Ⓑ Ⓒ Ⓓ Ⓔ
3	Ⓐ Ⓑ Ⓒ Ⓓ Ⓔ	13	Ⓐ Ⓑ Ⓒ Ⓓ Ⓔ	23	Ⓐ Ⓑ Ⓒ Ⓓ Ⓔ	33	Ⓐ Ⓑ Ⓒ Ⓓ Ⓔ
4	Ⓐ Ⓑ Ⓒ Ⓓ Ⓔ	14	Ⓐ Ⓑ Ⓒ Ⓓ Ⓔ	24	Ⓐ Ⓑ Ⓒ Ⓓ Ⓔ	34	Ⓐ Ⓑ Ⓒ Ⓓ Ⓔ
5	Ⓐ Ⓑ Ⓒ Ⓓ Ⓔ	15	Ⓐ Ⓑ Ⓒ Ⓓ Ⓔ	25	Ⓐ Ⓑ Ⓒ Ⓓ Ⓔ	35	Ⓐ Ⓑ Ⓒ Ⓓ Ⓔ
6	Ⓐ Ⓑ Ⓒ Ⓓ Ⓔ	16	Ⓐ Ⓑ Ⓒ Ⓓ Ⓔ	26	Ⓐ Ⓑ Ⓒ Ⓓ Ⓔ	36	Ⓐ Ⓑ Ⓒ Ⓓ Ⓔ
7	Ⓐ Ⓑ Ⓒ Ⓓ Ⓔ	17	Ⓐ Ⓑ Ⓒ Ⓓ Ⓔ	27	Ⓐ Ⓑ Ⓒ Ⓓ Ⓔ	37	Ⓐ Ⓑ Ⓒ Ⓓ Ⓔ
8	Ⓐ Ⓑ Ⓒ Ⓓ Ⓔ	18	Ⓐ Ⓑ Ⓒ Ⓓ Ⓔ	28	Ⓐ Ⓑ Ⓒ Ⓓ Ⓔ	38	Ⓐ Ⓑ Ⓒ Ⓓ Ⓔ
9	Ⓐ Ⓑ Ⓒ Ⓓ Ⓔ	19	Ⓐ Ⓑ Ⓒ Ⓓ Ⓔ	29	Ⓐ Ⓑ Ⓒ Ⓓ Ⓔ	39	Ⓐ Ⓑ Ⓒ Ⓓ Ⓔ
10	Ⓐ Ⓑ Ⓒ Ⓓ Ⓔ	20	Ⓐ Ⓑ Ⓒ Ⓓ Ⓔ	30	Ⓐ Ⓑ Ⓒ Ⓓ Ⓔ	40	Ⓐ Ⓑ Ⓒ Ⓓ Ⓔ

SECTION 9

1	Ⓐ Ⓑ Ⓒ Ⓓ Ⓔ	11	Ⓐ Ⓑ Ⓒ Ⓓ Ⓔ	21	Ⓐ Ⓑ Ⓒ Ⓓ Ⓔ	31	Ⓐ Ⓑ Ⓒ Ⓓ Ⓔ
2	Ⓐ Ⓑ Ⓒ Ⓓ Ⓔ	12	Ⓐ Ⓑ Ⓒ Ⓓ Ⓔ	22	Ⓐ Ⓑ Ⓒ Ⓓ Ⓔ	32	Ⓐ Ⓑ Ⓒ Ⓓ Ⓔ
3	Ⓐ Ⓑ Ⓒ Ⓓ Ⓔ	13	Ⓐ Ⓑ Ⓒ Ⓓ Ⓔ	23	Ⓐ Ⓑ Ⓒ Ⓓ Ⓔ	33	Ⓐ Ⓑ Ⓒ Ⓓ Ⓔ
4	Ⓐ Ⓑ Ⓒ Ⓓ Ⓔ	14	Ⓐ Ⓑ Ⓒ Ⓓ Ⓔ	24	Ⓐ Ⓑ Ⓒ Ⓓ Ⓔ	34	Ⓐ Ⓑ Ⓒ Ⓓ Ⓔ
5	Ⓐ Ⓑ Ⓒ Ⓓ Ⓔ	15	Ⓐ Ⓑ Ⓒ Ⓓ Ⓔ	25	Ⓐ Ⓑ Ⓒ Ⓓ Ⓔ	35	Ⓐ Ⓑ Ⓒ Ⓓ Ⓔ
6	Ⓐ Ⓑ Ⓒ Ⓓ Ⓔ	16	Ⓐ Ⓑ Ⓒ Ⓓ Ⓔ	26	Ⓐ Ⓑ Ⓒ Ⓓ Ⓔ	36	Ⓐ Ⓑ Ⓒ Ⓓ Ⓔ
7	Ⓐ Ⓑ Ⓒ Ⓓ Ⓔ	17	Ⓐ Ⓑ Ⓒ Ⓓ Ⓔ	27	Ⓐ Ⓑ Ⓒ Ⓓ Ⓔ	37	Ⓐ Ⓑ Ⓒ Ⓓ Ⓔ
8	Ⓐ Ⓑ Ⓒ Ⓓ Ⓔ	18	Ⓐ Ⓑ Ⓒ Ⓓ Ⓔ	28	Ⓐ Ⓑ Ⓒ Ⓓ Ⓔ	38	Ⓐ Ⓑ Ⓒ Ⓓ Ⓔ
9	Ⓐ Ⓑ Ⓒ Ⓓ Ⓔ	19	Ⓐ Ⓑ Ⓒ Ⓓ Ⓔ	29	Ⓐ Ⓑ Ⓒ Ⓓ Ⓔ	39	Ⓐ Ⓑ Ⓒ Ⓓ Ⓔ
10	Ⓐ Ⓑ Ⓒ Ⓓ Ⓔ	20	Ⓐ Ⓑ Ⓒ Ⓓ Ⓔ	30	Ⓐ Ⓑ Ⓒ Ⓓ Ⓔ	40	Ⓐ Ⓑ Ⓒ Ⓓ Ⓔ

SECTION 10

1	Ⓐ Ⓑ Ⓒ Ⓓ Ⓔ	11	Ⓐ Ⓑ Ⓒ Ⓓ Ⓔ	21	Ⓐ Ⓑ Ⓒ Ⓓ Ⓔ	31	Ⓐ Ⓑ Ⓒ Ⓓ Ⓔ
2	Ⓐ Ⓑ Ⓒ Ⓓ Ⓔ	12	Ⓐ Ⓑ Ⓒ Ⓓ Ⓔ	22	Ⓐ Ⓑ Ⓒ Ⓓ Ⓔ	32	Ⓐ Ⓑ Ⓒ Ⓓ Ⓔ
3	Ⓐ Ⓑ Ⓒ Ⓓ Ⓔ	13	Ⓐ Ⓑ Ⓒ Ⓓ Ⓔ	23	Ⓐ Ⓑ Ⓒ Ⓓ Ⓔ	33	Ⓐ Ⓑ Ⓒ Ⓓ Ⓔ
4	Ⓐ Ⓑ Ⓒ Ⓓ Ⓔ	14	Ⓐ Ⓑ Ⓒ Ⓓ Ⓔ	24	Ⓐ Ⓑ Ⓒ Ⓓ Ⓔ	34	Ⓐ Ⓑ Ⓒ Ⓓ Ⓔ
5	Ⓐ Ⓑ Ⓒ Ⓓ Ⓔ	15	Ⓐ Ⓑ Ⓒ Ⓓ Ⓔ	25	Ⓐ Ⓑ Ⓒ Ⓓ Ⓔ	35	Ⓐ Ⓑ Ⓒ Ⓓ Ⓔ
6	Ⓐ Ⓑ Ⓒ Ⓓ Ⓔ	16	Ⓐ Ⓑ Ⓒ Ⓓ Ⓔ	26	Ⓐ Ⓑ Ⓒ Ⓓ Ⓔ	36	Ⓐ Ⓑ Ⓒ Ⓓ Ⓔ
7	Ⓐ Ⓑ Ⓒ Ⓓ Ⓔ	17	Ⓐ Ⓑ Ⓒ Ⓓ Ⓔ	27	Ⓐ Ⓑ Ⓒ Ⓓ Ⓔ	37	Ⓐ Ⓑ Ⓒ Ⓓ Ⓔ
8	Ⓐ Ⓑ Ⓒ Ⓓ Ⓔ	18	Ⓐ Ⓑ Ⓒ Ⓓ Ⓔ	28	Ⓐ Ⓑ Ⓒ Ⓓ Ⓔ	38	Ⓐ Ⓑ Ⓒ Ⓓ Ⓔ
9	Ⓐ Ⓑ Ⓒ Ⓓ Ⓔ	19	Ⓐ Ⓑ Ⓒ Ⓓ Ⓔ	29	Ⓐ Ⓑ Ⓒ Ⓓ Ⓔ	39	Ⓐ Ⓑ Ⓒ Ⓓ Ⓔ
10	Ⓐ Ⓑ Ⓒ Ⓓ Ⓔ	20	Ⓐ Ⓑ Ⓒ Ⓓ Ⓔ	30	Ⓐ Ⓑ Ⓒ Ⓓ Ⓔ	40	Ⓐ Ⓑ Ⓒ Ⓓ Ⓔ

NOTES

AP Exams

Cracking the AP Biology Exam,
2004–2005 Edition
0-375-76393-7 • $18.00/C$27.00

Cracking the AP Calculus AB & BC Exam,
2004–2005 Edition
0-375-76381-3 • $19.00/C$28.50

Cracking the AP Chemistry Exam,
2004–2005 Edition
0-375-76382-1• $18.00/C$27.00

**Cracking the AP Computer Science
A & AB Exam ,** 2004-2005 Edition
0-375-76383-X • $19.00/C$28.50

**Cracking the AP Economics (Macro &
Micro) Exam,** 2004-2005 Edition
0-375-76384-8 • $18.00/C$27.00

Cracking the AP English Literature Exam,
2004–2005 Edition
0-375-76385-6 • $18.00/C$27.00

Cracking the AP European History Exam,
2004–2005 Edition
0-375-76386-4 • $18.00/C$27.00

Cracking the AP Physics B & C Exam,
2004–2005 Edition
0-375-76387-2 • $19.00/C$28.50

Cracking the AP Psychology Exam,
2004–2005 Edition
0-375-76388-0 • $18.00/C$27.00

Cracking the AP Spanish Exam,
2004–2005 Edition
0-375-76389-9 • $18.00/C$27.00

Cracking the AP Statistics Exam,
2004–2005 Edition
0-375-76390-2 • $19.00/C$28.50

**Cracking the AP U.S. Government
and Politics Exam,** 2004–2005 Edition
0-375-76391-0 • $18.00/C$27.00

Cracking the AP U.S. History Exam,
2004–2005 Edition
0-375-76392-9 • $18.00/C$27.00

Cracking the AP World History Exam,
2004–2005 Edition
0-375-76380-5 • $18.00/C$27.00

SAT Subject Tests

Cracking the SAT Biology E/M Subject Test,
2005-2006 Edition
0-375-76447-X • $19.00/C$27.00

Cracking the SAT Chemistry Subject Test,
2005-2006 Edition
0-375-76448-8 • $18.00/C$26.00

Cracking the SAT French Subject Test,
2005-2006 Edition
0-375-76449-6 • $18.00/C$26.00

Cracking the SAT Literature Subject Test,
2005-2006 Edition
0-375-76446-1 • $18.00/C$26.00

**Cracking the SAT Math 1 and 2
Subject Tests,** 2005-2006 Edition
0-375-76451-8 • $19.00/C$27.00

Cracking the SAT Physics Subject Test,
2005-2006 Edition
0-375-76452-6 • $19.00/C$27.00

Cracking the SAT Spanish Subject Test,
2005-2006 Edition
0-375-76453-4 • $18.00/C$26.00

**Cracking the SAT U.S. & World History
Subject Tests,** 2005-2006 Edition
0-375-76450-X • $19.00/C$27.00

Available at Bookstores Everywhere
PrincetonReview.com

Need More?

If you're looking to learn more about how to excel on the SAT, you're in the right place. Our expertise extends far beyond this test. But this isn't about us, it's about getting you into the college of your choice.

One way to increase the number of fat envelopes you receive is to have strong test scores. So, if you're still nervous—relax. Consider all of your options.

We consistently improve students' scores through our books, classroom courses, private tutoring, and online courses. Call **800-2Review** or visit PrincetonReview.com.

If you like our *Cracking the New SAT with CD*, check out:
- *The Best 357 Colleges*
- *Cracking the SAT Math 1 and 2 Subject Tests*
- *11 Practice Tests for the New SAT and PSAT*
- *Math Workout for the New SAT*
- *Cracking the SAT Biology Subject Test*